Mehmet Kalyoncu
Virginia 2007

INTERNATIONAL RELATIONS

AN INTRODUCTION

Is Turkey Going Crazy?

International-systemic
Domestic-systemic
Leadership.

David N. Farnsworth
Wichita State University

NELSON-HALL nh CHICAGO

COVER PAINTING:

White on Red, Elvarina Acosta, 1985
Oil on Canvas, 30"×22"

Project Editor: Richard Meade
Designer: Claudia von Hendricks
Copy Editors: Richard Meade, Kathy Willhoite
Typesetter: Interface Studio
Illustrator: Cynthia Schultz

LIBRARY OF CONGRESS CATALOGING-IN-PUBLICATION DATA

Farnsworth, David N. (David Nelson), 1929-
  International relations: an introduction/David N. Farnsworth.
   p.   cm.
  Bibliography: p.
  Includes index.
  ISBN 0-8304-1101-1
  1. International relations.   I. Title.
JX1391.F29 1988   87-35328
327 — dc19   CIP

Manufactured in the United States of America

10 9 8 7 6 5 4 3 2 1

™ The paper used in this book meets the minimum requirements of American National Standard for Information Sciences—Permanence of Paper for Printed Library Materials, ANSI Z39.48-1984.

Contents

PART I

Concepts and Principles of International Relations

INTRODUCTION: WHY STUDY INTERNATIONAL RELATIONS?

The complexity of the international system allows for many reasons why a person would be attracted to the study of international relations. But two general and compelling reasons are, first, the need to know more about the impact international events have on our lives and the possible results if nations lose control of those events; and, second, to discover the intellectual satisfaction students of international relations derive from understanding more about that which perplexes them.

The threat of nuclear war is the most obvious and most disturbing characteristic of the international environment. Such a war clearly could result in the deaths of millions and the destruction of our political, social, and economic systems, as well as having a devastating effect on the ecosystem. With such an omnipresent threat it may be scant comfort to discover how the nuclear arms race developed and the alternatives available to decision-makers to end it; yet the arms race can end only through greater knowledge about it. While less devastating than nuclear war, conventional wars are far more likely to occur within the present international system. The United States has engaged in two such wars,

in Korea and in Vietnam, since World War II. Avoiding wars of this nature is an important objective for all nations, and one which can be achieved only through an informed public.

But the possibility of war is not required to show that international events strongly affect our lives. Within the United States, international events help determine the allocation of scarce resources. The U.S. Congress, depending on how it perceives external threat, determines what portion of those resources will be spent on national defense. A perceived greater Soviet threat usually results in an increased defense budget which will create jobs in defense-related industries, but less money will be available for student loans, social welfare programs, and highway construction. The strength of the dollar relative to other currencies affects the U.S. balance of trade, interest rates at home, and the flow of foreign capital into the United States. The large deficit in the U.S. federal budget results in complaints from other countries as to the manner in which the U.S. manages its financial affairs. An economic boycott imposed on another country or the decision not to impose tariffs on imported products results in layoffs of American workers. American farmers experience good or bad times depending, in part, on the demand for their products abroad. If the dollar is strong, fewer farm products are sold abroad; conversely, a weak dollar will tend to increase exports. Thus, individuals, industry, and agriculture in the United States find their well-being directly affected by international events.

The second category of reasons for studying international relations is the need to know more about that which we do not understand. The international system and conflicts within it at times frighten even the most experienced observer, but these events are no less frightening if they are ignored or not understood to the extent they can be understood. A generally valid argument is that the more we know about something the less perplexing it becomes. At the least, the study of international relations can teach us that all conflict situations are not equally threatening. If we learn nothing more than to differentiate between international threats as to their seriousness, that alone can make the study of international relations worthwhile. If, in addition, we learn to distinguish between a nation's behavior that is based primarily on domestic concerns, as opposed to behavior based primarily on international motivations, this too can be an important contribution to our understanding of international relations. The discovery of any generalization about or pattern of domestic and international behavior contributes to our understanding of the international system and removes some of the frustration involved in observing international events. Put directly, the study of international relations is an important aspect of our intellectual and personal well-being.

While serious students of international relations realize that supportable generalizations have not yet been developed to explain all international behavior, they also know that much can be learned about international relations and that explanations for behavior in many instances can be developed. Even the unsolved mysteries of international behavior add to the excitement of studying international relations. A field of study that provided valid explanations for all behavior would be sterile and without challenges.

Although the study of international relations can be fascinating and exciting, many people do not follow even day-to-day international occurrences. The complexity and diversity of international relations attracts and challenges many students. But this complexity intimidates others and prevents them from learning more about the international system. Since the easiest means of coping with the threats and fears generated by international events is simply to ignore them, the limited knowledge that many persons possess about international relations is understandable. The perspective of those who take the ignorance-is-bliss approach seems to be that what they do not learn will not confound them. Others avoid the complexity of the system by dedicating themselves to a particular ideology that has an overall explanation for all behavior. Communist philosophy, for example, simply explains all conflict, domestic or international, as a product of class struggle, and a search for further explanation becomes unnecessary. Conspiratorial theories such as that the world is controlled by the giant multinational corporations or that U.S. foreign policy emanates from the Trilateral Commission also provide comfort through oversimplification.

Many persons dismiss the study of politics by labeling political activity as corrupt and thus beyond their control or not worthy of their attention. The domestic version of this attitude is the hackneyed statement that "you cannot fight city hall." Thus, why study that which you can do nothing about? Still others take the view that international events take place too far from home to have much effect on their lives. If interested in following politics at all, these individuals limit themselves to the domestic political scene. An illustration of this attitude is the infrequency with which a foreign policy problem becomes a major campaign issue in U.S. presidential elections. Studies of U.S. elections generally indicate that while foreign policy often is discussed during campaigns, domestic questions, particularly economic issues, are more apt to influence how citizens vote.

Any or all of these reasons for avoiding the study of international politics results in national publics inadequately informed and incapable of rational analysis of international events. Too much is at stake to ignore the importance of international relations in our lives.

This book attempts to take some of the confusion and fear out of studying international relations. This is done by analyzing central concepts such as power and nationalism, by looking at the various ways in which the international system can be organized, by describing the principal sources of conflict in the system, and by investigating the sources and transfers of the weapons of war. This book also follows the development of diplomacy and its use to control day-to-day conflict as well as conflict management. Institutions designed to limit or even resolve conflict such as international organizations and international law are also discussed in the quest for a better understanding of international relations.

Central concepts of International Relations:
1. Power
2. Nationalism

CHAPTER 1

Conflict and International Relations

Briefly defined, international relations are past and present interactions among the many actors of the international system. Nation-states are the system's most prominent actors, but many other actors also participate. The *study* of international relations is not only the examination of behavior among those actors; it also includes theories, generalizations, and concepts that explain how and why actors behave as they do. International relations can be analyzed from the level of the international system, which examines actions between actors, or from the perspective of national behavior, which examines the origins of interests actors project into the international system. A combination of analysis of behavior at both levels explains international behavior most fully.

International actors have developed, by their interactions, an international system through which they can promote their interests and manage the intensity of conflict, thus international relations do not take place in a state of anarchy. Because these are central characteristics of the international system, this book is organized around those dual themes: interest conflict and conflict management.

International conflict can come in many forms. Conflict may be a state of war, but not necessarily so, and an international crisis is conflict that has become so intense that it may serve as the bridge between peace and war. Wars and crises are extreme forms of conflict, but conflict ranges from acts of violence to routine disagreements occurring daily among the nation-states (Fox, 1984). Conflict can have many origins. Conflict may arise over a boundary dispute between two nations, or the arrest of a citizen of one nation in another nation. Conflict may be over a requested arms transfer or landing rights for a national airline. It may also arise out of economic problems. As the industrial nations negotiate trade arrangements and developing nations demand greater access to the world's markets, a growing aspect of international conflict is economic. Recognition that conflict is endemic in the international system does not mean, as Marxists argue, that conflict is a constructive element in that it brings about revolutionary change. It means only that conflict occurs and needs to be managed. Thus, as long as the international system is based on the nation-state and organized as it is, conflict, and thus conflict management, seem to be inevitable.

NATURE AND SCOPE OF INTERNATIONAL CONFLICT

The international system consists of more than 160 nation-states, hundreds of international organizations, numerous multinational corporations, nongovernmental international organizations, terrorist groups, liberation movements,

5

and various other actors. The cause for conflict among all actors is that no two have, or can be expected to have, the same set of interests. Since the societal and political structure of each nation-state differs, their domestic political systems make differing demands on their decision-makers and, in turn, they bring different demands to the international system. Within the resulting environment of international conflict, nations experience some satisfaction but no nation is wholly satisfied; demands far exceed resources available to any nation to fulfill all of its interests.

At the national level of analysis, even though Western democracies provide domestic interests better access to decision-makers than do totalitarian systems, the contention that demands made by nations are a product of the domestic system is not limited to democracies. Whether a democracy or not, any nation's decision-makers must arrive at decisions within the framework of demands being made by the interests within that nation. The patterns by which domestic interests make their demands upon decision-makers vary between political systems, but conflicts within a national political system about that nation's foreign policy take place in any type of domestic political system.

Because of internal disputes over policy, what appears as conflict between two nations—such as a U.S.-Soviet, Sino-Soviet, Argentine-Chilean, Syrian-Israeli or any competitive alignment among several nations—is extended into the domestic political systems of the nations involved. Thus, conflict between two or more states is actually a continuum of conflict within and between domestic systems operating through national bureaucracies.

Under these circumstances, pure categories of domestic decisions (decisions that affect only domestic interests) and foreign policy decisions (decisions that affect only interest demands between nations) seldom exist. Most conflict situations have both domestic and international implications.

In the United States, the State Department often sees policy choices differently than does the National Security Council or the Defense Department. The congressional leadership of the Republican and Democratic parties may also have differing views, and the congressional perspective may differ from that of the executive. While the president generally works toward developing consensus in foreign policy, he is seldom, if ever, successful except for brief periods during times of international crisis, such as during the months immediately following the attack on Pearl Harbor.

The Soviet Union behaves little differently. That nation's defense establishment, for example, has disputes with Communist party leadership. Within the party, foreign policy disputes occur between members of the Politburo and between the Politburo and other party institutions. During the period from 1981–85, which encompassed the

Fig. 1.1 Flow of Demands into International System

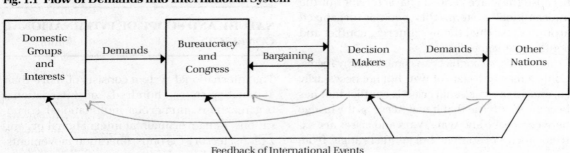

Feedback of International Events

illnesses and deaths of successive Soviet leaders—Leonid Brezhnev, Yuri Andropov, and Konstantin Chernenko—the Soviet Union had no central leadership to resolve domestic conflict. Within a system designed for strong central leadership, the absence of such leadership resulted in Soviet policy that appeared uncertain and drifting. To some extent, all nations share this behavior of bureaucratic conflict over policy and the need to resolve that conflict.

Conflict among the domestic decision-making institutions of a political system occurs because each decision-making unit views policy choices from its own perspective of the nation's interests. Developing a nation's foreign policy thus becomes the process of working out differences between the various bureaucratic units. This process of negotiation between units is similar, in many respects, to nations negotiating an international agreement. Either differences between the various units are resolved and policy is agreed to, or an impasse develops and the result is confusion or no action. This process of domestic bureaucratic bargaining indicates that, as with conflict, conflict management has domestic as well as international applications.

In this discussion of interests, the use of the term "national interest" has been avoided, since it is so closely associated with the Hans Morgenthau–realist school of international politics. Morgenthau defines national interest in terms of power. Policy goals that contribute to a nation's power, Morgenthau feels, are in the national interest, and those that do not therefore are not. But, to judge policy choices in this manner is of little aid to decision-makers. Conflicts and the need for a decision are of the moment, and if decision-makers must await the evaluation of history to find if a policy choice did or did not contribute to a nation's power, power as a standard is of little aid in making decisions. Also a problem exists in how to judge whether another policy alternative would have better served the national interest, that is, whether it would have made a greater contribution to the nation's

power. Morgenthau, by defining national interest in terms of power, has given us nothing by which to judge decisions as they are made.

At the moment a decision is needed, decision-makers must concern themselves only with what they consider to be their nation's interests and hope that their decision is not detrimental to their nation's well-being. That choice is, for the time being, one of that nation's interests. Therefore, interest is defined as including anything to which a nation's decision-makers agree to as a policy choice. Interest thus becomes synonymous with policy objective or goal.

CONFLICT AND INTERSTATE BEHAVIOR

International conflict thus far has been described as existing throughout the international system, as occurring among many international actors, as unavoidable within the present system, and as the pursuit of interests that are primarily a product of domestic conflict and demands. The next question is how does conflict affect nations and how do those nations, in turn, react to conflict?

Considering the complexity of the international system, the opportunity for conflict to develop is omnipresent; but it does not follow that every nation has some degree of conflict with every other nation. The degree of formal diplomatic contact through embassies illustrates this point. Of the many nation-states, only a few—the United States, the Soviet Union, a few Western European countries, and Japan—maintain embassies in virtually all the nations of the world. Most nations have only limited representation, with diplomats assigned only to their neighbors, a few of the major powers, and a delegation to the United Nations. In part, those nations maintain limited representation because they cannot afford additional embassies, but often they do not have representation because little or none is required in many countries. Without a reason for contact, conflict with other nations and the need for representation are limited. Thus, one of the limits on conflict in the international system is simply the lack of contact between nations. An exception to this argument is that, occasionally, two nations have such poor relations that they deliberately break diplomatic relations. In such instances, the lack of contact is due to intense conflict, not the absence of conflict.

If nations do have contact, no matter how friendly the relationship between two countries or among several nations in an alliance, some degree of conflict will occur. Perhaps the closest bilateral relationship among the Western countries is that between the United States and Great Britain. Both are democracies having open elections to select their leaders, they share a common language, many Americans have British ancestors, and they have many of the same nations as alliance partners. In spite of all this commonality, the two nations have had serious conflicts over policy. In the early 1960s Great Britain was particularly angry because the United States canceled the Skybolt missile project without first consulting them. The U.S. had promised the British the missile in order to extend the life of British manned bombers. During the Falklands War in 1982, the British government complained that the United States did not provide full diplomatic support for the British effort. The British government also, from time to time, charges that the United States takes Great Britain for granted and fails to consult with it over policy issues common to both nations. The British government, depending upon which party is in power, occasionally complains about U.S. policy toward the Soviet Union and U.S. interference in matters the British regard as purely European Community (EC) affairs.

The United States, in turn, has complaints about the British. During the early stages of the war in Vietnam, the United States criticized the British for failing to give the U.S. proper diplomatic support, and the U.S. has charged the British a number of times with not providing their fair share of support for NATO. The United States boycotted the 1980 Olympics and called for other countries to do likewise. The British sent their athletes to Moscow anyway. The relationship between the United States and Great Britain is not without significant disagreements. Among Western democracies in general, similar national political systems and close bilateral relations do not prevent conflict.

On the other hand, probably no relationship between two nations is so hostile that they do not find some interests in common. The United States and the Soviet Union disagree about an extensive list of issues, but, despite this, negotiations to settle these differences are frequently in session. The two countries have concluded a number of agreements in the last twenty-five years including the SALT treaties, the Helsinki Agreement, and treaties regulating weapons in space and on the seabed. Negotiations between the two nations usually are lengthy, but a mutuality of interests is occasionally found.

What this comparison of two sets of relationships indicates is that any two nations with contact will experience some level of conflict and some level of conflict management and resolution. A relationship probably can never be totally hostile or totally harmonious, and the relationship between any two or more nations falls someplace on a continuum that runs from conflict at one end to cooperation at the other.

Stating that conflict between any two countries exists on a continuum needs an additional dimension to make it even more descriptive; conflict and cooperation between countries also must be measured as to the degree of intensity. Two nations can have considerable conflict, but most of it may be minor and more in the category of bickering than serious disagreement. Conversely, two nations can have much in common, but have a single serious dispute that overshadows what is otherwise successful conflict management. In some instances, nations have friendly relations, but have little in the way of common interests; friendship in this instance would be based more on the lack of conflict than the presence of common interests. The United States, for example, has seemingly friendly relations with a number of African nations, but shares little trade and grants them little economic aid. During 1986 relations between the United States and Zimbabwe deteriorated rapidly, but the intensity of this conflict did not compare to the intensity of conflict between the United States and the Soviet Union. Intensity in both of these examples is the measure of violence that could follow if events moved beyond control of the disputing nations. Conflict among nations thus must be measured both as to amount and intensity.

While the discussion to this point has dealt with conflict relationships on a bilateral basis, nations usually have an alternative to pursuing their interests alone. Unless isolated within the international community for some reason, a nation often can join a coalition made up of nations with similar interests. The purpose of a coalition is to strengthen, through numbers, the demands that the coalition can agree to. In order to join, coalition members must be willing to sacrifice a degree of specificity in their interests, since the formation of a successful coalition requires compromise by its members in order to present a common set of interests to those outside. Also, to maintain itself a coalition must undergo constant diplomatic repair. Even a coalition as old and established as NATO must constantly be renegotiated among its members. Every few months, it seems, a news story appears posing the question, "Is NATO falling apart?" Such headlines simply serve to remind us that mem-

Fig. 1.2 Impact of Intensity on Conflict and Cooperation

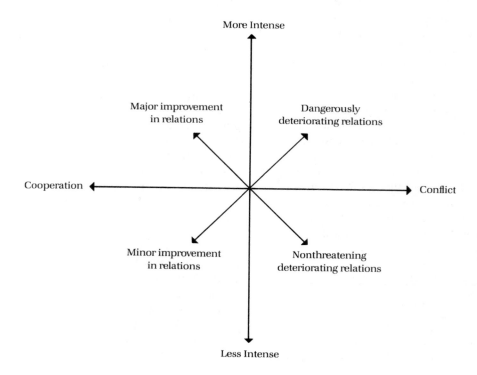

bers of a coalition disagree among themselves, and if their coalition is to survive it requires constant attention.

Even wartime coalitions formed to fight a common enemy experience internal conflicts. During World War II, the Allied coalition was presented publicly as united in the common cause of defeating the Axis. While no disagreement existed as to who the enemy was, the proper strategy to bring about his defeat was contentious throughout the war. Not only did Stalin insist on a second front in Europe long before the U.S. and Great Britain were ready, the British and Americans quarreled over where the invasion was to take place. Command problems between the U.S. and Great Britain existed throughout the war as well.

In the abstract, nations wish to avoid conflict; at least, that is the case if they can achieve their interests without opposition. But, since opposition is there, conflict cannot be avoided. In terms of violence in the international system, national leaders never proclaim anything but a desire for peace. Even when nations go to war, each participant usually claims to have done everything possible to avoid it and charges the other side with making war unavoidable. Occasionally, there are national leaders, such as Germany's Hitler, Libya's Qaddafi, and Uganda's Idi Amin who deliberately use violence as a means of settling conflicts and fulfilling interests, but they are the exception within the system. Since nations usually attempt to avoid war, if not conflict in general, and since conflict seems an inevitable result of any meaningful contact between nations, then the practical objective of nations is to control the level of conflict and successfully limit any crises that develop.

LIMITS ON CONFLICT

For the most part, nations resolve conflict without violence—through traditional diplomatic channels, international organizations, and the involvement of third parties or, on occasion, because of exhaustion with the conflict and the growing importance of other interests. Conflict resolution probably never means that a nation has received all that it wants, however. Typically, conflicting nations resolve their differences through a bargained settlement wholly satisfying to neither party but producing an agreement that both can accept. If, however, a nation is negotiating from a position of weakness, the settlement will probably last only until the weaker nation finds itself strong enough to renew its demands. One such situation, which resulted in tragic consequences for both nations, was the border agreement the Shah of Iran imposed on Iraq in 1975. The agreement clearly satisfied Iran's demands at the expense of Iraq. In 1980, following changes of government in both countries, Iraq saw Iran as weak and launched an attack. Iraq was not strong enough to bring about a quick victory, and the war has continued for years. An agreement that is not mutually bargained clearly does not contribute to conflict resolution.

Even when violence does occur, those nations not engaged in the clash ordinarily work toward confining it to as few nations as possible. The nations surrounding Iraq and Iran, though mostly supportive of Iraq, worked to limit the war to those two countries. The interests of the other Persian Gulf nations required them to make every effort to limit the war to prevent it from threatening their own oil shipments and from weakening OPEC. The Arab–Israeli wars have also been limited to the region, as were several wars between India and Pakistan.

A technique for limiting the duration of wars in the Third World is for no outside nations to resupply the combatants. The limited resources of most Third World nations usually prevents them from sustaining a major war effort over a long period of time. The Iraqi-Iranian War is an obvious exception. If war were to break out between major industrial nations, this limitation, of course, would not be a controlling factor, particularly if nuclear weapons were involved. A conventional war between industrial nations could be of long duration, but a nuclear war conceivably could last only a few hours.

For even a serious observer of the international scene, the impression is easily gained that, at any given time, much of the world is at war. The reasons for that impression are perhaps twofold. First, the focus of the world's press is on the violent events. Wars, hijackings, and terrorist acts are well covered, suggesting that the world as a whole is gripped in violence. A war between Third World countries, a frequent occurrence in the post–World War II period, immediately becomes the top story for the media worldwide. A less interesting news story and thus receiving far less media attention results from a conflict being resolved through negotiation. The bargaining process between nations when carried on through traditional diplomatic channels is not a visual event and thus is of little interest to television. Often, bargaining concerns a seemingly minor point of conflict, and, once resolved, is prevented from becoming more intense. This sort of preventive diplomacy is not considered a good news story. An additional factor is that since diplomats prefer to bargain in private in order to prevent public kibitzing, negotiators often deliberately keep a low profile to avoid the spotlight of the communications media. Whatever the reasons for limited reporting of peaceful settlement, much day-to-day conflict resolution goes unnoticed.

The second reason for the emphasis on violence is that the failure to resolve conflict peacefully often has long-term consequences. Resolving a conflict over trade policy between two countries is routine in most cases, and if negotiations fail the consequences likely would produce little tension within the international system. But a war, even if limited to conventional weapons and to two countries having only a limited capacity to wage war, could escalate into a more serious conflict involving additional nations. A confrontation involving the major powers is perhaps what the world fears most; such a confrontation could lead to World War III. Violence within the system thus poses an immediate threat, whereas use of the diplomatic process does not.

Since a number of wars are taking place in the international system at any given moment, many opportunities exist for the escalation of violence. If border conflicts, guerrilla wars, and conventional wars are totaled, thirty to forty such events are usually occurring simultaneously. While this involves a substantial number of nations, many of these violent situations are not international—they take place within a single nation and do not involve other nations in any serious manner. Thus, even though wars involving a number of nations are occurring at several locations in the international system, far more nations are at peace.

The international system, therefore, is not one of continual violent turmoil. Much of the system is at peace or, if not at peace in the tranquil sense, not involved in acts of violence. Conflicts are resolved, and usually to the extent that most nations, most of the time, do not resort to violence to fulfill their interests. No nation ever has its wide range of interests fully satisfied, nor does it expect to. Even in those instances in which a nation achieves more in a negotiated settlement than does its adversary, in other areas of interest it is probably not faring as well. If a score card could be kept on the success of nations in promoting their interests, the result would likely show that a nation wins some, loses some, but essentially has a draw overall; in balance, it usually is difficult to tell if a nation is ahead or behind other nations in the fulfillment of its interests. This sort of equilibrium in the fulfillment of interests is fortunate, since an international system in which each nation insisted upon total fulfillment of its demands might well be one of total anarchy and continual violence. It would, in fact, not be a system, for such an arrangement would indicate no management of conflict, a requisite of a political system.

Even if self-interest were the sole reason nations do not resort to violence—war is often just not worth the trouble—this in itself indicates recognition on the part of most members of the nation-state system that some order is desirable. In this respect, nations, when pursuing their interests, do not behave any differently than do domestic units pursuing their interests. Domestic groups also are willing to accept a degree of order as long as they feel that a nonviolent means of fulfilling at least a portion of their demands is available. Interest groups on the domestic level accept the political system in which they operate because they feel it serves their purposes to do so. Internationally, nation-states function similarly.

When comparisons are made between the international system and domestic political systems in regard to the stability of each, the international system often comes off badly. Too often evaluations are limited to only one aspect of a political system—the formal, structured institutions. Specifically, this means a legislative body, a chief executive, and perhaps an independent judiciary. The international system has no such institutions. If, however, a political system can be identified by its ability to resolve conflict rather than by formal institutional structures, there is evidence that a political system operates at the international level.

Additionally, when unfavorable comparisons are made between the international system and domestic political systems, the domestic systems used for the comparison are usually Western democracies. If the less stable political systems of the Third World are used in the comparison, differences between international and domestic systems in resolving conflict are much narrower (Alger, 1963). If less stable domestic systems are used in the comparison, peaceful settlement of conflicts on the domestic level is often not found, thus suggesting that many domestic political systems share with the international system the inability to find peaceful solutions to many conflicts. Many domestic political systems are not effective in resolving conflict as revolutions, civil wars, and coups d'etat indicate. Thus, in a sense, the international system is similar to an underdeveloped domestic political system.

DIFFERENT LEVELS OF STUDY OF INTERNATIONAL RELATIONS

Since conflict occurs at both domestic and international levels, the study of international relations requires the examination of conflict and conflict management at each level. The domestic level of analysis can be broken down into the domestic origins of interest demands as opposed to bureaucratic conflict among decision-makers over policy formulation; therefore, three overall levels of behavior can be distinguished for investigation. To ignore any of these levels of analysis is to neglect some important aspect of behavior related to the study of international relations.

The international-system level of analysis provides an opportunity to study interaction among the nation-states. It also provides an opportunity to look at how the system is organized or might be organized, and how it manages conflict situations. At this level, the broadest generalizations about international relations are made. At the domestic-system level, analysis centers on the source of interests within the system. Since each nation can be described behaviorally in terms of the set of interests it pursues, and since each nation has a unique set of interests, generalizations at this level are limited to the nation being investigated and the conflicts it has with other nations. The level of analysis pertaining to decision-makers looks at the decision-making process and the influences brought to bear on decision-makers. Since a nation's international behavior is determined at this level, it is here that the domestic and international patterns of behavior merge. Also at this level, issues lose their identity as either domestic or international

Levels of analysis
1. Int'l-system level
2. Domestic-system level → *Why does ? why it does?*
3. Decision maker level   *act the way*

1 / CONFLICT AND INTERNATIONAL RELATIONS **13**

issues. Each level of analysis provides knowledge about the behavior of nations, but the sorts of generalizations are more specific at the domestic and decision-making levels than at the international level.

CONFLICT MANAGEMENT

Up to this point, little has been said about conflict management other than to point out the frequency with which it occurs and that it usually serves the interests of a nation to minimize conflict. An additional constraint on conflict within the system is the diplomatic process. Diplomacy is both a process by which demands can be made between nations through agreed-upon procedures and a means of communication that can lead to bargaining and possible settlement of differences. The formality and protocol of diplomacy is intended to make the process as neutral as possible so that it does not contribute further to conflict. International organizations are an additional constraining influence on conflict. While international organizations occasionally can, through their procedures, settle disputes, such organizations also can, through their multilateral setting, contain a variety of differences between nations that would be more focused and perhaps more intense if the contact took place on a bilateral basis.

Established procedural arrangements are perhaps less important constraints on a nation than are the number of interests that a nation pursues. The result of having multiple interests is twofold. First, a nation cannot work toward the achievement of one interest without affecting its chances of achieving others. This assumes, of course, that any nation has finite energy it can put forth in fulfilling its interests, which means that if a nation places too great an emphasis on one policy objective less energy is available for other interests. Thus, a constraint on the pursuit of one interest is the amount of capability a nation chooses to divert from other interests.

Secondly, and a consequence of the uneven distribution of effort to achieve various policy objectives, a nation sets priorities, ranking the importance of its interests. Such priority lists may or may not be consciously drawn and may be discernible only from a nation's behavior, or the list may be the result of conscious choices made by decision-makers. Either way, a priority ranking of policy objectives is important because it reflects the effort a nation is willing to expend for any particular interest.

An example of a constraint on one interest by other interests is the long-term objective of United States policy toward Cuba. Virtually from the time Castro took over in Cuba in 1959, U.S. policy has been directed toward bringing about his downfall. Various alternatives are available to the United States to achieve this end, including the direct use of armed force, but that alternative has not been implemented even though the U.S. did support and train the refugee army that landed at the Bay of Pigs in 1961. Even if the Soviet Union did not come to Cuba's aid, which it might very well do if the U.S. were to invade Cuba, the damage to U.S. relationships with other Latin American states would be considerable. Although the United States does not have economic or diplomatic relations with Cuba, several Latin American nations do. Even those Latin American countries that still diplomatically and economically isolate Cuba share the Latin American view that military intervention by the United States in any Latin American country is unacceptable. Mexico is particularly sensitive to any such action, and the United States, even during a time of glut on the oil market, is dependent upon Mexican oil. If the flow of oil stopped, the cost to both Mexico and the United States might be too high a price to pay for Castro's removal. Instead, a softer policy is used—U.S. economic and diplomatic isolation of Cuba.

Another illustration of the impact priorities have on U.S. interests was the dispute between the United States and Panama over the Panama

Canal, an issue whose low U.S. ranking for years kept it from being settled. As a United States diplomatic official once stated, "Panama is always sixteenth on any list of the top fifteen issues" (Franck and Weisband, 1975–76, 171). In this instance, the U.S. wanted no change in the Canal Zone—it was satisfied with the current arrangement; thus, delay through low priority was an effective strategy. The issue was finally settled, that is, given a higher priority, in 1978, only after U.S. inaction resulted in the deterioration of U.S. relations with Latin America. Thus, institutional and practical considerations exert constraint on the pursuit of a nation's interests. If these constraints provide some control over a major power such as the United States, then the impact on less powerful nations is even greater.

One additional limitation on conflict needs to be mentioned. Earlier, the point was made that no two nations have like interest alignments. Neither do any two nations have the same capabilities available to them to promote their interests; capabilities limited by the physical, economic, and societal characteristics of that state. The armed forces of most Third World nations are often not a threat to even their immediate neighbors. Therefore, the expectations of all but a few states to achieve policy objectives through force, or the threat of force, is not credible. In addition to limits on the threat of force, only a few nations have the economic capacity to use the threat of economic sanctions to achieve policy ends. Even a major economic power such as the United States hesitates to impose tariffs on foreign imports for fear that other industrial nations will retaliate with tariffs on U.S. exports. Among Third World countries, only the members of the Organization of Petroleum Exporting Countries (OPEC) have successfully controlled the price of a commodity needed in the Western industrial nations, and that success was temporary.

A nation can expect to achieve the fulfillment of its demands only if those demands are credible with other nations, but less powerful nations can achieve their demands made on major states only

if the more powerful nations do not regard those demands as unreasonable. What is "reasonable" depends on what decision-makers in the major states are willing to accept. The powerful nations are constrained in what they can achieve because they "are each other's main competitors, and the main restraint on each other's arbitrary exercise of power over weaker neighbors" (Fox, 1984, 7). Depending on the circumstances, smaller nations can exercise their capabilities and fulfill their interests effectively even when opposed by more powerful nations. The war in Vietnam is an obvious example. The U.S., though the most powerful nation involved in that conflict, was unable, due to the circumstances under which that war was fought, to bring its full power to bear. The relationship between major and smaller nations is not a simple matter of major states always receiving what they want and the smaller nations receiving nothing.

On occasion, an obstacle to the fulfillment of an interest is that its expression goes unheeded within the system. Possibly, the demand is made and ignored, or it goes unheard because of poor communication. At times, nations or groups with international objectives may be demanding no more than to be heard. Terrorist groups often justify their actions on the grounds that they had no other means of bringing their cause to the world's attention. Since terrorist groups have no access to traditional diplomatic channels through which they can express their demands, a terrorist act serves that purpose. Nations, however, do have such access to the international system, but access is not equal for all nations, simply because some are "listened to" more carefully than others.

PERCEPTION AND INTERSTATE RELATIONS

Up to this point, nothing has been said about the differing perceptions nations have of one another and how those perceptions affect the manner in which demands are perceived. A demand made by one nation upon another, if perceived incorrectly, can intensify conflict independent from what the nation making the demand intended (Jervis, 1976). If one nation fails to communicate its demands successfully to another, the result is that the demand is misperceived either as less important than intended and perhaps ignored, or it is seen as more hostile than intended and results in overreaction. Either way, the nation making the demand has failed to achieve what it sought.

Even when the message appears to be perfectly clear, the image the receiving nation has of the sending nation can distort the message's meaning. A message coming from a normally friendly nation will probably be interpreted in a friendly fashion, even if that was not the intent of the sender. This seems, in large part, to be what is behind the British charge that the United States takes Great Britain for granted. Even when the British disagree with the U.S., the United States does not take the disagreement as seriously as the British feel the U.S. should.

The reverse relationship also produces a communications problem. A nation's message to a hostile nation might be interpreted as more hostile than the sender intended. Even if the message were intended to be conciliatory, the receiver is unlikely to interpret it as such, at least initially. When Sadat asked, in 1977, to appear before the Israeli Knesset in order to present a peace plan, the Israeli government was suspicious, but allowed him to come because to deny his request would place Israel in the position of rejecting a peaceful gesture. The visit began negotiations that resulted in a peace treaty between Egypt and Israel in 1979. Thus when messages are sent and demands made within the system, the manner in which a message is received and interpreted is dependent, to a great extent, on the relationships of the nations involved.

Although perceptions among nations are not static, ordinarily they change gradually. Occasionally, however, perceptions undergo sudden change. Perhaps the most dramatic change in perception during the post-World War II period was the mutual alteration of perception of the United States and China. Before the relaxation of tensions between the two countries which began in 1971, each saw the other as an enemy. The United States regarded China as at least as hostile as the Soviet Union. China was seen, due to the Korean War, the 1962 invasion of India, and Chinese support of North Vietnam during the Vietnam War, as an aggressor nation with expansionist tendencies. The U.S. assumed that at least some of the missiles China was developing would be aimed at U.S. targets. Although still not viewed as an ally, in the 1980s China is seen as a nation with far fewer interests that conflict with those of the United States. China is no longer viewed as aggressive, and no threat of war exists between the U.S. and China. Indeed, the perception of China has changed to such an extent that the United States has abrogated its mutual defense treaty with Taiwan, an inconceivable development before 1971.

Another aspect of misperception is for one nation to view its enemies as better organized and moving more purposefully than itself. Although a nation is aware of the conflicting interests and the bureaucratic differences occurring in its own domestic system, the probability that its opposition is having the same problems is less apparent. This makes the opposition appear more united than it is and therefore more threatening. Yet another problem stemming from misperception is the degree of familiarity a nation has with a policy problem. A nation's familiarity with the policy issues and interests within its own system makes it seem inconceivable that the messages it sends to other countries could be misunderstood.

Communication in the international system has at least one additional obstacle. When a national leader makes a policy statement, other nations must make a number of decisions as to how to interpret that statement. What was the intended audience? Was the statement intended largely to bolster the leader's position with his domestic audience and not intended to have international implications? Or was the statement intended as a statement of policy that other nations should heed? If the statement were dismissed as being for domestic consumption when, in fact, it was intended for the international audience, the failure of communication could be serious.

These are but a few of the results of misperception that can develop between nations sending or receiving information, but they serve to illustrate the risks involved in the communication of demands, especially if greater hostility is perceived than was intended. During times of crisis, nations must take particular care that this sort of communication failure does not occur.

CONCLUSION

International relations is the study of how nation-states and nonstate actors interact with one another. Conflict results because no two actors have identical interests, and cooperation results from actors prioritizing their interests since they do not have the resources to pursue all their interests with equal effort. Due to their need to control conflict, actors develop rules of behavior which result in a functioning and often effective international system; a system flawed by its inability to prevent violence on all occasions. Conflict comes in many different forms, with peaceful conflict management the rule rather than the exception. Conflict does not occur only between nation-states; it also occurs within nations over the making of foreign policy. The international system is further complicated by the different perspectives actors have of one another. International relations is, indeed, a complicated subject for study.

CHAPTER 2

Actors in the System

Nation-states are the principal actors in the international system, but the complexity of the system is intensified by the large number of nonstate actors. While there has been a substantial increase in the number of nation-states since World War II, the number of nonstate actors has increased even more rapidly. This chapter will trace the development of the nation-state system, characteristics that distinguish a nation-state from a nation or state, and some possible means of classifying nation-states before turning to an examination of nonstate actors.

RISE OF THE NATION–STATE

The nation-state system is a relatively recent development—if viewed in the context of overall diplomatic history. The city states of Greece and Italy were not nation-states; nor was the Roman Empire, Charlemagne's empire, or the Holy Roman Empire. While history labels them states or countries, they did not possess the characteristics that have become associated with the modern nation-state. They lacked, in particular, a sense of nationalism and legal sovereignty that is a part of the present system.

While a precise date of origin is difficult to fix in the development of an ongoing system, the nation-state system had its beginnings somewhere between the middle seventeenth and early eighteenth centuries. The date most commonly presented by historians is 1648, when the Peace of Westphalia was concluded, marking the end of the Thirty Years War. Some historians prefer the Peace of Utrecht in 1713 as being closer to the beginning date. Whichever date is used, the system is about three-hundred years old, a relatively young political system.

The principal early requisite for being a nation-state was that it not be subservient to the rulers of the Holy Roman Empire or to any other political entity. The Peace of Westphalia not only ended a protracted conflict, it also drew the final curtain on the Holy Roman Empire. Before the peace settlement, states in Europe had at least nominal loyalties to a higher authority than their own government. Great Britain was an exception, however, in that it had achieved its independent status by the sixteenth century. Great Britain had a monarch who owed loyalty to no higher authority and who was in control of the territory over which he or she ruled. France probably also had the characteristics of a nation-state before 1648. An important characteristic of the early nation-state system was its limitation to Europe. While there were political systems in other parts of the world, the nation-state system that eventually was dominant throughout the world was originally an exclusively European arrangement.

Some present-day European nations developed the characteristics of a nation-state more slowly than others, but by the mid-eighteenth century the system dominated Europe. The system spread slowly beyond Europe, and many nations, particularly those that achieved independence as a result of the breakup of colonial empires following World War II, did not achieve nation-state status until recently. Thus, the nation-state system developed unevenly, and the process of development is ongoing.

The characteristics of the modern nation-state may be simply stated. First, a reasonably precise portion of territory must exist—not that the boundaries must be drawn exactly, as many wars have been fought over just where those boundaries are, but that a portion of land is generally recognized as making up that nation-state. Second, naturally following the designation of territory, a population of people must be present on that territory. Third, a government controls and rules over that territory and population. Up to this point, these characteristics of a nation-state do not differ particularly from those of political arrangements that preceded the nation-state system. What was new was the development of nationalism and sovereignty.

Nationalism is one of many concepts found in the study of international relations that suffers from too many definitions. One scholar, tracing the multiple meanings of nationalism, found more than two hundred (Snyder, 1954). Many of the definitions do have common qualities, however. Nationalism exists in a country when its population feels that its history, political institutions, and culture are unique; this feeling, in turn, elicits a sense of loyalty to the nation and the political system. The development of this sense of uniqueness and loyalty over time is a product of the political socialization that individuals undergo within a political system.

It is no coincidence that nearly all the people living within the boundaries of a particular nation are loyal to its political system. Each individual, by virtue of growing up in a particular political culture, is socialized into accepting his or her national institutions and system. Each has been taught that nation's version of history and has been instructed on the virtues of that country's political system. If the socialization process is successful, which it usually is, the product will be an individual loyal to the state. Individuals may differ with their leaders over policy questions, but they are, with few exceptions, a part of the national consensus in support of the system as a whole.

This sense of support for the domestic system is essential to the survival of national leaders. While necessary to the maintenance of the system at all times, the support of the people is critical during times of national crisis. If such support is not forthcoming, few governments can survive a crisis, domestic or international. Nationalism was essential for the United States and Great Britain to carry on the war effort during World War II. Questioning the war as to its morality or need was rare in either country. When the Soviet Union was invaded by Germany in 1941, Stalin did not appeal to the Soviet people to defend the communist system but, rather, to defend "Mother Russia." This was clearly an appeal to traditional Russian nationalism, which Stalin apparently felt was a stronger binding force than communist ideology.

Political socialization is not equally successful in all countries. The stability of domestic governments is directly related to the degree of nationalism, that is, consensus in support of the system. It is not uncommon, however, to find in underdeveloped countries an abstract loyalty to the state that does not extend to the political institutions. Where this exists, revolutions and coups d'etat occur with some frequency. Stable political systems must have support both for the political system and the nation-state. Nationalism is thus the psychological basis of the nation-state, and, since nationalism develops in support of a particular nation, it is also what divides the world into many competitive nation-states. Without the support and loyalty of its people, no nation-state could survive.

The term nationalism is used other than as the

basis for domestic consensus, however. In fact, at times it is applied to situations that are directly contradictory to a definition based on support for the state. For example, perhaps the oldest active terrorist group extant is an organization of Armenians that opposes the Turkish government. This opposition seeks retribution for the genocide of Armenians carried out by Turkey during World War I. The activities of this group are described as expressing nationalism although it is directed against a nation-state, not in support of one. Another example includes the activities of the Kurds in Iraq, Iran, and Turkey. As an expression of their Kurdish nationalism, the Kurds have, at one time or another, fought against the governments of all three countries. Their most recent effort to establish a Kurdish state took place during the 1970s when they conducted open warfare against the Iraqi government. In this situation, nationalism is expressed as an attempt to establish a state in opposition to the political system of which the Kurds are nominally a part. The activities of the Basques in Spain and the Croatians in Yugoslavia provide similar examples.

An important aspect of nationalism in any country is the national myth. This myth develops from the history commonly shared by a country's citizens and serves as a means of building national consensus. The important element of any national myth is not whether it is historically accurate, but whether it is commonly accepted. Historians argue that each generation rewrites history, but it is equally important to point out that each nation writes its own history and rewrites it as the need arises. The perception of national heroes may change over time, and their exploits may be exaggerated, but a history of heroes and great victories is a common element in the development of any national myth. In the United States, for example, it is not difficult to find historical inaccuracies in the stories that make up the national myths concerning early leaders such as Washington and Jefferson, but the importance of these stories, accurate or not, is their contribution to national consensus.

In search of a national myth, newly independent nations that are struggling to develop stable political and economic systems often look to a time in their past when they were strong. If, today, Western economies dominate such a nation's economic system, that country may search its history for a time when it was a part of a great civilization and Western nations were no more than tribal societies. The Arab countries point to the Arab empire that stretched across the Middle East, North Africa, and into Spain and to its achievements in science and mathematics that long predated such developments in Europe. A recent occurrence of such behavior among Western countries is exemplified by Great Britain. While still regarded as a major state, the British tend to look to their days of empire when their influence was far greater than it now is.

In addition to a generally accepted history, the national myth also includes a sense of the future, which is usually projected as a time of security and prosperity. What a country lacks today is projected as being attainable in the future. If the country has a sense of being wronged in the past by other countries, then the projection is that these injustices will be corrected. A common past and future, presented as favorably as is credible, contributes to the sense of uniqueness so essential to nationalism.

In brief, then, nationalism is the overall support a population gives to a nation's political system. It is the sense of uniqueness that a people feel about their political system, history, and culture. In turn, nationalism is the psychological underpinning of the nation-state. Political systems existed before the development of nationalism, but the development of nationalism was essential to the development of the modern nation-state.

Often, various other elements are described as being aspects of building national unity, such as a common language, race, religion, or ethnic group. While some or all of these elements are found in many nation-states, many exceptions also exist. Several countries, such as India, Switzerland, Yugoslavia, and the Soviet Union, do not have a common language. Virtually all nations have an official national language, but in practice many nations have several languages, each spoken by sizeable groups, within their borders. India's effort to establish Hindi as its national language has actually been divisive rather than unifying. Many deaths have occurred in India among groups demonstrating to retain their own language rather than adopt Hindi. Some nations, such as Switzerland, have no common national language but are high-consensus nations nevertheless. Canada operates with two official national languages and, although having some problems in the past with demands from the French-speaking community, is a unified nation. The United States, while still predominantly a single-language nation, seems to be approaching becoming bilingual with Spanish as the second language.

A common race or ethnic group as a basis for nationalism also has many exceptions. The heterogeneous makeup of the superpowers, the United States and the Soviet Union, are prime examples. Although neither nation has any serious problem with national unity, as Russians approach becoming a minority within the Soviet Union some such problems may develop.

Much of Africa provides examples of different tribal groupings within a single country. When the European nations colonized Africa, colonies were created without regard to tribal boundaries. When those colonies gained their independence, tribal conflicts were included within the new nation-states. While several African countries have had problems in maintaining national unity due to tribal strife—Nigeria suffered through a civil war when the Ibos attempted to establish their own state—no boundaries among the African states have changed because of tribal demands for independence. Africa is estimated to have some 600 different tribal units included among its fifty-odd nations.

Generally, a common religion is not necessary for national unity, since many nations have successfully unified with several religions active within their boundaries. Some nations, however, utilize religion as the primary basis for unifying

the nation. Both Israel and Iran are theocracies, and the sense of nationalism in those countries is to a great extent based on belief in the national religion. The respective religions of those countries are used as a guide to policy-making as well. Some nations, such as Great Britain, have a national religion with the monarch as the head of the church, but other religions are tolerated, and those citizens who do not participate in the state religion are generally loyal to the government. Language, ethnicity, and religion may contribute to the sense of national unity, but they are not requisites.

The nationalism of nations that received their independence after World War II has been labeled the "new" nationalism. While their form of nationalism does not differ fundamentally from that found in the older, more established nation-states, this nationalism has some qualities that set it apart. This "new" nationalism grew for the most part out of those countries' colonial past. If the nationalism long established in Western Europe brought those countries to Latin America, Africa, and Asia in search of empire, the colonial powers, in turn, created a sense of nationalism in the colonies that made up those empires. This new nationalism called for independence from the colonizing nation and provided a sense of unity that often had not existed earlier. After independence, the new nationalism centered on a particular sense of purpose, that of economic independence from the West combined with political independence. This conflict between the older nationalism of the earlier-established nation-states and the new nationalism is a part of the ongoing struggle found between the industrialized nations and the developing nations.

THE IMPORTANCE OF SOVEREIGNTY

In addition to nationalism, another concept—sovereignty—also developed with the rise of the nation-state system. While sovereignty, both domestic and international, can be described as essentially a legal fiction, it has at its core the concept that the nation-state is authoritatively supreme. Domestically, this means that the government of the nation-state is the highest legal authority in the state; no appeal exists beyond the decision-making process of that state. Internationally, the concept of sovereignty is even more important. The sovereignty of the nation-state is not to be infringed upon by any other nation-state, and other nations are to accept domestic decisions as final and not interfere in internal affairs. Thus, in a legal sense, all nation-states are equal to all others regardless of size and power. Within the practical context of the international system, nations are not, of course, equal. As a reflection of this legal equality, in the General Assembly of the United Nations all nations are granted equal representation. Each nation, regardless of political importance, has one vote (except for the Soviet Union, which, due to a special arrangement, has three votes).

The French Revolution, in the latter part of the eighteenth century, introduced another important element into the nation-state system. During the turmoil of the revolution, the populace of a country for the first time became directly involved in defending the state. Before the revolution, European armies generally were made up of professional soldiers, either indigenous or hired mercenaries. The general population was not called upon to do battle for the state, and wars were usually distant from the common citizen's life. The French Revolution had shown that the people could overthrow a government; thus, when France was attacked by more conservative nations during the Revolutionary Wars in the 1790s, France was saved by the *levee en masse,* the virtually spontaneous development of a citizen army. Wars from that time on were no longer limited to professional and small armies, but included the general populace. This development intensified the sense of nationalism throughout Europe and increased involvement of the populace in aspects of the state other than fighting wars. In turn, the rulers could use this more

intense nationalism to call upon the people to defend and support the state.

Wars fought by professionals produced relatively few casualties compared to the casualties of later wars. As mass involvement of the people increased the size of armies, and as the technological developments of the industrial revolution introduced more destructive weapons, more destructive wars with many more casualties resulted. These developments culminated in the near-total commitment made by the nations involved in the world wars of the twentieth century.

Another result of increased citizen involvement with the state was the development of ideology to rally support for the government. Nationalism, when it includes an ideological commitment, is a powerful element of support for any government. Leading up to and following the Soviet revolution in 1917, Marxism became the rallying cry for left-wing revolutionaries, and, in the post–World War I period, fascism in Italy and National Socialism in Germany became the basis for fervent nationalism in those countries. While Marx intended his ideology to be the basis of an international movement, Stalin utilized the ideology to form national support within the Soviet Union. While not a clearly stated ideology, belief in democracy is an ideology of sorts and certainly serves as support for the political institutions of a democratic state.

Even though a state develops a sense of nationalism and claims national sovereignty, it must meet one additional requirement to be officially a member of the nation-state system. Full membership in the system comes when an unspecified number of states extend diplomatic recognition to the new state; in particular, recognition must include several of the major powers. Recognition of the new state is necessary in order to establish diplomatic contact through the exchange of ambassadors. Without such contact, and without the channels of communication between states that the diplomatic process offers, identity as a nation-state would mean little.

The Soviet Union was hampered in this regard

until 1933 because the United States refused to recognize the Soviet government following the 1917 revolution. The United States also delayed extending recognition to the communist government of China until 1979. While U.S. refusals to recognize communist governments placed some limits on those countries' participation in the international system, it did not prevent Soviet and Chinese diplomatic activity, since many other states recognized the new governments. These attempts to deny access to the diplomatic process were applied to new governments coming to power in old established nation-states and were only partially successful, but in the instance of the homelands that South Africa set up for various tribal groups, the absence of recognition by the rest of the nation-state system effectively prevented those new "nations" from participating in the international system both as new states and as new governments.

One distinction should be made at this point. Recognition can be given to either a new state or to a new government. In the instance of both China and the Soviet Union, the refusal to recognize applied to only the new governments, since the United States had long recognized the existence of the states of Russia and China. Both forms of recognition are prerequisites to the establishment of diplomatic relations, however.

While any two nations must diplomatically recognize one another before they have official contact, nations frequently develop other means of contact when such recognition is missing. The United States communicated with the Chinese communist government for years through their respective ambassadors to Poland. Technically, that contact was through the British ambassador to Poland since Great Britain recognized both the U.S. government and the Chinese communist government. The United States does not recognize the Castro government, but the U.S. maintains an American interests office in Havana, nevertheless. Thus, nations do establish contact by extraordinary methods when there is a need to do so.

With the advent of universal organizations, first the League of Nations and then the United Nations, membership in one of those organizations largely has replaced the piecemeal, nation-by-nation recognition of the past. Today, becoming a member of the United Nations is the equivalent of full membership in the nation-state system. Even though all UN members may not have bilateral relations with the new state, the number of votes necessary to become a member of the United Nations (two-thirds of the nations voting) is sufficient to gain acceptance as a part of the nation-state system.

IMPACT OF WORLD WAR II ON THE NATION-STATE SYSTEM

On the the eve of World War II, the world was divided into approximately sixty nation-states. Much of the remaining territory in the world was controlled by the Western European colonizing nations, with limited empires held by the United States and Japan. What territories remained were mandates of the League of Nations. The world thus was made up primarily of either nation-states or colonies of those nation-states. The war and its aftermath brought about a profound and significant change in this arrangement.

While World War I brought an end to the German and Turkish empires, it did not increase the number of nation-states. The colonies lost by the defeated nations were transferred to Great Britain, France, Japan, and Belgium; while designated mandates, they were administered much as if they were still colonies. World War II was fought far more extensively in the colonies than was World War I. In Asia, Japan occupied most of the British, French, and Dutch colonies. While not occupied, India was promised its independence after the war if it would resist Japanese invasion. British and French control over their empires in Africa was also weakened by the defeat of France in 1940 and early Axis victories in some British colonies. The myth of the colonial powers' invincibility as colonial masters was shattered, though the Axis nations were eventually defeated.

After the war, a process of decolonization began that has been nearly completed in the 1980s. The process began in the Middle East at the end of the war when Lebanon, Syria, and Jordan, former League mandates administered by either Great Britain or France, gained their independence. Israel became an independent Jewish state in 1948, occupying a part of the former British mandate of Palestine. The first colony to achieve independence in Asia outside the Middle East was the Philippines, which the United States granted independence in 1946, thus fulfilling a promise made in 1936. In 1947, Great Britain carried out its wartime promise and granted India its independence. Following India's independence, decolonization in Asia moved rapidly. Within a year, Pakistan, Ceylon (now Sri Lanka), and Burma were independent. The Dutch were unable to reestablish control over the Dutch East Indies, and the result was an independent Indonesia. Laos and Cambodia become independent in 1951. In 1957, Malaya (now Malaysia) and Singapore obtained their independence from the British. The territory in Asia to wait longest for independence was Vietnam. In 1954, the French withdrew from Vietnam with the territory divided into a communist north and an anti-communist south. The United States replaced the French effort, and after U.S. withdrawal in 1973 and the collapse of the South Vietnamese government in 1975, the country was placed under a single government.

In Africa the movement for independence moved more slowly. At the end of World War II, only four African nations were independent— Liberia, Egypt, Ethiopia, and the Union of South Africa. In 1951 Libya was granted independence by the United Nations, in frustration over lack of another acceptable alternative for the disposition of this former Italian colony. The main surge toward African independence began in

1956 with the independence of Sudan, followed by that of Tunisia, Morocco, and the Gold Coast (now Ghana). In 1958 France attempted to establish the French Community among its African colonies similar to the British Commonwealth. Guinea did not join and was given its independence. In 1960 the French Community broke up, with more than a dozen former French colonies receiving their independence. Also in 1960 the British granted independence to Nigeria, and the Belgians gave the Congo (now Zaire) its independence. The further breakup of the French and British African empires plus those of Belgium, Portugal, and Spain continued over the next fifteen years. By the 1980s most of Africa had obtained its independence; forty-seven new nation-states had been formed from the European-controlled colonies. Namibia was the only remaining area whose political future remained undecided. Today Africa includes nearly one-third of the world's independent nations.

Most of Latin America had been independent since the nineteenth century. The remaining colonies, mainly islands in the Caribbean, achieved their independence during the 1960s and 1970s. Decolonization in Latin America, Asia, and Africa probably would have occurred without the influence of events during World War II, but that war no doubt hastened the process.

In the forty years since the end of World War II, nearly one hundred new nations have been added to the international system. The original membership of the United Nations, 49 nations (51 votes due to the two additional votes for the Soviet Union), increased to a total of 157 nations (159 votes). The expansion of the nation-state system to nearly three times the number of countries independent in 1945 not only reflects a dramatic extension of the system into parts of the world where it hardly existed before; it also indicates an important change in the kinds of issues dealt with in the system. Economic questions, particularly those related to the problems of development of underdeveloped economies, have become major international issues in the United Nations and other forums where Third World countries can speak out. The breakup of the colonial empires resulted not only in the expansion of the nation-state system, but in different kinds of issues in conflict within the system.

The increase in the number of new nation-states does raise the question of why the breakup of empires resulted in so many new nation-states and why the colonial powers did not control and consolidate the movement more effectively than they did. The reason for this failure is that the colonizing nations not only did not prepare their colonies for independence, they did not intend to grant them independence. Consequently, the road to independence for a number of the colonies came only after violence and warfare. Even where there was little or no violence, independence came only after long-term pressure on the colonizers. The colonial nations did not so much guide their colonies to independence as agree to grant it when the political or military costs were too great to prevent it. The new nation-states retained in all but a few instances the boundaries of the former colony; thus, the nation-states that emerged from the empires were nearly as numerous as were the colonies. Little or no effort was made to consolidate the colonies into larger political units.

In western Africa, first the Portuguese and then later the British and French had landed on the coast and moved inland. The coastline alternated between British and French colonies after the Portuguese were largely forced out of west Africa. Colonial boundaries were established at the convenience of the colonizers rather than along the lines of traditional tribal territories. To attempt to readjust the boundaries along more rational political lines after independence would have been a task beyond the political capabilities of the new nations. The political fragmentation of Africa by the colonial powers thus carried over into the era of the new nation-states.

A number of attempts were made by the new nations to unite into larger political entities, attempts which failed, except for the combination of Tanganyika and Zanzibar into the single state of Tanzania. Singapore and Malaysia began as separate states, then united, but later split into two states again. Among the former French colonies in Africa, several attempts were made to create larger political units, but all failed. For a brief period from 1957 to 1961, Syria and Egypt attempted a political union which ultimately was dissolved.

The division of former colonies into additional political units has occurred, however; of these India is the most significant example. At the time of independence, colonial India was split into a Moslem state, Pakistan, and a Hindu state, India. In 1971, what was then the eastern portion of Pakistan split off and became the new state of Bangladesh. Rather than to consolidate into fewer states, the pattern has been to retain the old colonial boundaries or to split into more states, thus contributing to an even larger number of new nation-states.

An example of the impact expansion of the nation-state system has had is found in the United Nations. In the first session of the General Assembly in 1946, of the fifty-one votes twenty were from Latin America, five from the British Commonwealth, and about twelve from Western European nations. The Latin American nations were in virtually unanimous support of the United States; thus, the U.S. and its Western supporters controlled more than two-thirds of the votes necessary to carry a vote in the General Assembly. By the 1980s, political alignments in the General Assembly had changed to the point that the Western coalition no longer controlled a two-thirds majority; in fact, it could not muster one-third of the votes to stop a resolution. Many Latin American countries now supported arguments coming from other Third World nations, and most of the newly independent nations voted contrary to positions taken by Western nations. In addition to this development, the new majority preferred discussing its own economic problems with the industrialized nations, rather than the Cold War issues that had dominated the agenda of the United Nations up to the 1960s. The United Nations had changed both in size and in the questions discussed.

Conflicts between industrial nations and the Third World are by no means confined to the United Nations. The charge is often made by Third World nations that the former colonies continue to suffer from economic exploitation carried over from their colonial past. The Western industrial nations, including those which had small or no empires, are accused of practicing economic policies similar to those adhered to during the colonial era. The Cold War issues that once dominated the international political scene now share the world's attention with the economic problems of the Third World.

THE LABELING PROBLEM

Up to this point, nations have been classified as either economically developed or underdeveloped, with the latter group labeled as the Third World. More precise categorization is called for to better understand the present structure of the nation-state system.

While the label "Third World" is commonly used to describe all nations that are not economically advanced, the origins of the term are not economic but relate to earlier political alignments in the Cold War. During the 1950s and early 1960s, when East-West tensions peaked, the major issues on the world scene, as viewed by both Western and communist coalitions, were conflicts between those coalitions. In the West, the First World consisted of the industrialized, anticommunist nations; the Second World was the Soviet-led coalition; and the Third World constituted nations that were not aligned with either of the other two worlds. At that time, few nations were not aligned. When Cold War issues dominated international politics, the three categories of nations seemed appropriate.

As the number of newly independent nations grew, most took a position of nonalignment on Cold War issues. India under Nehru took the lead in proclaiming a neutral foreign policy that avoided alignment with either superpower. In the 1960s, within the United Nations this group of nonaligned nations was called the "Group of 77." This group still carries that label, but now has more than 120 members.

Though commonly used, the three-worlds means of classifying nations has two major shortcomings. First is the implication that these are three united coalitions, each with a solid basis of unity. The Western coalition has at its organizational military center the North Atlantic Treaty Organization (NATO, sixteen members), and the Organization of Economic Cooperation and Development (OECD, twenty-four members) and the General Agreement on Tariffs and Trade (GATT) its economic center; but all three organizations have had their internal problems. The European Community is also important to the economic organization of the Western coalition but its membership is more restricted (twelve members) than is that of OECD or GATT. The Soviet coalition also has its problems of maintaining unity. Opposition to Moscow's leadership— the most recent example is Poland in 1980 and 1981—indicate differences within the Soviet-led coalition.

The Third World is even less united than either of the other two worlds. Even if the Third World label is used only to describe that coalition's position on conflicts between East and West, there is considerable division among its members. Some members have close arrangements with one of the superpowers. Cuba is a member of the nonaligned group but depends on the Soviet Union for its military and economic well-being. India has a friendship treaty with the Soviet Union but receives economic aid from several Western countries as well. Countries such as Oman and Somalia have military arrangements with the United States. Angola and Ethiopia have Soviet and Cuban troops within their borders to maintain governments in power that are sympathetic to the Soviet Union. Many non-aligned countries in the Third World buy military equipment from either the West or the communist countries and, in some instances, from both sources. Others maintain small military establishments but receive economic assistance from whoever will provide it. Overall, nonalignment carries different meanings among the Third World countries; thus, those countries are divided as to policy toward the Western and communist coalitions. The nonaligned nations hold a conference on a three-year cycle, and unfailingly quarrel over policy toward the Western and communist coalitions.

The second problem in using the three-worlds classification is that, although its origin came from the position nation-states took on Cold War issues, it is now most commonly used to describe levels of economic development. Within this usage, the First World is the industrialized West, including Western Europe, the United States, Canada, and Japan, plus Australia and New Zealand. The Second World is, again, the economically advanced communist bloc nations. The Third World includes the economically less-developed nations and encompasses most of the nonaligned nations as well as underdeveloped nations that have alignments with the West, such as the Philippines, Thailand, and South Korea, and those Latin American countries that are signatories of the Rio Pact, a mutual defense arrangement with the United States.

An economics-based category of Third World nations includes such a variety of levels of development that it is often meaningless. Nations that are on the threshold of being economically developed, such as Brazil, Argentina, South Korea, and Taiwan, are sufficiently advanced economically that they are now often referred to as Newly Industrialized Countries (NICs). Other nations of the Third World, such as some OPEC members, have such a large income from oil that even though they have limited economic development they are not poor nations. Then there are nations that have some natural resource other than oil upon which the industrialized nations are heavily dependent. Their fortunes fluctuate with the market for their product in the industrial nations. Still another category includes nations that have a stable economy but little industry. Lastly, another group of Third World nations consists of those that are very poor, with little prospect of improving their lot without massive aid from the industrial nations. Thus, the Third World can be subdivided into several categories, or additional worlds. Under most circumstances, the Third World label for all underdeveloped nations is simply too general.

The World Bank meets the problem of categorizing nations by using six classifications based on income—1) low-income economies (about 50 countries), 2) middle-income economies, oil importers (about 40 countries), 3) middle-income economies, oil exporters (about 15 countries), 4) high-income economies, oil exporters (about 6 countries), 5) industrial market economies, (about 20 countries), and 6) centrally planned or nonmarket economies (about 10 nations). The first four World Bank classifications would be included in what is commonly referred to as the Third World. The fifth group would be the industrial West, and the sixth the communist coalition.

The Western world, with about twenty members, can also be subdivided by labeling the most economically advanced nations as post-industrial societies. These are nations that have advanced beyond the original industrial revolution into a new phase of industrialization. This stage of development includes advanced information processing, the presence of a broad-based technical and professional class, the extensive use of robotics and advanced technology to design and manufacture products, and a generally more service-oriented society. Only a few nations fit this category—Japan, the United States, and two or three Western European nations.

Numerous other means of classifying nations can be utilized. One is to rank nations as to population. This would place China first, followed by India, the Soviet Union, and the United States

Tab. 2.1 Ranking of Top 20 Nations in Population and Land Area

	Top 20 in Population (in millions)			Top 20 in Area (in 1,000 sq. mi.)	
1.	China	1,043	1.	USSR	8,650
2.	India	768	2.	Canada	3,850
3.	USSR	278	3.	China	3,696
4.	USA	239	4.	USA	3,623
5.	Indonesia	168	5.	Brazil	3,287
6.	Brazil	136	6.	Australia	2,966
7.	Japan	121	7.	India	1,183
8.	Pakistan	100	8.	Argentina	1,073
9.	Bangladesh	97	9.	Sudan	967
10.	Nigeria	96	10.	Algeria	919
11.	Mexico	78	11.	Zaire	905
12.	West Germany	61	12.	Saudi Arabia	865
13.	Vietnam	60	13.	Greenland	840
14.	Italy	57	14.	Mexico	756
15.	United Kingdom	57	15.	Indonesia	741
16.	France	55	16.	Libya	686
17.	Philippines	55	17.	Iran	636
18.	Thailand	51	18.	Mongolia	604
19.	Turkey	49	19.	Peru	496
20.	Egypt	49	20.	Chad	496

down to the least-populated nations such as the Maldives, Principe and Sao Tome, Dominica, Seychelles, and Liechtenstein. Nations can also be ranked according to their gross national product with the United States at the top, followed by the Soviet Union, Japan, West Germany, and France, and a large group of nations at the bottom with GNPs that are only a small fraction of those of the most productive nations. Another common ranking is based upon nations' per capita incomes. Using per capita income as the basis of classification, among the top nations is Kuwait and other oil exporting Persian Gulf states, as well as the advanced industrialized nations.

Each of the classification systems noted thus far has been based on a single variable; this presents problems since the rankings come out differently depending on which variable is used. A more complex system would be to use several variables such as the classification of nations

done by James Rosenau (Rosenau, 1966, 27-92). In an attempt to analyze nations' behavior on the basis of their respective characteristics, Rosenau employed three sets of variables: large-small in size, developed-underdeveloped economically, and open-closed political systems. This method provides eight possible categories. The United States is a large, developed, and open system and, depending on the differentiation between "large" and "small," perhaps such countries as West Germany, Great Britain, and France. Certainly, Canada and Australia would be examples if size is based on land area. If population is the index for size, this category would also include Japan. A large, underdeveloped, and open system would be India. With the recent reintroduction of democracy in Brazil it too would fit this second category, although Brazil might be included in the large, developed, and open category, depending on how one considers the level of Brazil's economic development. The Soviet Union would

Fig. 2.1 World Bank Economic Groupings

Key

Low-income economies

Middle-income oil importers

Middle-income oil exporters

High-income oil exporters

Industrial market economies

East European nonmarket economies

Not included in indicators

SOURCE: Christian Science Monitor
July 3, 1985, p.3.

World economic groupings

Map shows country groups on the basis of gross national product per capita and, in some cases, distinguishing economic characteristics.

Tab. 2.2 Rosenau Classification of Nations

Large-Open-Developed	Large-Closed-Developed
USA, United Kingdom, France, West Germany, Japan, Italy, and Spain	USSR, South Africa
Large-Open-Underdeveloped	Large-Closed-Underdeveloped
India, Brazil, Argentina, and Mexico	Bangladesh, China, Indonesia, Ethiopia, South Korea, Iran, Pakistan, Nigeria, and others
Small-Open-Developed	Small-Closed-Developed
Canada, Belgium, Denmark, Israel, The Netherlands, New Zealand, Sweden, Switzerland, and others	Bulgaria, Czechoslovakia, East Germany, Hungary, Poland, Saudi Arabia, Yugoslavia, and others
Small-Open-Underdeveloped	Small-Closed-Underdeveloped
Botswana, Colombia, Costa Rica, Ecuador, Jamaica, Peru, and others	Albania, Angola, Chad, Chile, Cuba, Guatemala, Iraq, North Korea, Morocco, Mozambique, Senegal, and others

be the prime example of a large, developed, and closed nation. Large, underdeveloped, and closed nations would include China, Indonesia, and Pakistan.

The small, developed, and open category would certainly include the Netherlands, Denmark, Austria, and Sweden. Except for New Zealand, probably no examples in this category would be found outside Western Europe and Scandinavia. Examples of small, developed, and closed nations would include Eastern European nations such as East Germany, Czechoslovakia, Hungary and, perhaps, South Korea. The small, underdeveloped, and open assessment would include such countries as Costa Rica, Jamaica, and Ivory Coast. Open political systems have been reintroduced in several Latin American countries such as Uruguay and Peru, and if their democratically chosen governments can remain

in power, they too would fit into this category.

The largest single category would be the small, underdeveloped, and closed nations. Dozens of examples exist here, including most of the African states, several in Latin America, such as Chile, Paraguay, Bolivia, and Nicaragua, and such Asian nations as Burma and Thailand.

A number of nations do not fit conveniently into any of the suggested categories, but this classification process does have the advantage of providing a broader base than do most means of categorizing nations. While Rosenau used these categories to predict how nations in each category would behave, they are also useful for viewing the nation-state system in general.

NONSTATE ACTORS IN THE INTERNATIONAL SYSTEM

While the nation-state system has expanded from a few European nations in the seventeenth century until, presently, virtually the entire world is divided into nation-states, an even higher rate of growth has occurred among nonstate actors. Nonstate actors exist in several forms; one category is international organizations, including such well-known intergovernmental organizations (IGOs) as the United Nations and the North Atlantic Treaty Organization, which are made up of nation-states, and nongovernmental organizations (NGOs) such as Amnesty International and the International Red Cross, which are composed of groups having no direct connection with national governments. The rise in the number of both IGOs and NGOs is explained by increased contact resulting from improved communications and a growing recognition that many problems can best be dealt with at the international level.

Another type of NGO exists as well—terrorist groups and liberation organizations. Finding even an approximate number for such actors is difficult; many such groups exist in name only and carry on little or no overt action. Others, such as the Palestinian Liberation Organization (PLO) have gained wide-spread international recognition as reflected in the UN's acceptance of the PLO as an official observer. While an estimate of active groups in this category of nonstate actors is difficult to make, an increase in the post–World War II period is unquestioned. The rise can be attributed to various groups of people who feel they have been deprived of their native land, excluded from the benefits of economic or political change, or wish to replace the government of a country. Multinational corporations (MNCs) must also be included as nonstate actors. The increase in economic interdependence among industrial nations and opportunities for investment in Third World nations has contributed heavily to the increased activity of MNCs.

IGOs AS ACTORS

Though the membership of IGOs is made up of nation-states, international organizations do not have the characteristics of a nation-state, and thus are nonstate actors. With few exceptions, representation in these organizations is based on the one-nation, one-vote concept of sovereign equality.

The broadest-based IGOs, both in membership and purpose, are the United Nations and its predecessor, the League of Nations. Each of these IGOs attempted to provide membership to virtually any nation which applied, though the United Nations had major membership problems during its early years when membership became a Cold War issue. Virtually any issue that is international in scope can and does come before the United Nations today. Although functioning under a broad agenda, the effectiveness of this IGO in resolving conflicts has been limited.

No broad-based or universal-membership IGOs existed until after World War I. In fact, few IGOs, regardless of their scope of purpose, existed

before the twentieth century. IGOs did not fit into the nation-state system until it was recognized by the European nations, following the Napoleonic period, that some issues could best be handled through a structured international arrangement. The Central Commission for the Navigation of the Rhine is credited with being the first IGO in the modern nation-state system. Its scope clearly was limited, as was true of all international organizations until the League of Nations, but it was a beginning. It, like every IGO since, had an international purpose, but was restricted from taking any action that infringed on national sovereignty. IGOs grew to a total of about fifty before World War I, largely as a result of needs brought about by the industrial revolution, which increased contact between nations. Between the world wars, the number of IGOs grew to nearly eighty. By the 1980s, nearly 350 IGOs were functioning. (Jacobson, 1979). All but the UN and League are limited in either membership or agenda.

Examples of specific-functioned IGOs with near-universal membership are the specialized agencies that are a part of the United Nations system, about a dozen in number. The oldest of these, the International Telecommunications

Tab. 2.3 IGOs by Purpose and Membership

		Nature of Purpose	
		General	*Specific*
Scope of Membership	*Global*	United Nations League of Nations	UNESCO World Health Organization Universal Postal Union
	Limited	Association of Southeast Asian Nations Organization of American States Organization of African Unity	NATO OECD OPEC Tin Council European Communities

Union (originally the International Telegraphic Union) was created in the late 1860s. The Universal Postal Union was developed later in the nineteenth century. Some, such as the International Labor Organization, came into existence under the League in the 1920s, but most of the specialized agencies had their start under the United Nations after World War II. The pattern of development of these IGOs is typical of the development of IGOs in general. They were created to handle specific problems such as international telecommunication, mail between countries, international labor problems, health issues (World Health Organization), maritime issues (Inter-Governmental Maritime Consultative Organization), international air travel (International Civil Aviation Organization), or international financial problems (International Bank for Reconstruction and Development, or as better known, the World Bank, and the International Monetary Fund). While limited in function, these IGOs often have nearly as many members as does the United Nations.

MILITARY AND ECONOMIC IGOs

While all nations do not belong to the United Nations or the specialized agencies associated with it, those organizations are essentially open to any nation-state that chooses to join. Other IGOs are more restricted in their membership and have either geographic regional qualifications or certain political standards for membership.

The best known of the military IGOs are NATO and the Warsaw Pact. These counterbalancing organizations have both regional and political qualifications for membership. NATO is theoretically made up of nations touching on the North Atlantic Ocean, but the basis for membership is more political than geographic. In existence since 1949, when the original membership was twelve, now sixteen, NATO includes those nations which have a major interest in Europe's security and which consider the Soviet Union to be a military threat. The Warsaw Pact, in existence since 1956, is the opposing military alliance whose members argue that it is needed because of the threat from NATO. It is made up of the Soviet Union and the Eastern European communist nations. (More on these alliances in chapter five.)

Organizations based on an effort to attain regional economic cooperation have sprung up almost exclusively since World War II. While not always successful, these actors play an important role in the international system. The most ambitious effort, and the most successful, is the European Community (EC). Begun in 1958 with six members, now twelve, this group of European democratic states has as its objective the integration of their twelve domestic economies. The EC has experienced problems, but overall is regarded as having come a long way toward achieving its economic objectives.

Eastern Europe also has an economic IGO. The Council for Mutual Economic Assistance (CEMA) or COMECON, is made up of the communist states of Europe, plus Mongolia, Cuba, and Vietnam. Several other nations have observer status with COMECON. A complaint occasionally voiced by members of COMECON is that the Soviet Union dominates the organization and uses it to control the economies of the other members.

Among the organizations of the underdeveloped nations created to achieve economic cooperation is the Association of Southeast Asian Nations (ASEAN). With six members from the region, the organization has achieved some economic integration, particularly in the area of tariffs. Other efforts among the underdeveloped nations to establish regional economic cooperation have been less successful. The Central American Common Market collapsed as a result of conflicts among its members, particularly between El Salvador and Honduras. The common market between Kenya, Uganda, and Tanzania suffered a similar fate due to the activities of Idi Amin while he was in power in Uganda.

Broader-purposed regional organizations such

as the Organization of American States (OAS) and the Organization of African Unity (OAU) continue to exist, in part, by avoiding the issues that might split the organizations. The OAS, established in 1949, is made up of all but a few nations in the Western Hemisphere. The organization has not been an economic success, but has had some diplomatic victories, especially in its earlier years. Latin America also established the Latin American Free Trade Association (LAFTA), but it has largely been ineffective. The OAU is composed of all African states except the Republic of South Africa and is dedicated to the abolition of colonialism in Africa. It considers apartheid in South Africa and South Africa's activities in Namibia as a part of that problem. On colonial issues, the organization has experienced unity and success. On the matter of disputes among the member states of the OAU, the organization has been ineffective.

NGOs AS ACTORS

NGOs are organizations based on nongovernmental groups that cross national boundaries and have grown in number in a pattern similar to that of IGOs. At the beginning of World War I, about 170 NGOs existed. By World War II, the number had grown to nearly 500, and by the late 1970s there were 2500 NGOs. The extensive growth of such organizations can be attributed to an increasing awareness that many areas of international cooperation can exist without involving the governments of nation-states. NGOs are mostly narrow in scope, and many have political purposes, though their membership does not represent governments.

One of the best known politically active NGOs is Amnesty International. Dedicated to the protection of human rights in general and the release of political prisoners in particular, the organization has gained considerable public attention as well as objections from governments that are its targets. Another well-known NGO is the International Olympic Committee (IOC). While not outwardly considered to be political, this NGO has nevertheless been the center of several international controversies. One of the IOC's decisions was allowing Taiwan to send teams to the Olympics, with the result that mainland China refused to participate. China returned to the games in 1984 after Taiwan was no longer allowed to represent China. During the 1976 games, several African countries boycotted the Olympics because New Zealand was allowed to attend. New Zealand had sports affiliations with the Republic of South Africa, and the African countries wanted a complete sports boycott of South Africa because of its policy of apartheid. In 1980, the United States boycotted the Olympics in Moscow to protest the Soviet invasion of Afghanistan. To retaliate, the Soviets refused to attend the games in Los Angeles in 1984. In the midst of these controversies was the IOC, an NGO that intended to be nonpolitical. Among other well-known NGOs are the International Red Cross, the Salvation Army, and the International Chamber of Commerce.

While the NGOs mentioned above are generally well known, most NGOs receive little public attention. The purposes of these organizations cover a wide range of subjects. Virtually every profession and academic discipline has an international association. Each major religion and nearly all denominations have an NGO. In industry, every product manufactured or type of industry seems to have an international organization. In the arts and literature, there are a number of NGOs. Health, science, education, and medicine have over 600 NGOs alone. Virtually every sport has an NGO as do each of the trade unions. In all, the combined purposes of the NGOs cover nearly every facet of the economy, social concerns, communication, educational endeavors, art, sports, health, and industry. The collective efforts of NGOs indicate a vast network of nongovernmental international cooperation and interdependence.

MULTINATIONAL CORPORATIONS AS ACTORS

As is the case with all international actors discussed so far, multinational corporations (MNCs) were an influence in the international system before World War II, but greatly expanded their activities after the war. This expanded influence is due both to increased economic interdependence among Western industrial nations and extended opportunities for investment in the Third World. The influence exerted by MNCs is most commonly associated with the Third World, but MNCs, in fact, not only originate in Western industrial nations, they are most active there as well.

A standard means of illustrating the influence of the MNCs is to compare the economic capabilities of nation-states with those of major MNCs. By ranking the top 100 nations and MNCs—the nations on the basis of their gross national product and the MNCs on the basis of their annual product or sales—a reasonably comparable analysis can be made. Several such lists have been compiled during the last twenty years with varying results, but certain patterns appear. The first twenty-some units listed are nation-states. At the top is the United States, followed by the Soviet Union, Japan, West Germany, and China. This top group includes a number of other European countries plus Canada, Brazil, Mexico, India, Argentina, Australia, and Saudi Arabia. The first MNC does not appear until approximately the second quartile. For a number of years, the first MNC listed was General Motors, but after the price of oil rose the top MNC became Exxon. When oil prices fell, General Motors was back as the top MNC. In the top fifty units on most lists, only about eight MNCs appear, including other major oil corporations such as Royal Dutch Shell, Mobil, Texaco, British Petroleum, and Standard Oil of California, plus the automotive corporations, General Motors and Ford. As the list

progresses, a higher percentage of MNCs appears in the bottom fifty. Overall, such lists include about forty MNCs and sixty nations. While the largest MNCs are American, in the overall listing only about forty percent are American-owned corporations. The remaining major MNCs are Western European and Japanese.

The listing of nations and MNCs in this manner makes some important points about actors in the international system, perhaps the most significant being that a substantial number of MNCs have an economic impact that is greater than that of all but the most industrialized states. In addition, many of the MNCs have the economic capacity to challenge policies of the less-developed states. The MNCs can, but do not necessarily, function as if creating their own foreign policy. Though each of the MNCs has a national home based on the location of its corporate headquarters, each, through its operations abroad, has considerable influence independent of its corporate national ties. It should also be pointed out, however, that any particular MNC spreads its economic influence over a number of countries, thus reducing the influence it has in any one country.

The top 430 MNCs have a collective international impact approaching $2 trillion a year, which ranks somewhere between the GNPs of the United States and the Soviet Union. Each of an estimated ninety nations has a smaller gross national product than the annual sales of any one of the top forty MNCs. MNCs approach controlling ten percent of the world's economic production (Papp, 1984, 60).

In the West, MNCs are viewed as an important means of assisting the Third World develop economically through the investments they make, the employment they provide, the technology they transmit, the marketing expertise they bring, and the income they generate. Third World countries, while accepting the presence of MNCs, generally fear that MNCs' awesome economic strength will infringe on their political independence and control over their own eco-

Tab. 2.4 Top 100 National GNPs and MNC Sales (1984 Figures)

Country or MNC	GNP or Annual Sales (in $ billions)	Country or MNC	GNP or Annual Sales (in $ billions)
1. USA	3,670	51. Pakistan	35
2. USSR	1,925	52. Philippines	35
3. Japan	1,248	53. Hong Kong	34
4. West Germany	679	54. AT&T (USA)	33
5. France	543	55. Egypt	33
6. United Kingdom	481	56. Iraq	31
7. Italy	367	57. Malaysia	30
8. Canada	331	58. Libya	30
9. China	318	59. United Arab Emirates	29
10. Brazil	227	60. General Electric (USA)	28
11. India	197	61. Kuwait	28
12. Australia	185	62. Standard Oil (Ind.) (USA)	27
13. Spain	172	63. Chevron (USA)	27
14. Iran	159	64. ENI (Italy)	26
15. Mexico	158	65. Bulgaria	25
16. Poland	143	66. Atlantic Richfield (USA)	25
17. The Netherlands	136	67. Toyota Motor (Japan)	24
18. Saudi Arabia	116	68. New Zealand	24
19. Switzerland	105	69. IRI (Italy)	23
20. Sweden	99	70. Unilever (UK/Netherlands)	22
21. East Germany	94	71. Israel	21
22. Exxon (USA)	91	72. Shell (USA)	21
23. Royal Dutch Shell (UK/Netherlands)	85	73. Elf-Aquitaine (France)	21
24. Indonesia	85	74. Chile	20
25. South Korea	85	75. Portugal	20
26. Czechoslovakia	84	76. Matsushita Elect. (Japan)	20
27. General Motors (USA)	84	77. Chrysler (USA)	20
28. Belgium	83	78. Pemex (Mexico)	19
29. Nigeria	74	79. Hitachi (Japan)	19
30. South Africa	74	80. Syria	19
31. Austria	69	81. Singapore	18
32. Argentina	67	82. Hungary	18
33. Turkey	58	83. U.S. Steel (USA)	18
34. Denmark	58	84. Francaise des Petroles (France)	18
35. Taiwan	58	85. Philips (Netherlands)	18
36. Venezuela	57	86. Nissan (Japan)	18
37. Norway	57	87. Peru	18
38. Mobil (USA)	56	88. Ireland	18
39. Finland	53	89. Petrobas (Brazil)	17
40. Ford (USA)	52	90. Sieman (West Germany)	17
41. British Petroleum (UK)	51	91. United Technology (USA)	16
42. Algeria	51	92. Cuba	16
43. Texaco (USA)	47	93. Volkswagenwerk (West Germany)	16
44. IBM (USA)	46	94. Phillips Petroleum (USA)	16
45. Romania	46	95. Occidental Petroleum (USA)	16
46. Thailand	43	96. Daimler-Benz (West Germany)	15
47. Yugoslavia	39	97. Bayer (West Germany)	15
48. Colombia	38	98. North Korea	15
49. Greece	37	99. Kuwait Petroleum (Kuwait)	15
50. DuPont (USA)	36	100. Nippon Oil (Japan)	15

SOURCE: *Fortune* and *Britannica Book of the Year 1987.*

nomies. They are concerned that MNCs' profits will not be used as additional investment capital in the Third World, but, rather, will go to the further advancement of Western economies. They also see MNCs as a means of exploitation of their raw materials to the benefit of the industrial nations. They view the technology received as inappropriate to their level of development, therefore of little help to their economies. They fear that foreign MNCs will inhibit the development of indigenous industries, will create unfair competition within the labor force, and what benefits they receive domestically will go to those persons who are already rich.

There is probably no nation in the world in which there are not several MNCs operating. Even the communist nations, in which the corporate structure as it is known in the West does not exist, have subsidiaries of Western MNCs. The MNCs have truly become major actors in the international system. The single most important problem that MNCs present within the international system is how they are controlled and by whom.

CONCLUSION

The foregoing discussion of actors has made a number of points about the changing nature of the international system. The most obvious observation, regardless of the category of actor, is the increase in numbers. In every category, increases were gradual before World War II, with substantial increases in numbers since the war. Another recurring theme is the increased importance of economic matters among the actors. Increased economic dependence and interdependence have provided considerable change in the system, also primarily since World War II. The increased role of MNCs further contributes to this development. Coupled with this is the rise of economic-development issues as the nation-state system expanded into the economically underdeveloped colonial areas of the world.

Nation-states continue to be the central actors of the international system, although several patterns of economic and political development exist among them. Even though IGOs have increased in numbers and influence since World War II, their ability to resolve conflict has not. NGOs present extensive international activity, and although often successful in their endeavors, have limited impact on conflict management among the nation-states.

One additional observation that has not been mentioned but that is appropriate to a discussion of changes in the international system is the reduction in the number of major states. While later discussions will trace the reasons for and impact of this change, it is worth noting that the present system has two superpowers, the United States and the Soviet Union, with a number of industrialized states labeled as major states which, however, do not compare to the superpowers in overall impact on the system. Before World War II, France, Great Britain, Italy, Germany, and Japan were all included among the major powers, and the international system did not include any nations that could be regarded as superpowers. The system of the post–World War II period does have major powers distinct from superpowers.

CHAPTER 3

Power and the Nation–State

The two previous chapters described the nature of conflict among actors in the international system and identified who those actors are. Concepts that help explain behavior among those actors is the next topic for discussion and is based on the assumption that a nation's success in fulfilling its policy goals is determined by its characteristics, both physical and political, relative to the characteristics of other nations. Collectively, those characteristics make up a nation's power which, in turn, serves as a unit of exchange between nations in fulfilling their demands.

A nation's foreign policy objective is not to obtain power as such, although the terminology used in the study of international politics often suggests that is so in phrases such as "struggle for power" or "power politics." Actually, nations seek power in order to translate that elusive commodity into whatever level of interest fulfillment they can achieve. Thus, when a nation is described as being more powerful than it once was, or as seeking greater power, such phrases are an abbreviated means of stating that that nation is or hopes to become better able to fulfill its interests. In this sense, power is to international politics what money is to the economic system. As with money, power is not in itself important, but its importance lies in how it is used and what it will obtain.

An analogy between money and power has limitations. Power is not as easily converted to interest fulfillment as is money, and, because power is the product of various national attributes, it is more difficult to measure than money. National goals carry no price tags to indicate how much power must be expended to achieve these goals, and, thus, they can be fulfilled only through bargaining among nations utilizing their relative conditions of power.

PROBLEMS OF DEFINING POWER

As was pointed out earlier in regard to the meaning of nationalism, power also suffers from too many definitions. Again, as in the many meanings of nationalism, the numerous efforts to define power contain common qualities. Nearly all definitions speak of power as the ability of a nation to bring about changes to its advantage relative to other nations. Karl Deutsch's definition of power is an appropriate illustration. "Power consists in accepting the least amount of nonautonomous change in one system while producing the largest amount of nonautonomous change in another" (Deutsch, 1953, 47). The principal problem encountered in using a measure of power to explain international behavior is that perceptions about what power is and how to measure it are vague and imprecise. One means of attempting to avoid such problems is to substitute for the term power another term such as capabilities, but this only introduces the problem of defining the new term. Another approach to understanding power is to create subcategories. Bachrach and Baratz suggest that power can be divided into five forms of behavior change. They argue that "in order for a power relation to exist . . . one of the parties [must] threaten to invoke sanctions." (Bachrach and Baratz, 1963, 633). For Bachrach and Baratz, an influence relationship differs from a power relationship only in that the exercise of influence involves no threatened sanctions. Such a distinction between power and influence is not uncommon in the literature on international relations, but these authors suggest further breakdowns as well. A change in behavior can also come about through the use of authority. If B complies with A's demands in this sort of relationship, it is because B "recognizes that the command is reasonable in terms of [B's] own values." A force relationship exists when one party uses some form of force to obtain compliance with its demands. A manipulative relationship is one in which one nation brings another into compliance with its wishes but the complying nation is not aware of its acquiescence. This breakdown of behavior into five categories—power, influence, authority, force, and manipulation—is helpful in illustrating the varieties of behavior usually covered by the term power alone.

POWER AS A RELATIONSHIP

Another problem with the analogy between power and money is that money can be saved, but power cannot be stored for future use. If a nation or group of nations want another nation or group of nations to take a particular action, power is a factor in that specific transaction and therefore can be analyzed only in terms of that transaction. Under these circumstances, a nation cannot possess power in isolation, but, rather, a

nation's power must be evaluated in terms of a relationship with other nations. Thus, to state that a particular nation is powerful must be followed with the question, "Relative to what?" Nations may not agree on their evaluations of their own or of other nations' power, but it is only in a comparative situation that power can be assessed.

The Middle East provides ample illustrations of this point. The question, "Is Israel a powerful nation?" can be answered only in terms of Israel's relationship with the nations that oppose or support it. Israel is more or less powerful than its Arab neighbors depending on which Arab nations are included. In each of the several wars between Israel and its Arab opponents, regardless of which Arab nations were involved, Israel has won. This can be used as one measure of Israel's power and as an indicator that Israel is more powerful than some of its neighbors, at least in situations when force is used. Such a comparison of power is limited to the use of military capabilities, however, and does not involve other national characteristics that contribute to a nation's power. Even when the comparison is limited to force, that comparison alone is not sufficient, since Israel's power cannot be evaluated without reference to the alignment of Israel and the Arab states with other nations.

The role of the superpowers is critical in analyzing the Arab-Israeli power relationship. Israel would certainly be less powerful than the Arab countries if the Soviet Union supported the Arab states and the United States withdrew its support of Israel. In turn, if the Soviet Union withdrew its support from the Arab nations it supports, Syria and Iraq, and the United States continued its support of Israel, Israel's position would be enhanced. Israel's power would also be enhanced when a hostile Arab state became embroiled in a war with a nation other than Israel, such as occurred with the Iranian-Iraqi war. Also, Israel's power would increase if it settled its differences with one of its enemies, as occurred when Israel signed a peace treaty with Egypt in 1979. Knowing that its southern flank was secure, did this encourage Israel to move into Lebanon in 1982? Thus, Israel is not powerful as a single entity; Israel's power relative to its enemies depends on the actions of others and the relationship Israel has with other nations.

To establish that power has meaning only in a relationship or a set of relationships is not alone sufficient to explain use of the concept in analyzing international behavior. How powerful a nation is in a relationship also depends on the specific situation in which power is being evaluated. United States involvement in Vietnam is a case in point. While there is the question as to whether the U.S. used its power in Vietnam to best advantage, could the U.S. have won the war if other policies had been followed, or was the war not winnable under any circumstances? There are various explanations for why the United States lost the war, and each relates to how the United States utilized the power available to it. But did losing the war mean that the United States was less powerful than North Vietnam and the Viet Cong? If this question is answered in the affirmative, did that, in turn, mean that the United States was less powerful than other nations with about the same power as that possessed by North Vietnam? Or, did losing the war mean that at that time, under the circumstances in which the war was fought, the United States was less powerful, that is, less effective, than its enemies? The United States had elements of power in which it was clearly superior to its enemies in Vietnam, such as a strong economy, which could not be used in that type of war to full advantage; and it possessed weapons, including nuclear weapons, that were not used. By almost any objective measure that could be used, the U.S. would be judged, overall, as more powerful than North Vietnam and the Viet Cong. During the war, the United States remained powerful in other relationships and situations but, due to policy choices and the nature of the war, was less powerful than its opponents in that specific situation (Baldwin, 1979). The Soviet involvement in Afghanistan parallels the U.S. situation in Vietnam to the extent that the Soviets

also are more powerful than their enemies in a general sense, but are unable to win the war due to the limitations the nature of that war has placed on the use of Soviet power.

The war in Vietnam can be used in another way to point out that power is situational. Both the Soviet Union and China provided support for North Vietnam and the Viet Cong. The Soviet Union, by conventional standards for evaluating power, is more powerful than China, but in that particular situation China exerted more influence than did its communist rival. This could be explained by pointing out that China is geographically closer to Vietnam and is a fellow Asian nation, but the situation changed dramatically after the war ended. By January 1979, when Vietnam invaded Cambodia with Soviet support, China had lost its influence with Vietnam. China opposed the invasion and in turn invaded Vietnam. Vietnam easily drove back the invading force, but China, once an ally of Vietnam, was now an enemy. The actual power of China and the Soviet Union had not changed significantly, but the situation in which the two nations exercised their power had.

In addition to power's relational and situational nature, there is an another perspective concerning power that needs to be pointed out. The general definition of power presented earlier stated that power was exercised when B changed its behavior because A had asked or demanded that B do so. The problem with this approach to the exercise of power is that events in the international system seldom, if ever, occur on a simple, bilateral, single-issue basis. It would be extremely unlikely that nations A and B would have only a single issue pending; ordinarily, two nations would have a variety of issues about which there is some conflict. Among the pending issues, B complied with A on one issue, but A may have complied with B on one or more different issues. On the range of issues between the two countries, each country may have given up something in one area to obtain a concession from the other country in another area, thus neither nation was exerting greater power over the

Fig. 3.1 Single issue, Bilateral Relationship Multi-Issue, Bilateral Relationship

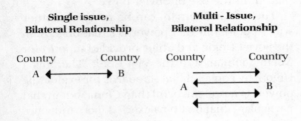

**Single issue,
Bilateral Relationship**

**Multi - Issue,
Bilateral Relationship**

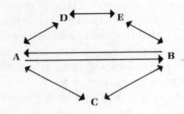

**Multi - Issue, Multilateral
Relationship**

other. An additional possibility is that even on a single-issue basis what appeared to be compliance with A's demand was an action by B that B had already planned to carry out before A made its request. Examination of the motivation behind B's compliance could reveal that A was not exercising its power, but only appeared to be doing so.

A factor related to the problem of measuring the exercise of power is how to assess what constitutes a diplomatic victory or defeat. Dean Acheson, the American secretary of state during the Truman presidency, described a diplomatic victory as one in which the United States obtained 51 percent of what it wanted and the other side received only 49 percent. His point was that even when a country feels that it has negotiated successfully, the margin of victory is usually very narrow. Applying this to the range of issues between countries A and B, victories and defeats would probably be narrow ones, and, likely, there would be no agreement between the

countries as to which country received the most in each of their areas of interest. Overall, both might think they received 51 percent of their demands, and both would be pleased with their relationship. Perhaps each would feel that it had received only 49 percent and be dissatisfied with the results. The relationship between two countries is not simply a case of one issue, but a mix of issues and confusion of perception as to what is victory and defeat.

If a relationship between two countries were limited to one issue, with one of the countries clearly more powerful than the other, then the weaker nation would be in the simple position of finding out what the stronger nation wanted and then granting it. But with a mix of issues, and since nations have different priorities for the interests they pursue, negotiation is possible between two countries even when one is clearly the more powerful. Consequently, power and the ability to exercise it is much more dispersed within the international system than is commonly thought (Bundy, 1977).

While the Acheson analysis of diplomatic victory and defeat does illustrate that the diplomatic outcome of negotiations is generally a close thing, the fifty-one, forty-nine percent example can be misleading in another respect. It implies that what one nation gains the other must lose to the same degree. Agreements are possible in which each nation receives more than half of what it wants. Diplomacy is not necessarily a zero-sum game in which a country can gain only by another country's losing. Since the measure of a diplomatic victory is imprecise, it is possible for two nations to go away from the bargaining table feeling that both made an advantageous agreement.

To this point, the discussion of power has concerned bilateral power. B's motivation for complying with A's demand may have been motivated by relationships outside the bilateral relationship. B may want something from C and makes concessions to A in an attempt to obtain A's support in making a demand on C. A and B could develop

Elements
of power :

1. *Population*   5. *Natural resources*
2. *Geography*
3. *Economic strength*
4. *Military strength*

3 / POWER AND THE NATION–STATE **41**

an alliance directed at C, with concessions between A and B necessary to form the coalition. The relationship of A and B thus does not exist in isolation from their diplomatic relations with other countries in the system. Diplomatic concerns and conflicts with countries C, D, E, etc., are also a consideration.

All of these possibilities concerning the variety of interests between nations and the motivation behind behavior make a simple, bilateral relationship highly unlikely in the international system. Similarly, any attempt to distinguish and measure the power a nation exercises on a single issue is complicated and obscured by the interplay of other issues and nations.

ELEMENTS OF POWER

When power is mentioned, the concept often is reduced to military capability alone. This restricted definition probably results from thinking about power in its most obvious form—the ability to exercise force and win wars. Of the breakdown of power into five means of changing another nation's behavior—power, influence, authority, force, and manipulation—only two of those means, power and force, involve the use of or the threat to use military capabilities. Military capabilities thus are essential to the exercise of some types of behavior change, but certainly not all of them.

Using military capability as a shortcut means of explaining the exercise of power also stems from the commonly held perception that nations most frequently obtain what they want through the use of force or the threat to exert force. This perspective ignores the subtleties of international politics and, in particular, ignores a number of capabilities a nation has available other than military power. The discussion which follows will analyze the elements of power, including military capability, as to how each contributes to a nation's power. A theme that will run through

this discussion will be that measuring each element's contribution to a nation's power presents problems, even though the assumption is that each element does make a contribution.

POPULATION

Assessing the impact of population on a nation's power provides a good illustration of the measurement problem. The size of a nation's population should be commensurate with that country's ability to effectively utilize its population. Ideally, a nation's population will be literate, skilled, ambitious, and will possess a high level of support for the nation's political system. A skilled population is needed to support a growing industrial base and to provide the weapons of war, if that should become necessary. A high level of support for the political system is necessary to obtain stability within the system. The population should be proportionate to the ability of the economic system to provide jobs in order to remove the politically destabilizing influence that comes from having too large a portion of the population unemployed. The rate of population increase should not exceed the rate of economic growth, since the failure of the economic system to produce a rising standard of living can also result in political unrest. Also, the mean age of the population will be high enough that there is not a disproportionate percentage of the population in or soon to enter the reproductive age; the lower the mean age of the population the more difficult it is to control the rate of population growth. These would be the characteristics of a model population, but, as with any model, no nation possesses those precise characteristics. China, as the world's most populous nation, is a case in point.

In 1983, China announced the result of its first modern attempt to conduct a census. Western estimates of China's population were between 900 and 950 million, with the Chinese government using a 750 million figure. The result of the census was that China had a population of 1.06 billion. Did the announcement of a population that exceeded all estimates diminish or enhance China's power? In spite of the population's unexpected size, China seems able to keep everyone fed, to avoid the famines of the past caused by local crop failures, and to prevent political unrest due to food shortages. China lacks the economic development to employ vast numbers in industry, but much of China's population remains in rural areas and thus is not directly dependent on industrialization for its well-being. No doubt coping with such a large population drains resources that China could otherwise devote to economic development. In an effort to hold down the population to 1.2 billion by the year 2000, the Chinese government has launched a vigorous campaign to restrict families to one child.

During Mao Tse-tung's rule, China's vast population was used as a threat. Traditionally, China's immense population caused concern among its more sparsely populated neighbors. If China wished to find more living space for its people, a vast land army could overwhelm any nearby country, with the possible exception of the Soviet Union. But Mao placed a nuclear-age interpretation on the military threat of China's population. He pointed out that the United States and the Soviet Union were more powerful than China because they were more highly industrialized. If a nuclear war occurred, the industry of all three countries would be destroyed, but, since there were so many Chinese, China would be more powerful than either the United States or the Soviet Union because more Chinese would survive than Soviets or Americans. Population would become a more important factor in a nation's power if the industrial base of all three countries were destroyed.

India, the world's second-most populous nation, also faces problems directly related to the size of its population. Unlike China, India has had difficulty feeding its 700 million people. Until the 1970s, Indian agriculture was neglected in favor of attempts to industrialize rapidly—a policy that experienced many failures. When development efforts were redirected to agriculture, the food problem in India improved and, coupled with favorable weather conditions, India is now food-sufficient. India also has a problem with population other than size and food. Domestic conflicts between cultures, religions, and ethnic groups have made it difficult to hold India together under a single political system.

The Soviet Union has yet a different population problem. Throughout Russian, and then Soviet history, Russians have been the major ethnic group, with all other ethnic groups collectively not as numerous. The Russian rate of population growth is not as high as the growth rate of the other ethnic groups, and probably during the 1990s Russians will become a minority. What effect this will have on control of the Soviet government is unknown, but until now the leadership of the country has been predominantly Russian. Canada and Australia present still another population problem. Both have vast land areas but have not had sufficient people to fully populate their countries. Efforts to attract immigrants to their countries have been only partially successful.

Nations can offset a lack of population through the use of technology and organization, particularly if there is a threat from other countries. Israel, with fewer than four million people, exists in an Arab world that outnumbers it thirtyfold. If population were the only determinant of power, then Israel should have been overrun years ago, but it survives by using advanced technology and greater political unity to offset the disadvantage of a population smaller than that of its enemies.

The underdeveloped countries present still another problem related to population. In the industrial countries, the rate of population growth is less than 1 percent a year. The rate of population increase in the underdeveloped countries averages about 2.3 percent a year, which, for many of these countries, exceeds their rate of economic growth (McNamara, 1984). Even in countries where there are serious efforts to limit the rate of growth, the problem will persist for many years, since a majority of the population in many Third World countries is under the age of eighteen and has not yet had an impact on the birth rate through the children they will produce.

Population thus can present many problems to a country. There can be too many people to feed adequately, and there can be too many people to provide with employment. Also, a country with too few people can have difficulty in developing the country even when natural resources and capital are available. Ethnic and religious differences may occur among the many groups that make up a nation. If the mean age of the population is low, it can hamper efforts to control the rate of population increase.

Population problems have been of sufficient concern worldwide that the United Nations has sponsored two international conferences on the subject—in Bucharest in 1974 and in Mexico City in 1984. The hope of both conferences was to find a response to the world's population problems other than war, starvation, and disease, the traditional checks on population growth. While the United Nations conferences were not directly concerned with how population problems erode a nation's power, the thrust of both conferences was the study of interrelated problems of how to cope with too great a population within an underdeveloped economic system. Both the issue of population and the issue of underdevelopment have an effect on how powerful a nation is in the international system.

The size of a nation's population is not always a problem, however. Industrialized nations need enough people to provide a work force for its factories and soldiers for its armed forces in times of war. There can be little doubt that population is a factor in how powerful a nation is within the international system. The difficulty lies in determining a means of measuring the impact a particular nation's population has on that nation's power.

GEOGRAPHY

The geographic location and topography of a country are also factors in a nation's power. Ideally, a nation will possess some or all of the following geographic characteristics. The size of the nation will be proportionate to the population so that a nation's territory is not an attractive target for overpopulated neighbors. Its borders will be marked by natural barriers such as high mountains or oceans to make its frontiers difficult to breach. The climate will be mild, neither extremely cold nor debilitatingly hot. The growing season should be long enough to provide crops the opportunity to mature. Natural resources should be sufficient in quantity and of diverse types so that the nation is not unduly dependent on other countries. An adequate portion of the land area can be cultivated so that the country is self-sufficient in cereal and feed grains. If mountain ranges exist within the country, they should not provide serious barriers to an internal transportation system or to the unity of the country politically.

A country with a large territory is not necessarily assured major-power status, however. Canada and Australia are among the largest nations in the world, but they not only are not major powers, they contain large portions of territory that are virtually uninhabitable. The Soviet Union and China, the two largest nations in the world, have experienced both advantages and disadvantages from their vast territory. In their history, both have suffered because their land area made political unity under one government difficult to achieve. On the other hand, both countries have utilized the vastness of their countries to absorb invaders until they were repelled or assimilated into the general population.

Land area can also have an effect on how a nation behaves toward the rest of the world. During the nineteenth century, the United States was so preoccupied with filling out its frontiers

Population has a relative impact of power which itself is a relative concept.

that all it wanted internationally was to be left alone to carry out internal development. At a time when a number of European countries were looking to Africa and Asia for empires, the United States was satisfied to fulfill its "manifest destiny" by developing a nation from the Atlantic to the Pacific. The United States, as did czarist Russia, created its empire from territories contiguous to it.

A nation's location can also affect its power. The United States, located between two vast oceans, could virtually ignore European politics during the century before World War I. Problems in Europe allowed little time for the major European powers to become involved in the Western Hemisphere, which left the United States free to pursue its own interests. The location and topography of some countries, however, often has placed them in jeopardy. Belgium, with its flat terrain, is a traditional battleground and invasion route between central Europe and France. Poland, also because of its flat terrain, has often suffered invading armies moving between Germany and Russia.

Topography can influence a nation's development in other ways as well. Brazil has mountain ranges so close to the Atlantic Ocean that until recently, it was limited in its development to the areas between the coast and the mountains. Brazil's new capital, Brasilia, was built to the west of the mountains in an effort to encourage development of the interior. More recently, an ambitious network of highways into the interior was constructed for the same reason. The Pyrenees mountains between France and Spain have provided a relatively more stable frontier between the two countries than would likely have been possible without such a barrier. The Alps have provided Switzerland with natural protection that makes that country too costly for even major powers to attack. Chile and Argentina are separated by the Andes, and the long frontier between the two countries has been a peaceful one, although the threat of war developed between them in the early 1980s. An exception

to this principle, however, would be the Golan Heights on the northern border of Israel with Syria. When Syria occupied the heights before the 1967 Six-Day War, this natural barrier was considered by Israel to be a threat. Israel's perception resulted from its having only flatlands on its side of the border. Now that the Golan Heights are divided between Israel and Syria, that frontier could develop, in time, into a more peaceful dividing line between the two countries.

Landlocked nations such as Paraguay, Bolivia, Burkina Faso (formerly Upper Volta), and Uganda suffer because they do not have direct access to an ocean. Conversely, for centuries Great Britain based its security on its being an island and built a large navy to increase the cost to any invading force. Some land areas occupy such strategic geographic locations that they attract the major powers. Examples include Gibraltar, the Suez Canal, Malta, and Singapore, all possessed at one time by Great Britain for their strategic value. The Panamanian isthmus is a similar example for the United States. More recently, the Straits of Hormuz at the entrance to the Persian Gulf has taken on increased strategic importance due to the importance of oil to the Western nations.

The strategic position of a nation can undergo dramatic change even though the geography remains the same. Before the development of nuclear weapons and long-range delivery systems, the United States viewed the Atlantic and Pacific Oceans as its protection from invasion and such formidable barriers for an enemy that a large standing army was unnecessary. As long as the United States had a large navy, it considered itself safe. With the development of long-range aircraft and intercontinental ballistic missiles, the geographic position of the United States took on a new perspective. Enemies of the U.S. were no longer an ocean away, but, rather, the Soviet Union was across Canada and the Arctic ice cap with weapons that could reach the U.S. thirty minutes after launch. The world's geography remained unchanged, but the manner in which the United States viewed its position changed.

While this change in geographic perspective was important in itself, the concept of distance has been altered for all nations as a result of technological change. Any point in the world is now minutes away from devastating weapons, not, as in the nineteenth century, days and weeks away from enemies with weapons of relatively minor destructive power. However, the same advanced technology that produced the nearness of destructive capability also produced the means for quicker communication and travel. The cliché about this being a small world is in fact a recognition of a change in geographic perspective.

While geographic factors are not the only elements that make up a nation's power, a school of thought—geopolitics—emerged between 1900 and World War II that attempted to explain international behavior by geography alone. Among the geopoliticians, the best known was Sir Halford MacKinder. He viewed Europe, Asia, and Africa as the world island and the other continents as satellites. The "heartland" of the world island was eastern Europe including European and much of Asian Soviet Union, Iran, Tibet, Mongolia, and parts of the Middle East. MacKinder argued that the following was the basic principle of who controlled the world:

> He who rules East Europe commands the Heartland of Eurasia;
> Who rules the Heartland, commands the World Island of Europe, Asia and Africa;
> And who rules the World Island commands the World.

Karl Haushofer, a German geographer and a close adviser to Hitler, was strongly influenced by the MacKinder thesis. Based on the principles of geopolitics, Haushofer advised Hitler to form a German-Soviet-Japanese alliance in order to control the world island. Haushofer advised Hitler not to invade the Soviet Union, since such an action would violate the MacKinder thesis.

The American version of geopolitics, an interpretation almost diametrically contradictory to MacKinder's, was expressed by Alfred T. Mahan, who argued that control of the oceans with a large two-ocean navy was the route to U.S. security, not control of the world island. A later version of the geopolitical position of the United States was offered by John Spykman just prior to the U.S. entering World War II. His view was that the U.S. was secure when it controlled the rimlands of Asia and Europe, as well as the Atlantic and Pacific Oceans. As interesting as geopolitics might be, its overriding fault is explaining international behavior with a single element of power—geography.

NATURAL RESOURCES

Closely related to geography as an element of power are the location and quantity of natural resources found within a country's borders. All nations are dependent on natural resources to heat homes, to provide the raw materials for industry, to produce electricity, and to manufacture weapons for their armed forces. All nations need fossil fuels to run their motor, rail, air, and water transportation systems, as well as to serve as the base for plastics and fertilizers. The presence of natural resources is not enough, however. The resources must be accessible and not unduly expensive to develop, and the nation must have the capability to take advantage of them.

No nation is self-sufficient in the natural resources it needs, but the Soviet Union comes as close as any nation to being so. Until the 1960s, when industrial development in the United States outstripped the resources available within the country, it also was considered to have most of the natural resources needed to be self-sufficient. Today, the United States is increasingly dependent on foreign markets for its raw materials. Athough the United States obtains some resources from countries nearby, such as bauxite from Jamaica, oil from Mexico, and nickel, zinc, and asbestos from Canada, many other resources come from countries some distance away. The United States imports industrial diamonds primarily from South Africa and Zaire, natural rubber from Indonesia and Malaysia, chromite and platinum from the Soviet Union and South Africa, ferro-chromium from South Africa and Zimbabwe, cobalt from Zaire and Belgium, manganese from Brazil, Gabon, Australia, and South Africa, columbium from Brazil and Canada, titanium from Australia and India, and tin from Malaysia, Thailand, and Bolivia. Eighty-five to one hundred percent of each of these resources is now imported by the United States, and each resource is essential to the ability of the U.S. to produce industrially.

As long as the aforementioned sources of raw materials are available, the United States does not have a problem. While political instability or a hostile government in any of those countries could disrupt the flow of resources, perhaps the greatest threat to the United States and other industrial countries comes from efforts by nations that export raw materials to control their products' prices. A complaint frequently voiced by the underdeveloped countries is that they have little control over the price of the resources they export and thus are at the economic mercy of the industrialized nations. To offset this disadvantageous position, several efforts have been made by raw-material exporting countries to form international cartels. The only such effort that has experienced success is the Organization of Petroleum Exporting Countries (OPEC), and this proved to be only temporary. Oil prices rose rapidly during the 1970s (from about $2.00 to $34.00 a barrel). When a glut of oil developed in the early 1980s, OPEC was unable to control production levels and the price tumbled to about $15.00 a barrel. Efforts to control oil prices were further complicated by the Iranian-Iraqi War. Iran sold as much oil as it could to finance its war effort; Iraq, due to the Iranian blockade, was unable to exceed its oil production quota. If such efforts to control the price of resources were to be successful in the future, they could provide

a serious threat to the industrial nations through spiraling costs for these products, as was the case when oil prices were at their peak.

During World War II, the United States suffered shortages of various resources, but the most serious were in tin and natural rubber. Both resources had come from what was now Japanese-occupied southeast Asia. When the Cold War developed, the United States initiated a system of strategic stockpiles of resources in order to avoid similar shortages in the event of another major war. Those stockpiles have since been sold off due to high maintenance costs and the probability that if a major war developed between the superpowers it would be of short duration; thus, natural resources would not play an important role. The development of such stockpiles did indicate a recognition of how important natural resources are to the survival of an industrialized nation, however. A recent effort to stockpile a strategic resource occurred in 1976 when the United States established the Strategic Petroleum Reserve by pumping oil into abandoned salt mines. In this instance, the stockpile was established in case of another oil sanction by Arab members of OPEC such as was initiated following the 1973 war between Israel and its Arab neighbors. The goal for the reserve was one billion barrels. The oil reserve met with opposition from Saudi Arabia, the Arab member of OPEC most closely aligned with the United States, and was not fully stocked.

Western Europe and Japan are dependent on imported natural resources to even a greater extent than is the United States. Even though the Soviet Union is well endowed with natural resources, it is dependent on other nations for other forms of resources such as technology and cereal grains. Although natural resources are often discussed in regard to their importance during wartime, the contribution of natural resources to power in peacetime is primarily to maintain a strong economy in the industrialized nations and to provide foreign currency for the countries that export resources. In peacetime,

Tab. 3.1 Worldwide Oil at a Glance

COUNTRY	Estimated Proved Reserves 1-1-1987 Oil (1,000 bbl)	Oil Production Estimated 1986 (1,000 b/d)	% change from 1985
Asia–Pacific			
Australia	1,712,800	472.0	− 16.9
Bangladesh	...	...	...
Brunei	1,420,900	170.0	+ 12.6
Burma	58,000	30.0	...
China, Taiwan	(c) 5,400	1.9	− 9.5
India	4,202,800	622.7	+ 0.9
Indonesia	8,300,000	1,243.8	+ 1.5
Japan	57,000	12.8	+ 20.8
Korea, South	...	...	...
Malaysia	2,820,500	503.3	+ 16.2
New Zealand	(c) 167,000	29.3	+ 54.2
Pakistan	96,000	41.0	+ 17.1
Papua New Guinea	(c) 65,000	...	...
Philippines	16,900	6.3	− 25.9
Singapore	...	...	...
Sri Lanka	...	...	...
Thailand	101,200	35.6	+ 1.7
Total Asia–Pacific	*19,023,500*	*3,168.7*	*+ 1.1*
Western Europe			
Austria	76,300	22.2	+ 0.9
Belgium	...	...	...
Cyprus	...	...	...
Denmark	440,000	74.7	+ 26.6
Finland	...	...	...
France	234,900	59.0	+ 15.7
Germany, West	316,00	80.0	− 1.2
Greece	26,000	26.4	− 1.5
Ireland	...	...	...
Italy–Sicily	721,750	49.0	− 22.5
Netherlands	194,900	79.0	+ 11.3
Norway	10,500,000	823.3	+ 5.0
Portugal	...	...	...
Spain	28,200	37.2	− 17.3
Sweden	...	...	...
Switzerland	...	...	...
Turkey	400,000	46.8	+ 11.4
United Kingdom	9,000,000	2,602.0	+ 2.8
Total Western Europe	*21,938,050*	*3,899.6*	*+ 3.9*
Middle East			
Abu Dhabi	31,000,000	949.0	+ 31.8
Bahrain	140,000	44.0	+ 4.8
Dubai	1,350,000	350.0	+ 0.6
Iran	48,800,000	1,806.3	− 20.0
Israel	700	1,787.7	+ 24.6
Jordan		0.1	...
Kuwait	91,916,000	...	...
Lebanon		1,202.0	+ 40.7
Neutral Zone	5,212,100	...	...
Oman	4,032,000	325.7	− 7.2
Qatar	3,154,000	540.8	+ 11.3
Ras al Khaimah	200,000	332.3	+ 11.1
Saudi Arabia	166,573,900	11.0	+ 22.2
Sharjah	500,000	4,719.7	+ 43.9
Syria	1,400,000	65.0	...
Yemen, North	500,000	185.0	+ 3.9
Yemen, South	...	...	...
Total Middle East	*401,878,700*	*12,328.6*	*+ 19.4*
Africa			
Algeria	8,800,000	600.7	− 7.4
Angola–Cabinda	1,149,400	280.7	+ 24.8
Benin	100,000	7.0	+ 1.4
Cameroon	540,000	180.0	+ 34.3
Congo	720,000	115.0	+ 16.2
Egypt	3,600,000	773.7	− 11.6
Ethiopia	...	...	...
Gabon	645,000	146.2	− 4.4
Ghana	2,350	0.3	− 40.0
Ivory Coast	125,000	20.0	− 28.6
Kenya	...	...	...
Liberia	...	...	...
Libya	21,300,000	1,030.7	− 2.0
Madagascar	...	...	...
Morocco	300	0.3	...
Mozambique	...	...	...
Nigeria	16,000,000	1,464.0	− 1.1
Senegal	...	...	...
Sierra Leone	...	...	...
Somalia	...	...	...
South Africa	...	...	...
Sudan	300,000	...	...
Tanzania	...	...	...
Togo	...	...	...
Tunisia	1,800,000	106.0	+ 1.9
Zaire	112,000	32.1	− 8.3
Zambia	...	...	...
Total Africa	*55,194,050*	*4,756.7*	*− 1.8*
Western Hemisphere			
Argentina	2,270,000	430.2	− 3.8
Barbados	500	1.8	− 5.3
Bolivia	149,000	18.7	− 11.0
Brazil	2,250,000	578.0	+ 5.7
Canada	6,850,000	1,475.3	+ 0.9
Chile	290,000	34.4	+ 4.2
Colombia	1,290,500	324.2	+ 83.2
Costa Rica	...	...	...
Dominican Republic	...	...	...
Ecuador	1,672,300	270.1	− 2.5
El Salvador	...	...	...
Guatemala	23,000	4.9	+ 11.4
Honduras	...	...	...
Jamaica	...	...	...
Martinique	...	...	...
Mexico	54,653,000	2,468.0	− 9.7
Netherlands Antilles	...	...	...
Nicaragua	...	...	...
Panama	...	...	...
Paraguay	...	...	...
Peru	546,000	179.0	− 5.8
Puerto Rico	...	...	...
Suriname	1,000	1.8	+ 50.0
Trinidad & Tobago	610,000	167.9	− 5.1
Uruguay	...	...	...
Venezuela	25,000,000	1,664.9	+ 6.9
Virgin Islands	...	...	...
United States	24,560,000	8,790.0	− 2.0
Total Western Hemisphere	*120,165,300*	*16,409.2*	*− 1.2*
Total non-Communist	*618,199,600*	*40,562.8*	*+ 4.9*
Communist Areas			
China	18,400,000	2,590.0	+ 3.8
USSR	59,000,000	12,300.0	+ 3.4
Others	1,850,000	427.0	− 5.7
Total Communist	*79,250,000*	*15,317.0*	*+ 3.2*
Total World	**697,449,600**	**55,879.8**	**+ 4.4**

SOURCE: *Oil and Gas Journal.*

the issue involved in evaluating the contribution of natural resources to a nation's power is whether a nation either possesses the necessary resources within its own boundaries or has access to them elsewhere.

ECONOMIC STRENGTH

A nation's Gross National Product (GNP) may be the single most reliable indicator of that nation's influence in the international system. It reflects a nation's ability to produce products for international trade and domestic consumption, and, along with a nation's technological development, it indicates the capacity a nation has for producing weapons, if called upon to do so. A nation's GNP also reflects generally the degree of economic development; the higher the GNP, the greater the development (Organski and Kugler, 1980). This last statement has limitations, however, since countries with large populations, such as India, China, and Indonesia, have higher GNPs than do several more highly industrialized nations with smaller populations.

Assessment and comparison of nations on the basis of their economic strength is complicated by the availability of several commonly used indices that can yield different rankings for nations. All such measures, however, except for the index of per capita income, rank the United States as the top economic power. Zbigniew Brzezinski, writing before he became national security adviser to President Carter, compared the power of the United States and the Soviet Union at different stages of the Cold War. (Brzezinski, 1972, 203–04). He compared the two countries on four bases—military capability, international image, stability of the domestic system, and economic strength. From one time period to another, which country was ahead in each category of power varied except for economic strength, in which the United States was judged to be well ahead of the Soviet Union

during all the time periods. Any attempt to update Brzezinski's evaluations undoubtedly would produce the same results. Among all the elements of power, perhaps the greatest impact the United States currently has on the international system is through its economy, which includes a GNP of about $4 trillion, the largest of any nation. (All figures on GNPs, except other estimates of the Soviet GNP, are taken from the *Britannica Book of the Year* 1986.)

One of the ironies concerning the international impact of the U.S. economy is that, although the largest single industrialized economic unit, the United States is also the leading exporter of agricultural products. The economies of the underdeveloped nations are, for the most part, based on agriculture; thus an industrial nation would not be expected to be a major exporter of agricultural products. Technological advances in the United States have included agricultural technology and allow the United States to produce a greater surplus of food, particularly cereal and feed grains, than any other country. These developments in agriculture also apply to the other four major exporting nations of cereal grains—France, Australia, Canada, and Argentina. All are industrialized nations except Argentina, which is generally classified as on the threshold of industrialization.

Although there are problems in arriving at an accurate estimate of the size of the Soviet economy, Western estimates place the Soviet GNP at about $2 trillion, about one-half the size of the U.S. economy. Japan, with less than half the population of the Soviet Union, has a GNP of $1.2 trillion. Since the Japanese economy is growing more rapidly than the economies of either the Soviet Union or the United States, Japan continues to improve its economic position relative to either of the superpowers. The major members of the European Community—Great Britain, France, West Germany, and Italy—have a combined GNP of nearly $2 trillion. As a total economic unit including the GNPs of all twelve members, the EC has a GNP of nearly $2.6 trillion. In brief, the economic impact of the major industrial countries, all of which are Western nations except for the Soviet Union, is enormous.

China, on the other hand, has a GNP approximately the size of Italy's. Italy does not yield the influence on the international scene that China does. Therefore, their respective power obviously is influenced by factors other than their economic output. Following those nations with the largest GNPs, there is a dramatic drop in the size of the economies of other economically developed nations on through the threshold nations and into the clearly underdeveloped nations of the world. With so much of the world's economic capacity concentrated in the industrialized nations, if that element of power alone were the criteria for power much of the world would be nearly powerless.

Per capita income is another frequently used measure of economic development. This indicator presents a problem when one considers a nation with a small population but a high level of industrialization. Examples are Sweden and Switzerland, which rank high among the industrialized nations in per capita income. Clearly, they are not more powerful than the larger industrial nations with lower per capita incomes. The greatest distortion provided by this index, however, is represented by Kuwait, the country with the world's highest per capita income (nearly $21,000). Obviously, Kuwait is not a particularly powerful nation. Such anomalies will appear in any index used, however, and serve only to warn that more than one index must be used to gain an appreciation of how powerful a nation is within the nation-state system.

Comparing nations on the basis of per capita income tends to magnify the underdevelopment of many nations. India, with a GNP of about $175 billion and a population of nearly 700 million, has a per capita income of only about $250 a year. Bangladesh, one of the world's poorest nations, has a per capita income of only $140 a year, the lowest figure for nations with larger populations.

Other indices for measuring economic capa-

bility are steel production, energy consumption, telephones per thousand population, and percentage of the population engaged in nonagricultural employment. These measures are, for the most part, specific measures of industrial development.

MILITARY STRENGTH

Of all the tangible elements of power discussed thus far, military capability is the most commonly used measure. Reasons for this frequent oversimplification of power are that the use of military strength to fulfill national interests is direct, thus easily understood, and that it is the easiest measure to quantify, and can be reduced to numbers and graphs. The use of military force or the threat to use it is seen as a means of achieving a nation's interests by forcing others to do what you want them to do. The assumption is that if your nation possesses more military capability than do its adversaries, then they must comply with your demands without regard for the other elements of power.

In practice, the use of military capabilities to achieve a nation's goals presents measurement problems not found in other elements. Military capability is what a nation can use if it goes to war, but, for the most part, the peacetime influence of arms is somewhat limited. Military strength thus is more a potential element of power than a direct means for achieving a nation's interests. Nations will respond to such potential, but, unlike economic strength, its peacetime function is essentially just being there. Even then, a nation's armaments, no matter what their quantity, are not a contribution to power unless opposing nations believe that, if sufficiently provoked, a nation will use them effectively. The development of nuclear weapons perhaps has further reduced the peacetime impact of military capability for those nations that possess such weapons. The potential use of such weapons has

Fig. 3.2 Soviet and U.S. Sources of Natural Resources

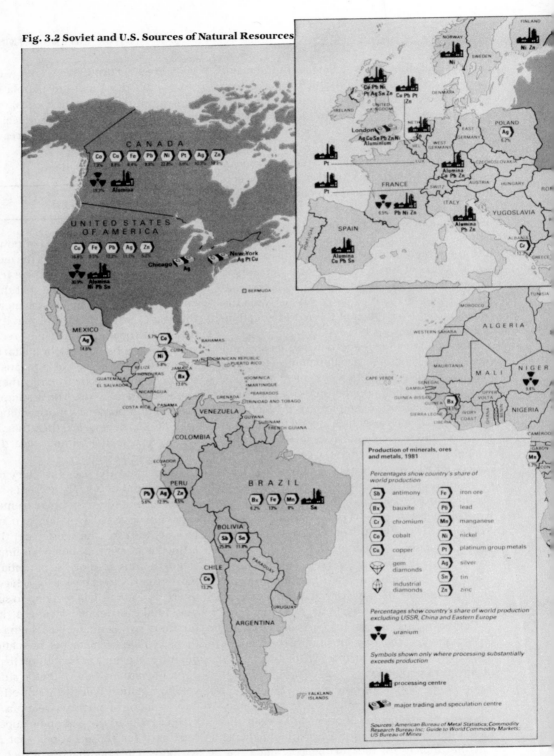

SOURCE: *The New State of the World Atlas*, Michael Kidron and Ronald Segal (Simon and Schuster, 1984), No. 11. Used with permission.

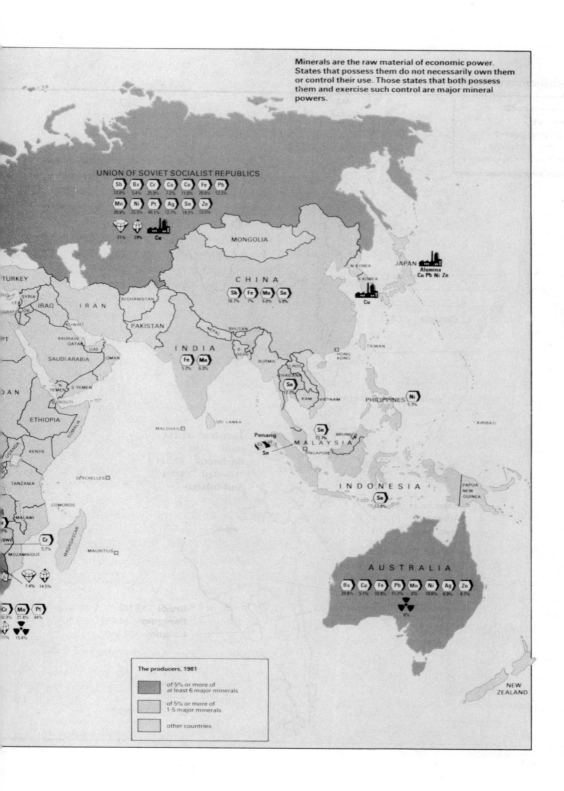

Minerals are the raw material of economic power. States that possess them do not necessarily own them or control their use. Those states that both possess them and exercise such control are major mineral powers.

UNION OF SOVIET SOCIALIST REPUBLICS

Sb	Bx	Cr	Co	Co	Fe	Pb
12.9%	5.4%	25.9%	7.2%	11.6%	26.6%	12.2%

Mn	Ni	Pt	Ag	Sn	Zn
39.9%	22.5%	49.1%	12.7%	14.3%	13.5%

21%   29%   Cu

MONGOLIA

N KOREA
S KOREA

JAPAN
Alumna
Cu Pb Ni Zn

Cu

CHINA

Sb	Fe	Mn	Sn
16.7%	7%	6.6%	5.9%

TURKEY

SYRIA
IRAQ   IRAN
AFGHANISTAN

KUWAIT
BAHRAIN
QATAR   PAKISTAN
UAE
SAUDI ARABIA   OMAN

NEPAL   BHUTAN

INDIA

Fe	Mn
5.2%	6.3%

BURMA

TAIWAN

HONG KONG

LAOS
THAILAND

Sn
12.7%

KAM   VIETNAM

PHILIPPINES

Ni
5.3%

N YEMEN
S YEMEN
DJIBOUTI

ETHIOPIA

SOMALIA

KENYA

MALDIVES

SRI LANKA

Penang

Sn

M A L A Y S I A
SINGAPORE

Sn
23.7%

BRUNEI

KIRIBATI

SEYCHELLES

TANZANIA

COMOROS

I N D O N E S I A

Sn
13.8%

PAPUA
NEW
GUINEA

MALAWI

MADAGASCAR

MOZAMBIQUE

Cr
5.7%

MAURITIUS

A U S T R A L I A

Bx	Co	Fe	Pb	Mn	Ni	Ag	Zn
29.9%	5.3%	10.9%	11.7%	6%	10.6%	6.9%	8.7%

6%

7.4%   14.5%

Cr	Mn	Pt
10.9%	27.4%	44%

11%   15.4%

NEW
ZEALAND

The producers, 1981

of 5% or more of
at least 6 major minerals

of 5% or more of
1-5 major minerals

other countries

Fig. 3.3 Distribution of World's Wealth

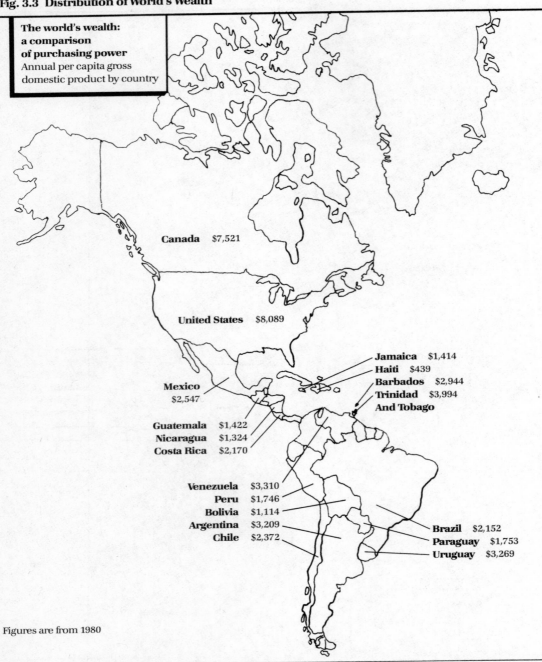

The world's wealth:
a comparison
of purchasing power
Annual per capita gross
domestic product by country

Canada $7,521

United States $8,089

Jamaica $1,414
Haiti $439
Barbados $2,944
Trinidad $3,994
And Tobago

Mexico
$2,547

Guatemala $1,422
Nicaragua $1,324
Costa Rica $2,170

Venezuela $3,310
Peru $1,746
Bolivia $1,114
Argentina $3,209
Chile $2,372

Brazil $2,152
Paraguay $1,753
Uruguay $3,269

Figures are from 1980

SOURCE: Christian Science Monitor
March 14, 1985, p. 19.

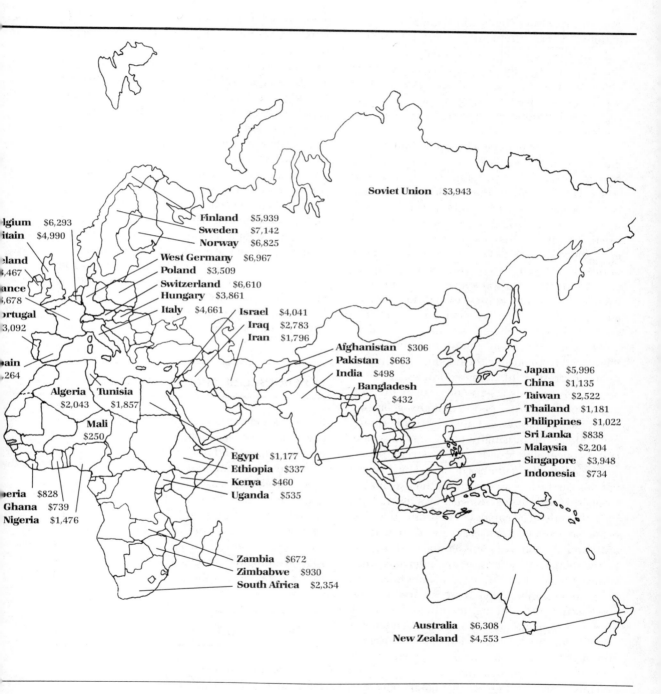

Soviet Union $3,943

lgium $6,293
itain $4,990

Finland $5,939
Sweden $7,142
Norway $6,825

eland
,467

ance
,678

West Germany $6,967
Poland $3,509
Switzerland $6,610
Hungary $3,861
Italy $4,661

ortugal
3,092

Israel $4,041
Iraq $2,783
Iran $1,796

Afghanistan $306
Pakistan $663
India $498
Bangladesh
$432

Japan $5,996
China $1,135
Taiwan $2,522
Thailand $1,181
Philippines $1,022
Sri Lanka $838
Malaysia $2,204
Singapore $3,948
Indonesia $734

ain
,264

Algeria $2,043
Tunisia $1,857

Mali
$250

Egypt $1,177
Ethiopia $337
Kenya $460
Uganda $535

eria $828
Ghana $739
Nigeria $1,476

Zambia $672
Zimbabwe $930
South Africa $2,354

Australia $6,308
New Zealand $4,553

such far-reaching implications that the international community knows that it is highly unlikely that nuclear weapons will be used or threatened in any but the most serious situations of conflict, and that the use of conventional arms by the superpowers in many situations will be restricted because their use might escalate into nuclear war.

Before the development of sophisticated satellites and other electronic means of monitoring each other's activities, armaments were easier to conceal. Now, only at the developmental stage can a nation expect to maintain secrecy about its weapons. If a country has the technological capability to conduct electronic and satellite intelligence-gathering, it can monitor the number of missile silos, aircraft on the runway, ships at sea and in port, and the above-ground military installations of any nation in the world. Virtually any nuclear explosion, whether a test or an accident, can be detected beyond a nation's borders and all communications within a nation can be monitored from outside the nation. Knowing the military strength of other countries does not necessarily provide a sense of security in itself, but it does prevent a nation from exaggerating its military capabilities. Thus, electronic spying can reduce the possibility of serious miscalculation concerning an adversary's strength.

The military capabilities of most Third World nations can be assessed without the use of electronic spying, however. Since only a few nations have the industrial capability to produce sophisticated armaments such as advanced combat aircraft and ground-to-air missiles, arms transfers by the industrial nations to the underdeveloped countries are relatively easy to monitor. Both governments and independent research groups, such as the International Institute of Strategic Studies which annually updates the armaments of all nations in its publication, *Military Balance*, appear to have reliable information on how well-armed any particular nation is.

Thus, uncertainties about military strength are not related so much to what or how many arms a nation possesses as they are to under what circumstances and how effectively a nation will use those arms. Earlier, the point was made that Israel overcomes its disadvantages in size and population relative to its enemies through training, organization, and technology. If military capability were based solely on the quantity of arms possessed, Israel should not have won any of the wars in which it has participated. Quantity of arms thus is not in itself a sufficient measure of a nation's military power. In peacetime, however, quantity is about the only measurement that can be taken with any accuracy; intangibles such as morale of the troops, their training, the organizational abilities of the nation, and the quality of military leadership are much more difficult to ascertain. In later chapters, when arms control efforts between the United States and the Soviet Union are discussed, this point is particularly important in comparing the relative military strength of those two nations.

INTANGIBLE ELEMENTS OF POWER

Intangible elements also are an important aspect of a nation's power. Though the tangible elements of power discussed above present problems in assessing their contribution to a nation's power, those variables at least have some means of being quantified. The intangible elements must be assessed mainly by impression and perception. They are also more apt to be subject to substantial changes over a relatively short period of time than are tangible elements. A good example of this is national morale.

NATIONAL MORALE

A few months after the United States withdrew from Vietnam in 1973, an opinion poll in the United States revealed that the only foreign countries a majority of the American public was willing to defend were the two countries that bordered on the United States, Mexico and Canada. Not even our NATO allies in Europe or Latin American countries other than Mexico could muster a majority of Americans in support of their defense. Coupled with this attitude that the United States should come to virtually no one's aid in case of attack was the disillusionment in the political system that came with the Watergate scandal in 1973 and 1974. National morale, at least in terms of confidence in the political system and involvement in international matters, was very low. At that time, NATO was concerned because American leadership was preoccupied with matters other than those pertaining to Western Europe. Many Europeans felt that the U.S. was making too much of Watergate, especially since it was distracting the U.S. from other more important matters. During this period of low confidence, the image of the United States abroad suffered.

Specific events and achievements can also have an impact on national morale. In 1969, when the United States placed men on the moon for the first time, morale in the United States was high. Great Britain, during and for a time after its successful operations in the Falkland Islands, had an upsurge in morale. When a nation's domestic economy is performing well or a nation has dynamic leadership, this also alters a nation's international image. Thus both domestic and international events have impact on how a nation sees itself and how others view it.

High national morale is critical to a nation's ability to conduct war. In World War II, German bombing of British cities was supposed to break the British will to resist, but the attacks actually contributed to the British resolve to fight the war. Allied bombing of German cities was supposed to break German morale, but never did so. The Japanese attack on Pearl Harbor, while a severe blow to the U.S. militarily, unified the American public behind the war effort. American bombing of North Vietnam was intended to force the North Vietnamese into making major concessions to the United States, but seemed instead to strengthen their resolve to resist. In each of these examples, the national publics already supported their governments, but in instances where a nation's public does not support a war, conduct of the war may go badly, such as occurred in Italy during World War II in spite of Italy's large armed forces.

NATIONAL LEADERSHIP

Conceivably, a nation could be rated highly on each element of power and yet, due to ineffectual leaders, have very little impact on the international system. Effective leadership takes maximum advantage of the elements of power available to it. If, however, the tangible elements of power for a nation are weak overall, no matter how effective the leadership, national leaders cannot make that nation a major power. Thus, a nation can lose or gain power through the effectiveness of its leadership within the bounds of what is realistic.

National leadership preoccupied with keeping itself in power can even place a country in jeopardy. One explanation for Argentina's occupation of the Falkland Islands in 1982 is that the military government thought such a move would unite the country behind what had become an unpopular government. When the war was lost, that leadership was blamed for the defeat and eventually forced out of office. Internationally, Argentina was seen as a less powerful nation after the war than before. Conversely, leadership that performs well in time of crisis can greatly enhance a nation's power. Israel's crushing defeat of its Arab adversaries in 1967 certainly elevated Israel's image. The 1973 war, due to the failure of Israeli leadership to mobilize Israel's armed forces when first warned of an attack, in turn reduced Israel's status internationally. Qaddafi's adventures in Chad, Uganda, and Sudan brought the leadership of Libya into question in the international community.

War is not, of course, the only circumstance in which national leadership is important. How leaders respond to economic crises is also important. If the leadership places restraints on the economy during a time of economic inflation, as West Germany has done periodically, the stability of the economy will increase a nation's power. If leaders fail to act or act unsuccessfully, as did leadership in the United States during the inflationary period of the late 1970s, the power of a nation can be affected adversely.

Leaders can be ineffective for various reasons. If the nation is in domestic turmoil, international problems tend to be neglected. When leaders are operating with only marginal support from the people, that lack of support will limit the leadership's ability to be decisive. Leadership can also simply be poorly organized and unable to make the decisions necessary to capitalize on opportunities.

National leaders operate within the context of perceptions and images of their country and other countries. Their task is to enhance their country's image and develop realistic images of other countries. Leaders may utilize a variety of styles of leadership and means of decision-making to be effective, but successful leaders must accomplish these ends. Overall, a nation's leadership can make a great deal of difference in how a nation translates its capabilities into interest fulfillment.

THE POLITICAL SYSTEM

National leaders must, of course, operate within the framework of a particular political system. An authoritarian or totalitarian leadership ordinarily can make decisions without the public and legislative debate found in a democracy. The question is, however, does a democracy suffer because of its consultative process of decision-making?

An assumption often made is that democracies take longer than more centralized political systems to make decisions and that opportunities are lost because of this delay. Another assumption is that the democratic process dilutes decisions, thus weakening a decision's impact, whereas authoritarian and totalitarian systems concentrate decision-making among the top leaders without the need for time-consuming consultations with lesser bureaucratic units, a legislative body, or the public.

There is no evidence, however, that democracies are slower in making decisions than centralized decision-making systems. Also, during times of international crisis, the immediacy of the problem often forces democratic leadership to bypass public debate. Far-ranging debates over foreign policy do take place in democracies, but, ordinarily, this occurs after decisions are made; the public reviews the decision, not whether it should be implemented. Nor do authoritarian and totalitarian leaders totally escape the need to consult with various bureaucratic units before a decision is made. Since decision-making in democratic and centralized systems is essentially the same in that each system must work out differences between its bureaucratic units. The issue is, which system can resolve those differences the fastest.

A note of caution pertaining to judging the efficiency of decision-making within a particular political system is in order. Because no country can be as familiar with the conflicts over policy in another country as it is with its own, it always seems that others have a more effective system of decision-making than you have. Also, even if authoritarian or totalitarian systems are more efficient in decision-making than democratic systems, the one advantage that democracies have is that on the broad parameters of policy, decision-makers often have the support of the public, whereas centralized systems do not necessarily have such support. On the other hand, although the Soviet Union is a closed society wherein public debate of policy is discouraged, there is little evidence that the Soviet people do not support the major themes of their government's foreign policy, such as the attitude that the United States is a threat.

A significant difference between political systems that does have a major effect on a nation's power lies in the stability of the domestic system. An unstable system cannot rally support for its decisions as readily as can a stable one. Even in democracies that are stable, election time tends to bring foreign policy decision-making to a near standstill. When the United States holds elections, the electorate turns inward for the issues that are debated, and foreign policy questions rarely are included among the major campaign issues. Short of an international crisis, the public debate of foreign policy is postponed until after the election, when leaders are restored to office or new officials elected. In 1984, Israel delayed deciding the issue of withdrawing its troops from Lebanon until elections were held. Following the elections, the decision was delayed further for an additional two-month period while a new national government was being formed.

The regularity of elections in the United States can also create problems internationally. Most democracies are parliamentary systems, thus having some flexibility as to when elections are held, but the United States holds elections by a fixed calendar. In October 1956, while the United States was engaged in a national election campaign, crises over both Egypt's nationalization of the Suez Canal and the Hungarian Revolution developed. In 1962, the Cuban missile crisis occurred in the midst of a congressional election campaign. The elections took place on schedule in spite of the need for national leaders to devote their attention to international problems. Whether crises at election time result in the United States' behaving differently than it would at other times is debatable, but crises during campaign

periods are, at the very least, inconvenient.

Regardless of the form of government, the principal contribution the political system makes to a nation's power is its ability to respond to international problems in a rational and prompt manner. A system that is unable, for whatever reason, to decide important matters or that makes unreasonable demands is certainly going to be less effective in the international system than a system that avoids such shortcomings.

ASSESSING THE ELEMENTS OF POWER

Throughout this discussion of the elements of power, two assertions have been made. The first is that each of the elements does, in some manner, affect a nation's power. The second is that the way in which a nation's power is affected by an element of power is often difficult to ascertain. The circumstances from one situation to another change, so that what an element contributes to power in one instance can even result in a reduction of power in another. Thus, the elements of power are not themselves power to a nation, but, rather, they present the opportunity to convert them into power. The conversion of elements of power into effective influence in the international system is the task of national leadership.

The above analysis of the elements of power can create confusion as to why power as a concept should even be studied if so many unanswered questions exist about its contribution to understanding international relations. Just what form of government contributes the most to a nation's power? On what basis can you decide that the size of a nation's population is weakening its power? In modern warfare, is any particular strategic position to be preferred over another?

The fundamental issue therefore becomes how to draw up an assessment of what the elements of power overall contribute to a nation's power. If each element is difficult to assess, a collective assessment of all elements presents an even more complex problem of measurement. Various formulas have been developed to provide a means of assessing a nation's overall power. One attempt uses the following formula:

$$Pp = (C + E + M) \times (S + W)$$

Pp represents perceived power, C represents population and territory, E economic capability, M military capability, S strategic objectives and W the will to pursue those objectives (Cline, 1975). Even this formula, which is designed to produce a numerical measurement of a nation's power, fails to avoid subjective judgments. The formula assumes that the population-geographic element is equal to military capabilities, that military capabilities are equal to economic capabilities, and that strategic objectives are equal to a nation's will. This formula faces the same problems that all attempts to come up with a precise measure of power face: the importance of particular elements of power will vary from situation to situation, and the elements are not necessarily of equal influence in any situation. Nor does the formula take into consideration which country or countries will be the adversaries in a particular situation. This formula, or any formula designed to measure power, reflects the problem faced by decision-makers throughout the world; they reflect several subjective judgments in assessing power, including deciding how much weight to give each element of power and how to come up with an overall assessment. If a reliable formula exists among the decision-makers who make such assessments, it is not a matter of public record.

The absence of a generally accepted formula for measuring power does not mean that power goes unmeasured either by observers of or decision-makers in the international system. Probably any formula for measuring power can be criticized, but it does not follow that attempts to measure power are not taking place. Since power cannot be measured with any precision, the result is perceptions or images of power.

In the absence of a generally accepted standard for evaluating a nation's power, each nation must develop its own means of evaluation both for its own power and the power of others. Whether the assessment or perception of power nations develop is accurate is not the issue, since nations react to one another on the basis of how powerful they think they and their opponents are at any given moment. Following an international event, the perceptions of power used during the crisis may be judged to have been inaccurate or unrealistic, but at the time of decision-making the assessment decision-makers made was realistic to them. Power, as is the case with relations between nations in general, is based on the perception nations have of one another.

Numerous examples of misperceptions exist in the history of any nation's foreign policy. The United States has reacted on various occasions to how powerful it thought the Soviet Union was at the time and later found those assessments to be inaccurate. Once in the mid-1950s, when the United States thought the Soviet Union was engaged in a massive buildup of long-range bombers, and then again in the early 1960s, when it was thought the Soviets were ahead in intercontinental ballistic missiles, the United States, on both occasions, made a major effort to catch up with the Soviet Union. Later, U.S. estimates of Soviet strength were found to be exaggerated, and the United States' image of its power and that of the Soviet Union had to be revised as a result. A more recent example is the reassessment of Soviet power made by the Reagan administration in the early 1980s which resulted in substantial increases in the defense budget, as opposed to the assessments made by the Carter administration, which called for lower military expenditures. Whether the Carter administration's original assessment was more accurate than the one made by the Reagan administration is not at issue. What is important is that each administration developed a defense budget and approached the Soviet Union from a different perspective as a result of different assessments of Soviet and U.S. power.

If nations do interact with one another on their perceived images of each other's power, then if those comparative images are reasonably close the international system should be relatively stable. That is, if the United States views Soviet power in about the same way as the Soviets see their own power, and vice versa, then the two nations have at least a common base from which to negotiate. The greatest danger within the system would occur when the two superpowers, or any nations in conflict, differed substantially in their assessments of one another and of themselves. Under such circumstances negotiations would be difficult.

DEPENDENCE AND INTERDEPENDENCE

Earlier, it was pointed out that in many transactions between nations it was possible that the nations involved could feel that each had obtained a substantial portion of what it was seeking and could be relatively satisfied with the outcome; that both winners and losers were not necessary in all transactions. Such outcomes would also indicate that for some transactions power is not the governing concept. Keohane and Nye have introduced concepts that apply to such situations. These concepts are dependence and interdependence. "Dependence means a state of being determined or significantly affected by external forces. Interdependence most simply defined, means mutual dependence" (Keohane and Nye, 1977, 6). Dependent relationships would typically, but not exclusively, be transactions between the industrialized nations and the underdeveloped nations. The industrialized nations must have the natural resources found in the underdeveloped nations, and the underdeveloped

nations need the markets for their resources found in the industrialized nations. Power, in the sense that either party to the transaction is coerced into a change of behavior, is not significantly involved. The parties involved need each other and all benefit from the relationship. Interdependence also includes transactions that are of mutual benefit to the parties involved. "Where there are reciprocal (although not necessarily symmetrical) costly effects of transactions, there is interdependence" (Keohane and Nye, 1977, 9). Such relationships are most apt to be found between the industrialized nations where trade and exchanges of technology will benefit all parties involved in the transaction.

Even though both dependent and interdependent relationships benefit to some extent all parties involved, it does not follow that these will be relationships without conflict. Conflict will most likely come from a dependent relationship, since the underdeveloped nations have little choice but to enter into the transaction, but interdependent relationships also produce conflict. The trade relationship between the United States and the European Community often involves conflict. The same observation is valid for the economic relationship between Japan and the United States.

Introducing the concepts of dependence and interdependence should make clear that the use of power in the international system is not necessarily a case of one country's gain being another country's loss. These concepts also emphasize that using power to explain the behavior of nations does not establish military strength as the singlemost important element of power. Economic factors are of increasing importance in the relations between nations.

CONCLUSION

Power has been defined as the ability of one nation to change the behavior of another. In most instances, however, the exercise of power is not on a bilateral, single-issue basis. What appears to be bilateral usually involves relationships with third parties, and what seems to be a single interest usually is related to various other interests. Nations are never powerful in isolation; thus, power can be measured and judged only within the context of specific relationships and in specific situations. Power is not a single element or capability but, rather, constitutes many elements, both tangible and intangible. Nations face the problem of having no common means of measuring power, but that obstacle in no way prevents them from developing perceptions of their power and the power of others. The instruments of power are many, but, in particular, bargaining, economic persuasion, and the use of or the threat to use force are the most prominent ones. Measuring the outcome of the use of power is also a problem because often a winner or loser is difficult to identify in the overall relationship of a nation with other nations.

Many relationships and outcomes do not result in winners or losers. Nations can have conflicts with other nations in which all benefit from the relationship. In relationships involving the Western industrial nations with one another, their interdependence results in a need for each nation to cooperate for their mutual well-being. The dependence relationship between the industrial nations and the developing nations also is mutually beneficial, but the developing nations often feel that their choices are limited even though the transaction benefits them.

CHAPTER 4

Organization of the System

Even though the international system often seems to be one of self-help—that is, a nation is its own best protector—differing patterns of behavior among the nation-states produce different arrangements or systems that limit and control conflict. These systems are not formal organizations but, rather, unwritten but generally understood rules under which a particular arrangement of the international system functions. Several means of organization are only theoretical, thus have never been operational systems internationally. Others, the ones that will be the focus of discussion in this chapter, are those that have functioned in some form during recent nation-state history. Since political behavior seldom follows precisely a model or theoretical explanation, the discussion of systems in this chapter will develop both the theoretical and the behavioral aspects of these systems.

As the various alternatives for organizing the international system are examined, the false impression can be given that the manner in which the overall international system behaves is by design, that somehow nations can choose the sort of system they wish to have and then develop the rules under which it will operate. Except for the system of collective security, which was designed and negotiated to serve as the heart of the League of Nations, the operating systems of international relations have been a result of a particular political environment produced by international behavior, not a conscious choice of nation-states. The number of major states, their forms of government, the distribution of power among those nations, the flexibility of coalition membership, and the type of diplomacy seem to be governing factors in how a system functions and what the rules of behavior are. A crucial aspect of any system is whether it is anarchic, that is, essentially a self-help system, or hierarchical, that is, displays at least some of the characteristics of an organized government (Waltz, 1979, 107–116).

Development of organizational models of the international system helps explain the behavior of nations when they function within a particular political environment. "In a systems theory, some part of the explanation of behaviors and outcomes is found in the system's structure" (Waltz, 1979, 73). If conditions within the international system change, then a different model may be more appropriate to describe behavior. A model thus is a means of analyzing the international system at a particular time or in a particular hypothetical arrangement.

The first system to be discussed is balance of power. To the realist school of international politics, this system was the only system possible, and any other arrangement was merely a variation on balance of power. Since, for the realist school, power is the central operational concept used in explaining international behavior, it follows that balancing power among the nation-states through competitive coalitions is the only manner in which stability can be introduced into the international system. The discussion here, however, treats balance of power as only one possible means of organizing the international system, and argues that other possibilities exist.

BALANCE OF POWER

Though balance of power will be discussed here as a system of organization, the term is often used in ways that are not consistent with its use as a system. For example, when used to describe the military relationship between the United States and the Soviet Union, the statement might be made that a balance of power exists between the two countries. Such a reference does not imply that a system of balance of power exists internationally, but, rather, that a particular condition exists in the international system—a condition of military equality between the United States and the Soviet Union. Another way in which balance of power is used is actually in contradiction with the term itself. This occurs when reference is made to the balance of power shifting to one side or the other. Under these circumstances, balance of power is used to describe either a balance or an imbalance in power relationships. That is, balance of power is used to describe any relationship between two countries or coalitions of nations. On other occasions, balance of power is used to describe a policy objective, that is, when a country wishes to achieve a balance of power with another country. As different students of international politics have pointed out, "Unfortunately for the scholar who wants to understand and evaluate, the meaning of balance of power is not so definitely established as those who glibly use the phrase seem to imply" (Claude, 1962, 12). Or, "The term is defined differently by different writers; it is used in varying senses, even if not defined exactly at

all; and, finally, it is the focal concept in several quite distinct theories of international relations" (Haas, 1953, 442).

Hans Morgenthau, though a proponent of balance of power as the organizational base of the international system, admitted that he used balance of power in several ways: "(1) As a policy aimed at a certain state of affairs, (2) as an actual state of affairs, (3) as an approximately equal distribution of power, (4) as any distribution of power" (Morgenthau, 1956, 167). With all these possibilities available to the realist school, then, balance of power is to it a term that can be used to describe a wide range of behavior.

As a system of organization, however, balance of power is utilized to describe a particular means of controlling conflict, primarily among the major states. In this context, a balance-of-power system is a system of two competing coalitions, each of which includes about the same number of major states with each of the major states of about equal power; the major states are not hierarchically organized. The underlying assumption of the balance-of-power system accepts the idea that conflict is inherent in international politics, but that the best means of limiting the outcomes of conflict is through an equilibrium of power between opposing coalitions. This assumption also includes the idea that nations start wars only when they feel they have an advantage, or when their situation is desperate and they turn to war as a final effort to save themselves. But, when confronted with power equal to their own, nations choose to avoid the prospect of a protracted, costly war of attrition. Thus, stability can be achieved in the international system when a balance of power develops among the major nations of the system. This aspect of the balance-of-power system does not include a means of resolving conflict among the opposing nations, but only attempts to limit the consequences of conflict.

Probably the most forceful challenge to this basic assumption of balance of power is that when nations are in balance or near balance, a time when the system is intended to be stable, the system is, in fact, at its greatest risk of going to war. A. F. K. Organski argues that the "relationship between peace and the balance of power appears to be exactly the opposite of what has been claimed. The periods of balance, real or imagined, are periods of warfare, while periods of known preponderance are periods of peace" (Organski, 1958, 292. See also Garnham, 1975; Rummel, 1972; Siverson and Sullivan, 1983, 473–494). The Organski approach to balance of power is that if one coalition of nations has a distinct advantage over the other, the stronger does not need to go to war since it can achieve what it wants with the use of threats. Since relationships between nations are always in a state of flux, balance can only be momentary; therefore, as one coalition of nations becomes stronger and the other weaker, the weaker will be the one most apt to go to war, because the longer it delays, the weaker it fears it will become. Thus, according to Organski, the assumption that the stronger coalition will start a war is erroneous. The conflicting arguments concerning the stability of the balance-of-power system thus are that a balance of power between coalitions will limit major wars or, in opposition, that balance is transitory, thus, dangerous because it tempts the weaker coalition in the relationship to go to war.

One aspect of this system that both arguments must take into account is that if the balance-of-power system is to function effectively, there must be a relatively common means of evaluating power. As was pointed out in the discussion of power in the previous chapter, there is no commonly agreed-upon means of assessing a nation's power; thus, the opportunity for miscalculation within or between the competing coalitions is always present. If the major states cannot agree that a balance has been achieved, then the system necessarily will fail to achieve its primary objective of limiting wars among major powers.

Since balance of power, if successful, requires coalitions that are approximately equal in power and since power relationships are always changing, membership in the coalitions must be flexible; that is, the major states that make up each of the coalitions must be willing to switch to the opposing coalition if the needs for balance call

---

Fig. 4.1 Model of Balance of Power

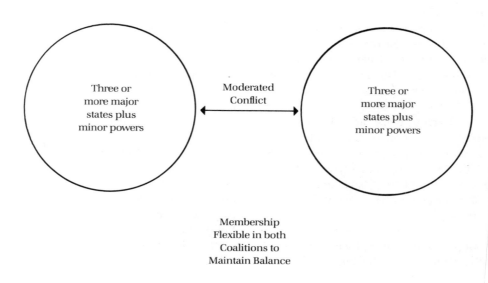

Three or more major states plus minor powers

Moderated Conflict

Three or more major states plus minor powers

Membership
Flexible in both
Coalitions to
Maintain Balance

for such a change. In order for the balance-of-power system to function, no nation's loyalty to its coalition can be stronger than its commitment to maintain a balance between the coalitions. If one of the coalitions is losing strength relative to the other coalition, then a major state belonging to the stronger coalition should leave that coalition and join the weaker coalition. If loyalties to the coalition are strong, then such shifts of membership become difficult to achieve. Thus, the stronger a coalition becomes, the more fragile its membership should be (Kaplan, 1959, 697).

This requirement carries with it expectations about the behavior of major states that is perhaps one of the flaws in the functional rules of a balance-of-power system. Nations are expected to behave in a fashion contrary to their natural inclination in that they are supposed to abandon a position of strength and move to a weaker coalition in the name of balance. Loyalties to allies and treaty commitments must give way to the search for balance. (Waltz, 1979, 125–127).

In order for a balance-of-power system to have this flexibility in membership, it must include a minimum number of at least five or six major states. With too few major states, a shift in membership would automatically create a new imbalance in favor of the coalition that just received a new member. During the nineteenth century, when a balance-of-power system was reputed to have functioned at various times, there were five major powers. France, Great Britain, Russia, Prussia, and the Austro-Hungarian Empire functioned as major powers throughout the century, and after 1870 Italy and a united Germany under Prussian leadership were added. Since the balance-of-power system of that century was limited to Europe, growing powers such as Japan and the United States were not part of the system, but even without their participation there were enough major powers to make the system functional.

While each of the major powers engaged in a balance-of-power system are theoretically committed to shifting coalition allegiances if called upon to do so, in practice all major states need not meet this requirement as long as at least one major state with sufficient power to substantially affect the balance is prepared to shift sides. In the balance-of-power system of the nineteenth century, Great Britain was often described as the balancer nation. In general, Great Britain was to shift to the weaker coalition as the political situation demanded, but how well Great Britain carried out its role is a matter of debate among historians.

The balance-of-power system is not intended to prevent all war, but, rather, to control wars if they break out. While wars are to be avoided if possible, if they occur they are to be limited both as to objectives and as to the number of nations that participate. A war is particularly acceptable within the system if necessary to maintain a balance, but, whatever its objective, wars are to be limited. The reasons for this restriction are twofold: first, major wars tend to produce significant changes, and if the terms of a peace settlement are harsh or the war damage too great this might weaken one or more of the major actors and thus restrict the ability of the system to function; second, major wars or harsh peace terms might create long-term animosities between major states and prevent them from belonging to the same coalition again. Either a reduction in the number of major states or less flexible membership is a threat to a balance-of-power system.

In the nineteenth century, major European powers were not always able to fulfill these requirements. During the Crimean War in the 1850s they successfully confined the fighting primarily to the Crimean Peninsula, even though the war involved three of the major powers— Russia, Great Britain, and France. Also, when the Franco-Prussian War broke out in 1870, the other major powers restricted the war to those two major states by maintaining their neutrality. But the impact of this war made it diplomatically impossible for France to serve again in the same alliance with Germany due to the hostility created by France's defeat and the peace settlement that Germany imposed on France. The balance-of-power system lost some of its flexibility as a result. By the beginning of the twentieth century, the opposing coalitions had become rigid in membership, and, in terms of the requirements of balance of power, this loss of flexibility made a major war more likely. Thus, one explanation for why World War I occurred was the rigidity of the coalitions in the years before the war began.

An extension of the rules of balance of power that no major actor be weakened and no long-term animosities be allowed to develop is the principle that major actors should not interfere in the internal affairs of another major actor. Such an act of interference could weaken or produce a long-term hostility among the major actors. The principle of national sovereignty was to be adhered to carefully.

The diplomatic method also must take a particular form in order to meet the needs of a balance-of-power system—generally, diplomacy is to be conducted in secret. Since the system requires that nations move freely and quickly when shifts in coalition membership are required, diplomatic secrecy is necessary. Open, public diplomacy tends to create public support behind a government's policies, but a closed, secret system of diplomacy avoids the delay involved in explaining policy shifts to a nation's public. Diplomacy in a balance-of-power system will thus be conducted by well-trained, professional diplomats who understand the rules of and the need for secret diplomacy, and who will not react to the emotional aspects of a situation, as might the public if it were involved.

If Europe during the nineteenth century is any indication of how a balance-of-power system functions, nations will keep diplomatic channels open at all times so that changes can be negotiated quickly. It also means that, since the system is closed to public observation, many international agreements will not only be negotiated in secret, their existence will also be held secret.

Evidence of this practice was apparent when treaties secretly negotiated among the major powers became public following World War I. Whatever conflict resolution results from a balance-of-power system comes from the negotiating process found in this traditional, closed diplomatic method.

The major states that operate within a balance-of-power system must have domestic systems that are similar; otherwise, agreement on the rules for operating the system would be difficult to arrive at. In addition, the coalitions must avoid ideological differences; if such occurred, it could introduce either long-term commitments to allies or sustained differences with ideologically different nations, and thus impair the movement of nations from one coalition to another. The introduction of ideology would also bring about a commitment from the public, thereby making even more difficult shifts in coalition membership.

In brief, the environment of a balance-of-power system is one of competitive coalitions with flexible membership among the major-power members. The assumption underlying the system is that when a balance of power occurs between the coalitions war is less likely, but if war does develop it must be limited so that none of the major actors are unduly injured. Conflict must be confined and controlled in order not to disturb the balance. To what degree Europe during the nineteenth century operated under a balance-of-power system is debatable, but, at a minimum, there is agreement that at times European diplomacy operated approximately within the rules of such a system.

BIPOLARITY

A system of bipolarity is often described as a variation on the balance-of-power system, though the operating rules for each are somewhat different. The one characteristic that the two systems have in common is that both are organized around competitive coalitions. The outstanding difference is that balance is not the policy objective for either coalition in a bipolar system. A balance-of-power system intends to achieve international stability through equality and reluctance to fight a war of attrition. Bipolarity does not strive for balance, but, rather, each coalition seeks to develop superiority over the other; each coalition would prefer that the other coalition not exist. In a bipolar system, if balance occurs it is incidental. A bipolar system can develop out of a balance-of-power system, particularly if a hierarchy develops among the major states and two of those nations emerge more powerful than the others. In addition, if the coalitions of balance of power lose their membership flexibility and commitment to balance is lost, the result is a bipolar system. In theory, bipolarity is hierarchical in nature, whereas balance of power lacks hierarchy and is more nearly anarchical.

The period since World War II has commonly been described as one of bipolarity, thus the operating rules of such a system are largely drawn from the diplomatic experience of that period. One significant change brought about by World War II that led to the development of a bipolar system was the reduction in the number of major powers in the international system. Only the United States and the Soviet Union increased their power as a result of the war, and each, in turn, assumed the leadership of competing, hierarchically organized, hostile alliances.

Unlike a balance-of-power system, where coalition leadership can be shared by several major states, bipolarity with two superpowers produces coalitions each of which is dominated by a single power. The coalitions of a bipolar system differ from those of a balance-of-power system in another manner as well. Commitments to the coalitions are long-term, and shifts in membership are rare. If a second-level nation shifted membership under balance of power, that event would be of little importance. But under bipolarity, where membership is not flex-

---

Fig. 4.2a Model of Tight Bipolarity

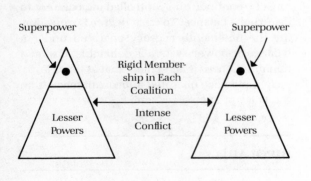

Hierarchically Organized
Coalitions

Fig. 4.2b Model of Loose Bipolarity

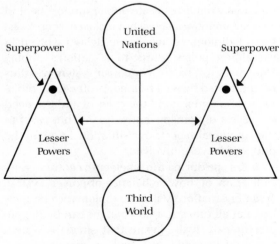

Intensity of Conflict Modified
by UN and Third World

ible, a shift in membership from one coalition to the other or to a nonaligned position is seen as an important change in the system. Under the present bipolar system, when Cuba left the Western coalition and aligned itself with the Soviet-led coalition, that event produced a reaction that is still an issue after nearly thirty years. Under a balance-of-power system, such an event would have received little notice.

Since in a bipolar system membership in either of the coalitions is long-term, the precautions of a balance-of-power system that allow for quick shifts in coalition membership are not necessary. Where ideological commitments are avoided in balance of power, in a bipolar system ideology is used to hold the coalitions intact. Whereas diplomacy was generally carried out in secret under balance of power, bipolar diplomacy is more open, and there is no need to avoid a commitment by the public that might make coalition shifts difficult. In bipolarity, since the objective of the coalition leader is to not allow any members to slip away, ideology and open diplomacy are means to bring national publics behind their governments' policies. Consequently, diplomacy in a bipolar system is apt to be conducted with considerable fanfare, as occurs when national leaders meet in summit conferences. The purpose of such conferences often seems to be to show that efforts are being made to resolve differences between the coalitions, but such conferences have, overall, produced few substantive results. Successful negotiations between the two coalitions do take place, but usually after a long period of quiet diplomacy carried on by special ambassadors, not heads of state.

According to the theory of bipolarity, the minimum objective of the coalition leaders is to avoid losing members either to the other coalition or to the ranks of the nonaligned. At best, the leaders of the coalitions will expand their coalition by adding new members. This can most easily be done by attracting as members nations that are among the nonaligned. The more difficult and more destabilizing task is to bring into the coalition a member of the other coalition.

Where it is a rule of balance of power not to intervene in the internal affairs of a major actor, the same is not always true under bipolarity. The likelihood of intervention under bipolarity depends, however, on the status of the nation within the system. Open intervention in the internal affairs of one superpower by the other superpower would be the riskiest form of intervention and would be avoided short of a major war between those nations. Intervention in the internal affairs of any member of a coalition by any member of the other coalition, particularly by the coalition leader, would be nearly as destabilizing to the system as would intervention in a coalition leader's affairs. Less risky would be intervention by a coalition member in the internal affairs of a nonaligned nation. Least risky would be intervention by the coalition leader in the internal affairs of a member of the same coalition. The purpose of this latter sort of intervention ordinarily would be to hold the coalition intact. Risk, in each instance, would be measured by the degree to which an act of intervention might result in overt opposition by the leader of the other coalition. For example, the Soviet Union only diplomatically opposed intervention by the United States in the Dominican Republic in 1965 and Grenada in 1983, and the United States only diplomatically protested Soviet interventions in Hungary in 1956 and Czechoslovakia in 1968. In none of these instances did the opposing coalition leader threaten military involvement.

In bipolarity, the same problem of measuring power exists as in a balance-of-power system, and as with balance of power, the distribution of power is critical to the functioning of the system. (See Waltz, 1979.) Without a common means for measuring power, the relationship between the two coalitions can be misinterpreted, particularly if one coalition departs markedly from the other's perception of the relationship. Even though balance is not the policy objective of either coalition, the competition between the coalitions can produce a balance, of sorts, as each attempts to keep up with or surpass the power of the other coalition. This has been the situation between the United States and the Soviet Union throughout the Cold War.

Within the present bipolar system, the distribution of power between the two coalitions often is uneven from one measurement of power to another. In the economic competition between the Western and Soviet coalitions, the Soviet coalition is far behind; the combined economies of Western Europe, Japan, and the United States far surpass what the Soviet bloc can assemble economically. In conventional military capabilities, the Soviet bloc may have an advantage over Western conventional forces. But the area where both coalitions in the present system must have equal certainty as to outcome is the realm of nuclear capability. Both coalition leaders must be convinced that if either uses its nuclear weapons the coalition that is attacked will have sufficient surviving weapons to destroy the attacker in turn. The superpowers do not have to possess a balance in nuclear weapons, but each must have sufficient numbers of such weapons to make deterrence and mutually assured destruction through a second-strike capability credible.

Another variable in bipolarity pertains to whether it takes a tight or loose form. A tight system of bipolarity would be one in which there are few nations, and certainly no major states, that are not members of the coalitions. With many countries not committed in the current system of bipolarity, the system that has operated since the late 1940s has always been loose, even though most of the major states have committed to one coalition or other.

The "something loose" with the greatest influence on the present system is made up of those nations that prefer nonalignment over membership in either of the coalitions. In terms of numbers alone, nearly two-thirds of the present nation-states are a part of this nonaligned group. This group is anticolonial, often anti-Western, and occasionally anti-Soviet. The nonaligned nations generally argue that the issues in dispute between the two major coalitions are not the issues that are of concern to them. The nonaligned nations thus are both a part of the loosening process in bipolarity and, as pointed out earlier, a potential source of new members for the committed coalitions. Since China is the one major state without a commitment to either coalition, it, too, is a major influence in the loosening of the bipolar system.

Factors other than nonaligned nations could also be the "something loose" in a bipolar system; a strong universal actor that could mediate effectively between the competing coalitions can also loosen a bipolar system. The United Nations was intended to play such a role, but even in its early years failed to do so and, since, has played only a minor role in arbitrating conflicts between the superpowers. Yet another means of loosening a bipolar system is for the coalitions themselves to become looser in organization. The hierarchical character of the coalitions could be challenged by coalition members' developing greater freedom of action independent of coalition leaders.

The most hopeful means of loosening a bipolar system comes from improved relations between the coalitions, and, most importantly, between the coalition leaders. In the current system, when détente developed between the superpowers during the early 1970s, the question was raised as to whether the Cold War had come to an end. The improved relationship deteriorated, however, and left little doubt that a system of bipolarity was still operative.

Bipolarity thus is a system based on competition between alliances or coalitions. As a system, it does not perceive balance as a policy objective but, rather, emphasizes competition. Deterrence, conventional and nuclear, is the nearest thing to an intended balance found in bipolarity. Nonalignment, a universal actor, or loosely organized coalitions can all serve to loosen a tight bipolar system. Membership in the coalitions is regarded by the coalition leaders as long-term, making withdrawal from a coalition difficult. Both coalitions attempt to recruit new members either from the ranks of the nonaligned or from the competing coalition. If nuclear weapons are present within the system, the system gains whatever level of stability it has to offer from deterrence and mutually assured destruction. (See Waltz, 1979, pp.170-183.)

MULTIPOLARITY

Multipolarity can be described as a system that is somewhere between balance of power and bipolarity. It, too, is a competitive-coalition system, but it differs from balance of power and bipolarity in that there are more than two coalitions. The anticipated behavior of a multipolar system is more difficult to place within a set of rules since, unlike balance of power and bipolarity, there has been no recent experience with such a system internationally.

In spite of this difficulty, approximate rules can be projected about such a system, especially if the view is taken that the present international system is, in economic terms, organized along multipolar lines. This approach accepts the idea that the international system is one of bipolarity militarily but of several poles economically. The United States, Japan, and the European Community are military allies but economically competitive. The Soviet bloc, in military or economic terms, is another pole. These poles of economic strength compete with one another, but they also have to maintain a degree of cooperation in order to carry on trade. The Soviet economic pole is not as involved in the system as the Western poles, but some trade and economic interaction does exist between them. China and the other Third World countries are yet another economic pole, but have a different impact on the world economy than do other economic poles due to their low level of industrialization.

Balance in a multipolar system can be achieved in two ways. One would be for nations to shift their membership to one of the weaker coalitions,

similar to what is expected system. This sort of action sense of loyalty to the coalition, a balance-of-power system. A second method of achieving balance would not require changes in coalition membership. Balance could be achieved through the realignment of the coalitions. If one coalition becomes too strong, then the remaining coalitions could coalesce to reestablish balance. These alignments of coalitions would have to be short-term, however, or a multipolar system could develop into a bipolar system. A common objective of both multipolarity and balance of power is that major actors not be weakened and that nations should act to that end.

The most likely manner in which a multipolar system could emerge in the international system is for various regional concentrations of nations to develop out of a bipolar or balance-of-power system. (Masters, 1961, 797). Such would be likely, however, only if the hierarchy of bipolar coalitions collapsed. One probable result of a multipolar system would be that there would be fewer uncommitted nations than exist in the present bipolar system, since a multipolar system would offer a greater number of alternatives for alignment.

How stable such a system would be depends on several factors. If the primary strength of the poles were economic, the system could be stable over an extended period of time because it would serve the interests of all poles to cooperate in order to maintain other poles as trading partners. If the poles were based on conventional military strength, then stability would depend on the ability of the coalitions to align for the sake of balance. If some, but not all, of the poles possessed nuclear weapons, the system would probably not be stable and would quickly be reduced to those poles that did possess such weapons. If all of the poles possessed nuclear weapons, the system could easily be one in which an uneasy deterrence existed among the poles with each having some control over the activities of the other poles through the threatened use of force.

Fig. 4.3 Model of Multipolarity

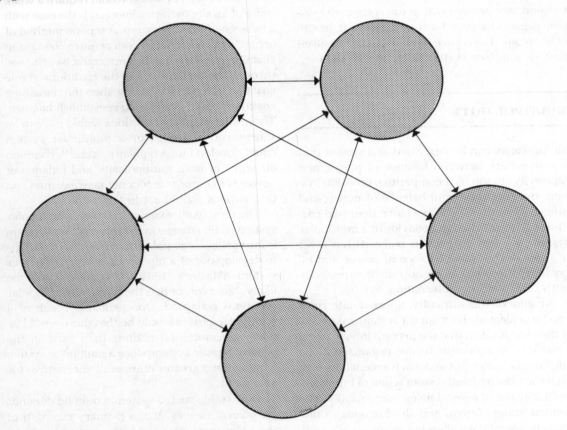

Flexible membership
in coalitions. Each
coalition probably
headed by a major power.

This could also be a system of limited movement and one in which the risks of nuclear war would be high.

COLLECTIVE SECURITY

Each of the three systems discussed has been a competitive-coalition system. Collective security is not but, rather, is based on a cooperative worldwide effort to maintain peace. Reduced to its simplest terms, a collective-security system is designed to frighten off a potential aggressor by providing it with an overwhelming preponderance of power and, if the deterrent fails, committing that power against the aggressor nation. While balance of power, and bipolarity for that matter, seek to avoid a preponderance of power in anyone's hands, collective security would place the control of overwhelming power in the hands of all nations acting together through a universal actor such as the League of Nations or the United Nations. Collective security rejects the balance-of-power premise that if overwhelming power is available to stop aggression, it can also be used to commit aggression (Claude, 1962, 112–113). Central to a collective-security system is the national commitment that if an act of aggression is committed by one nation against another, it is the duty of all nations to come to the aid of the victimized nation. In both balance of power and bipolarity, an alliance looks outward to prevent another coalition from gaining a power advantage. Collective security necessarily looks inward to the collective-security commitment to insure that the peace is not broken.

A collective-security system assumes that wars begin with an act of aggression; therefore, they can be prevented if aggression is deterred or punished. Collective security has failed as a deterrent when an act of aggression takes place, even if nations collectively bring overwhelming power to bear on the aggressor. But the system also has

failed if an act of aggression takes place and nations do not unite to bring overwhelming power to bear against the aggressor.

The League of Nations, created after World War I, was built around collective security. The planners of the organization felt that balance of power had failed to prevent World War I. Therefore a new system, collective security, was needed to avoid the disaster of another world war. In the immediate postwar period, the international system was dominated by the victorious Allies, and collective security was intended to keep the victors in a dominant position. The premise was that this could be done if the victors would cooperate with one another to punish any future aggressors. The post-World War II organization, the United Nations, was not organized around the concept of collective security to the extent that the League was, but it did make collective security available in its charter. Again, the intention was that the victors of the recently ended war would control the international system if only they would cooperate with one another. The Security Council of the United Nations was intended to be the institutional framework that allowed such cooperation, and the veto granted the major powers was intended to guarantee that any action by the Security Council had their unanimous support.

In a collective-security system, all nations must recognize and support the proposition that peace is indivisible and that if the peace is broken anywhere the security of all nations is threatened. While this rule applies to all nations, it is imperative that the major powers participate for the system to be successful. Thus, although regional alliances are frequently described as collective-security arrangements, they are not true collective-security efforts in that they fall short of a universal application of power. An alliance such as NATO is only regional, not global, and is designed to repel only designated aggressors: in NATO's case, the Soviet Union. Portugal discovered this limitation on NATO's collective effort when it sought but failed to receive NATO sup-

Fig. 4.4 Model of Collective Security System

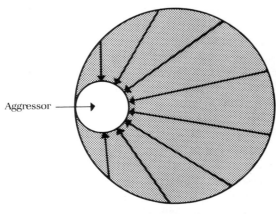

Aggressor

System-wide
commitment
to punish
aggressors.

port when India invaded Goa in 1961. Another example of the limited application of power by NATO was its unsuccessful effort to use the structure of NATO to settle differences between Greece and Turkey over Cyprus. Also, NATO differs from a collective-security system in that NATO is intended to offset Soviet power in eastern Europe, not to provide overwhelming power relative to the Soviet Union. In the context of alternative systems, NATO is a part of the western coalition in a bipolar system, not a regional version of a collective-security system.

In addition to the presumption that all nations accept the idea that peace is indivisible, a collective-security system requires that certain political-environmental conditions exist before it can function successfully. The most important of these requirements is that all nations must be vulnerable to the threat of overwhelming power; that is, power must be widely enough dispersed in the nation-state system that overwhelming power, or a meaningful threat of it, can be brought to bear against any nation. Obviously, this sort of distribution of power does not currently exist, particularly since only a few nations possess nuclear weapons. The size of the nuclear arsenals possessed by the superpowers makes those states formidable and very dangerous opponents, even if all the other nations of the system were to align themselves against either one of them. To make the superpowers vulnerable to collective security would require substantial arms reduction on their part. While arms reduction is important to collective security, it is not essential to either the balance-of-power or the bipolar systems. In a balance-of-power system, it could occur in order to obtain balance or, in a bipolar system, to maintain deterrence, but it is not necessary to the functioning of either system.

A strong universal actor also is necessary for the success of a collective-security system. The universal actor has the role of calling on members to participate in a collective-security action and must organize the punitive action against an aggressor. It also must decide when an act of aggression has taken place and what the sanc-

tions should be; economic as well as military sanctions can be imposed upon an aggressor nation. The presence of an effective collective-security system presents the opportunity for all states to settle their differences through the universal actor, to reduce their arms budgets, and to feel secure from acts of aggression by other nations. In spite of these objectives of the founders of the League and the United Nations, several problems of implementation have arisen in carrying out collective-security operations. Perhaps central to all of these problems is simply how to recognize when an act of aggression has occurred.

An act of aggression is a situation that everyone assumes will be recognized when it takes place but often is not obvious when an international crisis develops. In international politics, therefore, there is no functional definition of aggression. If a country attacks another country without warning, then that is generally regarded as an act of aggression. But even in this instance, the attacking nation might claim that its act was prompted by the other nation's preparations to attack and that what occurred was a preemptive act of self-defense, not an act of aggression. While the universal actor debates who the aggressor was, or tries to determine if an act of aggression has occurred, the war goes on. Both the League's covenant and the UN's charter committed these organizations to take action against aggression but neither document defined aggression. The UN General Assembly finally adopted a definition in 1974 which included first use of armed force, invasion into another country's territory, bombardment of another's territory, blockade of ports, stationing of armed forces in another country without permission, or support of irregular forces by one nation in the territory of another. While helpful, these instances of aggression are difficult to identify in actual situations. A related problem is the assumption that wars are started only by an act of aggression, when, in many instances, wars begin without such an act of moral clarity.

Illustrations of the denial that an attack was

an act of aggression abound in international politics. When China attacked India in 1962, the Chinese defended the action as the seizure of territory that had been taken from them when the British controlled India. In both 1956 and 1967, Israel argued that it attacked its Arab neighbors in order to prevent an attack by them. The United States invasion of Grenada in 1983 was justified as necessary to protect American citizens on the island. Even when the North Koreans invaded South Korea in 1950, North Korea claimed that it was only repulsing a South Korean attack.

Another problem with carrying out a collective-security action is the assumption that there will be a single aggressor or, at least, that only a few nations will be supporting the aggressive act. If the act of aggression is supported by a sufficient number of nations, or if too few nations join to punish the aggressors, then the aggressors will not face overwhelming power. The collective-security system would work best when there is a single, obvious, and quickly labeled aggressor.

The League and the United Nations encountered each of these problems at some point in their attempts to implement collective-security actions. When Japan occupied Manchuria in 1931, it took the Council of the League of Nations nearly a year to decide that aggression had taken place and that Japan was the guilty party. By that time, Japan had set up a puppet government in Manchuria and had consolidated its position. The League took no further action, but Japan did withdraw from the League in protest. When Italy invaded Ethiopia in 1935, the League labeled Italy an aggressor and imposed economic sanctions. The boycott was violated by several nations, including American oil companies, and Italy suffered little ill effect. When the Soviet Union invaded Finland in late 1939, the League named the Soviet Union as the aggressor and expelled it from the League. World War II had already begun, and the League's action was mainly a symbolic gesture by a dying organization. None of the League's attempts to carry out a collective-

security action even approached success.

The United Nations made its single effort toward a collective-security action when South Korea was invaded in June 1950. The Security Council of the United Nations did label North Korea the aggressor and, later, when China intervened, also included China as a part of the aggression. There was a call for the member states to take action against the aggressors, but only sixteen of the sixty members of the organization responded. Most of the troops from United Nations members came from the United States, and overwhelming force was never sent to Korea. The war eventually was fought to a stalemate, and a cease-fire line was agreed upon in 1953 that still exists more than thirty years later. At best, the Korean action can be described as only a partial implementation of collective security.

The United Nations, when called upon to use armed force, has, since Korea, avoided labeling any nation the aggressor as a prelude to its use of armed force. While the United Nations sent troops of member states to the Sinai in 1956 and 1975, the Congo in 1960, Cyprus in 1965, the Golan Heights in 1975, and Lebanon in 1977, those troops did not constitute overwhelming force and were not sent for the purpose of punishing an aggressor. Nor did they include forces from the superpowers, which would be necessary for overwhelming force to exist in the theoretical sense of all nations participating in a collective-security action. These post–Korean War uses of armed force by the UN were, in fact, labeled as peacekeeping operations, not collective-security actions, and were justified under a different section of the charter than that which dealt with collective security.

The result of the recent UN efforts to use armed force has been essentially to eliminate collective security as a means of controlling violence in the international system. In a political environment of bipolarity in which collective-security actions have been attempted, the stronger or more influential system has been bipolarity. The issues are East-West or North-South conflicts, and issues between these poles of interests are not resolved with overwhelming power, not even when the charge is aggression. (An example would be when the World Court found the United States guilty of mining Nicaraguan harbors and the General Assembly labeled the U.S. an aggressor for its air strike on Libya.) Collective security could conceivably work in a different political environment, but it has not been successful in the environments of the postwar periods of the two world wars.

CONCLUSION

While there are other means by which the international system could conceivably be organized, of the systems discussed—balance of power, both loose and tight bipolarity, multipolarity, and collective security—all but multipolarity have been attempted in recent history. None of these international systems takes into consideration, however, the sort of domestic systems that must exist in order for these international systems to function effectively. Each system has a set of rules and practices for the behavior of nations internationally, but rules for the domestic systems are lacking. In balance of power, since membership should be flexible, members of both coalitions would need to have similar domestic systems. In bipolarity, the domestic systems of members within each coalition need to be similar, but not similar to that of members of the other coalition, since switches in membership are rare. In the present system, the members of the Soviet bloc are all communist governments, and the Western coalition is composed of mostly democratic regimes, although at times the main requisite for membership in the Western coalition has been that a country be anticommunist but not necessarily democratic. Both Portugal and Greece, for example, were members of NATO at a time when they had nondemocratic governments. Based on the present system, the countries that are non-aligned in a bipolar system can have a variety of domestic systems, since unity among the non-aligned is not important to the functioning of the system.

Multipolarity, like bipolarity, could function only with a degree of commonality in domestic systems among the members of each pole. Collective security apparently cannot function if there is much diversity in domestic systems worldwide. This may be the single greatest problem in carrying out a collective-security operation, since the nations with authoritarian and totalitarian systems usually have been the nations that have opposed collective-security actions when they have been attempted.

The overall observation that can be drawn from this discussion of international systems is that the international environment is the determining factor in what sort of system functions at any given time. Domestic systems are also important because they, as a part of the environment, strongly affect the manner in which nations will align themselves and what coalitions can be formed. The international system operates under the general rules produced by a particular sort of system, but any system is continually in a state of change, and new systems and rules are always possible.

PART II

Sources of Conflict in the System

While conflict among nations is commonplace and the potential for disagreement exists between any two actors that interact, conflict in the present system is concentrated between and within the major coalitions of nation-states. In the current system of loose bipolarity, the principal arenas of intercoalitional conflict are between the Western and communist coalitions, and between the industrialized and the underdeveloped nations. A third arena of conflict is intracoalitional—the ongoing concern in the West to keep its coalition intact, especially economically, and the Soviets' need to maintain control over its coalition. This chapter will investigate the first of these areas of conflict, the development and nature of conflict between East and West.

CHAPTER 5

Sources of Conflict I: East–West Conflict

Since shortly after World War II, tensions between East and West have been labeled simply as the Cold War, a level of conflict that has not led to a shooting war between leaders of the coalitions but that occasionally has been controlled just short of it. Limited wars have occurred, and some have involved armed forces from one of the superpowers, but never forces from both in the same war. Conflict between the Western and communist coalitions has gone through cycles ranging from tense confrontation, where war seemed near at hand, to détente, with the expectation that the Cold War was coming to an end. Throughout these cycles, however, the elements of suspicion and mutual caution between the two coalitions remained.

The Cold War label for the tensions between the coalitions is generally accredited to Bernard Baruch. But whatever the label and its origin, the situation of two superpowers, the United States and the Soviet Union, in direct and often bitter competition is a product of the international environment following World War II. While it is often stated that wars resolve little, wars often do present the victors with the basis for new conflict. This was unquestionably true of World War II. The United States and the Soviet Union emerged as the world's superpowers. The other nations that had entered the war as great powers were either defeated, as were Germany, Japan, and Italy, or seriously weakened by their efforts

to win the war, as were Great Britain and France. The result was that only the United States and the Soviet Union, among the prewar major powers, improved their positions in the international system. They, in turn, dominated their respective areas of control in Europe and Asia, and, because of the manner in which the war ended, the United States and the Soviet Union faced one another across lines that ran through central Europe and Korea. While this was the political environment that came out of World War II, it does not explain how or why tensions and hostilities developed so rapidly between the two new superpowers following the war; they were, after all, co-victors and wartime allies.

When discussing a traditional, shooting war, ordinarily no difficulty exists in determining the beginning of hostilities. World War II began on September 1, 1939, when Germany invaded Poland, and within the next two days both France and Great Britain declared war on Germany. The United States entered the war officially on December 8, 1941, when it declared war on Japan; this action was followed shortly by a declaration of war on Germany. When discussing the Cold War, however, comparably precise dates are missing. If direct, hostile confrontation between the United States–led Western coalition and the Soviet Union is the criterion, then the beginning of the Cold War can be generally fixed as occurring shortly after the end of World War

II. If the criterion for a Cold War is an overall poor relationship between the Soviet Union and the Western democracies, then the Cold War began with the Communist Revolution in 1917.

INTERWAR RELATIONS

Following the revolution, diplomatic relations between the new communist government and other major states were strained, if not hostile. In March 1918, the Soviet government removed itself from World War I by concluding the Brest-Litovsk Treaty with Germany. In September, troops from Great Britain, France, Japan, and the United States landed in the Soviet Union for the stated purpose of preventing war supplies sent to Russia from falling into German hands. The Allies took the view that the new communist government was a tool of the Germans, since the German government had smuggled Lenin back into Russia, and that Allied military intervention might bring Russia back into the war and reopen the eastern front. The Soviets, however, saw the intervention of Allied troops, all from nations that the Soviets regarded as capitalist enemies, as a move to crush the revolution. Although clashes occurred between the interveners and the Soviet army, most of the Allied and all of the American troops were out of the Soviet Union by the end of 1919.

To increase Soviet suspicion of the outside world, Poland, reestablished as a nation by the Allies in 1918, invaded the Soviet Union in 1919. Poland seized a portion of the Soviet Union that was not recovered until 1939 when the Soviets invaded Poland. Also, while the Soviets were occupied with their civil war against the White Russians, Rumania seized Bessarabia, present-day Moldavia, U.S.S.R.; and the Baltic states—Estonia, Latvia, and Lithuania—were reestablished out of what had been, under the czar, Russian territory. The Soviet government interpreted all of these developments as indicative of the hostility that the outside world felt toward their revolution (Kennan, 1961).

Following the communist victory in the civil war, the Soviets chose to withdraw into isolation from what they perceived to be a hostile world. For quite different reasons, the United States also chose a policy of isolation following World War I. This mutual policy of isolation, and thus reduced contact, did not improve relations between the two countries, however. The United States and Great Britain had a range of disputes with the Soviet Union during the 1920s and the early 1930s over the seizure and nationalization, without compensation, of American and British property in the Soviet Union. The tensions between the United States and the Soviet Union were eased somewhat when the United States recognized the Soviet Union diplomatically following the election of Roosevelt in 1932 and the two countries negotiated the Litvinov agreements in 1936. These agreements were an attempt to settle American claims against the Soviet Union, although the U.S. Supreme Court later declared the agreements unconstitutional.

As early as 1924, Stalin supported a policy of "Socialism in one country." This policy suggested to the Western nations that the Soviet Union, at least temporarily, would not push for communist revolutions in other countries, even though the Soviets had organized the Communist International (Comintern) in 1919, an organization whose purpose was to promote revolution outside the Soviet Union. The Comintern continued to be a source of conflict between the Soviet Union and the West until 1943, when, as an expression of wartime cooperation, it was dissolved.

In 1934, the Soviet Union abandoned its policy of isolation and became a vigorous exponent of international cooperation. This shift in policy followed Hitler's rise to power in Germany and Japan's seizure of Manchuria. These perceived threats to Soviet security from Germany and Japan persuaded the Soviet government to seek a closer relationship with Western democracies.

As an aspect of this new policy of cooperation, the Soviet Union joined the League of Nations.

Within the League, the Soviet Union became a champion of collective security and disarmament. Outside the League, the Soviets extended aid to the Loyalists in the Spanish Civil War and concluded treaties of mutual assistance with France and Czechoslovakia. These attempts to gain protection from Germany and Japan through closer association with the Western democracies came to an end following the Munich Agreement in 1938. The Soviets saw France and Great Britain as selling out to Germany, abandoning Czechoslovakia, and rendering the mutual assistance pacts and collective security through the League of Nations useless. The alternative the Soviets now chose, since an antifascist alliance was not possible, was to work out an accommodation with the nations the Soviet Union feared most—Germany and Japan.

In August 1939, Germany and the Soviet Union concluded a Pact of Neutrality and Non-Aggression. Later, the Soviets signed a similar agreement with Japan. Nine days after the pact with Germany, Germany invaded Poland. A short time later, Soviet armies seized eastern Poland. Even though the German attack on Poland prompted Great Britain and France to declare war on Germany, the Soviet attack on Poland resulted only in even more strained relations between the West and the Soviet Union. The Soviet attack on Finland in November 1939 further worsened Soviet relations with the Western democracies and resulted in the expulsion of the Soviet Union from the long-since ineffective League of Nations.

TENSIONS DURING WORLD WAR II

Germany's attack on the Soviet Union in June 1941 abruptly changed the alignment of nations then participating in the war. Great Britain, which, since the fall of France in June 1940, had been without an ally, and the Soviet Union were now allies in the war against the European Axis powers. The United States joined the coalition six months later.

A common enemy does not necessarily produce friendship or cooperation, and the wartime alliance contained much dissent and disagreement over the conduct of the war. Stalin's demands for a second front in Europe as early as 1942 were a continuous source of friction between the wartime allies. The Western Allies argued that a successful landing in Europe could not be made until 1944, but the Soviets saw the delay as a deliberate effort to allow Germany to do as much damage to the Soviet Union as possible before the democracies launched a second front and brought the war to an end. When the second front came in 1944, the Soviet Union regarded it as coming so late that the Soviets had not only absorbed the wrath of Germany but were well on their way to winning the war without British and American assistance.

In addition to disagreements over the strategic conduct of the war, the Soviets charged that the United States and Great Britain did not allow the Soviets to participate in the decisions that allocated war materiel produced in the West. Even though the United States sent $11 billion in aid to the Soviet Union, the Soviets complained that their front did not receive the portion of war materiel it deserved. In addition, the United States charged that Soviet propaganda downplayed U.S. aid to the Soviet war effort.

A number of other issues were also in dispute during the war. The Soviets refused to enter the war against Japan until the week before Japan surrendered and then claimed they were a major factor in Japan's defeat. They also refused to allow American pilots to ferry American-built aircraft into the Soviet Union, and interned American crews forced down in Soviet territory after raids on Japan. In Europe, the Soviets placed so many obstacles in the way of shuttle bombing raids between Western and Soviet bases that the effort was canceled. When the Western Allies wanted to drop supplies to Polish rebels fighting the Germans in Warsaw, the Soviets refused permission. While publicly the antifascist nations presented a united effort during the war, privately relations were tense.

In February 1945, a summit conference of Allied leaders—Roosevelt, Churchill, and Stalin—was held at Yalta in the Crimea. The war in Europe was in its closing weeks, and the sort of world that was to exist in the postwar period needed to be decided upon. The conference was "a traumatic experience because it exposed in one massive revelation, for those who chose to read its lessons, what the United States had suppressed with remarkable success through three years of war. How could a democratic leadership reiterate the principles of the Atlantic Charter [a statement of postwar objectives made by Roosevelt and Churchill in August 1941] and admit publicly that these principles meant nothing to an ally whose defection would mean failure?" (Graebner, 1962). Soviet leadership had been difficult to negotiate with throughout the war and continued to be so at Yalta. The conference, however, did result in agreement on boundaries for occupation zones in Germany and on some details concerning the United Nations.

The war ended in May 1945, with the Soviet Union in control of Eastern Europe and with the Western allies confronting Soviet forces along a line that ran through central Europe. In July 1945, at Potsdam outside Berlin, the heads of state met again to discuss conflicts that were growing out of the military victory. The single biggest issue was how Germany was to be dealt with. Great Britain and the United States were also concerned with the future status of the Eastern European countries occupied by Soviet forces. A number of agreements were made at Yalta and Potsdam concerning these issues, but much of what was decided was never implemented.

In the absence of an overall agreement, the immediate effect of World War II was to bring the United States and the Soviet Union, two nations without a history of mutual cooperation, into direct and physical contact for the first time. In the past, efforts at expansion by the Soviet Union, and, earlier, Russia, had been blocked in the West by Germany and in the East by Japan. When World War II removed those two countries as obstacles, the Soviet Union moved into Eastern Europe, Manchuria, and North Korea. The United States had moved into Western Europe, Japan, and South Korea. While the actual boundaries of the Soviet Union and the United States were still far apart, their spheres of influence now converged.

DEVELOPMENT OF POSTWAR CONFRONTATION

The immediate problem following any war in which clear winners and losers exist is the sort of peace settlement the winners will impose upon the losers. The inability of the wartime allies to settle their differences at Yalta and Potsdam resulted in the creation of the Council of Foreign Ministers that was to continue the discussion of the problems facing Europe. The Council's first task was negotiating peace treaties with the European members of the Axis. The Council sidestepped the problem of a peace treaty with a Germany divided into occupation zones and went to work on treaties with Italy, Hungary, Rumania, and Bulgaria. The negotiations did not go well, since the Soviets from the beginning made it clear that they had no intention of relinquishing control of Eastern Europe. Once the United States and Great Britain accepted the Soviet presence in Eastern Europe, the peace treaties were concluded.

The only withdrawal by the Soviets from territory taken during the war occurred outside Europe in northern Iran. The northwest portion of Iran had been occupied by allied troops during the war in order to insure a route into the Soviet Union for war materiel. A 1942 Allied-Soviet agreement called for all foreign troops to

Fig. 5.1 Europe – 1938 Boundaries.   **81**

leave Iran within six months of the war's end. Only after considerable diplomatic pressure from the United States did the Soviets withdraw their forces, six months later, in May 1945.

Soviet pressure on Turkey, a neutral during most of the war, developed shortly after the war ended. In June 1945, the Soviet Union demanded that Turkey allow Soviet bases in Turkey and that it cede territory to the Soviet Union that the Soviets claimed had once been a part of Russia. Turkey rejected the demands with the strong support of the United States and Great Britain. In northwestern Greece, communist guerrilla warfare presented a serious threat to the newly restored noncommunist government. Initially, Great Britain aided the Greek government, but in February 1947 financial problems forced the British to withdraw their support.

The American response to the British withdrawal led to a policy statement known as the Truman Doctrine or the policy of containment. This new American doctrine was of major historic significance and has been an important component of U.S. foreign policy since that time. The Truman Doctrine stated that the United States would tolerate no further expansion of the Soviet Union; that the Soviet Union was to be contained to its current sphere of influence. (The content and background of containment policy was developed in "The Sources of Soviet Conduct," *Foreign Affairs*, 25 July 1947. The policy's author was listed as "X," although it was written by George Kennan, Director of the Policy Planning Board in the State Department. Secrecy as to who wrote the article allowed an explanation of a confrontational policy statement without an official statement and, since the purpose was to worsen relations as little as possible, was indicative that the Cold War was still in its developmental stages.) To carry out this policy, the United States promised aid to any country that was subject to Soviet pressure. The initial implementation of containment came when President Truman announced that the United States would take over British commitments and provide economic and military aid to Greece and Turkey.

Previous to the announcement of the Truman Doctrine, the Soviet Union had been tightening its hold on the Eastern European countries it occupied. Elections, agreed to at Yalta and in the peace treaties with Eastern European Axis members, were held, but the presence of Soviet troops in Eastern Europe and Soviet control of the machinery of government ensured the election of communist governments. The United States and Great Britain denounced the elections as shams, but the Soviets argued that by their definition of free elections, free elections had been held.

The next major development in the deteriorating relations between the Soviet Union and the West came in June 1947 when the United States announced the Marshall Plan, an aid program to rebuild Europe. Europe needed help and, for both altruistic and self-serving reasons, the United States was willing to assist. The Soviets saw some of these reasons as threatening to their interests. Strong emotional and ethnic ties many persons in the United States had with Europe was one motivation for establishing the plan, but the U.S. also needed Europe as a trading partner and did not want the war-weakened economies to be easy targets for communist takeover. The Marshall Plan thus was an important link in the newly announced containment of the Soviet Union. With the Cold War still in its developmental stage, the U.S. wished to minimize the sense of threat felt by the Soviets and offered aid to all war-torn nations of Europe, communist and noncommunist alike, in the hope that the Soviet Union would not allow Eastern Europe to participate. The Soviet Union quickly denounced the program, and, under Soviet pressure, so did all the countries under Soviet control; the Marshall Plan became economic aid to noncommunist Europe only. Aid began to flow to Europe by summer 1948, and it produced a startling recovery during the three years the program functioned. The Soviets countered with an economic aid program for Eastern Europe, the Molotov Plan, but since the Soviet Union lacked the economic resources available in the United States, this plan never enjoyed the Marshall Plan's success.

What was probably the most disturbing event for the United States during the early years of the Cold War came in February 1948, with the communist takeover of Czechoslovakia. The West had seen several Eastern European countries become communist states since the end of the war, but Czechoslovakia was the only country in Eastern Europe that the West regarded as a democracy. The comforting thought in the West had been that authoritarian and totalitarian countries might shift from one form of dictatorship to another, as had been the case with the rest of Eastern Europe, but a democracy could successfully resist communist pressures. In addition, Soviet troops were in the Eastern European countries that were now communist, but no Soviet troops were in Czechoslovakia. Therefore, when the Czech government fell to communism through domestic pressures, it was clear to the West that a democratic form of government alone was not adequate protection against a totalitarian takeover.

Even though relations between the United States and the Soviet Union were strained by 1948, there had not been a direct confrontation until the Soviets imposed a blockade on West Berlin in June 1948. When Germany was divided into four zones by the occupying nations, Berlin was also partitioned into four zones. A four-power body for the joint administration of Berlin called the Kommandatura governed Berlin, but each nation had its own sector. Since Berlin was in the Soviet occupation zone, access to Berlin for the Western allies had been worked out at the Potsdam Conference; several rail, highway, and canal routes, plus three air corridors to Berlin had been guaranteed by the Soviet Union. The Soviet blockade involved the closing of all but the air routes. The Soviets also withdrew from the Kommandatura.

The immediate Soviet explanation for blockading Berlin was that they were retaliating against a currency reform carried out in the Western zones of the city which the Soviets perceived as a move against them. The Soviets hoped the blockade would force the Western powers to abandon the city. The Soviet view seemed to be that a valid reason to tolerate a Western presence so deep in the Soviet sphere of influence no longer existed.

The blockade continued for nearly a year. After considerable effort on the part of the Western allies, particularly during the difficult 1948–49 winter, West Berlin was supplied by air transport. While the Soviets could easily block the surface routes into Berlin, short of shooting down Western aircraft the Soviets could not stop the airlift. The Soviets, no doubt, calculated that the million people of West Berlin could not be supplied exclusively by air. When the Western nations made clear that such a feat was possible, the Soviets called off the blockade in May 1949.

The division of Europe between Western and Soviet coalitions was essentially completed by 1949. The fall of Czechoslovakia had shown that a democratic form of government was insufficient to stop the spread of communism in Europe; therefore, a Western military commitment would be necessary. In 1948, when negotiations for a Western military alliance in Europe began, the armed forces of the democracies had been reduced to a fraction of their strength during World War II. Following the war, the Western powers had carried out the most extensive disarmament program in history. The United States had reduced its military manpower from nearly 12 million to about 1.5 million. Comparable reductions had taken place among the other Western allies, and West Germany had no army. The Western European nations were not capable of rebuilding their economies without outside help; thus, they certainly did not have the economic strength to rebuild their armed forces. The Soviet Union also reduced its military capabilities at the end of the war, but Western estimates were that the Red Army still contained four million men. The only offsetting force to this large conventional army was the atomic bomb monopoly the United States had held since 1945. Much of Western Europe wanted American atomic protection, and an alliance, the North Atlantic Treaty Organization (NATO), which included the United States and several Western European nations, resulted. The treaty was signed in April 1949. Four months later, the Soviet Union exploded its first atomic test device.

The charter members of NATO were Canada, Iceland, nine Western European countries including Great Britain, France and Italy, and, of course, the United States. In 1951 Greece and Turkey joined, and in 1955 West Germany did so. Spain became the sixteenth member in 1982. In 1950 the United States began a military aid program for NATO members known as the Mutual Defense Assistance Program so that they could rearm without undue strain on their economies. Rearming West Germany, which was implicit in granting West Germany membership in NATO, was particularly distasteful to the Soviet Union. Germany's invasion of Russia in 1914 and of the Soviet Union in 1941 were bitter memories to the Soviets. The Soviets countered West German membership by establishing the Warsaw Pact in 1956, a few months after West Germany entered NATO.

By the early 1950s the United States had firmly established the two pillars that were to be basic to its foreign policy for decades to come, notably economic and military aid and military alliances. This assistance and support were available to those countries that sought the means to resist the expansion of the Soviet Union and became the standard U.S. approach for forging an anticommunist coalition.

In the years after the creation of NATO and the Warsaw Pact, Europe endured many crises, but the dividing line between East and West was fixed and underwent no major alterations. Indeed, in 1948 Yugoslavia split with the Soviet Union but remained a communist state, although outside the Soviet coalition. The same nations that occupied Germany had also occupied Aus-

tria, and in 1955, following a treaty among those powers, the occupying forces left Austria with the understanding that Austria would be a neutral country and not join either coalition. Berlin intermittently became an issue for several years. In November 1958 the Soviets threatened to sign a separate peace treaty with East Germany, the nation resulting from the Soviet occupation zone, just as West Germany had resulted from the British, French, and American zones. None of the powers had concluded a peace treaty with either Germany, and if the Soviets made such a treaty with only the communist portion of prewar Germany, Soviet guarantees for Western access to West Berlin might cease to be in effect. The Western nations would either have to negotiate a new agreement with East Germany, a country they did not recognize diplomatically, or leave Berlin. A crisis was avoided when the Soviet threat was not carried out.

Berlin again became a crisis point in 1961, when the Soviets and East Germans constructed what became known as the Berlin Wall. The Soviet and East German intention was to stop the defection of East Germans using West Berlin as an escape route to the West. The drain of critical manpower was stopped, but a crisis developed. The Soviets did not reimpose a blockade on West Berlin, but did delay rail and motor transport. After a few weeks the tensions subsided, but the wall remained. During the Cuban missile crisis in October 1962, enough suspicion remained about Soviet intentions in Berlin that the United States suspected the Soviets of planning to use the missiles in Cuba as a bargaining chip to force the West to withdraw from Berlin. Since 1962, the situation in Berlin has not produced any additional major crises between the East and West.

No members of NATO have abandoned the alliance, and, in spite of several crises within the Warsaw Pact, only Albania has defected from the Soviet-led military arrangement. In June 1956, riots broke out in Poland, but the Soviets quieted the situation by releasing Gromulka, a Polish nationalist, who continued to include Poland in both the Soviet military and economic arrangements for Eastern Europe. In October 1956 a revolution developed in Hungary against the communist government and Soviet presence in Hungary. A new government was formed that withdrew Hungary from the Warsaw Pact, but soon the revolt was crushed by Soviet troops. The West took maximum propaganda advantage of the situation, but did not intervene directly. In 1968, following the removal of a Stalinist-style leader, Novotny, Czechoslovakia entered into a period of liberalization of domestic policies. The new leadership was careful to guarantee that Czechoslovakia would remain in the Warsaw Pact, but in August 1968 Soviet troops and troops from other Warsaw Pact nations intervened and established a government more aligned with Soviet policies for Eastern Europe. Again, the West did not become directly involved.

In 1981 Poland produced a new crisis for the Soviet coalition. An independent trade union, Solidarity, had been pressuring the ruling communist party for greater independence and government recognition. Also, the Polish government was facing economic problems in repaying its loans from Western banks. The Soviets ordered the Polish government to stop Solidarity's activities and to put its economic house in order. Pressure from the Soviet Union became so intense that many observers felt that the Soviets would invade Poland just as they had invaded Hungary and Czechoslovakia. After warnings from the Soviet Union that Poland must either manage its own problems or the Soviet Union would, the premier of Poland, General Jaruzelski, imposed martial law in December 1981. Solidarity was badly weakened, and the crisis took on a much lower level of intensity. The Western countries again took no direct action.

The several occasions when crises developed in the Soviet coalition with no Western intervention gave rise to what has become a rule of understanding between the West and East concerning behavior in Europe. When problems develop within one of the coalitions, they are to remain within the coalition. The opposing coalition is limited to verbal assaults only; no material or military support is allowed. This rule is clearly intended to prevent intracoalitional crises from becoming intercoalitional crises, which could be much more dangerous.

Europe has not, in the last twenty years, produced a major intercoalitional crisis. East-West relations are not necessarily improved so much as the United States and the Soviet Union have moved their confrontations to parts of the world other than Europe. The line through Europe that Churchill labeled the Iron Curtain has undergone no change for decades.

GLOBALIZATION OF THE CONFLICT

Until 1949, the Cold War was virtually confined to Europe. It broadened, however, when the Chinese Civil War came to an end in 1949 with the communists victorious, and when, in June 1950, the Korean War began with an attack on South Korea by North Korea. The Cold War became a shooting war for the United States when it and fifteen other countries created a United Nations military force to aid South Korea. In October 1950, China intervened and joined forces with the North Koreans. This war lasted until July 1953 and ended in a stalemate near the 38th Parallel, the line that divided North Korea and South Korea before the war began. While no Soviet troops were involved in the fighting in Korea, the Soviet Union was the main source of supply for the communist forces.

The principal result of the Korean War was a recognition by the United States that it now had a second major opponent in the Cold War—China. The policy of containment, originally applied only in Europe, now was extended to the Asian peripheries of both the Soviet Union and China. In Europe, the dividing line between communist and Western spheres of influence was clearly drawn, but such preciseness did not exist in Asia. The result was that, following the Korean War, several crises developed between the United States and China. The first major post-Korean crisis came over islands offshore from the Chinese mainland. The Chinese Nationalists controlled those islands, as they did the much larger island of Taiwan. The United States feared that the Chinese Communists would invade the offshore islands or even Taiwan, and to prevent this from occurring the United States placed its Seventh Fleet in the Formosa Straits. The invasion never took place, although a second crisis developed over the offshore islands in 1958. During the 1960 presidential campaign between Nixon and Kennedy, those islands were still considered of sufficient importance to be an issue. The question was whether both candidates were committed to the defense of the islands. They were.

During the decade after the Korean War, the Communist Chinese government engaged in several military operations along its southern and western borders that were not direct confrontations with Western nations but contributed to suspicions in the West of China's intentions. These conflicts were defended by China as necessary to reclaim territory taken from her when she was weak and divided. In 1959, China completed its occupation of Tibet, claiming it as a province, and in 1962 China invaded northeast and northwest India to retake territory expropriated from China when India was ruled by the British. By the early 1960s, China was regarded in the U.S. as perhaps an even more disruptive force in East-West relations than the Soviet Union.

The response of the United States to this expanded Cold War was, first, to significantly increase its defense budget and, second, to extend the policies that had been successful in Europe to the new areas of Cold War conflict. In his State of the Union address in January 1950, President Truman asked Congress to provide funds for technical assistance aid to the underdeveloped countries. This became known as the Point Four

Program, as it was the fourth point of the address. As foreign aid had been a successful tool of containment in Europe, the thinking went, surely it could be used successfully in other parts of the world. The United States also applied the second pillar of policy in Europe, the military alliance, to Asia. In September 1954, following the French withdrawal from Indo-China and the partitioning of Vietnam, the United States negotiated the Southeast Asia Treaty Organization (SEATO) in an attempt to provide a NATO-like alliance in that part of the world. Pakistan, Thailand, and the Philippines joined, but India and Indonesia refused to do so. Great Britain, France, Australia, and New Zealand were also members. Farther west, the United States helped develop the Central Treaty Organization (CENTO), known originally as the Baghdad Pact, in 1955. Pakistan also joined this organization, as did Turkey, Iran, and Great Britain. Iraq was the only Arab nation to join, but after a revolution in 1958 Iraq withdrew from the organization. Both SEATO and CENTO were dissolved in the 1970s. In addition, the United States negotiated security treaties with Taiwan (abrogated in 1979), Japan, South Korea, and the Philippines. These arrangements, plus the Rio Pact signed in 1947 between the United States and twenty Latin American countries, provided a total of forty-four allies to whose defense the United States was committed. The United States had security arrangements with virtually any nation that desired to join an anti-communist pact. While the policies that had been successful in Europe were faithfully applied elsewhere, they did not provide the same stability and clear lines of demarcation.

The Cold War was fought in an institutional arena as well. In the 1980s, the United Nations is not thought of as an important forum for major-power confrontation, but in the UN's earlier years issues before the organization were dominated by the Cold War environment. Then, as now, the United Nations reflected closely conflicts found in the international system. Until the 1960s, the U.S. controlled more than the necessary two-thirds vote to pass a resolution in the General

Assembly. Since the Soviets controlled only a few votes in that body, they attempted to bring Cold War issues before the Security Council, where the Soviet Union had the veto and could better protect itself from Western actions. The United States used the General Assembly extensively to promote its policies whenever possible, although that body's resolutions were only recommendations to members of the United Nations.

Early in the planning of the United Nations, both the United States and the Soviet Union made clear that they would not join the organization without a veto in the Security Council. Thus, they and Great Britain, France, and China were given that extraordinary voting right. The then eleven-, now fifteen-member, Security Council could be blocked by a negative vote from any one of those five nations, no matter how large the majority voting in favor of the measure. Since the charter of the UN required that all threats to international peace and security first come to the Security Council and that the General Assembly could not take up a particular problem until the Security Council released it to them, it was inevitable that the Security Council become the focus of Cold War activity in the UN. The Soviets blocked Western-sponsored measures with its veto, but the United States, since it controlled a majority of the votes in the Security Council, stopped Soviet-supported resolutions with a majority vote. By 1965, the Soviets had cast more than a hundred vetoes; the United States did not cast its first veto until 1970.

The confrontation in the Security Council covered a wide range of issues. Many of the Soviet vetoes were cast to prevent nations that the Soviets felt would vote with the West from joining the organization. The United States, by using its majority, prevented nations sympathetic to the Soviets from gaining membership. Issues such as arms control, colonialism, the Korean War, the Congo crisis, and problems in the Middle East also resulted in veto-inspired deadlocks in the Security Council. Since Soviet activities were so public in the UN, the United States also found it convenient to utilize the Soviet use of the veto

as a propaganda tool. Until 1970, when the U.S. first became dependent on the veto for protection against a new majority made up of Third World nations, the U.S. frequently pointed out that it seldomly used the veto while the Soviets used it extensively. Until the 1960s, the Security Council was both a focal point of Cold War diplomatic confrontation and a convenient institution for the United States to publicize Soviet intransigence.

A number of significant developments in the Cold War occurred during the 1960s, in both the location of confrontation and major changes in weaponry. During the 1960s, the United Nations gradually lost its importance as a place of Cold War conflict, and issues between the Third World nations and the industrialized nations became the focus of activity for the organization. Another development of the 1960s was the changed perception in the West of the relationship between China and the Soviet Union. Since the end of the Chinese Civil War, the Western view had been that China's policies were both expansionist and Moscow-directed. This meant that, from the Western perspective, China was a giant satellite of the Soviet Union following Moscow's master plan. In 1960, the Chinese split from the Soviet Union, accusing it of interfering in the internal affairs of China. Even though this split between the two largest communist states provided an unusual opportunity to the West, there was no change in United States policy toward China for more than a decade.

One situation preventing improved relations between the United States and China was U.S. involvement in Vietnam. China opposed U.S. presence and the U.S. accused China of strengthening the communist effort. The United States had supported the South Vietnamese government with economic and military aid since the partitioning of Vietnam in 1954, but did not introduce U.S. combat units until 1965. Both China and the Soviet Union assisted North Vietnam and the Viet Cong.

The war was also an obstacle to improved relations with the Soviet Union. The split between China and the Soviet Union made those two countries competitors, with each attempting to show that it was the more forceful supporter of communist allies. The Soviet Union pointed out to the United States that it could do little to improve their relationship as long as the U.S. carried on the war in Vietnam, and the U.S. government, in turn, found it difficult to gain domestic support to improve its relationship with countries supplying its enemies. When a period of détente developed between the United States and the Soviet Union and China in 1971 and 1972, it was possible because the United States gradually withdrew its forces from Vietnam and accomplished complete withdrawal in January 1973. The United States had entered the war in Vietnam in the name of containment. When the United States withdrew from the war, it was an admission that, in this instance, attempts to contain communism had failed.

Another development of the 1960s was extension of the Cold War into the Western Hemisphere. In 1959, Castro took over in Cuba. For a time, it was debated in the United States whether or not his was a communist government, but within a few months Washington decided that it was. The United States quickly isolated Cuba diplomatically and economically from the rest of the hemisphere. As the Soviet Union increased its military and economic aid to Cuba, Cuba became a major issue in East-West relations. In October 1962, the status of Cuba produced what is still generally regarded as the most serious crisis in the Cold War. The Soviet Union placed medium- and intermediate-range missiles in Cuba surreptitiously, and when the United States discovered the missiles, it imposed a naval blockade on Cuba and demanded that the missiles be withdrawn. After several tense days, the Soviets withdrew the missiles in exchange for a guarantee that the United States would not invade Cuba.

The presence of a communist government in Cuba had an important influence on U.S. policy toward other Latin American countries as well.

The United States already had a security treaty, the Rio Pact, with Latin America, but no economic aid package. In 1962, Kennedy initiated the Alliance for Progress, which provided the missing element of containment found elsewhere. Also, the United States used the Cuban situation as a precedent in preventing other communist governments from coming to power in Latin America. In 1965 the U.S. militarily intervened in the Dominican Republic following reports that a communist takeover was imminent. After the 1970 election of Allende in Chile, the U.S., which regarded his government as communist, used clandestine means to undermine Allende, who was overthrown in a military takeover in 1973. When the Sandinistas overthrew the Somoza regime in Nicaragua in 1979, the U.S., after an attempt to reconcile differences with the new government, treated Nicaragua as a client state of the Soviet Union. In neighboring El Salvador, the U.S. supported the government with economic and military aid in its fight against leftist guerrillas. The Cold War was being fought by the United States in the Western Hemisphere as well as in Europe and Asia.

The 1960s also introduced a major change in the weaponry of the Cold War arms race. The Soviets put up the first earth satellite in October 1957. While the satellite had no direct military value, this achievement had far-reaching military implications. Any missile that could put a satellite in orbit could also deliver a nuclear warhead over a long distance. The United States quickly demonstrated its own ability to develop an intercontinental ballistic missile (ICBM), and a new phase of the arms race was under way. In the 1960 election, missiles became an issue. Kennedy charged the Eisenhower administration with allowing the Soviet Union to move ahead of the United States in the deployment of ICBMs, thus creating a missile gap. Subsequently, it was learned that such a gap did not exist, but the United States, and to a lesser extent the Soviet Union, embarked on the deployment of hundreds of protected ICBMs. The Soviet Union made its major surge in the deployment of ICBMs in the 1970s.

During the 1960s the United States and the Soviet Union engaged in a peaceful, but highly competitive, race to explore space. The United States "won" the race when it placed a man on the moon in 1969, although research and exploration continued into the 1980s. While this sort of competition can be defended as scientific and nonmilitary, the technology needed to explore space also has implications for the development of weapons such as those involved in the Star Wars, or Strategic Defense Initiative, program of the mid-1980s. The 1960s had further broadened the Cold War, this time into space, and the effects of this competition were still in place in the 1980s.

Tensions between East and West have not been unremitting, however. Even the 1960s, a decade with many crises, produced two important agreements between the United States and the Soviet Union. In 1963 the two countries completed the negotiation of the Limited Nuclear Test Ban which prohibited all but underground nuclear tests. Over 130 countries had signed the agreement by the 1980s. In 1969 the two countries signed the Nonproliferation Treaty which prohibited nations with nuclear weapons from passing on the technology for building such weapons to nonnuclear nations. Also, countries without nuclear weapons pledged that they would not develop them. While not quite as popular as the test ban treaty, the Nonproliferation Treaty has been signed by nearly 120 nations. Besides such agreements, during three different periods East-West relations noticeably improved. In July 1955 a summit conference between Eisenhower and Khrushchev was held in Geneva. The conference produced little in the way of conflict resolution, but the mere convening of the conference resulted in a brief respite from Cold War tensions. This brief, roughly six-month-long period of reduced tensions was known as the "Spirit of Geneva." In 1959 a second period of relaxation known as the "Spirit of Camp David" came about in connection with Khrushchev's visit to the United States. This period of relaxed relations came to an end in May 1960 after an American U-2 aircraft was shot down some two thousand miles inside Soviet territory, and just before a summit meeting between Eisenhower and Khrushchev was to be held in Paris. The conference was canceled.

The third period was labeled détente and applied to United States relations with both China and the Soviet Union. In Europe, détente between the United States and the Soviet Union grew out of the diplomatic initiative of West Germany. One of the long-standing issues in Europe was the location of the eastern boundary of East Germany with Poland. A portion of prewar Germany had been annexed to Poland, but West Germany had never accepted the new boundary that ran along the Oder and Neisse rivers. In 1970 West Germany accepted the Oder-Neisse line as the boundary between East Germany and Poland and recognized the division of the remaining German territory into two Germanys, thus dropping its recurring demand that East and West Germany be reunited. This move also opened the way for the two Germanys to become members of the United Nations. This peace offensive by West Germany was known as *Ostpolitik.* In 1971 tensions were reduced further when the United States, the Soviet Union, France, and Great Britain signed an agreement on the status of Berlin. Détente in Asia began with the "nonpolitical" visit to China by the United States table tennis team in 1971 and progressed to open contact between the United States and China for the first time since the Chinese Civil War. (The U.S. and China for several years had had unofficial talks in Warsaw through their ambassadors to Poland.) The United States now was convinced that communism was polycentric and China was not under Soviet control.

This phase of the Cold War introduced a new

diplomatic challenge to the United States, the Soviet Union, and China. In November 1971 the Beijing government was granted the Chinese seat in the United Nations, and in February 1972 President Nixon visited China. Within less than six months, United States relations with China underwent a dramatic turnaround, and the image of China as a major Cold War opponent nearly disappeared. Formal diplomatic recognition of China by the United States did not come until 1979, but a vastly improved working relationship existed throughout the 1970s. United States–Soviet relations underwent improvement as well. Three months after Nixon's visit to China, he went to Moscow. While there, he and Brezhnev signed the SALT I (Strategic Arms Limitation Treaty) agreement, the negotiation of which had been going on intermittently for four years. Talks on other matters of mutual concern to the United States and the Soviet Union followed. Discussion of the status of Eastern Europe and human rights in those countries began—the Conference on Security and Cooperation in Europe—which, in 1975, resulted in the Helsinki Agreements. Mutual Balanced Force Reduction (MBFR) talks also were initiated, and, although still underway, have not produced an agreement.

The diplomatic triangle resulting from the politics of détente did not include improved Sino-Soviet relations, and United States policy-makers had to be careful to improve relations with both countries evenly. If the United States drew too near one country, the other feared that an alliance was being formed against it. United States-Soviet relations continued on a generally improved basis through the 1970s and included the negotiation of the SALT II agreement in 1979. This agreement was never ratified by the United States due to the Soviet invasion of Afghanistan in December 1979. The Soviet invasion essentially marked the end of the period of détente. United States relations with China, although occasionally strained over such issues as United States relations with Taiwan, continued on a generally improved basis.

By the 1980s, the United States–Soviet rela-

tionship had undergone even further changes. Each country had developed client states among the Third World nations which were not coalition members but were supported by one of the superpowers. In Africa, during the 1970s, Angola, Ethiopia, Somalia, and Mozambique signed friendship treaties with and became client states of the Soviet Union. In Asia the Soviet Union had similar arrangements with Vietnam and India. (Although India has never been regarded as a Soviet client state). In the Middle East, the Soviet Union had close client-state relations with Syria, South Yemen, and Iraq. Large contingents of Cuban troops were placed in Angola and Ethiopia, where they still remain in the late-1980s. Of these relationships, the ones with Somalia and Iraq were eventually severed, although Iraq and the Soviet Union reestablished good relations as the Iranian-Iraqi War wore on and Iraq needed Soviet arms. The United States developed client-state relationships with Oman and Saudi Arabia in the Persian Gulf. These relationships, plus United States activities in Central America and continued Soviet operations in Afghanistan, added up to considerable intrusion into the Third World by the Cold War opponents.

In 1979 Vietnam, with Soviet support, invaded Cambodia. This support of Hanoi by the Soviets, coupled with poor relations between China and Vietnam, further contributed to Chinese suspicions of the Soviet Union. China, its relationship with the United States improved, now viewed the Soviet Union as the nation it feared most. China saw its 4,000-mile border with the Soviet Union, Soviet presence in Outer Mongolia, and Soviet support of Vietnam on China's southern border as posing a major threat.

A further contribution to deteriorating relations between the superpowers came in Europe. The deployment by the United States of Pershing II missiles and ground-launched cruise missiles (GLCMs) was strongly opposed by the Soviet Union and led to Soviet suspension of arms control talks on both theater and strategic delivery systems. Those talks were resumed in 1985, however. Perhaps no other incident illustrated the ongoing tensions between the two countries better than when the Soviets shot down the Korean Airlines Flight 007 in October 1983. The accusations and recriminations that followed were symptomatic of the poor relations between the two superpowers.

PERSPECTIVES ON THE COLD WAR

The foregoing account of East-West conflict, while outlining major events, provides little explanation for the behavior of the nations involved. Investigating the question of what caused the Cold War is somewhat like searching for the cause of a shooting war. Did the Kaiser cause World War I by his treachery and aggression, or did the war come about as a result of the rigidity of the alliance system that preceded the war? Was that war planned, or was it an accident? Did the United States enter the war after serious provocation from Germany and on the moral plane of making the world safe for democracy, or did American bankers and munition-makers conspire to bring the United States into the war to protect their investments, as the Nye Committee of the U.S. House of Representatives concluded in the 1930s? Wars often elicit different explanations as to causes and outcomes, and the Cold War is no exception.

The explanations for the Cold War are channeled essentially into two general lines of argument. The first attributes the Cold War to the ideological differences between the Soviet-led, communist coalition and the anticommunist coalition. The second emphasizes that the differences between the Soviet Union and the West are historic in origin and the Cold War is the result of two major states competing with one another for dominance (Schweitzer, 1962). The first explanation will be referred to as the ideological model of the Cold War, and the second, the historic-power model.

The conclusion that many observers draw is that the Cold War is a mixture of the two expla-

nations; thus, neither model alone is adequate. But, for the moment, each of the explanations of behavior will be discussed separately to see how developments in the Cold War are explainable within the context of that model.

IDEOLOGICAL MODEL

The ideological explanation of the Cold War is based on the premise that nations behave as they do because of the ideologies they follow. The Soviet coalition is committed to the Marxist-Leninist ideology, which explains, in turn, both how the Soviet Union should behave and why the Western states behave as they do. The Western states are committed to democratic principles that reject the totalitarian structure of present communist nations, and they resist any attempt by the Soviets to spread communist ideology and revolution. Ideology thus provides a nation with a set of ideals, symbols, and slogans, and an explanation for why nations behave as they do. This view of ideology does not claim that ideologies are unchanging but that they provide a general set of principles that is both an explanation and a guide for future policy-making.

In reference to the Cold War, communist ideology, as set down by Marx and Lenin, proclaims the need to challenge the bourgeois, noncommunist political systems. The foundation of all societies, according to Marx, is the economic system. All other aspects of society are "superstructure"; thus, what happens politically is a result of the economy a nation has. In capitalist economic systems, the bourgeoisie is in control and exploits the working class; thus, the bourgeoisie must be destroyed or reformed. The communist appeal for a proletarian, classless society knows no international boundaries, and the call for the proletariat to revolt is a plea to the working class everywhere. A dictatorship which functions in the name of the proletariat is necessary temporarily in communist states until vestiges of bourgeois influence have been destroyed and capitalist nations are no longer a threat to communist systems. Coexistence with capitalist nations can only be a matter of temporary expediency. Marxist-Leninist philosophy should be the blueprint for the making of domestic and foreign policies, but until an international classless society is achieved, communist nations must be militarily strong, be dictatorships, and export their revolutions. From the Marxist-Leninist perspective, the West is at fault for the Cold War because it resists the inevitable communist takeover.

In contrast to the communist ideological approach, the political systems of the West are based on competitive political parties, not a one-party dictatorship, and democracies ideally promote the competition of ideas, not a prescribed set of principles. National elections are used to select leaders, and the concept of class is not the basis for organizing society. All Western states have vestiges of capitalism in their economic systems, but none is a pure system of capitalism, and they do not believe that the basis of political behavior is necessarily a product of economic behavior. Human rights are a guarantee that exists outside and transcends the needs of the political system. Democratic principles do not accept the claim that a dictatorship can be justified under any circumstances, even in the name of achieving a utopian, classless society. According to Western ideology, the Cold War is caused by the efforts of communist governments to subvert and destroy these principles. Ideologically, the perspectives of the communist and Western states are clearly at odds, and conflict between such views is inevitable. The Western states can and do explain Soviet expansion as an effort to spread the revolution, and the Soviets can and do explain Western containment of the Soviet Union on the grounds that capitalist nations, since controlled by the bourgeoisie, will always resist efforts to change their economic systems.

The Cold War began, if ideological conflict is the basis of the Cold War, when the communists took over in Russia in 1917. Even though communist ideology predates the revolution, a Cold War was not possible until a major state adopted communism as national policy. Until 1939 the Soviet Union was content to look inward and to consolidate its revolution. After 1939 the Soviet Union, in the context of Stalin's "ebb and flow" theory of communist expansion, moved from an ebb period into a flow period, which was made possible by conditions that existed both just before and after World War II. Before the war, the Soviets occupied the Baltic states and portions of Finland, and after the war they expanded into the countries of Eastern Europe and North Korea. The ideological model recognizes that the czars were also interested in expanding Russia and did so when presented with the opportunity, but expansion by the czars was to gain territory, not spread an ideology. Within the context of the ideological model of Soviet behavior, expansions of Soviet influence are for the purpose of extending their revolution, with territorial expansion being secondary.

A development such as the 1960 Sino-Soviet split can be viewed by the West at least two ways within the ideological model. One view would be that the split is only a ruse planned by the Soviet Union and China to mislead Western nations into thinking that the communist movement is divided. If ideology is the dominant factor in making policy, the Soviet Union and China would place the success of the communist revolution over any national interests that might divide them; thus, no meaningful split is possible. If, on the other hand, the split is serious, the division can only be the result of different interpretations of Marx and Lenin. Support for this approach rests in the fact that each has accused the other of being revisionist, that is, guilty of a false interpretation of Marx and Lenin. The split can be healed if the two nations negotiate away their ideological differences or if an international crisis should develop in which either seriously needed the other to defend the communist movement.

The Soviets justify intervention in the affairs

of Eastern European countries on the grounds that any effort to break away from the communist coalition can only be the result of capitalist influence imported from the West or left over from before the communist takeover; intervention is justified in the name of preserving the revolution. United States intervention in the affairs of the members of the Soviet Union's coalition would, from the Soviet perspective, be evidence that capitalist nations will not allow communism to take over peacefully, thus making conflict with the West inevitable. The West views Soviet intervention as examples of the use of force to maintain an inhumane form of government that stems from communist philosophy. The United States explains its intervention as necessary both to prevent communism from spreading and to help democratic governments. From either perspective, ideology is central to the action taken.

The basis of each of the two competing coalitions is a shared intracoalitional ideology. Certainly, all of the nations in the Soviet-led coalition are communist, but not all members of the United States-led coalition are democratic or capitalist. This particular discrepancy has been a policy problem for the United States. The United States has promoted the principle that democracies must be saved from communism, but what of the anticommunist nations that are not democracies? Should the Western coalition be ideologically pure and admit only democratic nations, or should any nation which is anticommunist be admitted? The United States has dealt with this dilemma by collecting virtually all the world's democracies into the coalition but excluding no country that wishes help in resisting communism. Either basis for the Western coalition can be justified on ideological grounds, the first basis being a set of principles the coalition is defending—democracy—and the second, a set of principles that is being rejected—communism.

If ideology is the basis of the Cold War, then the manner in which the conflict will end must also be explained in ideological terms. The conflict could end if either of the ideologies prevailed over the other. Since each coalition views the other as wishing to extend its philosophy to other nations, if one should be successful in the war for "men's minds," the Cold War would end. Another approach to explain a possible end is the convergence of the two ideologies. If Marxism-Leninism moderates and moves more toward a style of Western liberalism, and, at the same time, Western thought becomes more socialistic and collective, the two positions could come close enough together that no serious conflict would remain. With no ideological differences of consequence, assuming that ideology is what divides the East and West, the Cold War would end.

HISTORIC–POWER MODEL

The historic–power model of the Cold War relegates ideology to the role of a technique of control, domestically and internationally, rather than viewing it as a motivating force in the development of policy. In this model, ideology is used by nations only to explain actions and rally public support, but not as a blueprint for policy; ideology is made to fit policy rather than the other way around. If Marx did not provide an explanation or justification for a particular policy, then his theories must be revised so that they do. Since Marx did not discuss imperialism, Lenin found it necessary to do so in order to justify communist hostility toward such behavior in the West. If Marx did not discuss collective farms, since he was mostly interested in the means of industrial production, then he will be interpreted so that collective farms are acceptable. If the Soviet Union was too weak to extend its revolution in the 1920s and 1930s, then Stalin will provide an interpretation temporarily allowing for "Socialism in one country."

A nonideological explanation for the conflict between East and West is that as the hierarchically organized coalitions of the superpowers expand their spheres of influence, those spheres overlap and conflict intensifies. The two super-powers behave as they do because they are powerful, not because an ideology motivates them to resist one another. Soviet policy objec-tives do not differ markedly from that of czarist Russia; the only real difference is in how the policy is explained. Thus, the Cold War is the result of traditional Russian foreign policy; explained in Soviet terms, the conflict is the result of Western resistance to the Soviet efforts to expand. Conditions at the end of World War II, not ideology, produced the bipolar system of intensely competitive coalitions.

The expansion of the Soviet Union in Europe and Asia at the end of World War II, within the framework of the historic-power model, was made possible because of the vacuum left in those areas by the defeat of Germany and Japan, which provided the Soviets with the opportunity to fulfill czarist policy objectives of hegemony over areas near the Soviet Union. Soviet control of Eastern Europe is explained as fulfilling czar-ist objectives of uniting all of the Slavic peoples under Russian rule. The Soviet interest in Man-churia and Korea can be traced to traditional Russian interests that led to the Russo-Japanese War in 1904-05. Russian pressures on Turkey for access to the Mediterranean long predated the communist revolution. In short, Soviet foreign policy is more Russian than it is communist.

Alexis de Tocqueville is credited with predict-ing the Cold War in 1834, long before Marx wrote his doctrines. De Tocqueville wrote that the United States and Russia would one day be major states and opponents. He based his predic-tion on the direction in which each country was expanding, the United States west and Russia east, and believed that one day they would come into competition for territory. While the Cold War did not develop as de Tocqueville predicted, his was a nonideological view of competition between the United States and Russia, long before Russia was communist. Carrying the logic of the historic-power model one step further, the

Cold War would have occurred whether the Soviet Union was communist or not. The same differences could have developed between a non-communist Russia and the United States even if their political and economic systems were similar.

CONCLUSION

Events in the Cold War from time to time fit one model better than the other, or a single event suggests that both ideology and traditional national interests are involved. But each model does provide different explanations for what caused the Cold War, ideological differences or conflicting spheres of superpower influence. Each model presents a different beginning for the Cold War, either when the ideologies of the superpowers first differed or when the two nations became superpowers and were in direct confrontation with one another. Also, each model differs in its explanation of the origins of foreign policy, either ideology as a blueprint for making policy or the pragmatic needs of reacting to the policies of the other coalition with ideology primarily utilized as a means of policy explanation. In addition, each model suggests means by which the Cold War could end peace-fully, either through the resolution of ideologi-cal differences or the resolution of specific conflicts. The ideological model is more apt to place the East-West conflict on a moral plane than is the historic-power model. If differing ideology is the cause of conflict, then one ideol-ogy is morally superior to the other. But if con-flict between East and West is between two competing giants, then moral superiority is more difficult to establish. As a consequence, the two superpowers are apt to have mirror images of one another. Each is a conflict model, regardless of what means is used to explain the conflict; and regardless of the model, each superpower blames the other for the Cold War.

CHAPTER 6

Sources of Conflict II: North–South Conflict

For the first decade or so after World War II, from the Western perspective, important international events were associated with East–West relations. Events outside the Cold War framework either tended to be ignored or were reported in terms of their effect on East–West relations. Nations that were not aligned with either Cold War coalition were viewed only as possible new members of one of the superpower-led coalitions, rather than in terms of their own interests and conflicts. Even use of such terms as nonaligned or neutral to describe the policies of nations that participated in the international system outside East-West conflict described their behavior from a Cold War perspective. The nonaligned countries were in fact neutral only relative to the East–West struggle, but were very committed to the interests that were important to them. An example was Nehru's foreign policy for India, described in the West as neutral, but which to Nehru was the aggressive pursuit of India's interests. In addition to its policy of nonalignment, India wanted economic assistance in order to bring about industrial development, and Nehru was a leading opponent of colonialism. None of these policy areas were directly relevant to the Cold War confrontation. Particularly offensive to Nehru was the perspective of the Eisenhower administration that the Cold War was a moral struggle between good, as represented by the West, and evil, as exemplified by the communist countries. John

Foster Dulles, Eisenhower's secretary of state, on occasion lectured India to the effect that to remain neutral in such a struggle was in itself immoral. This view of international behavior illustrated the extent to which the West was preoccupied with East–West problems; it not only neglected the problems of the underdeveloped countries, but it displayed little understanding of them.

India is a particularly good example of the Third World's perspective on events in the international system. Since it was one of the first countries to gain its independence after World War II, it was in a position early on to take the lead in promoting nonalignment and opposing colonialism. Also, India as the largest single country in both area and population to gain its independence during decolonization after the war was more apt to gain the attention of the industrial nations than were smaller Third World nations. As a consequence, although a number of nations subscribed to nonalignment during the 1950s, a neutral foreign policy was most closely identified with Nehru and India. As were all former colonies, India was underdeveloped and therefore looked to the Western industrialized nations for help in meeting its need for industrial development and increased production of food.

India's foreign policy points up the main agenda items for much of the Third World—anticolonialism and nonalignment with a special emphasis on assistance for economic development. Economic underdevelopment is a condition found in over 80 percent of the nations which contain about 75 percent of the world's population. Since the industrialized nations are mostly Western and include the former colonial masters, those countries are the primary targets of anticolonial policy coming from the Third World. The Soviet Union is only occasionally a target, since it has had no empire, at least not in the nineteenth-century sense of overseas possessions. In addition, the Soviets, who also proclaim themselves to be anticolonial and certainly anti-Western, can openly support the anticolonial policies of the Third World countries, thus gaining favor among those countries.

Conflict between the industrial countries and the Third World, like East–West problems, has been summarized with a directional label and is most commonly referred to as the North-South conflict. This terminology stems from the location of the industrialized nations predominantly in the northern temperate zones, with the less developed countries lying to the south. Beyond their general location, terminology to categorize the so-called Third World is not so easily determined. In addition to being called Third World, they are sometimes labeled the lesser-developed countries (LDCs), the modernizing countries, or the underdeveloped nations. Reference to their level of development in the West usually refers to both their economic and political systems, although the countries themselves tend to use the term underdevelopment only in reference to their economic condition. Even though the Third World label for the underdeveloped nations originated with their refusal to align with either of the Cold War coalitions—the First World was the West and the Second, the communist coalition—it has become the most commonly used label for those nations seeking economic assistance from the industrial nations and will be the label used here.

Decolonization and the subsequent struggle for economic development have produced a wide range of conflict in the international system. Since the Soviets are only on the fringes of Third World developmental issues, this conflict occurs primarily between former colonies and other once-dependent territories and the Western industrial nations, including those Western nations that had small empires or none at all. The East-West and North-South conflicts have little in common, other than what is the West in East-West is the North in the North-South. The East-West struggle includes economic issues between the coalitions, but is most often placed in a diplomatic or military framework. North-South conflict concerns a very different set of issues and is primarily economic and anti-neocolonial, with military problems secondary. As Joan Spero summarizes these differences, the world's economic relationships are "the Western system of interdependence, the North-South system of dependence, and the East-West system of independence" (Spero, 1985, 13). The development and nature of North-South conflict is the subject of this chapter.

THE BREAKUP OF EMPIRE

In earlier chapters, political conditions following World War II were blamed for two major changes in the international system. The first was the reduction in the number of major states, which led to the development of an East–West bipolar relationship; the second was the breakup of the colonial empires, which produced a considerably expanded nation-state system. The breakup of empires not only increased the number of nation-states in the system, it also produced new arenas of conflict; initially, the conflict was over political independence for the colonies, but after independence was achieved the conflict moved to demands for economic assistance.

The colonial empires were primarily the possessions of Western European nations. Most of Africa, portions of Asia, especially south and southeast Asia, and islands in the Caribbean and South Pacific were all parts of those empires. The largest of the empires were held by Great Britain and France, with smaller ones possessed by Portugal, Spain, Belgium, Italy, the Netherlands, and the United States. Most of the dependent areas were held as colonies, but some were carry-overs of the mandate system of the League of Nations, such as Tanganyika and South West Africa in Africa, or Trans-Jordan, Syria, Lebanon, and Iraq in the Middle East. The mandates, however, were treated little differently than were the colonies, since the mandate authority appointed by the League was usually a colonial power. Some of the old mandates were converted to UN trusteeships before gaining their independence, but as trust territories they were administered much as they had been as mandates.

Since Latin America had driven out its colonial masters in the nineteenth century, only a small portion of Latin America was still held as colonies after World War II. Latin America had its political independence, but its economic relationship with the industrial nations, especially the United States, was similar to that found between colonies and colonial masters. Thus, as the colonies of Africa and Asia gained their political independence, Latin America soon came to realize that it had much in common with those former colonies—political independence had not translated into economic independence.

World War II speeded decolonialization in several ways. The desire for independence among the colonies long predated the war, but the war presented many colonies with a greater opportunity to express their nationalism than had existed earlier. During the war, the Netherlands, Belgium, and France were occupied by Germany, which left their colonies to local administrators to carry on colonial rule without support from home; Great Britain, the only major European colonial nation not occupied by Germany, was much too busy with its war effort to devote much attention to its empire. This situation especially increased the bargaining power of those colonies

important to the British war effort. This was particularly the case in India, where the British exchanged postwar independence for India's wartime support.

The Western nations saw the Japanese occupation of their possessions in Asia as aggression, but nationalists in the colonies often viewed the Japanese as liberators, and the Japanese frequently utilized nationalists to head puppet governments in the occupied colonies. In the Dutch East Indies, the Japanese set up an indigenous government under the leadership of Sukarno, who, after the war ended, continued as the leader of Indonesian nationalism and in 1949 led Indonesia to independence. The government established in the Philippines after the United States granted that country its independence in 1946 included a number of men who had cooperated with the Japanese during the occupation. During the war, nationalists in French Indo-China fought the Japanese under Ho Chi Minh's leadership, but after the war turned to fighting the French when Ho found that France would not grant the colony its independence peacefully. This launched a war that lasted, with a five-year respite in the late 1950s, for thirty years. The Japanese occupation of Burma also fostered new levels of nationalism and Burmese divisions fought alongside the Japanese during the war; Burma gained its independence in 1948. Overall, Japanese occupation provided the opportunity for nationalism in the colonies to become well-enough established that after the war the colonial nations were unable to regain their prewar control. Although Japan ultimately lost the war, the impact of early defeats suffered by the Western nations made it clear in Asia that the Western nations were vulnerable. By the late 1950s, the decolonization process in Asia was nearly complete.

In Africa the impact of the war on colonialism was more limited than it was in Asia, since the war there was between European nations; whoever occupied the colonies, there was no sense of being liberated. While Africa eventually

Fig. 6.1 New States from the Empires

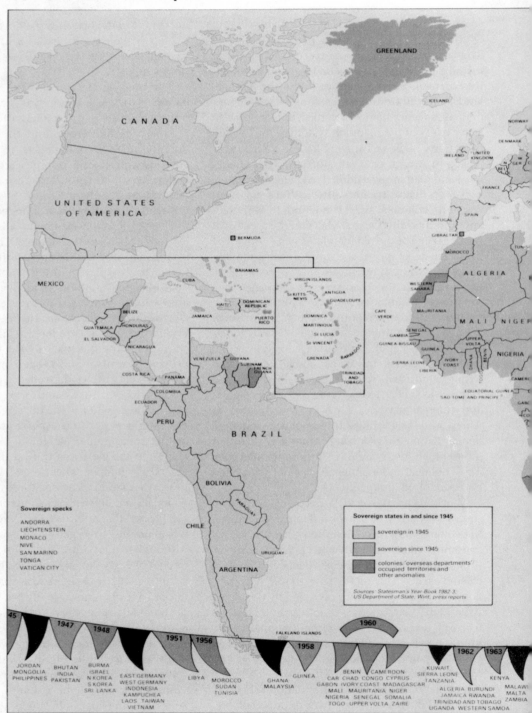

SOURCE: *The New State of the World Atlas*, Michael Kidron and Ronald Segal (Simon and Schuster, 1984), No. 1. Used with permission.

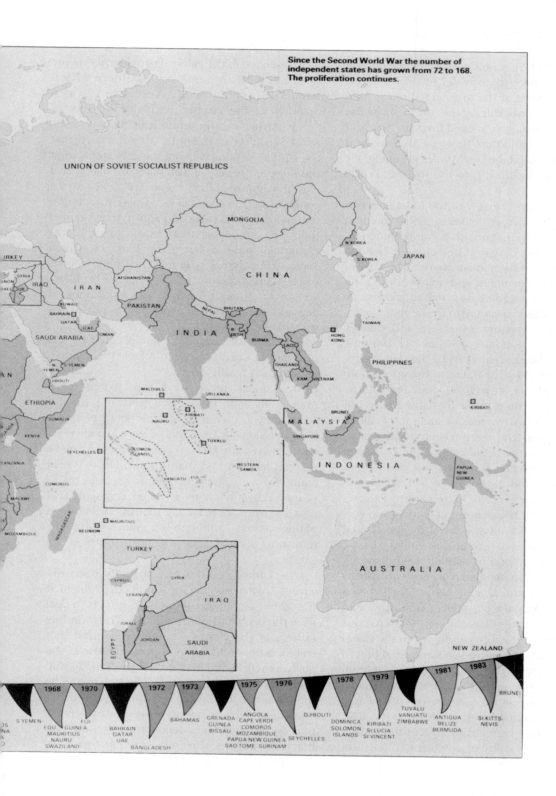

Since the Second World War the number of
independent states has grown from 72 to 168.
The proliferation continues.

UNION OF SOVIET SOCIALIST REPUBLICS

MONGOLIA

N KOREA

S KOREA   JAPAN

URKEY

LEBANON
ISRAEL SYRIA
JORDAN   IRAQ

IRAN

AFGHANISTAN

CHINA

KUWAIT

BAHRAIN
QATAR
UAE   OMAN

PAKISTAN

NEPAL BHUTAN

TAIWAN

SAUDI ARABIA

INDIA

B
DESH   BURMA

HONG
KONG

PHILIPPINES

N
YEMEN S YEMEN

DJIBOUTI

LAOS

THAILAND

KIRIBATI

ETHIOPIA

SOMALIA

MALDIVES

SRI LANKA

KAM VIETNAM

BRUNEI

KIRIBATI

KENYA

NAURU

KIRIBATI

M A L A Y S I A

SEYCHELLES

SOLOMON
ISLANDS

TUVALU

SINGAPORE

TANZANIA

WESTERN
SAMOA

I N D O N E S I A

PAPUA
NEW
GUINEA

COMOROS

VANUATU FIJI

MALAWI

MADAGASCAR

MAURITIUS

MOZAMBIQUE

REUNION

TURKEY

CYPRUS

SYRIA

LEBANON

IRAQ

ISRAEL

AUSTRALIA

EGYPT

JORDAN

SAUDI
ARABIA

NEW ZEALAND

1968 1970   1972 1973   1975 1976   1978 1979   1981 1983

BRUNEI

S YEMEN

EDU FIJI
GUINEA
MAURITIUS
NAURU
SWAZILAND

BAHRAIN
QATAR
UAE

BANGLADESH

BAHAMAS

GRENADA
GUINEA
BISSAU

ANGOLA
CAPE VERDE
COMOROS
MOZAMBIQUE
PAPUA NEW GUINEA
SAO TOME SURINAM

SEYCHELLES

DJIBOUTI

DOMINICA
SOLOMON
ISLANDS

KIRIBATI
St LUCIA
St VINCENT

TUVALU
VANUATU
ZIMBABWE

ANTIGUA
BELIZE
BERMUDA

St KITTS-
NEVIS

produced nearly fifty new nations, independence came more slowly than it did in Asia and the Middle East. Most of the African nations gained their independence during the 1960s. After the wave of independence moved through Asia and the Middle East and then through Africa, island possessions around the world were granted their independence, mostly during the 1970s and early 1980s.

While this brief review of the independence movement for former colonies fails to mention specifically many nations that gained independence after World War II (see chapter two for greater detail), it does illustrate the widespread nature of the movement and points out that no colonial empire escaped the breakup. In general, the decolonization began with the larger colonies and moved to the more obscure and smaller possessions. By the late 1980s nearly 100 new nations had been created from the empires.

By the late 1970s, as the movement for political independence neared an end, few of the earth's people could claim that they were not independent. Only two major remnants of colonialism remained. One was the United States presence in the Panama Canal Zone. The Canal Zone technically was not a colony, but the United States, under the authority of a 1903 treaty, governed "as if sovereign" in perpetuity. Panama claimed that this broad grant of control and economic exploitation of the canal by the United States, plus the existence of U.S. military bases, various military training schools, and discrimination against Panamanian workers, constituted classic colonialism. During the 1970s Panama gained the support of other Latin American countries and many African and Asian nations in its struggle to modify conditions in the Canal Zone. Sufficient pressure was generated that in 1977 new treaties were negotiated that agreed to turn full control of the canal over to Panama at the end of the century. While the entire Canal Zone was not immediately restored to Panama, the new treaties brought to an end the charge that the U.S. was guilty of practicing colonialism in Panama.

The second major colonial problem, as yet unresolved, involves Namibia in southern Africa. Namibia, formerly South West Africa, was a mandate of the League, with the Republic of South Africa as the administering authority. After World War II, South Africa argued that the United Nations was not a legal extension of the League; therefore, the mandate had ended with the demise of the League, and South Africa could now claim Namibia as its own. As colonies to the north of Namibia and South Africa gained their independence, their black governments demanded independence for Namibia, which South Africa refused to grant. The United Nations has been unsuccessful in resolving the problem, and, even though black Africa continues to demand Namibia's independence, South Africa remains in the territory.

The issue of Namibia is complicated by the presence of Cuban troops in Angola to the north of Namibia; South Africa refuses to withdraw from Namibia until the Cuban troops leave Angola. By late 1980s, however, the world's attention was on South Africa's policy of apartheid, not Namibia. Civil disobedience and guerrilla warfare in South Africa were explained by black African leaders and many other Third World countries as a struggle against colonialism as practiced by a white-minority government. This perspective is increasingly that of the Western nations as well, although the industrial nations took only limited action against South Africa earlier.

The United Nations has not only been unsuccessful in resolving the Namibian problem; it was generally unsuccessful in its efforts to deal with the problems of colonialism. The founding fathers of the United Nations recognized that colonialism would be an important issue in the postwar world and established the Trusteeship Council as the unit of the organization to handle the problem. While the Trusteeship Council's immediate purpose was to bring the areas under trusteeship to independence, the intention was that those nations with empires would turn their colonies over to the United Nations for disposition. This did not take place. The United Nations did have a part in negotiating Indonesia's independence in 1949 and provided the means by which the former Italian colonies became independent, but the remaining colonies became independent without UN assistance. Although the UN had a limited formal role in decolonization, it did serve as a forum for Third World countries to bring pressure on the colonial nations to give up their colonies.

Each of the colonial powers resisted relinquishing their empires and, on a number of occasions, used armed force in attempts to prevent independence. The British left Cyprus and Palestine only after extended terrorist attacks. The British also faced the Mau Mau movement in Kenya before that colony became independent. The Dutch left Indonesia only after it was demonstrated that they could not restore control over the colony following World War II. The French fought from 1946 to 1962 in efforts to hold first Indo-China and then Algeria. Even if the movements for independence did not result in open warfare or violence, nationalist leaders frequently were imprisoned for long periods. The breakup of the empires left behind many scars in the relationships between the former colonies and the former colonial rulers.

The colonial powers' differing styles of administering their colonies had a direct effect on how well prepared the different colonies were for independence. While it is debatable that any of the colonial powers was particularly effective in readying its colonies for independence, the British possibly provided the best preparation. The British administered their colonies through the tribal structure in Africa and the princely state system in India. Local administration was essentially vested in the people indigenous to the colony with the British directly involved only at the top administrative level. Thus, when independence was granted, only the top administrative officials had to be replaced and not the entire administrative infrastructure as was the case for other colonial powers. The French moved further into the administrative structure than did

the British, and the Dutch controlled their colonial administration down to the lowest levels. In Indonesia it was several years after independence before Sukarno could risk expelling the Dutch and run the country with only Indonesians. The Portuguese, who did not relinquish control of their African colonies until 1975, also maintained control far down into the administrative structure.

Other factors involved in how well colonies were prepared for independence were the varied sorts of political, educational, and judicial systems introduced into the colonies by the European nations. Here as well the British seem to have made the strongest effort. However, it cannot be said that any colonial power set up its colonial administration for the specific purpose of preparing its colonies for independence.

EXPLANATIONS FOR COLONIALISM

The breakup of colonial empires can be attributed to one of the causes of colonialism—nationalism. The proposition that nationalism overextended breeds nationalism is well illustrated by the demands of the colonies for independence. Western European nations had ventured abroad for centuries in search of wealth and prestige. Often the colonies were sources of raw materials for the industrial nations, but always they were seen as symbols of power. In extending their own spirit of nationalism into areas where it was unknown before, the empire-building nations created resentment and nationalism indigenous to the colonies themselves. The Western-developed concept of nationalism grew in the colonies until the demands for independence forced the European nations holding empires to relinquish their control.

Colonies were sometimes profitable for the colonizing nations although generally not. In addition to the direct cost of administering their colonies, protecting and controlling the colonies became a major cause of warfare in the nineteenth century; thus, colonies were more often than not a drain on the national treasury. But the colonial powers took pride in controlling territories often many times the size of the homeland. The British boast that the "sun never sets on the British empire" was not an economic defense of empire, but rather a manifestation of prestige. The demands of late empire-builders, Germany and Italy, for their "place in the sun" also seems to have been essentially a search for the prestige an empire would afford them.

While nationalism, economic gain, and prestige were among the reasons offered for building empires, the one defense of colonialism that was based on seemingly unselfish motives was that it was the duty of the more advanced nations to bring Western civilization to the colonies. This paternalistic approach to colonialism perhaps is best labeled as the "White Man's Burden" explanation of colonialism. Closely associated with the civilizing argument was the felt need to Christianize those parts of the world that had not accepted Christianity. Missionaries were often the vanguard of later economic and political control of a prospective colony. Still another defense of colonialism was the need to relieve population pressures in overcrowded European cities. The number of persons who went to the colonies was usually negligible, although the British did emigrate in large numbers to the older commonwealth nations such as Canada and Australia, and of course to the United States; however, as a means of population relief, colonies overall played a minor role. Thus, although the colonial nations had various explanations for their development of empire, the only one that was consistently credible was that empire produced pride and prestige.

The Marxists have a very different explanation for colonialism. The arguments presented up to this point concerning the origins of empires assume that the countries that embarked on empire-building did so as a policy choice; nations could choose either to develop an empire, or not to do so. Lenin in his book, *Imperialism: The Highest Stage of Capitalism,* argued that imperialism was unavoidable for capitalist nations and was the final stage of capitalism before the inevitable revolution of the proletariat. Lenin described imperialism as the "development and direct continuation of the essential qualities of capitalism in general," and stated that the "briefest possible definition of imperialism [is] the monopoly stage of capitalism." Lenin believed that at that stage, since the proletariat could not consume all it produced due to profits taken by the bourgeoisie, the capitalist nations would have to sell their surplus products overseas in order to maintain profit margins for the bourgeoisie. In order to accomplish this, capitalist nations would become expansionist economically, and political control would follow. Thus, according to Lenin, imperialism is the result of domestic overproduction and underconsumption, therefore inescapable for capitalist nations.

J. A. Hobson, a British economist, presented a theory of imperialism that also was based on overproduction-underconsumption, but he did not argue that imperialism was unavoidable for capitalist nations. According to Hobson, the national policy of a nation could either alleviate the situation of overproduction through a redistribution of income so that the working class could consume more of what they produced, or the country could choose to turn to imperialism to find markets abroad to dispose of the surpluses. Hobson felt that imperialism was not necessarily profitable, but he did feel that the main cause of imperialism was economic. (Hobson, 1938.)

It is interesting to note that, according to present Soviet theory, the last stage of capitalism is no longer imperialism. The countries that once had overseas empires have now lost them, but not one of those nations has undergone a proletarian revolution. The Soviets argue that the capitalist nations have found yet another last stage of capitalism, which is cooperation among the capitalist nations. The European Community is an example of such an effort.

This discussion of colonialism and imperialism

uses the two terms interchangeably, although some writers make a distinction between them. When they are defined differently, the term imperialism is used to describe any territory that is incorporated into the empire-building country so that the new area becomes an integral part of the nation. An area is colonial until it is incorporated. In this context, the United States is an empire, as is the Soviet Union, since both extensively annexed contiguous territory which was integrated into their political systems. "A colonial relationship is created when one nation establishes and maintains political domination over a geographically external political unit inhabited by people of any race and any stage of cultural development," but the colonial relationship ends "whenever the subject people becomes fully self-governing . . . [or] a subject people becomes assimilated into the political structure of the colonial power on equal terms" (Snyder, 1962, 45). While such distinctions between colonialism and imperialism do have some relevance to developments in the international system, at present the two terms are used interchangeably.

Up to the time the empires broke up, the terms colonialism and imperialism were usually used narrowly in reference to overseas possessions controlled by industrialized nations. Since the colonies are now largely independent, those terms have taken on a broader meaning. The Third World, with the diversity one would expect to find among approximately 130 nations, has common agreement on few issues, but one that it does agree upon is that its nations are still victims of colonialism. In this instance, colonialism refers to the economic relationship that followed the achievement of political independence. The Third World has found that the advantages of political independence are seriously diminished without corresponding economic independence from the Western industrial nations. In order to obtain this goal, the Third World is demanding that a number of changes be made in the economic relationship between the Third World and the industrialized nations, changes that would result in a major reordering of the world's economy and which have become the basis for much of the North-South conflict.

These demands for economic change come from a broader range of countries than those that were once colonies, mandates, or UN trust territories. It also includes those countries that for various reasons escaped colonization, such as Thailand, Ethiopia, and Liberia, or obtained their independence during or after World War I, such as Saudi Arabia or North Yemen, as well as the Latin American countries that obtained their independence even earlier.

Although generally underdeveloped, the Third World countries vary considerably in economic development and thus have different development needs. Some are wealthy in a natural resource such as oil, copper, or bauxite that may reduce their need for outside assistance. This group of nations is more apt to need technical assistance as opposed to capital investment. The economic development of other nations, such as Argentina, South Korea, and Brazil, has brought them to the threshold of categorization as industrialized nations. These countries are, in fact, sometimes referred to as newly industrialized countries or NICs. Still others, such as Bangladesh, Mali, and Haiti, are among the world's poorest, with little prospect of raising their citizens' standard of living. Most Third World countries fall in between those countries with good prospects and those whose future is bleak. The common goal of all, even those with substantial markets for their raw materials, is to achieve economic development as rapidly as possible and in this way achieve economic independence.

Though the Third World countries have a number of problems that are not thought of in the West as economic, the Third World's view is that if it can develop economically its other problems will either take care of themselves or be more easily managed. The Third World countries contend that problems such as over-population, corruption, and political instability are a consequence of their economic under-development, which stems from past and present economic exploitation by Western industrial nations. This relationship with the West is generally described by the Third World countries as neocolonialism—the economic aftermath of the colonial era. In their anticolonial policies, the Third World countries are presented with a paradox. They are united in their demand that the international economy be reformed, but the countries that control that economy are the same ones from which the Third World must seek economic assistance. In general, their desire for development is what is referred to as the "revolution of rising expectations." Political independence is only the first step in this revolution; economic development is the second.

DOMESTIC CONDITIONS IN THIRD WORLD COUNTRIES

In the broadest terms, Third World nations are embarked on nation-building. This involves more than developing an advanced economy; it also includes solving their major social problems and securing a stable political system. Earlier, a nation-state was defined as a specific area of territory with a population of citizens, an established set of political institutions, and a sense of nationalism and loyalty to that political system on the part of its citizens. Many Third World countries have difficulty in meeting those general qualifications.

An initial problem often is that a Third World nation does not have well-defined territorial boundaries. The present boundaries of most Third World countries are those established when they were colonies for the convenience of the colonial powers. Many of these boundaries were the result of a colonial power's expanding until it came into conflict with another colonial power. For example, at the Berlin Conference of 1885, central Africa was divided between France

and Great Britain on the basis of where their spheres of influence met. The possibility that one day the colonies would be independent nations and need politically logical boundaries was not a consideration. In Africa, where boundaries are a particular problem, the new nations have generally left colonial boundaries intact in order to avoid the myriad disputes that would arise if adjustments were once started. While Africa has not entirely avoided boundary disputes, they have been few, considering the possibilities. Latin America has few boundary disputes today, but settling the boundaries for those countries required more than a century of arbitration and wars. The only major exception is the present boundary dispute between Venezuela and Guyana. This, too, is a disagreement left over from a colonial border drawn by Great Britain and Spain. The cause of the war between India and China in 1962 was the boundary between those two countries drawn by the British, and the current dispute between Morocco and Algeria is over the boundary drawn by France when it possessed both territories.

The manner in which the colonial masters established borders has also created a problem for national unity and the development of a sense of nationalism. In Africa, where boundaries often cut through traditional tribal areas and where various tribes are located within one nation-state, creating a sense of nationalism is difficult. In the absence of strong national loyalties, tribal conflict is commonplace, and establishing stable political institutions under these circumstances is difficult. Political parties, if they exist, often are based on tribal affiliation, and national leadership frequently rests with a dominant tribe. When a coup occurs, it often is one tribal group overthrowing another. The fundamental problem, however, as seen by the Third World countries, is the development of a stable economic system that can meet the needs of their people. Once that is achieved, they feel, stable political institutions will develop.

The strategies for achieving political and economic stability differ among Third World nations. Some Third World nations, such as Mozambique and South Yemen, label their governments Marxist and plan to use the communist model for development. Since Marx was interested only in the industrial capitalist nations, his theories offer little in the way of a guide for economic development. Central planning is about as far as Marxist ideology is carried in direct application to the Third World nations, and this sort of central control of economic development is commonly found in the Third World whether a particular country labels itself Marxist or not. Thus, to label a Third World country Marxist often has little meaning.

Other countries, such as Kenya and Ivory Coast, openly pattern their development after the capitalist nations. Many countries in the Third World appear to have no particular approach to development but, rather, accept whatever economic opportunities are offered them. In spite of the diversity found in Third World countries, a number of conditions are common to those countries regardless of their level of development, their label for their political systems, or the nature of their associations with the industrialized nations. These conditions, whether a carry over from colonialism, a consequence of neocolonialism, or a product of internal conditions, are, overall, the obstacles to development of the Third World. These obstacles, which are domestic situations, have also produced the main policy conflicts between the Third World and the Western industrial nations, one of which is how to control population growth.

OVERPOPULATED AND UNDERFED

One consequence of an underdeveloped economy is that much of the labor force is either underemployed or unemployed. The two possible solutions to this problem are economic growth, to produce the needed jobs, or, alternatively, population control so that there will not be a labor surplus. A second problem resulting from overpopulation is growing sufficient food so that everyone will be fed adequately. If a nation cannot grow its own food, then food must be imported from nations with food surpluses. While several countries have food surpluses available for export, for those countries that already have the problem of raising funds for development, paying for imported food is yet an additional economic burden.

The rate of population growth (birth rate minus death rate) in the industrialized nations for the 1980–85 period was .64 percent a year, which, assuming the rate of growth to be constant, means that the population will double in those countries in about 110 years. In the industrial nations of Europe, both Eastern and Western, the rate of growth is even lower, .4 percent, and it will take about 175 years to double the population. West Germany and East Germany are losing population with a −.4 and −.2 percent rate of growth, respectively. But in the Third World countries, the rate of growth is about 2 percent per year, and the population will double in those countries in about 35 years. Based on these projections, the present population ratio of 3 to 1 between underdeveloped and developed nations, respectively, will become 5 to 1 by 2025, and by 2100, 7 to 1. (1982 United Nations projections).

In a breakdown of the Third World by region, the growth rate in Latin America is 2.3 percent, in Africa 3 percent, and in Asia, excluding Japan, about 1.8 percent. Since 1950 the general pattern of population change has been for Africa to steadily increase its rate of growth, Latin America to decrease its rate since 1970, and Asia to steadily decline in its rate of increase from its peak in the late 1960s. The Third World as a whole has declined from a rate of population growth of nearly 2.5 percent in the early 1970s to 2 percent in the late 1980s. While a number of these countries are Catholic or Moslem—both religions encourage large families—the difference in the rate of growth between Third World countries with one of those two as the dominant religion compared with countries where neither is the national religion is small. For example, Latin America is predominantly Catholic and its growth rate is lower than Africa's. African Moslem countries have a slightly higher growth rate than do the non-Moslem black African countries.

The rate of population growth is more closely related to economic conditions than religion, since the largest difference in the rate of growth is between the industrial nations and the underdeveloped countries, not countries with differing religions. If the fundamental reason for a high rate of population growth in Third World countries is economic underdevelopment, then the characteristics of an underdeveloped economy must produce conditions that make large families economically necessary.

One such characteristic exists in the agricultural sector of Third World countries. In most of the Third World countries, agriculture is not highly mechanized and thus labor-intensive. A large family provides the necessary labor and serves as a substitute for modern agricultural methods. In countries without a social security system, which the Third World countries generally cannot afford, a large family will provide security in one's old age. A large family thus may exist for economic reasons, and not only because of religious principles or a lack of knowledge about birth control.

From the perspective of the industrial nations, a vigorous educational program of family planning is the most direct solution to the population problem. Such a program would relieve population pressures where the economy has difficulty keeping up with population increase, and would increase that country's standard of living. Even in Third World nations that have an expanding economy, if the rate of economic growth is equal to the rate of population increase, the standard of living remains the same. While there are years in which many Third World countries have had economic growth that has exceeded

their rate of population growth, the average rate of economic growth is about 2 percent a year, which is about equal to the rate of population growth. Many Third World countries have embarked on educational programs of birth control, but thus far, those programs have had limited impact on slowing population growth.

Among the Third World countries, China has made perhaps the greatest effort to restrict the size of families and has introduced an extensive campaign encouraging families to have only one child. Even if this program is successful, China's population of 1.06 billion people will increase to 1.4 billion by 2025 (World Bank estimate). The reason for this seeming contradiction between limited families and continued population growth is the low median age in China and the Third World countries in general. In these countries, with a higher percentage of their population of child-bearing age than found in the developed countries, even with smaller families the population will continue to grow for a number of years.

Another factor in the high rate of population growth in the Third World is that population increases are not a result of a rising birth rate but, rather, a product of reduced death rates. Birth rates have always been high, but high infant mortality and disease limited the size of the population. Improved medical facilities, international campaigns against disease such as the World Health Organization's successful campaign to eradicate smallpox, and better infant care have been the major contributors to population growth.

Even though medical standards in most Third World countries are still well below those found in the industrialized nations, the declining death rate is evidence that improvements have been made. A return to the Malthusian population controls of disease, war, and starvation certainly is not being suggested by anyone as a means of controlling population growth, but it is important to point out that if the population is to remain stable a lower death rate will have to be compensated for with a lower birth rate.

While many Third World countries have programs of education for family planning, the Third World offers another, more radical, solution to the population problem. Fundamental to the Third World's argument is that the solution to overpopulation rests with industrialization, not birth control. If the industrialized nations would provide the lesser developed nations with the aid to which they are entitled, the resulting industrialization would take care of the population problem. Third World nations point out that the industrialized nations themselves once had a high rate of population growth, but the rate of growth declined as those nations became industrialized. The need for large farm families declined because of mechanization, and large families generally were not needed for old-age security as social security systems were introduced. It has also been found that as women receive more education and enter the labor force the size of families declines.

An even more radical version of this approach is the charge that the industrial nations promote family planning in order to avoid meeting their responsibilities to the Third World. A high rate of population growth places increased pressure on the industrial nations to provide the Third World with economic assistance, but if population is controlled by noneconomic means demands on the industrial nations will decrease. Thus, family planning is viewed as a part of a conspiracy by the industrialized nations to maintain current neocolonial relationships and avoid any fundamental reform of the international economy. It would not only be less expensive for the industrial nations if the population problem were resolved through family planning rather than through economic development, the industrial nations would not have to give up any of the economic advantages they currently enjoy. This line of reasoning was widely voiced at the 1974 United Nations–sponsored population conference held in Bucharest. At that conference, the Third World countries also argued that any attempt to impose birth control policies on them as a condition for receiving economic aid was an infringement upon their sovereignty. In addition, they suggested that the world could support a considerably larger population if resources were more equally distributed and more effectively exploited. They argued that this was particularly true of food, which was the subject of a second United Nations–sponsored conference held in Rome a month later.

The world presently produces sufficient food so that its population can be fed adequately, but there are food shortages and starvation in the world, nevertheless. The problem is uneven food distributions, and, while there are surpluses in some countries, others with shortages either cannot afford to buy the food needed or have such a poorly developed distribution system that the food cannot be delivered to the needy. Although a higher percentage of the work force in the Third World is engaged in agriculture than is the case for industrial nations, the more advanced agricultural methods and technology are found in the industrial nations; thus, on a per-acre basis, the land is more productive in the industrial nations.

The so-called green revolution—the introduction of dwarf strains of wheat and rice—has had an important effect on food production in the Third World, however. Countries in Latin America and Asia have, in particular, benefited to the point that food shortages have been eliminated in many of those countries. India, a country heavily dependent on grain imports from the United States in the late 1960s, is now nearly self-sufficient in grain. However, this improvement in India's food supply is explained, in part, by favorable monsoon rains for the past several years, and drought or flooding might reintroduce shortages.

Africa, on the other hand, has not benefited from the green revolution. Grains grown in Africa are not among the new dwarf strains. This, coupled with a drought that began in parts of Africa in the early 1970s and that has since

Fig. 6.2 Map of Food Power

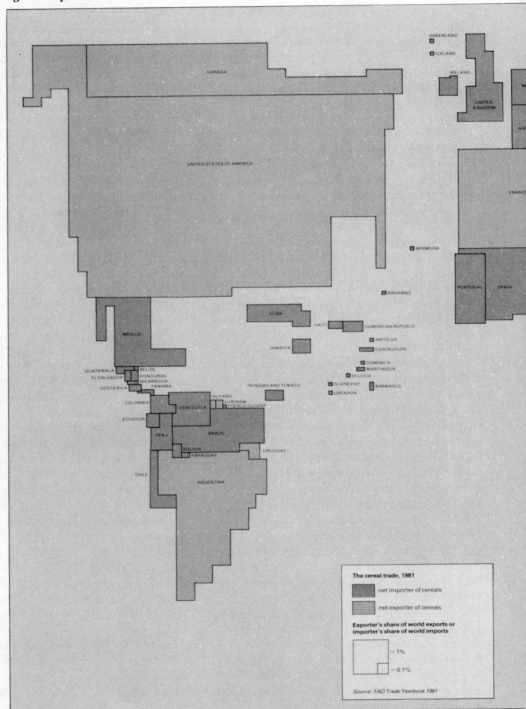

The cereal trade, 1981

net importer of cereals

net exporter of cereals

Exporter's share of world exports or
importer's share of world imports

= 1%

= 0.1%

Source: FAO Trade Yearbook 1981

SOURCE: *The New State of the World Atlas*, Michael Kidron and Ronald Segal (Simon and Schuster, 1984), No. 14. Used with permission.

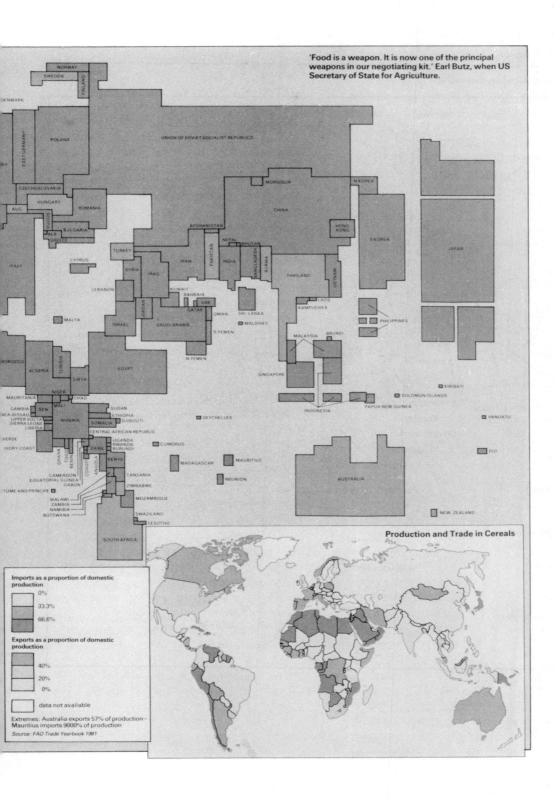

'Food is a weapon. It is now one of the principal weapons in our negotiating kit.' Earl Butz, when US Secretary of State for Agriculture.

Production and Trade in Cereals

Imports as a proportion of domestic production

- 0%
- 33.3%
- 66.6%

Exports as a proportion of domestic production

- 40%
- 20%
- 0%
- data not available

Extremes: Australia exports 57% of production—Mauritius imports 9000% of production

Source: FAO Trade Yearbook 1981

Fig. 6.3 Map of African Drought

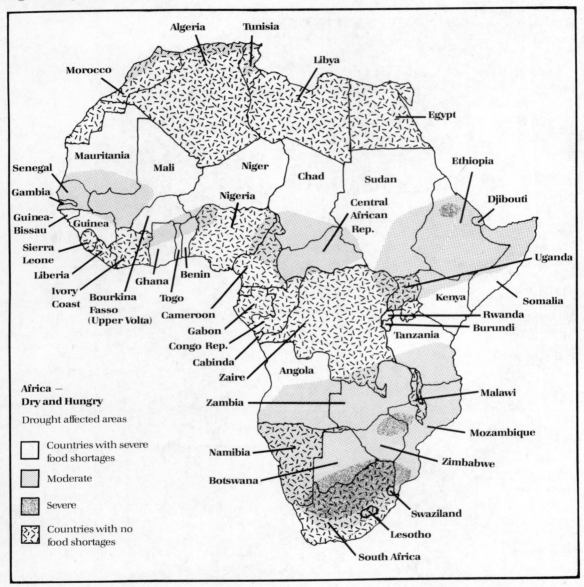

Africa —
Dry and Hungry

Drought affected areas

☐ Countries with severe food shortages

☐ Moderate

☐ Severe

☐ Countries with no food shortages

spread to portions of southern Africa, has introduced the most serious food shortage in Africa's recent history. While much of black Africa is experiencing serious food shortages, in the late 1980s famine conditions existed in about a dozen countries along a belt from Senegal and Mauritania in West Africa to Ethiopia, Kenya, and Somalia in East Africa. In southern Africa, Zambia, Tanzania, and Mozambique also had severe food shortages. Though food production in Africa has increased over the last twenty years, the increase has been at a rate 1 percent less than the rate of population increase. The problem is so severe that Africa is the only region in the world where food production on a per capita basis has dropped. In the early 1960s, when many African countries became independent, Africa produced 95 percent of the food it needed. In the mid-1980s, food production meets only 75 percent of needs, and all African nations, except South Africa, must import food. (Christian Science Monitor, November 27, 1984, 24-25.). Outside Africa, increased food production has not always kept up with increases in population. Mexico, a country that was once self-sufficient in food, now must import one-fourth of its food.

The countries that have food surpluses, and in the instance of the United States the capability for producing even more, are nearly all industrialized nations. Two-thirds of wheat production in the United States is exported, although more than half of that amount goes to other than Third World countries. Thus, when a Third World nation imports food it probably does so from a Western industrialized nation, thereby establishing yet another dependent relationship with the West.

While the industrial nations do provide free famine relief in Africa and the United States has its Food for Peace program that provides subsidies for countries with food shortages, generally the Third World nations must pay for the food they require. Controlling the rate of population growth and obtaining an adequate food supply clearly are closely related issues. As the

Fig. 6.4 Top Ten U.S. Wheat Buyers for Marketing Year 1984-85 (June-May)

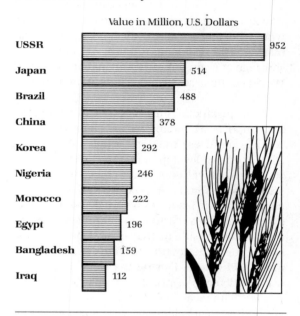

Value in Million, U.S. Dollars

USSR	952
Japan	514
Brazil	488
China	378
Korea	292
Nigeria	246
Morocco	222
Egypt	196
Bangladesh	159
Iraq	112

SOURCE: Washington Post National Weekly Edition August 11, 1986

demand for food increases and the additional need cannot be met through increased domestic production, the choice is to either import or allow people to go hungry. The Third World nations have many demands on their capital, and the more that is spent for food imports the less there is for economic development.

An additional aspect of this problem that goes beyond the economics of the situation is that the Third World charges that more food would be available if the industrial nations curbed their wastefulness. This is not so much an allegation that the people in industrialized nations eat too much or that too much edible food goes into the garbage as it is that too much grain is expended in the production of meat. The estimate is that grain consumption for each American is about one ton a year as compared to 400 pounds per person in Third World countries. Obviously, most of this ton of grain is not actually consumed by each American but is fed to animals for the production of meat. If Americans, so the Third World argument goes, consumed less meat there would be more grain available on the world market. The problem, in truth, has not been a shortage of grain but rather an inability of Third World countries to produce it or, if imported, to pay for it.

While producing sufficient food or paying for food imports are immediate problems for Third World countries, the long range problem is where to find development capital. Their economies are not well enough developed to generate investment capital domestically in the amounts needed. Even in instances where domestic capital exists, high rates of inflation and unstable economies often result in that capital being transferred out of the country for more secure investments elsewhere. During the early 1980s, this was particularly a problem for Argentina and Mexico. The means of obtaining outside capital are limited to developing a favorable balance of trade, attracting private capital by establishing good investment opportunities for MNCs, generating grants of aid from other countries, and receiving loans from other countries, international agencies, or private banks. Each of these means requires the cooperation of the industrial nations.

ONE–PRODUCT ECONOMIES

The principal means currently available to Third World countries for achieving a favorable balance of trade is through trade with the industrial nations, and the Third World products most in demand in the West are raw materials and commodities. While this sort of trade is considerable, unfortunately the economies of many Third World countries are overly dependent on one crop or natural resource for their income from foreign trade. Third World countries subject to

this sort of dependency often find themselves victims of economic recession when prices for that single product fall. If the price of tin falls in the industrial nations, then Malaysia and Bolivia, countries whose principal export is tin, suffer. If the price of bauxite falls, Jamaica suffers. If the price of sugar falls, Cuba and the Dominican Republic suffer. If the price of coffee falls, Brazil and Colombia suffer. If the price of oil falls, Mexico, Venezuela, Nigeria, Indonesia, and the Arab petroleum-exporting nations suffer. If the price of copper falls, Chile and Zambia suffer. In the early 1980s when the price of copper was low, Zambia found itself selling copper at a price lower than the cost to produce it; the net effect of this situation was that Zambia was subsidizing the economies of countries importing Zambian copper. To cease exporting copper would have brought the Zambian economy to a halt; it was therefore better to sell at a loss. With any commodity, if prices decline income falls, and funds available for development are adversely affected. The result is that countries exporting these and other commodities and resources feel that they are the victims of what they regard as a neocolonial trade relationship in which they must import from the industrialized nations consumer products and items needed to develop, but they have no control over the prices charged for either the products they import or those they export. Prices in both instances are determined by market demands in the industrial nations.

The countries that export commodities and natural resources to the industrial nations feel that the price they receive should be based on the ultimate contribution their products make to the economies of the industrial nations, not on the market demands of those countries. One way in which this could be accomplished would be for the exporters and importers to negotiate agreements that would guarantee prices and markets. Such agreements could be used to raise the prices on those resources and commodities and stop the roller-coaster effect of price changes. The Western industrial nations have not acquiesced to this demand, although international sugar and coffee agreements have been negotiated which assign quotas to countries selling those commodities, thus providing reliable markets for those products, but no guaranteed prices. For example, in 1985 when the price of sugar from the Caribbean sugar-producing nations fell to 2.5 cents a pound, those countries complained that the price decline was due to U.S. government protection of domestic sugar producers. The price of sugar in the U.S. was 21 cents at the time. The sugar-producing countries were also complaining that the U.S. was cutting their sugar quotas as an additional protection for the domestic industry.

In the absence of Western cooperation in controlling prices, the exporting nations have established international cartels whose purpose is to increase prices for Third World materials and commodities. While cartels have not developed among the sugar and coffee exporting nations, perhaps because of the current commodity agreements, such an effort was carried out by the banana-exporting countries (Council of Banana Exporting Countries). The effort was largely a failure. In raw materials, international cartels were created for copper, tin, and bauxite. The copper cartel, the International Committee of Copper Exporting Countries (CIPEC), included the four major exporting nations—Chile, Peru, Zaire, and Zambia—but the effort failed because those countries did not hold to the prices agreed upon. First one country and then another would sell at a lower price until the cartel was broken. The cartel for tin, the Tin Council, suffered a similar fate. Jamaica provided the leadership in putting together the International Bauxite Association (IBA) with eleven nations in membership. For a time, in the late 1970s, IBA enjoyed success, but the Western nations developed alternative suppliers and during the recession of the early 1980s, the cartel all but collapsed. The only cartel that experienced any long range success was the oil cartel, the Organization of Petroleum Exporting Countries (OPEC). That organization was successful in raising the price of oil from less than $2 a barrel to $34 a barrel between 1970 and 1978. As world demand for oil declined in the early 1980s, the price of oil fell, and OPEC was forced to impose production quotas on its members. The war between Iraq and Iran further cut production and both factors combined to slow the decline in the price of oil, although in 1984 Nigeria, a member of OPEC, and Great Britain and Norway, nonmembers, sold oil for less than the fixed price. The OPEC quota system quickly broke down and prices fell to under $14 a barrel. By the late 1980s OPEC had lost much of the clout it once had internationally and became again subject to the prices the industrial nations were willing to pay.

Due to the number and quantity of raw materials and commodities imported by the industrial nations from the Third World, the West is vulnerable, at least in the short term, to cartels formed by Third World exporters—if cartel members will cooperate. Since such cooperation has been lacking, no cartels are presently successful. Economic uncertainty thus comes to

Fig. 6.5 Raw Sugar Prices

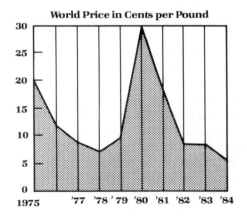

World Price in Cents per Pound

SOURCE: International Sugar Organization and Coffee, Sugar and Cocoa Exchange, Inc.

Third World countries because they either do not have anything to sell that the industrialized nations want, or, if they do have a product in demand by the industrial nations, they have little control over its price. While the discussion has centered on raw materials and commodities imported from Third World countries, the picture for the Third World concerning items it manufactures is even bleaker. Of the Third World's manufactured items imported by the West, three-fourths come from seven newly industrialized countries (NICs)—South Korea, Taiwan, Singapore, Hong Kong, Brazil, Mexico, and Argentina—leaving little market for other Third World nations. Achieving a favorable balance of trade under these circumstances as a means for creating development capital is very difficult for most of the Third World.

ARMED FORCES AND ARMS PURCHASES

A further drain on development funds is the money the Third World countries spend on maintaining and equipping their armed forces. This particular point must be made with a note of caution, however, because the percentage of the gross national product spent on the military by Third World countries varies considerably. Many spend no more than 1 percent of their GNP, but a number of countries spend considerably more. Latin America as a whole spent only 1.5 percent of its GNP on its armed forces in 1983, but Chile spent 4.5 percent and Cuba 6.1 percent. Africa, overall, spent 4.5 percent, but Ethiopia spent 10.9 percent; Somali, 9.1 percent; Zambia, 14.7 percent; and Zimbabwe, 6.4 percent. Among the Arab nations in Africa, Morocco spent 8.2 percent, and, before the October War in 1973, Egypt was reported to be spending 25 percent of its GNP on its military. In 1983 the Egyptian percentage was down to 8.3 percent. Libya's 1983 expenditure was 17.5 percent. The highest rate of expenditure is found in the Middle East, how-ever, where, overall, 15.7 percent of GNPs is spent on the military. In 1983 Syria spent 13 percent; Jordan, 14.9 percent; Oman, 27.9 percent; and Israel, 29 percent. North Yemen, one of the world's poorest nations, spent 15.4 percent of its GNP on its military, and South Yemen spent 17.4 percent. In Asia the percentage of the GNP expended for the military is 3.6 percent, although North Korea spent 16.7 percent; South Korea spent 5.8 percent; China, 8.6 percent; Malaysia, 5.2 percent; Pakistan, 5.4 percent; and India, 3.5 percent. Vietnam probably spends the highest percentage in Asia, but no figures are available for that country. (Percentages taken from U.S. Arms Control and Disarmament Agency, *World Military Expenditures and Arms Transfers*, *1985* (Washington, D.C.: Arms Control and Disarmament Agency, 1985), and *Military Balance*, compiled by the International Institute of Strategic Studies.)

Nearly all Third World countries who allocate high percentages of their GNP to their militaries are involved in conflicts with their neighbors or have domestic guerrilla opposition. Chile is concerned about Argentina's intentions involving disputes pending between the two countries, as well as being worried about internal opposition to the Pinochet government. Cuba's high percentage stems from its concern with hostility from the United States and from maintaining large contingents of troops in Ethiopia and Angola, as well as carrying on support of leftist forces in Central America. Ethiopia is fighting against as many as six guerrilla forces, and Somalia is concerned about Ethiopia's intentions in the Ogaden desert. Morocco is fighting the Polasario in the old Spanish Sahara. North and South Yemen have shared a hostile frontier for some years, as have North and South Korea. The Arab-Israeli dispute largely accounts for the high military budgets in the Middle East. In the Persian Gulf, the cost of the war between Iraq and Iran is unknown, but clearly has financially drained both countries. Concern about the Iranian-Iraqi War's spreading has spurred other countries in the region to increase spending on their militaries as well. Vietnam continues extensive military operations in Cambodia. While each of these countries has an explanation for their large military budgets, those budgets have served to limit the funds available for development. Many Third World countries do not report their military expenditures, but based on the size of their militaries and the cost of the equipment they have purchased, the amount expended must take an important part of their gross national products.

A portion of a nation's military budget is of course spent within the domestic economy but, since Third World countries must purchase most of their military equipment from the industrialized nations, either East or West, such purchases result in the transfer of considerable funds to the industrialized nations. In the 1950s and 1960s the Third World countries were willing to accept military hardware that was obsolescent, thus holding down the cost of such purchases. During the 1970s and 1980s, however, the demand grew for the latest models in aircraft, missiles, and tanks, and the more modern equipment was correspondingly more expensive. The rationale offered by the exporting countries for meeting the military equipment demands of the Third World nations is, "If we do not sell to them, someone else will." The result is a highly competitive market among the industrial nations for Third World arms contracts.

The largest exporter of arms is the Soviet Union, with the United States a close second. In 1984 the Soviets delivered arms valued at $8.6 billion to Third World countries, and the United States delivered $4.8 billion worth. Contracts for future deliveries concluded in that year were $10.6 billion for the Soviet Union and $7.7 billion for the United States. The Soviet Union has led the United States in arms transfers to as well as contracts with, Third World countries each year since 1977, except in 1983 when the United States signed new agreements valued at $9.4 billion and the Soviets $4.8 billion. France, Great Britain, and other Western European countries are also substantial exporters of arms to Third World countries.

The United States does have restrictions on the types of arms it will sell. During the Carter administration, Congress passed a prohibition on selling advanced military equipment to Third World countries without congressional approval. This restriction primarily affected the export of recent models of fighter aircraft to other than NATO allies. The U.S. did have one fighter, the F-5, which was designed for export that was not classified as advanced equipment; over 2000 were sold to other countries. The U.S. argued that the F-5 better suited the needs of Third World countries than did more advanced aircraft since the F-5 was less costly to purchase and maintain. Such an aircraft did not satisfy some U.S. customers, however. When Brazil and Peru wanted aircraft more advanced than the F-5, the United States refused to sell. Peru purchased aircraft from the Soviet Union, and Brazil bought its aircraft from France. These examples of aircraft purchases not only illustrate the growing demand among Third World countries for more advanced military equipment; they also point up the intense competition among the arms-exporting nations. But, whichever nation supplies the arms, the funds for those purchases must come from resources that could otherwise go toward development. An encouraging note is that while arms sales to Third World countries increased steadily during the 1970s, the amount of money spent on arms by the Third World, when discounted for inflation, remained level during the early 1980s.

INSTABILITY OF DOMESTIC SYSTEMS

One aspect of behavior by military forces in Third World countries that is less pronounced in the Western industrial countries is their extensive role in domestic politics. As in all countries, the militaries of the Third World function both to protect those countries from foreign enemies and to maintain domestic peace. But in many Third World nations the armed forces are also the single most important political group and enjoy a near-monopoly control over the means to exercise force. In the absence of a democratic tradition, the militaries of many Third World countries see themselves as a legitimate alternative to democratically chosen governments. In Latin America, in particular, the military views its role as the guardian of national values, and if these are violated it is the obligation of the military to intervene. The military does not see this as necessarily contradictory to democratic values, however. If democracy fails to provide a stable, well-run government, the military feels obligated to intervene as an interim solution to instability, until a democratic government is strong enough to run the country. When the democratically elected Allende government was overthrown by the Chilean military in 1973, it justified its actions on the grounds that it was protecting democratic values. This takeover occurred even though the military in Chile did not have a tradition of intervention in the democratic process and had not interfered in a civilian-run government for over forty years. On the occasions when the military has removed democratic governments in Nigeria, the Nigerian military has claimed that these actions were not antidemocratic but were carried out in the name of providing stability until democracy could be restored.

Even among the few democratic governments found in the Third World, democracy is not necessarily a solution to their problems of stability and development. India, the largest democracy in the world, has successfully conducted several national elections, but, even in this instance, India lived under a dictatorship of sorts from 1975 to 1977, when Prime Minister Indira Gandhi declared a state of national emergency and imposed martial law. Democratic values were deeply enough ingrained in the Indian political culture that democracy was restored, however. The democratically elected government of Ferdinand

Marcos in the Philippines eventually evolved into military control and martial law. In Pakistan, democratic governments have twice been replaced with military rule: first, after the speaker of the Pakistani parliament was killed during a "debate" and, second, in 1977, when the military overthrew a democratic government that had been elected in 1971. Ghana started as a democracy, but the military took over. In Asia and Africa the few democracies that have come to power are often shortlived and frequently are replaced by the military. In the Middle East, only Israel can be regarded as having a democratic system.

In the late 1970s military governments far outnumbered democracies in Latin America. Argentina, Brazil, and Chile, the three major countries of South America, all had military governments. At that time, the only South American countries with democratically elected governments were Venezuela and Colombia. By the mid-1980s, however, democratic regimes had been elected in Argentina and Brazil, as well as Uruguay, Bolivia, Ecuador, and Peru. Only Chile, Paraguay, Guyana, and Suriname, among the South American countries, still had military governments. In Latin America outside of South America, Mexico, with its own special brand of one-party democracy, has had regularly scheduled elections since 1928. In Central America, Costa Rica is a functioning democracy, with other states having held elections but, at best, having established only fledgling democracies. Overall, however, by the mid-1980s significant gains had been made in establishing democratically chosen governments in Latin America. The test for democratic procedures, in Latin America and elsewhere, comes when the elected leader's term of office expires. Does he leave office, or does he manipulate the constitution and extend his term of office?

While authoritarian governments found in Third World countries are often militarily run, other forms of nondemocratic regimes are also encountered. A number of the newly independent countries were ruled by the persons who

Fig. 6.6 Civilian Governments in Latin America

Belize (1981)

Guatemala (1985)

Honduras (1981)

El Salvador (1984)

Nicaragua

Costa Rica (1948)

Panama (1984)

Colombia (1957)

Venezuela (1958)

Guyana (1970)

Suriname

Ecuador (1979)

Brazil (1985)

Peru (1980)

Bolivia (1982)

Paraguay

Chili

Argentina (1983)

Uruguay (1985)

LATIN AMERICA
Civilian and military governments

Countries still under military rule

Countries under civilian rule

Dates indicate when civilian leader took office

SOURCE: Christian Science Monitor
May 1, 1987, p.12.

led them to independence. This was the case in Kenya, where Jomo Kenyatta ran the country until his death. Habib Bourguiba is the only leader Tunisia has had in its thirty years of independence. King Hassan of Morocco has been that country's only leader, and Tanzania, which gained its independence in 1961, was led only by Julius Nyerere until his retirement in 1985. While such leadership may conduct elections of sorts, their regimes are usually one-party arrangements. When such leaders eventually leave office, a period of instability often follows since a regularized process for selecting their successor has not been established.

The generalization that emerges concerning the forms of government found in the Third World countries is that, while democracies do exist, the most common form is military or civilian dictatorship. The Third World nations place the blame for their instability and authoritarianism on their colonial past and on their lack of economic development. They argue that democracy cannot be imposed on a former colony that did not experience democratic practices when it was ruled by outsiders, and that it will take time for democratic traditions to develop. They also point out that such traditions developed in the Western democracies over several generations. Even in the instance of the United States, the electorate was limited in the beginning and was broadened as economic development took place. Thus, democracy is viewed by much of the Third World as a luxury that accompanies economic development. This perspective on democracy leads to conflict with the West, however. In the West the instability found among Third World governments is seen as a major obstacle to economic development, which can best be resolved through a democratic form of government.

The rejection of democracy, at least temporarily, is further justified in much of the Third World on the grounds that democracy is in contradiction with the need for central planning of economies. Democracy is a slow and often chaotic means of making decisions, so it is

argued, and development must take place more rapidly in the Third World than it did in the Western democracies. The industrial revolution of the developed nations took place over more than a century; the Third World countries cannot wait that long. Central control and planning are necessary to shorten the development period, and democracy will not provide the centralized leadership needed for rapid development.

Corruption, commonly found among the Third World countries, is also a hindrance to economic development. One explanation for corruption at the lower levels of administration is that bureaucracies are deliberately large in order to provide employment for as many persons as possible; thus, the pay is low, and small bribes and petty corruption help provide a living wage. Corruption at higher levels is another matter, however, particularly if it occurs under a democratic government. Democracy is seen, especially by the military, as a less disciplined form of government and therefore more corrupt than dictatorship; thus, a central system controlled by the military is necessary. The immediate rationale for the military's takeover in Nigeria in 1984 was that it was necessary to stop the corruption of the civilian, democratic government, and, shortly before Indira Gandhi was assassinated, she sharply attacked corrupt officials for their damage to the development of India. Someday, corruption will be eliminated and democracy will be possible, so the Third World argument goes, but only after a stable economic system has been established.

The North-South conflict also includes different perspectives concerning what constitutes human rights and how they can be guaranteed. When Western democracies and international human rights organizations charge Third World countries with human rights violations, the Third World's response is that the rights granted in democracies were possible only after they had achieved strong economic systems. An additional problem is that what is meant by human rights differs somewhat between the Western countries and the Third World. When human rights are discussed by the Western nations, the reference is usually to civil and political rights: that is, the right to vote; the right to a fair trial and associated procedural rights of due process; and the First Amendment freedoms of free speech, a free press, and the right of assembly. The Third World countries view human rights within the context of economic rights—the right to a job, the right to adequate housing, and the right to a degree of economic security. The civil and political rights found in the democracies, the Third World argues, can and will develop after the more basic economic rights have been granted.

The characteristics of Third World countries discussed thus far have all shared one important element. They all are domestic problems that have resulted in international conflict with the industrialized nations. The perspective of the economically developed nations is that the causes of the North-South conflict are found in the domestic systems of the Third World countries; therefore, reform of those systems is necessary and should come at the initiative of Third World governments. Domestic consequences of these problems are a low standard of living, poor housing, low levels of education, high unemployment, and low-level technology. Externally, the results are a neocolonial or dependency relationship with Western industrial nations. The Third World would grant that there is strong linkage between its domestic problems and international conflict, but, in their view, the causes of those problems came from outside their domestic systems and are a result of past colonial practices and present-day neocolonialism; thus they can be rectified by outside assistance which should come from the industrial nations that have exploited the resources of the Third World. Therefore, the Third World makes demands for economic assistance and international economic reform, but the developed nations do not respond adequately, in the Third World's view. Third World countries charge that the Western nations are insensitive to their problems and that

the Third World has difficulty in even gaining a hearing before the industrial nations. The best opportunity for the Third World to make its agenda known has occurred in international forums where both Western and Third World representatives are present, particularly at the United Nations, where the Third World has been its most outspoken.

INTERNATIONAL FORUMS AND THE THIRD WORLD

While a number of generalizations have been made about the Third World, those countries are so diverse in both their domestic and international behavior that any generalization involves a number of exceptions. This diversity means that the Third World is a coalition of nations only in the loosest sense, but sufficient commonality of interests exists that those countries collectively have developed forums for making their demands known to the rest of the world. In the instance of the United Nations' General Assembly, the Third World captured control of an already-established institution, but, in other instances, they developed new forums in which to voice their concerns.

Whereas the United States was able to command a working majority in the General Assembly up to the 1960s, after that time the advent of new members into the body resulted in control passing to the Third World. Thus, for over twenty years that body has given the Third World an opportunity to "have its say." The Third World utilized the General Assembly to speed decolonization which resulted in further increasing Third World membership and voting strength in the UN. While the West generally dismisses the demands made there as repetition of Third World rhetoric, the United States has, on occasion, reacted angrily to the charges leveled at it. The U.S. reaction is dependent, however, on who is serving as United States ambassador to the

United Nations. During the tenure of Ambassadors Moynihan and Kirkpatrick, the United States argued back, but during Ambassador Young's tenure at the UN the response was more generally sympathetic to the Third World. Other United States ambassadors have been mostly silent or have presented muted responses.

If one of the objectives of the Third World is to gain the attention of the industrial West through constant renewal of charges of past and present exploitation, its policy has met with some success. The rallying cry of the Third World is for a New International Economic Order (NIEO). This demand is based on the fact that nearly 75 percent of the world's population is found in the Third World, but the Third World produces only 20 percent of the world's GNP. While the Third World's demand for a new economic order is an umbrella for several more specific reforms of the international economic system, fundamentally it is a demand for a reallocation of the world's resources. Just how far this reallocation should go is not clear, even to the Third World, but the Third World is united in its demand for changes.

Though the UN has been centrally important to Third World efforts in making its demands known, the first meeting of Third World nations occurred outside the structure of the United Nations at Bandung, Indonesia in 1955. Twenty-nine countries attended this conference, including China. Chou En-Lai, China's foreign minister, emerged from the meeting as the titular leader of the Third World, which led to speculation in the West that China was forming a coalition of Third World nations to use against the West. China soon retreated into a more traditional Chinese foreign policy of isolationism and did not exploit its close ties with the Third World. Without China's leadership, the movement's early leaders became Jawaharlal Nehru of India and Marshal Tito of Yugoslavia. The Bandung conference was of historic significance since it was the first occasion that a major international conference was held with no industrial nations

present. The conference condemned colonialism and generally disassociated the nations in attendance from the West, thus creating an agenda for Third World countries—anticolonialism and nonalignment.

The strength of the Third World within the United Nations is illustrated by the techniques used to bring its demands for economic reforms to the world's attention. Perhaps the first important victory for the Third World came in 1964 with the first United Nations Conference on Trade and Development (UNCTAD), which was called by the General Assembly over the objections of the Western nations. Subsequently, UNCTAD conferences were held in 1968, 1972, 1976, 1979, and 1983. The agenda of each of these conferences was dominated by Third World economic concerns. The 1976 meeting, held in Nairobi, concentrated on the problems of commodity pricing and the structuring of Third World debt. At the 1979 meeting in Manila, the Third World nations were still concerned with restructuring their debts, stabilizing prices on the commodities they export, and expanding trade with the industrial countries. The agenda has remained about the same for recent UNCTAD meetings, which indicates that much of what the Third World wants from the industrialized nations has not been granted. At the most recent UNCTAD conference, held in 1983, the Third World countries asked for, but failed to receive, $100 billion of assistance over a two-year period to ease their debt burden and compensate for falling income from exports due to the worldwide recession. The meetings usually end with a resolution calling for continued and more extensive North-South dialogue (Gosovic, 1972).

Within the UNCTAD conferences, the General Assembly, and other United Nations agencies such as the International Monetary Fund and the International Development Association, the caucusing group for the Third World is known as the Group of 77. When the group was created in 1965, it had 77 members, but, by the late 1980s, there were nearly 130 member nations, although the group retains its original title. The Group of 77 strives to develop as united a voice for the Third World as is possible within such a diverse coalition.

The membership of the Group of 77 includes a few nations that have close ties with the West and are not considered to be nonaligned; otherwise, it closely parallels the membership of the nonaligned nations conference, which exists outside the structure of the UN and is scheduled to be held every three years. Following the 1955 Bandung conference, another Third World meeting was not organized until 1961. This conference, officially labeled as the first nonaligned conference, was held in Belgrade, Yugoslavia. Though it formalized the nonalignment nature of its attendees, it did not deal with the economic problems of the nonaligned countries. Twenty-four nations attended. At the next such conference, held in Cairo in 1964, disputes among the nonaligned dominated, but the conference had grown to forty-seven nations. The third conference was not held until 1970 (the 1967 meeting was canceled), but perhaps the most important meeting for the Third World was the fourth conference, held in Algiers in 1973. Seventy-six countries attended this meeting. This conference dealt with a variety of items, but it coincided with several important international events that contributed to a rising morale among Third World countries. The conference expressed its support of the Arab countries in their fight against Israel and endorsed the oil boycott the Arab exporting nations had imposed on the Western nations supporting Israel. The successes of OPEC were greeted with enthusiasm by the Third World, even though it could ill afford to pay the higher oil prices themselves. In spite of this new financial burden, the Third World for the first time saw the industrial nations suffer from an economic action taken by Third World countries. This conference also marked the beginning of the anti-Israeli position of the nonaligned nations,

which since has proven to be a unifying factor among the Third World countries. The conference also expressed the feeling that the UNCTAD conferences (three had been held) were not meeting the needs of the Third World for economic change. As a result, out of this conference came the initial structure of the Third World demand for a new international economic order.

In addition to the usual themes of anticolonialism, nonalignment, and economic reform, the 1979 meeting of nonaligned nations in Havana illustrated the problems found among those nations as to what constituted nonalignment. To a Western observer, Cuba's membership in a conference of nonaligned nations hardly seems appropriate due to Cuba's close alignment with the Soviet Union. At that conference, Castro argued that Soviet interests and Third World interests were one and the same; therefore, alignment with the Soviet Union was a natural consequence of the fight against colonialism. The conference as a whole, however, stated that colonialism must be fought wherever it was found, and, by implication, the Soviets could also be guilty of colonialism. At the 1983 meeting of the conference held in New Delhi (scheduled for Baghdad in 1982, but moved and postponed due to the Iranian-Iraqi War), the tone toward the West set by Indira Gandhi was more moderate. The agenda for the 1986 meeting held in Harare, Zimbabwe was dominated by the issue of apartheid in South Africa, a practice seen by the Third World as colonialism at its worst.

The nonaligned movement does in fact break down into three general groups of nations. The first are those countries that take a pro-Soviet stance such as that expressed by Castro in 1979. A second group sees Western capitalism as the proper route to development; while these countries may maintain close economic ties with the West, they usually do not have military commitments. The third and largest group genuinely pursues nonalignment with neither of the major industrial coalitions. Theoretically, no nation that has a political commitment to one of the super-powers or allows one of them to have military bases in its country will be admitted to the non-aligned group. In practice, these restrictions are applied to countries associated militarily with the United States; association with the Soviet Union is not regarded as a prohibition to membership. This inconsistency points out that North-South conflict is between Western industrial nations and the Third World; Soviet bloc nations are only on the periphery.

At the UN, the Third World nations brought their agenda before the Western nations through any institution or situation that served their purposes. In 1974 the Third World was successful in calling a special sesson of the General Assembly devoted solely to its economic problems. The West opposed the special session and left its preparation to the Third World. The special session, building on the agenda of economic demands that emerged from the Algiers meeting of non-aligned nations, produced the Declaration of the Establishment of a New International Economic Order (NIEO). Later that year, the General Assembly adopted the Charter of Economic Rights and Duties of States, which was a further expansion of the Third World's demands for economic reform. Another special session of the General Assembly was called in 1975, the subject again was development and economic cooperation. Yet another special session of the General Assembly was held in 1979 to deal with the question of technology transfer to the Third World. The Third World has also been active within the Economic and Social Council (ECOSOC) at the United Nations. As with the General Assembly, the Third World membership dominates ECOSOC's agenda. By the 1980s the demands of the Third World seemed to be fully articulated, but not met, and they all fell under the general concept of reforming the international economic system. The demand that called for a new international economic order dealt with a number of specific complaints and what the industrialized nations should do

about them. Those specific issues will be discussed next.

THE NIEO AGENDA

While the most broadly stated demand of the Third World is that the Western nations provide economic assistance for Third World development, that assistance can come in various forms and from different sources. The most direct aid industrial nations can give is bilateral, which means the transfer of monetary grants or credits. The Third World regards the present level of such aid as far from adequate and would like to see contributions to Third World development increased considerably.

ECONOMIC AID

In spite of Third World protestations to the contrary the Western nations feel they have provided the Third World with substantial amounts of economic assistance. "Economic aid was used [by the Western nations to assist the Third World] because it dovetailed with the desire of the developed market states to maintain the existing structure of international economic relations and at the same time to garner political influence in the developing world by responding to Southern desires for development" (Spero, 1985, 179). The Third World accepts Western aid because it needs it, but it does not necessarily approve of the motivations behind that aid.

The United Nations, through UNCTAD, has set as a goal for the industrial countries that they give 1 percent of their national income, or .7 percent of their GNP, annually to the development of the Third World. While the United States has given the largest amount of economic aid to foreign countries of any of the industrial countries, the percentage of the national income involved averages annually less than .3 percent. Only four Western nations—the Netherlands, Norway, Sweden and Denmark—meet or exceed the goal set by UNCTAD. Other Western European countries fall somewhere in between the U.S. percentage and the UNCTAD goal.

In 1982 the Western nations granted the Third World about $18.5 billion in bilateral economic aid. The OPEC countries, which were a major source of aid to the Third World before oil prices fell, provided $5.5 billion down from $8.7 billion in 1980 with additional declines since 1982. The Soviet Union and East European nations channeled $2.8 billion to the Third World in 1982, for a total of $26.8 billion in bilateral aid from all sources. Multilateral agencies such as the World Bank granted $7.5 billion in aid. When credits and loans from governmental and private sources, mainly Western, are added, the Third World received about $93.1 billion in aid in some form. Although these figures are impressive, the amounts from Western sources had been declining since 1980. (OECD, 1983, 51). p. 51).

Tab. 6.1 Economic Assistance to Third World from Developed Nations 1985

As Percentage of GNP		Per Capita	
Norway	1.20%	Norway	$191
Netherlands	1.00	Denmark	137
Denmark	.89	Sweden	129
Sweden	.85	Netherlands	116
France	.72	France	93
Australia	.49	Canada	68
Canada	.48	Switzerland	66
Germany	.43	Germany	63
Italy	.40	Australia	49
United Kingdom	.32	Japan	46
Switzerland	.30	Italy	42
Japan	.29	United States	40
United States	.23	United Kingdom	28

SOURCE: Organization for Economic Cooperation and Development, 1986

The decline in aid programs to the Third World can be explained in part by the worldwide recession of the early 1980s. Certainly the OPEC nations reduced their aid for that reason, coupled with the fall in oil prices, but in the West, policy issues were also involved. The reduction in Western aid is in part a product of Western disillusionment with the ability of the Third World to use aid it receives effectively. Western economies continued to expand at a more rapid rate than those of Third World countries, and, in spite of Western economic aid, the Third World accumulated substantial foreign debt due to large imports of food and energy. Why provide additional aid when what has been provided has helped so little? The Marshall Plan was highly successful in Europe, but aid for the Third World has fallen far short of expectations. Also, if the Western nations gave aid to the Third World to gain influence and allies, little has been gained. The Third World is still critical of the West without showing the same level of criticism for the West's Cold War opponents. The evolution of U.S. foreign aid reflects these changes in attitude about assistance to the Third World.

Before the late 1950s U.S. aid went to Europe almost exclusively, but as economic and military assistance to Europe declined, economic aid to the Third World increased. By the 1960s U.S. aid had completed its transition from a basically European-oriented program to one in which nearly all U.S. aid was going to the Third World. During the 1950s, three-fourths of U.S. aid going to Europe was military, but by the mid-1960s three-fourths of Third World aid was economic. During this period the United States also was successful in encouraging other industrialized nations to increase their aid to the Third World. U.S. military aid to the Third World went primarily to those countries that had joined such U.S.-sponsored alliances as SEATO and CENTO during the mid-1950s. Even though those alliances were dissolved in the 1970s, military aid still goes to selected Third World countries. In addition to military aid, the U.S. aid program also includes grants, technical assistance, and low-interest loans and credits.

While the U.S. Congress often discusses foreign aid in terms of the importance of overcoming poverty in the Third World, aid programs have, to a great extent, been justified as a means of combating communism or maintaining a balance between Third World nations in conflict, not as meeting an obligation to aid the Third World in its development. This justification for aid on ideological or political grounds is not well received in the Third World. In spite of disagreements as to why the aid should be given, by the 1980s the United States had provided aid to some 125 Third World countries. The amount of aid received by a number of nations is modest, however, particularly in black Africa; the U.S. has left economic and technical assistance for Africa to the former colonial masters in Western Europe, particularly Great Britain and France.

The United States aid program underwent another transition in the 1970s. Appropriations for foreign aid programs always signaled an annual fight in Congress, but the program received increased opposition during the 1970s. Congressional opposition was so serious, that for four years during the early 1980s, Congress passed no new foreign aid authorizations, but, rather, appropriated funds for the program based on earlier authorizations. Foreign aid has no domestic constituency to speak of, and thus is an easy target when the budget is tight. The program has never received long-range authorization of funds, which has made it difficult to develop and finance projects that called for funds over several years. Congress has reduced development aid, and the only reason funding has not fallen further is due to U.S. commitments to Israel and, after the 1979 peace treaty between Egypt and Israel, to Egypt. By far the largest aid package, both economic and military, goes to Israel, with Egypt receiving about two-thirds as much as Israel does. In 1984 Israel received over

$3 billion in assistance, $1.7 billion of which was in military aid. Considering the anti-Israeli position of the Third World countries and the Arab nations' opposition to Egypt's entering into a peace treaty with Israel, this sort of distribution of U.S. aid is strongly opposed by the Third World.

In 1985 Congress finally passed a new foreign aid bill totaling $12.8 billion. While the total amount was higher than previous aid bills, half was in military aid, two-thirds of which went to Israel, Egypt, Turkey, and Greece. Half the $3.8 billion for the economic support fund, which is used to support the economies of countries considered vital to the security of the United States, was earmarked for Israel and Egypt. $2.1 billion was assigned to development aid. While the bill

Fig. 6.7 U.S. 1984 Aid Program

How Senate would allocate $12.8 billion in foreign aid

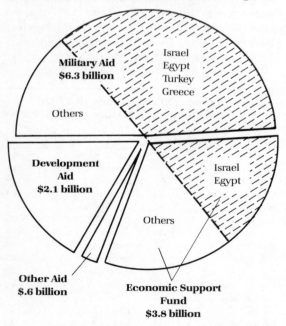

SOURCE: Christian Science Monitor
May 17, 1985, p.3.

Fig. 6.8 Total U.S. Security Assistance FY 1984

Top 20 recipients

in Millions of Dollars

Republic of Korea	$231.8	2.5%
El Salvador	$316.6	3.4%
Spain	$415.0	4.4%
All others		4.9%
Greece	$501.4	5.3%
Pakistan	$856.8	5.6%
Turkey	$525.8	9.1%
Sudan	$166.5	1.8%
Portugal	147.9	1.6
Costa Rica	139.1	1.5
Jordan	136.7	1.5
Honduras	117.4	1.3
Tunisia	113.1	1.2
Thailand	106.2	1.1
Philippines	101.5	1.1
Somalia	68.0	.7
Jamaica	59.2	.6
Oman	55.1	.6
Liberia	47.8	.5
Egypt	$2,219.6	23.6%
Israel	$2,610.0	27.7%

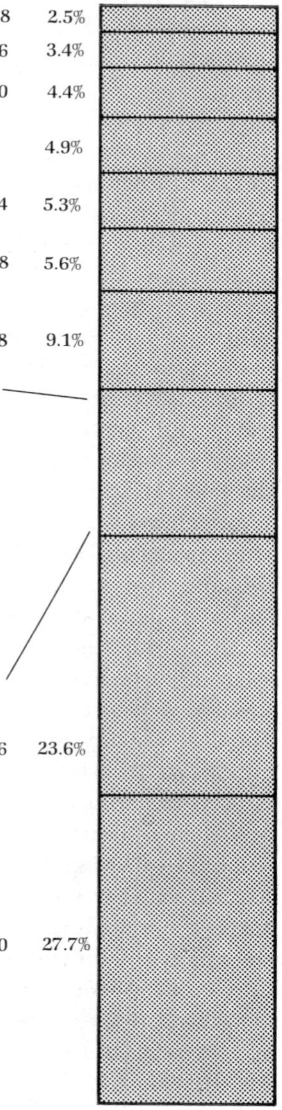

SOURCE: Christian Science Monitor
May 23, 1985, p.19.

was touted as providing aid to 123 countries, most of the recipients received small amounts. In 1984, over 97 percent of U.S. aid went to 20 allies or client states. Also in 1984, in separate legislation, the U.S. provided about $1.64 billion to development banks (including the World Bank) and international organizations. From the perspective of the Third World, the United States foreign aid program is too small, includes too much military aid, and is misdirected both as to the countries receiving it and the projects it finances.

The Third World has expressed its preference that aid from the industrial nations be funneled through international organizations rather than extended on a bilateral basis. Those countries feel that they would have more control over the aid's distribution through organizations to which they belong. This proposal has been rejected by the industrial nations, although Western nations do contribute funds to multilateral agencies that grant aid to the Third World.

CHANGES IN TRADE PATTERNS

As an alternative to obtaining development funds from direct economic assistance, the Third World could generate development capital through a favorable balance in international trade. A favorable balance of trade would provide the foreign currency needed to purchase machinery and technology for development. This would, however, be possible only if the Western nations revised their trade patterns with the Third World. But, the industrial nations point out, Third World countries spend too much of their scarce funding on oil purchases, modern weapons, and whatever consumer items they choose to buy. Greater austerity in making these purchases would aid development; they should put their own houses in order before asking for international trade

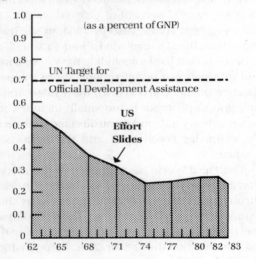

Fig. 6.9 Decline in U.S. Development Aid

SOURCE: Christian Science Monitor
May 17, 1985, p.18.

reforms. The Western nations point out that, since the increased cost of oil is the result of actions by other Third World nations, the additional expense should be met by subsidies from those countries that benefit from the higher oil prices. While oil-rich Arab countries have provided some funds to offset the higher cost of oil, those funds usually go to other, less fortunate Arab or Moslem countries, not the Third World in general. The Third World nevertheless feels that there is much the industrial world can do to improve the world's trade patterns for the benefit of the Third World.

The new international economic order calls for several changes that pertain to trade between the Third World and the industrial nations. The primary objective of these changes is to allow Third World nations to break out of a trade relationship in which they provide raw materials and commodities to the industrial nations at prices they feel are too low. They, in turn, are forced to buy from those nations manufactured items at prices which the Third World thinks are too

high. One manner in which this could be resolved is through the indexing of Third World exports with the manufactured items of the industrial nations. This proposal is similar to the plea of the American farmer in the 1950s for parity between farm products and industrial items. Farmers wanted the pricing of their products calculated on the costs of industrial items, which would have the effect of keeping farm prices higher. The Third World nations feel, as did the American farmers, that a more equitable system should be devised to avoid the situation in which both the prices on their products and the prices placed on the manufactured items they must purchase are fixed by someone else. If the prices for Third World exports are indexed with what those countries must import, the income they receive from their exports would be more stable and they would in turn be less susceptible to economic recessions in the industrial countries. As the Third World perceives the situation, such an arrangement would correct the problem created when prices on Third World exports fall, because the cost of manufactured items seems never to suffer a similar decline. The industrial nations have thus far rejected the concept of indexing.

Another change in trade patterns sought by the Third World is the establishment of additional commodity agreements with the industrial nations. This would enable the Third World nations to better anticipate their market in the industrial nations and would also help to stabilize prices through presale agreements. In connection with this effort, the Third World has also asked the industrial nations to establish buffer stockpiles of their products which could be built up when the market demand was low, further stabilizing prices. The OPEC nations have not supported buffer stocks of oil, however, as they fear that such an arrangement would make the industrial nations less susceptible to boycotts or production reductions.

The Third World also seeks better access to the markets of the industrial nations; this would require the industrial nations to lower tariffs and import quotas on the items sold by the Third World nations. The Third World contends that the present arrangement of tariffs and quotas is designed to allow only its commodities and raw materials into the markets of the indus trial nations; virtually anything else the Third World wants to sell has trade restrictions placed upon it. Since the General Agreement on Tariffs and Trade (GATT) is the framework devised by the industrial nations to deal with trade problems, the Third World wants GATT to carry out a broad-based reduction in tariffs and quotas that is more favorable to them. Within GATT, the industrial nations already have reduced tariffs for the Third World, but the Third World nations do not feel those reductions are sufficient.

Yet another demand from the Third World is that special drawing rights (SDRs), which are used among the industrial nations, be established for Third World use. SDRs were developed to facilitate trade by providing for easy convertibility of currencies. For the Third World nations, such a development would make their generally weak currencies more readily convertible, but an even greater advantage would be the expanded credit new SDRs would provide. Overall, the Third World has had little success in changing the world's trade patterns and arrangements.

COMMODITIES, RESOURCES, AND MNCs

The Third World nations also want greater control over their natural resources. The manner in which Mexico handled this problem seems to be a model for the Third World. In the Mexican Constitution of 1917, all natural resources were declared to be the property of the state. When Pemex was established as the state oil corporation in 1938 and the property of foreign oil firms was nationalized, Mexico paid for the facilities of those firms but not for the oil leases. Compensation for the leases was not necessary, Mexico claimed, since resources already belonged

to the state. If this practice became commonplace in the Third World countries, then when foreign property involving an extractive industry was nationalized, the cost of compensation would not be as great. Even without nationalization, if mineral rights were state-owned, the Third World countries would have more control over resources that now are controlled by multinational corporations (MNCs).

The Third World would also like additional controls over MNCs that operate within their borders, but attempts at the United Nations to negotiate such an agreement have failed. From the Western perspective, MNCs provide considerable aid to the Third World: MNCs are a means of transmitting technology; they provide jobs in countries where unemployment is a problem; they bring Western marketing practices to the Third World; and they provide much needed capital. To the Third World, however, MNCs are often seen as a means for the industrial nations to exploit their markets and resources. An overall generalization at the heart of the conflict concerning trade and MNCs is that the Third World wants considerable international regulation of the world's economy through changed trade patterns, regulation of MNCs, control over their own resources, and the right to nationalize foreign-owned property more readily. The industrial nations want a free and largely unregulated international market.

Natural resources are an issue between the Third World and the industrial nations in yet another way. The largely unexplored resources of the seabed and the question of who will control them has become an important North-South issue. The long-running United Nations Conference on the Law of the Seas dealt with many issues including territorial waters and economic zones, but the issue that struck at the heart of North-South conflict was control of the natural resources on the seabed.

The position of the industrial nations is that both private developers and an international seabed resources agency should have access to the development of the seabed's resources. The profits from such an international agency would go for the economic development of the Third World. The Third World argues that if Western corporations were allowed to explore and develop the seabed, no funds would be forthcoming from the Western nations to finance the efforts of an international agency. The Third World won this argument within the Law of the Seas Conference, but its victory would seem to be without benefit, since in 1982 the United States, along with most of the other Western nations, refused to sign the treaty that emerged from the conference. Without Western support, the seabed resources agency has little chance of success. The principal objection voiced by the Western nations to giving exclusive control over seabed resources to an international agency was that the Third World nations wish to limit access to resources found in their countries through international cartels, control over MNCs, and nationalization of those resources; in addition, they also want to control any new sources of resources that might be discovered on the seabed.

RESTRUCTURING THE DEBT

In the late 1980s, the total foreign debt of the Third World nations was nearing $800 billion in medium- and long-term debt, with about another $100 billion in short-term debt. About 60 percent of this debt is owed to private banks. The top debtor nation in the Third World was Brazil, with a debt of over $105 billion, followed by Mexico with nearly $100 billion and Argentina with a debt of about $50 billion. These debt-ridden countries are also the ones having the greatest difficulty in paying the interest on the debt, managing the short-term debt, and making payments on the longer-term debt. Other Third World countries having trouble with their foreign indebtedness included Venezuela, Chile,

and the Philippines. While the debt problem would appear to be concentrated among the Latin American countries—a total of $350 billion was owed by Latin America—it certainly was not limited to those countries. Zaire, Zambia, Nigeria, and several other African countries also had difficulty servicing their debts. Even though countries with large debts are the ones most often mentioned in the Western press, Third World countries with small GNPs and populations and debts of only $2 to $5 billion were also having problems meeting their debt payments. Countries

---

Fig. 6.10 Major Debtor Nations in Third World

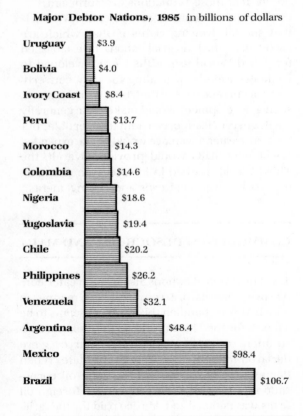

Major Debtor Nations, 1985 in billions of dollars

Uruguay	$3.9
Bolivia	$4.0
Ivory Coast	$8.4
Peru	$13.7
Morocco	$14.3
Colombia	$14.6
Nigeria	$18.6
Yugoslavia	$19.4
Chile	$20.2
Philippines	$26.2
Venezuela	$32.1
Argentina	$48.4
Mexico	$98.4
Brazil	$106.7

SOURCE: Christian Science Monitor
November 5, 1986, p.3.

in this category are Bolivia, Dominican Republic, Panama, and Uruguay.

Much of the Third World's foreign debt was accumulated during the 1970s. This was a time when private Western banks held large deposits of petrodollars from Arab members of OPEC and public sources for loans were cutting back on funding. The Third World needed money to meet energy and food costs, and Western banks had the funds available and were attracted to the Third World by an anticipated high return on their investment. The Third World nations having the greatest need and presenting the best opportunity for investment were the NICs. Thus, the foreign debt in those countries grew rapidly. Mexico, as an example, had a foreign debt of $25 billion when Lopez Portillo became president in 1976; when he left the presidency in 1982, Mexico's debt was nearly $85 billion.

Finding someone to blame for the debt situation in Mexico and elsewhere has not helped resolve the problem, but the most commonly offered explanations are mismanagement of the borrowed funds (often heard as the basis of Mexico's problem); money loaned for projects that failed to yield projected revenue; the fall in prices for Third World exports due to recessions in Western economies; the fall in price and quantity of oil exported; high interest rates, especially in the United States; the strength of the dollar relative to the Third World currencies; and an over-extension of credit to the Third World by Western banks. There certainly seems to be sufficient blame to go around and justification for blaming both the industrial and Third World nations. (Cline, 1983).

Third World debt has produced several financial crises when first one debtor nation and then another appeared to be about to default on its loans. Western banks, which had overextended themselves with Third World loans, could ill afford to absorb the loss if a loan were defaulted upon; the country threatening default could ill-afford to have its international credit rating

destroyed. Thus, the International Monetary Fund (IMF), at the point of a country's being near default, would intervene and work out a short-term solution which usually consisted of arranging loans to meet immediate obligations. In addition, the IMF often imposed restrictions on the debtor nations calling for an austerity program, in particular requiring a reduction in imports by the debtor nation in order to improve the trade balance. When the IMF made such arrangements for Brazil in 1983, the result was a slowdown in the Brazilian economy and a rise in unemployment, which typically is the short-term result when the IMF intervenes. By 1986, however, Brazil had lowered inflation considerably and the IMF-imposed austerity plan appeared to have worked well. The Third World is asking for longer-term relief than is provided by IMF bailouts, however; its requests center around a lowering of interest rates so that the debtor nations can more easily make payments on their debts, and an extension of their loans' payback period. The Western countries are prone to insist on austerity programs as a more reasonable means of meeting the problem. The Third World countries see economic austerity as compounding their problems through unemployment, a slowdown in their economies, and political unrest. By 1985 several of the Latin American debtor nations were openly saying what had been feared in financial circles for some time—much of the Third World's debt may be unpayable regardless of what arrangements are made.

CONCLUSION

Conflicts between the industrial nations and the Third World are numerous, but nearly all center on economic issues. The thrust of the Third World's argument is that funds must come from the industrial nations in order for the Third World to develop and that the industrial nations have an obligation to meet those needs. As the Third World sees it, the international economy is in need of major reforms to allow the Third World to escape its present dependency on the industrial nations. The international economy not only needs to be changed; it also needs to be more strictly regulated to the advantage of the Third World. The industrial nations support a largely unregulated international economy and a free market, which the Third World argues leaves it in its present position of dependency. While some limited concessions have been granted the Third World by the industrial nations, the issues of North-South conflict remain largely unresolved.

CHAPTER 7

Sources of Conflict III: Intracoalitional Conflict

For decision-makers in the United States, foreign policy is divided into three major areas. The first is to manage, control, and, if possible, improve the relationship the United States has with the Soviet Union and its allies; the second is to maintain or improve U.S. relations with the loosely knit Third World; the third is to keep the Western coalition intact and in good repair. In brief, as leader of the Western coalition, the United States must develop policy in its relationship with other coalitions and with the members of the coalition of which the U.S. is a member. These assignments do not differ, except perhaps in magnitude, from those of decision-makers of any nation. Unless a country pursues a policy of "going it alone," all must contend with both intercoalitional and intracoalitional conflict.

The focus of the two previous chapters was conflict between coalitions—between the Western and Soviet coalitions, and between the Western coalition and the Third World. The directional labels attached to those areas of conflict were East-West and North-South. The discussion of North-South conflict also included many of the conflicts that exist among Third World countries. What remains to be discussed is conflict within both the Western coalition and the communist coalition. If directional labels are attached to this sort of conflict, they are West-West and East-East.

PROBLEMS OF COALITIONS

The formation of a coalition between two or more nations carries with it sacrifice and risk. Since some degree of conflict exists between any two nations that have contact, a coalition is possible only when it is to the advantage of the nations involved to modify their interests so that a coalition can be formed. The more nations involved in a coalition, the wider the range of interests, thus the greater the need for modification of interests by members. If a potential member is not willing to make such sacrifices, the alternative is to remain outside the coalition, as Sweden chose to do in 1949, when it decided not to join NATO and instead developed a separate military force. When SEATO and CENTO were organized, India, Indonesia, and various Arab nations refused membership, since to join would have required more change than they were willing to adopt. Once countries are part of a coalition, the sacrifice of specificity of interests must continue in order for the coalition to remain viable. If a member nation is unwilling to do this, it has little recourse but to withdraw from the coalition or limit its participation therein. Examples of the latter option is France's reduced participation in NATO and both France's and Great Britain's reservations about the extent of their participation in the European Community (EC).

Eastern European members of the Soviet-led coalition complain about the sacrifices they must make in order to be an ally of the Soviet Union; particularly, they complain about integration of their economies into the Soviet economy. Since the Eastern European nations appear not to have available to them the alternative of withdrawal from the Soviet-led coalition, their only recourse is to complain.

The purpose of any coalition is to maximize the impact of interests common to the coalition members, the assumption being that the more nations that can agree on policy objectives, the more forcefully their demands can be made. In a coalition, differences among the members will continue to exist; thus, the diplomatic objective of coalition members is to repair the coalition on a continuing basis. Such diplomacy is difficult, however, and coalitions fail with some frequency. When SEATO failed in its primary objective, which was to prevent South Vietnam, Laos, and Cambodia from going communist, the coalition was eliminated. The purpose for CENTO was to provide an anticommunist coalition on the southern borders of the Soviet Union, but the keystone of the coalition was Iran. When the shah fell from power, Iran withdrew from the organization and the heart of the alliance was gone. Subsequently, in September 1979, the coalition was dissolved.

The assumption that a coalition will garner all the members it can in order to add strength to its demands has limitations. The European Community (EC) takes care to add members only when the additions will not weaken the economic structure of the community. The purpose of this coalition is to produce an integrated economy that is collectively stronger than the several economies of its members; thus, to add a member that would economically weaken the overall economic strength of the organization would be self-defeating. Both Portugal and Spain wanted EC membership for some time before the community deemed them economically strong enough to join. Clearly, as was illustrated in the last chapter concerning the coalition of nonaligned nations, a coalition can lose much of its effectiveness when it encompasses many diverse interests. The members of the European Community wish to avoid such a fate.

The creation of a coalition also can result in the formation of a countercoalition. This is most likely to occur when the basis of the coalition is military in nature, such as the development of the Warsaw Pact following the creation of NATO. Coalitions based on economic cooperation are not so prone to result in the creation of a countercoalition, although in the early stages of the European Community an opposing Western European organization, the European Free Trade Association (EFTA), came into being.

The structure of political parties in the United States is a domestic equivalent of international coalitions in that each of the two major parties is a coalition of interests. If each interest that operates within the structure of the parties were to make its demands individually rather than through the party structure, the demands made upon decision-makers would proliferate, and each would have less impact. Presumably, however, demands made by the political parties carry greater force than they would if exerted by each interest separately.

Perhaps the principal difference between domestic and international coalitions of interests is the degree to which there is formal agreement. Domestically, coalitions of interests do not have formal documents that bring them together; the commonality of interests is sufficient in a nation in which a high level of political consensus exists. In the international system, where political consensus is low, coalitions ordinarily are formed through formal treaties.

Thus, a number of problems are involved in the creation and maintenance of coalitions. Common interests must be found on which to base the coalition, and the members must be willing to modify their individual interests in order to make the coalition function. How large a coalition should be to effectively achieve its objectives and how many members it should contain are judgments all coalitions must make. The interests of members must not be widely diverse, or the coalition will not be effective. Once formed into a coalition, the members must continue to modify their interests, or the coalition will collapse. The diplomacy of maintaining a coalition is an ongoing problem for its members, particularly those nations that serve as leaders, such as the United States and the Soviet Union. All coalitions have centripetal forces, the common interests that brought about the coalition and hold it together, and centrifugal forces, the conflicts within the coalition that tend to pull it apart.

WEST–WEST CONFLICT

One of the problems involved in using directional labels to identify coalitions is that the West in East-West and the North in North-South are essentially the same coalition, but the members are identified on a different basis. In East-West conflict, the Western coalition is seen as mainly a military alliance of anticommunist Western nations. In the instance of North-South conflict, the Northern coalition is seen as the Western industrialized nations with economic relationships holding them together. The West-West conflict discussed here will deal with both military and economic problems involved in maintaining this dual-named coalition. Since the Western coalition is both a military and economic alliance, and since its members are both economic competitors and economically interdependent, the opportunities for conflict are numerous.

CONFLICT WITHIN NATO

The most important military alliance among the Western nations is the North Atlantic Treaty Organization (NATO). The common interest that made this coalition possible was concern in the late 1940s that the Soviets might use their superior conventional military power against Western Europe. Western Europe's view was that this threat could be countered only if the United States agreed to extend its atomic umbrella to include Western Europe. The alliance, agreed to in April 1949, was a twenty-year commitment with provisions for renewal for an indefinite period. To supplement U.S. atomic protection, conventional armed forces in Western Europe were to be rebuilt with U.S. assistance. This arms buildup considerably improved the military standing of Western Europe, but to avoid the impression that the alliance was only an anti-Soviet move, a more positive rationale was offered in that the alliance's purpose was presented as an effort to strengthen the sense of community among nations bordering on or near the North Atlantic Ocean. The myth of a North Atlantic community as a basis for NATO was essentially negated when Greece and Turkey joined NATO in 1951. Those nations were far from the North Atlantic Ocean but did meet the qualification of being anti-Soviet. West Germany became a member in 1955, and Spain became a member in 1982; NATO had a total of sixteen members in the late 1980s.

The NATO coalition has been subject to considerable stress since 1949, and the addition of West Germany produced one of a number of divisive conflicts. West Germany easily met the qualification of being anticommunist and its manpower was greatly needed to bolster NATO's land forces, but some Western European members of NATO, particularly France, found it undesirable to rearm West Germany so soon after World War II. France had suffered three German invasions in 70 years and did not want to face yet another German army. As an alternative to a new German army, France proposed the European Defense Community (EDC), which would create a European army made up of forces from West Germany, France, Italy, the Netherlands, Belgium, and Luxembourg. No national units in this unified

Fig. 7.1 NATO and the Warsaw Pact

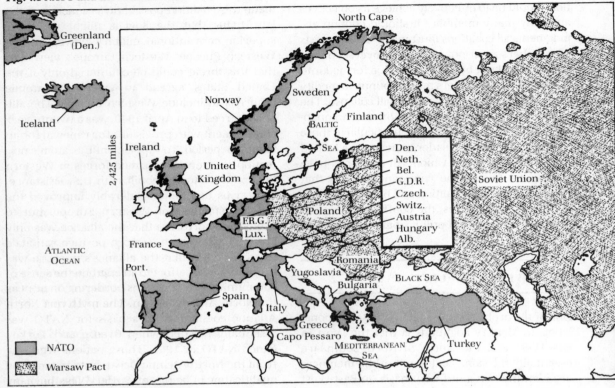

SOURCE: *Atlas of NATO*, 1985, p.3. (U.S. Dept. of State)

army would be larger than battalion strength, which would allow NATO to include the strength of German manpower, but there would be no German army to arouse French fears.

A treaty to implement EDC was negotiated; after all other potential members had agreed to it, in August 1954 the French National Assembly rejected the proposal. EDC had become the victim of a National Assembly so divided that a majority of support for virtually any measure was impossible. Thus, although the French government had proposed and promoted EDC, it was France that killed the plan. In early 1955 West Germany entered NATO as a full member.

A much weaker version of EDC eventually appeared as the Western European Union (WEU). WEU included Great Britain, along with the six countries that were to have been members of EDC. WEU did not include a European army, but was dedicated to promoting greater unity in Western Europe. WEU has never played a significant role in the Western coalition.

From the beginning, NATO encountered the problem of member states' failing to meet their commitments of armed forces. France was expected to make a major contribution to NATO land forces, but failed to meet its commitments, first because of forces sent to Indo-China and then, later, to Algeria. When Charles de Gaulle assumed power in France in 1958, he expressed support for NATO, but only if France could remain an independent military force. Initially, de Gaulle refused to allow U.S. aircraft armed with nuclear weapons to operate from French bases; later, all French naval forces were removed from NATO command; and then, in 1965, France refused to participate in a multinational seagoing nuclear force (MLF). In May 1966 de Gaulle withdrew French land forces from NATO and ordered NATO headquarters, located near Paris, out of France within one year. The headquarters were relocated in Brussels. France remained as a political member of NATO but no longer participated in any military aspects of the organization. France, however, did commit itself to fight alongside NATO in the event of war with the Warsaw Pact.

MLF proved divisive for NATO beyond the French opposition. In 1960 the United States had proposed NATO control of nuclear weapons independent of the British and American national nuclear stockpiles. In 1961, due to opposition within NATO to a NATO-controlled land nuclear force, the plan was narrowed to a seagoing force. By this time, France had developed its own nuclear weapons and was working on the development of delivery systems. De Gaulle had long resented the close relationship that existed between the United States and Great Britain and, in particular, resented U.S. assistance to Great Britain when the British developed nuclear weapons. Also, when Great Britain built submarines capable of launching long-range ballistic missiles, the United States provided the British with missiles. The French received no U.S. help with either of these weapon systems. As a reflection of France's growing independence, the French rejected MLF in 1964 on the grounds that France preferred a nuclear force solely under French control. Other NATO countries gave MLF only minimal support and the proposal was dropped.

Colonialism has also caused conflicts within

NATO, the most serious of which was the Suez crisis in 1956. Both the British and French resented U.S. opposition to their armed attempt to retake the Suez Canal and felt that the United States owed them support as a NATO ally. When India marched into the Portuguese colony of Goa in 1961, Portugal felt that since it was a member of NATO the invasion was an attack on NATO-protected territory. NATO took no action. As a consequence, Portugal threatened to evict the United States from its bases in the Portuguese-controlled Azores, but did not do so.

Conflict in Cyprus has also resulted in a long-term split within NATO, in this instance between Greece and Turkey. The island's population is about 80 percent Greek Cypriot and 12 percent Turkish Cypriot. From the time Cyprus gained its independence from Great Britain in 1960 considerable strain existed between the two ethnic groups. The Greek Cypriots, along with the Greek government, supported the union of Cyprus with Greece (*enosis*). Turkey, which saw itself as the protector of Turkish Cypriots, opposed such a move. As a result of fighting between the two ethnic groups, the United Nations sent a peacekeeping force to Cyprus in 1964. This held the issue of *enosis* in abeyance until 1974, when a Greek-supported overthrow of the Cypriot government occurred and a government supporting *enosis* came to power. To prevent the union from occurring, Turkey invaded the island and expanded considerably the area controlled by Turkish Cypriots. Greece felt that NATO and the United States should force Turkey to withdraw from Cyprus. When NATO failed in its attempts to reconcile differences between Greece and Turkey, Greece withdrew from the military structure of NATO in protest, but was readmitted in 1980. The Greek Papandreau government, elected in 1982, threatened during the election campaign to pull Greece out of NATO, but has taken no such action. The Turkish forces remain on Cyprus.

All of these divisive problems—contributions to NATO, French withdrawal of its forces from

Fig. 7.2 NATO Members and Other Mutual Security Pacts

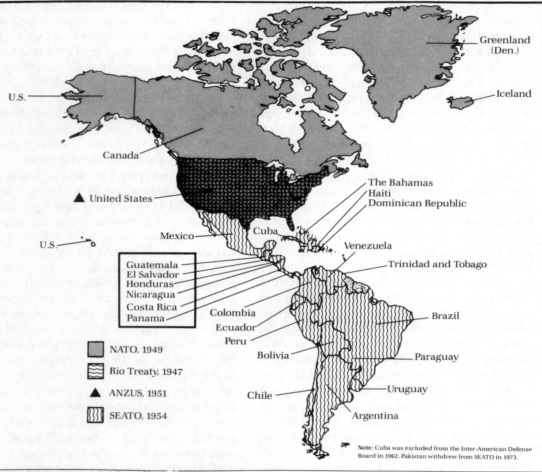

Greenland (Den.)

Iceland

U.S.

Canada

▲ United States

The Bahamas
Haiti
Dominican Republic

Mexico — Cuba

Venezuela

Trinidad and Tobago

Guatemala
El Salvador
Honduras
Nicaragua
Costa Rica
Panama

U.S.

Colombia
Ecuador
Peru

Brazil

Bolivia

Paraguay

Chile

Uruguay

Argentina

NATO, 1949

Rio Treaty, 1947

▲ ANZUS, 1951

SEATO, 1954

Note: Cuba was excluded from the Inter-American Defense Board in 1962. Pakistan withdrew from SEATO in 1973.

SOURCE: *Atlas of NATO*, 1985, p. 20. (U.S. Dept. of State)

NATO, control of nuclear weapons, colonial issues, and Cyprus—had, by the late 1960s, challenged the sense of unity that had once existed within NATO. Added to this was the growing feeling in Western Europe that perhaps the Soviet Union could be accommodated within acceptable limits without a military coalition. In the mid-1960s, de Gaulle promoted détente between France and the Soviet bloc with some apparent success. The NATO treaty contained the provision that a country could withdraw from the alliance if it gave notice to that effect during the year before the treaty's twentieth anniversary in April 1969. Some members of NATO discussed withdrawal, although no countries took any formal action. The Soviets unintentionally came to NATO's rescue when Warsaw Pact forces invaded Czechoslovakia in August 1968, thus reuniting NATO by revitalizing the sense of Soviet threat.

During the late 1960s and 1970s, preoccupation of the United States with the Vietnam War and the Middle East brought complaints from European NATO members that the U.S. was neglecting problems in Western Europe. During the Vietnam War, the U.S. drained its European

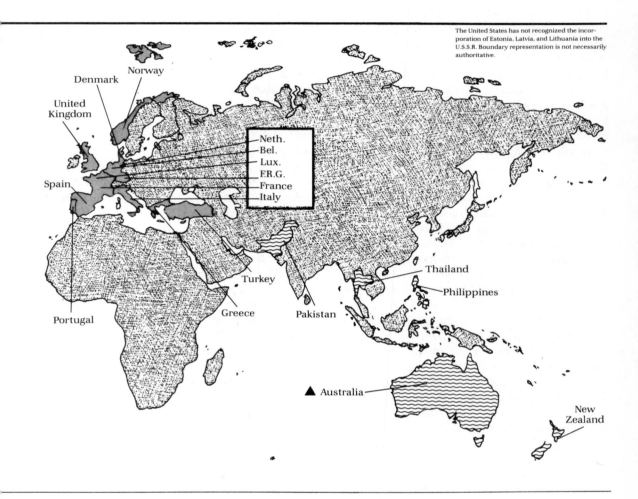

The United States has not recognized the incorporation of Estonia, Latvia, and Lithuania into the U.S.S.R. Boundary representation is not necessarily authoritative.

forces of manpower and materiel. Also, the morale of the U.S. forces in Europe was low and the desertion rate at an all-time high. Western Europe felt that the United States was expending its resources in a war it could not win, and confidence in the U.S. commitment to Europe was questioned. When the United States withdrew from Vietnam in early 1973, NATO hoped that the U.S. would return to its task of coalition maintenance in Europe; instead, it focused its attention on the Middle East. European NATO countries were particularly upset when the United States conducted a resupply airlift to

Israel during the 1973 October War. The United States used military stockpiles in Europe in support of Israel and flew over NATO countries, both without consulting with NATO. NATO felt it was well down on the list of U.S. foreign policy priorities.

At that time, force levels for NATO did not become as significant an issue as the circumstances would suggest. In 1973 Mutual Balanced Force Reduction talks (MBFR) began between the Soviet Union and the United States that could have led to not only a reduction of Soviet and U.S. forces in central Europe, but also a reduction in forces provided by other members of NATO. Any concern about force levels within NATO was muted until the outcome of these talks was determined. The talks, in fact, produced no reductions though still going on in the late 1980s.

The next important split among the NATO allies came when, in the late 1970s, the Soviet Union expanded its intermediate-range ballistic missile force which had the capability of hitting all of Western Europe. Great Britain and West Germany campaigned for the deployment of more and newer missiles within NATO to counter the growing Soviet strike capabilities. The smaller NATO countries wanted to wait to see if talks then going on concerning theater nuclear forces would produce results that would make such a deployment unnecessary. This latter group of nations was led by the Netherlands.

The United States, which would have to provide the new weapons, was similarly divided, with the Pentagon supporting deployment and the Arms Control and Disarmament Agency and President Carter preferring to wait for results from the arms control talks. In December 1979 the members of NATO agreed to the deployment, and the U.S. agreed to provide 108 Pershing II missiles and 464 ground-launched cruise missiles (GLCM). Belgium and the Netherlands accepted the decision with reservations. All Pershing IIs were to be placed in West Germany, but, at the insistence of West Germany, the GLCMs were to be deployed in several countries. While 96 GLCMs would go to West Germany, 160 were to be placed in Great Britain, 112 in Italy, and 48 each in Belgium and the Netherlands. When deployment began in 1983, demonstrations opposing the missiles were widespread in NATO countries. The Soviet Union carried on an aggressive propaganda campaign to prevent deployment, which included breaking off arms control talks in protest. Still indicating its resistance to this expansion of theater nuclear forces, Belgium in 1984 postponed the deployment of its allocation of GLCMs pending the outcome of arms control talks that were scheduled to resume in early 1985. In March 1985, after much pressure from

the United States and other NATO members, the Belgian parliament, by a narrow vote, did agree to deploy the GLCMs. The Netherlands, however, said that it would not accept its GLCMs if the Soviets did not build its SS-20 theater weapon force above 378 missiles. The United States insisted that the Soviet Union had already deployed missiles above that figure. Late in 1985, the Dutch finally did agree to accept their quota of GLCMs.

Still one more major issue continued to plague NATO in the late 1980s. The size of defense budgets of European NATO members had been an issue throughout NATO's history. In an effort to increase the level of those budgets, in 1978 NATO agreed to the Long-Term Defense Program which called for a 3 percent increase above inflation in each member's defense spending. All of NATO, except the United States and Great Britain, failed by wide margins to meet this commitment. NATO recognized that Warsaw Pact forces were numerically ahead of NATO, but those countries that fell short of the commitment blamed domestic resistance for their failure.

In the late 1980s, despite occasional predictions of its demise, NATO was still intact. The coalition continued to require constant attention in order for it to remain so. In addition to European members occasionally questioning U.S. commitment to NATO and the U.S. questioning whether European members are carrying their fair share of NATO's financial burden, conflicts also arise over military strategy for the defense of Europe, the extent to which national forces should be integrated, and how West European relations with the Soviet bloc should be managed. Coalition maintenance is a major policy issue for all members of NATO.

ECONOMIC CONFLICT IN THE WEST

Discussing conflict and cooperation over military matters among the Western countries is comparatively simple in that institutionally, all major

Western bloc nations except Japan are members of NATO and, NATO's opponent is clearly the Warsaw Pact. The discussion of Western conflict and cooperation over economic issues is somewhat more complicated and involves the operations of several institutions and a more complex set of relationships than is found in NATO.

Economic issues and arrangements among the Western nations were rarely discussed by scholars studying international relations until the last decade. Earlier, the attitude seemed to be that issues of those sorts were not political in nature, thus were outside the purview of international politics. Currently, it is recognized that economic matters are highly political and that more and more diplomatic time is being spent on economic relationships. Additional reasons for this neglect of international economics were that for a number of years the focus of attention was on the Cold War, and, until détente in the early 1970s, little attention was directed elsewhere. Also, until the 1970s, the United States had dominated the international economic system with unquestionably the world's strongest economy, thus providing clarity to the organization of the world's economy. This, combined with virtually continuous economic growth among the Western nations, made for basically good economic relations among those countries. Little attention was given to a relationship that seemed to be going well. A shift in emphasis away from Cold War problems and a recognition that the United States was no longer as economically dominant as it once has resulted in a more confused and complicated economic system and greater attention being devoted to economic matters.

THE BRETTON WOODS AGREEMENT AND ITS AFTERMATH

The basic arrangement that governed economic relations between the Western nations from the end of World War II until the early 1970s was agreed to at the Bretton Woods Conference in 1944. At that conference an agreement was concluded on a system of fixed exchange rates for Western currencies, and nations agreed to maintain their currencies, in terms of gold, within 1 percent of the fixed rate. This produced a system of easy convertibility among Western currencies as long as the fixed exchange rate reflected accurately the value of a currency. The Bretton Woods agreement also encouraged freer trade among the Western nations. The International Monetary Fund (IMF) was created to oversee the system and, if problems arose, it could provide short-term assistance to countries in economic trouble. Since voting strength within IMF was based on the amount each country contributed to the fund and since the United States was by far the largest contributor, the United States had considerable control over these economic arrangements. At that time, Western Europe and Japan, exhausted by the war, were incapable of being more assertive and accepted the dominant role played by the United States.

The negotiators at Bretton Woods underestimated the economic needs of Western Europe and the demand for funds was more than IMF could provide. In addition, the Western world's gold supply was not sufficient to accommodate the needs of an economic system in which the stability of currencies was based on gold. In 1947, after an international economic crisis developed, currencies that were to have been based on gold alone were instead based on the dollar backed by gold. This placed the United States in an even more critical role than it had been assigned by the original Bretton Woods agreement. (Spero, 1985, 36–48).

Under this arrangement, the number of dollars a Western country had in its possession was an indicator of the health of its economy. But a country could obtain dollars in only two ways: the first was to receive direct grants of dollars from the U.S. foreign aid program; the second was to have a favorable balance of payments with the United States so that more dollars were coming in than going out. The United States had a favorable balance of trade with Western

Europe, but not a favorable balance of payments. The favorable trade balance was more than offset by U.S. investments in Europe, the cost of maintaining U.S. troops in Europe, and American tourists. From 1947 to the late 1950s the U.S. deliberately allowed this condition to exist so that dollars would flow to other Western countries. The International Bank for Reconstruction and Development (IBRD, or the World Bank) was also a source of funds for the Western nations, but here too the funds came largely from the United States.

The management of international trade was clearly an important aspect of relations between the Western nations and the removal of trade barriers was central to the well-being of those countries. The Bretton Woods agreement called for free trade, or at least freer trade, through lower tariffs and fewer quota restrictions. Discussions about an international organization to govern international trade, begun in 1943, were concluded in 1947. The proposal that emerged, the Havana Charter, called for the establishment of the International Trade Organization (ITO). President Truman, faced with serious opposition in the U.S., never presented the proposal to Congress, and ITO died, since the organization would have little meaning without U.S. participation. A stop-gap arrangement, the General Agreement on Tariff and Trade (GATT), was put into effect in 1947 and, with the failure of ITO, was expanded in order to carry out many of the objectives originally set for ITO. In essence, GATT placed on a multilateral basis the reciprocal trade agreements that the U.S. had been negotiating since 1934. Those agreements were bilateral and called for specific reductions in tariffs. They also contained "most-favored-nation" clauses, which meant that the best tariff rate granted by the U.S. to any nation would also be extended to all other nations with which the U.S. had reciprocal trade agreements. Because of GATT's multilateral basis, such trade advantages would be more widespread; thus, international trade barriers could be reduced and the

goal of free trade more nearly achieved.

GATT has provided the framework for several rounds of talks between the Western nations on an item-by-item reduction in tariffs. It is also through GATT that the so-called Kennedy Round, which approached tariff reduction on an across-the-board percentage basis, took place. The Kennedy Round was particularly important to the U.S. because it increased U.S. access to the European Community. This round of reductions was especially difficult to negotiate, and the talks lasted for four years. GATT's successes, for the most part, have been limited to the industrial Western nations. As pointed out in the last chapter, the Third World nations now would like the GATT arrangement applied to their problems.

By the late 1950s the recovery of Western Europe and Japan was nearly complete. The United States had redirected its grants of economic aid to other parts of the world, and the U.S. wanted to stop its subsidization of the Western economies through unfavorable trade balances. The dollar was weakening relative to the other Western currencies, as would be expected when the economies of other industrial nations gained strength.

One consequence of a weakened dollar was a steady decline in U.S. gold reserves. The dollar had weakened to the point that in 1960 the first of several postwar runs on the dollar occurred in the world's money markets. Problems for the dollar continued throughout the 1960s, and the U.S. balance of payments was increasingly unfavorable. Even with the creation in 1968 of Special Drawing Rights (SDRs), a means of creating artificial international reserve units and increasing liquidity without using the dollar for that purpose, the status of the dollar did not improve.

SDRs were a product of what was known as the Group of Ten (West European nations plus the United States), which would manage SDRs and control the amount issued. SDRs were based on the five major Western currencies (the U.S. dollar, the West German mark, the French franc, the British pound, and the Japanese yen), and while SDRs could fluctuate in value, they would not be as susceptible to economic changes as would any single currency. Each country that was a part of the agreement had to accept SDRs up to a certain amount in lieu of a specific hard currency. While an important advancement in international economic policy, SDRs alone could not solve the balance of payments problem.

In order to improve its ability to export, the United States wanted the dollar devaluated relative to the other Western currencies, but Western Europe and Japan had no interest in giving up their trade advantages. Even though the Western nations threatened to in turn devaluate their currencies if the U.S. devaluated its currency, in August 1971 the Bretton Woods arrangement came to an end when President Nixon announced that the dollar would no longer be convertible into gold; therefore, the price of gold was no longer fixed and could fluctuate on the open market. This also meant that the Western currencies, including the dollar, would "float," depending on how strong or weak each currency was. Though the dollar was no longer the means for stabilizing Western currencies, other aspects of Bretton Woods continued. GATT, IMF, and the World Bank continued to be important to the international economic system, but these institutions were increasingly turning their attention to the economic problems of the Third World.

What had by then developed was a Western economic system in which the United States was still the strongest single economic unit, but the system was not dominated by the U.S. economy to the extent it once was; the system had evolved into interdependence among the industrialized nations. The principal difficulty emerging from this change was the absence of a clear-cut leader for the economic system, and efforts among the Western countries to provide economic order to the post–Bretton Woods system often failed. While the Western nations were still attempting to fashion a new arrangement that would fit the era of interdependence, the price of oil began to spiral, causing more confusion. A high rate of

inflation in the United States further contributed to the falling value of the dollar. The one reality that economic interdependence made clear was that no nation had the degree of control over its domestic economy that it once thought it had, and the higher cost of oil had made the economies of all nations vulnerable to a successful international cartel. Whereas tariffs once could be imposed by domestic decision-makers with relatively little reaction from other countries, now protective tariffs would likely bring on serious reprisals from countries hurt by the tariff. Inflation could not be confined to one nation, and the weakening of one nation's currency, even if caused by domestic problems, was a threat to other nations. Banking was no longer a domestic matter, but, rather, international loans made by any Western bank contributed to interdependence among the Western nations. The failure of a major bank in any Western country had impact throughout the Western world.

The degree to which this interdependence exists is illustrated by Western European reaction to the U.S. budget deficit. After the dollar weakened during the 1970s, in the 1980s the Reagan administration was able to control inflation, oil prices fell, and the United States experienced modest recovery from the recession of 1981-82. The result of these developments was that the dollar climbed rapidly against other Western currencies. This first appeared to be good news for the United States, but the strengthened dollar further increased the U.S. trade deficit. Imports into the U.S. climbed, since other countries could now sell their products to the United States cheaper than before whereas products exported by the United States now cost more in other countries. The result was that the balance-of-payments deficit for the United States rose to $25 billion a month in late 1984 and early 1985; the trade deficit for 1985 was $149 billion. During 1986 the dollar declined in value, but the U.S. trade deficit for the year increased to nearly $180 billion.

Expanded Western European exports to the

United States was good news for those countries, but Western Europe still had complaints over the manner in which the U.S. was managing its domestic economy. The economic recovery the United States experienced had not extended to other Western nations. Western Europe felt that the reason for this was the large budget deficit in the United States. To meet the deficit the United States had to borrow, forcing interest rates higher in the United States than in Europe. This resulted in capital flowing from Western Europe to the U.S., producing a shortage of capital in those countries which retarded recovery in Western Europe. Western Europe felt that if the Reagan administration would reduce the deficit, interest rates would go down and capital would stay in Western Europe.

While Japan is included when the term "Western nations" is used, that country, unlike the Western European nations, has long had a special economic relationship with the United States. During the postwar recovery period the United States allowed Japan to maintain a protectionist economy, while U.S. markets were open to Japanese exports. China, Japan's traditional market, was closed with the communists in power, and in order to aid Japanese recovery the U.S. became Japan's principal overseas market.

With Japanese recovery complete, the United States wanted the Japanese market opened to U.S. exports, but Japan was reluctant to give up its trade advantage. Japan did not see its protectionist policies as unusual but rather a reflection of traditional Japanese economic values which stressed protectionism. The Japanese view was that Japan was discriminated against economically, particularly by the European Economic Community, and that it had little obligation to provide other Western nations access to its markets. Japan felt strongly its obligation to protect its weaker industries and agriculture. The Japanese, as have Western Europeans, pointed out that the United States continued to protect industries, particularly those considered to be strate-

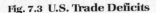

Fig. 7.3 U.S. Trade Deficits

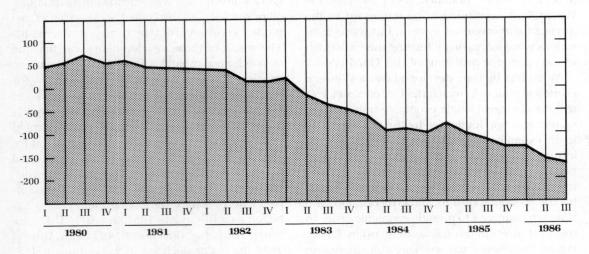

SOURCE: Washington Post National Weekly Edition,
November 17, 1986, p.9.

gic; thus, protectionism was not dead in the United States either. Also, implicit in the Japanese defense of their economic policies was the contention that the Japanese trade advantage existed in part because they simply were more efficient and quality conscious in their industrial output. Since the Nixon administration, U.S. presidents have attempted to persuade Japan to open its markets to U.S. products, with little success. Japan did limit temporarily the number of cars and steel tonnage it exported to the United States, but, overall, Japan has been slow to respond to demands by the United States to reduce its exports or weaken its protectionist policies.

Another aspect of the economic relationship between the United States and Japan is the degree to which Japan takes responsibility for its own defense. After World War II the United States imposed a democratic government on Japan, and in the new constitution, limited Japan to self-defense armed forces. The United States took responsibility for the defense of Japan, and the defense pact the United States negotiated with Japan is unique in that it is the only U.S. military commitment that is not reciprocal; the U.S. is pledged to defend Japan, but Japan is not committed to defend the U.S. Out of this limited military role, Japan developed the political limitation that no more than 1 percent of its GNP would go to defense spending; the U.S. spends about 7 percent of its GNP on the military. An important consequence of a small defense budget is that more of the national product is available for capital investment. But if Japan took a greater responsibility for its defense, the United States would be in a more competitive position relative to Japan. In spite of promises made by the Japanese government to increase defense spending, the 1986 budget still did not exceed the 1 percent self-imposed limit. Japan's principal exports to the United States remained cars and steel, and the principal United States export to Japan continued to be agricultural products, notably soy-

beans. In 1984 the United States had a $35 billion trade deficit with Japan.

ECONOMIC COALITIONS IN WESTERN EUROPE

When foreign aid began to flow to Europe under the Marshall Plan, the recipient nations could have requested aid on a bilateral basis and, by negotiating with the United States separately, become competitors with one another for that aid. Instead, with U.S. encouragement, they developed the Organization of European Economic Cooperation (OEEC); eventually, nearly all noncommunist nations in Europe belonged. The United States and Canada were associate members. The immediate purpose of OEEC was to coordinate its members' requests for American aid, but in the longer term, the OEEC was to work toward liberalizing trade restrictions among the West European nations.

From the start there were conflicting views as to how OEEC was to be structured. The French wanted a strong centralized organization with a supranational character, but the British promoted a looser structure based on the voluntary cooperation of the members. The British approach prevailed, but later the French provided the leadership that led some members of OEEC into the European Coal and Steel Community and the European Economic Community, both of which had a supranational character.

By 1961 U.S. aid to Europe had ended. The OEEC still had a purpose in regard to trade and thus a successor organization, the Organization of European Cooperation and Development (OECD), was created. The OECD had the added responsibility of coordinating European aid to the Third World. The United States continued to be active in OECD, just as it was in OEEC, and in 1964 promoted Japan's membership in the organization. OECD, along with GATT, are the economic organizations that include nearly all Western nations in their membership.

The purpose of economic organizations among the Western nations is not so much to protect against an external threat, as is the case with the West's military coalitions, but to recognize that all members of an economic coalition can benefit from cooperation. In Western Europe, however, there have been two distinct approaches to expressing this cooperation: the supranational approach (decisions by a central authority that transcend national decisions) and the mutual-cooperation approach (decisions arrived at through diplomatic consensus). The objective of both approaches is the same, however, and that is to bring about greater economic integration. The beginning effort toward economic integration with a supranational character came in 1950 when France proposed the Schuman Plan. This plan called for the removal of all trade restraints on steel and the materials necessary to produce steel. It also called for the use of only the most efficient units of production found in the member states; less efficient units were to be closed down. Decisions as to which would produce and which would be closed rested with a supranational authority. The objective of the plan was to revive the steel industry in Western Europe and produce steel more competitively for the world market. The production of steel was considered to be central to the economic well-being of any industrial nation; thus it was the logical beginning effort of economic integration in Western Europe.

The argument over the supranational nature of the organization prevented the plan from gaining wider support in Western Europe than it did. Ultimately, only France, West Germany, Italy, Belgium, the Netherlands, and Luxembourg joined the European Coal and Steel Community (ECSC), the organization that implemented the Schuman Plan. ECSC began its operations in 1952. The British not only objected to the supranational character of ECSC, but, since British trade ties were much closer to the Common-

wealth than to the European continent, felt they had little to gain by joining. In addition, the British feared that if they were to join they would suffer considerable economic dislocation, especially in their depressed coal industry. The Scandinavian countries, Austria, and Switzerland supported Great Britain in rejecting the supranational character of ECSC.

ECSC proved to be so successful that the concept of economic integration through a supranational authority was expanded into a broader economic community. The European Economic Community (EEC) was formed by the Treaty of Rome in 1957, and operations began in 1958. The membership of EEC was the same as that of ECSC. The principal supranational body in ECSC was the High Authority; the equivalent in the EEC was the Commission. Each nation had representation on these bodies roughly equivalent to a member's economic capabilities. Each of the organizations had institutions that acted as controls on the supranational bodies, but for the most part, decisions were not overturned.

The objective of EEC, more commonly known as the Common Market, was an extension of the logic underlying ECSC—economic integration in order to be more efficient and competitive. Over a ten-year period dating from 1958, all tariff and other trade restraints existing between member states were to be reduced gradually until they were eliminated. At the same time a uniform tariff wall around the six members would be developed. During the transition period, nations below an agreed-upon tariff level would raise their tariff, and those above the level would reduce their tariff. Economic integration would also include the free movement of labor and capital among the member states. Common policies on transportation and agriculture were to be developed later. When these objectives were reached, the EEC nations would have: 1) a customs union with no tariffs between them and a common external tariff; and 2) a common market, where before there were six separate economies.

The customs union was established in less

Fig. 7.4 Institutions of the EEC

EUROPEAN INSTITUTIONS

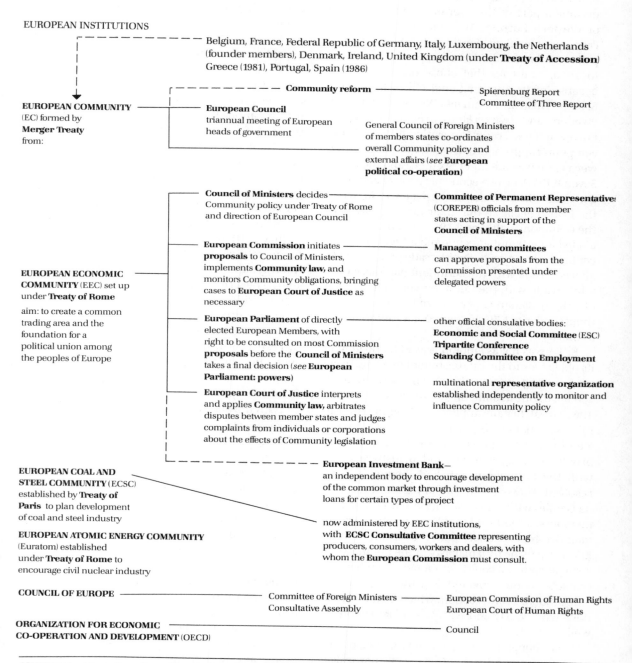

Belgium, France, Federal Republic of Germany, Italy, Luxembourg, the Netherlands (founder members), Denmark, Ireland, United Kingdom (under **Treaty of Accession**) Greece (1981), Portugal, Spain (1986)

EUROPEAN COMMUNITY (EC) formed by **Merger Treaty** from:

————— **Community reform** —————
Spierenburg Report
Committee of Three Report

European Council
triannual meeting of European heads of government

General Council of Foreign Ministers of members states co-ordinates overall Community policy and external affairs (*see* **European political co-operation**)

EUROPEAN ECONOMIC COMMUNITY (EEC) set up under **Treaty of Rome**

aim: to create a common trading area and the foundation for a political union among the peoples of Europe

Council of Ministers decides Community policy under Treaty of Rome and direction of European Council

Committee of Permanent Representatives (COREPER) officials from member states acting in support of the **Council of Ministers**

European Commission initiates **proposals** to Council of Ministers, implements **Community law**, and monitors Community obligations, bringing cases to **European Court of Justice** as necessary

Management committees can approve proposals from the Commission presented under delegated powers

European Parliament of directly elected European Members, with right to be consulted on most Commission **proposals** before the **Council of Ministers** takes a final decision (*see* **European Parliament: powers**)

other official consulative bodies:
Economic and Social Committee (ESC)
Tripartite Conference
Standing Committee on Employment

multinational **representative organization** established independently to monitor and influence Community policy

European Court of Justice interprets and applies **Community law,** arbitrates disputes between member states and judges complaints from individuals or corporations about the effects of Community legislation

EUROPEAN COAL AND STEEL COMMUNITY (ECSC) established by **Treaty of Paris** to plan development of coal and steel industry

European Investment Bank—
an independent body to encourage development of the common market through investment loans for certain types of project

now administered by EEC institutions, with **ECSC Consultative Committee** representing producers, consumers, workers and dealers, with whom the **European Commission** must consult.

EUROPEAN ATOMIC ENERGY COMMUNITY (Euratom) established under **Treaty of Rome** to encourage civil nuclear industry

COUNCIL OF EUROPE —————
Committee of Foreign Ministers —————
Consultative Assembly

European Commission of Human Rights
European Court of Human Rights

ORGANIZATION FOR ECONOMIC CO-OPERATION AND DEVELOPMENT (OECD)
Council

SOURCE: Brian Morris, Peggy Crane, Klaus Boehm, *The European Community* (Bloomington: Indiana University Press, 1981).

time than projected—about eight years—and EEC became a part of the overall economic growth of Western Europe. At the same time, the arrangement evoked considerable conflict over policy, which resulted in a competitive coalition. In 1959, countries that chose not to join EEC because of its supranational character—Great Britain, Austria, Denmark, Norway, Portugal, Sweden, and Switzerland—organized into the European Free Trade Association (EFTA). These competing approaches to economic cooperation were known as the Inner Six (EEC) and the Outer Seven (EFTA). British economic policy had undergone considerable change between 1950, when the British declared that their interests lay with the Commonwealth, and 1959, when Great Britain led an attempt at economic integration with continental countries. British trade patterns were altered; trade with the continent had increased, while trade with the Commonwealth had fallen off. Great Britain was now willing to try something similar to EEC, but without a supranational authority.

EFTA was not as ambitious as EEC and limited its objectives to the establishment of a free trade area among its members. This was quickly achieved, but in spite of this success, in August 1961 Great Britain applied for membership in EEC. Negotiations on British membership were lengthy, but by the end of 1962, such difficult problems as agriculture and British relations with the Commonwealth had seemingly been resolved. However, in January 1963, President de Gaulle, without consultation with other EEC members, announced that France vetoed British membership. Though policy decisions within EEC were made by a majority of the Commission, a single country could veto a new member. De Gaulle's action reflected a growing policy of independent French action, which included relations with NATO and with the Soviet Union, as well as the EEC.

Even though France had been a strong proponent of a supranational EEC, de Gaulle now called for fundamental changes in EEC that would place greater control in the hands of individual members. In July 1965 France suspended all consultation with EEC and withdrew its ambassador to the organization. These actions were prompted in part by the failure of EEC to agree to a common agricultural policy (CAP) that would have been of major benefit to France as Western Europe's major agricultural nation. Also in 1965 the six nations that made up the membership of three different European communities—EEC, ECSC and EURATOM (established in 1958 to manage energy needs)—agreed to place executive control of all three communities under a single European Commission; the decision was carried out in 1967. The combined communities were known as the European Communities (EC).

In May 1967 Great Britain made another bid for membership in EC; at this time, Denmark, Norway, and Ireland also applied for membership. The French refused to negotiate British membership on the grounds that the British economy was too weak for EC membership. Since Great Britain had not been formally vetoed by France, British membership was held in abeyance, but in November 1967 de Gaulle did announce France's veto. No action was taken on the other applications for membership.

With the question of British membership temporarily settled, EEC turned to other matters. Although a common agricultural policy had been agreed upon in 1965, the issue of the distribution of subsidy costs for agriculture had never been resolved. France continued to push for a settlement.

All was not conflict within EC by any means. In order to develop the level of economic integration achieved by EC in a decade required a great deal of cooperation among member states, but economic integration had slowed by the late 1960s, and those in the community that hoped economic union would be followed by political union of the member states were disheartened. There was even talk of reversing some of the economic advances made thus far. This situation existed until 1971, when the question of British membership came up again, and this time France withheld its veto. Pompidou was now president of France, and, although he followed de Gaulle's policies in many other respects, he did not stand in the way of British membership. A period of adjustment followed as Great Britain altered its tariffs and agricultural policy to comply with those of EC. Great Britain formally became a member in January 1973. Denmark and Ireland also entered EC after holding plebiscites, but in Norway the vote went against membership. EC now had nine members. In late 1974, after Great Britain had been a member for less than two years, the British asked to renegotiate the costs of its belonging to EC. In 1980 it was successful in obtaining some reductions, but in the mid-1980s Great Britain was still asking for further concessions, particularly in its contributions to agricultural subsidies.

A noneconomic issue that divided EC was the call from the United States to boycott the 1980 Olympics in Moscow in protest of the Soviet invasion of Afghanistan; only West Germany complied with the request. Relations with the United States were further damaged when the United States, during the Iranian hostage crisis, asked EC for an economic boycott of Iran; EC imposed only limited sanctions. EC also differed with the United States over policy in the Middle East and offered a separate proposal for peace.

In 1981 Greece became the tenth member of EC but without the disruption that had followed British membership. After long EC review as to the strength of their economies, Portugal and Spain became the eleventh and twelfth members of EC in 1986. During the early 1980s, EC continued to have internal problems, especially over agricultural policy and British complaints over its contribution. Unemployment was high in EC, and the recession of the early 1980s persisted. Disagreements with the United States over tariff rates, which had occurred often in the past, and complaints over the impact on Europe of the U.S. budget deficit continued. The most persistent problem in EC–United States relations was EC's

common agricultural policy (CAP). The United States saw the policy as protectionist and argued that high EC subsidies not only made it difficult for U.S. farm products to be sold to EC, but that CAP also created unfair competition in other markets as well. EC explained that all industrialized nations subsidize the agricultural sector of their economies, and that the subsidies given by EC were about the same as those provided in the United States. The basic problem facing both EC and the United States, so EC argued, was that markets could no longer absorb all that the two of them produced.

One issue that pointed out how different the relationship between the United States and Western Europe can be, depending on whether the issue is perceived as economic or military, occurred in 1982, when the Reagan administration imposed a boycott on any U.S. products being exported to the Soviet Union for use in the construction of a gas pipeline from western Siberia to Western Europe. The boycott was not only on equipment manufactured in the United States; it was also placed on items produced by U.S. subsidiaries overseas. President Reagan saw the matter in security terms; by buying natural gas from the Soviet Union, Western Europe would become subject to Soviet threats to stop shipments. Also, the United States felt that the Soviet Union would obtain technology from the imported equipment that would help Soviet industry. Western Europe viewed the matter in economic terms. If they bought natural gas from the Soviet Union, they could reduce their oil imports from OPEC. Contrary to the U.S. view that trade with the Soviet Union only serves to strengthen our enemies, Western Europe viewed the pipeline as a means of making the Soviet Union dependent on the Western economies as an important source of foreign currencies. In addition, the Soviet Union would have more hard currency with which to trade with the West.

Western Europe was particularly unhappy that the boycott was applied to European subsidiaries of U.S. corporations. Europe saw this as an attempt to apply United States law in other countries, an infringement on their sovereignty. This was not a new conflict in U.S.–EC relations, in that the United States earlier had attempted to restrict shipments to the Soviet Union of other products produced by overseas subsidiaries, and EC had reacted in a similar fashion on those occasions. The conflict was resolved when the U.S. called off the boycott after Western Europe refused to join it. The U.S. apparently felt that to continue the sanctions alone was costing too much in goodwill in Western Europe.

In the late 1980s, the Western relationships—GATT, NATO, EC, United States–Japanese relations and United States–EC relations—continue to need repair both at the economic and security levels. The coalitions seem to be sound, however, and in order for them to survive, conflict within them is more than matched by cooperation among the Western nations. Interdependence within the West has grown and each country seems to recognize that continued cooperation is beneficial to all. U.S. leadership of the Western military and economic coalitions is not as dominant as it once was, but the United States continues to be the strongest nation in the West militarily and to have the world's biggest economy.

EAST–EAST CONFLICT

The structure of, and conflict within, coalitions in the communist world bears only a superficial resemblance to those of Western coalitions. The communist nations do have a military alliance, the Warsaw Pact, and they also have the Council for Mutual Economic Assistance (CMEA), better known as COMECON, which is an attempt at economic integration. These organizations differ from their counterparts in the West in that: 1) neither the Warsaw Pact nor COMECON are as open about conflict that occurs among the membership as are their Western equivalents; and 2) both organizations are centered around the

interests of only one member, the Soviet Union.

Whereas the Western organizations have evolved from coalitions dominated by the military and economic strength of the United States into coalitions that are interdependent, particularly in economic matters, such is not the case for the Soviet-led coalitions. Decisions that determine policy for both the Warsaw Pact and COMECON come from Moscow. Soviet dominance within the coalitions does not, however, prevent less powerful members from complaining about this relationship. Soviet dominance is challenged, particularly in regard to economic matters, at virtually all meetings of representatives to COMECON. Western attention usually focuses upon the occasions when the Soviet Union directly intervenes in the internal affairs of Eastern European countries, such as use of the Warsaw Pact to intervene in Hungary in 1956 and Czechoslovakia in 1968; and Soviet demands in 1981 and 1982 that the Polish government control Solidarity and limit economic reforms. Lesser conflicts are seldom covered in the Western press, thus giving the impression that the Soviets go mostly unchallenged. Such is not the case.

CONFLICT WITHIN COMECON

Following World War II, the Soviet Union's initial objective in Eastern Europe was to consolidate its political and military control in order to create a geographic buffer between the Soviet Union and Western Europe. This was achieved after Soviet-monitored elections were held in Eastern Europe in 1946 and 1947, followed by the communist takeover of Czechoslovakia in 1948. Once secure in their control of Eastern Europe, the Soviets turned to economic objectives. The Soviets felt that if the West were denied access to Eastern European markets, this would compound the economic problems of the war-damaged Western European countries. Cutting off Eastern Europe from the West also fit the

Soviet Union's internal economic needs as well, in that the Eastern European economies could be used to help rebuild the Soviet Union. The Soviet Union had had little international trade before World War II, but in the postwar period the Soviets controlled a bloc of nations whose trade could be directed to Soviet advantage. Before World War II, only 10 percent of Eastern Europe's trade was among what was to become the Soviet-bloc nations; nearly three-fourths of its trade had been with the West. The Soviets were so successful in redirecting Eastern Europe's trade patterns that by 1953 nearly two-thirds of Eastern Europe's trade was within the Soviet-led coalition. Trade with the West was down to 15 percent.

The Soviets did not formalize their economic dominance until 1949, when COMECON was established. After the Soviet Union rejected Marshall Plan aid and forced Poland and Czechoslovakia to do likewise, COMECON was presented to Eastern Europe as an alternative to economic assistance from the West. The original membership of COMECON included the Soviet Union, Poland, Czechoslovakia, Hungary, Rumania, and Bulgaria. Albania was added later in 1949, but has taken no active part in COMECON since 1961. East Germany was added in 1950 and Mongolia in 1962. Cuba and Vietnam became members later, for a total membership in 1987 of ten countries. Other Third World nations—Afghanistan, Angola, Ethiopia, Laos, Mozambique, Nicaragua, and South Yemen—that are client states of the Soviet Union have observer status. Yugoslavia also has observer status. Even though the membership of COMECON was expanded beyond Eastern Europe, the central purpose of the organization continues to be the economic relationship of Eastern Europe with the Soviet Union.

Even before COMECON was formed, the Soviet Union exploited the economies of former Axis powers in Eastern Europe through reparations. In all, an estimated $20 billion was extracted from East Germany, Hungary, Rumania, and Bulgaria; the bulk of the reparations came from East Germany. After the formation of COMECON, Soviet economic exploitation of the relationship took a different form; the Soviets wanted the economies of Eastern Europe integrated into their own, but Eastern Europe largely wanted economies independent of the Soviet Union. The economies of Eastern Europe and the Soviet Union showed good growth rates during the 1950s and 1960s, but as the rate slowed during the 1970s, Eastern Europe became more outspoken in its complaints about the arrangement imposed upon it by the Soviet Union.

COMECON holds plenary sessions once or twice a year, and it is from those sessions that Western observers learn much of what is known about conflict within the coalition. The plenary session of COMECON in 1969, which celebrated the twentieth anniversary of the founding of COMECON, was a summit conference of communist leaders and had as its major purpose to speed up the economic integration of the member states. The Soviet, Polish, and Bulgarian delegations supported integration, but the Rumanian delegates argued in favor of mutual cooperation rather than integration. Rumania claimed that integration would curtail national independence and introduce a form of Western monopoly under the guise of socialist economic integration. East Germany and Czechoslovakia also opposed increased integration for a different reason. As the two most highly industrialized nations in Eastern Europe, they feared that in an integrated economy they would be held back by the less-industrialized members of COMECON. Consideration of the proposed integration plan was postponed at the 1969 meeting, but it was adopted at the next summit meeting of communist leaders held in 1971. The plan, with the title "A Comprehensive Program for the Further Deepening and Perfecting of Cooperation and for Developing Socialist Economic Integration among the Member Countries of CMEA," called for economic integration over a fifteen- to twenty-year period.

The economic integration of COMECON is not comparable to that of EC. In Eastern Europe prices are fixed by the state, and currencies are not convertible, even with other COMECON currencies; thus, tariff reductions and a customs union are not possible. Without currency convertibility, members of COMECON must trade among themselves on a barter basis. If Eastern European currencies were convertible, then items which the state priced artificially high could be imported at lower prices from other countries, and items priced artificially low could be bought by other countries at bargain prices. Thus, barter trade is necessary unless members of COMECON are willing to forego central state planning.

Eastern European nations have long been anxious to trade with the West, but since their currencies are not convertible, they must pay for Western imports with hard currencies which they obtain by selling to the West. The low quality of many items manufactured in Eastern Europe means they find little market in the West, thus providing a major restriction on East-West trade. The Soviets obtain much of their Western hard currency from precious metals or energy sold to the West, but Eastern Europe has little to offer in this regard.

The "Comprehensive Program" rekindled the fear for some members of COMECON that they would lose their economic national identity. Rumania again was the most outspoken in this respect. The plan was intended to forestall the national economic reform efforts of the Eastern European countries that had been taking place since the mid-1960s. Those reforms were seen by conservative Soviet leadership as a move toward a form of capitalism in that prices were, in part, based on market demands, not the fixed prices of the past. The Soviets saw a mixed economy, part socialist and part capitalist, as a threat to the entire socialist economic system. Except in Hungary and Czechoslovakia, the reforms were limited, and little meaningful change took place. Reforms in Czechoslovakia were rescinded abuptly with the military invasion by Soviet and other Warsaw Pact forces in August 1968. Czechoslovakia, unlike Hungary in 1956, had

pledged to stay in the Warsaw Pact in spite of political and economic changes. Apparently the Soviets did not believe those assurances and feared that the loss of economic control would ultimately mean the loss of a military ally. Also, the Soviets must have been concerned about the precedent Czech economic reforms established for other Eastern European countries and the Soviet people. Economic reform in other COMECON countries also came to a halt. The 1971 program was designed to get the economies going again, but without any basic changes that would be a threat to the socialist system.

The problem of trade between COMECON members, particularly between the Soviet Union and Eastern Europe, grew to substantial proportions by the 1980s, and the situation was compounded by the near collapse of the Polish economy in 1981. In both 1980 and 1981 Poland failed to meet its coal commitments to other COMECON members, as well as falling short of its quota for machinery, sulfur, and consumer goods. All East European members of COMECON, except East Germany, experienced a drop in productivity in 1981, but Poland had the largest decrease by far (*Economist,* May 29, 1982, 87-88.) The economic situation was serious enough that a five-year integration program that was to have begun in 1981 was postponed.

In 1971, when oil prices were beginning their rise in the noncommunist world, the Soviet Union promised Eastern Europe continued low prices for Soviet energy and raw-material exports. By the 1980s the Soviet Union wanted to change the arrangement. The first summit meeting of COMECON since 1971 was scheduled for May 1983, but was called off because there was no agreement on an agenda. The Soviet Union wanted to increase the price of its oil and rather than increasing shipments of oil to Eastern Europe as promised, was reported to be reducing shipments. The estimate was that Eastern Europe needed an increase of 3 to 5 percent annually in Soviet oil shipments in order to meet domestic needs. The Soviet Union also was demanding partial payment in hard currencies for its oil from some COMECON members, such as East Germany and Czechoslovakia, which had greater access to hard currencies than did other members of COMECON. Since those countries had benefited from the barter arrangements for oil in the past, they wanted that system to continue without the involvement of hard currencies. Eastern Europe feared that the Soviet Union would use the 1983 summit conference to announce these changes, and they pressed successfully for calling off the conference. Even though the Soviet Union had failed to meet its commitments concerning oil, it did continue to deliver oil to Eastern Europe at prices well below the OPEC price.

Rumania also was having economic problems and, with the possible exception of Poland, had the most troubled economy in Eastern Europe. Rumania was pressing for a special package of economic aid from the Soviet Union, including a reduction in the cost of food it imported. Since all members of COMECON were experiencing food shortages, the Rumanian requests were rejected.

After several postponements, the summit meeting of top party and government leaders of COMECON was finally held at Moscow in June 1984. Several agreements came out of the conference, designed to bring about further integration of COMECON's economies. An innovative and, for communist governments, unusual agreement emerged that allowed for direct contact between factories of member countries. The hope was that this would improve the quality of products and increase the market for Eastern European goods in the West.

Later in the year the regular meeting of COMECON convened in Havana. At both Moscow and Havana the less-developed members of COMECON—Cuba, Mongolia, and Vietnam—asked for additional aid and trade to speed their industrialization. In this respect, these meetings resembled meetings where Western industrial nations meet with Third World countries. The next regular meeting of COMECON in 1985 reflected inreased unity among the members of COMECON, but several members complained of the slowness with which decisions made at the previous year's summit were being implemented.

The two major problems for COMECON are: 1) Soviet domination and the suppression of other nations' interests; and 2) the weakness of the Soviet economy and a reluctance on the part of Soviet leadership to reform their economic system. The Soviets want COMECON to have the supranational authority of EC, but under Soviet control. They also want to reduce any Eastern European dependence on the West and point to Poland's debt problems as an example of what happens if a nation borrows from the West. Soviet dominance over the economies of Eastern Europe can easily be overstated, however. By the

---

Tab. 7.1 Soviet Trade with Eastern European Countries (in millions of dollars, current prices)

Country	Exports			Imports		
	1981	1982	1983	1981	1982	1983
Bulgaria	5,030.7	5,617.3	6,337.4	4,251.4	4,931.3	5,811.3
Czecholovakia	5,039.6	5,804.6	6,752.3	4,720.5	5,441.7	6,233.5
East Germany	6,355.0	7,382.5	7,817.5	5,927.8	6,642.6	7,585.1
Hungary	3,802.7	4,263.3	4,666.7	3,795.5	4,308.4	4,608.1
Poland	5,671.0	5,534.8	6,065.4	3,703.9	4,711.6	5,504.7
Romania	2,046.0	1,637.1	1,885.5	1,924.1	1.935.9	1.915.1

SOURCE: USSR Foreign Trade Statistics/Moscow from *Britannica Book of the Year 1985*.

late 1970s, Hungary and East Germany had introduced economic reforms that do not appear to conform to Soviet orthodoxy, but the Soviets have taken no action to reverse those changes. Also, both countries have expanded their trade with the West. The Soviets seem to have accepted this increased contact with the West, and apparently wish only to have their share of the benefits, not put an end to it. The Soviets, perhaps due to Poland's economic problems, show no inclination to interfere in those COMECON countries that are doing well, as long as there is no military or economic threat to the Soviet Union. The Eastern European countries are anxious to avoid further economic integration with the Soviet Union, contending that the Soviets take only their best products, especially in payment for oil. Overall, COMECON is a coalition with problems, but its membership works toward its survival.

CONCLUSION

The primary purpose served by a discussion of intracoalitional problems is to illustrate the general problems involved in holding coalitions together. All coalitions have internal stresses and conflict, but they also have positive elements that work toward holding the coalitions together. Not all coalitions survive, even among the Western nations. Western military coalitions, such as CENTO and SEATO, have collapsed, but NATO remains in good condition. But even NATO is beset with recurring problems concerning mili-

tary strategy, continued commitment to NATO by its members, concern over U.S. interest in foreign policy problems other than Western Europe, and how the costs of NATO will be met. Even introducing new weapons into NATO, such as the Pershing II and GLCM, can pose a threat to the alliance.

The Western economic coalition, while interdependent and mutually cooperative, exhibits strains resulting from established or threatened restraints on trade. The Western economic giants disagree over policy, particularly concerning agriculture and how the West should respond to Soviet efforts to trade with the West. Japan is often on the defensive because of criticism of its trade policies. Overriding these problems is a strong sense of mutual need for cooperation among the Western countries.

Soviet-led military and economic coalitions also display stress in maintaining their existence. While those coalitions are dominated by the Soviet Union to a greater extent than are the coalitions of which the U.S. is a part, members of the Warsaw Pact and COMECON do have an opportunity to express themselves and, in the case of some Eastern European countries, launch economic changes presently tolerated by the Soviet Union.

Coalitions are an important part of the international system, but they also demand considerable attention if they are to remain intact. The problems are continuous, but the industrialized nations of both the East and West find coalitions beneficial to the promotion of their interests and worth the time and effort they require.

PART III

Protecting and Promoting Interests

CHAPTER 8

The Importance of Image

The last three chapters have identified the major sources of conflict in the international system. Within the context of those arenas of conflict, each nation inescapably produces an image that it projects to other nations. The images or perceptions that nations' publics and decision-makers develop provide the basis upon which nations react to one another; thus, they govern how effective a nation is in achieving its policy goals and fulfilling its interests. However powerful a nation may be in the abstract, that nation is only as effective as the image it projects to other countries. A nation's image is not constant, however, and different countries hold different images of the same country. To some extent, how a country perceives another nation depends on how closely their interests align. The closer the alignment, the more favorable the image will be.

Though economic capabilities may be the common factor on which many countries base their image of the United States, those capabilities are perceived differently depending upon whether a nation is from the Third World, the Soviet coalition, or other Western alliances. In turn, these images will ordinarily differ from the image U.S. policy-makers have of the United States. Thus, various images or perceptions exist of the same country, depending on whether it is self-image, the image that friends or enemies hold, or simply the image held by countries that respect another nation's power but fear how it will be used.

The danger of violence in the international system is greatest when images of conflicting nations differ substantially. If country A holds an image of itself and of country B that differs substantially from B's self-image and view of A, the risk of misunderstanding escalates. If A is fearful of B's intentions, but B has no harmful intentions toward A, this can be as dangerous as if B had such intentions. Thus, since image is the basis on which other nations react and since image affects the ability of a nation to achieve its interests, image management is important for every nation's decision-makers.

To argue that images can be managed does not mean that a nation has more than limited control over how others will see it. Environmental conditions such as size, location, and natural resources limit the degree to which a nation can control its image internationally, no matter how effective its decision-makers are in image management. A small nation with economic problems will not be able to convince other countries that it is an economic giant, no matter how it tries. This chapter will discuss images and perception in two ways: 1) by discussing the images that the superpowers hold of themselves and of each other, and the image others hold of those nations; 2) by discussing the techniques a country can use in shaping its image.

IMAGES BETWEEN THE UNITED STATES AND THE SOVIET UNION

When observers discuss U.S.–Soviet relations, it often emerges that the basis of disagreements is formed by differing perceptions of those two countries and their policy objectives. One can also assume that when the decision-makers of either superpower are attempting to make a policy choice and assess the other country's objectives, more than one perception is included in the deliberations. One of the flaws that can occur when making decisions is that these differing perceptions are not identified; to not identify them can produce a poor decision, that is, a decision that will not fulfill the interests intended.

U.S. self-image is, as for any nation, strongly influenced by its history. What has occurred in the past produces a system of values and prioritizes them as to what is important in assessing foreign policy objectives. Past experiences will also produce a belief system or standard for judging what is moral and immoral in international behavior. For example, high on the list of immoral behavior in the U.S. value system is aggression— aggression is behavior the United States should avoid and an action for which other countries should be punished. Further, the belief system in the United States supports democracy as the best means of governing and considers intervention in the affairs of other countries to be undesirable, except on invitation by another country to assist in resisting aggression. The use of such terms as aggression, democracy, and nonintervention does not mean that the United States has firm, working definitions for those terms; nor does it mean that there will not be extensive domestic debate about when one of those values has been violated. It does mean,

however, that the United States considers those to be acts for which a nation should be punished, as with aggression; promoted, as with democracy; or avoided, as with intervention.

The strong aversion in the United States to aggression is, no doubt, a product of World War II. Whereas before the war the central value to be adhered to in the making of foreign policy was isolationism, that course of action did not prevent U.S. involvement in World War II or avoid the sense of guilt that if the United States had taken a more active role in opposing acts of aggression during the 1930s, World War II might have been avoided. World War II changed the basic values underlying U.S. policy from that of leaving Asia and Europe to work out their own problems to one of responsibility for aiding any country suffering an act of aggression. If a determined alliance of antifascist nations might have stopped an aggressive Nazi Germany in the 1930s, then that error will not be committed again. After World War II, the Soviet Union was perceived as the world's new aggressor nation which could be stopped through a determined alliance of anticommunist nations. This doctrine is manifested in NATO, the Rio Pact, and various bilateral agreements today, and earlier through SEATO and CENTO.

Democracy is itself a value system, and one that the United States feels is appropriate to all nations. As seen earlier, the Third World is viewed as including far too many nondemocratic political systems in which human rights are not protected. Thus, the United States is accused of trying to export its basic political values, even to countries not yet ready for them. An extension of this democratic value system is a capitalist economic system which allows for only a minimum of regulation and control by the government. This sort of economic system is based on the assumption that economic freedom produces a healthier economy and is what makes the United States the strongest nation economically in the world. The United States views its foreign aid program as promoting the various elements of the image that the United States holds of itself. Economic and military aid is extended to countries to keep them from adopting communist systems through either ideological or military aggression, to assist countries to develop a capitalist economic system, and to aid in the development of democracy. The activities of MNCs headquartered in the United States do not, from the U.S. perspective, exploit the nations in which MNCs operate, but, rather, contribute to the development of those countries. Western banks extend loans to other countries, both to legitimately make money and to contribute to other nations' development. Nations receiving U.S. loans and aid may view those activities as economic or cultural imperialism, but that is a part of the image they hold of the United States, not a part of U.S. self-image.

Thus, a generally accepted self-image of the United States is that of a democracy willing to deter aggression and, if necessary, punish aggressors; not willing to intervene uninvited in the affairs of other countries; and providing economic and political freedom for its citizens and encouraging the same for other countries. This view is, of course, idealized, and many exceptions to these principles occur in U.S. foreign policy. The U.S. was accused by foreign governments—including many that ordinarily were friendly toward the United States, and many of its own citizens—of violating these principles by committing aggression in Vietnam. Defenders of U.S. policy point out that the United States was invited to participate by the South Vietnamese government and that our involvement was the fulfillment of an international obligation under SEATO; thus no basic national values were violated. Intervention in the Dominican Republic in 1965 was justified as preventing ideological aggression in the Western Hemisphere. The invasion of Grenada in 1983 was defended on the same grounds. Also, the United States is charged with not always punishing acts of aggression committed by other countries. Argentina considered the British invasion of the Falkland Islands to be aggression, since the islands were originally Argentine territory; the United States supported Great Britain, thus tacitly giving support to the British claim to the islands over that of Argentina. The United States provided no direct assistance to either Hungary in 1956 or Czechoslovakia in 1968 when the Soviets invaded those countries, and the grain embargo and Olympics boycott had no apparent effect on Soviet aggression in Afghanistan. Thus, basic national values are not always promoted effectively.

It is also true that the economy of the United States is far from being purely capitalistic. There is considerable regulation of the economy by government, although relatively little actual government ownership. The entire population of the country has not benefited from the strength of the economy, and access to the political system is more limited for minority groups than for mainstream Americans. But despite qualifications of the generalizations that are a part of the U.S. self-image, those generalizations are what the United States hopes to project abroad. What is illustrated by pointing out the differences between the generalizations a nation holds about itself and the specific examples of behavior that fail to support those generalizations is that a nation's self-image is a combination of what it wishes its values to be and its interpretation of what is factual about itself. Decision-makers react to both conceptions in making decisions (Holsti, 1962, 245).

In contrast to the United States, the Soviet Union sees itself as a country attempting to carry out a revolution, but surrounded by enemies of that revolution. The Marxist-Leninist ideology officially is the guide for that revolution, and it is the overall value system to which the Soviet Union is committed. Within this perspective, the enemy is any noncommunist nation, but particularly the major capitalistic economic powers. The Soviets view the revolution as succeeding in spite of its enemies, but they are aware that the Soviet Union must always be vigilant for external and internal enemies. They point to the substantial economic progress the Soviet Union has made in the relatively short period of 70 years since the revolution began, as compared to the longer period of industrial development among the capitalist nations. They, too, are committed to spreading their principles of government to other countries willing to cooperate with them. This means that they will arm their allies and support national liberation fronts that are fighting noncommunist governments. In addition, the Soviet Union is willing to intervene in those countries that are a part of its coalition in the name of maintaining buffers of territory on Soviet borders. The Soviets do not see their intervention in Afghanistan in any different light from that in which they viewed their actions in Hungary and Czechoslovakia. All three countries border on the Soviet Union and must be secure from Soviet enemies. They see Eastern Europe as a necessary buffer against the West and an essential asset to the Soviet economic system.

The Soviets view capitalism as corrupt; thus, capitalist countries, though now economically strong, ultimately face a crisis that will lead to their collapse. The Soviets recognize that, in spite of their economic progress, they are behind the capitalist nations in economic development, but blame their failures on the the hostile actions of Soviet enemies. Such acts necessitate the Soviets' developing a strong military costing huge sums, thus further impeding their economic progress. Soviet leadership seems well aware that agricultural production in the Soviet Union is an embarrassment, but it uses to Soviet advantage the vast natural resources of the country. Oil shipments at below world-market prices are one means the Soviets have utilized to keep its allies in line. Whether the leadership recognizes the need for economic reforms within the Soviet system is difficult to assess, but this would appear to be a center of debate among Soviet leaders.

These self-images held by the United States and the Soviet Union do have elements in common. Both nations express a need to maintain a strong military, both see economic strength as an important aspect of international influence, both feel a sense of threat from the outside, and both are willing to intervene in the internal affairs of other countries under certain circumstances. Each country sees itself as morally correct, and, as will be illustrated below, each sees the other as the enemy. To an extent, they have mirror images of one another. But self-image is only one aspect of the international perspective of either the United States or the Soviet Union. They also have images of each other which are equally important.

Just how great a threat the Soviet Union is to the United States has been a matter of debate among U.S. policy makers for some time. In the United States, at least two general perceptions of the Soviet Union exist, with variations in between. While the extent of the Soviet threat has yet to be resolved, the origins of these perceptions lie in the late 1940s, when the United States first perceived the Soviet Union as an enemy. One perspective is the hard-line, or hawkish, view; the other is the soft-line, or dovish, image.

The hard-liners see the Soviet Union as bent on world domination through the extension of the communist ideology into other countries. The hard-line view is based on the assumption that any Soviet gain is a loss for the United States, and that the Soviet Union will expand its control whenever given the opportunity. Consequently, the policy of the United States should be to see that no such opportunities arise. This view also sees the communist movement as essentially Moscow-directed, and does not take seriously the splits that exist in the Soviet-led coalition or differences between the Soviet Union and China. A modified hard-line view is that the Soviet Union is expansionistic, but behaves thusly as an extension of traditional Russian interests and not of ideology; therefore, the Soviet Union can be controlled through strength and tough-minded negotiations, if negotiations are worthwhile at all.

Such an image of the Soviet Union calls for the United States to confront the Soviet Union whenever necessary. The liberation, or rollback, policy suggested by Eisenhower during the 1952 presidential campaign is an example of one proposed hard-line policy. Under such a policy, the United States certainly should not trade with the Soviets or in any way provide technology to the Soviet Union, and should punish any country that does so.

The image of the Soviet Union on which United States policy was based after World War II was a slightly softer version of this hard-line view. The Soviets had to be watched closely because they would take any opportunity to expand if the United States allowed them to do so. Thus, the United States had to contain the Soviets within their present borders, but not risk a major war by attempting to reclaim countries that had already come under communist control. Soviet military strength had to be counterbalanced by a strong military in the United States and Western Europe. Trade with the Soviet Union was possible, but should be limited to what served U.S. interests, such as grain sales. Both the hardline and the softer hard-line image views the Soviet Union as capable of a nuclear first strike against the United States. The policy result of this perspective for the United States is a nuclear arsenal capable of absorbing a first strike from the Soviet Union. The United States assumes that if nuclear war comes the Soviet Union is the country that will start it.

The soft-line image of the Soviet Union sees Soviet military capabilities as a projection of fear of invasion and of a hostile world, not as an instrument for world conquest. Policy toward the Soviet Union should be based on placating those fears, not on increasing them. The communist movement is not monolithic and Moscow-controlled; thus, communism can come in different forms in different communist nations. The Soviets take advantage of trouble spots in the world, but do not necessarily create them. The United States should not be the world's policeman, but should provide controlled restraint when dealing with the Soviet Union. Expanded East-West trade would help reduce Soviet fears of the West and make the Soviets better citizens of the world community.

What this review of differing United States images of the Soviet Union illustrates is that the United States views the Soviet Union in different ways at different times, or differently depending on what the policy choice is. If relations between the two countries are poor, the hardline image is more apt to come into play, whereas if relations improve the soft-line image emerges. Also, more widely divergent perceptions of the Soviet Union seem to be held by the American public than exist among U.S. decision makers.

Specific developments can have an important impact on images. The end of the war in Vietnam marked important changes in the U.S. self-image. The U.S. virtually abandoned the concept of world policeman for a decade following withdrawal, but it was resurrected by the Reagan administration. The conflicts in El Salvador and Nicaragua produce varying U.S. images of the Soviet Union. The hard-line image is that the Soviet Union is the instigator of the conflict, which continues only because of Soviet and Soviet-supported Cuban activity. The softer-line image is that the conflict is an outgrowth of domestic problems in those countries and the Soviet Union is only operating on the periphery of the situation.

The fourth dimension of this perception (the other three being the two self-images and the United States' image of the Soviet Union) is the Soviet image of the United States. The Soviets do not share our rather benevolent view of ourselves any more than we share their view of themselves as a beleaguered, revolutionary nation. Even though Soviet leadership has renounced first strike on their part and has asked the United States to do likewise, occasionally the United States reminds the Soviet Union that, in spite of a reluctance to go to war, the United States will launch a first strike if sufficiently provoked. Since we refuse to renounce first strike, a nuclear war can begin only through U.S. initiative, the Soviets maintain. Thus, like the United States, the Soviet Union must have sufficient nuclear weapons to absorb an attack and have enough nuclear weapons survive that it can counter-attack. The Soviets see any attempt by the United States to promote human rights in the Soviet Union as interference in Soviet affairs. The efforts of the United States to encourage the Soviet Union to allow more Soviet Jews to emigrate and to release dissident Andrei Sakharov are seen by the Soviet Union as forms of such interference.

The Soviets, if their public pronouncements are to be believed, see the deployment of new nuclear delivery systems in Western Europe as an indication of the aggressive intent of the United States. They view NATO not as a defensive alliance but as a threat to the Soviet Union. The economic activities of the West are seen as discriminatory toward the Soviet Union, and East-West trade is viewed as constrained by unreasonable Western restrictions. The Soviets see themselves as quite tolerant of the activities of Western nations. On the issue of West Berlin, for example, they see themselves as allowing a Western island of control well inside their sphere of influence—a situation the West would not permit in Western Europe. The West, of course, argues that its presence in West Berlin is not a product of Soviet tolerance, but the result of Western determination and resolution in defending its right to be there.

Clearly, the self-images held by the United States and the Soviet Union differ markedly from the images they hold of each other. It is also clear that those images of self undergo considerable change within a general framework of values and beliefs, depending on what is going on domestically in the two countries and internationally. It is based on these changing images that the two countries develop policy toward one another.

THE THIRD WORLD IMAGES OF MAJOR POWERS

Whatever the varying images between the superpowers may be, a very different set of images is held by the Third World. Various aspects of these images of industrial nations were discussed in the earlier chapter on North-South conflict; therefore, only a summary will be given here. Central to the Third World perspective is concern with the industrial nations' economic, rather than military, capabilities; the Third World generally views Cold War conflict as secondary to its own needs for economic development. Consequently, the Third World generally opposes the superpowers' arms buildup, since it feels this siphons off resources that could otherwise be directed toward Third World development.

No matter how friendly or hostile its relationship with the industrial nations may be, any Third World country is aware of its economic vulnerability and the considerable economic capability of the industrialized nations. The industrialized Western nations, particularly the United States, are seen as economic giants that often are unaware of the havoc their actions produce in the Third World. Thus, the Third World feels exploited, whether by design or not, by the trade patterns the industrial nations have established. It also feels that the industrialized nations, Western and communist, regard the economic needs of the Third World as lower in priority than East-West, West-West, or East-East demands. From the Third World perspective, changes in the world's economy will not take place and the industrialized nations will not fulfill their obligations to the Third World until pressured into doing so. Therefore, the Third World must go to great lengths to gain the attention of the industrial nations. These attitudes are directed mainly at the Western industrialized nations, since those nations include the former colonial masters and are, from the Third World perspective, the perpetrators of neocolonial behavior. The Soviet Union is not without blame, however, in that the Third World increasingly is taking the view that any industrialized power is capable of practicing neocolonialism.

The Western powers, of course, reject the Third World's image of them, and, particularly, they have a more limited view of the economic responsibilities assigned them by the Third World. Many of the Third World's problems, the industrialized nations feel, could be resolved if those nations would carry out domestic economic and political reforms; the Third World is too prone to blame its problems on others and ignore its own policy choices. The Western democracies particularly criticize corruption, the violation of human rights, and nondemocratic political systems found in the Third World. The economic assistance that comes from the industrial nations, and which the Third World regards as only a fraction of what it deserves, is, from the Western perspective, generous and given with the best of intentions. In the United States, a portion of the public and the Congress feel that the aid program is a "give-away" and should be curtailed, that the U.S. is too generous, that aid is not appreciated, and that recipients often criticize the United States while accepting aid. If aid does not gain friends and allies, then why give it? The image in the United States of the Third World is such that additional aid to the developing world has little public or congressional support.

THE UNITED STATES AND ITS NEIGHBORS

Images held by other nations often can be in such sharp contrast with a nation's self-image that issues existing between them are difficult to communicate, as is well illustrated in U.S.-Soviet relations. This also can be the situation between countries that are neighbors and thought of as allies. Americans are accustomed to thinking of the only two nations geographically contiguous to the United States, Canada and Mexico, as friends and admirers. Thus, Americans are surprised to discover anti-American feelings at both public and governmental levels in those countries. Canada sees the United States as an economic power of such magnitude that, if Canada does not exercise great caution, the Canadian

economy will become a mere satellite of the U.S. economy. Canada falls just short of charging the United States with treating Canada as an economic colony. Canadian complaints about acid rain are based on the view that the United States is not sufficiently concerned about the well-being of its neighbors to take action to protect them. As a Third World nation, Mexico sees the United States as having little understanding of Mexico's developmental problems. Attempts to restrict the flow of illegal aliens to the United States are viewed in Mexico as a direct economic threat to Mexico, and Mexico is particularly fearful of becoming overly dependent on the United States market for its oil. Such a dependency would, from Mexico's perspective, create a neo-colonial relationship. Overall, neighbors of the United States feel that there is little concern for their well-being in the United States. These images result in neighbors that tend to overreact to U.S. policy choices and, since the U.S. tends to take them for granted, U.S. failure to respond to its neighbors' needs.

Since images nations hold of one another and of themselves are the bases on which policy is made, the degree to which countries can control those images is central to the success of their foreign policy. A nation can use its image to cultivate friendships or to instill fear in others, but the purpose of doing either is to fulfill its own interests. The techniques available to a nation to develop and control its image will be examined next.

TECHNIQUES FOR DEVELOPING IMAGES

While nations cannot control much of how other nations see them, they do have several means by which their images and the images of others can be affected. Many governments have a public information office for the dissemination of propaganda to educate about or distort an image to advantage. The manner in which a nation conducts its diplomacy and its willingness to negotiate can change an image as can any decision a nation makes that has an impact on other nations. Nations gather intelligence, both covertly and overtly, for the purpose of sharpening their images of others. How these techniques are utilized is an important part of behavior in the international system.

USE OF PROPAGANDA

The initial problem involved in a discussion of propaganda is to overcome the popular connotation of the term itself. "My country and its friends have information services to educate the people of other countries; our enemies have propaganda machines which tell lies." While not necessarily so, propaganda generally is viewed as deliberate distortions designed to serve the interests of the nation telling the story.

While the term "propaganda" has its origins in efforts of the Catholic Church during the seventeenth century to "propagate" the faith, its negative connation undoubtedly emerged from its use during the two World Wars. The first large-scale effort to use propaganda to alter national images came during World War I. The British, following the German invasion of Belgium in 1914, accused the Germans of numerous heinous atrocities. After the war, most of the accusations were found to be untrue, but the campaign was effective in swinging opinion in the United States to the side of the Allies and leaving no doubt that if the United States entered the war it would be on the Allies' side. In World War II, the German propaganda ministry, under the guidance of Joseph Goebbels, became the master of the "Big Lie" technique. This technique operates on the assumption that the most difficult statement to disprove is one that has no vestige of truth in it. These wartime distortions led to the popular view that all propaganda is made up of lies. The "Big Lie" is, of course, only one of several techniques employed by those engaged in propaganda. Most propaganda today is simply a careful ordering of facts interpreted to present a particular image.

Propaganda, in the broader sense, is a means by which a nation presents its interests to audiences in other countries, develops its own image, and shapes the images of other countries for its own purposes. It is not a means of decision-making, but it attempts to affect decision-makers through the publics which are its targets. The importance of propaganda in international politics is reflected by the number of terms that refer to propaganda activities. Reference to the Cold War as a "war of ideas" or "a battle for men's minds" and engaging in "psychological warfare" all refer to propaganda.

Except for the active use of propaganda before World War II by Nazi Germany and the Soviet Comintern, propaganda was not used extensively during peacetime until the Cold War developed. Presently, all major states and many of the smaller countries maintain propaganda agencies, usually labeled information services. Even those countries that cannot afford such agencies have press attachés in their embassies. The British Information Service is one of the oldest such agencies, but the United States Information Agency (USIA) is perhaps the best known. The USIA was created after World War II and owes its heritage to the wartime Office of War Information (OWI). Numerous countries have more limited information operations, and even multinational information agencies have developed when a particular need has arisen. The Arab countries long complained that their side of the Arab-Israeli conflict was not being told in the West. As a consequence, those Arab nations most directly involved in the conflict established an information agency to present their story abroad, although the effectiveness of the agency was hindered when it developed problems that reflected splits among Arab sponsors. The European Communities also set up their own information service separate from the national agencies of member states. Its primary activity has been in the United States.

One of the issues dividing Western nations and the Third World within the United Nations Educational, Scientific, and Cultural Organization (UNESCO) has been the demand of the Third World to have its own news service. The Third World complains that the world's major news services originate in Western nations and that those services present a negative image of Third World countries by reporting essentially only revolutions, coups, natural disasters, and the details of poverty. Under the Third World plan, the Western news services would be limited in their access to the Third World, and news coming from the Third World would come primarily from the Third World's own service. The Western nations label this censorship, but the Third World claims that this development is necessary to improve the Third World's image. This new reporting service would be controlled as to what could be reported and, seemingly, would closely resemble a propaganda bureau for the Third World.

The United States probably ranks as the country having the most difficulty deciding what its propaganda agency should do, what approach should be taken to propaganda, and even whether there should be such an agency. The dilemma seems to stem from the question of whether it is proper for a democracy to engage in such activity. During the 1950s and 1960s, this issue was reflected in congressional suspicion of what the USIA was doing, which resulted in budget cuts and investigations of the agency. Congress also prohibits the agency from any domestic activity in the United States. Because of this restriction, it took an act of Congress before the USIA-made film of John Kennedy's funeral, *Years of Lightning, Day of Drums,* could be shown in the United States. In spite of these occasional attacks, the USIA does now seem to be firmly established as a part of federal bureaucracy.

Since propaganda usually seeks a broad audience, the mass media is the device by which it is most often disseminated. Radio is the most widely used mass media, although, in some instances, television can be used. The short distances between Israel and its Arab neighbors make it possible for each to watch the other's telecasts and news reports. The situation in the two Berlins offers a similar opportunity. Also, telecasts out of Havana can be viewed in Miami, and vice versa. Radio presents the opportunity for a much larger audience, however. The Soviet Union has an extensive system of broadcasts throughout the world, particularly in the Third World, and has coverage in more countries for more broadcast hours per year than does the United States. One could say that a "broadcast gap" exists between the two countries. The Voice of America is the United States' general broadcast service and, for broadcasts to Eastern Europe and the Soviet Union in particular, Radio Free Europe and Radio Liberty suffice. Radio Havana beams its broadcasts throughout Latin America, and Radio Cairo has been active in the Middle East since the late 1950s. In the 1960s the target of Egyptian propaganda was Jordan, but Libya is the primary target of the 1980s. The objectives of broadcasting to other nations vary, but the long-term purpose is to present the sender's version of world events and, if the target is a hostile nation, to debunk that country's representation of those events.

If a country chooses to do so, it can employ countermeasures to stop foreign propaganda from entering the country. The Soviets frequently "jam" Western broadcasts beamed at the Soviet Union, and mailings that are regarded as propaganda are confiscated. A more heavy-handed technique is to allow mobs that could be controlled by local police to destroy USIA libraries. Many USIA libraries are located in Third World countries and are more accessible for the venting of anti-American feeling than is the U.S. embassy.

Occasionally, propaganda has an adverse effect on the sending nation's image. Perhaps the best-known instance of this occurred during the Hungarian Revolution. Hungarian revolutionaries claimed that the United States promised them direct assistance, but no aid was received. On investigation, it was found that such promises were made by Radio Free Europe, which at that time was thought to be a privately supported broadcast, but no such promises were made in official Voice of America broadcasts. A few years later, it was learned that Radio Free Europe was secretly financed by the U.S. government, a disclosure which opened up once more the issue of false promises.

Whatever the means used to transmit propaganda, the message must be communicated in such a way that it is understood by the intended audience. The message must be simple, credible, and relevant. The message is often repeated, on the assumption that repetition is one means of effective communication. The message can be a straight newscast, it may be in the form of entertainment, or it can be deliberate distortion and misinformation. All are techniques used by those engaged in the transmission of propaganda.

Even though not commonly regarded as propaganda, an effort to educate certainly can be that; truthful and objective statements are a particularly effective propaganda technique. Propaganda can be true or false or any gradation in between. Propaganda can be slanted, selective in its facts, and varied in its interpretations, but the purpose of its dissemination is to affect images in the manner intended by those who are disseminating the propaganda.

DIPLOMACY AS AN IMAGE-BUILDER

The manner in which a nation conducts its diplomacy is also an important means by which a national image is developed. One means of utilizing diplomacy for image-building is for a nation, whether it intended to do so or not, to profess its willingness to negotiate seriously its differences with other nations. If negotiations are successful, that country can claim credit; if not successful, then it can charge the failure to other

parties to the negotiations. However the negotiations turn out, the image is protected. Whereas propaganda generally attempts to affect images held by the public at large, with decision-makers a secondary target, the diplomatic method is contact between decision-makers, with the general public observing the process and drawing conclusions from it.

A recent example of a substantial image change resulting from diplomacy emerged from the lengthy talks that led to the peace treaty between Israel and Egypt. When negotiations between Egypt and Israel began shortly after the 1973 October War, they were conducted through a third party, with Secretary of State Kissinger conducting shuttle diplomacy between the two countries. The result was a phased withdrawal of Israel from part of the Sinai. Other efforts at negotiation largely failed until November 1977, when President Anwar Sadat of Egypt announced that he would personally visit Israel if that would open up direct negotiations. The offer was accepted, and Sadat spoke to the Israeli Knesset. Little was accomplished in the negotiations that followed, and in August 1978 President Carter invited President Sadat and Prime Minister Begin to Camp David in an effort to break the deadlock. That conference took place in September and produced the basis for a peace treaty signed in March 1979. This sequence of events altered considerably Egypt's international image. From the time Egypt began purchasing Soviet arms in 1955, Egypt was viewed as a Soviet client state, particularly after signing a fifteen-year friendship treaty with the Soviet Union in 1971. But, by 1979, Sadat had broken off the client-state relationship with the Soviet Union, established good relations with the United States, signed a peace treaty with Israel, and was co-winner, along with Begin, of the Nobel Peace Prize. Egypt's image was now that of a friend of the United States and no longer that of a nation belligerent toward Israel.

Other dramatic changes in image through diplomacy include the manner in which the United States altered its view of the communist government in China. Until 1971 Gallup polls had consistently shown that about 80 percent of the American public opposed improving relations with China. Following the visit of the U.S. table tennis team in August 1971, the seating of China at the United Nations in November, and Nixon's visit to China in February 1972, the percentages in the Gallup poll reversed: over 80 percent of the American public approved of the change in policy. Even the manner in which China was referred to changed. At the peak of hostility between China and the United States, China was generally referred to as "Red China" or "Communist China," as contrasted with Nationalist China on Taiwan. After improved relations, reference was to the "Peking government" and eventually simply "China." The government of Taiwan was no longer seen as an alternative government for all of China. China's image changed from that of a country hostile to the United States, and equally as dangerous as the Soviet Union, to a country noted for being anti-Soviet, possible to negotiate with, and interested in closer ties with the United States.

Another example of a major change in image resulting from diplomacy is the status of arms control talks between the United States and the Soviet Union. The world view of relations between the superpowers seems to be based on whether those countries are engaged in arms talks. When talks are not in progress, the relationship is perceived as poor, but the relationship is seen as good when talks are going on. When talks were broken off by the Soviets in 1983 over the U.S. deployment in Europe of theater nuclear weapons, the image was that the relationship had deteriorated, but it was seen as improving when talks were resumed in March, 1985. These changes in image occur generally without regard to how well the talks themselves are progressing. Except for special events such as the summit conferences in November 1985 and October 1986, other aspects of U.S.-Soviet relations are secondary to the formation of images that come out of arms talks.

A more gradual shift in image than those already discussed is the change that has taken place in the U.S. view of the United Nations. In its early years, the United Nations was viewed with optimism and hope that it would be an important forum for international conflict resolution. As Cold War conflicts dominated the organization, the image was altered; it was felt that the United Nations could still fulfill the ideals of its founders if it were not for the obstinacy of the Soviets. Later, as Third World issues became the focus of the organization, the American public and decision-makers seemed to give up on the United Nations as an important conflict-resolving institution. This change in image resulted in diplomacy between the major powers shifting from the United Nations to other means of diplomatic contact. The superpowers reverted to bilateral negotiations and away from the multilateral opportunities of the United Nations.

Occasionally, a single major event can bring about an important change in a nation's image, such as Israel experienced following the 1973 October War. Before the war, Israel was regarded, particularly in the United States, as all but invincible to the Arab threat and tightly united with a strong sense of national purpose. Even though Israel eventually won the 1973 war, its early defeats destroyed the illusion of invincibility. Also, following the war, domestic consensus broke down, and dissension concerning national policy became the dominant characteristic of Israeli politics. The war, which lasted less than a month, produced major changes in how Israel was viewed. Diplomats and national leaders thus have a degree of control over the image their country projects, but events and circumstances can bring about change that is beyond their control.

INTELLIGENCE-GATHERING

Though decision-makers bring to policy-making their own perceptions of issues and countries, they also need to garner as much external information as possible. Images of one's friends and enemies exist no matter how limited the information upon which those images are based, but the purpose of intelligence-gathering agencies is to provide additional information to make those images as accurate as possible. Decision-makers filter and interpret the information made available to them through their own perceptions. Since the experiences of decision-makers vary to some degree, they rarely share the same images; consequently, decisions necessarily reflect the compromises made to reconcile differences in image. The gathering of intelligence will be discussed first; the section following will discuss the impact of decision-makers' images on policy-making.

WHO GATHERS THE INFORMATION

Virtually every nation has some means of gathering intelligence. In totalitarian states, state security and external intelligence-gathering tend to be linked together as means of gathering information, as is the case for the Soviets' principal intelligence-gathering agencies, the KGB and the GRU. In addition, Soviet agencies make no distinction between intelligence gathering at the domestic and international levels. In the United States, however, the Central Intelligence Agency (CIA) is, by law, restricted from intelligence gathering inside the United States—the Federal Bureau of Investigation is responsible for domestic security—although the CIA is occasionally charged with violating that prohibition. During domestic protests in the U.S. against the Vietnam War, the CIA was accused of infiltrating the antiwar movement. The defense offered by the CIA for such activity was that it needed to find out if financial support for the movement was coming from other countries. The British also have different agencies responsible for domestic and external intelligence gathering. Many smaller countries cannot afford to maintain for-

eign intelligence-gathering agencies, although some, such as Israel and its Mossad, do have overseas networks for the gathering of intelligence. Nearly all countries have some sort of internal security agency to gather intelligence, however. Intelligence must be gathered by any government whether there is an administrative agency set up for that purpose or not. The larger nations have large, but generally undisclosed, budgets to finance their intelligence-gathering operations. The United States faces problems in this regard, since budgets hidden from the public are considered by many to contradict the idea of an open society. This has been partially resolved by assigning congressional committees on intelligence the task of monitoring the budgets and activities of the intelligence-gathering agencies, although the committees maintain secrecy in the process.

Much of what is regarded as intelligence can be gathered openly by methods which are traditionally not regarded as spying: through monitoring other countries' print and electronic media, through travel in other countries, through information from contacts with foreign government officials, and through use of a country's diplomatic missions to make observations. While it is difficult to assign percentages to the amount of intelligence collected by either covert or overt methods, much of the information gathered does come from public sources. Whatever the method used, the task of an intelligence-gathering agency is to collect and interpret a vast amount of information.

The United States has several agencies whose task it is to gather intelligence for decision-makers. In addition to the CIA, other well-known agencies include the Defense Intelligence Agency (DIA), the National Security Agency (NSA), and the State Department's Bureau of Intelligence and Research. The bureaucracy in Washington also includes about a dozen additional, lesser-known agencies. The techniques for gathering intelligence vary with the agencies. For example, the National Security Agency's principal means of gathering intelligence is electronic; this involves worldwide surveillance through the use of satellites and across-the-horizon devices for monitoring radio traffic. The information gathered by the Bureau of Intelligence and Research comes primarily from U.S. embassies and consulates, and from other overtly available sources. In addition, the CIA maintains a network of offices throughout the world which often operate out of the embassies. While the methods vary, the purpose of all intelligence-gathering agencies is to find out as much as possible about what is going on in the world. This information is then passed on to the decision-makers to aid them in forming the images they need to make policy.

DECISION-MAKERS AND IMAGE

The two general aspects of images that have been discussed thus far are: 1) nations—that is, their publics and decision-makers—develop perceptions of themselves and of others, and these images are a major determinant in how nations react to one another; and 2) various means are available to domestic decision-makers that to some extent control images, but events and environment limit the degree to which images can be manipulated. The next aspect of images that needs to be discussed is the impact that images held by policy-makers have on the decisions they make.

An ideal model of decision-making includes the following: 1) identify the issue about which a decision needs to be made and determine the objectives your country wishes to achieve; 2) identify the alternative actions that a country can take, assess how other nations will react to each of the alternatives, and estimate the risks involved in each alternative; 3) in the process of evaluating the alternatives, gather as much information as possible to aid in those evaluations; 4) choose the alternative that best achieves your country's objectives, balanced with the minimum of negative effects of implementing that course of action; 5) decide how the course of action will

be executed and plan for contingencies that may arise. The ideal model of decision-making also assumes that decisions can and will be made that have long-range and far-reaching application. This model, in short, assumes rationality which means that decision-makers will be neutral going into the search for the best alternative, or, if not neutral, will identify their values and beliefs and not let them interfere with arriving at a rational decision. This model also assumes that the information needed to make a rational decision can be collected and, after collection, will provide an

Fig. 8.1 Rational Model of Decision Making

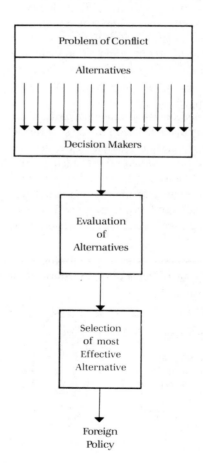

adequate basis for making a decision.

With any model, what actually transpires is somewhat different from the ideal. The first step in decision-making is identifying that a problem exists; it does not exist until the decision-makers decide that it does. An issue is not a problem if it is judged to be unimportant, presents no immediate need for action, or is postponed in the hope that it will resolve itself even if nothing is done. But once a problem is recognized as needing attention, decisions must be made; even if the choice is to do nothing, that too is a decision. Whatever is decided must be decided on the basis of the information available, and, since complete information is not possible, what is considered adequate information on which to base a decision is a judgment that decision-makers must make. Even when it is decided that sufficient information exists to make a decision, that information is not going to be evaluated in the same manner by each of the decision-makers since they apply varying images to the information.

To begin with, intelligence-gathering agencies do not provide decision-makers with raw, unprocessed data. The agencies interpret the information they collect and establish an intelligence estimate before it is passed on to the decision-makers. Estimates among the intelligence-gathering agencies differ, and they vie with one another in selling their estimates to decision-makers. The charge has been made that agencies will, on occasion, provide intelligence that is designed to please the decision-makers to whom it is passed. During the Vietnam War, such a charge was leveled at the Defense Intelligence Agency (DIA), which is an organizational part of the Defense Department. The DIA was accused of providing estimates concerning progress of the war that the Pentagon wanted to hear. The result was that the DIA and the CIA often had different interpretations about how that war was progressing and whether the United States was winning. Since each of the intelligence-gathering agencies, then as now, places its own estimate on the information it gathers—that is, each presents a different image—an initial step in making a decision is to attempt to resolve differences that exist among those estimates.

Information thus has already been filtered through the images or perceptions of the information gatherers before it is received by the decision-makers who must choose a policy alternative. The decision-makers, in turn, filter the information through their own perceptions of reality. After so much processing, the possibility of decision-makers' receiving unbiased information is nearly nonexistent. The problem of rational decision-making is compounded further when judging how well decision-makers control the influence of their belief systems and images. Under these circumstances, judging whether a

Fig. 8.2 Role of Perception in Decision Making

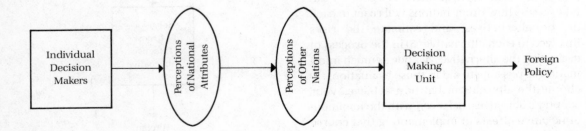

decision is rational becomes a question of whether observers of the process agree or disagree with the decision; those who agree tend to see the decision as rational, and those who disagree with the policy choice tend to see it as irrational.

Another problem lies in assessing how much information is necessary in order to make long-range decisions. Ordinarily, decisions are made on the basis of decision-makers' ability to predict the outcome of the policy choice they make. Since information is not complete, the tendency is to choose shorter-range alternatives that fit the limitations of the information. Decisions are, as a result, incremental and thus fall short of the long-range decisions expected in the rational model. Decisions tend to cover the immediate and unavoidable, but not the totality of the issue at hand (Lindblom, 1968; Janis and Mann, 1977).

A similar problem in decision-making pertains to how carefully each of the alternatives has been analyzed. Decision-makers have a tendency to select the first workable alternative as their policy choice. More than one alternative may be workable, and the first workable alternative may not be the best. An additional problem is that decision-makers may filter out important information that does not fit their images. Rather than change their images, as would be called for in rational decision-making, the information contradictory to established perceptions is ignored or is distorted in such a way that it does fit (Jervis, 1976).

While images or perceptions are an important aspect of how information is processed at various stages in the decision-making process, another aspect of processing information is that decision-makers are limited as to the number of interpretations or problems they can handle. For the issue or problem that is under consideration, the information, or at least its interpretations, may be contradictory. The effect is to overload the decision-makers, not with too much information, but with too many interpretations. The

pattern also exists that all problems cannot receive adequate attention. In the United States, for example, certain areas of policy are emphasized at any given time, and others are neglected. In the late 1980s, Africa receives little attention, and the Middle East and Central America receive a great deal of attention. Western Europe, after a decade of neglect, has begun to receive more attention from the United States as a result of nuclear theater weapons and Western trade issues. Decisions thus tend to be limited to those areas that are currently receiving attention.

Since information undergoes different interpretations and different issues receive differing amounts of attention, policy alternatives are not reviewed with the objectivity and thoroughness called for in the ideal model of decision-making. The question remains as to how policy can emerge from this situation.

One perspective that has received widespread attention among scholars is that policy emerges from resolving conflicts among the bureaucratic units that are concerned with a particular policy question. This model of decision-making emphasizes that the various units involved in the policy-making process—or, more precisely, the people who make up those units—have perspectives that reflect the interests and concerns of the unit. In general terms, the State Department is apt to view events and actions differently than does the Defense Department. The staff of the National Security Council may have yet another perspective. Within each of these units, there is likely to be a further variety of perceptions. Within the State Department, for example, the various bureaus may differ in their interpretations, and the economic officers may hold different views from the political officers.

Each of the units defends its position as being a rational choice, but arrives at its position on the basis of the interests and perspective of the unit. These differences must be bargained away. The policy that emerges from this bargaining process is not arrived at by rational means, but, rather, it is what has become acceptable to the units involved in the bargaining process.

CONCLUSION

Recognizing the significance of perceptions or images is important in understanding the behavior of nations within the international system. Self-image and the image of others significantly affect the policy choices nations make. Images are the filters through which nations interpret the events that take place in the international system, as well as the means by which individuals and governmental units react to other individuals and governmental units within a domestic political system. Images are the reality of the moment but can be changed as new information becomes available. Nations have some control over the image they have in the international system through propaganda, diplomacy, intelligence-gathering, and policy-making. Domestically, differing images among decision-makers set up conflict among bureaucratic units. That conflict must be dealt with in order to make policy; thus, decision-making is not the fulfillment of a rational model of decision-making but rather is a process of resolving bureaucratic conflict.

CHAPTER 9

Diplomacy and Bargaining

Diplomacy is a system of communication among nations through which they express and defend their interests, state their grievances, and issue threats and ultimatums. It is a channel of contact for clarifying positions, probing for information, and convincing another country to support your country's position. It is a process by which common interests are discovered and coalitions formed. Diplomacy is also a means by which conflict can be resolved through negotiation and bargaining. It is often formal in nature, but informal diplomatic contact is not unusual. This process among nations has aspects that are open to public review, but much of diplomacy is confidential. Even when the public is aware that negotiations are taking place, the specifics of bargaining are seldom revealed.

The foregoing description of diplomacy indicates two broad characteristics. The first is that diplomacy is an institution—with formal rules and principles, protected by international law and developed for the purpose of guaranteeing communication and representation between nations. The second is the use to which that institution is put in the way of interest presentation, conflict management, and conflict resolution. Both characteristics require that each nation have a corps of diplomats, usually professionals, and both require an established arrangement for the exchange of representatives between nations.

DIPLOMACY AS AN INSTITUTION

The beginning of the institutional development of diplomacy preceded by centuries the establishment of the nation-state system. Emissaries and messages were exchanged between countries long before even the Greek city-states developed, but the process was not formalized until the fifteenth century, when the Italian city-states developed the practice of exchanging ambassadors and establishing permanent diplomatic missions. This development also led to the need for professional diplomats. Much of what these early professionals did was serve as commercial attachés, still a part of a diplomat's duties today, but their duties also included representation of their home state in a broader sense as well.

The development of the nation-state system in the seventeenth century brought with it a need to formalize further the institutionalization of diplomacy. During the negotiation of the Peace of Westphalia between 1646 and 1648, since the rules of diplomatic contact were not fully developed, more time was spent on the procedures of negotiation than on the negotiation of the peace settlement. At Westphalia, procedural conflicts often appeared to be almost childish in nature, but they reflected the importance of working out the problems of status and equality in diplomatic contact. If all nation-states possess sovereign equality, then no emissary holds either lower or higher rank than another; therefore, such seemingly simple matters as to when ambassadors arrive at or leave a negotiating session and the order in which ambassadors proceed when diplomatic processions are held caused conflict until rules governing such matters were agreed to. Then, as now, formal diplomatic conferences required rules that establish the framework for negotiations before the negotiators can turn to substantive issues.

If these sorts of problems could arise when there were only a dozen or so nation-states in the system, as was the case in the middle of the seventeenth century, the potential for conflict was greatly increased as the system expanded. Through the late seventeenth and eighteenth centuries, whenever diplomats gathered together to negotiate, squabbles over protocol were commonplace. It was not until the early nineteenth century at the Congress of Vienna (1815) and the Congress of Aix-la-Chapelle (1818) that many of the procedural questions of diplomatic contact were resolved. One important step was to standardize diplomatic ranks, a precedence of ranks that is still accepted today. The highest rank was ambassador extraordinary and plenipotentiary, which meant that the ambassador had the full authority to represent his country and negotiate in its behalf; of equal rank were representatives from the Vatican, papal nuncios. Next were envoys extraordinary and ministers plenipotentiary, followed by ministers resident. Diplomats holding any one of these ranks could be sent by a head of state to another head of state as his representative. The fourth rank was chargé d'affaires, the individual who is in charge of the embassy in the absence of the ambassador or minister. This rank of diplomat is accredited by one foreign minister or secretary of state to another instead of between heads of state.

Until the twentieth century, the rank of ambassador was reserved for exchanges between major states; thus, few ambassadors were appointed. Otherwise, the highest-ranking diplomat exchanged usually was a minister. Until the nineteenth century, even such diplomatically active countries as Great Britain and France appointed only four or five ambassadors. The United States, which in the nineteenth century thought much of diplomatic ceremony and protocol to be undemocratic, did not appoint its first ambassadors until 1893; the use of the rank of minister was considered more egalitarian in that it avoided some of the diplomatic formality and pomp. During the twentieth century, more and more countries upgraded to the rank of ambassador the top diplomats they exchanged, until nations that were offered an emissary with a rank lower than ambassador felt insulted. A few ministers were still exchanged as late as the 1950s, but today only ambassadors are appointed, regardless of the obscurity of the nation. The rank of minister is still used, however, for appointments where the diplomat is not the chief of mission in another nation.

The clarification of ranks was helpful in that some diplomats carried higher precedence than others by virtue of their rank, but there were still problems of precedence within each rank. Rank, procedure, and protection for diplomats were updated in the 1961 Vienna Convention on Diplomatic Relations. Protections and functions of consular officials were updated and formalized in the Vienna Convention on Consular Relations in 1963.

From the perspective of the major states, the problem of precedence within ranks could best be resolved if countries were ranked according to their order of international importance, but it was unlikely that any group of nations could agree on what that order should be. Ultimately, the rule developed that precedence among ambassadors stationed in a particular national capital was decided on the basis of the amount of time an ambassador had been stationed there. The person who had been there the longest became the doyen, or dean, of the diplomatic corps, and precedence descended by seniority. The dean could be from a small nation, but the rule remained the same even though major states might take lower precedence than some of the minor nations. In Washington, for many years the dean of the diplomatic corps was the ambassador from Nicaragua. After that ambassador was removed following the overthrow of the Somoza regime in 1979, the dean became the Soviet ambassador, Dobrynin, who had held his post since 1962. When Dobrynin was recalled to Moscow in 1986, the Swedish ambassador became dean.

Language can also be an obstacle to the negotiation of substantive matters, and, although no international agreements govern the use of language, a style of diplomatic communication has developed. Among diplomats, language has evolved in which even ultimatums and threats of war would appear to the casual reader to be much less threatening than intended. The purpose of using language that appears to understate what is intended is to make the message clear without the language's creating problems in its own right. Diplomatic messages therefore are courteous, yet impersonal, and carefully worded so that the message is transmitted as accurately as possible. Diplomatic language is so well established today that any departure from it would lead to misunderstanding.

These considerations—rank, precedence, and language—are all matters of protocol and comprise only a small part of the courtesy and care in the international system to prevent procedure from becoming an obstacle to the negotiation of substantive issues. Most nations recognize the importance of such procedures by having a chief of protocol in their foreign office (or, as in the United States, their state department).

Such matters as a state visit by one head of state to another require great care in adherence to protocol. As with other aspects of protocol, state visits have predictable and established procedures so that negotiations will not be inter-

fered with by irrelevant disputes. On his arrival, the visiting head of state will receive a twenty-one gun salute. The host head of state will give a dinner for the visitor, and the visiting head of state will reciprocate with a dinner at his country's embassy. The guest list and seating arrangements on such occasions are carefully prepared so that no one will be offended. The visit will end after approximately three days with a carefully worded communiqué concerning the results of the visit. If the talks are successful, they may be described as "fruitful"; if not, they may be summarized as "frank." If it is an official state visit, a stay of less than three days could be viewed as an affront. An example of such was President Carter's visit to Nigeria in 1978. The Nigerian head of state had made an official state visit to Washington a few months earlier, and Carter was returning the visit on a swing through Africa. Carter was scheduled to spend only one full day in Nigeria, which the Nigerian government found to be a slight, as protocol had not been followed.

A certain protocol also is followed when a new ambassador is appointed. The sending government will quietly inquire of the host government as to the acceptability of a particular person. If that person is acceptable, the appointment is made, and the new ambassador, armed with a letter of credence, is sent to the host country. Sometime after arrival, the new ambassador presents his or her letter of credence to the head of state, and, in accepting the letter, the head of state formally accredits the new ambassador. This process may appear unduly ceremonial, but it protects both governments from embarrassment and formally establishes the ambassador as his or her country's representative.

Another important dimension of the institutional aspect of diplomacy is the matter of privileges and immunities accorded diplomats. Once permanent representation was established between nation-states, protections for personnel staffing the embassies and consulates had to be developed. Effective representation could hardly take place if the host government were free to harass ambassadors and their staff. Also, if the host government were to harass foreign diplomats, the sending governments could, in turn, harass the diplomats from the host nation. Without protection, diplomats could become hostages if war broke out or a crisis developed between the sending and host governments. From these possibilities, all of which could be used to restrict the ability of a nation to have representation in other countries, came the practice of privileges and immunities which grants diplomats and their families (at one time even their servants) freedom from the laws of the host country. This immunity applies to both civil and criminal law; diplomats can refuse to pay traffic tickets, may break a lease, or even commit a major crime and not be prosecuted under local law.

The media in the United States occasionally are critical of extending to noncitizens exemption from domestic law that citizens must obey. The city of New York for many years has complained about the unpaid traffic tickets issued to delegates to the United Nations. In retaliation, New York police began towing diplomats' vehicles if they were double-parked (the main cause for the tickets) or in some other manner blocking traffic. The fines were still not paid, but the towing charges had to be paid to recover the vehicle. Such disrespect for local traffic laws seems to be a widespread practice, not only in the United States, but in capitals throughout the world. While extending such immunity to foreign diplomats may be annoying, the practice is reciprocal; the same immunities are extended U.S. diplomats stationed abroad. Although easily attacked on nationalistic grounds, the defense of such privileges is the need to have diplomats free to represent their countries as effectively as possible.

While most violations are misdemeanors, problems do arise when felonies are committed. An incident in Washington a number of years ago involved the son of the Irish ambassador who fatally injured a woman with his automobile. He had received a number of traffic violations in the past but was exempted from paying those tickets and from prosecution in the fatal accident as well. He was returned home, and the Irish government paid an indemnity to the woman's family in the amount that the courts could have granted in a case of wrongful death. However, while paying the indemnity, the Irish government made clear that under international law governing the privileges and immunities of diplomats it had no obligation to do so. In another instance, a foreign diplomat committed a murder in Denmark. The Danish government requested the diplomat's country to waive his diplomatic status, which the sending country did, and the diplomat was tried under Danish law. The sending government is under no obligation to grant such a waiver, however. In other cases, the son of the Ghanian ambassador to the United Nations was accused of rape and could not be prosecuted, and the son of the Brazilian ambassador to the United States was accused of assault, but also was not prosecuted.

While such flagrant breaches of domestic law do occur from time to time, the felony diplomats are most frequently accused of committing is espionage. Diplomatic delegations often include intelligence-gathering agents, and, while the overt gathering of intelligence is a recognized function of an embassy staff, espionage is a violation of the law in every nation. If caught, an agent with diplomatic protections cannot be prosecuted, but the host government can declare the agent to be *persona non grata*. While protesting that the charges are false, the sending government will nevertheless order the accused back home. The usual practice is that within a short time that country will reciprocate by making similar charges against diplomats from the accusing nation. Such actions have become commonplace among nations actively engaged in the Cold War, notably the Soviet Union and the United States. The largest groups of diplomats so accused have been assigned in London and Mexico City, however, and in both instances Soviet embassy staffs were involved. But even declaring a diplomat *persona non grata* is within the spirit of maximizing the representative nature of a diplomat. By declaring a diplomat to be no longer welcome, the host government is stating that that diplomat's ability to represent his country has been seriously impaired.

To restrict spying activities, a nation can limit the travel of diplomats stationed in its country, and both the United States and the Soviet Union do so. For some time, the United States applied such restrictions only to Soviet diplomats, but eventually the restrictions were extended to Eastern European diplomats as well. Other countries have, on occasion, virtually restricted to their capitals diplomats of countries with which they have poor relations. This, however, is often done to show disfavor with the policies of the sending government rather than to prevent the diplomats from observing something they should not.

Diplomats do have certain obligations in return for the privileges and immunities they receive. Under international law they are expected to obey local law; their immunity only prevents them from being prosecuted. Also, diplomats are expected to not interfere in the domestic political system of the country in which they are stationed. While they may publicly defend their country's policies, they are not to criticize publically the policies of the host government. Expressing preference for a candidate in an election is regarded as particularly inappropriate. An example of the latter occurred during the 1946 presidential election campaign in Argentina in which Juan Perón was a candidate. Perón had been head of state during World War II, and the United States had had poor relations with Argentina due to that country's pro-Axis leanings. The American ambassador openly expressed his opposition to Perón. Perón won the election and the ambassador subsequently was withdrawn.

In addition to the immunities extended to diplomats, embassy buildings and their contents are also beyond the jurisdiction of local authorities. If a crime occurs in an embassy, local police cannot enter the building without permission from the chief of mission. If a fire breaks out in an embassy or consulate, firemen cannot fight the fire without permission. A few years ago, a fire occurred in the Soviet embassy in Washington which was serious enough that the local fire department was allowed in. Although there was no evidence that the files were violated, the Soviets accused the CIA of setting the fire in order to have agents disguised as firemen go through the embassy's files.

If diplomatic relations between the host and sending country are severed, the embassy and its files are to be sealed and protected by a neutral nation until normal relations are restored. In addition, the host nation has the obligation to protect embassy buildings from terrorist attack or demonstrating mobs. When the U.S. embassy in Pakistan was destroyed by a mob in 1979, the United States protested that the Pakistani government was slow in coming to the embassy's aid.

Embassies are not only to be protected by the host government; they may, under international law, be used to harbor persons seeking political asylum. The host government cannot enter an embassy to seize those who have been granted political asylum, but neither is the host government obligated to allow those persons to leave the country. The result has been a number of instances in which political refugees spend long periods of time restricted to embassy grounds. Perhaps the best-known instance of such long-term confinement was that of Cardinal Mindszenty who was granted asylum in the U.S. embassy in Budapest during the Hungarian Revolution in 1956, where he remained until 1971.

Despite the absence of enforcement procedures to punish violators, the principles and practices of diplomacy are adhered to within the international community with only occasional lapses, most of which are minor. The major recent exception to that observation was the seizure in November 1979 of the U.S. embassy and its staff in Teheran. In its revolutionary fervor, Iran violated virtually every principle of diplomatic privilege and immunity. The hostages were held for 444 days and were released only after protracted negotiations between the United States and Iran. Short of war, the United States had few options in the matter despite the gravity of Iran's violations of international law. The Iranian embassy staff in Washington could have been seized, but then the United States would have been guilty of the same violations as was Iran. The United States did take the case to the International Court of Justice (ICJ) and won, but the ICJ is without enforcement powers, and the decision could not be implemented. A rescue operation was attempted, but failed. The only other option proved to be negotiation.

The embassy staffs of the major states often are quite large. Some U.S. embassy staffs in Europe number as many as five hundred; the embassy in Teheran, until shortly before the seizure of the hostages, had more than a thousand personnel. While the top official in a United States embassy is the ambassador, there is also a deputy chief of mission (DCM), who ordinarily becomes the chargé d'affaire in the ambassador's absence. Other personnel include political, economic, and cultural officers; counselors; military, air, and naval attachés; first and second secretaries; and attachés from the Agriculture and Commerce Departments. While many of these positions are filled by the State Department's foreign service, the attachés represent the interests of other departments such as Defense, Agriculture, and Commerce. Many of the people working in the embassy have clerical, secretarial, and minor administrative duties and do not have diplomatic status; people in these lower-level positions often are citizens of the host country. In general, embassies are considered to be secure even though foreign nationals work in the buildings. This assumption was severely shaken in early 1987 when U.S. Marine guards, which are attached to U.S. embassies throughout the world, were accused of allowing unauthorized Soviet citizens to enter the U.S. embassy in Moscow. In addition to the embassy, many nations have consulates located in cities other than the capital of the country to handle administrative matters pertaining to business and to assist the sending nation's citizens in the area.

With respect to diplomacy as an institution, the point needs to be made that the diplomats whom a nation sends to foreign countries are only one portion of the personnel involved in diplomatic communication. Ambassadors and their staffs must have diplomats to negotiate with, and those people are the personnel who staff the foreign policy-making bureaucratic units of the host governments. Included are heads of state, foreign ministers, foreign ministry personnel, and foreign service officers who alternate between assignments at home and overseas. In the United States, members of the foreign service spend about as much time stationed in Washington as they do abroad.

ACTIVITIES OF DIPLOMATS

In the past, when ocean crossings took weeks and no rapid means of communication between capitals existed, embassy staffs played a more important role in negotiations than they do today. In earlier times, when ambassadors or ministers negotiated, they could not check with their governments without unacceptable delays; thus, they were granted a wide range of discretion in decision-making. The terms used to describe a top diplomat's authority—extraordinary and plenipotentiary—had far greater meaning than at present. Today, with rapid travel and instant communication, when ambassadors negotiate they can receive instructions from their home government at every turn. Thus, they often function more as messengers than as negotiators. Furthermore, when major issues are negotiated the ambassador frequently is bypassed altogether, and the foreign minister or a special emissary flies in to carry on negotiations. A recent example was when Robert McFarlane, then U.S. national security adviser, largely bypassed traditional diplomatic channels when he visited Iran in 1986 prior to the sale of arms to that country.

Before World War II, U.S. secretaries of state infrequently traveled abroad. Since the war, on-the-spot negotiations by a secretary of state are routine. The most-traveled secretaries of state have been John Foster Dulles and Henry Kissinger, but all postwar secretaries frequently have negotiated with their counterparts abroad. Kissinger, both as national security adviser and secretary of state, spent so much time in the Middle East that he introduced a new style of diplomacy—shuttle diplomacy—as he shifted from one capital to another in search of solutions to Middle Eastern problems. Use is also made of lesser officials in the State Department for overseas negotiations, and special negotiators are appointed to carry on major negotiations such as those concerning arms reduction or trade. SALT I and SALT II were negotiated by specially appointed ambassadors from both the United States and the Soviet Union, just as were the Helsinki Agreements, the Limited Nuclear Test Ban, and the Nonproliferation Treaty. U.S. negotiators of the Panama Canal Treaties were several specially appointed ambassadors; the last of these was Ellsworth Bunker, who had a reputation for being an excellent troubleshooter and was given several such special negotiating assignments. In all of these instances, the regular ambassadors to the countries involved in the negotiations played a relatively minor role.

The post–World War II style of diplomacy also includes heads of state meeting together more frequently than in the past, which has further diminished the negotiating role of the ambassador and his staff. While the observation has frequently been made that use of diplomacy has declined since World War II, a more accurate assessment is that diplomacy has changed but is no less a part of the system than it ever was.

The declining role of ambassadors as negotiators has led to the suggestion that embassies may be obsolete and the exchange of diplomats no longer necessary, particularly since many of the functions of an embassy can be carried on

through parliamentary diplomacy—the formal and informal contacts made available through membership in the United Nations and other international organizations. Whatever the UN's shortcomings, the organization is an ongoing international conference with a permanent staff, and it provides any member with the opportunity to make contact with representatives of virtually every nation in the world. This multi-lateral-embassy character of the United Nations is, however, infrequently utilized by the major states, which ordinarily use more traditional bilateral means of making contact. The smaller and less-developed nations, many of which cannot afford a widespread network of embassies, are more apt to rely on international organizations for diplomatic exchanges.

In addition to changes in the channels used for diplomatic contact, diplomacy has also changed in the degree to which it is open to public scrutiny. The old, or pre–World War I, diplomacy had several characteristics, but secrecy was the aspect of that form of diplomacy advocates look back on with the greatest nostalgia.

In the nineteenth and early-twentieth centuries, professional diplomats negotiated many international agreements in secret, and often the agreements themselves were kept secret unless

Tab. 9.1 Post–World War II U.S.–Soviet Summit Conferences

Principal Participants	Location	Date
Eisenhower–Khrushchev	Geneva	July, 1955
Eisenhower–Khrushchev	Washington (Camp David)	Sept., 1959
Kennedy–Khrushchev	Vienna	June, 1961
Johnson–Kosygin	Glassboro, New Jersey	May, 1967
Nixon–Brezhnev	Moscow	May, 1972
Nixon–Brezhnev	Washington	June, 1973
Ford–Brezhnev	Vladivostok	Nov., 1974
Carter–Brezhnev	Geneva	June, 1979
Reagan–Gorbachev	Geneva	Nov., 1985
Reagan–Gorbachev	Reykjavik	Oct., 1986

their implementation forced them to be made public. Even among the European democracies, there was no sense of obligation to keep the press or the public informed concerning diplomatic matters. Harold Nicolson, a British diplomat, summarized this period of diplomacy as follows: "Such, therefore, were some of the distinctive characteristics of the old diplomacy—the conception of Europe as a centre of international gravity; the idea that the Great Powers, constituting the Concert of Europe, were more important and more responsible than the Small Powers; the existence in every country of a trained diplomatic service possessing common standards of professional conduct; and the assumption that negotiation must always be a process rather than an episode, and that at every stage it must remain confidential" (Nicolson, 1955, 74). This style of diplomacy is still defended by many today on the grounds that the public is incapable of understanding diplomatic maneuvering and that negotiations make more progress when the public is not kibitzing.

An early vigorous attack on secrecy in diplomacy came from President Woodrow Wilson, who saw it as inconsistent with democratic principles. Following World War I, secret diplomacy fell into disrepute when wartime agreements made among the European allies allocating war spoils became public due to the Soviets' revealing the contents of czarist Russia's archives. The new, open diplomacy was characterized by Wilson's well-known phrase, "open covenents, openly arrived at." This was a plea not only for no more secret agreements, but also for no more secret negotiations. Nor was the new diplomacy restricted to professional diplomats. Heads of state and other political leaders began to take a more direct part in the diplomatic process, and the creation of the League of Nations introduced multilateral contacts on a greater scale than before. The international system also experienced more in the way of informal diplomatic contacts between nations. In effect, the new diplomacy was an extension into the international system

of domestic democratic principles, but it also was a product of improved methods of telecommunication. Remarks made by a head of state or a foreign minister at a news conference, messages sent by an American president to Congress, or a speech by any high government official could be used to bypass traditional diplomatic channels when the intention was to "send a message." Secretary of State Marshall's announcement of the Marshall Plan during his 1947 commencement address at Harvard, Khrushchev's impromptu news conference in Paris in May 1960 after the Paris summit conference was canceled, the use of an American television reporter to serve as an intermediary with the Soviets during the Cuban missile crisis, and President Reagan's use of news conferences to announce foreign policy decisions are all examples of diplomacy by informal and nontraditional means.

The degree to which diplomatic negotiations are known to national publics under the new diplomacy fall somewhat short of full disclosure, however. The process is more open in the sense that the public is generally aware when important negotiations are taking place; also, the end result of the negotiations is usually made public. However, the actual bargaining process does not become a part of the public record now any more than it did under the old diplomacy. Heads of state meet with great public fanfare, as observed in the several meetings between American presidents and Soviet leaders since World War II, but the conversations between them are confidential. Wilson's phrase could be more accurately stated as "open covenants, most of the time, arrived at through closed negotiations, although generally not secretly held."

In this environment of new diplomacy in which ambassadors and their embassy staffs are frequently bypassed by higher ranking diplomats or in which contact is made through international organizations rather than an embassy, embassies might indeed be obsolete if it were not for the important duties they perform that often relate to negotiations. Minimally, the ambassador and his staff provide their country with a symbolic presence at formal receptions, are active in the diplomatic corps, and hold a reception on their nation's independence day. They also attend such ceremonial events as the celebration of the host nation's independence day, state funerals, and the opening of the host nation's legislative body, if it has one. Such activities are the diplomatic equivalent of "showing the flag" and unfortunately are what many laypeople see as the limit of a diplomat's activity. These ceremonial and social occasions are not without benefit, however, in that they often allow diplomats to communicate with each other and members of the host government on a more relaxed level than do contacts through formal channels. This sort of activity, in itself, is regarded by many nations as sufficiently important that they provide their ambassadors with sizeable entertainment budgets.

The United States, perhaps because of its diplomatic egalitarian tradition, has never provided adequate budgets for American ambassadors to meet their social obligations in the major capitals where such demands are greatest. Since few professional diplomats can afford to provide personal funds to make up the shortfall in their entertainment budgets, persons appointed to major posts are usually wealthy contributors to the president's campaign fund. The ambassadorship from the United States to Great Britain traditionally has been such an appointment. Since the Soviet post is so important and sensitive, it has been filled with a career diplomat, however. While it varies from one administration to another, about one-fourth to two-fifths of all U.S. ambassadors are political, as opposed to professional, appointees. During the Carter administration, the number of political appointees fell below one-fourth, but about two-fifths of Reagan's ambassadorial appointments were political.

The representative function of an embassy, of course, includes other than ceremonial and social aspects. A diplomat has the duty to establish a relationship with the host government essentially for two reasons. The first is to provide him or her with the contacts through which he or she can make his nation's interests known to the host government. Since the host government is aware of this, one means it has of showing disfavor with an ambassador's country is to never be available for appointments and to avoid contact even at social functions. Without such contacts, a diplomat cannot, of course, be effective. While major negotiations rarely include the ambassador in present-day diplomacy, day-to-day routine negotiation of differences is carried out by the ambassador; thus, establishing a good working relationship with the host government is important. Although there is no means of estimating how many minor disputes an embassy staff resolves that might otherwise become major conflicts, the amount of such negotiation is significant.

The second reason for maintaining contact with the host government is to carry out the important function of keeping track of what is going on in the host nation. Earlier, during the discussion of international images, the point was made that a major source of information on which images are based comes from embassy staffs in foreign capitals. Information such as whether the government is stable, which party is likely to win the next election, or which persons are in favor or disfavor can be provided by the embassy. The military attachés can report on the readiness of the host nation's armed forces. The agricultural attaché can report on how well the grain harvest went or if bad weather threatens a future crop. The state of the host country's economy can be followed by the economic officers in the embassy. The gathering of such information is not considered to be spying, since it is collected by diplomats trained to interpret what is around them and what they learn by having good contacts in the host government. Also important are contacts outside the government such as those with political opposition leaders, local news reporters, and leading business people. Since the embassy's negotiating function is much more limited today than it once was, messages sent home currently are its principal means of influencing policy. When Iranian revolutionaries seized the American embassy, they charged that the embassy was a "nest of spies" and produced captured documents in support of their accusation. What was revealed by those documents was essentially what would normally be found in an embassy's files concerning conditions in Iran at the time.

When writing their memoirs, diplomats often complain that the advice they sent home was not followed or, worse yet, seemingly ignored; but to the decision-making units at home, the embassy is only one source of information. The at-home decision-makers feel, since they have more sources of information than does the embassy, that they take a broader perspective of policy. In addition, they tend to see the embassy as identifying too closely with the country in which it is located. This attitude stems from the limitations that are unavoidably placed on an embassy's activities. The embassy is dealing with a single country on a continuing basis and is in no position to possess the broad range of information available to decision-makers at home. The recommendations an ambassador makes may be a most reasonable solution to a problem with the host government, but his or her solution could cause problems with other countries about which he or she knows little. Another factor is that the reputations of ambassadors differ depending on the reliability of their reports. Ambassadors with reputations for dependability obviously will be paid greater heed when decisions are made than will those with reputations for being unreliable. Yet another limiting factor on the influence of an embassy's reports is who receives the information and recommendations it sends home. In the United States, information goes to the country desk officer, the lowest level of administrative structure in the State Department, but if not passed up through the decision-making structure, the embassy's perspective cannot be considered.

Another responsibility of diplomats is to protect their countries' citizens and, if they have problems with the local law, see that those citizens

Fig. 9.1 U.S. Noncareer Ambassadorial Appointments

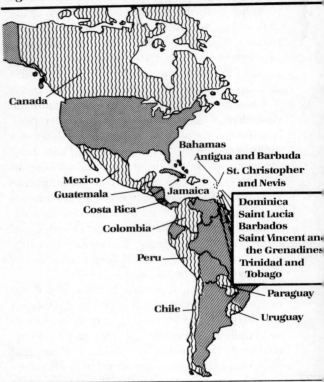

SOURCE: Christian Science Monitor
November 29, 1984, p.3

are accorded the rights guaranteed them under international law. The embassy is to see that they receive a fair trial and, if convicted, that they do not receive unusual punishment. U.S. diplomats have, on occasion, been criticized for the manner in which they carry out this function, but since the standard of justice in other countries is often inferior to that found in the United States, the legal protections American citizens receive may meet the standards of local or even international law but not those of the United States. The embassy also is available to those who lose their passports or are robbed and need emergency assistance. The embassy helps business people from its country make contact with

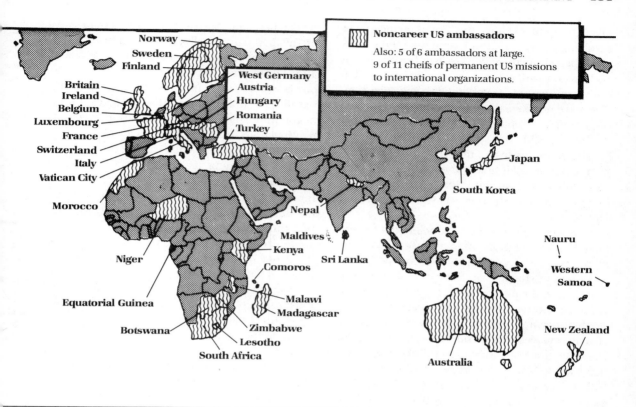

Norway
Sweden
Finland

Britain
Ireland
Belgium
Luxembourg
France
Switzerland
Italy
Vatican City

Morocco

Niger

Equatorial Guinea

Botswana

Lesotho

South Africa

West Germany
Austria
Hungary
Romania
Turkey

Nepal

Maldives
Kenya
Comoros

Sri Lanka

Malawi
Madagascar
Zimbabwe

Australia

Japan

South Korea

Nauru

Western
Samoa

New Zealand

Noncareer US ambassadors
Also: 5 of 6 ambassadors at large.
9 of 11 cheifs of permanent US missions
to international organizations.

those with whom they hope to carry on trade.

Thus, even if the embassies now are seldom directly involved in major negotiations, they do serve important functions in symbolic representation, the presentation of interests, minor negotiations, the gathering of information, recommendation of policy, and the protection of their citizens in the host country.

DIPLOMACY AS BARGAINING

One scholar of international politics has observed that there are five functions of diplomacy: 1) conflict management; 2) solving problems between nations; 3) improving communication between governments concerning issues; 4) negotiation of international agreements; and 5) overall program management (Poullada, 1974, 194–202.) While negotiation is listed as only one function of diplomacy, all of the others involve the use of negotiation in performing those functions. Thus, whatever the diplomatic activity, negotiations are centrally involved.

Negotiations between nations involving major conflicts ordinarily take what seems to the outside observer an inordinately long time, but the reason for protracted negotiation is that more than a solution to a problem is at stake. It not only takes time to explore the possible means of resolving a conflict; at the same time the means must be found to maximize the fulfillment of each nation's interests. To accomplish these dual objectives, nations negotiate with great caution. The bargaining process goes through various stages, and each party must in the end feel that the best possible bargain was obtained in order for it to stand the test of time. No negotiated bargain is successful if one of the parties feels that, had it only tried harder, a better solution—one in which more of its interests were met—could have been found.

When an agreement is concluded through negotiation the public often assesses the agreement in terms of which party "won." Who won or gained the most from the agreement usually depends on the perspective of those making the judgment; few international agreements are straightforward victories in which one party clearly receives more from the agreement than does the other. An exception to this generalization was the Munich Agreement negotiated among Hitler, Chamberlain, and Daladier in September 1938 which granted Germany the Sudetenland portion of Czechoslovakia. This agreement has become synonymous with appeasement; that is, the concessions made by Chamberlain and Daladier were not balanced by concessions on Hitler's part. Since Hitler received all that he wanted and the others gained nothing but delay in the start of World War II, history has judged it to be a bad agreement. Diplomats and national leaders remember the lessons of the Munich Agreement well and any agreement that is labelled appeasement is doomed to failure. Most international agreements, however, are close victories in which one party gains only a narrow margin over the other, or both parties conclude that the benefits are about equal. Unless a nation is under a realistic threat of military or economic sanctions or unless a nation has just lost a war to the country with which it is negotiating, there is no reason, other than bad judgment, for any nation to enter into a disadvantageous agreement.

The bargaining process is further complicated by the fact that, actually, two sets of negotiations are going on at the same time. One set of negotiations takes place between the nations involved, but a second set of negotiations is progressing within the domestic political systems of the negotiating nations. The domestic decision-making units must bargain away their differences as to what they will accept from the international bargaining. If a bargain is not acceptable to the domestic political system, then no matter how well the international negotiations progress the domestic system will have effectively nullified those negotiations.

If negotiators arrive at an international agreement not immediately acceptable to major domestic decision-making units, the head of state, if he or she wants the agreement to be approved, must then enter into a second round of negotiations, this time with the noncomplying bureaucratic units. If, in the United States, the State Department cannot convince the Defense Department that a particular defense agreement is in the U.S. interest, the agreement will fail. If the Senate does not approve of a treaty or the Congress refuses to pass implementing legislation for a treaty, the agreement will fail. Thus, while bargaining with another country, negotiators must bargain within the context of what is acceptable to the domestic system. This complex process takes time and care.

Negotiations thus must go through several stages, both at the domestic and the international levels, before a bargain can be struck. The first stage is for a nation to make the domestic decision that negotiations serve its best interest. Such decisions had to be made in both the United States and the Soviet Union prior to the resumption of arms control talks in March 1985. This domestic decision often parallels quiet, if not secret, contact between the potential negotiators. Preliminary talks serve several purposes. They may be held in order for one nation to persuade another that negotiations are desirable for both, or to avoid the appearance that one nation is seeking negotiations which, if publicly known, could be interpreted as a sign of weakness. The preliminary talks may also be a probing action between potential negotiators to find out if all parties are committed to good-faith bargaining. This initial probing can be accomplished through clandestine meetings, through third parties who serve as intermediaries, through the hallway diplomacy offered in international organizations, or through quiet contact by means of traditional bilateral channels. Whatever the means, the purpose is to avoid a commitment to negotiations until evidence exists that substantive talks are potentially worthwhile.

An example of this sort of secret negotiation—to find out if more substantive negotiations were possible—was Kissinger's visit to Beijing preceding Nixon's first visit to China in February 1972. Kissinger, while visiting Pakistan, was reported to be ill and to have gone to a mountain resort to recuperate; he was, in fact, in China negotiating arrangements for Nixon's visit. Elaborate efforts were made to maintain the secrecy of his mission. To have handled the matter openly would have made it difficult for either country to cancel Nixon's visit if preliminary talks were not successful.

Preliminary talks also provide an opportunity to avoid entering into negotiations that the other party will use for other than conflict management. Nations may use negotiations only for propaganda purposes—to indicate that they are the party seeking a settlement—when they have no intention of arriving at an agreement. Since all publicized negotiations are exploited to some extent for propaganda purposes, negotiators have the difficult task of assessing whether propaganda is the primary or only secondary reason for negotiating. Negotiations also can be used to mislead another nation into a false sense of improved relations in order to catch it off guard militarily or diplomatically. Possibly, the objective of negotiations is simply to gain information that would otherwise not be available. The latter is a charge the Soviets have made concerning

arms control talks: that the United States uses the talks to learn the specifics of the Soviet strategic arsenal. A nation may also agree to negotiations only because to refuse to do so would project a bad image to the international system. Both the United States and the Soviet Union find themselves in this situation when one challenges the other to negotiate strategic arms control or troop reductions in Europe. Neither can reject at least discussing the other's offer without suffering image problems.

Nations must also be cautious about entering into negotiations with another country because of the impact those negotiations will have on nations other than the one being negotiated with. Two recent examples illustrate this. After the development of détente in the early 1970s, the United States had to be cautious about how close a relationship it developed with either the Soviet Union or China. If the United States seemed to be drawing too close to one of the communist states, the other felt that a powerful alignment was being formed against it. Thus, in the present alignment among these three nations, Sino-U.S. negotiations always have an impact on U.S.-Soviet relations, just as negotiations between the United States and the Soviet Union can cause China to feel threatened. Consequently, the United States has to provide a balance when improving relations with either of the two major communist states. The second example is Egypt's negotiating position when it set out in 1977 to improve relations with Israel. Egypt knew that its relationship with other Arab states would be affected adversely; thus, Egypt had to negotiate cautiously in order to minimize the damage. Following the negotiations, for a time Egypt was isolated from the rest of the Arab world until, particularly after Sadat's death, the more conservative Arab states reestablished contact with Egypt.

As one would expect, the problems associated with opening negotiations ordinarily are greater between nations with a history of conflict than between nations with a relatively peaceful past. This is especially the case when there are no precedents for the participants, as occurred in the negotiations that led to the ending of both the Korean War and the Vietnam War. The Korean War was a collective security action in which aggressor nations, theoretically, were to suffer the effects of overwhelming power being brought to bear upon them by an international organization; they were to be crushed, not negotiated with. The Vietnam War presented the problem of the United States' negotiating with North Vietnam, which claimed it had no troops involved in the fighting and which was a nation the United States did not recognize, and the Viet Cong, which was not a nation but an insurgency group negotiating through its political arm, the National Liberation Front.

The Korean War lasted three years, but the final two years were a military stalemate while negotiations to end the war took place. The forces in the south were under United Nations command; never before had this type of military force been assembled. The UN command included South Korean forces, but the overwhelming non-Korean force was U.S., and the UN commander was American. The forces in the north were North Korean and Chinese. Since North Korea was initially labeled the aggressor by the United Nations (China was so labeled later), and since China claimed that its forces in Korea were volunteers, the formal parties in the negotiations were North Korea and the United Nations. The parties dominating the negotiations, however, were the United States and China. Thus, technically, the negotiations were between an international organization and a nonmember (North Korea) of that organization. Since the negotiations had no precedents, procedure and status were often in dispute, an example of which was North Korea's insistence that the talks be held in the small sliver of South Korean territory that North Korea occupied. The negotiations were marked by numerous incidents, some almost childish, on the part of the communist negotiators in their efforts to gain status. Each day's battlefield developments were used by the parties as

negotiating points. The talks eventually resulted in a cease-fire (still in effect in the late 1980s), after President Eisenhower notified the communist forces that the United States would consider the use of nuclear weapons in Korea if the talks did not result in an end to the war.

As with the Korean War, the location of the talks to end the Vietnam War was a problem, but in this instance negotiations took place far away from the battlefield. Each party submitted a list of possible locations for the talks, and each rejected the other's list. A compromise between the parties resulted in an agreement to hold the talks in Paris, the logical location because of France's past experience in Vietnam, but a location not on either party's initial list. The impression left was that if either party had placed Paris on its original list and the other had not, the party that did not include Paris would have been compelled to reject the location. When neither party included Paris on its original list, a compromise was possible.

After agreement on location, the talks were delayed for weeks over discussion of the shape of the table around which the negotiations would take place. Squabbling over the shape of the table was widely ridiculed in the media at the time, but the issue was symbolic of a more meaningful issue that had to be resolved before negotiations could progress. The North Vietnamese and the National Liberation Front wanted a table with four sides that would indicate there were four parties to the negotiations—the two of them and the United States and South Vietnam. The United States wanted a table that indicated a two-sided negotiating situation, with the United States and South Vietnam on one side and North Vietnam and the National Liberation Front on the other. The United States did not recognize the National Liberation Front as a legitimate representative and wanted to deal with it only through the North Vietnamese. Actually, more than one table was involved, as the location of two side tables that would separate the negotiators was also a part of the discussion. Ultimately, an arrangement of the tables acceptable to all parties was arrived at, and the talks began. The talks started in 1968 and were not concluded until January 1973. When the talks began to make progress in late 1972, ironically, the negotiations were then limited to talks between the American negotiator, Henry Kissinger, and the North Vietnamese negotiator, Le Duc Tho. Both the National Liberation Front and the South Vietnamese government complained of being bypassed in this arrangement.

Negotiations to end a stalemated war are perhaps the most difficult sort of negotiation to conclude successfully. When enemies are present at the negotiating table and no one has established a clear military advantage, negotiations can go on for years until one party, for whatever reason, concludes that ending the war is preferable to stalemate. This was the case in both Korea and Vietnam, just as in the negotiations between Egypt and Israel. "Peace feelers" are sent out by first one party and then another for months before negotiations begin. Decisions concerning the location of the talks, the parties that will participate in the talks, and overall points of negotiation can require an additional lengthy period before discussion of a peace settlement even begins.

Location can be an important factor in other sorts of negotiations as well. Talks between the United States and the Soviet Union often take place in Geneva, recognized by both parties as neutral ground. When the negotiation of arms talks have not been successful there, other locations have been used such as Vienna and Helsinki. Appearance is important in bargaining, and the impression that neither party has gone to the other to negotiate a bargain is critical; thus the need for an agreed-upon neutral place to negotiate.

In less hostile relationships, preliminary maneuvering and arguments over location are largely avoided, and the process of setting up the negotiations takes far less time. Negotiations between friendly countries can be long-term,

however, as the United States has learned when negotiating with the European Community concerning tariff reductions; but when friendly nations are negotiating, much more time is spent on substantive issues than on procedural ones.

THE BARGAINING PROCESS

The discussion of bargaining thus far has concerned the activities that lead up to the negotiation of substantive issues. What happens in the bargaining process when substantive issues are discussed is another matter. As mentioned earlier, aspects of the diplomatic process are conducted publicly; ordinarily, the public knows that negotiations are going on, knows who is participating in the talks, and knows the general issues being discussed. Occasionally, the positions of the negotiating parties are known, but only in a general sense. What is seldom known at the time the negotiations are underway is how the bargaining takes place and what offers and counteroffers are being made. In the course of bargaining, offers may be made that deliberately overstate or understate the position a negotiator is taking; the use of exaggeration, particularly in the beginning stages of bargaining, is a common tactic. It may be used to prompt the other side to make concessions, but the strategy underlying those offers might not be understood by observers who are not diplomats. If every offer made in negotiations were subject to public review, the negotiators would find it difficult to change their position as the talks progressed. The essence of the bargaining process is to encourage negotiators to alter their offers until a solution can be found, and public review of each negotiating position could so limit flexibility that a stalemate would result.

The question remains, however, as to the nature of bargaining, since bargaining can be described in different ways. One approach is to compare it to a debate between the negotiating parties during which each presents its argument and attempts to persuade the other to accept its position. Bargaining certainly has aspects of a debate, especially in the early stages when the parties are establishing their positions, and particularly if the conflict being discussed is based on misunderstandings which can best be resolved by face-to-face contact (Burton, 1972, 5–29). This method of negotiation—alleviating misunderstandings— is perhaps the easiest form of bargaining; but in most instances, after positions have been revealed, misunderstandings eliminated, and interests explained, what has been clarified is that the negotiating parties have a conflict that must be bargained further. Conflict usually is not simply a misunderstanding, but a result of differing policy objectives among the negotiating parties. One note of caution, however, is that radical governments often find it necessary to introduce a good deal of revolutionary rhetoric before settling down to serious negotiation. Radical Third World governments often use this approach, as does the Soviet Union on occasion. Negotiations usually progress more effectively if such rhetoric is ignored by the other parties.

If bargaining can be compared to a debate, it also has aspects of a game—in some instances a zero-sum game and others a nonzero-sum game. The Munich Agreement is an example of a negotiating zero-sum game in that German gains were French and British losses. A nonzero-sum, or variable-sum, game is more typical of diplomatic bargaining, however, because that sort of game allows for situations where negotiating parties can gain without anyone suffering compensating losses. The playing of any type of diplomatic game involves the use of threats, promises, rewards, and sanctions—military or economic—in an attempt to bring the other side around to a desired position. If these tools are used by the negotiating parties, they must be credible. If the promise of economic aid is offered, the nation making the offer must be able and willing to subsequently grant the assistance. The United States

offered Israel and Egypt military and economic aid in exchange for a peace treaty between those two countries. If the United States offer had not been credible the negotiations would never have succeeded. If the United States had made the offer and then after a time withdrew the aid, future offers of aid in negotiations would not have been credible. If a country threatens military sanctions, it must be willing to carry them out. This is an aspect of the often-cited argument of Clausewitz—that war is diplomacy by other means.

An instance in which a threat was not credible, therefore ineffective, was Khrushchev's threat to sign a peace treaty with East Germany if the West did not make certain concessions. Since all agreements concerning West Berlin were between the United States and the Soviet Union, an East German–Soviet peace treaty would mean the Western powers would either have to withdraw from West Berlin or be forced to negotiate with East Germany—a country they did not recognize—concerning access to the city. The threat was made three times between 1958 and 1962, with a deadline given each time. On each occasion, the deadline passed without a peace treaty.

Sanctions do not necessarily have to be stated in order to exert an impact on negotiations. When the superpowers negotiate with less-powerful nations, the military capabilities each possesses need not be mentioned in order to become an implied aspect of the bargaining. The economic assistance the United States is capable of granting a nation is always apparent even if not stated. Thus, negotiations that appear to be based purely on the persuasion of the arguments can never be totally free of such implications.

Negotiations are heavily dependent on timing. Obviously, timing is important at the start of negotiations, since no discussion can take place until all parties are seriously ready for them. A conflict situation can exist for many years before the nations involved conclude that the "time is right" to negotiate. As the negotiations progress, timing is important as to when proposals will be introduced. If the negotiations are moving slowly, when is the right time to make a "last" offer or to propose a recess in the talks in the hope that at a later date some flexibility will be introduced into the talks? When is a recess appropriate so that the home governments can review and revise their proposals without the pressure of negotiations in progress? All major negotiations between the United States and the Soviet Union have included several recesses.

Another kind of timing is important as well— timing in the sense of patience exhibited by a nation during protracted negotiations. In negotiating with the Soviet Union, the United States must have "staying power" to match that of the Soviets. Timing is also important in threatening to break off negotiations if further progress is not made. How committed is the other party to the position it has taken? Will it change its position in order to prevent the talks from collapsing? Timing is also involved in deciding when a nation should change its chief negotiator or, possibly, the entire negotiating team. Individual negotiators may weary of their assignment, and a replacement thus may bring a new perspective and enthusiasm to the talks.

Timing is also involved in the decision to set time limits on talks which are not progressing and then to adjourn *sine die.* Imposing a deadline on negotiations may break a stalemate in order to avoid failure, but, once imposed, a deadline is difficult to extend and could cut off negotiations prematurely. An example of a proposed deadline leading to the successful negotiation of an agreement occurred during the SALT I talks. Discussions had been underway for several years when, in early 1972, a visit by President Nixon to the Soviet Union was announced. Since Nixon and Brezhnev wanted to sign the agreement while Nixon was in Moscow, a deadline was imposed on the negotiators. Even though they were still negotiating while on the airplane as they brought the agreement to Moscow, the agreement was concluded in time. Timing is a

factor in the decision to split an issue. If negotiation of a total package proves to be impossible, when is it appropriate to divide the conflict so that at least some portion of it can be resolved? Until the late 1950s, the United States and the Soviet Union negotiated comprehensive arms control agreements. When agreement on such a plan was not forthcoming, the overall issue was broken down into negotiations on testing, nonproliferation, and strategic weapons, a split that proved successful. The issues blocking the negotiation of a comprehensive plan were thus bypassed. These limited agreements are often criticized for not doing more, but they are, in the minds of the negotiators, the alternative to doing nothing. Kissinger's negotiation of Middle Eastern problems were criticized on the same grounds. When Kissinger became aware that an overall settlement was not possible, he split the problem of Arab-Israeli relations and negotiated those parts possible to negotiate.

Explaining to the domestic political system the bargain that is concluded also involves timing. The United States is unlikely to conclude a major international agreement in the midst of a presidential election campaign. Once the American political system becomes preoccupied with an election, there is little interest in external matters. During the 1976 presidential campaign Panama insisted that negotiating sessions on the Panama Canal treaties be held. The United States agreed to the request but no progress was made, and the sessions were shorter than usual. After the election was over and Carter was in office, the timing was then right, and the treaties were concluded in August 1977. An equivalent period of international disinterest on the part of the Soviet Union occurs when its national leader is ill or when there has been a recent change in leadership.

One further observation should be made concerning the contribution of bargaining to international conflict management. Negotiations are not necessarily a failure if they do not produce an agreement. When nations are engaged in negotiations, there ordinarily exists a hope that a bargain can be struck. While this attitude of optimism exists, the chances of a conflict escalating are certainly lessened compared with what might occur in the absence of negotiations. If of no other value, negotiations provide a "cooling off" period and a time for evaluation. Even when the search for a common ground on which to base an agreement results in nothing more than the discovery that there is no commonality, such a result has at least clarified the range of conflict.

CONLUSION

Diplomacy is a complex process requiring time and patience. It is often viewed by national pub-

lics as slow and unnecessarily secretive, but deliberation and confidentiality are essential to successful negotiations. International law provides considerable protection and process to diplomacy in order to guarantee that extraneous matters do not interfere—protections that are generally adhered to throughout the international system. Diplomacy can be exercised in many forums ranging from the United Nations to informal contacts through third parties. But whatever the arrangement, it is the principal means by which nations communicate with one another and thus is necessary and well-established in international relations.

CHAPTER 10

Surprise and Crisis

The subjects of this chapter—surprise and crisis—are special situations that arise in the international system that do not fit accepted, routine, and anticipated behavior patterns of the system. While they often occur in the same time frame, the terms are not synonymous. A surprise can occur in the system without a resulting crisis, and a crisis can develop over an extended period of time and therefore not be a surprise. Nevertheless, many crises do come as a surprise, just as many crises follow a surprising event. Thus, of the examples discussed in this chapter, some will illustrate surprise, others crisis, and still others will illustrate both.

The last chapter discussed diplomacy and the next chapter discusses the use of force. A discussion of surprise and crisis is taken up at this time because either surprise or crisis can place extraordinary demands on the diplomatic process and often introduce a special form of diplomacy—crisis management. Also, since many surprises involve the unexpected use of force, a discussion of surprise and crisis is appropriate to either a discussion of diplomacy or a discussion of the use of force.

Crisis diplomacy differs from normal diplomatic relations in that a nation's decision-makers usually must make decisions quickly and the results of a bad decision are perceived of as immediate and serious; the luxury of extended deliberation is lost. If a poor decision is made, the opportunities to recover from that decision are much more limited in crisis situations. In short, a crisis is seen by decision-makers as a period of high threat with increased time constraints. Surprise, since it does not necessarily involve a crisis, is an unexpected event that may or may not intensify conflict, but coupled with crisis, which is a period of increased conflict, produces periods of highest tension in international relations.

Regardless of whether a crisis is a surprise or not, it is a crisis because it runs counter to the current arrangement of the international system (Morrow, 1986, 1131). For the nation or nations that carry out a specific action which results in a crisis, the purpose for the action is to bring about a change in the international system that is to their advantage, not necessarily to produce a crisis (Young, 1968, 63–69). For the nation or nations that feel threatened by that action, a crisis exists because they have temporarily lost control of at least a portion of their foreign policies. Thus, crises ordinarily are the result of some nations' attempting to fulfill a policy objective of which a crisis can be an unintended byproduct; crisis results when other nations react in opposition to that action.

Too often when surprise and crisis are discussed examples are limited to those instances involving military action—a declaration of war, an invasion, or a threat of military activity. An international economic crisis can have an equally devastating effect on the system, and a major source of surprise can be an unexpected diplomatic initiative that involves neither military nor economic aspects. The important characteristic of both surprise and crisis is their disruption of the system, not the particular instrument of power used to accomplish this.

Military crises, however, are the events that are most apt to gain the world's attention. No doubt this is because the use or potential use of violence within the system carries with it the possibility of death and destruction, whereas other sorts of crises usually do not. A possible second reason for the emphasis on military activity is that it is easier for the news media to report military activity since such activity is calculated and highly visual. Economic crises are more complicated, thus more difficult to report, and are more apt to result from a lack of planning or from poor planning than from an intentional act. The visual aspects involved in reporting economic events are usually limited to graphs or percentages of growth or decline. Diplomatic surprises and crises are even less visual and often are presented on television by a reporter reading a script explaining the development. The news media, however, is not alone in its emphasis on military surprises and crises. Scholars also tend to devote more attention to military than economic and diplomatic surprises and crises. This is probably because military operations produce a more immediate change in the international system than do other sources of crisis and surprise; as in news reporting, they are the more apparently dramatic events of the system.

A crisis may also produce at least a temporary change in a nation's decision-making process. Rather than using routine channels of decision-making which may be too slow for the occasion, special units often are established to speed up the process. How decision-makers manage a crisis is perhaps the most critical form of decision-making for a nation. During a crisis, decision-makers' minimal objectives are to develop a counterstrategy that will avoid the use of force and protect that nation's interests; crisis management thus is essentially damage control. At best, the counterstrategy will produce a diplomatic or military victory.

In an earlier chapter in which images were discussed a central theme concerned the importance of images that nations develop of themselves and of others. As long as diplomatic relations between two nations function on a routine basis and events generally fit into the images that each holds of the other, serious problems do not develop even if the respective images are not altered to fit new information. When an important event does not fit those images, it produces at least surprise, if not crisis. How decision-makers adjust to this challenge to their images is an important aspect of crisis management. A crisis or surprise does not necessarily force decision-makers to change their images, however. The event may fit their images, but be a surprise only in the timing of its occurrence.

Surprise is accurately described as an unexpected event, but surprise is a relative term in that it seldom indicates total lack of anticipation. In the instance of military surprise, "There is always some warning. . . . Pure bolts-from-the-blue hardly ever occur. Sudden attacks happen after prolonged political conflict. They often do not occur at the peak of tension, but they are usually preceded by periods in which the defender's leaders believe that war is possible. And they often follow a number of false alarms" (Betts, 1980, 571–572). In retrospect, warning signs were usually there, but for various reasons were misinterpreted. Because of this, after virtually all surprises, revisionists will argue that a surprise should not have been a surprise. Closely akin to this sort of reassessment by hindsight is that, since many alternatives are debated during crisis decision-making, someone is invariably in the position of having offered an alternative that, if followed, might have prevented the surprise or avoided the crisis. After the event, that decision-maker can say "I told you so."

An organizational failure somewhere in the decision-making process often is another important reason an event produces a surprise. A surprise, after all, is an attempt to change the system in some way, and since it runs counter to accepted images and patterns of behavior, if decision-makers interpret events only within the context of what is normal, a surprise can be used against them successfully. Not to alter images, that is, to reject the possibility of surprise, is a serious error in decision-making.

Ordinarily, misleading images come from two sources. The first is that the information or intelligence that is the basis of the image is wrong, thus producing an image that does not allow for the events that take place. A second source of a misleading image is that the intelligence is correct, but decision-makers are so wedded to a particular perspective that they cannot alter it to fit new information. The Vietnam War presents several instances of this flaw in decision-making. Information designed to please decision-makers can be particularly harmful, since it reinforces misconceptions rather than challenges them.

Intelligence-gatherers also can err by being too deliberate in their collection of information, and insisting on too much confirmation before passing it along to decision-makers. The gathering of intelligence rarely comes from a single or all-revealing source, but rather results from many sources and consists of many bits of information that must be interpreted and verified. This process takes time and may not be completed soon enough to give adequate warning of surprise. On the other hand, intelligence agencies can pass along information that has not been sufficiently verified and in that way mislead decision-makers.

The failure to anticipate surprises and crises can also be attributed to an overall organizational failing. The pressure of responding to day-to-day events can consume all the time of decision-makers and thus prevent them from analyzing the general direction those events are taking. Such preoccupation with specific events can lead to overlooking a pending surprise that could otherwise have been anticipated. A closely related problem is the overall effect of frequent crises on decision-makers. A frequently made observation about decision-making in the United States during the intense years of the Cold War was that crises were so frequent that being in a state of crisis had become the normal environment for policy-making. When a state of crisis becomes normal, decision-makers will treat crisis management little differently than routine decision-making; thus they may lose their ability to distinguish between what is serious and what is routine.

Even without the above-mentioned organizational failures, surprise events are difficult to predict or react to in time. Although most surprises have warnings, many warnings prove to be false; thus, a valid warning, when it comes, is less apt to be taken seriously. Since the attacker controls the timing of attack, if the defender takes a warning seriously and is prepared, the attacker can postpone the surprise. The warning was valid, but since no attack took place, subsequent warnings, due to alert fatigue, are likely not to be taken as seriously as previous ones. Intelligence reports predicting the surprise are correct, and the decision-makers take the right action, but the result may be to make the attack more successful when it does come. Repeated warnings tend to cause those in command to become skeptical about the seriousness of the situation (Betts, 1980, 557).

Thus, with respect to surprise and crisis in international politics, an event can be viewed as a crisis, a surprise, or both. A crisis or surprise can be the product of military, economic, or diplomatic developments or any combination of these. During a crisis, nations often adopt an ad hoc decision-making process. Images are often affected by surprise and crisis, but distortions in images are usually the product of poor intelligence-gathering or inappropriate use of intelligence by decision-makers. An international surprise often comes after warnings have been given, but, for various reasons, are not heeded. Surprise, particularly military surprise, often succeeds and thus is an attractive means of achieving a policy objective. With these general characteristics of crisis and surprise in mind, it is now appropriate to look at several major surprises and crises produced during and since World War II to see how these characteristics apply to specific cases.

SURPRISE IN WORLD WAR II

The most effective strategy in conducting a war is to surprise your enemy; thus, central to military planning is anticipating or conducting surprises. World War II produced several major military surprises, but the ones discussed here are those that brought about important changes in the alignment of nations engaged in the war. Most of those surprises were, until late in the war, instigated by the Axis powers. The surprise of Japan's invasion of China in July 1937 marked the first of the Axis nations of World War II to go to war. Germany's invasion of Poland in September 1939 resulted in the collapse of Poland and the formal beginning of World War II when France and Great Britain declared war on Germany. Even though the war had started months earlier, Germany's invasion of France and the lowland countries in May 1940 came as a surprise which resulted in their occupation and removal as belligerents. Germany's invasion of the Soviet Union in June 1941 was also a surprise and provided Great Britain with a badly needed ally. The surprise that had the greatest effect on the United States, however, was the Japanese attack on Pearl Harbor on December 7, 1941. The United States not only went to war against Japan but also declared war against the other Axis nations as well. Each of these surprises produced military crises and had important political implications as well.

None of these crises came without warning,

however. Japan began moving against China in 1931 when it occupied Manchuria, a province of China, and attacked Shanghai. Months before going to war with China in 1937, Japan increased its military pressure on the northeastern provinces of China. Political tensions preceded the attack, and Japan had already shown its willingness to exploit the military and political weakness of China, but the actual beginning of the war was a surprise. The German attack on Poland also was preceded by warning. For some time, Germany had been demanding a corridor through Polish territory to connect East Prussia with the rest of Germany. Poland rejected the German demands but indicated a willingness to negotiate the problem. The principal obstacle to launching an attack was German concern as to how the Soviets would react; before attacking Poland, Germany needed Soviet acceptance. On August 23, 1939, Germany and the Soviet Union signed the Ribbentrop-Molotov Agreement that formally was a nonaggression pact but in fact was an agreement to partition Poland. On September 1, Germany invaded Poland from the West, and, a short time later, the Soviet Union invaded from the East.

The nonaggression pact was a diplomatic surprise that allowed a subsequent military surprise which, in turn, marked the beginning of World War II. The military gains for both Germany and the Soviet Union were substantial, but Germany paid a high cost for the diplomatic surprise. Germany made the agreement without consulting with either Italy or Japan. Neglecting Italy had only short-term repercussions, but Japan was not so easily placated. At the time of the Ribbentrop-Molotov Agreement, Japan saw the Soviet Union as a greater threat than the United States. Nevertheless, Japan followed Germany's lead and signed a nonaggression pact of its own with the Soviet Union. The cost to Hitler came when he broke his pact by invading the Soviet Union in 1941 and Japan successfully resisted German efforts to bring it into the war against the Soviet Union. Both Japan and the Soviet Union honored the agreement until the closing days of the war. Following its nonaggression pact with the Soviet Union, Japan turned its expansionist efforts elsewhere—to the south, rather than to the west—which brought it into greater conflict with the United States.

There were warnings before both the diplomatic surprise (the Ribbentrop-Molotov agreement) and the military surprise (the invasion of Poland) but both were surprises for the British and French. Warnings came to both governments, but they either felt that Germany would never be able to resolve its differences with the Soviet Union, its archenemy at the time, or that the crisis between Germany and Poland was not yet at the critical point that called for military action.

When Germany invaded the Soviet Union less than two years later, in June 1941, for a time Stalin found it difficult to believe that Hitler had betrayed the nonaggression pact. Again, there were warnings before the attack, but Stalin was so wedded to the perception that he had settled his differences with Hitler that he did little to prepare for the attack. Stalin was aware of German reconnaissance flights over Soviet territory and of German troop movements, but refused to interpret those actions as a possible prelude to invasion.

The surprise in World War II that had the most profound effect on the United States was the attack on Pearl Harbor. It was an event that forty-five years later is still subject to interpretation and revisionism.

PEARL HARBOR

The attack on Pearl Harbor was perceived in the United States as an act of treachery, a stab in the back, and "a day that will live in infamy." Japanese envoys in Washington were supposed to inform Secretary of State Cordell Hull before the attack began that Japan rejected what it perceived to be a U.S. ultimatum. But because of delays in decoding the message from Japan, the envoys arrived late at the meeting, and after the attack had begun. Hull strongly expressed his outrage over the surprise attack to the Japanese envoys, but to the Japanese a military surprise was not an act of treachery; rather, it was an advantageous way of beginning a war. Japan began the Russo-Japanese War in 1904 with a surprise naval attack, and the model of that victory had become a part of Japanese naval tradition. Surprise was so essential to the Pearl Harbor operation that the Japanese commander had been instructed to withdraw if detected before he could launch his aircraft.

There were warnings before the attack. Japanese codes had been broken in 1940, and U.S. leaders thought they had a good picture of what was going on in Japan. American intelligence was aware that a massive military operation was under way, but the decoded transmissions gave no clue as to what was to be the target. U.S. commanders in Hawaii and Washington thought the target would be the Philippines, not Pearl Harbor, however. This confidence in their choice of Japanese targets was perhaps the most serious error made during the period of warnings before the attack, an example of being too committed to a particular viewpoint.

Hawaii was placed on alert twice before the attack, but the combination of anticipating the attack elsewhere and alert fatigue produced little preparation for an attack when it did take place. Much has been made of a warning issued to the commanders in Hawaii that arrived after the attack began, but if it had arrived before the attack there is little reason to believe that Pearl Harbor would have been any better prepared. The attack on the Philippines came more than eight hours after the attack on Pearl Harbor, but the Japanese attack was successful even though there had been advance preparation. The most serious charge brought by revisionists is that President Roosevelt knew that Pearl Harbor was the target, but that he had withheld warning in order to bring the United States into the war as an ally of Great Britain. This charge remains only speculation, however.

The immediate effect of the surprise attack was the loss of most of the battleships in the Pacific fleet. At the time, battleships were thought by many to be the most powerful weapons system yet developed; but as the war progressed, battleships played a minor role compared to aircraft carriers. No carriers were lost in the attack. The attack gave the United States a battle cry— "Remember Pearl Harbor!"—and a resolve to fight for the total destruction of the Japanese empire. While the attack itself was successful, the long-range effects were disastrous for Japan.

Not only did the major surprises of World War II have an important effect on the manner in which the war progressed, those surprises also had an effect on the decision-making processes of the democratic governments involved in the war. Great Britain, in effect, suspended its political party system and formed a national government with all parties included in the cabinet. In the United States, Congress did little during the war except appropriate the funds the president asked for to conduct the war. The normal legislative checks on the executive were, for all practical purposes, suspended for the duration of the war. In order to provide the centralized decision-making needed to conduct the war, both Roosevelt and Churchill became virtually wartime dictators.

SURPRISES AND CRISES OF THE COLD WAR

The advantage surprise grants the initiating nation makes it an attractive policy choice. The confrontations of the Cold War have produced many opportunities for surprises and subsequent crises, including a number that were not military. The status of West Berlin from 1948 until the early 1960s was often a point of crisis which began with the surprise Soviet blockade. None of these crises involved the use of force, although the threat of force was often present. The first military surprise of the Cold War was the Korean War. The Korean War produced two significant surprises—the attack by North Korea on South Korea on June 24–25, 1950, and the intervention of Chinese communist forces in October 1950. As seems to be the pattern with surprises, prior warnings occurred before both surprises.

The warning that North Korea was preparing an attack was dismissed by the United States on the grounds that North Korea had yet to try less direct means of unifying Korea under its leadership. Washington saw an invasion as a last-resort means for North Korea to obtain the unification of Korea, which if it came would likely be part of a general war with the Soviet Union and not a localized, limited war. This reaction points up another cause for the ineffectiveness of warnings. Often decision-makers create a scenario about how a problem will develop, and, even if there is warning, they expect the next predicted step in that scenario to occur. Invasion was not the anticipated next step. In addition, alert fatigue was a factor. Several invasion alerts had been issued, and so, when a valid warning came, South Korea did not believe it (Betts, 1982, 52–55).

After early military setbacks, the tide of war turned in favor of the United Nations forces in September 1950. As UN forces approached the 38th Parallel that marked the boundary between North Korea and South Korea, both the Soviet Union and China warned that the parallel must not be crossed. The parallel was crossed. The decision to do so was made by the United States, although other allies such as Great Britain warned against it. As UN forces moved northward toward the Yalu River, the boundary between North Korea and China, China warned the United States through the Indian ambassador in Beijing that if American forces moved any nearer the Yalu River China would intervene. Washington saw China as too weak, following the conclusion of China's civil war in 1949, to take on a major military operation.

Reports of Chinese troops in North Korea were confirmed in late October when Chinese prisoners were first taken, but the possibility of large Chinese units in North Korea was rejected. China heightened its surprise by delaying use of its major units for a period of time, thus making reports that such units were moving into North Korea appear false. In late November, a month after the first Chinese prisoners were taken, China utilized its forces in full strength, and UN forces were pushed back deep into South Korea. The Chinese surprise had been successful. The decision to cross the 38th Parallel and the failure to recognize the presence of large Chinese units in North Korea are criticized on the grounds that the United States seriously underestimated China's resolve to protect its borders. As an example of surprise, the intervention of China in the war is typical of the outcome of military surprise; warnings are seldom interpreted correctly. By the next spring, after the front lines moved north and south as each side mounted additional offensives, the front eventually stabilized near the 38th Parallel, where it remained until the war ended in stalemate in July 1953.

THE CUBAN MISSILE CRISIS

Each of the military surprises discussed thus far resulted in the start of a war or added new belligerents to an existing war. The Cuban missile crisis was a surprise and crisis of a different sort. In fact, it is inaccurate to describe that confrontation as solely a military crisis, since it contained both diplomatic and military aspects. The only loss of life was the pilot of a U.S. reconnaissance aircraft shot down over Cuba, although, under international law, the blockade of Cuba by the U.S. Navy was an act of war. Regardless of the nature of the crisis, few observers of international politics would dispute the idea that the crisis was the most serious confrontation between the United States and the Soviet Union in the Cold War. During the crisis, nuclear war seemed nearer than at any other time. Since it is generally viewed as an American victory, it has, cor-

rectly or not, become a model in the United States of the proper manner in which to manage a crisis.

The Cuban missile crisis spanned a relatively short period of time—October 13–28, 1962—but developments leading up to the crisis took place over several months. Relations between Cuba and the United States had deteriorated steadily virtually from the time Castro came to power in Cuba in January 1959, but had become especially strained following the unsuccessful CIA-planned Bay of Pigs operation in April 1961. Although the Soviet Union had been providing Cuba with economic and military aid, the United States did not see Cuba as a military threat; none of the Soviet-supplied weaponry was regarded as offensive in nature. The crisis evolved when the Soviets began the deployment of medium- and intermediate-range ballistic missiles in Cuba. These weapons had sufficient range to deliver nuclear warheads to all but the northwest corner of the United States.

While the possibility of missiles in Cuba was a surprise to the United States, it was an unusual surprise in the sense that it developed gradually. While Washington had been receiving reports of missiles arriving in Cuba for several weeks before the crisis developed, those reports mainly came from Cuban refugees who were neither impartial nor trained observers and thus were not a solid intelligence source on which to base action. Additional verification was required before any response could be made. Thus, warnings occurred, although it took time to verify the reports. In part, the crisis evolved gradually because the missiles could not be deployed immediately on arrival; launching sites had to be constructed before they became operational. The time required to carry this out allowed the United States the opportunity to develop a counterstrategy.

The presence of missiles in Cuba had important military implications, for their presence provided the Soviet Union with a quick means of countering the intercontinental missile advantage then enjoyed by the United States. The number of missiles the Soviet Union placed in Cuba constituted one-third of the Soviet missiles that could strike the United States from either the Soviet Union or Cuba. But the presence of Soviet missiles in Cuba also had a substantial effect on U.S.-Soviet diplomatic relations, as well. The basic understanding between the two superpowers that neither would interfere in the internal affairs of the other's coalition had been violated. Soviet support of the Castro government was a violation in itself, but to place offensive weapons within the Western coalition was the equivalent of the United States' placing missiles in an Eastern European country that had defected from the Soviet coalition. The Soviets had much to gain if the United States did not react strongly, and could always withdraw the missiles if the United States objected strenuously. The Soviets had taken the initiative, and now it was up to the United States to respond.

The American people were not aware that a crisis was at hand until President Kennedy informed them in a television address on the evening of October 22. Deliberations in the White House had been so tightly guarded that the news media was uncertain as to what the president was going to discuss in his address. While many speculated that the subject would be Cuba, others felt that he was going to announce yet another crisis over Berlin.

Even though the crisis began for the American people on the 22nd, it had begun for the White House on the 13th, when evidence that missiles were being brought into Cuba became so convincing that a reconnaissance flight over Cuba was agreed to. The flight was delayed for three days because of bureaucratic conflict between the CIA and the Air Force concerning which group would conduct the flight. Was it an intelligence operation or a military mission? The compromise was to use a CIA U-2 reconnaissance aircraft flown by an Air Force pilot. Once the aerial photographs confirmed that sites were being prepared for the missiles, a counterstrategy was selected.

While various alternatives were considered, including an invasion of Cuba, the one selected was a naval blockade. This course of action was considered by the decision-makers as the use of the least force necessary to achieve their objectives. This alternative had one important limitation, however. A blockade would only prevent new weapons from coming in, whereas the overall objective for the United States was the removal of the missiles already there. Negotiations with the Soviets would be necessary to achieve removal.

Consideration of alternatives did not take place through the ordinary channels of decision-making. President Kennedy established a special, high-level group—the Executive Committee of the National Security Council, or EXCOM—that cut across the formal organizational units of government. This group included the secretaries of defense and state and the attorney general; the vice president; the director of the CIA; the chairman of the joint chiefs of staff; various members of the White House staff, including the national security adviser; and a few additional experts in foreign policy. The deliberations of EXCOM were conducted in the strictest secrecy, which was difficult to maintain since a congressional election campaign was in full swing and some members of EXCOM would ordinarily be on the campaign trail. President Kennedy, before the crisis was announced to the American public, cut short a campaign tour by claiming illness.

Not until only a few hours before announcing to the American public the presence of offensive missiles in Cuba and U.S. countermeasures did President Kennedy attempt to build a consensus of support for his strategy outside the EXCOM group. Initially, he briefed congressional leaders on what he was planning and received their support for the proposed action. At about the same time, a number of ambassadors, primarily from Latin America and Western Europe, were called to the State Department and briefed. Special envoys were sent to London, Bonn, Paris, and NATO so that important heads of state in Europe would be informed about what the United States planned to do. The Soviet ambassador to the United States was briefed shortly before Kennedy went on the air, and the U.S. ambassador in Moscow informed the Soviet government directly. The president successfully developed support for his policy and, while providing the Soviets with a surprise, did not violate protocol by waiting until the public announcement to inform Congress, allies, and the Soviets of U.S. countermeasures.

The blockade was established and a period of high tension followed. Several diplomatic messages between Washington and Moscow were transmitted through both traditional and non-traditional channels, and by October 26 Soviet ships bearing contraband (which the United States defined as missiles, bombers, and support equipment) had turned back before reaching the blockade. The Soviets also agreed to withdraw the contraband material already in Cuba and the crisis came to an end.

Although the crisis was over and the United States was generally regarded as having achieved an important victory over the Soviet Union, the ramifications of that crisis are still felt in the 1980s. The United States achieved what it set out to do—namely, remove all offensive weapons from Cuba. For the United States to accomplish this, the Soviet Union had to retreat, which it did. Since management of this crisis was successful for the United States, what were the lessons of crisis management learned from the Cuban missile crisis? First, the United States showed great resolve and strongly indicated to the Soviet Union that the situation created by Soviet actions was unacceptable to the United States. The intelligence gathered proved to be reliable and the U.S. chose the alternative that required the least use of force to achieve its objective. The United States showed a willingness to negotiate, but made clear that it would accept nothing less than the withdrawal of the missiles. Second, the United States had a strategic advantage over the Soviet Union. Neither country was willing to launch a general war over the missiles; therefore, the regional military dominance exercised by the United States was of great importance. Cuba is geographically close to the United States, and the United States clearly could utilize its military

force much more easily than could the distant Soviet Union. In addition, the United States had a distinct advantage in the size of its surface navy and could effectively carry out a blockade. Third, the United States provided the Soviets with a means to retreat gracefully. In exchange for the withdrawal of the missiles, the United States gave its pledge not to invade Cuba. Khrushchev then could say that the only reason the missiles were sent to Cuba was to prevent a U.S. invasion and that the missiles could be withdrawn now that the United States promised not to invade. Khrushchev later argued that the withdrawal of U.S. missiles from Turkey (which Kennedy had ordered before the missile crisis) was also a U.S. concession.

The outcome of this crisis was, no doubt, a victory for the United States, but the confrontational position the United States assumed had long-range effects on Soviet policy. At the time of the crisis, the Soviets recognized that their surface navy was too small to challenge the U.S. Navy. Since the missile crisis, the Soviets have built up their navy until it has more ships than any other navy in the world. The quality of that navy compared to that of the U.S. navy is another matter, however. While several lessons learned about crisis management during the missile crisis would seem to be applicable to any crisis, to use the management of that crisis as a model for managing future crises could indeed be a serious error if similar theater advantages did not exist.

TECHNOLOGICAL SURPRISE

Surprises sometimes have their origin in technological developments. The dropping of the first atomic bomb, a weapon the world did not know existed until it was released on Hiroshima in August 1945, certainly qualified as a surprise. It was not only a surprise to Japan; what was also a surprise was this weapon's effect upon postwar relationships among the victors. When Truman

man informed Stalin at Potsdam in July 1945 that the United States had successfully tested an atomic bomb, Stalin's reaction was matter-of-fact. Stalin may have reacted in this manner because he did not realize the full implications of the weapon; or his reaction may have meant he already knew about the bomb from his own intelligence sources and did not want to reveal how much impact this surprise had had on the Soviet Union. To offset the U.S. atomic monopoly after the war ended, the Soviets retained a large conventional armed force. As the Cold War progressed, the Soviets utilized the strategy that their conventional forces could occupy all of Europe even if the United States attacked the population and industrial centers of the Soviet Union with atomic weapons. The effect of the bomb on U.S. strategy was to reduce conventional forces and bring about heavy reliance on atomic weapons.

The second surprise concerning atomic weapons was provided by the Soviet Union. In the late 1940s, the United States was confident that the Soviet Union would need considerable time to develop its own atomic weapons, but in August 1949 the Soviets exploded their first atomic device. A similar sequence of events occurred when the United States exploded its first hydrogen bomb in the early 1950s, which was followed in about a year with a Soviet hydrogen bomb test. These developments and counterdevelopments of weapons systems came as surprises, but they were not followed by a period of diplomatic or military crisis. A substantial time period occurs between the successful testing of a device, which initiates the surprise, and its deployment as an operational weapon. This allows nations time to adjust to changes in the international system brought about by a particular technological development; thus, no period of crisis occurs.

One surprise resulting from a technological development that did produce a crisis of sorts, however, was the Soviet launching of Sputnik, the first earth satellite, in October 1957. Such an achievement was one of the goals of the United Nations International Geophysical Year, which was dedicated to peaceful scientific research, but any country possessing a rocket that could place a satellite in orbit also had the capability to launch a nuclear warhead over great distances. The Soviets had been behind he United States in developing the atomic and hydrogen bombs, but this time the Soviets were first. The United States followed with its own satellite only three months later, but being beaten by the Soviets resulted in a national reevaluation of the American educational system to ascertain how such a thing was possible. The United States also developed a space program and a new government agency—the National Aeronautics and Space Administration (NASA)—and a reallocation of resources to finance both. Sputnik created a crisis, but it was a domestic U.S. crisis, not international in scope.

Other technological developments that have produced surprise include the development of an antiballistic missile (ABM) system during the late 1960s. This development was sufficiently upsetting to the international system, especially to the concept of deterrence, that it became the principal concern of the SALT I agreement, which sharply curtailed its deployment. A projected development that could have an even more extensive impact on deterrence is what commonly has been called "star wars" but labelled strategic defense initiative (SDI) by the Reagan administration. If successful, this system would destroy incoming missiles and warheads and thus basically alter the nuclear relationship among the superpowers. SDI produced surprise even before development of the new defense system began and has had an important effect on arms talks between the United States and the Soviet Union.

THE VIETNAM WAR

The war in Vietnam produced surprises in several ways. The surprises of this war will be dealt with here in only general terms, since the war spanned a twelve-year period and involved many decisions concerning U.S. involvement. One important overall aspect of surprise was U.S. failure to win the war by escalating its war effort on an incremental basis. The administration operated on the assumption that the enemy did not have the capability to counterescalate, but on each occasion it did. The Pentagon Papers, published while the war was at its peak, revealed that Johnson and his advisors were so committed to this view of the enemy that intelligence reports to the contrary were ignored (Janis, 1982, 97-101). The Defense Intelligence Agency (DIA) was accused of another error that further produced surprise. While some intelligence-gathering agencies, including the CIA, were issuing reports that were pessimistic about the outcome of an escalation policy, the DIA was producing reports that supported the policy choices of the administration.

Certainly among the surprises of the war was the degree to which it was opposed domestically. Demonstrations against the war were widespread in the United States during the late 1960s and early 1970s. When the 1968 Democratic National Convention was held in Chicago, demonstrations against the war were as important a news story as was the nomination of the Democratic presidential candidate. Many young men refused to serve in the armed forces and the desertion rate in the armed forces showed a notable increase. This opposition eventually permeated all age groups and the war became a serious political liability to whomever occupied the White House.

Perhaps the single greatest surprise of the Vietnam War was that the United States' attempt to implement its longstanding policy of containment failed. The Johnson administration remained faithful throughout the war to the concept that communist expansion in Vietnam had to be resisted. Confidence in that policy was so great that when the enemy was not defeated after a decision to escalate, the proposed solution was to further escalate. Consistent with the policy of containment, the Johnson administration made

clear that the United States did not intend to occupy North Vietnam, but intended only to prevent South Vietnam from becoming communist. The bombing targets in North Vietnam were retricted; no population centers were to be bombed nor harbors mined (Gelb, 1979). To continue the application of containment in Vietnam was also seen as essential in order to maintain confidence in U.S. commitments elsewhere in the world. This was so even when American allies in Europe opposed U.S. escalation in Vietnam and when resistance to the war increased in the United States.

The surprises of Vietnam thus happened to an administration that was overly committed to a policy of containment and to a particular view of how the enemy could be defeated. Commitment to containment overrode intelligence reports that the policy was not achieving its intended goals, and escalation of the war was seen as the only means by which containment could be made to work.

SURPRISE AND THE SOVIET UNION

The Soviet Union has used its armed forces on several occasions to produce surprise. One such instance was when the Soviet Union sent the Red Army into Hungary in 1956. When the Hungarian revolution began, Soviet forces in Hungary were insufficient to put down the revolt, and the Soviets were forced to withdraw from Budapest. Worldwide, the impression was that the Soviet Union had suffered a major defeat. While it was a surprise that the Soviets had given up one of their satellite nations without more of a struggle, it did appear that Hungary was out of the Warsaw Pact and had effectively broken with the Soviet Union. This euphoria was shattered after a few days when the real surprise was revealed, as Soviet forces returned in greater numbers and crushed the revolution. A crisis then developed, but not one that in any way reversed the Soviet intervention. Short of armed intervention by the

West, which probably would have resulted in a general war in Europe, the Soviet intervention was an accomplished fact and the Soviet Union had only to wait until tensions subsided.

The Soviets produced another surprise in Eastern Europe in August 1961 when they supported East Germany in erecting the Berlin Wall. East German citizens had easy access to East Berlin, and, once in East Berlin, they could ride public transportation to West Berlin, declare themselves refugees, and then be flown out to West Germany. East Germany suffered not only the loss of citizens, but the people who were leaving were those better educated, which had a detrimental effect on the East German economy. The wall prevented all physical contact between the two cities and virtually stopped the flow of refugees. This development, like the Soviet action in Hungary, also was a fact of life once the wall was up, there was little the West could do in response. The wall did have a negative short-range economic effect on East Berlin, since about 50,000 East Berliners worked in West Berlin, and, because of the wall, those people could no longer go to their jobs. A lesser number of West Berliners also lost their jobs in East Berlin. The East German government and the Soviets were willing to make this sacrifice in order to stop the flow of refugees. The East German economy, which had not been doing well, began to improve and today is one of the strongest economies in Eastern Europe.

The surprise of the Berlin Wall was planned well by the East Germans and Soviets. August is the traditional month for vacations in Europe, and many Western governmental officials were among the vacationers. In addition, construction of the wall began on a Saturday when those who were not on vacation were away for the weekend. The Western governments consequently did not respond for two days; but even then, unless they were willing to use armed force, there was little that could be done other than protest the action.

Yet another surprise was the invasion of Czechoslovakia by the other members of the Warsaw Pact in August 1968. NATO knew that the Warsaw Pact was concentrating troops, but the numbers were insufficient to be a prelude to an invasion of Western Europe. Since many observers thought that the Soviet Union could settle its differences with Czechoslovakia without an invasion, the invasion was a surprise. The invasion was a surprise in the West also because of how well it was carried out. In a twenty-four hour period, all of Czechoslovakia was occupied in a well-coordinated operation. There was speculation at the time that NATO, if called upon to carry out a similar operation, could not have done it as well.

The Soviets provided another surprise when their forces moved into Afghanistan in December 1979. The Soviets saw this intervention in much the same light as the interventions in Hungary and Czechoslovakia, that is, an action taken to prevent a fellow communist country from defecting. The Soviet invasion of Afghanistan was a surprise in the West for two reasons. The first was that, although Afghanistan had had several changes in government during the 1970s, it was not viewed as part of the Soviet coalition; therefore, the Soviet Union would have no need to intervene. The second surprising element was that the Soviets committed their own troops to combat in Afghanistan. On those earlier occasions when the Soviets had taken military actions that involved combat, surrogate forces had been used. In Korea, the communist forces were Chinese and North Korean, and the combat forces committed to Angola and Ethiopia were Cuban.

SURPRISE AND CRISIS IN THE MIDDLE EAST

Since World War II, the Middle East has provided more than its share of surprises and crises. Most have been military in nature, but at least one, Sadat's peace initiative toward Israel, was a diplomatic surprise. The Israelis have been responsible for many of the military surprises, but Egypt and Syria provided a major surprise when they launched the October 1973 War. Iraq's attack on Iran in September 1980 was a major surprise which also was not of Israel's making. With the exception of the Iraqi-Iranian war, military crises that have followed military surprises have lasted only a few days or weeks. In each such surprise and crisis, the single greatest problem for the international system has been to confine the military conflicts to the region and to limit the activities of the superpowers.

The effectiveness of military surprise was first demonstrated by modern Israel in its four-day Sinai campaign in October 1956. The invasion was prompted by several disputes pending between Egypt and Israel. Shortly before the attack, Egypt nationalized the Suez Canal and Israeli shipping was no longer allowed to use it. The Gulf of Aqaba was also closed by Egypt, thus preventing Israeli access to the Red Sea from its southern port of Eilat. Fedayeen (commando) raids, originating in the Egyptian-controlled Gaza Strip into bordering Israeli territory, were occurring with some frequency. Also, Egypt moved major units of its armed forces across the Sinai and up to the Egyptian-Israeli border. Israel decided to resolve all of these problems with a military surprise that involved the occupation of the Sinai up to within a short distance from the Suez Canal. The canal was to be retaken by British and French forces.

This military surprise came after months of tension in the region; thus, when military action did come, it was less surprising than was the degree of success experienced by the Israelis. Israeli armored columns easily bypassed major Egyptian units and quickly achieved their objectives near the canal. Even though the British and French were forced by U.S. and Soviet pressure to withdraw before they could occupy all of the canal, the Israeli aspect of the operation was successful. While the Israeli portion of the operation was a surprise, the Anglo-French invasion was

not. The latter force landed after a period of preparation and Egypt had ample warning.

The next major surprise attack launched by Israel occurred in June 1967. This war, the Six-Day War, was broader in scope and involved Jordan and Syria as well as Egypt and Israel. In the few days' duration of this war, Israel defeated all three of its Arab opponents. Again, the war was preceded by a lengthy period of tension; thus, an attack was not totally unexpected. Israel did what it could, however, to mislead the Arab states into thinking that a war was not imminent, since diplomatic methods had not yet been exhausted. Also, since war was likely, Israel tried by various means to confuse the Arab nations as to which nation might be attacked first. Critical to the Israeli plan was destruction of the Egyptian air force in the opening hours of the war. In order to accomplish this, considerable deception was necessary. When the attack came, the surprise was complete and the attack successful.

Egypt and Syria provided a surprise of their own in October 1973 when they launched a surprise attack against Israel. Since this war lasted longer than had earlier Arab-Israeli wars, it carried a greater risk of outside involvement and allowed the United States and the Soviet Union to become involved. This produced a crisis that went beyond the regional conflict.

Israel suffered heavy losses in the first few days of the war due to the effectiveness of the Arab surprise. But why was the attack a surprise when tensions were high in the region once again and an attack was not unlikely? The answer lies in the usual reasons why surprise works—preconceptions that did not allow for imagining an Arab surprise attack and either misinterpreting intelligence reports or not acting on those reports properly. The United States and Israel held images of Egypt and Syria that failed to include the possibility of a surprise attack. Soviet technicians had been withdrawn from Egypt in 1972 at Sadat's demand, and this was interpreted as meaning that Sadat would not launch an attack without more support from the Soviet Union than he had. Also, détente was at its height, which the Israelis interpreted to mean that Sadat was unlikely to receive Soviet support in the immediate future. A further complicating factor in recognizing the possibility of a surprise attack was that the Israelis, after two easy victories over its Arab enemies in 1956 and 1967, may have been overconfident concerning their ability to repulse an Arab onslaught.

The old nemesis of those who expect a surprise attack—alert fatigue—was also a factor. The Israeli armed forces had been placed on alert several times during the previous six months; thus, a new alert was treated as routine. Preparations for an attack in both Syria and Egypt were reported by Israeli intelligence, but these developments were not regarded as related. The Arab countries had not coordinated their military operations in the past; therefore, a coordinated attack was seen as unlikely. The Israeli explanation for activities in Egypt and Syria was that the Arabs were preparing for an Israeli attack. To increase the element of surprise, the Egyptians and Syrians launched their attack on Yom Kippur, a high Jewish holiday. Many Israeli troops along the Suez Canal, where Israeli forces had been since 1967, were on holiday leave. The surprise was a success, catching Israel off-guard despite the atmosphere of tension and preparations. Israel eventually drove the attackers back deep into their own territory, but surprise had once more been initially successful.

Even before the October War ended, a new surprise awaited the supporters of Israel. This was an economic surprise in the form of an oil embargo that the Arab oil-exporting nations placed on nations that supported Israel. The Arab members of OPEC, in an effort to modify the pro-Israeli policies of the United States and the Netherlands, curtailed oil production, placed an embargo on exports to those two countries, and raised prices. Later, Portugal, Rhodesia, and South Africa were added to the list of embargoed nations. The non-Arab members of OPEC did not join in the embargo, but they did raise their oil prices to conform with Arab members' prices. While Japan and most of Western Europe were not direct targets of the embargo, they did have to pay the higher prices and confront the shortage of oil brought about by reductions in production. The effect of this economic surprise was near panic in the industrial nations. Only France, which had had a pro-Arab policy since the Six-Day War, was largely unaffected. Gas rationing was imposed in some countries, speed limits were reduced, and thermostats were turned down. Japan, almost totally dependent on foreign oil, quickly issued a statement declaring its neutrality in the Arab-Israeli conflict, which the Arab states rejected. A new statement by Japan declaring a moderately pro-Arab position was found to be acceptable to the Arab nations.

Some warning existed that such an oil embargo would be imposed. After the Six-Day War, an embargo was considered, but economic conditions prevented such a move at that time. By 1973 the economic position of the oil-exporting nations had improved. The industrial nations were more dependent on OPEC oil than before, and production of oil was scarcely keeping up with demand. Those conditions made it possible for the Arab members of OPEC to both raise prices and make a political statement.

The embargo against the United States was lifted in early March 1974, and the embargo against the Netherlands was lifted the following July. Neither country abandoned its pro-Israeli policy, but the United States did declare a more "even-handed" policy for the Middle East. The other three nations stayed on the embargo list for some time; South Africa is still on the list. The long-range effect of the embargo was a continued rise in the price of oil until a surplus of oil on the world market developed in the early 1980s, forcing oil prices down. The overall effect of the embargo and higher prices on the balance of payments for the industrial nations was substantial. The Arab oil-exporting countries had effectively made their newly discovered economic power felt in the industrial world.

Still another surprise that came out of the Middle East was a diplomatic one when Sadat initiated a peace proposal to Israel in November 1977. This particular surprise produced no crisis, since it was an act of conciliation, although it did isolate Egypt from other Arab countries for a time. Of all of those discussed in this chapter, this surprise probably comes the closest to being total. Sadat's move was possible because he was firmly in control of the authoritarian Egyptian political system; surprise is ordinarily easier for leaders of such systems to achieve as opposed to leaders of more open societies. Also, in 1977 it was easier for Sadat to approach Israel, since Egypt felt that the honor of its armed forces had been restored by their respectable showing during the 1973 war. In 1977, Sadat did not appear to be offering negotiations from a position of weakness, as would have been the case before the 1973 war.

Sadat, in his view, had hinted strongly about wanting a peace settlement long before his 1977 proposal. He felt that he had made a peace proposal to Israel in February 1971, but that Israel had not taken it seriously. (Handel, 1981, 255–264). The 1977 proposal was more carefully prepared and was made after Sadat was assured of a positive Israeli response. This proposal contained provisions that would be attractive to Israel and could lead to an overall peace settlement between the two countries. The 1971 proposal was neither of those things. Sadat's offer to go to Israel and speak to the Knesset was accepted, and the visit opened the difficult negotiations that ultimately produced the March 1979 peace treaty between Egypt and Israel.

OTHER SURPRISES

The United States is also capable of surprises in international politics. Certainly ranking among the greatest diplomatic surprises of the post-World War II era was Nixon's effort to reestab-lish diplomatic relations with China. Such a move took considerable diplomatic preparation through sending various signals to China indicating that the United States was willing to make such a move. Those signals included continued progress toward ending United States involvement in Vietnam and messages through third parties who had diplomatic relations with both the United States and China. In the last six months of 1969 the United States removed travel restrictions for scholars, students, and journalists who wished to travel to China; indicated that the United States was willing to renew ambassadorial talks in Warsaw; removed nuclear weapons from Okinawa; and ceased United States naval patrols between Taiwan and the mainland. Nixon also began to refer to China for the first time as the People's Republic of China (Handel, 1981, 185–195). Such signals continued throughout 1970 and 1971, but the diplomatic contacts through third parties continued in the strictest secrecy. Pakistan was the channel for much of this contact. In July 1971, Kissinger, while on a visit to Pakistan, paid a secret visit to Beijing. Kissinger was in Beijing July 9-11, and the talks went well. On July 15 Nixon revealed the trip and the surprise of improving relations with China in a television address. The diplomatic path to better relatons was now open.

The United States has been the victim of surprise as well. The seizure of American hostages in the United States Embassy in Teheran in November 1979 is a prime example. All terrorist acts are a form of surprise, but the Iranian hostage situation was unusual in that it had the open support of the Iranian government. It also illustrates the vulnerability of any nation to such acts and a nation's limited ability to develop a counterstrategy.

Some acts of surprise leave little opportunity for other nations to act; once they occur they are accomplised facts. An example was the downing of the Korean Airlines Flight 007 by a Soviet fighter in October 1984. Little could be done by other countries beyond expressing moral outrage. To have done more could have created even more serious incidents and escalated the situation into a crisis confrontation. The killing in March 1985 of an American intelligence officer in East Germany who was attached to a military liaison mission is another example. Retaliation remained on a relatively minor level in order to prevent a crisis that could have jeopardized major U.S. interests. Still another example was the Iraqi attack on the *U.S.S. Stark* in May 1987. Since the U.S. nominally supported Iraq in its war with Iran, and Iraq explained the incident as an accident, any retaliation by the U.S. seemed inappropriate. The success experienced by countries who utilize surprise makes it a tempting means of achieving policy objectives. The success of surprise also places nations potentially to be victimized by surprise constantly on alert. But, despite precautions, surprise is often successful. NATO assumes that if war comes in Europe it will be a surprise Soviet attack. This necessitates special emphasis on gathering intelligence in the Warsaw Pact nations to learn if any unusual preparations are taking place. When the Warsaw Pact conducts military maneuvers, NATO goes on alert, since maneuvers could serve as deception for an invasion of Western Europe. The strategy of NATO's defense of Western Europe is to avoid surprise through the effective use of intelligence, anticipate where and when attack is most likely, and place major units far enough away from the borders that the effects of surprise will be minimal. To guard against surprises, however, decision-makers must know the limitations of intelligence-gathering. Information is never complete, nor is its interpretation obvious. Thus, surprise is always possible.

CONCLUSION

The discussion in this chapter has included both surprise followed by crisis and surprises that do not produce crisis. Various types of surprise have also been discussed such as military, diplomatic, and economic surprises. One category that has not been discussed is crisis that does not start from a surprise, but rather develops over months or years. These crises have been discussed elsewhere, but include such examples as famine in Africa, the debt problems of the Third World countries, and the world's expanding population. Surprise is not a prerequisite for a serious crisis.

The instances of surprise discussed in this chapter are all examples of a lack of intelligence or its misinterpretation that could have prevented a surprise or crisis. They also illustrate that while surprise is initially successful, a resulting crisis may work to the disadvantage of the initiator. Such was the the plight of the Soviet Union during the Cuban missile crisis. Crisis places great demands on the diplomatic process which are not always met, but diplomacy is greatly needed when a crisis develops. Military crisis produces the most immediate tensions, but economic and technological crises can have even greater long-term effects. This discussion also illustrates the frequency with which major events in the international system begin with a surprise and the high incidence of crises that have occurred in the international system.

CHAPTER 11

The Use of Force

The most commonly thought of circumstance for the use of force is in open warfare between two or more nations; but force is also used between nations in armed interventions, outside support for liberation movements, the use of surrogate forces, and terrorism. Domestically, force is employed in civil wars, coups, liberation movements, and the suppression of opposition. But force does not need to be used to exist as a factor in international relations. Its mere presence allows nations to utilize the threat of force to compel others to take some action or to deter them from a certain action. This chapter will discuss how force or its threat is used in the international system and how its use has changed in the twentieth century, particularly since the Second World War.

WAR AND DIPLOMACY

When war breaks out in the international system, the assumption is generally made that all peaceful alternatives have been pursued and rejected, and that the only remaining alternative is war. This assumption often is not valid. As pointed out in the last chapter, before the Korean War began, the United States felt that North Korea had various means still available to achieve its goals before war might occur, but North Korea launched

its attack, nevertheless. At the start of World War II, Germany had hardly begun to look for diplomatic solutions to its disputes with Poland before invading. World War I began with the major states of Europe frantically seeking a diplomatic solution while they collectively drifted into war. Dipomacy may fail to prevent many wars, but it does not follow that diplomatic alternatives are always exhausted before war breaks out.

One approach to the relationship between war and diplomacy is expressed by the nineteenth century military historian, Carl von Clausewitz—that war is the exercise of diplomacy by other means (von Clausewitz, 1976). Obviously war is not diplomacy, but von Clausewitz's observation makes clear that war, or any other use of force, and diplomacy are choices available to a nation in pursuing its policy goals. When force is used, it means that at least one nation has chosen force rather than diplomacy to achieve its interests.

A second assumption often made is that war reflects the failure of controls developed among nations to limit conflict. Even when war occurs between two or more nations, those controls are functioning with some degree of success if they isolate the war to the initial belligerents and maintain normal relations among most of the nations in the system. The degree to which international controls have been successful in limiting the use of force is reflected in the fact that all wars since World War II have been localized; thus, while at any given time some nations are at war, most nations are at peace.

The extent to which the world has been at peace since World War II is illustrated by the fact that the two superpowers have not had a direct clash of arms, and no two Western industrial nations have had an armed conflict. The single armed clash among major powers during this period was the Korean War which involved China, a major underdeveloped nation, on one side, and several Western industrial nations, including the United States, on the other. Diplomatically, this military confrontation was softened by China's claiming that its forces were volunteers, and by the Western forces operating as a United Nations force rather than as national armies.

WHERE FORCE IS USED

The absence of wars between industrial nations, communist or Western, since World War II means that within the framework of the three major groupings of nations—communist, Western and Third World—post–World War II inter-state wars have either been between Third World countries or between a Third World country and an industrial nation. One scholar who tabulated the use of force between 1955 and 1979, at both the level of war and lesser levels, found 120 incidents; all but six occurred in the lesser-developed countries (Sivard, 1979). International controls thus have been successful in preventing some types of war and limiting the scope of others. Clearly, however, the principal location for the use of force is in the Third World.

Even though many instances of the use of force occur between Third World countries, the frequency with which force has been used in the Third World by the industrial nations has resulted in those countries being increasingly fearful of the major states' military power. The industrial nations have both the economic and military capabilities to inflict serious damage on virtually any Third World nation. The vulnerability of the Third World and the frequent use of force there has resulted in the Third World countries overreacting, perhaps with good cause, to actions by the major states.

A number of the post–World War II wars between the Third World and the industrial nations were wars of independence—wars between colonies and colonial powers. By the late 1980s colonial wars had ended now that virtually all traditional nineteenth-century empires are gone. Even with that type of war ended in the Third World, newly independent nations have a number of problems remaining that produce armed conflict between them. Boundary disputes, for example, are the basis for armed conflict between Algeria and Morocco, Iran and Iraq, and Libya and Chad. If the boundaries drawn up by the colonial powers are rejected by a newly independent nation, the potential for war with its neighbors, who also are likely to be newly independent, is great. The boundaries in Africa are particularly susceptible to this sort of dispute, but to the credit of the African nations much less armed conflict has resulted over such disputes than has been potentially possible.

Another explanation for the frequency of war in the Third World is based on the theory that armed conflict is more apt to occur under uncertain economic conditions than during periods of economic stability. Third World countries are engaged in the important struggle of developing viable economies, and thus are in a state of economic uncertainty and change which more easily leads to war. Still another possible explanation for the frequency of war in the Third World relates to conditions in the international system over which the Third World has no control. Except for China, all nations possessing nuclear weapons are industrial nations, and although only a few industrial nations possess nuclear weapons most of the others are allied with nations that do. Since any use of force by a nuclear power must be calculated in terms of whether an action will lead to nuclear war, those nations possessing nuclear weapons and their industrial allies must use force with great caution. The nuclear powers have the military capability to enter a conventional, that is, a non-nuclear, war with one another, but such a war is avoided because the risks are too great that it will escalate into full-scale nuclear exchange. The only "safe" wars are those that do not involve another nuclear power or, at least, minimize the possibility of a confrontation with another nuclear power. The Third World offers the location for such "safe" wars.

As for the use of armed force in situations other than international war—civil wars and guerrilla-style wars—the Third World also has a high incidence of such events. Of the wars occurring in the post-World War II period, this sort of warfare—wars limited to a single state—is the one most frequently found. Of the 25 to 40 wars of all kinds (an exact number is difficult to ascertain since those persons who conduct such inventories use different counting methods) occurring in the mid-1980s, all but five or so have been internal wars (*The Defense Monitor*, vol. 12, no. 1, 1983, 1).

Civil wars have been more frequent since 1945 than earlier in the twentieth century and during the nineteenth century. They constitute the form of war that has increased most. This is partially attributable to the expansion of the nation-state system since the Second World War—with more nations, there will be more civil wars—as well as the instability of the governments of those new nations. Singer's project on the correlates of war (Small and Singer, 1982) found that of the 106 civil wars between 1816 and 1980, 40 began between 1948 and 1980. On the basis of these figures, the period from 1816 to 1948 averaged .5 civil wars a year, but the period from 1948 to 1980 produced 1.25 civil wars per year. The number of nation-states in

the international system more than doubled from 1816 to 1948, and more than doubled again from 1948 to 1980. If the number of civil wars per national actor for the pre–1948 period is compared to per actor incidence of civil wars for the 1948–1980 period, a slight decline in the number of civil wars occurred.

Still another perspective concerning wars within Third World nations is that when wars occurred in colonies before the breakup of empires, those were not seen as civil wars but as colonial wars (or, as Small and Singer categorize such conflicts, extrasystemic wars). Now, however, the use of force within a newly independent country is defined as a civil war. The location of the conflict has not changed so much as have the circumstances.

WAR—FREQUENCY AND SEVERITY

Providing a common definition of war is difficult, but, minimally, war means that the organized armed forces of at least one country are engaged in armed conflict with another armed force. If the second armed force is that of another country, the war is interstate in nature, but if the second armed force is internal it is a domestic conflict. Some studies and inventories of war require that to be defined as a war the conflict must produce a certain minimum number of casualties; otherwise, such events as border incidents, riots, or terrorist attacks could be included as wars. The Small and Singer study uses one thousand fatalities as the minimum number to constitute a war, although higher minimum numbers are used in other inventories. What seems to be a working definition of war is simply the use of force that produces at least a specified, though arbitrary, number of fatalities.

That humankind has often engaged in warfare is hardly a revelation. In 55 centuries of recorded history, one estimate claims that approximately 14,500 wars have occurred. (Grieves, 1977, 7).

Quincy Wright, in his study of war (Wright, 1942), recorded 278 interstate wars from 1480 to 1940. (Wright used a legalistic definition of war and counted only declared wars.) Small and Singer found that 224 wars (declared and undeclared) occurred between 1816 and 1980. They classified wars into three categories: 1) interstate—wars between two or more sovereign states, 2) extrasystemic—wars between sovereign states and nonstate actors, and 3) civil—wars involving groups within a single nation. Their study included 67 interstate wars, 51 extrasystemic wars, and 106 civil wars. Excluding civil wars, since they are not international in nature, international wars occurred in all but 20 of the 165 years covered by the study.

How to count the number of wars in any given time period might, at first impression, appear to be a simple enough task, since it would seem that a nation is either at war or not; however, several problems arise in conducting an inventory of wars. An initial problem exists in comparing the results of various inventories of war, since each inventory covers a different time period and defines differently how much force or how many casualties must be involved in order for a situation to be a war. If a certain minimum number of casualties must occur before fighting constitutes war, obtaining reliable data on casualties is a problem. In the nineteenth century, wars were apt to be fought in set-piece battles. Casualties were easier to count than, for example, casualties in modern guerrilla wars, especially when conducted in jungles where there is little visual contact with the enemy. The question of how many casualties were suffered by the Viet Cong and the North Vietnamese—the body-count issue—was a problem throughout the Vietnam War. Related to an accurate count of casualties is the problem of when to count civilian casualties as combat deaths and what constitutes civilian status. In guerrilla warfare, distinguishing between a combatant and a civilian is particularly difficult. Nations engaged in war in the nineteenth century and earlier more clearly distinguished between combatants and noncombatants; thus fewer civilian casualties occurred earlier than in the twentieth century. In twentieth-century wars, civilian casualties have gone up considerably both in numbers and as a percentage of total casualties.

Also, in the earlier years of the nation-state system, wars carried a more precise legal definition and were less frequently fought without a formal declaration; but, since the Second World War, virtually all wars have been undeclared. The Korean War and the Vietnam War were undeclared, all of the Arab-Israeli conflicts were undeclared, and internal wars with outside assistance have all been undeclared wars. When no declaration of war exists, the question is, how severe must fighting be between organized military units before the conflict is classified as a war. Is a nation at war, regardless of the casualties suffered, if the domestic economy continues to function on a peacetime basis (as was the situation for the United States during the Korean War and the Vietnam War)? How serious must a guerrilla movement's activities be before a nation is considered to be at war? If the targets of guerrillas and terrorists are primarily civilians and the seriousness of an armed conflict is judged in terms of military casualties (Small and Singer's minimum of 1000 fatalities applies to military, not civilian, deaths), when does such a conflict become a war? These problems of defining wars are resolved differently by those persons doing the various inventories.

The 118 international wars (interstate and extrasystemic wars) Small and Singer tabulated are, to some extent, the failure of international controls, since the conflicts were not resolved peacefully; but international controls bear little, if any, responsibility for most of the civil wars. While civil wars can come about because of external actions that destabilize the domestic political system, civil wars are primarily the result of the domestic political system's failure to resolve internal conflict. Although a higher percentage of wars are now civil wars, the Small and Singer study indicates that the number of wars overall has not increased over time but has remained relatively level. Taking into account the increased number of nation-states now as opposed to earlier years, the per–nation-state incidence of interstate war, as with civil war, has declined.

The number of wars, however, is not the only indicator of whether the incidence of armed conflict on the international level is increasing. While the number of wars shows a lower incidence per nation in the post–World War II period, the severity of war, measured in terms of casualties, has been much higher in the twentieth century than earlier. The combat fatalities of the 118 international wars reported by Small and Singer totaled 31 million. Nearly half (15 million) occurred during World War II, 9 million during World War I, and 2 million during the Korean War. The war in Vietnam produced 1.2 million fatalities. Thus, those four wars, all fought in the twentieth century, produced 27 million fatalities, with all the remaining 114 wars accounting for the other 4 million deaths; wars, obviously, have become more severe.

These totals are combat fatalities only and do not include civilian deaths. If civilian casualties are included, then the total fatalities for World War II number 37 million. Of the combined civilian and military casualties, the Soviet Union suffered an estimated 8 million combat and 12 million civilian fatalities; the civilian lives lost in Cambodia from 1975-1979 under the Pol Pot regime are estimated to have been 2 million; and Nigeria, by one estimate, suffered 1 million combat deaths and 1 million civilian deaths during the Biafran War from 1967 to 1970 (Sivard, 1982, 15). All of these figures are estimates, however, and vary depending on the source.

The 37 million fatalities of World War II, except for fatalities at Hiroshima and Nagasaki, resulted from conventional, as opposed to nuclear, means. The atomic bombs dropped on Hiroshima and Nagasaki produced from 130,000 fatalities, according to U.S. estimates, to 300,000

fatalities, by Japanese estimates. Whichever estimate is used, atomic bombs produced less than 1 percent of the fatalities of World War II. This would indicate that humankind had increased considerably its capabilities to kill even before the development of nuclear weapons.

Two factors are involved in the increase in wartime fatalities. One is the development of mass citizen armies in the late eighteenth century. The second is that by the twentieth century these mass armies faced automatic weapons, improved artillery, aircraft, and tanks, all of which helped produce greater casualties than could earlier weapons. While improved weaponry has increased casualties among combatants, civilian deaths are only in small part a product of combat in the field; more frequently, civilians are victims of aerial bombing, genocide, starvation, and disease. Deaths among civilians rose dramatically once nations industrialized and attacks on industrial centers (to reduce war production) and civilians (to weaken the enemy's will to resist) became accepted targets.

Estimates of fatalities in a nuclear exchange between the United States and the Soviet Union depend on many factors, such as whether only missile sites would be hit or whether the population centers would also be targeted. The number of deaths from radiation over the years following an attack is also subject to widely varying estimates. If the attack produced a years-long nuclear winter, then millions more would starve, since the land would be unproductive. Total fatalities, if all these possibilities occurred, would be in the billions, far exceeding the casualties of even the most destructive wars of the past.

THE DURATION AND INTENSITY OF WAR

Other indicators of how prevalent war is in the international system are how much time states are engaged in war and which nations suffer the most casualties. Evidence produced by the Small and Singer study (wars from 1816 to 1980) concerning those topics indicates that the major states are the ones most apt to be engaged in war and to suffer the highest number of casualties. Among the top ten nations in terms of months at war, only two, Turkey and North Vietnam, are not major states. North Vietnam is an anomaly, however, in that its months at war were primarily the result of its lengthy war of independence; whereas, for the major states, several wars are included in their totals. During the 165 years covered in the study, the country at war the greatest portion of time was France, with 604 months (50 years and 4 months); Great Britain was next, with 410 war months (34 years and 2 months); Turkey was third, with 341 months (28 years and 5 months); the Soviet Union/Russia was fourth, with 286 months (23 years and 10 months); The United States was fifth, with 262 months (21 years and 10 months); and Germany/Prussia, a nation often thought of as an instigator of war in modern times, was tenth with 139 months (11 years and 7 months). There was no greater concentration of war months during the twentieth century than in the nineteenth century for the major states.

In summation, wars, overall, are not becoming more frequent in the international system,

Tab. 11.1 Top 10 Nations Months at War 1816–1980 (Current Military Powers)

Country	Time at War (Months)
1. France	604 (50 yr., 4 mo.)
2. Great Britain	410 (34 yr., 2 mo.)
3. Turkey/Ottoman Empire	341 (28 yr., 5 mo.)
4. Soviet Union/Russia	286 (23 yr., 10 mo.)
5. United States	262 (21 yr., 10 mo.)
6. China	208 (17 yr., 4 mo.)
7. Japan	198 (16 yr., 6 mo.)
8. Vietnam	191 (15 yr., 11 mo.)
9. Italy	155 (12 yr., 11 mo.)
10. Germany/Prussia	139 (11 yr., 7 mo.)

SOURCE: Melvin Small and J. David Singer, *Resort to Arms: International and Civil Wars 1816-1980* (Beverly Hills: Sage Publications, 1982).

but the severity of war in terms of casualties has increased in the twentieth century. While the major states since 1816 have been more apt to be at war than other states, this has not been true since World War II. In the postwar period, most wars have been fought in the Third World, and civil wars have increased as a percentage of total wars.

WHO IS MOST APT TO GO TO WAR

An assumption often made is that democracies are peace-loving and that authoritarian regimes seek war. An extension of that assumption is that democracies are usually the victims of aggression and that the aggressors are authoritarian states; thus, authoritarian and totalitarian nations are more apt to be at war than are democracies. Studies show, however, that democracies are as likely to be at war as are nations with other forms of government. As was indicated above in the discussion about which nations spent the greatest number of months at war, the major democratic states were as apt to be at war as the major powers that were authoritarian (Wright, 1942; Chan, 1984, 617–648; Russett and Monsen, 1975, 5–31; Weede, 1984, 649–664). Germany, an authoritarian state for much of the period included in the Small and Singer study, spent substantially fewer months at war than did the major Western democracies. Also, the combined war months of Russia/Soviet Union, a country that has had little experience with democracy, were fewer than those of either France or Great Britain. The overall record of time at war would indicate that democracies are as prone toward war as are authoritarian states; therefore, the form of government apparently has little bearing on a nation's proclivity for war. It should be pointed out, however, that for both France and Great Britain, much of their time at war was involvement in colonial wars; whereas, Prussia/Germany and Russia/Soviet Union had small empires and therefore little opportunity for colonial wars. The number of months of war does not indicate which side is fighting a just war, however. Democracies may be more apt to feel that they are fighting for a righteous cause or to defend their form of government, but states with other forms of government also claim, when at war, that theirs is the morally correct side of the conflict. There is no statistical means of measuring morality in war.

Accounting for why the major states are the ones most apt to be at war is not difficult, since they tend to be the larger and economically more powerful states in the international system with the greater capability to wage war. Regardless of whether they are democratic or not, the generalization applies. As concerns nations other than the major states, war, as mentioned earlier, is more apt to occur among those that have recently received their independence. This observation not only applies to the large number of nations that gained their independence since World War II, but Quincy Wright (1942) drew the same conclusion about new nations well before the rapid expansion of the nation-state system following World War II. This generalization does not apply to all Third World nations equally, however. The poorest of the Third World nations are less apt to go to war than are the better-off, developing nations. Perhaps the explanation for this is that nations can be too poor, that is, not have the economic capability, to wage war. Also, the geographically larger Third World states are more apt to be at war than are the smaller ones. Thus, of the attributes of nations, the form of government does not seem to be a significant factor in determining whether a nation will be at war, but a nation's size and economic capabilities do seem to be.

EXPLANATIONS FOR WAR

One of the very basic issues of human behavior is the question of why wars occur. Despite the death and destruction of war and the pronounce-ment of nations that they are peace-loving, nations continue to fight wars. As is the situation with any important question that has not been resolved, many theories exist. Each explains some wars, but no theory is accepted as an overall explanation. Here those explanations will be reduced to a few general categories, the first of which is the human-nature argument.

WAR AND HUMAN NATURE

The most commonly heard explanation for war is that it is human nature to fight. Once people found that they could injure their fellow men and capture their possessions, violence among humans has existed; even though tribal cultures exist that reject the use of violence, they are atypical, because the nature of people is to be aggressive. When organized political units developed, that violence grew into warfare. If war is human nature, then it can never be eliminated.

Another approach, somewhat less pessimistic, is that humankind's inclination toward violence is learned, not natural; learned behavior can be altered and people can be trained to be peaceful. A variation on this assumption is an argument sometimes heard in the women's movement, that it is only the male who is warlike, and, since males are usually the decision-makers, that is why nations go to war. If women, since they are more oriented toward peace than are males, were making the decisions, war would be less likely. A further variation on the "war-is-natural" argument is that if humans are violent by nature, they can carry out mass destruction only if they have machines and weapons; therefore, war would at least be reduced in its severity if no one possessed weapons. This argument supporting disarmament accepts humankind's inclination toward violence as unalterable and focuses on limiting the ability to cause harm to others.

The social-Darwinism approach to war also assumes something about the nature of humankind. This argument accepts that the strong will naturally use their strength to subjugate the weak. Both Hitler and Mussolini argued that it was proper that strong nations survive and that aggression is acceptable behavior when carried out by the strong to eliminate the weak.

NATIONALISM AND EXCITATION THEORY

After the argument that human nature is the cause of war, nationalism seems to be the most frequently offered explanation. At the most general level, the reason nationalism is a cause of wars is that without the willingness of people to support war, no war could be fought. Nationalism was defined earlier as the unique attitude of support a citizen feels toward his or her country which becomes the psychological underpinning of governments and nation-states. When one blames nationalism for wars, however, additional aspects of nationalism must be mentioned. Nationalism can also include an irrational support for one's country and its policies. A "my country right or wrong" attitude leads to uncritical acceptance of a nation's policies regardless of their morality. A government must have the support of its citizens in order for its decisions to be effective, but the dark side of nationalism is apparent when that support is unquestioned and irrational.

Nationalism, rational or not, is the basis for a nation's attempt to recover territory it claims, now under control of another nation. Alsace and Lorraine, presently provinces of France, have been passed back and forth between France and Germany several times, with each claiming the territory as part of its nation. Transylvania has been at times a part of Rumania and at other times part of Hungary. During and after World War II, the Soviet Union claimed territory from Finland, Poland, Czechoslovakia, and Rumania, as well as occupying the Baltic states of Lithuania, Estonia, and Latvia. All this occurred in the name of reclaiming what was considered by the Soviets to be lost Russian territory. China reco-

vered Tibet on the grounds that it was legitimately a province of China, and invaded India in 1962 to reclaim territory China claimed was rightfully its own. Iraq justified its invasion of Iran in 1980 on the grounds of reclaiming Iraqi territory taken unfairly by Iran in a 1975 treaty. Other claims to territory controlled by another nation include conflict among Kenya, Ethiopia, and Somalia over the Ogaden Desert; the IRA in Northern Ireland; Venezuelan claims of Guyanian territory; and China's claims to portions of the Soviet Union. With the exception of the Irish Republican Army (IRA) in Northern Ireland, these irredentist movements involve sparsely populated and generally remote territories of little economic value; therefore, the basis of the claims can best be explained as nationalism. Nationalism can also be a cause of wars when a portion of the population within a nation, usually an ethnic group, expresses its nationalism by demanding that it be allowed to form its own separate state.

Closely related to nationalism as an explanation for war is the theory that wars are a product of excitation. Nations are involved in competition over arms, economic markets, overseas possessions, or territory, or are involved in a crisis for whatever reason. In circumstances in which a strong sense of nationalism exists, governments and their peoples become increasingly emotional over the issues at hand. As the crisis escalates, emotion replaces reason, the implications and possible results of a war are lost to nationalistic fervor, communication between nations breaks down, no alternative but war seems apparent, and war results. This explanation comes close to being no-fault war in that the nations involved do not intend for a war to occur. This sequence of events is very similar to those preceding World War I.

Explaining war through emotional escalation relates to various other factors that contribute to the development of wars. Perhaps the most important is the breakdown of communication between nations as a crisis becomes more intense. Such a breakdown does not necessarily mean that nations are no longer attempting to communicate with one another, but only that the messages sent are not perceived correctly and are viewed as more hostile than the sender intends. The possibility exists, as some studies indicate, that during the week prior to the outbreak of World War I so many messages were sent that there was an information overload; there simply was not time enough to interpret and understand all of the information being injected into the diplomatic process. The emotional escalation of a crisis illustrates the serious consequences of misperception, which becomes a critical problem during times of crisis. When the messages sent between nations are filtered through hostile perceptions, a message that is intended to be conciliatory may be perceived as hostile and thus intensify the crisis. Once that level of misperception develops, war is difficult to avoid.

POWER RELATIONSHIPS AS A CAUSE OF WAR

In an earlier chapter, the discussion of alternative means of organizing the international system included certain types of relationships that are conducive to war. In a balance-of-power system, the assumption is that two coalitions of approximately equal size are unlikely to go to war with one another, but if a significant imbalance develops, war is apt to occur. This approach argues that wars are caused by an imbalance; equilibrium will prevent war, but disequilibrium makes war more likely. One explanation for World War I is that the balance-of-power system lost its flexibility, and changes in power relationships could not be compensated for. When this rigidity in coalition membership developed, an imbalance resulted and war between the coalitions resulted.

The bipolar system practiced since World War II also has an explanation for what causes wars. Under this system, war is more likely, from the U.S. perspective, if the Soviet Union has an advantage in weaponry. From the Soviet perspective, if the United States has an advantage in weapons, war is more apt to occur. Both nations work to gain an advantage and in the process produce a balance of sorts. Balance is unintended, but results because neither coalition will allow the other an advantage. In this line of reasoning, balance or an advantage for your coalition will prevent war, but an advantage for the opposing coalition makes war likely. Analysis of both balance of power and bipolarity indicates that a possible cause of war is a set of particular conditions that can exist in the manner in which the international system is organized.

One other aspect of the international system that is mentioned as a cause of war is its self-help nature. This does not pertain to how the system is organized, but rather to the nature of the system itself. Since the use of deadly force has not been entrusted to a central authority within the system, and since international law and international organizations do not have the capabilities to protect a nation from other nations, each nation must provide its own protection. A nation, therefore, must be prepared to go to war in self-defense. No country has ever admitted that the war it was fighting was anything other than self-defense; therefore, whether justified or not, nations go to war in the name of self-defense.

A collective-security system attempts to resolve the problem of self-help that nations face. If nations band together to aid the victim of aggression, an international collective effort, not self-help, punishes the aggressor. This system is predicated on the assumptions that wars start with an act of aggression and that the international system can readily recognize who is committing such an act.

DOMINO THEORY OF WAR

The domino theory of how nations expand is usually explained as a particular aspect of containment policy, but it also carries an assumption about how wars develop. President Eisenhower introduced the concept, arguing that if the United States did not take a strong stand against communist pressure in one country, then that country would not only become communist, it would expose its neighbors to communist pressure as well. One by one, countries would fall to communism like a row of dominos standing on end if one domino were pushed over. This approach to stopping communist expansion assumes that aggression breeds aggression; therefore wars can be prevented through national commitment to resist aggression through strength and resolve.

Another aspect of the argument that wars breed wars is related to the cause of World War II. The Treaty of Versailles, so the argument goes, was unnecessarily punitive and gave Hitler a platform for his rise to power. Hitler claimed that the German army had not been defeated; thus, Germany lost the war due to betrayal by the left wing and by Jews. The allies had, in turn, imposed an unfair peace settlement on Germany, and those responsible, both domestically and internationally, had to be punished. Hitler's *Mein Kampf* outlined how Germany would seek its revenge. This version of the domino theory suggests that the results of World War I made World War II inevitable. If the arguments of these two versions of the domino theory are valid, the lessons to be learned as to how to avoid war are that a nation should stand up to its enemies; but, if war occurs, the winner should be reasonable in the peace settlement to avoid creating the basis for another war.

THE PRESENCE OF ARMS

Arms as a factor in bringing about war has already been discussed in two ways: first, as to how arms relate to the intensity of war (the greater the number and sophistication of weapons, the higher the casualties; second, as a

possible cause of war (arms races are one means of exciting governments and peoples to the point that they are willing to go to war). Arms are blamed for wars in other ways as well. If nations arm to find security within the international system, then the arms that a hostile nation possesses threaten that security. What each nation sees as an adequate level of arms is seen by the other as a threat. Escalation and counterescalation results, and an arms race is on. Arms races, as is the case with a breakdown in communications, may not directly cause wars, but many wars are preceded by an arms race (Richardson, 1960; Art and Waltz, 1971). An arms race is particularly dangerous when decision makers can justify arms expenditures only by the ultimate use of those arms in war.

Another view of the role of arms is that they are a symptom, not a cause, of conflict. Nations arm because they are in conflict with another nation or nations and feel threatened, but arms in themselves do not bring about conflict. If this point is valid, the way to stop an arms race is to resolve underlying conflict, not to reduce arms. On occasion, however, as an arms race progresses, the original conflict is largely forgotten, and the main issue becomes the arms race itself. Thus, under these circumstances, arms can begin as a symptom of conflict but ultimately become a cause of conflict.

DEMANDS OF THE DOMESTIC SYSTEM

All causes of war discussed to this point have primarily been the result of behavior between states operating at the systemic level. Another general category of causes of war flows from developments in the domestic political system. These arguments can be subdivided into causes that are inevitable, according to communist theorists, and causes that originate in the domestic system but are policy choices and therefore not inevitable.

Marxist theorists disagree more frequently than would be expected from those who reason from the same premise, but they do have some generally agreed-upon principles as to the causes of war. Marx argued that the capitalist system—that is, the private ownership of property and the means of production—produced a class system which was the sole cause of conflict, domestic and international. Reasoning from that basic assumption, Lenin and others came up with several causes of war.

One type of war is that between capitalist states. Such wars are fought over world markets through which capitalist economic systems can dispose of surplus products. Wars for these markets are labeled by Marxists as wars of imperialism, and such wars, according to Lenin, are inevitable as long as there are bourgeois-controlled states. Lenin labeled World War I the first of the great imperialist wars.

According to Lenin, a second cause of international wars is conflict between competing economic systems, that is, wars fought between capitalist and communist societies. These wars, Marxists contend, are started by the capitalist nations because they will not tolerate the inevitable peaceful success of communist economic systems. The aggressive act most nearly fitting into this category of war was the German invasion of the Soviet Union in 1941. If war were to occur between the Western coalition and the communist coalition today, the Soviets would no doubt explain it as a war between opposing economic systems.

A third Marxist category of wars is colonial war. This type of war is between capitalist nations and their colonies or areas they are attempting to colonize. This sort of warfare, as with the others, is also an economic imperative, since the capitalist nations must maintain their colonial markets in order to postpone the inevitable collapse of their economic systems.

All three of these categories of war are forms of international warfare and are caused by domestic class conflict. A fourth Marxist category of war is the civil war that occurs when the proletariat rises up and destroys the bourgeoisie. Unlike noncommunist theorists who tend to judge war's justness on a war-by-war basis, the Marxist views war as just only when the proletariat (the working class) is resisting the bourgeoisie (the exploiting class). Such wars are, of course, just only for the proletariat, not the bourgeoisie. All civil wars do not lead to the overthrow of the bourgeoisie, but such wars can be just if they weaken the position of the ruling class. Wars of national liberation, guerrilla warfare, and terrorism are included in this category of warfare if justified as part of the class struggle.

While Marxists explain war in terms of domestic economic conditions, non-Marxist Western thought also has domestic causes for war. One explanation for the Vietnam War, at least an explanation for how it was fought, is based on domestic considerations of U.S. presidents (Ellsberg, 1971, 217–274). According to Daniel Ellsberg, both the decision to enter the war and the decision to restrain U.S. efforts in fighting it were domestically based. Ellsberg argues that following the "loss" of China in 1949 and the subsequent recriminations of the McCarthy period, no U.S. president could afford politically to allow another country to be lost to communism without a fight, but neither was any president willing to sustain the casualties and subsequent domestic repercussions necessary to win such a war. Thus, the United States was not caught in a quagmire from which presidents could not escape, but rather, stalemate was a deliberate policy. Escalation of U.S. efforts was enough to maintain the stalemate, but never enough to win the war.

The domestic equivalent of a Vietnam-style war for the Soviet Union would be the domestic and intracoalitional effects of the Soviet Union's failing to come to the aid of a national liberation movement. Not to do so would raise doubts among Soviet allies about how reliable the Soviets were, but to do so would increase the strain on an already struggling domestic economy. Under these circumstances, the Soviets would probably intervene, but the level of intervention would be restrained to some extent, just as it was for the United States in Vietnam. Evidence that such a hypothesis is valid is that the Soviets have sent only about 110,000 troops to Afghanistan when they are militarily capable of making a greater commitment.

While the Vietnam War can serve as an example of a war that was fought in a particular manner for domestic as well as international reasons, an argument can also be made that wars in general emanate from the domestic political system. The reasoning for this explanation of war is that nations tend to go to war internationally to resolve, at least temporarily, domestic conflict. A populace's nationalism will rise to an international threat, whether real or created by its government, and internal differences will be forgotten; internal conflict will be externalized through war with another country. The classic illustration used to support this argument was Secretary of State Seward's suggestion to Lincoln early in the American Civil War that the United States declare war on Great Britain or France in order to reunite the country. The United States was having problems with both countries at the time. Since Seward's recommendation was not implemented, the proposition was not tested.

A variation on the Seward suggestion is a perspective on the results of the U.S. entering World War II. Before entering the war, the United States had for several years been in deep economic depression and had made only limited recovery when it began to rearm in preparation for World War II. When war arrived, demands on the nation's industrial base were so great that the depression vanished. Thus, World War II, not the policies of the New Deal, brought the United States out of the Great Depression. This perspective does not suggest that the U.S. entered the war to speed economic recovery, but that the results of doing so may not be lost on future decision-makers.

Another suggested domestic cause of wars is the existence of the so-called military-industrial complex. Perhaps the two most famous farewell presidential addresses were Washington's, in which he warned against long-term foreign alliances, and Eisenhower's, in which he warned against a domestic military-industrial complex. Eisenhower cautioned that, unless watched by Congress and the American people, an alliance between professional military people and the leaders of the weapons industry could allow those groups to control government policy and produce unneeded weapons because it was in their mutual best interests to do so. This argument does not attribute wars to the symbiotic relationship between the military and the defense industry so much as it suggests that high levels of arms which result from the demands of these two powerful groups might lead to war. C. Wright Mills carried this conjecture a step further and applied the military-industrial-complex approach to the Soviet Union as well as to the United States. Mills argued that the two complexes control policy within the two superpowers and that they encourage hostility between the United States and the Soviet Union in order to justify increased defense spending (Mills, 1958). Eisenhower's warning was limited to not allowing the military-industrial complex excessive political influence, but Mills saw the military-industrial complexes as encouraging policies that could lead to war.

The validity of the argument that domestic conflict leads to international war has been called into question by a number of scholars, but the results of efforts to test this hypothesis are mixed. Some of the literature does support the argument that society is more integrated when there is external conflict (North, Koch, and Zinnes, 1960, 355–374). But efforts to verify statistically that internal conflict is followed by external conflict show no statistical correlation (Rummel, 1963, 17; Tantor, 1966; Huntington, 1962, 40–41). One quantitative study does find some relationship between internal conflict and external wars, however (Wilkenfeld, 1968). This does not mean that external conflict is never used to bring about internal cohesion, but that there is no established pattern of such behavior. Nor do these results imply that nations' behavior is not motivated, at least in part, by what is going on in the domestic political system. The overall observation thus is that domestic considerations are a factor, but not the only factor, in why nations go to war.

While the evidence does not support a strong link between internal conflict and its being externalized into an interstate war, it is, however, often the case that internal conflict presents other countries with the opportunity to become involved in another nation's domestic problems. The various interventions by the superpowers and other nations since World War II were all preceded by periods of internal crisis within the country in which the intervention took place. Any country suffering from serious internal divisions is susceptible to outside interference; thus, an internal conflict can, at the initiative of a second nation, evolve into an international war.

This discussion of the causes of war illustrates the problems involved in determining what causes a particular war. World War I has been used as an example of several different causes of war, but during the war, the Allies had little doubt as to the cause of the war—the Kaiser had planned and carried out an aggressive war. After the emotional phase of fixing blame had passed, a number of other theories about the war's causes emerged. Those mentioned above include the rigidity of the competing coalitions, the arms race that preceded the war, competing nationalistic fervor, excitation, and the breakdown in communication. To Lenin, World War I was a result of class conflict and the first of the great imperialist wars. Several suggested causes for World War II also exist, although Hitler's desire to dominate Europe is still the most widely accepted. A domestic cause was the economic chaos that Germany experienced during the Great Depression, which allowed Hitler to capitalize on Germany's economic problems as a stepping stone to power;

thus, in more stable times, Hitler might not have come to power. Other suggested causes include what some observers saw as the unjust peace imposed on Germany by the Allies after World War I, followed by the allies' appeasement policies toward Germany before World War II; the Allies were willing to impose a harsh peace, but not willing to enforce it. To the Marxists, World War II was, until the German invasion of the Soviet Union, a second great imperialist war; after the invasion, it was the Great Patriotic War. Different explanations for the Vietnam War also exist. The quagmire theory is that the United States wandered into the war as a manifestation of the policy of containment, incrementally escalated its involvement, but could not find a way to win the war. A counterthesis is that the United States had a deliberate policy of stalemate because domestic considerations limited U.S. efforts to win the war.

The conclusion to be drawn is that wars may have various causes and that it is difficult to determine that a war was fought for a single reason. A reasonable observation is that wars may occur for more than one reason, and the larger the war the more difficult it is to find its causes.

FORMS OF FORCE

The discussion that follows attempts to divide the use of force into categories and to provide examples. The only categories of war identified so far—those used by Small and Singer—have been interstate, extrasystemic, and civil wars. A further breakdown of levels of force and the circumstances for their use is possible.

TOTAL WAR

World War II is often described as a total war. Whether it was or not depends, of course, on how total war is defined. The war was not total in the sense that all nations of the world were involved, though most were. All major states, plus their colonies, were involved; all Latin American countries declared war against at least one Axis nation; and nearly all of the smaller nations of Europe, Asia, and Africa were brought into the war. The United Nations (the Allied wartime coalition) numbered 49 nations, and the Axis powers totaled 6. Only a handful of wartime neutrals remained—Sweden, Switzerland, Ireland, Spain, Portugal, and Thailand.

The fighting during World War II took place primarily in the Eastern Hemisphere, but where combat occurred, little or no restriction existed on how the war was fought. Virtually all types of weapons, excluding poison gas, were used. Nonmilitary targets were often hit deliberately, and civilian casualties were high. Industry in all the major states was reorganized to maximize the production of war supplies and manpower was redistributed, with women making up a high percentage of the work force while eligible men served in the armed forces. The societal efforts of the major powers were almost totally focused on conduct of the war. The objective of the war, on the Allied side, was unconditional surrender of the Axis nations; that is, the Allies demanded total victory. The Japanese were allowed to retain their emperor; otherwise, the Allied objective was achieved. If World War II was not total war—geographically, in use of weapons, target selection, societal effort, and war objectives—it was the conflict most nearly approaching total war the world has yet endured.

What is meant by total war has changed since World War II and the development of nuclear weapons. The World War II example involved a total societal commitment in support of the war, but, in the late 1980s, total war is defined in terms of the use of nuclear weapons rather than societal change. Since it is generally asssumed that a nuclear war between the superpowers would be of short duration, time would not permit a reorganization of society. Presently, "total" refers to the degree of physical and human destruction, not societal reorganization.

LIMITED WARS

If World War II came close to being a total war and was the most recent war that could possibly qualify as one, then all interstate wars since then necessarily have to have been limited in some way. One limitation has been in the number of casualties. The two million fatalities of the Korean War and the undetermined but heavy loss of life in the Iraqi-Iranian War would indicate that in some post–World War II wars little effort was made to control casualties. The United States, however, did limit the number of troops it sent to Korea and in that manner limited casualties. The British, so it appears, attempted to hold down casualties during the Falklands War, but they also went to considerable lengths in World War II to limit their casualties in order to avoid the repetition of slaughtering a generation of males, as occurred in World War I. Most post–World War II limited wars have been limited in casualties when compared to major wars of the past.

A limitation on the types of weapons used has been placed on all post–World War II wars. Virtually all modern conventional weapons have been used in those wars, but a strict prohibition on the use of nuclear weapons is an accepted restriction. Certainly, the British had nuclear weapons available during the Falklands War, but did not use them, although a controversy carried over from the war as to whether the British had nuclear weapons aboard any of their ships in the war zone. Even the use of certain types of conventional weapons in limited wars has been questioned. In the Vietnam War, the United States was criticized for using napalm, a weapon developed and used in World War II and the Korean

War, and nonfatal poison gas. The Iraqis have been accused of using fatal poison gas in their war with Iran, as have the Soviets in their operations in Afghanistan. Thus, while there certainly is no agreed-upon list of weapons that can be used in limited wars, some conventional weapons are considered in world opinion to be inhumane and inappropriate for limited wars.

One clear limitation on post–World War II interstate wars is geographic; the wars, for the most part, have not spread beyond the initial participants. This is true despite the absence of declarations of war that under international law would clarify which nations are legal belligerents. The absence of declarations of war does have a beneficial side effect, however—if a war is not official, then no need exists for an official peace settlement to end a legal state of war.

Though all interstate wars since World War II have taken place in the Third World, those wars have been limited successfully to the initial parties. Only India and Pakistan have been involved in their several wars. None of the wars involving Israel and the Arab countries has expanded beyond the countries involved in Israel's war of independence in 1948. Morocco and Algeria have been in conflict over boundaries and the Spanish Sahara without other nations becoming involved (although Mauritania did engage in the fighting in Spanish Sahara for a short time). Even in the Korean War, which expanded to include many outside nations, the fighting was carefully limited to the Korean peninsula; and no Chinese Nationalist forces were allowed to participate in order to avoid reopening the Chinese Civil War. The Iraqi-Iranian War has not brought in any other combatants, although various countries have provided military and diplomatic support to one or the other of the belligerents. In general, wars of an interstate nature in the Third World have been controlled as to participants. This also means that major states generally have not militarily participated directly in wars between Third World nations.

ARMED INTERVENTION BY MAJOR POWERS—DIRECT AND SURROGATE FORCES

While not at war with one another at any time since World War II, the major powers have conducted a number of direct armed interventions in other countries. With the exception of Soviet interventions in Eastern Europe, all have occurred in Third World countries. Most have been mentioned in earlier discussions; therefore, only a brief mention is necessary here. The United States intervened with its armed forces in the Dominican Republic in 1965, in Lebanon in 1958, and in Grenada in 1983. If the war in Vietnam is regarded as a civil war, as it is by many, then that too was a direct U.S. military intervention in the internal conflict of a Third World nation. As an extension of its operations in Vietnam, the United States also intervened in Cambodia (now Kampuchea) in 1970 and secretly in Laos for several years during the Vietnam War. The Soviets directly intervened in Afghanistan in 1979. France sent troops to Zaire in 1978 to repel an armed force that had invaded Shaba province from Angola. France also sent troops to Chad in 1982 to protect that government from Libyan-backed rebels. France, Italy, the United States, and Great Britain provided forces for the international contingent sent into Lebanon in 1983.

While each of these situations directly involved the armed forces of major states, the major powers—particularly the superpowers—also often intervene by indirect means. The United States used surrogate forces in Guatemala in 1954 and again at the Bay of Pigs in 1961 by organizing and training refugee armies to carry out the operations. The Guatemalan operation was successful, but the Bay of Pigs was a military disaster. The Soviets have used surrogate forces—Cuban troops—in Angola and Ethiopia. Since the

Soviet Union provides Vietnam with substantial economic and military assistance, the presence of the Vietnamese army in Kampuchea can also be interpreted as a Soviet-sponsored surrogate force.

The major powers have, on a number of occasions, used their armed forces to establish a presence. The stationing of armed forces or substantial contingents of military advisers in a particular country for political purposes is a form of intervention, even though those forces are not involved in combat and may be there at the invitation of the host government. The Soviet Union has contingents of military advisers in Angola and Ethiopia along with the Cuban troops, as well as military advisers in Guinea, Mali, Algeria, Libya, Iraq, Syria, India, South Yemen, Zambia, Tanzania, Mozambique, Congo, Madagascar, Nigeria, and Peru. In addition, the Soviets have naval facilities in several of those countries (*Atlas of NATO*, 1985). Military maneuvers conducted by the United States in Honduras and Egypt, where the forces remain for weeks or months, serve as a form of military intervention, as do U.S. military arrangements with Oman and Kenya. In order to maintain political stability, the French have troop contingents in several of their former colonies, including Gabon, Central African Republic, Djibouti, Senegal, and Ivory Coast.

ARMED INTERVENTION BY THIRD WORLD COUNTRIES

In a number of instances, Third World countries have used their armed forces to intervene in the internal affairs of another country. While this form of intervention usually takes place in another Third World nation, the Falklands War is an exception. Among post–World War II wars, the Falklands War is unique because a Third World nation—Argentina—intervened in territory controlled by a major Western state—Great Britain.

The usual pattern is the reverse. Yet another problem in classifying that war is that Argentina is a nation on the threshold of being a developed nation and is hardly typical of the Third World in general; therefore, the Falklands War could be classified as a war between two developed states, also an unusual occurrence in the post–World War II period. To the Argentineans, however, this was a war to reclaim territory held by a colonial power and thus was a colonial war.

The typical pattern of intervention by a Third World country, however, is in another Third World country. Even the Korean War, since it started with the invasion of South Korea by North Korea, fits this category of wars if the two Koreas are thought of as separate nations rather than as one divided nation. Another important example of Third World intervention is the Vietnamese presence since 1979 in Kampuchea and lesser operations in Laos. An armed conflict related to the Vietnamese interventions, also involving Third World countries, was the abortive Chinese incursion into Vietnam in 1979. Other illustrations of armed intervention by a Third World country include the Turkish invasion of Cyprus in 1974; and, after the French had crushed an invasion of Zaire from Angolan territory in 1977, a second invasion in the same region in 1978, which was stopped by Moroccan and Senegalese troops.

The Arab countries also have intervened in other Arab countries. Egypt committed its armed forces to combat in North Yemen's civil war for several years prior to the 1967 Six-Day War, at which time the troops were withdrawn to help defend Egypt. Syrian armed forces were sent into Lebanon in 1975—where they still remain, under the auspices of the Arab League—for the purpose of stabilizing the political situation there.

With the possible exception of South Korea, each of the countries that suffered intervention by another Third World country did so during a period of internal crisis. The Third World countries that conducted these armed interventions, as is the case for the major states when they intervene, have suffered few reprisals for their actions.

GUERRILLA WARFARE AND NATIONAL LIBERATION FRONTS

The tactics of guerrilla warfare have long been a part of human conflict. The style of warfare conducted by the American Indian, used against Napoleon in Spain, and employed by Philippine nationalists after the Spanish-American War are all examples of guerrilla tactics. This style of warfare increased after World War II primarily as a means of speeding along the decolonization process, but later became a means utilized by rebel groups to destabilize governments when those groups possessed insufficient force to conduct a conventional-style civil war. Thus, guerrilla wars have changed from being a form of colonial warfare to being a form of civil war and, since World War II, have been fought almost exclusively in colonies and Third World countries.

In recent years, guerrilla warfare and the efforts of national liberation fronts have become virtually synonymous. National liberation fronts are usually Marxist-oriented, but not exclusively so. Regardless of what label is used, the objective of such a movement is to gain control of the government through the unconventional use of force, that is, by means other than organized military units engaged in open warfare. In any given year since World War II, several such wars have been underway.

A guerrilla-style war ordinarily develops through several stages. Acts of terrorism are the initial stage, followed by small-unit, armed attacks on civilian or minor military targets. As the movement gains strength, the size of the units increases, and larger-scale operations, including brief, open battles are possible. At this stage, the guerrilla units fight briefly, then retreat to safe areas to regroup; but the choice of targets rests with the guerrillas. In the latter stages of guerrilla warfare, still larger units are organized, and the war evolves into large-unit conventional combat. Guerrilla warfare thus is a war of escalation both as to unit size and the importance of targets. These progressively more aggressive steps were originally outlined by Mao Tse-tung during the Chinese Civil War and were further refined by the North Vietnamese general, Vo Nguyen Giap, who served as the military leader of the fight against, first, France, and then the United States. Guerrilla movements do not necessarily progress through all of these stages, however; guerrilla warfare is not an inevitable process. Not all such movements are successful, although they have a high rate of success.

Many of the worst atrocities of the post–World War II period have been carried out by guerrillas or by forces fighting them. The use of terror, particularly against civilian targets, has made guerrilla warfare especially brutal, and some of the most prolonged wars have been guerrilla wars fought to gain independence from a colonial power. Since the colonial powers were also industrial nations with considerable military capability, they could carry on a war against a guerrilla force until they either won or lost their resolve to continue. A purely military defeat of an industrial power by a guerrilla force was generally not possible; thus, if a guerrilla movement could sustain its operations long enough, domestic political support of the war in the colonial power often would wane.

The Mau-Mau rebellion in Kenya from 1952 to 1960 is an example of a guerrilla movement that was partially defeated by the British, but Kenya nevertheless gained its independence in 1963 during the overall dissolution of the British empire. Guerrilla movements in Portugal's African colonies—Angola, Mozambique, and Portuguese Guinea—fought the Portuguese for several years until, in 1974, the dictatorship in

Portugal collapsed and a new democratic government granted the colonies their independence. In this instance, the prolonged fighting not only produced independence for the colonies; it was also a major cause in the downfall of a colonial power's government. The French fought two major colonial wars against guerrilla forces, first in Vietnam from 1946 to 1954, and then in Algeria from 1954 to 1962. France lost both wars. The long years of fighting resulted in a political crisis in France that led to the collapse of the Fourth Republic in 1958 and General deGaulle's rise to power. U.S. efforts in Vietnam also produced a political crisis that led to President Johnson's decision to not run for reelection. Industrial nations, although not defeated militarily, have, on occasion, undergone important domestic changes as a result of their attempts to resist guerrilla movements.

In addition to the collapse of the Mau-Mau movement, other guerrilla movements have also failed. In Malaya, in 1948, a guerrilla force made up primarily of ethnic Chinese communists began a twelve-year fight against British and other commonwealth forces. Malaya, present-day Malaysia, received its independence in 1957, but not under the leadership of the guerrilla forces. Although substantially reduced in size, a small force operated in northern Malaysia until its surrender in 1987.

The manner in which the British prevented a communist government from coming to power in Malaysia was used as a model by the United States in its efforts in Vietnam. The British tactics were not successful a second time, however. Some guerrilla movements in Latin America have also been defeated. The attempt by Che Guevera to establish a guerrilla movement in Bolivia ended in his death, and the Colombian government was successful in defeating guerrilla forces that operated in that country. The armed force known as M-19 has become an increasing threat to the Colombian government again in the late 1980s, however. Also, Uruguay was successful in destroying an urban guerrilla movement, the Tupamaros. Other Latin American guerrilla wars, such as Castro's in Cuba and the Sandinistas' in Nicaragua, have been successful, however.

British support after 1957 of the Malaysian government's resistance against a guerrilla force is but one example of an outside nation supporting a Third World country's efforts to fight a guerrilla force. The largest such effort was, of course, the U.S. effort in Vietnam. The Soviets' operations in Afghanistan in support of the Afghan government is another example. The Soviet and Cuban military assistance to the governments of Angola and Ethiopia has also been justified by the Soviets as necessary to fight guerrilla forces. For a time, the United States sent aid to guerrillas (UNITA) fighting the Angolan government until Congress stopped such assistance on the grounds that it might lead the U.S. into another Vietnam-type war. South Africa continues to send aid to those guerrillas. Under the Reagan administration, substantial U.S. aid has been given the Contras, a guerrilla movement fighting the Sandinista government in Nicaragua. An ongoing example of U.S. support for a government fighting a guerrilla force is the economic and military aid extended El Salvador.

Devising successful tactics to use against guerrilla fighters has been a problem for any country that has attempted to fight a guerrilla movement. The Soviets have used many of the same methods in Afghanistan that the United States used in Vietnam, but with little more success. The advantages a guerrilla force has in choosing targets and the place of combat is reflected in the United States' attempt during the Vietnam War to maintain a manpower ratio of ten to one over guerrilla forces. Whether that ratio was ever obtained was one of the issues of the General Westmoreland-CBS lawsuit. If the enemy force was larger than Westmoreland claimed, then that ratio of advantage was never reached. The issue in the trial was whether Westmoreland had lied about the size of the enemy's forces; but whether he did or not, the trial and the war itself pointed out the problems involved in estimating the strength, both in numbers and morale, of a guerrilla force.

TERRORISM

Terrorism has been described as a phase of a guerrilla movement, but, of the hundreds of terrorist groups operating in the world today, most do not move beyond the terrorism stage of guerrilla activity. The objectives of such groups vary. They may want their own nation, as do the Basques, the Armenians, and the Palestinians; they may want a revolutionary change, as do the Baader-Meinhof group in West Germany and the Red Guard in Italy; or they may want to control the government of a country, the objective of the Islamic Jihad (Holy War) terrorist organization in Lebanon. Although many organizations demanding political change are not active in terrorist activities, those that are have introduced considerable violence into the international system. Bombings of civilian targets have been a particularly tragic aspect of such groups' activities. Political assassinations and kidnappings are also widely used techniques of terrorists. In the late 1960s and the 1970s, hijacking commercial aircraft was a frequent terrorist act, but increased security substantially reduced that sort of terrorist operation. Aerial hijackings do still occur, however, as when a Shiite Moslem group seized TWA Flight 847 out of Athens in June 1985. Terrorism is clearly the use of force to achieve political objectives, but the activities of most terrorist movements cannot be classified as a war, since their activities do not produce the minimum number of fatalities established by Small and Singer. The activities of groups such as the Provisional Wing of the IRA in Northern Ireland and the operations of various terrorist groups in the Lebanese civil war, however, have produced substantial fatalities, but most of those casualties have been suffered by civilians rather than recognized armed forces. Whether constituting war

or not, terrorist attacks are the most rapidly expanding use of force in the international system. In the decade from 1968 to 1979, terrorist attacks tripled. (Papp, 1984, 82).

While persons engaged in terrorist activities are commonly referred to as terrorists, particularly in the industrial nations, to their supporters they are freedom fighters fighting bravely for what they believe. But, whatever they are called, they are people who feel that they have no other means available to achieve their objectives. Thus, incidents of terrorism can be seen as acts of the desperate who feel they have no other choice but to use terror as a weapon. Beyond those who sympathize with the political objectives and tactics of such groups, the violence they utilize is viewed as an atrocity, since many of the acts of violence seem to have no purpose other than to bring attention to a group's cause.

A number of terrorist attacks have gained worldwide attention. Perhaps the most widely known was the attack by the Black Septemberists on the Israeli Olympic team in Munich in 1972. More recently, suicidal attacks by members of the Islamic Jihad on a U.S. Marine post near Beirut and twice on the U.S. embassy in Beirut have gained considerable attention. Terrorist attacks seem to have declined in frequency during the early 1980s, but they also seem to have become more spectacular (Alexander and Meyers 1982, Livingstone, 1982). To combat these activities, some nations have developed special military units, such as the British Special Air Services and the West German Group Nine. Israel and the United States also have special units trained for that purpose.

Until the 1980's, terrorist activity was generally regarded as the work of small bands of dedicated political fanatics, most of which received no training in planning and carrying out missions. The major exception to this view was the training and weapons terrorist groups within the Palestinian Liberation Organization received. Financing for these operations came either from the Soviet Union or sympathetic Arab states. But even then, terrorist acts carried out by these groups were not viewed as the indirect acts of a state. Their operations were usually directed against Israel, and when Israel retaliated with air attacks, it was against those groups' bases and not against the states that financed them.

By the 1980s, however, states that provided aid to terrorist groups were being held directly responsible for activities of those groups. The U.S. air attack on Libya in 1986 was explained as retaliation for terrorist acts committed by persons trained and sheltered in Libya. Iran and Syria were also blamed for their support of terrorist activities. The United States held Iran responsible for the kidnapping of Westerners by groups supported by Iran. After it was convinced that the Syrian government had financed an attempted bombing of an Israeli commercial aircraft, Great Britain broke diplomatic relations with Syria. State-sponsored terrorism had become a major source of conflict between the Western nations and a few Third World countries.

CONCLUSION

The purpose of the discussion in this chapter has been to show that while violence exists in the international system and within the nations that make up that system, war is a less frequent occurrence than generally thought; on a per actor basis, the incidence of war has probably declined. Certain types of use of force such as guerrilla activity and the use of terror have expanded, but warfare in general has not increased. The threat to use force is present at all times in the international system because many nations maintain large armed forces. Occasionally a nation will use that force to intervene in another country's affairs, but most such incidents do not involve combat. Moving armed forces into or near trouble spots is also frequent, but such operations are generally limited to the major powers.

Though the incidence of warfare has not increased, wars of the twentieth century have tended to be more severe and produce more casualties than wars of earlier centuries. Perhaps the greatest fear of humankind is a nuclear war that could destroy civilization as it is now known, if not wipe out the human species.

The explanations for why wars occur are numerous, and range from a violent human nature, through economic explanations to excitation, arms races, and an imbalance of power. No explanation explains all wars.

CHAPTER 12

Use of Economic Intervention

Chapters five through seven discussed the sources of international conflict; a significant portion of that discussion centered on economic conflict. Economic problems were prominent whether the conflict originated from East-West, North-South, West-West, or East-East relationships. The causes of this conflict vary, but two major sources are: 1) differing levels of economic development and capabilities, particularly disparities found between industrialized and Third World countries; and 2) differing means of organizing a nation's economic system, as exemplified by contrasts between communist and Western nations. But economic conflict also exists among the Western nations that have roughly equal levels of development and similar means of organizing their economic systems, which points out that economic conflict exists even among nations whose economies are interdependent.

Within this context of conflict, many opportunities exist for a nation to use its economic capabilities to influence the behavior of other nations with both rewards and sanctions. This chapter will discuss how nations use those instruments of policy to achieve foreign policy objectives. These instruments are generally utilized by economically advanced nations to either punish or reward other nations for their behavior, but they are not the exclusive domain of those nations.

WEAPONS OF ECONOMIC CONFLICT

Nations, if their economies are strong enough, have a variety of economic weapons at their disposal. The most commonly used is the tariff. Tariffs—fees or taxes levied on imported items—raise the cost of an imported product, thus making that item less competitive with a similar product produced domestically. When the term "protectionism" is used, it usually refers to a country's maintaining or raising tariffs to protect domestic industries. Tariffs can be applied discriminately to give trade advantages to some nations and to punish others.

Nations justify their tariff structures in various ways. On occasion, a tariff is defended as protecting growing industries that are not yet strong enough to compete with foreign producers. Tariffs also may be imposed to protect established domestic industries that are having economic difficulties, such as the steel, textile, and automobile industries in the United States. Tariffs may be established or raised to reduce a nation's negative balance of payments; the higher the tariff, the less attractive it is to import. Tariffs also may be increased in retaliation because another country has raised its tariffs. Whatever the motivation for increasing tariffs, the demand for doing so often comes from within the domestic economy; some sector of the economy feels it needs protection from foreign competition. Even though tariffs do raise revenue—in the nineteenth century they were a large portion of any government's budget—today they are such a limited source of funds that tariffs are seldom justified on the basis of needed revenue.

A number of nontariff sanctions can also be imposed. While many post–World War II economic conferences have led to the reduction of tariffs, recent conferences have devoted considerable attention to nontariff trade barriers such as customs procedures, health standards, tax advantages granted domestic industries, currency convertibility, and safety standards such as those imposed on automobiles imported into the United States. Nations may also establish quotas or quantitative limits on how much of a particular product may be imported, or embargo certain items or all items imported from a particular nation. (Baldwin, 1985, 40–50). An example is the system of sugar quotas the United States extends to the sugar-producing countries of Latin America. If the United States wishes to punish one of those countries, the quota is reduced, or, as in the case of Cuba under Castro, eliminated.

Severe economic sanctions, such as the reduction or elimination of quotas or the imposition of embargoes, usually are imposed for political, not economic reasons, and often are directed at a nation with which conflict extends well beyond any economic differences. If they can afford to extend economic aid to other nations, nations also may utilize their foreign aid, lending capability, granting of credits, and investment policies to punish or reward other nations. The policy objective in imposing economic sanctions can range from gaining a limited economic advantage to an attempt to bring down a government. The stronger the economy of a nation imposing economic sanctions, the more dependent other nations are upon that economy and the more effective will its economic sanctions be. The eco-

nomic rewards and punishments just described are those available during peacetime; wartime economic sanctions can be even more severe.

During both world wars, the Allies attempted to strangle Germany economically by imposing a naval blockade. The purpose was not only to prevent Germany's receiving any materials that would aid its war effort, but also to create food shortages and perhaps starve Germany into capitulation. In addition during World War II, the Allies blacklisted any firms operating outside the Axis nations that had Axis connections. For example, many firms operating in Argentina were blacklisted both during and after the war for having Axis connections. The Allies also engaged in preemptive buying of materials in neutral countries in order to prevent those materials from being sold to one of the Axis powers. Raw materials were purchased by outbidding Axis buyers, even when those materials were of no use to the Allied war effort. Such buying was particularly important in Spain, a country to which both Germany and the Allies had access. Other European neutrals, such as Sweden, were forced to sell to Germany because the Allies had no geographic access to those countries and Germany threatened to take what it needed if it were not provided.

In peacetime, it is not easy to draw a distinction between a nation's engagement in routine economic competition and a nation's use of economic capabilities to modify another nation's behavior. Even though the declared objective of the world's major trading nations is to achieve free trade, international economic transactions still have many restrictions imposed upon them. Restrictions on trade have been reduced, but those remaining could be viewed as the use of economic instruments for political purposes. For example, what is seen as routine trade transactions by industrial nations is often perceived by Third World countries as the maintenance of a colonial-style trade relationship, with the industrial nations using the strength of their economies to continue that relationship. A number of specific examples of the use of economic sanctions to alter the behavior of other nations do exist, however, and these examples will be the primary subjects of this chapter. Certain observations about the world's economic condition need to be made, however, before turning to instances in which economic sanctions have been used, for it is within the context of those conditions that sanctions and rewards succeed or fail. The choice of sanctions depends on the sort of economic relationship nations have with one another.

SANCTIONS AND WORLD ECONOMIC CONDITIONS

Of the international relationships among major groups of nations in the present international system, the one most heavily dominated by trade and economics is the North-South relationship. This relationship is primarily a dependent one, with the South or Third World having little control over how it will be treated. Third World countries are heavily dependent on the industrial nations, both for markets for their raw materials and the degree to which the markets of the industrial nations are open to manufactured goods from the Third World. These lesser-developed countries must also depend on the industrial nations for their developmental capital in either the form of direct aid or loans. Even the international lending agencies are dominated by the Western industrial nations. Overall, the generally weak economies of the Third World make those countries particularly vulnerable to the trade and aid policies of the developed nations.

If an industrial nation imposes restrictions on its economic relationship with the Third World, the Third World often has only limited means to retaliate. The major exception was the temporary success of OPEC as a producers' cartel when OPEC was able to shift control of oil prices from the buyer to the producer. Only a few Third World nations have a surplus of oil for export, however, and OPEC's successes of the 1970s were drastically diminished during the oil glut of the 1980s.

The Third World nations are not, however, helpless victims with no alternatives when economic sanctions are imposed upon them by a Western nation, and those nations need not be members of an effective cartel such as OPEC in order to protect themselves. Western nations often do not agree on economic policy, and restrictions imposed by one or more Western nations frequently are not acceptable to all. Third World nations thus often have alternative Western nations with which to trade. A second alternative for the Third World is to turn to the Soviet bloc for assistance. Economic sanctions imposed by the United States on Cuba, Nicaragua, and Afghanistan were countered when those countries sought closer ties with the Soviet Union. The situation can also be reversed. Egypt and Somalia, both at one time dependent on Soviet aid, subsequently turned to the United States for assistance after relations with the Soviet Union deteriorated. Regardless of which bloc, Western or Soviet, Third World countries turn to for aid and trade, the relationship remains a dependent one and thus subject to the whims of the industrial nations.

One additional weapon available to Third World nations is to nationalize or threaten to nationalize property owned by multinational corporations headquartered in a major industrial state. Nationalization can be self-defeating, however, because such an action may limit investment by other MNCs that fear they, too, may be subject to nationalization. In addition, the home state of the MNC that has had its property nationalized can retaliate in other ways, such as refusing future economic assistance. The United States has a law requiring that aid be cut off from any nation not providing adequate compensation when U.S.-owned property is nationalized.

In contrast with this dependent relationship, the relationship between the Western industrial nations is one of interdependence. The strength of the Western economies is far from equal, but they all boast advanced economies. This strengthens their mutual bargaining power, thus avoiding the dependent relationship of the Third World. An indication of both the interdependence and strength of the Western industrial nations has been the various rounds of negotiations among those countries to reduce trade barriers. Negotiations usually are long, with each side taking a tough position. Such talks would not be possible if potential advantages did not exist for all concerned.

The result of interdependence is cooperation for mutual advantage through such organizations as the General Agreement on Tariffs and Trade (GATT) and the Organization of Economic Cooper-

ation and Development (OECD). In spite of considerable effort to reduce trade barriers, the Western industrial nations are not free from aspects of protectionism, and a truly free trade environment has not yet been achieved. Thus, negotiations among those countries to regulate economic conflict and to achieve further reductions in trade barriers continue to be important.

The need for cooperation among the industrial nations is expressed not only through various international organizations established for that purpose, but also through such efforts as the annual economic summit meeting held by the leaders of the strongest of the Western economies (the United States, Great Britain, France, West Germany, Italy, Canada, and Japan). The 1985 economic summit, held in Bonn, devoted

Fig. 12.1 7-Nation Economic Summits
Participants: Britain, Canada, France, Italy, Japan, the United States, and West Germany.

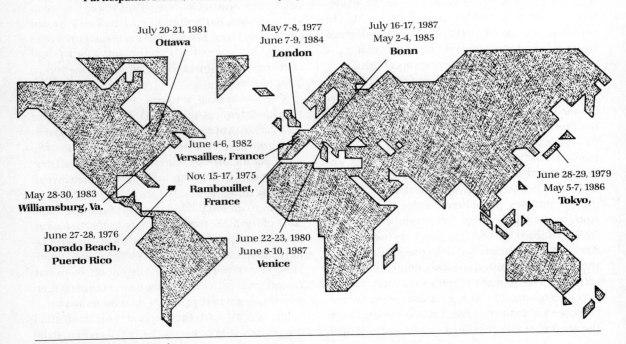

much of its time to the subject of growing demands in the United States for tariff protection, particularly against Japanese imports, and to complaints by the United States that the EC's Common Agriculture Policy (CAP) discriminated against U.S. agricultural exports. A summary communiqué at the end of the conference conceded that a degree of protectionism still exists in all the Western economies. The agenda for the 1986 conference held in Tokyo was essentially the same as that of the Bonn conference. Efforts among these nations to impose economic sanctions on one another are generally avoided, however, for if one of the Western countries were to raise tariffs that action would undoubtedly lead to strong and effective retaliation whereby all in-volved would suffer.

Among the Eastern European communist nations, the Soviet Union is the only member with an economy strong enough to impose its will on the other members; thus, the Soviets can and have imposed sanctions on other members. The Eastern European countries can bargain with the Soviet Union and express their disfavor with Soviet economic policy, but they have limited means to retaliate; the Soviet–East European relationship is therefore a dependent one. As a result of Soviet domination of the Eastern European economies, the communist bloc's economic organization, COMECON, has only a superficial resemblance to the economic cooperation found in the European Community.

The East-West economic relationship involves considerable use of negative sanctions and is the relationship in which economic sanctions are most likely to be imposed as a deliberate policy choice. While the Third World feels that many trade sanctions are imposed on it as carryovers from the past, sanctions imposed on Eastern bloc nations by the Western states are official policies clearly intended to damage the Soviet bloc's economies and harm their military capabilities. The Western nations, particularly the United States, restrict the transfer of advanced technology to the Soviet Union because of its strategic value to the Soviets; nonstrategic technology transfers are evaluated in terms of whether they have any military implications. While the Western nations disagree on how extensive trade should be with the Eastern bloc, they are in agreement that the West should not allow trade to aid the Soviets militarily. In addition, the Soviets are denied many other trade advantages granted noncommunist nations, and the United States has tied trade concessions for the Soviet Union to noneconomic issues such as an expanded emigration of Jews from the Soviet Union.

It is within these general patterns of economic relationships that economic sanctions and rewards are used in the international system. Based on these characteristics, and since the strongest economies are the Western ones, the use of economic sanctions for political purposes would most likely be imposed by Western industrial countries against Third World and communist countries. These latter two groups of nations have limited economic capacity to retaliate; thus they are the countries most vulnerable to sanctions. The use of economic sanctions, regardless of which nations utilize them, has had only limited success, however, as will be illustrated below.

Before turning to instances in which economic capabilities are used in an attempt to alter another nation's behavior, a few observations about the economic role of the United States in the international system are in order. Even though the United States no longer has the overall economic dominance it possessed for much of the post–World War II period, much of the change in the U.S. economic position is the result of the development of the Western European and Japanese economies, as opposed to a decline in the U.S. economy. The Bretton Woods agreement, which placed the United States in a central, dominant position in the international monetary policy, collapsed in 1971, but the influence of the United States in monetary policy remains substantial. The negative balance of payments for the United States has become even more serious in the

1980s than in the 1970s, but the United States continues to possess the world's largest single economy, about twice the size of that of its nearest rival, the Soviet Union. The use of U.S. economic power as an instrument of foreign policy continues to be a tempting and common occurrence within the international system. As a result, the United States is the country most likely to use economic measures to influence other nations and has indeed done so more often since World War II than all other countries combined. (One estimate is that 60 percent of uses of economic sanctions since World War II have been initiated by the United States.)

In the United States, as in other nations, international economic policy is governed to a great extent by domestic interests. The United States can successfully embargo advanced technology to the Soviet Union because there are adequate markets for that technology elsewhere, thus arousing no adverse reaction from domestic interests; but the embargo of grain shipments to the Soviet Union, as in 1979, when no alternative markets were available, resulted in strong pro-

tests from domestic interests. American farmers charged that they were being forced to bear the full load of punishing the Soviet Union for its invasion of Afghanistan; if the Carter administration wanted to take retaliatory action against the Soviets, it was suggested that an embargo should be spread throughout the domestic economy to reduce the impact on any single industry. After the grain embargo had been in effect for one year, the Reagan administration gave in to this pressure and dropped the embargo. The Soviet Union may have been vulnerable to an embargo of grain, but the presidency was vulnerable to domestic political pressures. The domestic demands won out.

Domestic considerations are an important aspect of any foreign policy decision, and, increasingly, virtually any foreign policy question has a strong economic element. This certainly includes U.S. policy toward the Soviet Union and conduct of the Cold War. The Cold War has been waged in various arenas, and the economic arena has been one of the most important.

THE ECONOMIC COLD WAR

The first move taken by the United States after World War II in its economic offensive against the Soviet Union was to rebuild Western European economies as bulwarks against communist expansion. This was the underlying motive of the European Recovery Act of 1948 and subsequent aid plans, both economic and military. Soviet retaliation was limited to preventing traditional prewar trade between Eastern and Western Europe in an effort to further weaken Western Europe's economic position. While the U.S. aid programs did not directly affect European communist countries, as the Cold War intensified, the United States extended its economic offensive by taking direct action against the Soviet Union and Eastern Europe. In 1949, the U.S. Congress passed the Export Control Act, which authorized the

Fig.12.2 US Trade Deficit

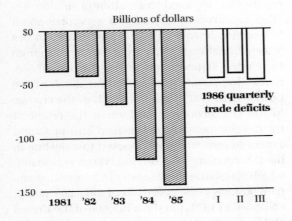

SOURCE: Christian Science Monitor
November 26, 1986, p.3.

president to limit or prohibit all exports to communist countries and provided for a licensing system regulated by the Department of Commerce for any exports not prohibited. During the Korean War, more than a thousand items were embargoed by the United States (Goldman, 1975, 49).

The U.S. had difficulty in convincing its NATO allies and Japan that they, too, should abide by the U.S. list of embargoed items. Western allies wanted a restricted meaning of *strategic*, whereas the United States defined as strategic anything that might aid the communist countries militarily or economically. In order to encourage its allies to comply with its perspective, the U.S. Congress passed the Mutual Defense Assistance Control Act of 1951 (more commonly known as the Battle Act). This act authorized the president to deny assistance to any country that shipped strategic items to communist countries. While Western Europe and Japan resented this sort of coercion, they were so heavily dependent on U.S. economic aid and military protection that they were forced to comply. Under pressure from its allies, the United States did shorten the list of embargoed items following the Korean War. The dispute over what items should be considered strategic has continued into the 1980s. One form this conflict continues to take is resentment in Western Europe over restrictions the U.S. imposes on subsidiaries of U.S. MNCs operating in Europe. The Western European countries feel that U.S. law should not apply to firms operating in their countries.

Early in the Cold War, the United States also put pressure on the Soviet Union to pay back the $11 billion lend-lease debt accumulated during World War II. Legislation passed in 1934, designed to promote payment of World War I debts, was used by the United States after World War II to collect debts accumulated during that war. This legislation denied credit to any nation in default on a debt to the United States. In order to protect its allies from these sanctions, Congress exempted any nation that belonged to the International Monetary Fund or the World Bank.

The Soviet Union belonged to neither. The Soviets argued that only communist countries were being asked to repay the lend-lease debt and that this was particularly unfair since the Soviet Union had suffered so much during the war. The United States and the Soviet Union have negotiated this issue off and on; though at times seeming near resolution, the issue still has not been resolved in the late 1980s.

Domestic concerns over trade with communist countries led to further restrictions when Congress passed the Trade Agreements Extension Act of 1951, which withdrew any trade concessions previously granted communist countries. The embargoes, debt problems, credit restrictions, and trade limitations became important instruments of the United States in waging the Cold War against the Soviet bloc nations. Although other Western nations have since increased their trade with the Soviet bloc somewhat more than has the United States, East-West trade is still not a significant part of worldwide trade, and the United States continues to impose many of its earlier restrictions on that trade. As late as 1962, Congress amended the Export Control Act so as to continue restrictions on items that would significantly benefit the Soviet Union economically. The Johnson administration's attempt in 1966 to expand East-West trade—the East-West Trade Relations Act—was never voted on by Congress, as Soviet activities relative to the Vietnam War and Soviet involvement in the Middle East created too much opposition in Congress. The approval of wheat sales to the Soviet Union in October 1963 was the only major concession to expanded trade between the United States and the Soviet Union during the 1960s. The United States did provide credit for that purchase and subsequent purchases of U.S. grain.

The United States does not, however, apply economic sanctions equally to all communist countries. In its effort to split the communist coalition and establish some dependence on the West, the U.S. provided special trade concessions and loans to Poland. With the rise of the Solidarity movement of the early 1980s, the policy appeared to be succeeding, but when martial law was imposed by the Polish government the Reagan administration withdrew the concessions. The effort to split Poland from the Soviet bloc had failed or, at least, had suffered a major setback. Trade concessions granted Yugoslavia by the West were more successful, however. The ability of Yugoslavia to remain independent of the Soviet Union after the split between Tito and Stalin in 1948 was due largely to a willingness in the West to open markets and credits to Yugoslavia.

In October 1972, as the Nixon administration was bringing United States involvement in Vietnam to an end, the United States and the Soviet Union signed an agreement on commerce and on the lend-lease debt. The agreement appeared to offer solutions to all the major outstanding economic problems between the two countries. The Soviets agreed to pay back a negotiated figure of about $700 million of the lend-lease debt over a thirty-year period and to allow American businessmen limited access to the Soviet market. President Nixon agreed to grant expanded credit to the Soviet Union through the Export-Import Bank and promised the Soviets most-favored-nation status in trade. The agreement required congressional approval, however, and before the implementing legislation could be reviewed by Congress a number of problems developed, not the least of which was that the 1973 grain deal did not proceed as planned. (Spero, 1985, 348–351, 369–371).

Grain sales by the United States to the Soviet Union were controversial from their inception. Arguments in favor of such sales emphasize that American farmers need overseas markets for their economic well-being and that the Soviet Union is a major market that should not be boycotted because of the nature of the Soviet system. Also, it was pointed out that grain sales to the Soviet Union reduce the U.S. balance-of-payments deficit, and if the United States did not sell the Soviets grain, the Soviets would purchase it from

other Western grain-exporting nations. The counterargument is that the grain shipments help the Soviets mask the failings of the Soviet agricultural system. Whenever the Soviet Union has a particularly bad harvest, as in 1963 and 1972, instead of suffering the domestic political consequences, the Soviets simply purchase grain from the United States. This sort of trade thus is aiding the principal enemy of the United States, and any domestic benefits in the United States are not worth the cost.

After the United States sold the Soviets 19 million tons of grain following their 1972 crop failure, grain shipments to the Soviets were subject to another criticism. The Soviets had contracted for the grain at a specific price, but before the grain could be shipped by the major exporting firms the price of wheat and other grains rose dramatically. The actual cost of the grain was now about $700 million more than the contract price. The U.S. government picked up the difference. The net effect was that the United States was subsidizing the feeding of the Soviet people. Previous grain sales to the Soviet Union had been taken from the vast grain surplus in the United States, and large overseas sales had had little effect on the domestic price of grain; by 1973, however, the large amount of grain sold to the Soviet Union, India, and other countries had reduced the domestic surplus to the point that that year's sale had had direct effect on domestic prices. The Nixon administration had not anticipated this change in the market; thus the difference between the contract price and the market price. The 1973 grain deal was also criticized in the United States because the rise in the cost of grain contributed to domestic inflation of food prices. In order to prevent recurrence of these problems, in 1975 a grain agreement was negotiated between the United States and the Soviet Union which committed the Soviets to purchase a minimum of six million tons of grain each year, but not more than eight million tons without U.S. permission. This, it was hoped, would reduce the effect on domestic grain prices of future grain shipments to the Soviet Union.

The Nixon administration saw the steps taken in the 1972 U.S.-Soviet commercial agreement as important to the development of détente. The administration was not abandoning the use of economic persuasion in its dealings with the Soviet Union, but rather had changed tactics. The United States was still using its economic strength in an effort to change the behavior of another nation, but not in a punitive way. If the Soviet Union were to become more involved in trade with Western countries, the Soviets might be less hostile toward the West and easier to negotiate with on other matters. If interdependence worked among the Western nations, it might work with the Soviet Union. The Trade Reform Act of 1973, which included the implementing legislation for the agreement with the Soviets, granted the Soviet Union most-favored-nation status and would have provided credit guarantees through the Export-Import Bank. Of the two major provisions, the credits had the greater economic impact, since they would have allowed the Soviets to purchase U.S. goods they had been unable to purchase in the past due to a shortage of foreign currency. The Soviets did have access to credit in the other Western countries by 1972, but this legislation provided an important opening to the U.S. market. The most-favored-nation provision was of more political significance than economic importance. The Soviets had available mainly raw materials to export to the United States, and most-favored-nation status would have little effect on those exports. Most-favored-nation status for the Soviet Union was important symbolically as acceptance into world trade arrangements, however.

The provisions of the Trade Reform Act that pertained to U.S.-Soviet trade relations never went into effect. The legislation was caught up in an executive-congressional conflict and was debated in Congress for nearly two years. In the midst of the debate, the Watergate scandal occurred, and President Nixon resigned. This was a period when anything coming from the executive was closely questioned by Congress, and Congress added provisions to the legislation that were opposed by both the administration and the Soviets, and that ultimately made the agreement unacceptable to the Soviet Union.

The congressionally added provision that drew the most public attention was the Jackson-Vanik amendment, which linked Jewish emigration from the Soviet Union with trade concessions. In October 1974, Senator Jackson announced that the Soviet Union had agreed to allow 60,000 Jews to emigrate annually in exchange for the trade concessions. The linkage of the two issues appeared to have been successful, and Secretary of State Kissinger, who opposed the linkage, agreed that the Soviets were willing to accept the Jackson-Vanik amendment. In December, however, Congress placed a $300 million limit on the Export-Import Bank credits and prohibited any credits for the production, transportation, and distribution of energy. This was too much for the Soviets, and they now claimed that they had never accepted the linkage of emigration and trade concessions and charged the United States with attempting to interfere in Soviet internal affairs. The next month, the United States and the Soviet Union announced that the 1972 commercial agreement was canceled. The lend-lease debt settlement was also declared null and void. Policy changes which had showed hope and begun with promise were scrapped and the U.S. returned to the 1960s policy of isolating the Soviet Union economically. A combination of scandal, ill-advised congressional initiative, and domestic demands resulted in the collapse of the agreements.

The Soviets were not hurt by the cancelation of the agreements as much as it appeared. Since the economic sanctions imposed by the United States on East-West trade are more stringent than those imposed by the other Western industrial countries, the Soviets could always find an alternative in the West to trading with the United States. Even during the 1979 grain embargo, the Soviets were able to purchase grain from Western sources other than the United States; costs to the Soviet Union in finding new grain sources were not so great that they deterred the Soviets from continuing operations in Afghanistan. In the matter of technology and finance, when the gas pipeline from western Siberia to Western Europe was proposed, the Soviets found financial and technical aid to build the pipeline in Western Europe despite U.S. objections. Since, in the past, the Soviet Union had not been dependent on trade with the United States, when the 1972 agreements failed, the Soviets lost little.

SANCTIONS AMONG THE WESTERN NATIONS

With respect to economic relations among the Western industrial nations, it is sometimes difficult to distinguish routine economic competition among government-regulated economies from the use of sanctions by one nation against another. The United States charges the European Community (EC) with protectionism in regard to the EC's Common Agricultural Program (CAP) and claims that government subsidies to EC farmers are greater than those granted the American farmer, and that EC indirectly assists agriculture by providing subsidies for food exports. As a consequence, U.S. food exports to EC have declined, and the U.S. is finding it increasingly difficult to compete with EC for other markets. In retaliation, the U.S. Congress, at the executive's request, appropriated $2 billion to subsidize food exports in order for the United States to remain competitive. Use of those subsidies began with a grain sale to Algeria in June 1985. The issue seems to be whether EC behavior is routine and within the context of what remains in the way of protectionism among the Western countries or whether EC has an active policy of protectionism in regard to U.S. agricultural products.

These EC policies and countermeasures by the United States are examples of behavior the Western industrial nations attempt to avoid. The more

common practice among those nations is either to ask for voluntary restrictions on exports that are harming another country's economy or to carry on negotiations to resolve the problem. An example of the first practice was the understanding between the United States and Japan to voluntarily limit the number of Japanese-produced automobiles sold in the United States; an example of the second was the Tokyo Round or Multilateral Trade Negotiations (MTN).

MTN, which began with discussions in OECD in 1971, formally commenced in Tokyo in September 1973 with nearly one hundred nations participating. The Trade Reform Act that President Nixon submitted to Congress in early 1973 not only contained provisions to implement the U.S.-Soviet trade agreement, it also contained authorization for the president to engage in the Tokyo negotiations. The legislation would give the president a broad range of authority to reduce tariffs, eliminate nontariff barriers to trade, and grant Third World countries trade preferences. The provisions in the legislation concerning the Soviet Union and congressional preoccupation with Watergate delayed the bill, but it was finally passed as the Trade Act in February 1975; it was essentially the same bill as introduced without provisions pertaining to Soviet trade. Even though the Tokyo Round had been under way for some time when the bill was finally passed, the conference could make little progress until the U.S. president had congressional authorization to negotiate trade reform.

Although the purpose of the Tokyo Round was to reduce trade obstacles, the negotiations had been agreed to before the economic shock of rising oil prices and worldwide recession and inflation. With these developments, the mood in Tokyo was one of protectionism, that is, an increase in trade barriers, rather than a commitment to greater free trade. When economies are expanding and unemployment is low, as was the case during the 1960s, the domestic demands for protection from outside competition are few; but all that had changed in the 1970s. When the negotiations were concluded in April 1979, more than five years after they had begun, protectionist demands had been contained, tariffs were reduced, and limits were placed on nontariff barriers to trade. Problems in the trade of agricultural products remained unresolved, however. The one aspect of protectionism that did develop from these negotiations was the voluntary export restraint agreement (VER), but, as its name specifies, such agreements are voluntary and thus differ from traditional trade quotas.

The Tokyo Round is illustrative of the use of diplomacy as opposed to economic sanctions among the industrial nations to resolve economic problems. Domestic demands for protection continue to be heard in the United States for such industries as steel and automobiles, but such sanctions have not been implemented, although Congress was working on protectionist legislation in 1987.

ECONOMIC AID AND FOREIGN POLICY

Since the European Recovery Act of 1948, the United States has spent billions of dollars in economic assistance to over 100 countries. Even though the U.S. foreign aid program was reviewed in some detail in an earlier chapter, additional generalizations can be made here concerning the use of the program as sanction and reward.

By granting economic aid to other Western nations in the late 1940s and 1950s, the United States was clearly using the strongest instrument of policy available to it in the immediate postwar period—its economy. The success of that aid led to similar efforts in providing aid to the developing nations. Here the task was much greater. The West European countries and Japan already had the economic infrastructure on which to build an advanced economy; the task was essentially that of rebuilding economies damaged by World War II. The developing countries did not yet have an economic foundation, and the problem was that of building, not rebuilding, economies. In

addition, as the developing nations increased in number, there were far more nations needing aid than were involved in the earlier economic efforts directed toward the industrial nations.

During the late 1960s and 1970s, an often-heard criticism of the U.S. aid program to the Third World countries was that it was spread over so many countries that it was of only limited benefit to any single one. The successes of this phase of the aid program were few, although Taiwan and South Korea did develop strong economies as a result of U.S. aid. A second criticism, and one being heard in the late 1980s, is that the United States directs far too few of its resources toward the Third World. The U.S. Congress, however, considers that the level of aid is as high as it can be politically and still meet the needs of domestic programs, which have higher priority. Also, Congress does not feel that it should increase aid to countries that are often critical of U.S. policy and do not seem to appreciate the aid they are receiving.

The result of this congressional view of foreign aid is that any appropriation for assistance to Third World countries results in a hard-fought legislative battle. The aid program has declined as a percentage of the gross national product, and major recipients are countries closely aligned with the United States. That is, the United States uses its aid program primarily for policy gains, not because of a sense of obligation to the Third World. The United States views trade with the Third World in a similar context. The Third World wants greater access to the U.S. market, but the United States does not see any economic benefit in meeting this demand.

ECONOMIC AID AS A REWARD

Both the United States and the Soviet Union have been selective in the economic aid they extend to other countries, although the Soviets have limited their aid to fewer countries than has the United States. In Eastern Europe, the Soviets have either controlled the economies of nations to force compliance with Soviet policy or punished those that did not cooperate. Yugoslavia was alternately punished and rewarded after the Tito-Stalin split in 1948. The split resulted from Tito's refusal to accept Moscow's directives, and Stalin imposed an economic boycott on Yugoslavia. As is the case with many such efforts by major economic powers, Tito established trade relations with other countries; in this instance it was Great Britain and Italy and, later, other Western countries, including the United States. In 1955, Khrushchev extended assistance to Yugoslavia once again, but each time Tito expressed a policy line independent of the Soviet Union Khrushchev threatened to cut off economic aid. By the early 1960s, however, the Soviet Union, recognizing that increased pressure might force Tito to seek even closer relations with the West, accepted Tito's independent policies. The Soviet policy of economic sanctions and rewards to bring Yugoslavia under Moscow's leadership had failed.

In the late 1950s and the early 1960s, the Soviets were more successful in their relationship with Finland. Finland was more vulnerable to Soviet military and economic pressures than was Yugoslavia; however, Finland was able to avoid becoming a communist state. This bargained political and economic relationship with the Soviet Union, without becoming a communist state or a Soviet satellite, is what is commonly referred to as "Finlandization."

In their relations with Third World countries, both the United States and the Soviet Union have been far more generous with their aid to countries whose policies closely align with theirs than to those whose policies do not align. When economic assistance is used as an instrument of policy, this sort of behavior is what would be expected. After Khrushchev came to power in 1953 and the Soviet Union began granting aid to noncommunist countries, the major Third World recipients of Soviet aid were Afghanistan, India, China, Indonesia, Burma, Egypt, and Syria. Soviet

policy, if the purpose of that policy was to gain client states, failed in several instances; but in the late 1980s Afghanistan, India, and Syria continue to be major recipients of Soviet aid. Angola and Ethiopia have been added to the list. Iraq and Nicaragua receive Soviet aid to a lesser degree.

While both the United States and the Soviet Union use military and economic assistance to attract client nations, making a distinction between the two forms of aid often is difficult. Any military aid a country receives frees funds for economic development, just as denying a country military assistance may force a country to spend more of its developmental funds on its armed forces. U.S. aid to Israel is an example of the problem of making a distinction between military and economic aid. Much of the economic aid granted Israel goes to making payments on past purchases of military equipment.

The Third World countries fall into three categories as possible recipients of U.S. aid. One group not only does not receive aid but has economic sanctions imposed upon them. This group of Third World countries includes mainly client states of the Soviet Union. A second group receives little or no aid, either because of its anti-U.S. policies or because those nations in it are of no strategic importance to the United States. The third group has a client-state relationship with the United States. It is, of course, among the countries of this latter group that the United States aid program is most active.

The most notable use of U.S. economic and military aid to control conflict and to secure client-state relationships is the aid granted Egypt and Israel. Israel has long been dependent on U.S. aid, but if it agreed to a peace settlement the United States promised to increase Israel's aid package. Egypt was particularly susceptible to such an offer, since it had received little aid from the Soviet Union since 1971 and was not interested in reestablishing a close relationship with the Soviets. Also, if Egypt were to enter a peace settlement with Israel it would need aid to replace that which it would undoubtedly lose from the oil-rich Arab countries, notably Saudi Arabia. Egypt could not afford a peace settlement without a U.S. aid commitment.

In providing aid to Egypt, a longstanding enemy of Israel, the United States had to be careful not to alienate Israel, and avoided such an eventuality by providing Israel with more aid than it provided Egypt. Between 1979 and late 1983, the United States granted Egypt $9.5 billion in military and economic aid. Total U.S. aid for Israel from 1979 through 1984 was $ 15.3 billion. Of about $65 billion in foreign aid granted by the United States in the six years from 1979 through 1984, Israel and Egypt received approximately $27 billion, or about 40 percent of the total aid program. The strategy of providing aid to both sides in a conflict in this instance has apparently been successful. It not only brought about a peace treaty between Israel and Egypt, it has made both countries dependent on U.S. aid and placed the United States in a position to punish either nation if it failed to live up to the peace settlement.

The U.S. relationship with Pakistan is an example of a different use of U.S. economic and military assistance—aid provided to a country because of its strategic position. During the 1950s and early 1960s, Pakistan was a U.S. ally, but that relationship deteriorated after the 1965 and 1971 wars between Pakistan and India. The United States stopped all military support and much of its economic aid following the 1965 war to punish Pakistan for using its U.S.-supplied equipment against India. The United States argued that the equipment was sent Pakistan as an ally in anti-Soviet coalitions (CENTO and SEATO) and not for use against India. When Pakistan's armed forces performed poorly in the 1971 war, Pakistan blamed the United States for not having provided it with up-to-date equipment for such a long period. As the U.S.-Pakistani relationship deteriorated, Pakistan established a close relationship with China. This was before Sino-U.S. détente, and so further damaged U.S.-Pakistani relations.

The relationship between the United States and Pakistan did not improve during the early 1970s when Sino-American relations improved. SEATO and CENTO were both abolished, and it was not until the Soviet invasion of Afghanistan in late 1979 that Pakistan became strategically important to the United States again. With a hostile Islamic government in power in Iran, the only geographic contact with the Afghan rebels was through Pakistan. Also, the United States did not want Soviet expansion into Afghanistan to be extended into Pakistan and used economic rewards as a means of reestablishing a relationship with Pakistan. The aid package first offered Pakistan totaled $400 million, which General Zia, Pakistan's head of state, rejected as "peanuts" and far short of what Pakistan deserved after so many years of neglect. Pakistan was aware of its bargaining position and, although badly in need of aid, was not willing to come to terms cheaply. Eventually, the United States and Pakistan agreed to a five-year military and economic aid package totaling about $3 billion. After Israel and Egypt, Pakistan became the third-largest recipient of U.S. aid.

The United States has also dramatically reversed its economic policy toward China. The United States maintained a complete diplomatic and economic boycott of China from the communist takeover in 1949 until Sino-U.S. relations turned around after 1971. Following the Chinese Civil War, much of the impetus for isolating China came from domestic forces in the United States, and any U.S. leader advocating better relations with China ran the risk of being charged with communist leanings. Americans not only saw China as an enemy, but as an enemy even more hostile toward the United States than was the Soviet Union. This perception was so strongly implanted in U.S. policy that the United States maintained its isolation of China for more than a decade after China broke with the Soviet Union in 1960. After the policy shift in 1971, China did not become a recipient of U.S. economic and military aid, however, although trade and credit restrictions were relaxed considerably. The U.S. did commence arms sales to China in 1987, however.

Yet another country toward which U.S. economic policy was reversed is Nicaragua. After the Sandinista government came to power in 1979, the Carter administration asked Congress to appropriate economic aid for Nicaragua, which it did. The Sandinistas were suspicious of the United States because of its past support for the Somoza regime, but Nicaragua was in dire need of assistance in rebuilding the country after the revolution, and aid from the United States was both sought and accepted. In 1981, the Reagan administration cut off all economic aid to Nicaragua and eventually, in May 1985, suspended all trade between the two countries. The change in policy was explained as retaliation for the aid the Sandinistas were giving leftist rebels in El Salvador. United States policy shifted from the use of economic aid to obtain good relations with a new revolutionary government to a policy of economic sanctions against that same government in an attempt either to produce a major shift in policy or to bring down the government.

USE OF ECONOMIC SANCTIONS IN THE THIRD WORLD

In the instances of Pakistan, China, and Nicaragua—all Third World countries—economic rewards were either preceded or followed by economic sanctions. But neither rewards nor sanctions produced any important change in the recipient's policy or form of government. The United States has used economic strength against other Third World governments as well, often in an attempt to bring down a government. The best known is the U.S. effort to isolate Cuba economically.

After Castro came to power in Cuba in early 1959, the United States and Cuba went through an uneasy, but not openly hostile, period until Castro began confiscating American-owned property. In addition to planning and attempting an abortive invasion of Cuba at the Bay of Pigs using a refugee army, the United States also imposed economic sanctions on Cuba. The United States reduced, and then eliminated, the Cuban sugar quota, and embargoed the shipment of arms to Cuba. As the tension between the two countries escalated, the United States imposed a trade boycott on Cuba exempting only food and medicine. Later, food and medicine were embargoed. The United States also brought pressure on other countries to embargo Cuba, and successfully promoted a diplomatic and economic boycott of Cuba in the Organization of American States. These U.S. moves all took place in the early 1960s, and many are still in effect in the late 1980s. But were they successful?

If the purpose of attempting to isolate Cuba economically was to bring down the Castro government, then the sanctions were not successful, since Castro remains in power. If their purpose was to seriously damage the Cuban economy, then they succeeded, temporarily. When traditional markets with the United States were cut off, Cuba suffered for a time, but established new markets with communist-bloc nations. In return for supplying Cuba with modern military equipment and economic aid, the Soviets obtained surrogate armed forces for Soviet operations in Africa. These developments certainly were not intended results of U.S. sanctions. Eventually, much of Latin America grew weary of the diplomatic and economic boycott, reestablished diplomatic relations with Cuba, and resumed trade. In the late 1980s, Cuba continues to struggle economically, and support of Cuba is an economic drain on the Soviet Union, but Cuba does provide the Soviet Union a base of operations in Latin America. The United States-imposed sanctions were not, in any reasonable overall assessment, successful.

The United States has also imposed economic sanctions on Vietnam in the post-Vietnam War period. During the war, the United States maintained a total economic boycott of North Vietnam; but Western allies such as Great Britain and

France did not, and the United States often complained of merchant vessels from those countries delivering cargo to the north. In the south, however, the United States provided substantial economic aid in addition to the large outlay of military assistance. After the United States withdrew the last of its armed forces in early 1973, aid to South Vietnam became more difficult to pass in Congress, but aid continued. It was not until shortly before South Vietnam fell that Congress rejected a $700 million aid package for South Vietnam. Thus, neither economic nor military assistance was successful in preventing a communist takeover of South Vietnam.

Even though previously a boycott of North Vietnam had been in effect, the 1973 agreement between Hanoi and Washington that ended U.S. involvement in Vietnam included economic assistance. This assistance was, in the view of the United States, tied to North Vietnam's abiding by the settlement, which included a cessation of hostilities in the south. In 1975, the north completed its occupation of the south in violation of the agreement, and the United States, in turn, withheld the promised aid. The present Vietnamese government occasionally mentions that the United States has not delivered on the aid promise and cites this as a U.S. violation of the agreement. Vietnam's economy has recovered poorly from the war, and the lack of aid from the United States is, no doubt, a factor. Additional factors contributing to Vietnam's weak economy, however, are poor relations with China, a former ally, and the cost of Vietnam's invasion of Cambodia. But, like Cuba, Vietnam receives substantial Soviet aid that has prevented its economic problems from becoming critical.

Iran has also been subject to U.S. economic sanctions. In 1979, as a consequence of the seizure of U.S. embassy personnel in Teheran, the United States retaliated by imposing economic sanctions on Iran. The United States stopped importing Iranian oil and seized Iranian assets. The assets were valued at about $11.1 billion. In April 1980, after various diplomatic efforts failed to effect the hostages' release, the United States embargoed all exports to Iran except food and medicine and broke diplomatic relations. An attempt by the United States to impose an economic boycott on Iran through a Security Council resolution failed when the Soviet Union cast its veto. A further attempt to harm Iran economically by asking Western European allies and Japan to embargo their trade with Iran was only partially successful. Since the United States imported only a small amount of oil from Iran, it could easily replace that oil with imports from other countries, but Japan was heavily dependent on Iranian oil and continued its purchases. Western Europe also was reluctant to forego the oil contracts it had with Iran, for to do so would have meant higher prices for oil purchased elsewhere. The British did agree to a boycott, but only concerning new business; earlier commitments would be carried out. Thus, United States efforts to bring about a general Western boycott of Iran met with very limited success.

To seize the assets of another country is a very severe economic sanction, but in many instances such a move means little. Third World countries, in general, do not have sufficient assets abroad so that their seizure would impose an economic threat. Iran was one of the few Third World countries with sufficient assets in the United States to make their seizure important.

In spite of the many countermoves by the United States, most of which were economic, bargaining between the United States and Iran went on for months without success. The frozen assets took on new importance in September 1980, when Iraq and Iran went to war. Iran then needed money and dropped various demands it had been making as a condition for the release of the hostages. The hostages were released in January 1981 after an agreement on the assets was concluded. Iran recovered only a fraction of its funds, however, as a number of outstanding claims existed against Iran. Iran received immediately $2.8 billion, but $3.7 billion went to pay off loans owed to U.S. banks, $1.4 billion was reserved to pay other sorts of loans, and $32 billion was held back for future claims by U.S. companies which suffered losses at the hands of the Iranian government. Economic sanctions had been successful, but only after the war with Iraq had forced Iran into concessions. After the hostages were released, the Reagan administration continued the sanctions and pressed other Western countries to do so as well. New emphasis was placed on the sanctions when the Reagan administration charged Iran with sponsoring terrorism. But the U.S. position with its allies was weakened considerably when it was discovered in November 1986 that the U.S. was violating its own policy by selling arms to Iran.

A more recent U.S. attempt to influence the behavior of a Third World nation through the use of economic sanctions occurred after terrorist attacks on the Rome and Vienna airports on December 27, 1985. The Reagan administration accused Libya's Qaddafi of supporting and training the terrorists that carried out the attacks and, in retaliation, expanded economic sanctions imposed a few months earlier into a total economic boycott. The U.S. had carried on only limited trade with Libya even before the limited sanctions were imposed; therefore, broader sanctions had little effect on Libya.

SANCTIONS AND INTERNATIONAL ORGANIZATIONS

International organizations have, on occasion, also used economic sanctions in attempts to alter the behavior of nations. While the League of Nations utilized economic sanctions sparingly, in 1936 the organization did place an embargo on oil shipments to Italy to punish that country for its invasion of Ethiopia. So many violations of the embargo occurred, particularly by the United States, that Italy, although having had only a small amount of domestic oil production, suffered little.

The principal effort of the United Nations to punish a nation through economic sanctions was the trade embargo it placed on Rhodesia in 1966. The UN took this action following Rhodesia's unilateral declaration of independence in 1965. The new government of Rhodesia was a white-minority government, and sanctions were imposed to force Rhodesia to include blacks in the government; only 5 percent of the population was white. Great Britain had imposed sanctions on Rhodesia earlier, but that move had failed to bring Rhodesia back under British control. The UN embargo included oil exports to Rhodesia and twelve principal Rhodesian exports. Most of Rhodesia's overseas assets were also frozen. As when the United States first imposed economic sanctions on Cuba, Rhodesia's economy initially suffered, but by transferring its trade to South Africa Rhodesia was able to defy the United Nations' demands. The white-minority government remained in power until 1980, when guerrillas fighting the government forced elections. The country was renamed Zimbabwe after a black government came to power. The change the United Nations had wished to achieve took place, but not as a result of its economic sanctions.

Economic sanctions by an international organization can take a form other than trade embargoes, however. Management by the International Monetary Fund of Third World debts is a sanction in the sense that the debtor nations' economies come under the control of an outside agency. Those Third World countries that borrowed heavily during the 1970s were in serious economic straits in the early 1980s due to recession and inflation. Most of the borrowing was from private Western banks, and as those banks developed more caution in making loans to many of the Third World countries, old debts could not be covered by new long-term loans. In 1983, 33 countries had to have their debts either rescheduled or restructured. Most of the refinancing of debts was done through the International Monetary Fund, but IMF insisted on economic austerity before it allowed additional credits and loans to the nations involved. The IMF-imposed sanctions resulted in higher unemployment and a further slowdown in the domestic economies of many Third World countries. As a result, such controls often met with domestic opposition, although the debtor nations had little choice but to accept the IMF plan if additional credits and loans were forthcoming. The IMF perhaps did not see these controls as sanctions, but they seemed such to the debtor nations.

CONCLUSION

An overall assessment of using economic sanctions to change the behavior of another nation shows mixed results. Among the successes would have to be included Soviet control over Eastern Europe. The Soviets successfully control the economies of Eastern Europe, but the Soviets have had to pay a price. The Eastern European countries are generally uneasy with the relationship, and Soviet economic gains over the years, with such a closed economic system, have been small. The use of Soviet economic sanctions against Yugoslavia failed, however. The Soviet experience in Eastern Europe would indicate that control over other countries' economies works best when you also have military and political control as well. The United States was success-ful in its use of economic sanctions with Iran, but only after a crisis of fourteen months. The sanctions might never have succeeded if the Iraqi-Iranian War had not forced Iran into making concessions.

United States sanctions against China and Cuba did not succeed. Sino-American relations improved greatly, but not because China was forced into the new relationship. The sanctions against Cuba succeeded only in forcing Cuba into an ever-closer relationship with the Soviet Union, a development that has further eroded U.S.-Cuban relations. In the process of furthering economic sanctions against Cuba, the United States lost prestige and influence in the remainder of Latin America. Economic sanctions against Nicaragua have also resulted in little change in the behavior of that new government. The Sandinista leadership has moved gradually closer to the Soviet Union, as did Cuba in the early days of the Castro government. Economic sanctions among the Western countries are used occasionally, but with generally unfavorable results. The IMF-imposed controls on some Third World countries have shown some success in improving their economies, however. The overall assessment that must be made concerning economic sanctions is that they are effective under only limited and controlled circumstances which occur infrequently in the international system.

CHAPTER 13

Arms—Distribution and Transfers

The principal instruments of policy available to a nation are those discussed in the last two chapters—the use of and the threat to use force or economic rewards and sanctions. A nation's ability to *use* force is not only dependent on the quantity and quality of its armaments but also the suitability of those weapons to the situation in which they will be used. The effectiveness of a *threat* to use force is dependent on that nation's reputation concerning the use of force as well as the size and quality of its arsenal. As a general rule, the threat to use force is usually ineffective against a nation that has a larger stockpile of weapons than does the nation making the threat. Therefore, the distribution of armaments among the nation-states is an important factor in how effective a nation is in achieving its interests. In turn, the distribution of weapons is dependent on which countries have the industrial capability to manufacture their own weapons and, of those nations, which are willing to sell weapons to other countries. The often close relationship between economic and military coercion was also discussed earlier, thus force and economic capabilities are not necessarily independent instruments of policy.

MAJOR ISSUES CONCERNING ARMS

While arms are widely distributed among virtually all nation-states, major arms manufacturers, particularly those producing more sophisticated weapons, are located in a relatively few industrial countries. This not only means that few nations are capable of producing their own weapons systems, but that many nations are dependent on the industrial nations for their armaments.

The arms-producing nations transfer to other countries weapons worth billions of dollars each year, not only for the revenue the transactions will bring, but also for the influence such transfers provide; arms transfers are both a business transaction and an important instrument of foreign policy. Arms transfers are also the transmittal of potential force from one nation to another. Arms transfers do carry risks, however, since they can destabilize a conflict situation by giving an advantage to one party. On the other hand, an arms sale can stabilize a regional conflict by producing an approximate equality of armaments, if it is possible for the parties involved to recognize that an equality has been achieved. Thus, an arms deal could be the prelude to an arms race, or it could be a stabilizer. To the different parties involved, each with its own perception, it could be seen as both.

Virtually all nations express a desire to limit armaments, but few arms *control* agreements exist, and those are primarily applicable to nuclear weapons; no arms *reduction* agreement is currently operative. Also, although conventional arms have received considerable diplomatic attention, no major multilateral agreement regulating conventional arms exists. In spite of slow progress in controlling armaments, the accumulation of arms is of great concern to laymen and national leaders alike. In addition to the moral questions involved in the death and destruction war can produce, armaments present a nation with two specific problems of policy. First, can the nation afford their cost? Second, how can nations manage the increased potential of war when arms are available? For nations with nuclear arsenals, these problems are much more serious than for nations possessing only conventional weapons.

Within the argument that arms do not cause wars but are only symptoms reflecting conflicts among nations, the level of arms a nation possesses is merely a barometer used to gauge tensions. Arms, from this perspective, are neutral; it is the political environment that is dangerous. The counterargument is that the presence of arms makes it easier to go to war when tensions exist; conversely, when stockpiles are limited, war is less apt to occur. Little doubt exists, however, that if war does come, the larger the stockpiles of arms, the more destructive the war can become.

These general observations concerning armaments lead to four major areas of discussion. The first topic is the origin and expense of arms. How large are national arms budgets, and are military expenditures increasing? What portion of nations' GNPs and national budgets is diverted to arma-

ments? The second subject is arms transfers. Since many nations obtain their arms by importing them, which countries are arms exporters and which are importers? How important are arms transfers in international trade? The countries that export arms occasionally place limitations on the arms they transfer, both as to the types of arms and expectations as to how those weapons may be used when transferred. What are those limitations? Thus, this area of discussion concerns who produces arms, who sells arms, who buys them, and what sorts of weapon systems are available for sale.

The third area of discussion is the comparison of the arms capabilities of nations. Perspective is especially important to this discussion, since no nation views its armaments in the same fashion as other nations view them. This is illustrated by the longstanding dispute as to the military capabilities of NATO and the Warsaw Pact. Which coalition leads in the arms competition between them? What type of war should each alliance be prepared to fight? What weapons and how many are needed to fight that sort of war? In comparing the military capabilities of opposing coalitions or even two particular nations, the easiest comparison is of the total stockpiles of arms that each possesses. Which side has the most combat aircraft or the most submarines? Which army has the larger number of men under arms? A simple bar graph is all that is necessary when numbers alone are compared. Problems arise, however, when the comparison is extended to a country's ability to use those weapons, the quality of the weapons, the portion of those armaments that are combat-ready, or the circumstances under which the weapons will be used. These kinds of comparisons go beyond a comparison of numbers and involve subjective judgments about which disagreements exist.

The fourth area of discussion concerns the diplomatic effort that has gone into arms control and arms reduction. Any arms agreement, if freely entered into by the nations involved, has to have a common basis that the agreement benefits all who enter it. Agreement must exist as to the level of arms possessed by each party and at least an approximate agreement on how those levels compare among the parties to the agreement. Thus, discussion of this final area—arms control and arms reduction—cannot be undertaken meaningfully without an understanding of the first three areas of discussion: who makes the arms, who buys and sells them, and how the levels of arms compare. The first two topics, the distribution of arms and arms transfers, will be discussed in this chapter; the last two topics, the comparison of arms stockpiles and efforts to control them, will be discussed in the following chapter.

ARMS AND POLICY GOALS

A nation's success in achieving its policy goals and its level of armaments may have little correlation. Translating military power into diplomatic or even military success is difficult and often impossible. Since World War II, the United States has faced a number of situations in which its military capabilities far outweighed those of its opponents, and yet it was unable to dominate. The war in Vietnam has become the standard example of such a situation. Although militarily superior to Cuba, the United States has been unable to force Castro from office; and the North Koreans were never punished for their invasion of South Korea or even for their seizure of the *USS Pueblo* in 1968. Hostage situations, in particular, point up the limitations of either conventional or nuclear weapons. During both the Iranian hostage situation, from late 1979 to early 1981, and the kidnapping of Westerners by terrorist groups in Lebanon, the Western military powers found little use for their military might in resolving those crises.

The use of military capabilities in an economic crisis is also extremely limited. The OPEC nations proved their capacity to seriously harm the West-ern nations economically without any military action by the OPEC nations or military response by the industrial nations. Even if military action had been directed at the OPEC nations, the unstated threat was that the OPEC nations could quickly destroy the oil fields in retaliation, which would have placed the oil-importing nations in a worse position than paying higher oil prices. What situations such as these illustrate is that military capability is not applicable to all situations, thus seemingly weaker nations sometimes have power that transcends military capabilities.

WORLD MILITARY EXPENDITURES

In 1985 world military expenditures were $940 billion. Based on a world GNP of over $16 trillion, this means that about 6 percent of the world's total goods and services went to military spending. Members of NATO and the Warsaw Pact spent 77 percent of the world's military expenditures (a ratio of three to one over Third World nations), but the developing countries had more people under arms (17 million) than did the developed countries (10.5 million). About three-fourths of the world's population is in the developing nations, thus on a population basis, a substantially smaller portion of the Third World's population was under arms than in the developed nations. The developed countries have a collective GNP about three times that of the Third World, but the percentage of GNP spent on armed forces is about the same for both groups.

Another measure of military spending is the percentage of a national government's budget dedicated to the military. In 1983 approximately 19 percent of national budgets went to armed forces. The developed nations spent a slightly higher percentage on their military than did the developing countries, but by less than 1 percent. Each of these percentages—the annual percentage of GNP and the percentage of national budgets—varied little during the decade from 1973 to 1983.

In that decade, military spending in current dollars increased about 160 percent, but in constant dollars, when inflation is figured in, the increase was about 33 percent. This percentage of real growth in military expenditures is about the same as the growth of the world's economy during the same period.

A further breakdown of figures on military spending indicates that a greater difference exists between the behavior of the developed and developing nations than these general figures and percentages suggest. During the decade from 1974 to 1983, in constant dollars the developing countries increased their military spending by more than did the developed countries (51 percent and 27 percent, respectively). However, the percentage of increase for the developing countries fell from 12 percent a year early in the decade to about 3 percent annual increase late in the decade. In 1983 military expenditures in the Third World actually experienced a slight drop, due mostly to a decrease in military spending in the Middle East. The percentage of increase for the developed countries rose from 2 percent a year early in the decade to over 4.5 percent late in the decade. Thus, while the overall percentage of increase during the decade is higher for the developing countries than that of the developed countries, by the 1980s the developing countries were increasing their military budgets at a slower rate than were the developed countries. This slowdown in increase has given rise to the argument that the Third World market for arms is nearly saturated, and that those countries are controlling increases in arms purchases either because they feel the arms they have are adequate for their defense or because the need for economic development is being given a higher priority.

Before proceeding further, a note of caution must be given about the preciseness of the figures used to analyze military spending. The percentages and figures cited above were principally drawn from an annual publication of the Arms Control and Disarmament Agency (ACDA) entitled

World Military Expenditures and Arms Transfers. The figures presented in this publication differ in varying degrees from those presented in other

---

Fig. 13.1 World Military Expenditures, 1973-1985

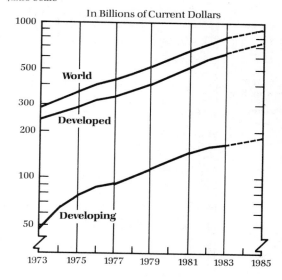

Ratio Scale*

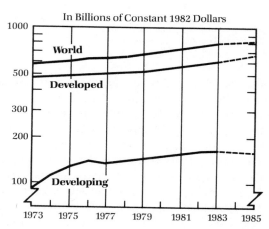

*On a ratio (or semi-log) scale, an equal slope anywhere on the chart means an equal growth rate.

SOURCE: *Military Expenditures and Arms Transfer,* 1985, p. 3 (Arms Control and Disarmament Agency)

Fig. 13.2 Leading Countries in Military Expenditures

Military Expenditures, 1983

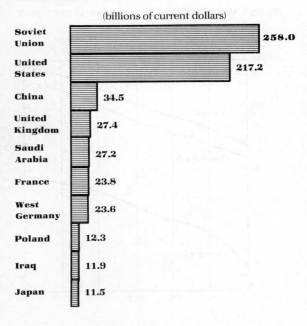

(billions of current dollars)

Country	Expenditure
Soviet Union	258.0
United States	217.2
China	34.5
United Kingdom	27.4
Saudi Arabia	27.2
France	23.8
West Germany	23.6
Poland	12.3
Iraq	11.9
Japan	11.5

SOURCE: *Military Expenditures and Arms Transfer,* 1985, p. 5. (Arms Control and Disarmament Agency)

and the figures used here, unless otherwise cited, will be from ACDA publications.

As would be expected, a further breakdown of military expenditures reveals a substantial variation in spending among nations. In 1983, 10 countries spent less than 1 percent of their GNP on their military. All but Iceland were Third World countries. This group also included two of the more advanced Third World countries, Mexico and Brazil. Twenty-nine countries spent between 1 percent and 2 percent. All but eight were Third World countries. As the percentage of spending increases, the number of developed nations in each category also increases. However, among the 19 countries in the top category—those spending more than 10 percent of their GNPs on their military—all but the Soviet Union and Israel are Third World nations. Thus, the Third World offers more percentage extremes in spending than do the developed nations overall.

The largest spenders among the Third World countries are in the Middle East. Of the top 10 military spenders in 1982, in terms of percentage of national budget, six are located in the Middle East. The four remaining countries are the Soviet Union, China, Angola, and Afghanistan. The Middle Eastern countries and the percentages of their respective national budgets are: Oman, 49.1; United Arab Emirates, 36.4; South Yemen, 32.0; Syria, 29.8; Saudi Arabia, 29.6; and Jordan, 29.5. Two Middle Eastern countries one would expect to be on the list of high spenders, but which are not, are Iraq and Israel. ACDA offered no figures on Iraq's national budget, and in Israel's case the ACDA lists the percentage of Israel's national budget spent on arms as less than the percentage of Israel's GNP spent on arms. Since the national budget is ordinarily only a fraction of the GNP, the portion of the national budget spent on arms will, in most cases, be higher than the percentage of the GNP spent on arms. But, due to the substantial amount of U.S. military aid to Israel and heavy deficit spending on the military, Israel's military expenditures are only 24.2 percent of the national budget, but 29 percent of the GNP.

summaries that attempt to measure the same expenditures. For example, Sivard's study, *World Military and Social Expenditures 1983* and *Military Balance* (MB), published by the International Institute of Strategic Studies, offer slightly different figures. Differences in calculations can be accounted for in part on the basis that exact figures are not available for closed societies, and data must be based on estimates which vary. The ACDA admits that much of its data "are subject to considerable margins of error, particularly for countries that have restrictive data disclosure policies or developing national statistical systems." This is the case for the other publications as well. The figures and percentages do not differ markedly from one data set to another, however,

Tab. 13.1 Military Spending by Percentage of GNP

ME/GNP* (%)	GNP Per Capita (1982 dollars)					
	Under $200	$200-499	$500-999	$1,000-2,999	$3,000-9,999	$10,000 and over
10% and over	Laos† Vietnam† Kampuchea†	Yemen (Aden) Cape Verde†	Angola Yemen (Sanaa) Zambia† Nicaragua	Iraq North Korea Jordan Syria Mongolia†	Israel Oman Libya Soviet Union	Saudi Arabia Qatar†
5-9.99%	Samalia Ethiopia	China Guyana† Mauritania Guinea† Pakistan Afghanistan†	Egypt Morocco Zimbabwe Peru Honduras†	Lebanon Taiwan Albania† South Korea Cuba† Malaysia Iran	Bulgaria East Germany Greece Czechoslovakia Singapore Poland United Kingdom	United Arab Emirates United States
2-4.99%	Burma Burkina Faso Mali Benin Chad† Bangladesh	Guinea-Bissau† Lesotho Mozambique† India Burundi Equatorial Guinea† Liberia Tanzania Togo Senegal Madagascar Kenya	El Salvador Thailand Swaziland Botswana Indonesia Nigeria Cameroon	Turkey Chile South Africa Yugoslavia Congo Portugal Uruguay Tunisia Algeria Argentina Guatemala	Romania Hungary France Cyprus Belgium Netherlands Trinidad and Tobago Italy Gabon Suriname New Zealand Spain	Kuwait Bahrain West Germany Sweden Norway Australia Denmark Canada
1-1.99%	Zaire Nepal	Central African Republic Sao Tome & Principe Malawi Sri Lanka Haiti Rwanda Uganda	Bolivia† Philippines Sudan Ivory Coast Papua New Guinea	Panama† Paraguay Ecuador Dominican Republic Jamaica Fiji† Colombia	Ireland Austria Venezuela Malta Japan	Switzerland Finland Luxembourg
Under 1%		Sierra Leone Niger The Gambia	Costa Rica	Brazil Mexico Ghana† Mauritius	Barbados	Iceland

*Countries are listed within blocks in descending order of ME/GNP
†Ranking is based on a rough approximation of one or more variables for which 1983 data or reliable estimates are not available

SOURCE: *Military Expenditures and Arms Transfer*, 1985, p. 7.
(Arms Control and Disarmament Agency)

The growth rate of military expenditures in the Middle East for the decade 1973–1982 was 11.4 percent annually, substantially higher than that of any other geographic region, and total expenditures were 15.7 percent of GNPs in 1983.

Fig. 13.3 Military Expenditures by Region, 1973-1983

Ratio Scale   In billions of constant 1982 dollars

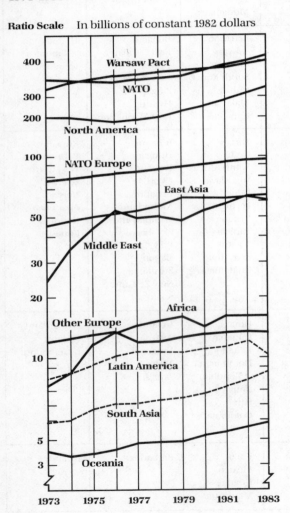

SOURCE: *Military Expenditures and Arms Transfer*, 1985, p.4. (Arms Control and Disarmament Agency)

Other Third World regions were between 1.5 percent and 8 percent. The rate of annual increase for North America was only 1.9 percent. This percentage is misleading, however, since North America has a low percentage of increase before 1981, but shows a high increase in 1981 and 1982. *Military Balance* offers somewhat different figures for 1982, most of which are higher percentages than those offered by ACDA. For example, *Military Balance* lists 15 countries that spend more than 27 percent of their budgets on their military; ten were Third World countries, and five of those were Middle Eastern countries. Some major differences in the two lists were Israel and Pakistan, with 44.6 percent and 45.6 percent respectively in *Military Balance*, about 15 percentage points higher than on the ACDA list. Despite different percentages, both lists indicate that the Middle East has the highest percentage of military spending in the Third World. A further indication of this concentration of spending in the Middle East is that the six highest spenders on a per capita basis worldwide are Saudi Arabia, Qatar, Oman, United Arab Emirates, Israel, and Kuwait, all Middle Eastern countries.

Substantial budgets for the military in Third World countries are justified in several ways. To maintain national security is certainly the overall justification, but that general rationale can be broken down into more specific arguments. Since many Third World countries have military governments, the military is also the bureaucracy of the country; many military officers function more as administrators than as military men in their day-to-day assignments. In this context, at least a part of the military budget goes toward running the country. In many Third World countries, whether dictatorships or not, the military is, as a profession, a modernizing influence and training ground, especially for junior officers. Thus, without the military the process of modernization might be slowed. But whether the military is in power or not, it is a major political group in most Third World countries, and any

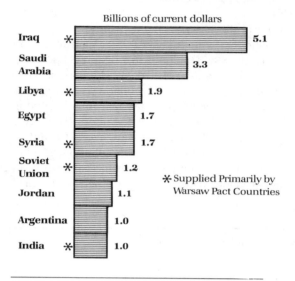

Fig. 13.4 Leading Arms Importing Countries, 1983

Billions of current dollars

Iraq ✱	5.1
Saudi Arabia	3.3
Libya ✱	1.9
Egypt	1.7
Syria ✱	1.7
Soviet Union ✱	1.2
Jordan	1.1
Argentina	1.0
India ✱	1.0

✱ Supplied Primarily by Warsaw Pact Countries

SOURCE: *Military Expenditures and Arms Transfer*, 1985, p.9. (Arms Control and Disarmament Agency)

attempt to reduce that influence through budget reductions could lead to a military coup. The military may also be seen as a job corps of sorts, providing employment for those who would otherwise be unemployed. In some Third World countries, portions of the military are used as a domestic Peace Corps in combating illiteracy and low health standards. These more positive uses of the military do not exist in all Third World countries, needless to say.

The military is more often justified simply on the more traditional grounds of being necessary for domestic and international protection. In the more politically stable Western nations, the military is seldom utilized to maintain domestic peace—local law enforcement agencies carry out that function—but in many Third World countries the military does maintain domestic stability. The frequency of coups in Third World countries further intensifies the domestic need to protect the government through a strong military. The tendency, therefore, is for military governments to

increase the military budget in order to remain strong and maintain their domestic political influence.

All of the factors thus far mentioned justifying Third World military budgets stem from the domestic political system, but the highest military budgets in the Third World are justified on the basis of external threat. The presence of Iraq and Iran in the top ten in percentage of national budget for the military is to be expected, because they have been at war since 1980. The ongoing dispute between North Yemen and South Yemen explains their high budgets. Pakistan's presence on the list is explainable because of the threat from Afghanistan and because of Indo-Pakistani differences. Taiwan, on the MB list, has a high budget because of tensions with China, just as South Korea, also on the MB list, has longstanding problems with North Korea. The presence of several Middle Eastern countries on both lists can be explained as a result of Arab-Israeli problems and problems in the Persian Gulf. The simple generalization that emerges is that arms expenditures are highest where tensions are high.

ARMS TRANSFERS—HOW MUCH?

Broadly speaking, arms transfers involve any means by which one country provides arms to another country. The arms may be purchased in what is essentially a commercial transaction, although usually the government of the exporting nation must approve such transactions. A second method is for an arms transfer to be financed by the exporting government through loans and credits. A third means of transferring arms is an out-and-out grant, in which one nation gives arms to another country. Some arms transactions utilize more than one of these methods. Presently, however, most arms transfers involve some financial consideration.

The calculation of how much is transferred is complicated by another factor as well. Although the ACDA reports the transfer of all weapons, they do not include such important support items as training and construction. Some estimators include only major weapons systems such as tanks, aircraft, missiles, and warships in their summaries. A further complication is the occasional Soviet practice of selling weapons at discounts up to 40 percent in order to undersell the competition or attract a client state. This means that some arms sales are not reported at their full value. (Pierre, 1982, 78.)

Although overall figures are available for the years up to 1985, 1983 is the latest year for which a nation-by-nation breakdown on arms transfers

is available. Since the ACDA, at times, presents the 1983 figures differently than it does the 1982 figures, data for both years will occasionally be used in discussing arms transfers.

The total amount spent on arms transfers in 1983 was $37.3 billion; $28.7 billion (81 percent) were transfers to Third World nations. The remaining amount of $8.6 billion were transfers among the developed nations, mainly among NATO and Warsaw Pact members. Forty-two percent of all arms transfers went to Middle Eastern countries, and 51 percent of transfers to Third World countries went to that region. In dollar value, arms transfers to the Third World

Fig. 13.5 Arms Exports as a Percent of the World Arms Export Trade, 1973-1984

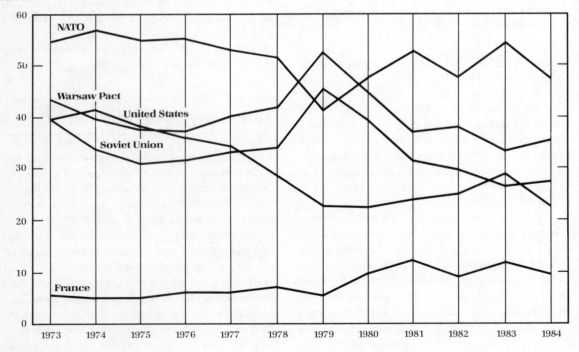

SOURCE: *Military Expenditures and Arms Transfer*, 1985, p. 10 (Arms Control and Disarmament Agency)

in 1983 were four times the amount in 1973; when discounted for inflation, the figure doubled. In 1983, arms transfers to Third World countries declined by 4.6 percent over the previous year, however.

WHO TRANSFERS ARMS

The ACDA calculates that 44 countries exported arms in 1982, up from 32 countries in 1972. The dollar amounts for many of these countries, however, are not large. In 1972, 10 countries exported arms exceeding $100 million, and, in 1982, 29 countries had arms exports exceeding that figure. The United States and the Soviet Union, as would be expected, are the largest transferers of arms. Which one is the largest changes from year to year and sometimes depends on how arms exports are measured. Another problem in calculating arms exports is that some sources calculate new contracts concluded in a particular year while others use the dollar amounts of arms delivered. The ACDA uses the arms-delivered measure, and, accordingly, the United States led the Soviet Union in arms transfers until 1977. From 1977 through 1982, the Soviet Union surpassed the U.S. in deliveries, but in 1983 the United States delivered more ($10.6 billion) than did the Soviets ($7.8 billion). In 1984, however, the Soviets returned to first place in arms transfers with $9.4 billion to $7.7 billion for the United States.

In new contracts during 1983, the value for the United States was $9.8 billion, and for the Soviet Union $4.2 billion. The figures for new contracts do not include any grants for arms, however. The largest single difference between the two countries is that arms exports accounted for 13 percent of the Soviet Union's total exports in 1982, but only 4.4 percent of total exports for

the United States. While the percentages vary from year to year, the range for transfers by the two superpowers in recent years ordinarily has been between 55 percent and 58 percent of all arms transferred; in 1982 it was 55 percent. Due to increases in the number of nations exporting arms, in 1984 their combined sales for the first time went under 50 percent of the total of world's arms transfers.

With approximately one-half of the arms market serviced by nations other than the superpowers, several other countries necessarily have substantial arms sales. In 1982, France had 8.8 percent of the market. France sells arms to a number of countries, but its largest customers are Iraq, Saudi Arabia, and Morocco; Great Brit-

Fig. 13.6 Shares of World Arms Exports, 1983

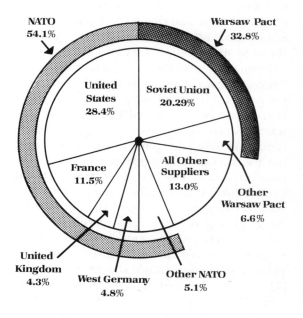

SOURCE:*Military Expenditures and Arms Transfer,* 1985, p. 10. (Arms Control and Disarmament Agency)

ain had 5.5 percent of the market, and its largest customers are Saudi Arabia and Jordan; West Germany had 2.0 percent; other NATO countries had 5.4 percent, and Warsaw Pact nations other than the Soviet Union had 8.2 percent. All other suppliers (non–NATO and non–Warsaw Pact) had about 14 percent of the market, including, in descending order of exports, China, Brazil, Spain (joined NATO in 1982), North Korea, South Korea, Israel, Egypt, Libya, Sweden, and Yugoslavia. As this second-level list of arms exporters indicates, several are from the Third World, an indication of the growing arms industry in some of those countries. Arms transfers from such countries as Egypt and Libya are primarily the reexport of arms, however, and not the result of domestically produced arms. Non–NATO Western industrial states such as Sweden, Austria, and Switzerland export only small quantities of arms. What clearly has developed in the arms trade is that several sources are available to any country that wishes to import arms and that the competition for arms markets is particularly fierce among the Western countries and between the Western and communist nations.

From the late 1950s up to the late 1980s, the figures on arms transfers indicate that although the rate of increase in arms transfers to Third World countries has slowed, the amount in constant dollars has grown considerably and the percentage of total sales going to the Third World has also increased. Two reasons can be cited for these increases. The first is increased tension among Third World nations, and the second is the growing demand by Third World countries for more sophisticated, thus more expensive, weapons. These two reasons are closely related in that when regional tension exists and one party receives sophisticated weaponry, the other side also feels obliged to do likewise. The time when the superpowers would dispose of their obsolescent equipment at relatively low prices, as in the 1950s and early 1960s, has long since passed.

SOVIET ARMS CUSTOMERS

In 1982, the top 10 importers of arms received about 53 percent of all arms transferred. The Soviet Union and other Warsaw Pact nations were the primary suppliers to six of those nations (Iraq, Libya, Syria, India, Algeria, and Cuba) for a total of $12.3 billion. The other four—Saudi Arabia, Egypt, Iran, and Israel—whose total was $9.0 billion, received their arms principally from Western sources. The Soviet Union suspended arms shipments to Iraq in 1979 due to anticommunist policies of the new Iraqi military government, but after the Iraqi–Iranian War began in 1980, and resupply of Iraqi forces became critical, the Soviets resumed shipments. During the five-year period from 1978–1982, Iraq imported $13.6 billion in weapons, about $8 billion of which came from Warsaw Pact nations. Western European countries transferred about $2.5 billion to Iraq in that time period. The quantity of arms purchased by Libya ($11.5 billion, 1978–1982; $7 billion from the Warsaw Pact) exceeds what the Libyan armed forces can absorb, thus giving rise to speculation that Libya stockpiles arms for reshipment to countries it wishes to support. Shipments to Syria ($9.8 billion, 1978–1982; $8.7 billion from Warsaw Pact nations) are for the purpose of maintaining that country as the sole remaining Arab state on Israel's borders that is a likely opponent for Israel in a new war. Algeria receives large shipments of arms ($3.8 billion from 1978–1982; $3.2 billion from the Warsaw Pact nations) to maintain its support of the Polisario in its fight against Morocco, a country with which Algeria also has a boundary dispute. Cuba receives Soviet arms support in exchange for the use of Cuban troops in Soviet client states in Africa and to maintain a Soviet outpost in Latin America. From 1978 to 1982, Cuba received $2.7 billion in arms transfers, all from Warsaw Pact nations.

India is a special case, since it is not a Soviet

client state. The Soviet Union is India's principal source of arms, but France and Great Britain also transfer arms to India. From 1978 to 1982, India received $3.6 billion in arms transfers, $2.9 billion of which came from Warsaw Pact nations. A further unique feature of Soviet arms transfer to India is the Soviet-built assembly plant for MiG combat aircraft. No other such facility exists outside the Soviet Union.

The Soviet Union also ships arms to a number of other countries including members of the Warsaw Pact. The cost of the Soviet arms going to Eastern Europe is particularly difficult to calculate, both because of the closed political systems of the Warsaw Pact nations and because of the difficulty in figuring the exchange rates between the bloc nations. ACDA estimates are, however, that the Soviet Union transferred $6.3 billion to those countries from 1978 to 1982. In Latin America, in addition to Cuba, Peru ($525 million between 1978 and 1982) is a major purchaser of Soviet arms; in Asia, it is Vietnam. Although Vietnam is not included among the top ten importers of Soviet arms, the value of the arms transfer to Vietnam may be higher than estimated, since figuring the cost of Soviet arms received by Vietnam is subject to the same problems encountered with respect to Eastern Europe. ACDA estimates that the Soviet Union transferred $3.6 billion to Vietnam from 1972 through 1978. In Africa, the Soviet Union's various client states, such as Angola ($950 million, 1978–1982) and Ethiopia ($2.2 billion, 1978–1982), are also recipients of Soviet arms transfers.

During the 1960s, the Soviet Union used a number of incentives to induce arms transfers. The Soviets offered arms at discounts, provided long-term credits at low interest rates, and allowed payment in soft currencies. The Soviets have also, on occasion, accepted a barter arrangement of food or fiber commodities in exchange for arms. Some Soviet loans for the purchase of arms proved to be poor investments, however, since Egypt and Indonesia have not

repaid their loans; and some countries received their arms as grants, as did North Vietnam during its war with the United States. The purpose of such loans and grants, however, was to gain client nations and influence, not solely to make a good economic investment. In the 1970s, the Soviets experienced hard currency problems and tightened the terms for making arms transfers or sought out those countries that could afford to pay cash, such as Libya, Iraq, and Algeria. (Pierre, 1982, 78–79.)

The Soviets do have some important advantages over the Western countries in arms trade. Western equipment generally costs more than its Soviet equivalent, and, because the quantity of arms production is higher in the Soviet Union, the Soviets can promise more rapid delivery than can Western producers. Although Soviet equipment is ordinarily not as sophisticated as Western equipment, it usually meets the needs of a developing country.

While Soviet policy seems to be to transfer arms to any country sympathetic to Soviet foreign policy, the United States has attempted at times to place policy restrictions on its arms exports, even to countries that are closely aligned with the United States. But for both countries "arms sales are far more than an economic occurrence, a military relationship or an arms control challenge—*arms sales are foreign policy writ large*" (Pierre, 1982, 3). The transfer of arms can buy influence, be of economic benefit, secure an ally, frustrate another country's foreign policy, or simply prevent a competitor from making a sale.

UNINTENDED OUTCOMES

Both of the superpowers have experienced frustrations in their arms transfers. The United States sold Iran, under the Shah, large quantities of arms only to see a hostile government come to power. If the attempted rescue mission of the hostages in April 1980 had developed into combat, the mission would have faced U.S.–made weapons. In the Iraqi–Iranian War, U.S. arms are being used to fight Iraq, which the United States nominally supports. Also, the United States provided arms to both Pakistan and India before their brief wars in 1965 and 1971, yet afterward derived only poorer relations with both nations.

A particularly frustrating result of arms transfers was the outcome of the Vietnam War. When South Vietnam collapsed in April 1975, large stores of U.S.–supplied weapons fell into the hands of the victors. Those arms were then integrated into Vietnam's armed forces. The Soviets have had their frustrations as well. The weapons transferred to Egypt from 1955 until the early 1970s did not prevent a break between the two countries. Indonesia, after receiving substantial shipments of arms from the Soviet Union, first aligned itself with China; then, after a military coup in 1965, became pro–Western. After supporting Somalia with arms transfers in its fight with Ethiopia, the Soviets switched sides and shipped weapons to Ethiopia.

NATO AND WESTERN EUROPEAN TRANSFERS

Among the Western nations the least controversial of all arms transfers are those that take place within NATO. But even in this case, problems can develop. The controversy does not concern the fact that the arms transfers take place, as is often the case with transfers to Third World countries, but relates to the question of which country's weapons will be used by NATO. During the early years of NATO, when U.S. grants of aid were rearming NATO members, the equipment transferred was largely U.S.–made. By the 1980s, U.S. grants to the economically advanced members of NATO had long since ended, and several members produced their own weapons. Each NATO producer hopes to sell its weapons sys-

tems to other NATO countries and, in particular, hopes to have them adopted as standard NATO weapons. The result is either considerable controversy before a weapons system is agreed upon by NATO or no agreement on a standard weapons system. The latter is usually the outcome. For example, West Germany developed the Leopard tank and hoped to have it adopted as NATO's main battle tank. This never occurred, since the United States, Great Britain, and France each had a tank to promote. NATO could not agree on which to adopt, and, thus, each of these states uses its own tank. The members of NATO that do not manufacture a main battle tank usually purchase the West German tank.

A recent change in intra–NATO arms transfers is the development of multinational weapons systems. While this method of maneuvering around the national-origin problem has been applied to only a few weapons systems, it has been used in the development of a new multipurpose combat aircraft. West Germany, Italy, and Great Britain aided in the development of the *Tornado* that is used in each country's air forces. Previously, the West German and Italian air forces used either U.S.-built aircraft or U.S.–designed aircraft built in Europe under license, and the British used mainly aircraft produced in Britain. The joint development of weapons systems is motivated not so much by a desire to reduce competition within NATO as to reduce expenditures for each country by several countries' sharing developmental costs. The effect of such developments, however, is to reduce competition and conflict among NATO members.

The selection of combat aircraft for NATO members that do not manufacture their own presents yet another problem. When The Netherlands, Belgium, Denmark, and Norway decided to replace their obsolescent U.S.–built fighter aircraft, a scramble occurred among Western nations for the 348-aircraft contract. The French presented their Mirage F1, the Swedes offered their Viggen, and the United States lobbied for two fighters, the F–16 and the F–17. After fly-off competition and fierce lobbying of the potential recipient nations by the manufacturers, in 1975 the contract went to the General Dynamics F–16. One explanation offered for rejection of the Viggen was that Sweden was outside NATO and thus could cut off production if it disagreed with NATO policy. The French fighter was considered to be near the end of its development, having first flown in 1966, and could be improved little over time. The U.S. fighters were both new designs. The F–16 was selected only after coproduction arrangements were worked out so that a substantial portion was done in the countries that would receive the aircraft. In 1983, a similar arrangement was developed with Turkey for 160 of the same aircraft.

The contract between the United States and Turkey for coproduction of the F–16 was the largest contract within NATO and Western Europe during 1983 and 1984, although there were a number of other substantial contracts, including one in which West Germany sold Switzerland 210 Leopard tanks at a cost of over $2 billion. The general characteristic of arms transfers within Western Europe is that arms transfers are numerous, particularly for missiles and less expensive weapon systems, but major items such as tanks and aircraft are transferred only if no domestic production of the item exists. The result is considerable arms trade among the members of NATO, but little common agreement on weaponry to be deployed within NATO; from 1978 through 1982, weapons worth $13.6 billion were transferred among NATO members, with $10.2 billion coming from the United States.

Although most members of NATO finance their own armed forces, the poorer members continue to receive U.S. military assistance, much of which is used for arms purchases from the United States. In fiscal year 1983, Turkey and Spain each received $402 million, Greece received $281 million, and Portugal received $111 million. Because of conflicts between Greece and Turkey over Cyprus and Turkish claims to Greek-controlled islands near the Turkish main-

land, fiscal year 1983 aid reflected U.S. policy of granting aid to Greece and Turkey on a 7 to 10 ratio respectively in order to not upset the military alignment between the two countries even though they are nominal allies.

U.S. TRANSFERS TO THE MIDDLE EAST

Although Western Europe continues to be an important market for U.S. arms transfers, the United States makes its biggest sales to Third World countries. Any major arms transfer to those countries carries with it an element of controversy, since the importing nations receive arms in what is often a tense political situation. Regardless of which nation is exporting the weapons, an arms transfer seldom takes place without the charge that it upsets the current weapons balance in the region.

One of the United States' biggest arms customers is Israel. The U.S. had supported Israel diplomatically since it became independent in 1948, but did not supply it arms in any quantity until 1967. Until the Six–Day War, France was Israel's principal source of arms, but the French considered Israel the aggressor in that war and adopted a pro–Arab stance and suspended all arms shipments to Israel. This shift in policy secured France's oil supply from Algeria, an Arab country hostile to Israel. The United States then became Israel's principal source of arms.

Though Israel is a major importer of arms, it also exports arms, although its exports do not include such major items as combat aircraft and tanks. The most controversial Israeli arms sales have been those made to South Africa and Chile, when those countries were subject to Western arms embargoes (Pierre, 1982, 161). Israel wanted to export its Kfir fighter aircraft, but the United States objected because the aircraft is powered by a U.S.–built engine. The United States does not allow the reexport of its military equipment to a third state, even if the item is only a component of a domestically manufactured weapons system. Later, the United States dropped that objection to the export of the Kfir, but found other reasons to restrict its export; to date, few Kfirs have been exported. This problem also arose when Sweden wished to export its Viggen to Iran, since the Viggen also has U.S.–made components.

The United States began reequipping the Israeli air force after the Six Day War with the sale of 50 F–4s and 75 A–4s, both first-line aircraft at the time. Additional aircraft of these types were sold to Israel for a number of years and became mainstays of the Israeli air force. Israel was the only country outside NATO to receive such advanced aircraft during the 1960s and early 1970s. Later, Israel became the first country, including NATO countries, to receive the F–15, perhaps the best aircraft of its type in the world.

Secretary of State Kissinger, who frequently used arms transfers as a means of persuading other nations to comply with U.S. requests, promised Israel F–15s as a part of the arms package Israel received when it accepted the 1975 Sinai disengagement agreement. The original order was for 25 aircraft, but additional orders were permitted later. Israel was also sold the even newer, but not necessarily more advanced, F–16. The United States had already agreed to sell the F–16 to Israel before the Camp David agreement in 1978, but delivery dates were advanced and the number to be sold increased as a part of the arms package used to induce Israel to sign the agreement. By the late 1980s, the Israeli air force possessed some of the most advanced aircraft in the world.

Israel, of course, receives military equipment other than aircraft from the United States, but type of combat aircraft has become the measure of sophistication for the weapons a nation receives. The United States also sells tanks to Israel, some of which were airlifted to Israel in U.S. aircraft during the critical days of the October 1973 war, as well as missiles and various other weapons systems. In fiscal year 1983, Israel received $1.7 billion in U.S. military assistance in addition to loans to pay for past purchases.

The United States also sells arms to other countries in the Middle East, including nations counted among Israel's enemies. The U.S. arms deals that were the most upsetting to Israel were transfers made to Saudi Arabia. From 1978 through 1982, the United States sold the Saudis arms valued at $3.5 billion. In addition, the Saudis bought heavily from France, Great Britain, and West Germany. The most controversial of these transfers occurred in 1978 when the U.S. agreed to sell Saudi Arabia 60 F–15s; until then, Israel had been the only country to receive that aircraft. Israel objected strongly to the sale, and in order to placate Israel the United States sold Israel additional F–15s and initiated sales of the F–16. Congress was concerned about the sale of F–15s to Saudi Arabia, but, after the Carter administration assured it that the capabilities of the aircraft were limited to defense only, Congress allowed the sale to proceed. The Reagan administration revived the controversy in 1981, when long-range fuel tanks were provided for the Saudi F–15s, so that now Israel was within easy range of Saudi bases. The Reagan administration also sold bomb racks and missiles for the F–15s and AWACS (long-range surveillance aircraft) and aerial tanker aircraft to support F–15 combat operations. Israel again objected, but the United States justified upgrading the capabilities of the Saudi F–15s as necessary because of the threat posed by Iran. The Shah was still in power when F–15s were first sold to Saudi Arabia, but by 1981 Iran was a nation hostile toward the United States.

The greatest single policy reversal for the United States in the Middle East came in 1979 with the fall of the Shah of Iran. After Great Britain withdrew from the Persian Gulf in 1968, the U.S. strategy was that Iran would provide security in the region. By the mid–1970s, Iran was the single-largest importer of U.S. arms, although only a marginally larger customer than Saudi Arabia. Even before the Islamic government came to power, the Shah's growing military capability worried the Saudis, who pressed the United States for additional arms. Both Iran and Saudi Arabia could afford the cost, since this period was the high point of oil income. Iran became the only country to receive F–14s, the first-line fighter of the U.S. Navy (the F–15 and F–16 are U.S. Air Force aircraft). While most of Iran's military equipment was purchased from the United States, its tanks were purchased from Great Britain.

The United States also has made substantial arms transfers to two other Middle Eastern nations, Egypt and Jordan. The controversy surrounding the arms arrangements with Egypt as a part of the Camp David agreements has already been discussed, but arms transfers to Jordan were also troublesome. Jordan suffered a humiliating defeat in the 1967 war with Israel; it lost the West Bank and its entire air force in less than three days. Jordan received its arms from Western sources, and, when resupplied, continued to do so (from 1978 through 1982 Jordan divided its arms purchases among the United States, France, and Great Britain). King Hussein, in particular, wanted an air defense system to prevent the easy destruction of his new air force. Because Israel objected, the United States refused to sell Jordan such a system, and in 1975 Hussein began discussions with the Soviet Union for one of their air defense systems. The United States then sold Jordan 500 Hawk surface-to-air missiles, but with the restriction that they have permanent sites and not be mobile. This restriction was intended to overcome Israeli objections to the sale.

DEVELOPMENT OF U.S. TRANSFER POLICY

U.S. policy on arms transfers has undergone considerable change since the years prior to World War II. Until shortly before the U.S. entered World War II, it maintained, under the Neutrality Acts of the 1930s, that any country purchasing arms from the United States must pay cash and pick up the arms in their own ships. This policy followed from the perception that the United States had entered World War I to protect the loans American banks made to France and Great Britain and to retaliate for the sinking of U.S. ships carrying munitions to the Allies. Until the Lend–Lease Act was passed by Congress, U.S. policy was that it would sell arms to any country as long as the terms were "cash and carry." After the United States entered World War II, labeling itself the "arsenal of democracy," it financed a massive arms transfer program to any country fighting the Axis nations. This program actually began in March 1941 with the Lend–Lease Program, nine months before the United States officially entered the war. When the war ended, so did the arms shipments until the intensity of the Cold War led to the creation of NATO in 1949, followed by the Mutual Security Act of 1951 and the Military Assistance Program, the purpose of which was to rearm the members of NATO. An earlier and smaller program of military aid was directed to Greece and Turkey. U.S. arms transfers during the 1950s were predominantly directed toward Europe, except for military assistance sent to South Korea and Taiwan. The Soviets, during this same period, were concentrating on arming their Eastern European allies, although China, North Korea, Syria, Egypt, and Indonesia also received Soviet arms. During the 1960s, an increasing number of Third World countries received arms transfers from the United States—the United States, at the time, had a total of 45 treaty allies, many of which were Third World countries.

Following the Lend–Lease Act, Congress passed no major legislation governing arms transfers until the Foreign Military Sales Act in 1968. When U.S. arms were going essentially to Western nations, Congress saw no need to regulate the transactions, but, by the late 1960s, arms transfers were going primarily to Third World nations, and Congress was raising questions about the ethics of some of those transfers. The two principal features of the legislation were: 1) the executive was required to consider foreign policy objectives in making arms transfers; and 2) arms transfers to governments guilty of human rights violations were to stop. This legislation brought about little change in arms transfer policy, however. The shipment of sophisticated weapons to Israel and Iran during the Nixon and Ford administrations resulted in further efforts by Congress to place legislative restraints on arms transfers. Thus, Congress, at this time at the peak of its challenge to the executive in foreign policy-making, attached the Nelson amendment to the fiscal year 1975 foreign aid bill. The amendment required the president to report to Congress any arms sale exceeding $25 million and gave Congress the authority to stop the sale. In 1976, Congress passed the Arms Export Control Act, which further expanded and clarified the congressional role in reviewing arms sales. Congress had always had the authority to stop grants to finance arms transfers, since those required an appropriation; now Congress was directly involved in all major arms transfers.

Shortly after taking office in 1977, the Carter administration developed policy guidelines that committed the United States to reduce transfers and pledged that the U.S. would not be the first to transfer a new weapons system into a region. The new guidelines also stated that no new weapons systems would be exported until they were deployed to U.S. forces, that the human rights policies of recipient nations would be considered before selling them arms, that weapons sold by the United States could not be resold to a third party, and that both the State and Defense Departments would review arm sales for their policy implications before transfers were made. NATO was exempted from the guidelines; thus, the policy statement was directed primarily at arms transfers to Third World countries. The human rights requisite for arms transfers was the most controversial aspect of the Carter policy.

When President Reagan took office in 1981, legislative restrictions remained in effect, and the Carter guidelines were discarded. In a statement in July 1981, President Reagan made clear that his would be a flexible arms transfer policy and that it would be used to help deter aggression, support allies, foster regional stability, and aid U.S. weapons production capabilities. These were not policy guidelines but, rather, were goals that indicated the abandonment of the Carter policy of looking at a nation's human rights policies before selling it arms. The Reagan administration essentially returned to the old policy of arms transfers to friends and allies, regardless of their domestic policies. An additional difference in the policies of the two presidents was that Carter had prohibited "the development or significant modification of advanced weapons systems solely for export," whereas the Reagan policy neither imposed such a restriction nor prevented the United States from being the first to introduce a new weapons system into a region. Arms transfers to Latin America illustrate well the differences in application of the Carter and Reagan approaches.

HUMAN RIGHTS AND U.S. EXPORTS

The provision of the Arms Export Control Act of 1976 that prohibited the export of arms to any country guilty of "gross violation of human rights" would appear to be a straightforward guideline for arms transfers. Its application to specific arms transfers proved to be troublesome, however. In order to give Congress the information it needed to evaluate arms transfers, the act required the administration to make an annual country-by-country report on human rights conditions. The first such report, issued in March 1977 shortly after Carter took office, revealed that in the 82 countries receiving some form of U.S. military assistance only a few outside Western Europe had not committed some violations of human rights. Since the Third World countries generally have authoritarian regimes, the results of this report were not surprising. The Carter administration then had to make the difficult decision as to how serious those violations had to be before arms exports would be cut off or reduced.

The first countries to receive a reduction in aid were Argentina, Uruguay, and Ethiopia. The action taken toward Ethiopia meant little, however, since that country was already turning to the Soviet Union for its military assistance. Argentina also had other sources of military aid and turned to France and Great Britain. Thus, during the Falklands War in 1982, the British not only faced French and American weapons, but also some of their own. In 1979 when the United States asked Argentina to join in the Soviet grain embargo, Argentina refused, probably in retaliation for the arms sanctions. Brazil, which was cited in the report for human rights violations but had no sanctions imposed on it, refused any further military assistance from the United States and denounced U.S. interference and moral judgments. Later, Chile, El Salvador, and Guatemala were limited in the arms they could receive from the U.S. Other countries also guilty of human rights violations, such as South Korea, the Philippines, and Iran, were considered too important to U.S. interests to have aid reduced.

These decisions during the Carter administration to reduce aid to nations violating human rights were accompanied by decisions to deny the export of certain types of aircraft to some countries on the grounds that their export either would violate the Carter guidelines that advanced weapons system would not be exported to Third World countries or would introduce a new weapons system to a region. The countries denied new types of aircraft included Iran, South Korea, Pakistan, and Taiwan. The administration also refused Israel's request to coproduce the F–16. Egypt was denied F–16s but was allowed F–5s (this aircraft was not considered to be an advanced weapons system). A number of other countries were denied lesser weapon systems, but some new recipients of U.S. arms, such as

Sudan, were added. In all, several hundred requests totaling about $1 billion in weapons were turned down in the first fifteen months of the Carter administration. (Pierre, 1982, 34–35, 55–56).

Most of the targets of the Carter human rights policy were Latin American countries. This was probably because those countries were seen by the U.S. as less important strategically than countries on the periphery of communist nations; therefore, arms embargoes or reductions would not be so costly politically. The policy did not bring about any changes of government in Latin America that would be more protective of human rights, but, ironically, after President Reagan rejected the Carter guidelines, a number of new democracies emerged in Latin America. During the Carter administration, the one country that did change its government was Iran, and it had not been subject to sanctions; that change was not to the United States' advantage. Effective or not, the human rights guideline was dropped when the Reagan administration came into office.

ARMS TRANSFERS AND THE REAGAN ADMINISTRATION

In Reagan's first three months in office, his administration offered arms transfers totaling $15 billion and reestablished military assistance to the embargoed countries, except South Africa. The arms embargo on South Africa was the result of a United Nations resolution and was not U.S. policy alone. Another change introduced by the Reagan administration was the increased level of sophistication of weapons exported. This was reflected in the type of aircraft the United States was now willing to sell to Third World countries.

For nearly twenty years, the F–5 had been the most modern combat aircraft the U.S. sold in the Third World. This aircraft was designed for export and, while an effective defensive aircraft, was less sophisticated than some other types manufactured in the United States. The F–5 also was less expensive to purchase and cheaper to maintain. Thus, whenever a Third World country requested an arms transfer of combat aircraft from the United States, the F–5 was offered. If the country asked for a more sophisticated aircraft, the United States refused. Even during the Vietnam War, the South Vietnamese received F–5s rather than more advanced aircraft. In all, over 2000 F–5s were exported. Until the Reagan administration, the only exceptions to this policy of selling low-cost combat aircraft to Third World countries were Saudi Arabia and Iran. The U.S. felt that the sale of F–5s tended not to upset a regional balance, thus was less controversial than would be the sale of more advanced aircraft. Occasionally, when the United States denied a country more sophisticated aircraft, that country would look elsewhere. Such was the case when Brazil bought aircraft from France and Peru purchased aircraft from the Soviet Union. The Reagan administration abandoned this limitation on the export of advanced aircraft and sold the advanced F–16 to Pakistan, Thailand, Venezuela, and South Korea. Sales of advanced aircraft to one country in a region where they have not been sold before often leads to requests by other countries either in that region or other regions for similar aircraft. The agreement to sell Pakistan F–16s prompted India to buy aircraft from France and to upgrade the fighters assembled in the MiG facility. Formerly, the MiG–21 was assembled there, but the Soviets now are providing components of a new design, the MiG–29. After the United States no longer limited fighter exports to F–5s, requests for more advanced aircraft were numerous.

There is a strong domestic motivation for the U.S. to sell advanced aircraft to other countries, other than the fact that the more sophisticated aircraft bring in more revenue. The cost of developing a modern combat aircraft runs into billions of dollars, and those costs are spread over the number of units produced; the more units produced, the lower the cost per unit. Since each of the advanced aircraft is also purchased for the U.S. armed forces, the lower unit cost makes those aircraft less expensive to U.S. air forces.

The effect of the Reagan administration's more aggressive policy in promoting arms transfers has been to increase the U.S. portion of the arms market. As pointed out earlier in this chapter, during the Reagan administration the United States surpassed the Soviet Union in arms transfers for the first time in several years.

CONCLUSION

A report prepared by the Congressional Research Service in 1984 states that when inflation is discounted, Third World countries are spending less on arms transfers than they did in 1976; the market for arms in the Third World may have peaked. The reasons offered for this are mounting Third World debt and declining oil prices. As would be expected, since the largest purchasers of arms have been those countries with large oil incomes, as those incomes decline there is less to spend on arms. Another speculation is that the arsenals of Third World countries are almost full, and thus the high demand of the 1970s for sophisticated weapons has been met. The degree to which nations spend their national budgets and GNPs on their militaries, the amounts involved in arms transfers, and the political problems that arise from those transfers has been discussed. The next chapter will consider comparisons of stockpiles between the major coalitions—their nuclear arsenals, in particular—and the diplomatic efforts to limit those stockpiles.

CHAPTER 14

Arms—Comparison, Control, and Reduction

Even as the superpowers created their nuclear and conventional arsenals, they repeatedly expressed their desire to place limits on those stockpiles through international agreements. Several such agreements have been forthcoming and others are under negotiation, but none of the agreements has been a comprehensive arms control plan. Each agreement has dealt with a limited aspect of arms control. Collectively, these agreements have not reduced the level of superpower arms, but some have placed limits on the number of certain weapons the superpowers can possess. SALT II, adhered to but not ratified by the superpowers, placed a limit on delivery systems, but the production of nuclear warheads and the ongoing introduction of advanced weapons technology, such as strategic defense initiative (SDI), are not controlled by this or any other agreement.

Consensus among negotiating nations as to how their respective levels of arms compare is a requisite to any arms control agreement. Each superpower—through the use of sophisticated surveillance satellites and other techniques—can count with reasonable accuracy the number of missiles, aircraft, or other major weapons systems possessed by the other coalition; thus, the problems of making comparisons is not so much not knowing the size of the other side's stockpile as it is a lack of agreement as to its capabilities and the needs each nation has for those weapons.

Disagreement not only exists between the superpowers concerning interpretation of their arsenals. Disagreement also exists within the U.S. decision-making agencies as to how to interpret the data. It is reasonable to assume that the Soviet system also contains such disagreements, both about the U.S. arsenal and the Soviet Union's own weapons. In the United States this sort of disagreement is often oversimplified by identifying decision-makers as either hawks or doves—with the hawks viewing new weapons as necessary to keep up with the other side and doves viewing present levels of weaponry as sufficient—when in fact various perspectives exist for interpreting the effectiveness of stockpiles and the diverse situations in which they might be used.

SOVIET AND U.S. MILITARY SPENDING

Comparing the military budgets of the United States and the Soviet Union is one means of illustrating the problems encountered in making comparisons between U.S. and Soviet military capabilities. In 1982, the U.S. Arms Control and Disarmament Agency (ACDA) estimated the Soviet Union's military budget as $257 billion or about 15 percent of the Soviet GNP. The military budget for the United States in 1982 was $196 billion. The U.S. military budget was 6.4 percent of the GNP in 1972; it fell to 5.1 percent in 1978 and

1979, and then rose again to 6.4 percent in 1982. In 1972, the Soviet military budget had been nearly 70 percent of its national budget and had fallen gradually to 44 percent in 1982. The U.S. military budget had been 33 percent of the national budget in 1972, had declined to 23 percent in 1978, and had risen to 25 percent in 1982. Based on these figures, the Soviet Union spends more and takes a larger percentage of its GNP and its national budget for its military than does the United States. None of this establishes a trend in spending, however, or indicates which country is ahead in the Cold War arms race, because the figures must be interpreted as to the effect such spending has on arms acquisition and efficiency.

A possible indicator of a trend would be whether either country is making important changes in its budget. By Fiscal Year 1985, the United States had increased its spending to $293 billion,

or 7.1 percent of GNP, and had established an increase over inflation in military spending each year since 1981 for an overall real increase of about 7 percent in three years. Administration projections are that U.S. military spending will increase to 33 percent of the federal budget by 1988. Recent CIA estimates conclude that the Soviet military spending rate in constant currency has increased about 2 percent a year in recent years. The Defense Intelligence Agency (DIA), however, estimates the rate of real increase for the Soviet Union to have been at between 5 and 8 percent each year (*Christian Science Monitor*, February 27, 1985, 8). The CIA estimate would indicate that Soviet spending is increasing at about the same rate the Soviet economy is growing, both slowly. The DIA estimate would indicate that the Soviet Union is making a greater effort than ever before in supporting its military and is exceeding economic growth by several percentage points. If the CIA estimates are used, the U.S. is increasing its defense budget over inflation at about the same percentage rate as is the Soviet Union. If the DIA estimates are used, the United States is falling even further behind the Soviet Union. Since both the CIA and the DIA have access to essentially the same raw intelligence data, the difference is in interpretation of that data. In comparing budgets alone, then, the Soviet Union poses less of a threat if the CIA estimates are used as the basis for making decisions in the United States than if the DIA estimates are used. But how can such different estimates come from the same data?

One reason lies in converting the buying power of the ruble into dollars and deciding how many weapons and how much manpower each budget will provide. The Soviets have lower labor costs than has the United States; thus, their budget goes further when purchasing military equipment. Also, the Soviets spend a higher percentage of their budget on the purchase of new equipment. Consequently, with a larger budget and a higher percentage of the budget going to the acquisition of equipment, a long-range projection

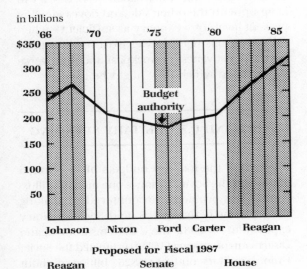

Fig. 14.1 Defense Budget Trends
(in constant 1986 dollars)

in billions

Johnson   Nixon   Ford   Carter   Reagan

Proposed for Fiscal 1987

Reagan	Senate	House
$320 billion	295 billion	285 billion

SOURCE: Christian Science Monitor
August 12, 1986, p.3

Tab. 14.1 Relative Standings in US–Soviet High–Tech Race (technologies with potential military significance)

1. Aerodynamics/fluid dynamics	US, USSR equal
2. Computers and software	US superior and growing
3. Conventional warheads	US, USSR equal
4. Directed energy (lasers)	US, USSR equal
5. Electro-optical sensors	US superior
6. Guidance and navigation	US superior
7. Life sciences	US superior
8. New materials	US superior, but Soviets gaining
9. Micro-electronics	US superior
10. Nuclear warheads	US, USSR equal
11. Optics	US, USSR equal
12. Power sources and storage	US, USSR equal
13. Production/manufacturing	US superior
14. Propulsion	US superior, but Soviets gaining
15. Radar sensors	US superior, but Soviets gaining
16. Robotics, artificial intelligence	US superior
17. Signal processing	US superior
18. Signature reduction (stealth)	US superior
19. Submarine detection	US superior but Soviets gaining
20. Telecommunications (includes fiber optics)	US superior

SOURCE: *Christian Science Monitor*, April 24, 1986, p. 133.

would indicate the Soviets moving further ahead in major conventional weapons such as aircraft, tanks, artillery, and manpower. But does that place the Soviet Union ahead of the United States militarily? In 1986 the Pentagon announced that in twenty important basic areas of technology the United States was ahead in fourteen and behind in none (*Christian Science Monitor*, April 24, 1986, 13). In the technology of weapons deployed, according to the Pentagon, the United States is ahead in seventeen categories, even in ten, and behind in five (*Christian Science Monitor*, February 27, 1985, 3-4). This evaluation would indicate that the United States is ahead at least in the technology of weapons even if behind in levels of military equipment. On the basis of these

factors—size of budget, amounts going to the purchase of new equipment, and weapons technology—the issue of which country is ahead in the arms race remains unresolved.

SOVIET AND U.S. CONVENTIONAL WEAPONS

If budgets are difficult to compare, so are the weapons they fund. Perhaps even more than nuclear weapons, conventional weapons present a range of problems when respective arsenals are analyzed. The first issue is not the weapons themselves, but where they are likely to be used, since different locations for a war create different demands for weapons.

In any potential theater of operations, when the armies of the superpowers are compared, the Soviet Union has, by various measures, a substantial advantage over the United States. The U.S. Army has 16 divisions, whereas the Soviet Army has about 200 divisions. The Soviet Union has approximately four times as many tanks as does the United States and more than twice as many combat aircraft; in addition, the Soviet Union is geographically much closer to the European theater of operations, where general land war is most likely, and thus could deploy its forces more rapidly than could the United States. This sort of comparison is an example of the use of statistics that are correct but fail to give an accurate picture of relative capabilities to conduct a major war, particularly in Europe. It is these sorts of statistics, rather than a reasoned comparison of forces, that are used to justify larger defense budgets in the United States, and, perhaps, in the Soviet Union as well.

If war with conventional forces alone or with conventional forces in combination with the use of theater nuclear weapons would occur in Europe, the assumption is that the first few days would be critical and the forces already deployed or capable of being rapidly deployed would be the deciding factor. The United States has only five divisions in Europe, and, although additional combat-ready troops could be deployed to Europe, it would take a number of days to do so. This would leave the impression that the position of the United States in Europe relative to the Soviet Union is even more disadvantageous than the across-the-board comparison made above would indicate.

The war in Europe would be between NATO forces and the Warsaw Pact forces, however, not just between the forces of the superpowers. Many of the 200 Soviet divisions are category 2 or 3, which means that they are at partial strength, or cadres, and would have to be fleshed out with reserves, which would take time. Also, about one-fourth of the Soviet divisions are on the Sino-Soviet border and not quickly deployable in Europe. (Figures on U.S. and Soviet conventional forces are drawn from *Military Balance, 1984–1985*.) In case of war, NATO's estimate is that the Soviets and other Warsaw Pact nations could have 112 divisions in place or rapidly deployed. The United States and other NATO countries could deploy 88 divisions (NATO, 1984, 8). NATO's totals do not include French or Spanish divisions, since neither country, though members of NATO, has forces under NATO's integrated command. The French maintain three armored divisions in West Germany, however, and have stated that if war occurs they will join in the defense of Western Europe. Nor do these division totals reflect the fact that Warsaw Pact divisions have fewer people in them than do U.S. and West German divisions—the manpower ratio is about four to three. To offset this, the Warsaw Pact divisions have about the same number of tanks and combat soldiers as do Western divisions; U.S. and German divisions have more support troops than do the Warsaw Pact divisions.

In 1982, ACDA estimated the total armed forces of NATO and the Warsaw Pact, including U.S. and Soviet forces not in Europe, to be 5.38 million men and 5.80 million men, respectively.

The NATO estimates of total manpower in the two alliances in 1983 were 5.33 million men in NATO's armed forces and 6.22 million in the Warsaw Pact armies. The overall effect of this is that the Warsaw Pact has a numerical advantage but not as great an advantage as the beginning of this discussion indicated.

This statement concerning marginal superiority of Warsaw Pact nations applies as well to other means of measuring military capability. In total manpower in Europe alone, NATO has about 3.5 million soldiers, and the Warsaw Pact about 4 million. The Warsaw Pact totals include all Soviet forces that are at a level of high readiness in much of European Soviet Union and all forces in Eastern Europe. NATO has about 15,000 tanks in Europe, and the Warsaw Pact about 27,000. In combat aircraft, the Warsaw Pact has 7,500 and NATO 3,700, but in the critical area of fighter-bombers NATO is behind only slightly, 2,250 to 1,960 (NATO, 1984, 8; Department of State, 1985, 3).

The Warsaw Pact advantage in tanks is offset to some extent by a large NATO reserve of antitank weapons. The assumption is that the Warsaw Pact would be the aggressor, and since the tank is primarily an offensive weapon the best means of offsetting the Soviet advantage in tanks is not to use more tanks but to employ antitank weapons. Yet another issue is the reliability of the Soviets' allies. Would NATO allies of the United States be more reliable in defending Western Europe than Soviet allies would be when attacking Western Europe? Such questions are unanswerable short of war but must be considered in assessing what is sufficient to defend Western Europe. Nor does any of this consider the Chinese reaction if a general war were to break out in Western Europe. If China were to remain neutral, Soviet forces on the Sino-Soviet frontier could be transferred to the West, but if China entered the war, demands on Soviet forces would be even greater than the 52 divisions already on the Sino-Soviet border. The comparison of NATO and

Warsaw Pact forces quickly becomes much more complicated than the comparison of numbers alone would indicate.

SOVIET AND U.S. NUCLEAR FORCES

Among NATO and Warsaw Pact nations, even though Great Britain and France have nuclear weapons and delivery systems, when nuclear weapons are compared usually only the Soviet and U.S. arsenals are used. At least, that was the case until 1984, at which time the Soviets insisted that the British and French weapons be included among European theater weapons. In terms of strategic nuclear weapons, however, the Soviet

Tab. 14.2 Balance of Conventional Forces in Europe

Manpower (in thousands)	NATO	Warsaw Pact
Total ground forces: Includes French plus US and Canadian forces stationed in Europe; excludes Spain	2,979	2,809
Divisions*		
Divisions deployed in Europe, manned in peacetime	33	78⅓
Total divisions, war mobilized: Potential number of divisions if all draft-age citizens were mobilized	133	176⅓
Ground Force Equipment		
Main battle tanks	20,333	52,600
Artillery, multiple rocket launchers	9,414	30,500 est.
Antitank guns	364	1,684 est.

*Warsaw Pact divisions are much smaller than NATO divisions, so ratios are calculated according to manpower rather than division numbers.

SOURCE: Christian Science Monitor
November 5, 1986, p. 9.

and U.S. stockpiles alone continue to be compared. The overall problems of comparing nuclear stockpiles are, as with conventional weapons, related to issues of interpreting the data rather than not having the data. A central problem pertains to how to compare the different delivery systems of nuclear weapons.

Each side has three primary means of delivering nuclear weapons. These are land-based intercontinental ballistic missiles (ICBMs), usually in hardened, well-protected silos; submarine-launched ballistic missiles (SLBMs); and manned aircraft. A fourth method of delivery, a combination of these systems, is the nonballistic cruise missile; it is essentially a pilotless aircraft, which can be launched from aircraft, surface vessels, submarines, or from the ground.

The Soviet Union has about 1400 ICBMs, and the United States 1000. The Soviets not only have more missiles, but they can deliver more megatonnage and warheads than can the U.S. (a megaton is the equivalent of one million tons of TNT). This is offset, in part, by the greater accuracy of U.S. missiles; smaller warheads can be used if they land closer to their target. Soviet missiles are becoming more accurate, however, and the accuracy advantage for the U.S. is now limited mainly to an advantage over older Soviet missiles. In addition, undamaged Soviet silos can be reloaded, and U.S. silos cannot.

In regard to submarine-launched ballistic missiles, the Soviet advantage is about 1000 to 600. SLBMs, for either country, are not as accurate as ICBMs, although the new U.S. SLBM, the Trident II, is as accurate as ICBMs. This is important in the negotiation of arms control agreements, since being less accurate overall limits the targets for SLBMs; they are not, for example, accurate enough in most cases to be used reliably against ICBM sites and thus would probably be used against larger targets such as cities and industrial complexes. U.S. SLBMs are more accurate than Soviet SLBMs in general and substantially more accurate than older Soviet SLBMs.

The effectiveness of the Soviet SLBM arsenal is reduced further by maintenance problems with Soviet submarines that bear SLBMs. Because of these problems, the Soviets can keep at sea a smaller percentage of their submarines than can the United States. The U.S. advantage in this regard is substantial, since the Soviets reportedly maintain only 12–15 percent of their submarines on station, and the United States 45–50 percent. Also, Soviet submarines are noisier and thus easier to detect than U.S. submarines, and the United States has developed more sophisticated methods of conducting antisubmarine warfare (ASW) than have the Soviets. The Soviets are reported to be improving their ASW technology, however.

In manned strategic bombers, the United States has an advantage with about 300, whereas the Soviets have only about half that number. If, however, the Soviet Backfire bomber is counted—the Soviets insist that it should not be because of its limited range—the Soviets have a slight advantage in long-range bombers. If U.S. tactical aircraft in Europe capable of delivering nuclear weapons on targets in the Soviet Union are counted, the United States has a considerable advantage. The United States has deployed more air-launched cruise missiles than have the Soviets, although the Soviets are pushing development in that area.

A further complication arises when comparing the total Soviet and U.S. nuclear stockpiles of warheads and throw-weight. The Soviets have more than twice the throw-weight possessed by the United States, but the U.S. can deliver more strategic warheads by a margin of about 11,000 to 9,000. The Soviets can deliver more warheads by means of ICBMs than can the United States, but the United States can deliver more weapons by means of bombers and SLBMs than can the Soviet Union. These relationships are the result of deliberate U.S. and Soviet policies. The United States has spread its efforts over the three methods of launching an attack—bombers, ICBMs,

and SLBMs—which are commonly known as triad. The Soviets have concentrated their efforts on the development of ICBMs.

The reason more warheads than delivery systems exist is that each country has MIRVed substantial numbers of their missiles. (MIRV stands for multiple independently targetable reentry vehicle, which means a missile can have several warheads and each warhead can be directed to a different target). The MIRVed U.S. ICBM is the Minuteman III, which carries three warheads, but MIRVed U.S. SLBMs carry from eight to fourteen warheads each. While the Soviets have MIRVed their ICBMs even more extensively than has the United States, they have not done so with their SLBMs. The Soviets, however, are currently deploying three new MIRVed SLBMs (SS-N-18, SS-N-20, and SS-N-23) which will increase the number of warheads they can deliver from submarines. Some U.S. strategic bombers can carry twelve air-launched cruise missiles, and others can carry several nuclear bombs. The United States has more warheads which have greater accuracy, but the Soviets have more delivery systems and bigger warheads.

This discussion of strategic weapons reviews only weapons systems currently in the inventories of the superpowers. Several new weapons systems are being developed or have just begun to be deployed. In 1986, the United States began deploying its new B–1B bomber that is to replace at least some of the older B–52s. The Soviets also have a new bomber, the Blackjack. In addition, the U.S. has a long-range development program for a stealth bomber that is to be virtually undetectable on radar. The United States has two new missile systems that will be deployed by the late 1980s, the Trident II, an SLBM, and the MX, an ICBM. The Soviets have new ICBMs and SLBMs under development as well. Whether these new systems will change the relationship between the superpowers or whether the new systems will balance each other is widely debated but largely unknown.

The issue of which country is ahead in the nuclear arms race can become even more complicated when considering intermediate nuclear forces (INF) or theater nuclear forces. The INFs are targeted mainly in Europe, with the Soviets having about 400 missiles (SS–20s) with 1200 warheads; the United States, when deployment is completed, will have 108 Pershing IIs and 456 ground-launched cruise missiles (GLCMs) in Europe, each with one warhead. This would give the Soviets a two-to-one advantage if it were not that some, perhaps up to one-third, of the Soviet INF are directed at China and not Western Europe. In total tactical warheads, the United States has about 15,000, and the Soviet Union about 13,000. While estimates on the number of tactical weapons possessed by each side varies, the estimates generally agree that the United States has a lead.

One further complication is how to count the British and French nuclear forces. The British have 64 MIRVed SLBMs with about 250 warheads and a small bomber force capable of delivering nuclear bombs. The French have 80 SLBMs which only recently were MIRVed, nearly 100 bombers, and a small force of intermediate range missiles that can reach the Soviet Union. The Soviets insist that these forces should be included in the Western INF, in this way justifying the Soviets' deploying more SS–20s. The United States argues that the British and French nuclear forces should not be counted, that those forces are not under U.S. control, and that they have not been counted during previous U.S.–Soviet negotiations concerning nuclear weapons. In U.S.–Soviet talks concerning theater nuclear weapons, this has been a particularly difficult negotiating point.

The purpose of reviewing the conventional and nuclear arsenals of the United States and the Soviet Union is twofold. The first is to reveal the extent and variety of those stockpiles, and the second is to illustrate the complexities of comparing those weapons—which country is ahead

in the arms race remains unresolved and is perhaps irresolvable.

MAD AND NUT

The Soviet and U.S. nuclear stockpiles are rationalized by the superpowers within the context of deterrence—the policy that has governed U.S.–Soviet relations since each country developed a creditable counterforce. Deterrence, or mutually assured destruction (MAD), is based on the assurance that if either the United States or the Soviet Union launched a first strike, enough of the other's weapons would survive to destroy the attacker. The result of this approach to maintaining the peace is that each country has accumulated a stockpile of nuclear weapons far in excess of the number needed to destroy the other. It is frequently pointed out that each country possesses sufficient nuclear weapons to destroy one another twelve times over.

Why the excess, if only weapons to destroy each other once is enough? While it is difficult to determine who is ahead in the arms race or whether rough equality exists between the two countries, from the point of view of deterrence an equality of arms is not necessary. What is important is that the country considering a first-strike be convinced that sufficient nuclear weapons in the other country's arsenal will survive an attack that the attacking nation will in turn be destroyed. Under these circumstances, many nuclear weapons possessed by the nation first attacked will never be used but will be destroyed in the initial assault. Each nation must, therefore, have a surplus of nuclear weapons sufficient to convince the other country that enough delivery systems and warheads will survive in order for it to effectively retaliate. The difficulty is, of course, that each of the superpowers argues that the first attack will come from the other; thus, each feels it must have an excess of nuclear weapons in order to make deterrence a creditable policy.

During the late 1940s when the United States was the only nation with atomic bombs, the Soviet counterthreat—an early version of deterrence—was that it could occupy Western Europe with its superior conventional forces even after Soviet cities and industry had been destroyed. After 1949, as the Soviets developed a nuclear stockpile, the Soviet retaliatory threat of conventional weapons shifted to nuclear weapons. MAD thus became the theoretical basis on which peace between the superpowers has been maintained for thirty-five years.

Another facet of MAD during the early years of nuclear standoff was that if war were to come the targets would most likely be Soviet and U.S. cities. CEPs (circular error probability or the maximum radius from a target in which at least half of the nuclear weapons aimed at that target will land) could thus be the size of a city. The larger the bomb, the greater the CEP could be and still destroy the targeted city. Some bombs in the 20–30 megaton range were deployed, and the Soviets tested one device that was estimated to be at least 57 megatons. This was the equivalent of 57 million tons of TNT, compared to the Hiroshima bomb that was no more than 15 kilotons or 15,000 tons of TNT. The delivery systems of early MAD were manned bombers, and as the first ICBMs were developed they were not even as accurate as nuclear bombs dropped from aircraft. As ICBMs became more accurate and then were MIRVed, more specific targets could be hit, such as missile silos, and each missile could strike several targets in a particular region, as would be found in a complex of missile silos. Such missile accuracy added a new dimension to deterrence.

The United States, as a conscious policy choice, chose to go for more accurate ICBMs and smaller warheads, as opposed to the Soviet policy of building large missiles to carry large warheads to compensate for their lesser accuracy. The United States developed MIRVed missiles first and with

this technological breakthrough was able to maintain the strategic advantage it had had over the Soviet Union since the late 1940s. By 1970, the Soviets passed the United States in the number of ICBMs and eventually developed a MIRV system of their own, thus greatly expanding the number of deliverable warheads. Since the beginning of deterrence the United States had been concerned about Soviet attacks on its cities and strategic nuclear forces, but the MIRVing of Soviet ICBMs now made it possible for the Soviets to attack only U.S. retaliatory forces. If the United States lost its ability to retaliate, then the war would be lost and cities in neither country would have to be hit. The loss of a nation's ability to retaliate is the "window of vulnerability" President Reagan has spoken about.

The fact of missile sites, rather than cities, as targets gave rise to a new doctrine of nuclear war known as nuclear utilization theory (NUT) or damage limitation nuclear conflict, which encompasses the strategy of something less than an all-out nuclear attack. A nuclear attack could involve only a portion of the weapons available and strike only selected targets, particularly missile sites, or be limited to only a region of the world and not be a massive strike against another country. NUT argues that nuclear weapons can be used in strategic alternatives other than massive retaliation or all-out first-strike. If only a limited use of nuclear weapons can force the other side to sue for peace, so much the better. The principal criticism of NUT is that the concept of limited nuclear war is impractical; a nuclear war probably could not be fought at any level of intensity other than complete nuclear involvement. To plan otherwise weakens the concept of deterrence since it suggests that a nuclear war is winnable.

It is within this context of respective weaknesses and strengths in conventional and nuclear weapons, and different perspectives as to how a nuclear or conventional war between the superpowers might take place, that negotiations concerning arms control occur. But before turning to discussion of those negotiations, one more problem concerning nuclear weapons must be mentioned—proliferation.

NUCLEAR WEAPONS AND PROLIFERATION

Much of the discussion concerning nuclear weapons has been confined to the arsenals of the superpowers, but there are four other members of the so-called nuclear club. The United States and the Soviet Union were the first members in 1945 and 1949, respectively; Great Britain became a member in 1952, France in 1960, China in 1964, followed by India in 1974. India claims it has no nuclear weapons, but has only tested a nuclear device. While the British, French, and Chinese nuclear weapons could do considerable damage to any country one of them might attack, their stockpiles are small compared to those of either of the superpowers. As current alignments exist, the nations with secondary stockpiles of nuclear weapons are a problem only to the Soviet Union, since each of those countries is currently friendly toward the United States.

A second problem for the international community concerns nuclear proliferation; a substantial number of nations without nuclear weapons possess the scientific knowledge to build them. In addition to several countries in Europe that have the ability but have made the decision not to do so, other countries with the ability to build nuclear weapons that have not rejected the possibility are Brazil, Argentina, South Korea, Taiwan, Pakistan, Nigeria, South Africa, and Israel. Though denied by Israel, speculation runs high that it possesses a secret arsenal of unassembled nuclear weapons and may have had them as long ago as the early 1970s. Estimates concerning this stockpile range from 25 to 140 such weapons. Also, it has long been rumored that Israel and South Africa have a secret agreement to develop and test nuclear weapons.

A major obstacle to the development of nuclear weapons in the Third World is cost. Several oil-rich countries, even if they do not have the scientific community to develop the bomb, can provide the funds for other Third World countries to do so. Other countries have expressed a willingness to sacrifice whatever is necessary to obtain nuclear weapons. Now that India has tested a nuclear device, General Zia of Pakistan has said that even if his people must "eat grass" to fund the development of nuclear weapons, such is necessary to protect Pakistan from India. If it is confirmed that Israel has nuclear weapons, Arab countries might be willing to do what is necessary to obtain nuclear weapons as well. Regional conflicts could, under these circumstances, become regional nuclear confrontations.

These problems of proliferation have been considered by the international community, and the result was the Non–Proliferation Treaty of 1968. Over 120 nations have signed the treaty, which commits them, if they have nuclear weapons, to not aid another country in developing them; if they do not have nuclear weapons, they are committed not to develop them. A number of the potential developers of nuclear weapons, particularly in the Third World, have not signed the treaty. The potential for expansion of the nuclear club beyond its present membership is substantial.

ARMS NEGOTIATION—PAST AND PRESENT

The underlying assumption of arms *control* negotiations simply stated is that nations are less likely to go to war if their armaments are balanced with those of potential opponents. Arms *reduction* negotiations are conducted on the same assumption, plus the corollary that nations are less inclined to go to war if they have fewer arms. The assumption of *disarmament* negotiations is that if all arms are prohibited, then nations are not apt to go to war if they have nothing to fight with, no matter how serious the conflict between them. Since no disarmament agreements have ever been negotiated, the discussion here will center on arms control and arms reduction negotiations. A pragmatic reason for any limitation on arms, unrelated to a theory of conflict, is simply that it saves money.

Assuming a genuine interest by negotiating parties in arriving at an agreement, the fundamental problems of negotiating arms agreements are: for arms control, arriving at which weapons will be included and a ceiling for those weapons; and, for arms reduction, a level to which arms can be reduced. The issue in either instance is to arrive at a level of arms mutually agreeable to the negotiating parties. By comparison, in theory at least, negotiating a disarmament agreement is simple, since no level of armaments has to be negotiated. If all parties disarm, then balance is not an issue and no ratio of arms is needed. In practice, however, disarmament is not currently politically feasible in the international system, but arms control and reduction agreements are. At least, under current conditions the superpowers are willing to talk about arms control and reduction, but not about disarmament. Thus, the simplest approach is not possible politically, but the more difficult negotiating situation is politically feasible. All three approaches—arms control, arms reduction, and disarmament— would be more easily negotiated if conflicts involving issues other than arms were settled or, at least, if tensions were reduced before arms were discussed. The situation seldom exists in which arms are discussed seriously when tensions are high.

While the concept of arms control and disarmament was a matter of philosophical discussion in the nineteenth century and even earlier, no agreements were forthcoming. During the nineteenth century, the achievement most closely approaching an arms control agreement was the Rush–Bagot Agreement of 1817 between the United States and Great Britain to not fortify the U.S.–Canadian border. That agreement continues in force today. The first Hague Conference of 1899 included arms reduction on its agenda, but no agreement was forthcoming. In fact, the subject was given little consideration at the conference. Thus, most of the history of arms talks has occurred in the twentieth century.

It is not often that one diplomatic event can illustrate so much about a particular subject, in this case arms reduction, as does the Washington Naval Conference of 1921–1922. As is usually the case following a war, after World War I the former belligerents carried out considerable arms reduction—the losers because they were forced to do so by the victors, and the victors because a need no longer existed for such a high level of arms. The victors did this unilaterally, however, and no arms reduction agreement governed the reductions. In one category of arms, not only did no arms reduction take place among the victors, but an arms race developed; following the war, the major naval powers continued to build up their navies. The fuel for this postwar naval arms race was tension among the naval powers in the Pacific and Asia. In an effort to halt this, the United States sponsored a conference on naval arms control which was held in late 1921 and early 1922.

The conference produced three agreements, the best known being the Five-Power Naval Treaty which established a ratio among the naval powers concerning capital ships (battleships and battle cruisers). Today an agreement of this sort would seem archaic, but at the time, capital ships were the single most destructive—and most expensive—weapons system in existence. Even though the United States called the conference more as an economy measure than out of a fear of war, the conference was successful. The ratio established in the five-power agreement was 5:5:3:1.67:1.67, respectively, among the United States, Great Britain, Japan, France, and Italy. These quotas were then multiplied by three to determine the number of capital vessels each nation could have. Each of the major naval powers had to reduce the number of capital ships it possessed in order to be in accordance with the treaty. The tonnage of capital ships and the size of guns they could carry were also controlled by the agreement. In addition, the naval powers were limited as to the size and number of aircraft carriers—a weapons system in the early stages of development—they could have in their navies. This agreement overcame one of the most difficult problems of arms negotiations—it established a formula for limiting the numbers of a particular weapons system. Before this could be accomplished, however, a nine-power agreement (the same five nations plus four lesser powers) and a four-power agreement (the major naval powers except for Italy) were negotiated which resolved the political conflicts in Asia and the Pacific. The second obstacle to arms reduction had been overcome as well—the political conflict that precipitated the naval arms race.

The Washington conference was a success in that the naval arms race was halted temporarily. Other efforts at arms control during the interwar period were not successful, perhaps because they occurred too long after the end of World War I and the memories of the cost of war were fading, or because no other major conference was held until after the Great Depression began and dictatorships took over the governments of some major states. Further efforts to limit naval arms in categories of ships other than capital vessels were undertaken at the London Naval Conferences in 1930 and 1935, but they brought forth no effective agreements. Japan felt it was operating at a disadvantage as a result of the Washington agreement and rejected all new proposals. Shortly before the 1935 London conference, Japan served notice that it would no longer abide by the 1922 agreement, making all further efforts at naval arms control futile. The League's major effort to bring about general arms control met a similar fate in 1933. In late 1932, after years of planning and delay, the World Disarmament Conference convened in Geneva. Hitler came to power in January 1933

and subsequently withdrew Germany from the conference which collapsed. The League also failed in other efforts to control arms, including efforts to effect a moratorium on arms production and to regulate arms exports.

Some symbolic gestures occurred during the interwar period. They fell short of being arms control agreements, but were efforts to minimize the chances of war. In 1928, the Kellogg–Briand agreement, signed by fifteen nations, renounced war as an instrument of national policy, except in instances of self-defense. Earlier, in 1925, the Locarno treaties, signed by various European powers, guaranteed boundaries and secured assistance from France should Poland and Czechoslovakia be attacked. None of these efforts seemed to slow the development of dictatorships during the 1930s or delay the coming of World War II.

After World War II, the international community went through a second massive arms reduction program, but again this was done without an international agreement. The United Nations was new, and, initially, the only arms issue it was concerned with was controlling development of the atomic bomb. Since only the United States had the bomb, the issue was narrowed to how to control the U.S. stockpile of atomic weapons and prevent other countries from developing the bomb. The United States dominated the United Nations during its early years; thus, it fell to the United States to propose a means to control this new weapon. The U.S. response was the Baruch Plan in which the U.S. would agree to destroy its stockpile if other countries would submit to international inspection and agree to not build atomic weapons. The United Nations Atomic Energy Agency, the institution established to discuss the Baruch Plan, was immediately deadlocked over the issue of which would come first, inspection or destruction of the stockpile. The U.S., of course, wanted a system of international inspection established before it destroyed its stockpile; the Soviets wanted the stockpile eliminated before inspection was established. In various forms, this conflict remained in arms talks until the 1970s.

The Baruch Plan also provided an illustration of another longstanding aspect of postwar arms talks. The United States wanted the talks limited to atomic weapons alone, since it was in that area that the United States held superiority and had the stronger negotiating position. But from the perspective of the Soviets, they wanted conventional arms to be discussed along with atomic weapons, since their large conventional force was their means of offsetting the U.S. atomic monopoly and reflected their negotiating strength. The United States was successful in limiting the talks to atomic weapons, but the U.N. brought forth no agreement. It would be reasonable to conclude that neither nation was interested in an agreement at that time except under conditions clearly unacceptable to the other side. The Soviets certainly were not going to allow inspections that might prevent the development of a Soviet atomic bomb, and the United States would settle for nothing less.

By the Eisenhower years, both the United States and the Soviet Union had hydrogen or fusion bombs. The Eisenhower administration also ushered in negotiations between the U.S. and the Soviet Union concerning a comprehensive arms reduction program. These discussions included both conventional and nuclear weapons and the manufacture and stockpiling of each. Now that the Soviets had nuclear weapons, there was no longer any point in separating conventional and nuclear arms talks. Deadlocks in the negotiations eventually led to their failure, primarily because each side included in its proposals conditions that were clearly unacceptable to the other side. The United States continued to insist upon on-site inspections in the Soviet Union, and the Soviet Union insisted that the United States give up its overseas bases.

The Eisenhower administration did produce one rather unheralded, but precedent-setting, agreement with the Soviets. This was the Antarctic Treaty of 1959 (entered into force in 1961), which removed the Antarctic from militarization with either conventional or nuclear weapons. Twenty-six nations have ratified the treaty, which includes all nations that have claims in the Antarctic. This was the first of several agreements that established limited controls on arms.

Another limited plan that failed to gain approval was Eisenhower's Open Skies Plan. As an alternative to on-site inspections, in 1955 Eisenhower proposed that substantial areas of the Soviet Union and the United States be open to aerial surveillance by the other nation. The Soviets rejected the plan, and it eventually was outmoded when spy satellites were developed. The Rapacki Plan proposed by Poland in 1957, which called for no nuclear weapons in Central Europe, also failed.

By the time the Kennedy administration took office, the comprehensive approach to negotiations with the Soviets had been abandoned, and the principal public issue concerning arms became nuclear testing. U.S.–Soviet talks on the issue were held in Geneva under the auspices of the U.N. Disarmament Commission. While these talks, which began in 1961, included a number of nations other than the superpowers, and issues other than nuclear testing, the focus of the negotiations was a test ban between the United States and the Soviet Union. Worldwide, strong demands developed that tests be stopped because they were polluting the atmosphere with radioactive fallout. This was coupled with the testing of bigger and bigger bombs and the fear that a catastrophe could result from a test accident. Kennedy pushed for a nuclear test ban, and a limited one went into effect in 1963.

The Limited Test Ban Treaty prohibited atmospheric, outer-space, or underwater tests; underground tests were allowed. A total of nearly 120 countries have ratified the agreement. Since underground tests were allowed, this agreement did not slow testing as such, but it did sharply reduce the amount of radioactive waste placed in the atmosphere. China and France did not sign the agreement, or the nonproliferation treaty that came later, and continued atmospheric testing.

Although France still has not signed either agreement, since 1974 it has conducted only underground tests. Further efforts to negotiate limits on underground testing produced the Threshold Test Ban Treaty and the Peaceful Nuclear Explosions Treaty in 1974, but neither treaty had been ratified by the superpowers by the late 1980s. Other limitations on nuclear weapons have been approved, however.

In 1967, the Outer Space Treaty, which bans nuclear weapons in space, went into effect. The Non–Proliferation Treaty gained approval in

---

Tab. 14.3 Arms Control and Disarmament Agreements

The historical record of official negotiations on disarmament shows limited results so far. For more than three decades the major emphasis has been on nuclear weapons, but no agreement has yet been reached on the "discontinuance of all test explosions of nuclear weapons" (a pledge of the signers of the Limited Test Ban Treaty of 1963), nor on measures for the "cessation of the muclear arms race" (a pledge of the signers of the NPT in 1968). Furthermore, the last three US–USSR treaties that were signed (SALT II and two nuclear test ban treaties) have not been ratified. (The limits of SALT II, however, are mutually observed.)

The US and USSR currently have two sets of negotiations underway relating to control of nuclear weapons: the strategic arms reduction talks (START) for long-range missiles and the intermediate-range nuclear force (INF) negotiations on weapons in Europe.

Nuclear Weapons

To prevent the spread of nuclear weapons—
Antarctic Treaty, 1959   **26 states[1]**
Bans any military uses of Antarctica and specifically prohibits nuclear tests and nuclear waste.

Outer Space Treaty, 1967   **83 states[1]**
Bans nuclear weapons in Earth orbit and their stationing in outer space.

Latin American Nuclear–Free Zone Treaty, 1967
22 states[1]
Bans testing, possession, deployment, of nuclear weapons and requires safeguards on facilities. All Latin American states except Argentina, Brazil, Chile, Cuba are parties to the treaty.

Non–Proliferation Treaty, 1968   **119 states[1]**
Bans transfer of weapons or weapons technology to non-nuclear-weapons states. Requires safeguards on their facilities. Commits nuclear-weapon states to negotiations to halt the arms race.

Seabed Treaty, 1971   **71 states[1]**
Bans nuclear weapons on the seabed beyond a 12–mile coastal limit.

To reduce the risk of nuclear war—
Hot Line and Modernization Agreements, 1963
US–USSR
Establishes direct radio and wire-telegraph links between Moscow and Washington to ensure communication between heads of government in times of crisis. A second agreement in 1971 provided for satellite communication circuits.

Accidents Measures Agreement, 1971   **US–USSR**
Pledges US and USSR to improve safeguards against accidental or unauthorized use of nuclear weapons.

Prevention of Nuclear War Agreement, 1973   **US–USSR**
Requires consultation between the two countries if there is a danger of nuclear war.

To limit nuclear testing—
Limited Test Ban Treaty, 1963   **111 states[1]**
Bans nuclear weapons tests in the atmosphere, outer space, or underwater. Bans underground explosions which cause release of radioactive debris beyond the state's borders.

Threshold Test Ban Treaty, 1974   **US–USSR[2]**
Bans underground tests having a yield above 150 kilotons (150,000 tons of TNT equivalent).

Peaceful Nuclear Explosions Treaty, 1974   **US–USSR[2]**
Bans "group explosions" with aggregate yield over 1,500 kilotons and requires on-site observers of group explosions with yield over 150 kilotons.

To limit nulcear weapons—
ABM Treaty (SALT I) and Protocol, 1972   **US–USSR**
Limits anti-ballistic missile systems to two deployment areas on each side. Subsequently, in Protocol of 1974, each side restricted to one deployment area.

SALT I Interim Agreement, 1972   **US–USSR**
Freezes the number of strategic ballistic missile launchers, and permits an increase in SLBM launchers up to an agreed level only with equivalent dismantling of older ICBM or SLBM launchers.

SALT II, 1979   **US–USSR[2]**
Limits numbers of strategic nuclear delivery vehicles, launchers of MIRVed missiles, bombers with long-range cruise missiles, warheads on existing ICBMs, etc. Bans testing or deploying new ICBMs.

Tab. 14.3 Arms Control and Disarmament Agreements (continued)

Other Weapons

To prohibit use of gas—
Geneva Protocol, 1925   **118 states**
Bans the use in war of asphyxiating, poisonous, or other gases and of bacteriological methods of warfare.

To prohibit biological weapons—
Biological Weapons Convention, 1972   **92 states**
Bans the development, production, and stockpiling of biological and toxin weapons; requires the destruction of stocks.

1. Number of accessions and ratifications,   2. Not yet ratified.   3. Convention enters into force December 1983. The US is not a signatory.

To prohibit techniques changing the environment—
Environmental Modification Convention, 1977 36 states
Bans military or other hostile use of techniques to change weather or climate patterns, ocean currents, ozone layer, or ecological balance.

To control use of inhumane weapons—
Inhumane Weapons Convention, 1981   **22 states[3]**
Bans use of fragmentation bombs not detectable in the human body; bans use against civilians of mines, booby traps, and incendiary weapons; requires record-keeping on mines.

SOURCE: Ruth Sivard, *World Military and Social Expenditures*, 1983.

1968 (entered into force in 1970), and in 1971, the Seabed Treaty, which prohibited nuclear weapons on the seabed beyond a twelve-mile limit, was approved. The Biological Weapons Convention, signed in 1972 (entered into force in 1975), prohibited the development, production, and stockpiling of biological weapons. This agreement, plus the Geneva Protocol of 1925, which banned poisonous gas, and the Environmental Modification Convention of 1977 (entered into force, 1978), which prohibits military techniques from changing the environment, were the only arms agreements that did not relate directly to nuclear weapons. The only agreement related to nuclear weapons that did not include the United States and the Soviet Union was the Latin American Nuclear–Free Zone Treaty of 1967 (entered into force, 1968) which prohibited any nuclear weapons in that region. Several major Latin American states, including Argentina. Brazil, Chile, and Cuba, are not parties to the treaty, however. All of these agreements are multilateral and include many signatory nations.

The United States and the Soviet Union have entered into additional agreements on a bilateral basis which do not pertain to weapons directly, but are intended to reduce the chance of war. In 1963, following the Cuban Missile Crisis, during which there was no communications link between Washington and Moscow, the two countries entered into the "hot line" agreement that established a teletype connection between the two governments. This arrangement has been modernized by two subsequent agreements. They also entered a Nuclear Accidents Agreement in 1971 to prevent an accident from leading to a nuclear exchange. In 1973, the two countries entered into a Prevention of Nuclear War Agreement, which was designed to prevent the two countries from drifting into war during a time of crisis.

A matter about which no formal agreement exists, but which is accepted by both powers, is the use of spy satellites each places over the territory of the other. While each would strongly protest the overflight of its territory by the other side's aircraft, neither protests the overflight of satellites. Apparently, the intelligence gathered by such satellites is of greater importance than their mutual objections to the spy satellites of the other side. The collection of intelligence in this fashion, at least in part, provides verification of stockpiles of weapons and how well each side is living up to agreements.

The nuclear agreements are clearly limited in what they do. In some instances, they prohibit that which is already not being done (no nuclear weapons in Antarctica or on the seabed). In other instances, the agreements can be tested only if a serious crisis should develop; therefore, no means exists of judging their effectiveness beforehand. In still other cases, the agreements have been violated. Several nations, for example, have been charged with using chemical weapons or poisonous gas, thus violating the Biological Weapons Convention.

Overall, the agreements pertaining to nuclear weapons thus far discussed limit the testing of nuclear weapons and the places where they can be deployed, but do not limit delivery systems or nuclear weapons themselves. The first such agreement of this sort was the result of the Strategic Arms Limitations Talks (SALT), which began in 1968 and produced the ABM Treaty and the SALT I Interim Agreement in 1972.

STRATEGIC ARMS TALKS

The diplomatic atmosphere of the 1950s and the 1960s was such that any agreement could be arrived at only after protracted and difficult negotiations; when talks broke down, each side blamed the other for the collapse. Overseas bases and on-site inspections were obstacles to broadly based arms agreements until the mid 1960s. When the United States developed weapons systems that could strike the Soviet Union from the continental U.S., overseas bases were less important strategically; spy satellites made on-site inspections unnecessary. Other complicated issues continued to make negotiations difficult, however. The negotiation of SALT I illustrated some of those problems.

During the late 1960s, the United States developed an antiballistic missile (ABM), the Safeguard, and began to construct a site near Grand Forks, North Dakota to deploy it. This missile was designed to intercept and destroy incoming Soviet ICBMs, and the location of the site was an indication that the United States had decided that the Minuteman ICBM silos scattered over north-

central United States, rather than U.S. cities, would be the first Soviet targets. The decision to build the base and to spend $6 billion on its construction were indications that the United States thought it could successfully intercept Soviet missiles. The Soviets earlier had constructed an ABM base to protect Moscow. If the systems worked as designed and if many such sites were constructed—the North Dakota site had only 100 ABMs, and the Moscow base only 64—the logic of MAD and deterrence would no longer be valid if either side decided that its ABMs could destroy enough incoming missiles to make nuclear war something other than an act of suicide.

The system had been tested against only one ICBM at a time, however, and, while successful, might not work if hundreds of ICBMs were launched. Also, no means existed to intercept SLBMs which could be in flight a much shorter time than the ICBMs. Even if the ABM were successful, it would be several years before enough ABM bases could be built to destroy Soviet missiles in substantial numbers. Successful or not, the cost of ABM bases would place the arms race on a new level of expenditures. The combination of the threat to deterrence and the potentially increased cost of the arms race made negotiations between the United States and the Soviet Union possible.

It was in this atmosphere of weapons development that the SALT talks began. An additional factor that made an agreement possible was the Nixon administration's acceptance of "sufficiency" relative to the Soviet Union. The United States had had nuclear superiority over the Soviets until the late 1960s, but the Soviets had been deploying ICBMs at a more rapid rate than had the United States. The United States became willing to accept approximate equality with the Soviets as long as mutually assured destruction was maintained. SALT I thus was based on the approximate equality of delivery systems between the superpowers.

What is commonly described as the SALT I Treaty is actually two agreements—the ABM treaty and an interim agreement on missile delivery systems. The ABM treaty allowed each country to build no more than two ABM bases and was amended in 1974 to allow only one base each. The United States did complete the ABM base under construction, but deactivated it six weeks after it became operational, on the grounds that it alone would have little effect on a large number of incoming missiles.

The interim agreement established for the first time the number of strategic missiles each side could possess. The United States had 1054 ICBMs and 656 SLBMs for a total of 1710 delivery systems; the Soviets had 1618 ICBMs and 740 SLBMs for a total of 2358 delivery systems. Each side was committed to not going over its current level. Within those limits, each side could convert ICBMs to SLBMs, if it chose to do so. The United States could convert 54 older liquid-fuel Titan IIs to SLBMs, and the Soviets could convert 210 older missiles to SLBMs. SLBMs were limited both by the number each side could have and by the number of submarines that could launch SLBMs. The United States could have 41 such submarines, and the Soviets could have 62. The Soviets' numerical advantage in delivery systems was more than offset by MIRVed U.S. missiles. The United States was allowed 550 MIRVed Minutemen and nearly 500 MIRVed SLBMs. The Soviets had not yet MIRVed any of their missiles, but limits were placed on the number they could MIRV when they developed such a system.

Because of disagreements about how to count manned aircraft, a type of delivery system in which the U.S. had a distinct advantage, the agreement included only missiles. While no disagreement existed over counting strategic bombers as delivery systems, the Soviets wanted to include U.S. tactical aircraft based in Western Europe; the United States objected. Since they could not agree on which manned aircraft should be included in the agreement, what could not be agreed to was simply left out. The interim agreement did establish a ceiling for the number of missile delivery systems, but it did not resolve other issues. In addition to excluding aircraft from the agreement, no limitation was placed on warheads, except to limit the number that could be placed on missiles.

Since SALT I was to expire in five years, the plan was for SALT II to be completed by 1977. When a new agreement was not ready by that date, the two powers agreed to extend SALT I. U.S.–Soviet relations deteriorated after President Carter took office in early 1977, but, in spite of cooling relations, Carter and Brezhnev signed the SALT II treaty in June 1979.

Several items held up agreement on SALT II. One issue was the ceiling on delivery systems. President Ford and Chairman Brezhnev had agreed in 1975 to a ceiling of 2500 for each country. Unlike SALT I, SALT II allows the two countries the same number of delivery systems, since strategic bombers were included and the Soviets now were MIRVing their missiles. When the Carter administration took office in early 1977, it proposed lowering the ceiling on delivery systems to as low as 1700. The Soviets thought that figure too low and charged the United States with reneging on commitment. The final agreement carried the provision that initially each country would have 2400 delivery systems and would, within two years, lower the number of 2250. SALT II also allowed each country to develop and deploy one new missile system.

The Soviets were slightly under the 2400 ceiling but would have to retire some older missiles to reach the 2250 figure. If the Soviets deployed a new missile system, additional missiles would have to be scrapped. For the United States, the 2250 figure presented no problem. Even including manned bombers, the U.S. had a total of about 2100 delivery systems. If the 54 Titan IIs were retired, as the U.S. had been planning, the United States could deploy about 200 new ICBMs and still be within the limit. It was for this reason that President Carter called for the deployment of 200 MX missiles (renamed the Peacemaker during the Reagan administration) that at the time were in the developmental stage.

Another problem encountered during the negotiations was how to count the newly developed U.S. cruise missile. The Soviets wanted each counted as a delivery system, but the U.S. insisted they be considered as warheads or bombs, not as delivery systems. Ultimately, the Soviets dropped their demand, but already-deployed bombers were limited to no more than 20 cruise missiles each, and any new bomber to no more than 28. Disagreement over the new Soviet Backfire bomber centered around whether it had strategic capabilities; the Soviets insisted that it did not have sufficient range to be counted as a strategic delivery system. The Soviets won on this point, but the United States did receive a guarantee from Brezhnev that no more than 30 would be produced each year.

SALT II clearly was a much more complex treaty than was SALT I. Even though there were other negotiating problems, the central issue was the matter of sublimits for each delivery system; it was here that the treaty became most complex. Of the 2250 delivery systems each side could possess, no more than 820 ICBMs and no more than 1200 SLBMs and ICBMs combined could be MIRVed. This meant that if more than 380 SLBMs were MIRVed, then fewer than 820 ICBMs could be MIRVed. Also, there could not be more than a total of 1320 MIRVed SLBMs, ICBMs, and bombers with cruise missiles. This meant that the remaining 930 delivery systems had to be either single-warheaded SLBMs or ICBMs or bombers without cruise missiles. Limits were also placed on the number of warheads the MIRVed missiles could carry. ICBMs could carry no more than ten warheads, and SLBMs were allowed no more than fourteen. This did not reduce the number of warheads each side could deliver at that time, but it did mean that there would be ceiling on future deployment of warheads.

The agreement allowed the United States to deploy air-launched cruise missiles (ALCM) immediately, but postponed the deployment of sea or ground-launched cruise missiles in Western Europe until after 1981. This postponement, plus the omission of the Backfire bomber from the agreement, were two aspects of SALT II often attacked by U.S. opponents. Another point of opposition was that the total number of delivery systems was so high that if the Soviet Union were to attack, too few U.S. delivery systems would survive to make a creditable counterforce.

After the treaty was signed, President Carter submitted it to the Senate for advise and consent. Since SALT II was a complex agreement, it was subject to various interpretations as to how it would affect the strategic abilities of the United States and the Soviet Union. The Senate Foreign Relations Committee recommended it favorably, but before the Senate could consider the treaty the Soviets invaded Afghanistan, and Carter asked that the Senate give the agreement no further consideration. Even though SALT II was not formally ratified, the U.S. and the Soviet Union agreed to abide by the treaty. At various times, both countries have accused the other of treaty violations, and President Reagan, particularly, has been critical of what his administration considers violations of both SALT I and SALT II. President Reagan described SALT II as "fatally flawed" during the 1980 presidential campaign, but did maintain its provisions in force after he took office.

The Reagan administration has accused the Soviet Union of violating SALT I in various ways, but the most important accusation concerns a major radar site constructed in south-central Siberia. SALT I allows each country to maintain a system of radar stations to detect incoming missiles, but those stations are to be located near the territorial edges of each nation. Radar facilities at those locations have only a limited purpose in directing an attack, thus are primarily defensive in nature, but major radar facilities deep in a nation's territory can be used for both detecting and directing an attack. The location of a major radar station deep in Soviet territory, even though the Soviets claim it has only defensive functions, would be a violation of the treaty.

As SALT I was to be an interim agreement

until SALT II was concluded, SALT II was to be a prelude to SALT III. When President Reagan took office, he dropped the SALT III label and renamed the talks the Strategic Arms Reduction Talks (START). The START talks commenced in 1982 and were divided into two separate sets of negotiations. One pertained to strategic arms, and the other dealt with nuclear weapons in Europe, or intermediate nuclear forces (INF).

The weapons under consideration at the INF talks had more range than tactical or battlefield nuclear weapons, but did not have sufficient range to be classified as strategic weapons. The fundamental problem emerging in these talks is that all of Europe, including European Soviet Union, can be struck with either INF nuclear weapons or strategic nuclear weapons, but the United States can be hit by only strategic weapons. It is within this context that the Soviets insist on including French and British nuclear weapons as part of NATO's INF, while opposing the deployment of additional INF nuclear weapons in Western Europe. In an attempt to arouse Western Europe's opposition to the deployment of additional INF missiles among the NATO countries, the Soviet Union emphasized Western Europe's vulnerability to all nuclear weapons and the potential that Europe could become the main battleground in the event of a nuclear exchange.

Even though strategic arms talks were under way at the same time, the center of controversy was the INF negotiations. The Carter administration, along with NATO, had agreed to begin deployment of ground-launched cruise missiles (GLCMs) and Pershing IIs in Europe in 1984. Under SALT II, this could be done any time after 1981. The Soviets objected strongly to their development, although the Soviets had been deploying their SS–20s inside the Soviet Union. When the deployment of the new NATO weapons began in 1984, the Soviets broke off the INF talks. Later, to further protest the deployment, the Soviets broke off negotiations concerning strategic nuclear weapons as well.

Little progress toward an agreement had been made before the talks were suspended. The United States was asking for a dramatic reduction in strategic weapons and a reduction of Soviet INF missiles down to the level the United States believed existed in Western Europe. The Soviets seemed to be interested in only an extended and gradual reduction of strategic weapons and no reduction in SS–20s, although they might have been willing to retire some of their older theater missiles. By 1985, with the deployment of Pershing IIs and GLCMs well underway, the Soviets apparently realized that they could not stop their deployment and agreed to new arms talks. The talks resumed in March 1985, but the sessions produced no immediate diplomatic breakthroughs.

As the new negotiations commenced, the Soviets were particularly critical of President Reagan's decision to begin the development of a strategic defense initiative (SDI), or Star Wars defense system. The Soviets insisted that an SDI defense system would violate the provisions of SALT I banning the deployment of additional ABM systems. Like the ABM system, SDI would be designed to destroy incoming missiles; in this instance, however, the missiles would be destroyed by energy-transfer satellites and ABMs placed in space. This system was also criticized in the United States on much the same grounds on which the earlier ABM system was criticized. If it could be developed, and doubt existed that it could be, its development would be very expensive. If made operational, it might destroy many incoming missiles, but enough enemy warheads would survive to cause unacceptable damage. As was the possibility with the ABM system, SDI might also destroy the concept of deterrence and make war more likely.

When Gorbachev and Reagan met at Reykjavik in October 1986, the Soviet leader insisted that the SDI development cease before he would agree to an arms reduction agreement. Both leaders accepted drastic cuts in strategic weapons, but the summit conference ended in no agreement when President Reagan insisted that SDI development would continue. Following this conference, however, a major diplomatic breakthrough developed concerning an INF agreement and one is expected at the Washington summit conference scheduled for December 1987.

CONCLUSION

The talks that began in 1985, as in all past negotiations concerning nuclear weapons, centered on how the nuclear weapons of each side compared. Which country was ahead in the nuclear arms race, or was there approximate parity between the two superpowers? If parity existed, where would the cuts in weapons take place? If new agreements are reached, they will come only after long and difficult negotiations.

PART IV

Restraints on Conflict

In earlier chapters, although sources of conflict in the international system were discussed extensively, the means within the system for controlling and limiting conflict was not. Part IV will provide such a discussion. It is important to keep in mind that control of international conflict, as is the case with the causes of such conflict, does not take place only in the international system; domestic systems also provide restraints on conflict. The next chapter, therefore, will synthesize the aspects of behavior in both the international system and domestic systems that place limits on conflict among nations. The subsequent two chapters will examine the institutional efforts to control conflict—international organizations and international law.

CHAPTER 15

International and Domestic Restraints on Conflict

Though the international system often appears to be one of self-help, nations are not without restraints on their actions. The observation was made earlier that any nation in contact with other nations experiences some degree of conflict with them, but that that conflict only occasionally results in violence. This would indicate that nations in most instances are not willing, often perhaps because they lack the political resources, to pursue their interests to the point of violent conflict. A logical extension of that observation is that no two nations are so hostile toward one another that some cooperation does not exist between them. Either aspect of national behavior—accepted limits on conflict or some degree of cooperation—indicates that there are constraints (legal, moral, or practical) on a nation's activities. The legal and moral restraints of the system are perhaps not as well developed as the practical ones, but even when nations do not allow conflict to escalate simply because it is not practical to do so, those nations are accepting a degree of restraint. Major international conflict is often avoided simply because the cost is too great relative to a nation's other interests. Under these circumstances, restraint is used not for moral or ethical reasons, but is based on practicality and convenience.

Whatever the source of international norms, norms that restrain and limit conflict are involved when the following occurs: first, when

nations are punished or isolated in some manner within the international system for their behavior, and second, when that punishment is for the violation of what is considered by most nations to be a consistent pattern of behavior.

THE RESTRAINT OF INTERNATIONAL NORMS

Whether an international morality exists and whether it is observed by most, or any, nations has long been debated. While the system as a whole certainly does not adhere to a generally accepted set of moral principles, norms of behavior exist that nations are expected to follow and generally do. Whether these norms collectively constitute a morality is questionable, but they do impose limits on the activities of nations. These norms may be conformed to simply because it is convenient, or out of international courtesy more than out of a sense of obligation, but they are generally followed.

Rather than describing these norms as international morality, these restraints are more appropriately labeled as the limit of behavior tolerated by world opinion. While world opinion rarely generates any direct action against a country that violates the norms, most nations are restrained because they do not wish to be held in disfavor by the international community at large. Such disfavor complicates what would otherwise be routine relations and, on occasion, leads to formal sanctions. Even though, as was pointed out in an earlier chapter, economic sanctions are usually not successful in forcing nations into major changes of policy, they can be a major inconvenience.

Examples of penalties for violating these norms would be the manner in which the international system has isolated such renegade national leaders as Muammar al-Qaddafi of Libya, because of his support of terrorists, his meddling in the internal affairs of nearby states, and his allowing a mob to storm the U.S. embassy in 1979; Idi Amin of Uganda, because of his harsh policies directed against selected tribal groups in Uganda and his invasion of Tanzania; and Ayatollah Khomeini of Iran, because of his attempts to export his fundamentalist religious policies through terrorism and his support of those who seized the U.S. diplomats and held them hostage. The isolation of these national leaders was never complete, although their behavior cost them support throughout the international system. Even though Iran was subjected to enormous international pressures during the hostage crisis, its isolation was as much a domestic policy to keep out foreign influence as it was a product of world opinion.

> There are probably few nations in the world that would have been willing to sustain the battering of national pride and national interest to which Iran was subjected in the long months of the [hostage] crisis. In one sense, this campaign was a convincing demonstration of the powers of moral and political persuasion that can be mustered by the world community. Unfortunately, it was also a demonstration of the inherent limitations of international public opinion to deal with a renegade nation in a state of revolutionary euphoria (Sick, 1985, 218).

Additional punishment received by Iran and other such countries includes a reluctance by MNCs to invest in those countries because of their erratic and often anti–Western policies, and many states have isolated them diplomatically and economically.

While these leaders often justified their actions as domestic policy—therefore claimed by them to be of no concern to the international community—they were guilty of violating several international norms. These included interfering in the internal affairs of other countries (Libya); violating the accepted standards for the treatment of foreign diplomats (Iran and Libya); genocide of certain groups (Uganda); promoting terrorism (Iran and Libya); and committing aggression (Uganda). Another nation and its leader isolated within the system was Kampuchea under Pol Pot. He was seen as committing indiscriminate genocide among the general population. An additional example is the world's reaction to South Africa's policy of apartheid. The United Nations has imposed limited sanctions on South Africa and deprived it of its vote in the General Assembly, and Western industrial nations are increasingly enforcing bilateral economic sanctions. World opinion in opposition to apartheid has placed great stress on the South African government and may, eventually, result in fundamental changes in the political system.

While renegade countries, in some instances, have economic or arms sanctions imposed upon them, their isolation from the system is effected through general world opinion rather than through formal sanctions. The direction of pressures put upon nations by other nations is usually for maintenance of the status quo; disruption of the system is to be avoided. Nations labeled as radical and renegade are, by definition, those that are not behaving according to the established rules—rules which call for nations to settle their conflicts by negotiations through established channels.

Even when the pressures of world opinion and traditional diplomacy fail and an interstate war breaks out, as has occurred numerous times since World War II, the expectation is for uninvolved countries to isolate the conflict to the immediate participants. As was pointed out in the chapter on the use of force, this norm has generally been applied. With the exception of domestic guerrilla movements, wars in the Third World typically have been brief, usually of only a few days' or weeks' duration. The arms stockpiles of Third World countries, so heavily dependent on outside resupply and spare parts, often are quickly exhausted. Virtually the only interstate wars between Third World countries that have not been stopped after a brief flurry of combat have been the Iraqi–Iranian War and the Vietnamese invasion of Kampuchea, although the latter has settled into a guerrilla-style war. It seems that, whatever the conflict, it is in the interests of most nations to restrain it as much as possible. This is the case even for the participants, particularly if they are Third World nations, since they have limited resources with which to conduct a war.

Attempts at formal control of conflict through law and institutions exists within the international system, but what appear to be the most effective restraints on nations are the limitations of resources and the pressures brought to bear on those nations in violation of international norms.

DETERRENCE AS A LIMITATION

Referring to the United States and the Soviet Union as superpowers suggests that their position in the international system is such that, except for restraints on one another, either power can do pretty much as it pleases. But, in practice, the very status they possess in the international system is a constraint on their activities.

The concept of deterrence is aimed specifically at preventing nuclear war, but it also has effects on other international activities of the superpowers. Since a major policy change by a state possessing nuclear weapons is perceived by other states as more threatening than would be the same action taken by a nonnuclear state, the superpowers must act with a degree of caution so that others will not misinterpret their actions and overreact. The net effect of deterrence and its resultant large stockpiles of nuclear weapons may be that the superpowers accept more limitations on what they do internationally because they possess nuclear weapons than if they did not possess them. Thus, in the context of deterrence, nuclear weapons tend to restrict and control conflict rather than expand it.

While deterrence is employed to prevent a first strike by one of the superpowers, it has also prevented major confrontations between the United States and the Soviet Union, particularly in Central Europe. Each country appears to have an understanding of what would provoke the other into a European war. The line between East and West is clearly drawn, and if either crossed the line militarily the assumption is that a general war would break out. This implicit understanding has prevented the Soviets from taking direct action in any of the Western nations, and the West has not intervened directly in Eastern Europe when the opportunity presented itself. It seems safe to assume that such opportunities to intervene in the affairs of the other side's coalition would more likely be acted upon if both coalitions did not possess nuclear weapons and did not have a clear understanding of the limits of their spheres of influence.

DETERRENCE AND THE PRISONERS' DILEMMA

A means used by specialists in international relations for analyzing conflict and cooperation between the superpowers is to compare those nations' problems with those presented in the Prisoners' Dilemma Game. This game is an application of game theory to the study of international politics based on what is described as a mixed-motive or nonzero-sum game. This sort of game assumes that a gain for one side does not have to be offset by a corresponding loss by the other side; pursuit of a particular alternative can be beneficial to or a mutual loss to both parties.

The Prisoners' Dilemma Game involves two individuals who have been arrested for a capital crime but are told by the police that insufficient evidence exists to convict them of that crime. The accused are not allowed to communicate with one another, and each is told that if he or she confesses and his partner does not he or she will go free, but his cohort will be sentenced to a 40-year prison term. If both prisoners confess at about the same time, however, both will receive a 20-year sentence. Since there is insufficient evidence to convict them of the major crime without a confession, if neither confesses each will serve a one-year term on a lesser charge. Each prisoner thus knows that if he or she does not confess, he or she will serve either 1 year or 40 years in prison. If he or she confesses, then he or she will either serve no time in prison or 20 years.

Much of the literature on the Prisoners' Dilemma Game concentrates on what is rational behavior for the prisoners. Cooperation between the prisoners, that is, no confession by either, would provide a short sentence and be of the greatest benefit to them collectively. But to not confess carries the risk of a 40-year sentence if the other confesses; thus, perhaps a confession is the safest route, since that action would guarantee avoiding the harshest sentence. Cooperation with one another provides the greatest collective good, but taking independent action does, at least, avoid the worst of the alternatives. What is rational under these circumstances is difficult to determine; equally difficult to determine is the consequence of applying the Prisoners' Dilemma Game to U.S.–Soviet relations.

This game has obvious flaws when applied to international politics. The first is that nations do not exist in isolation, and, even in the greatest of crises, they have some communication with one another; therefore, unlike the prisoners, nations can talk to one another in even the worst of circumstances. Whether effective communication always takes place when attempted is another matter, however. A second problem is that relations between nations are not based on a single event, but are a process of many events and decisions, and thus are an ongoing learning and communicative process. For example, when the Prisoners' Dilemma Game is played several times by the same people, cooperation becomes more likely than when played only once.

The Prisoners' Dilemma Game can be applied to specific issues in U.S.–Soviet relations. One such issue would be the Strategic Defense Initiative (SDI). If one side develops such a weapons system and the other does not, a substantial advantage is gained by the initiating side, the equivalent of one prisoner's confessing and the other not. If both develop an SDI system, it would be at great cost and have dubious operational reliability, thus similar to both prisoners' confessing at about the same time and serving a 20-year sentence. If the nations cooperate and neither develops the system, then the sense of security that the new system might provide would not develop, but the cost and risks of developing and operating the system would be avoided and deterrence would remain intact. This would be the equivalent of neither prisoner confessing.

The Prisoners' Dilemma Game can be applied more broadly as well. A number of authors have applied the game to arms negotiations between the United States and the Soviet Union to illus-

Fig. 15.1 Prisoners' Dilemma

		First Prisoner	
		Confess	Not Confess
Second Prisoner	Confess	20 years each	First–40 years Second–Goes Free
	Not Confess	First–Goes Free Second–40 years	1 year each

Fig. 15.2 Dilemma of SDI Development

| | | USA | |
		Develop	Not Develop
USSR	Develop	High cost, loss of deterrence	Soviet advantage
	Not Develop	USA advantage	continuation of deterrence

trate the advantages of cooperation. If both nations cooperate and arms stockpiles are reduced, that action would be similar to the Prisoners' Dilemma Game's alternative of neither prisoner's confessing, and both nations would benefit. If both nations continued the arms race, each would continue to suffer the tensions and expense of maintaining high levels of arms, the equivalent of each prisoner's receiving 20-year sentences. If one superpower continued to arm, but the other did not, it would be similar to one prisoner's confessing and the other's receiving a 40-year sentence.

The same sort of comparison can be made as to whether either the United States or the Soviet Union would benefit from launching a nuclear assault. If one launched and totally destroyed the other, the aggressor would suffer little or no damage. If neither attacked, that is, neither confessed, the tensions between the two countries would continue, but neither country would suffer damage. If deterrence and MAD existed, and one superpower launched an attack, both would suffer great damage, but perhaps not as much as would be the case if one nation could not retaliate (the equivalent of both prisoners' confessing at about the same time).

A number of games have been developed to analyze international relations and virtually all indicate the importance of cooperation in the management of international affairs. The application of game theory to international behavior shows that cooperation is a viable alternative in

promoting and protecting a nation's interests and that international politics is not necessarily a zero-sum game where only one side benefits.

LIMITS IN A NON-NUCLEAR WORLD

Nuclear weapons are justly feared for the devastation and death they would create if a nuclear exchange took place, but what has been suggested is that their existence has prevented a general war between the superpowers. Providing evidence to support such a proposition is difficult at best, except to point out that no direct violent confrontations between the U.S. and the Soviet Union have occurred in the more than 40 years since World War II ended and the two nations emerged as the most powerful nations in the international system. Possibly, no war between the two countries would have occurred even if neither had nuclear weapons, but it does seem that a major war would be less likely in an international system in which deterrence is present than in one where it is not. This is not to suggest, however, that if the present levels of nuclear weapons have prevented a nuclear exchange, then even more such weapons will make the world safer still. Deterrence is based on second-strike capability and the relative size of the stockpiles, not on how many weapons can be manufactured.

This approach to nuclear weapons as a restraint on conflict gives rise to speculation as to what sort of international system would presently exist if nuclear weapons had never been developed. If a general war between the two superpowers would be more likely if no nuclear weapons existed, the consequences of a conventional war, while initially less destructive than a nuclear exchange, would be devastating, nevertheless. Even if neither side launched a deliberate attack on the other, a drift into war would be easier when the results were not as horrendous, virtually guaranteed, and immediate as they are under the present system of deterrence. Certainly, devising a system of deterrence between the superpowers with only conventional weapons would be more difficult than is the case with nuclear weapons.

It also seems reasonable to assume that if no nuclear weapons existed, other elements of power such as economic capabilities would be more important in the international system. Would it not be the case that nations with large populations, such as China and India, would play a more significant role in the international system than they do presently? In the event of a major war involving only conventional weapons, large land armies would likely be more important than they would be in a nuclear war, and the most populous countries could provide such armies. While military interventions by the superpowers presently are restricted to the Third World and to within the coalitions the superpowers head, interventions in the opposing coalitions of the Cold War would seem to be a more tempting policy choice than would be the case when the results are as predictable as they are when nuclear weapons are present.

In an international system without nuclear weapons, both the United States and the Soviet Union would probably build up their conventional armaments to a much higher level than now exists. During the Eisenhower years, when nuclear arms were promoted by the United States as a less expensive means of obtaining national security than developing both conventional and nuclear arms, without nuclear weapons the U.S. would simply have spent more on conventional arms. The Soviet Union, no doubt, would have done likewise. The world's experience with conventional arms races has been that most resulted in war, which possibly would be the outcome of a conventional arms race between the United States and the Soviet Union. What all this suggests is that the international system, unless organized in a dramatically different fashion after World War II, would have been even more unstable without nuclear weapons than with them.

SUPERPOWER RESTRAINT IN THE THIRD WORLD

Surrogate confrontation, as used by the superpowers in the Third World, lessens the possibility of direct conflict between the superpowers and, as long as no Third World country has nuclear weapons, limits the possibility of nuclear war. While it is not a commonly accepted perspective that the U.S. and the Soviet Union purposefully exercise restraint in their dealings with one another, they do seem to avoid undue escalation of conflicts in the Third World where one or the other has staked out a claim. In Afghanistan, the United States has not confronted the Soviets directly; U.S. actions have been limited to diplomatic pressures and clandestine activities. U.S. policy in this instance may be the result of its having no easy geographic access to Afghanistan, but it also may be because the Soviets established a political foothold there long before they actually invaded the country, and to confront the Soviets now would be a fight in the wrong place at the wrong time.

During the Vietnam War, the Soviets supplied the North Vietnamese but fell short of support that could have produced a major-power confrontation. When asked by the United States to aid in ending the war, the Soviets, rather than arguing their commitment to a national liberation movement, argued that their hands were tied because of their competition with the Chinese. Even if not a true statement of their feelings, their explanations for supporting North Vietnam were means of avoiding a direct confrontation with the United States. In 1985 and 1986, Cuban relations with the Soviet Union were strained, reportedly, because Castro felt the

Soviets were not adequately supporting Nicaragua. The Soviets provided the Sandinistas with economic and military aid, but it fell far short of the amount of aid Cuba was receiving, or the aid Nicaragua felt it needed. The United States has tolerated the Soviet-supported Vietnamese operations in Kampuchea, but has drawn the line on that conflict's spilling over into Thailand. Perhaps the Soviets simply do not have the resources to fully support every anti-Western movement, but neither the United States nor the Soviet Union has been willing to support a Third World country to the extent that such support could produce a superpower confrontation.

In the Middle East, both the United States and the Soviet Union operate through their surrogate forces and with an unwritten rule that neither nation allows its surrogates to totally defeat the other's surrogate forces. The United States has on several occasions, beginning in the 1948 war, restrained Israel from maximizing its military victories over the Arab forces; the Soviets have never armed the Arab armies to the point that they could destroy Israel. The risk involved in the superpowers' exercising this sort of restraint is that one or both will miscalculate and initiate a major confrontation. Without the present exercise of such restraint, every Third World crisis could become a superpower confrontation.

Similarly, the superpowers, as well as the other major powers, have the potential to exercise two additional restraints on Third World countries. First, in spite of their general desire to be economically independent of major industrial powers, Western or communist, they have no alternative but to turn to those countries for both economic and military assistance. This places the major states in the position of being able to restrict the activities of many of the Third World countries through the levels of assistance they are willing to provide.

The larger the debts the Third World countries accumulate with the industrial nations, the greater is the control exerted by the lending countries. Since the major international lending agencies and the International Monetary Fund, as well as much of the bilateral aid, are controlled by the Western industrial nations, the Third World nations are essentially under whatever economic restraints the Western states wish to impose upon them. The debtor nations can threaten to default on their loans, but where would financing come from in the future if they once did so? Argentina and Brazil may chafe under the IMF-imposed economic reforms, but neither country has a reasonable alternative to complying with IMF guidelines. A particularly vivid illustration of restraint by a major state on smaller nations is the economic and military aid the United States grants Egypt and Israel, aid tied to the maintenance of peace between those two countries. Many Third World countries genuinely want a new international economic order which would reallocate the world's resources, but as long as the present economic system exists, the industrial nations are in a position to control the markets and the loans that the Third World countries need.

Secondly, if the superpowers do not want Third World countries to have nuclear capabilities, they can do a great deal to prevent it. Minimally, they can refuse to transmit technology or radioactive materials that would aid a Third World country in the development of such weapons. Some Third World countries probably are able to develop nuclear weapons without the help of the industrial nations, but the most expeditious means of obtaining the technology is through transfers from those countries that already have it.

While no member of the nuclear club has knowingly transmitted to a nonmember information for making a nuclear weapon since the United States helped Great Britain develop their nuclear weapons in the early 1950s, and the Soviets possibly assisted China in the development of their bomb, the Western nations have aided some nonmembers, including Third World countries, in the building of nuclear reactors for the production of electricity. The waste products produced by such reactors can be refined to weapons-grade level and used in the production of nuclear weapons. Thus, even though such assistance may not be direct aid in the development of a nuclear weapon, it can be indirect aid. Even in such cases, international controls exist over how radioactive waste material from reactors can be used.

Nations receiving assistance in the development of their nuclear reactors are usually asked by the providing nation to promise not to develop nuclear weapons and to abide by the provisions of the nonproliferation treaty. In addition, a United Nations agency, the International Atomic Energy Agency (IAEA), has the responsibility of monitoring the waste products from nuclear reactors so that those products will not be diverted to weapons. The success of that agency in carrying out its charge is questionable, however. It is interesting to note that only Western nations have provided Third World countries with assistance in the building of nuclear reactors, while the Soviet Union has not done so.

The Third World countries not only are dependent on the industrial nations for their nuclear technology, but also are heavily dependent on them for their conventional weapons. If the industrial nations choose to use it, they have the capability to restrict the Third World nations in the quantity and types of weapons they possess; they may also choose to make distinctions, tolerating greater nuclear development by some nations than by others. No nation, for example, took action against India when it exploded a nuclear device; however, Iraq was prevented from working on the development of nuclear weapons when the Israelis used an air strike to destroy a nuclear reactor near Baghdad in June 1981. Though the air strike was carried out by a U.S. surrogate, not by the United States itself, it was a demonstration of the limits to which Third World nations may be allowed to go.

DOMESTIC INTERESTS AS RESTRAINTS

In most instances, a nation's punishment for violating international norms is neither particularly severe nor necessarily effective. Pressures are exerted in the direction of cooperation, but the penalties for noncooperation are limited. With such limited international restraints over a nation's activities, most control that prevents conflict among nations from escalating more than it does appears to come from within domestic political systems.

A concept presented earlier was that nations can best be identified by their interests. All nations have physical characteristics such as territory, population, and governmental structure; but when a nation is interacting with other states, its interests distinguish it from other nations. While it is valid to point out certain general interests that all nations have in common, such as maintaining national security and striving for a sound economy, it is the means used to further those interests that provoke conflict among nations (Krasner, 1978).

A nation's interests are many, but, each country has limited resources to expend; the more expended on a particular interest, the less there is available to further other interests. Due to this limitation, a nation's decision-makers must establish priorities which determine the degree to which each interest will be pursued. Ordinarily, unless one interest is overwhelmingly dominant, and in peacetime that is rare, no one interest is promoted to the extent of pushing the nation to violence. The dispersal of political resources among many interests and the absence of a dominant interest result in its not being worthwhile for a nation to take overly aggressive action in the promotion of a particular interest.

Another aspect of national behavior that limits the effort a nation will expend to achieve a particular interest is that pushing too hard for one interest could make it more difficult to persuade other nations to cooperate on other matters. The use of persuasion beyond what other countries consider appropriate might result in that interest's being fulfilled, but, in so doing, alienate those nations and make it more difficult to fulfill other interests.

What the multiplicity of a nation's interests indicates for the international system is that as long as no one interest dominates a nation's priorities and as long as its demands are not outrageous, conflicts will be limited, and the normal pattern of fulfilling some interests, fulfilling others in part, and not fulfilling others will occur.

RESTRAINT OF PUBLIC OPINION

If the opinions of other nations exert some restraint on a nation's activities, then certainly it is to be expected that domestic public opinion has an effect on a nation's policies. Even in nondemocratic countries, national leaders are aware of the limits imposed by their public's opinion. If that were not the case, then national leaders would not direct so much effort toward shaping and controlling domestic public opinion.

Public opinion is usually expressed in general terms, however, and is seldom more than a statement of favor toward or rejection of a particular policy, thus having little effect on the specifics of a decision. Public opinion therefore sets broad limits on policy; parameters within which policy may be made without arousing major public opposition. The reason public opinion does no more than set limits on policy is that, even in democracies where citizens have the responsibility of selecting their leaders by ballot, the "majority of citizens hold pictures of the world that are at best sketchy, blurred, and without detail...." (Robinson, 1967, 1; see also Scammon and Wattenberg, 1970, 299). This imprecise view of the world does not mean that the public does

not have opinions, but that those opinions are based on relatively little information.

Such complex issues as SALT II and the Panama Canal Treaties evoked strong opinions from the American public, but opinion surveys made at the time those treaties were before the U.S. Senate revealed that the public knew little about their content. This limited knowledge about foreign policy also indicates that domestic problems are seen as having a more immediate impact on most people's lives than foreign policy issues. This means that democratic leaders who wish to remain in office must balance off domestic and foreign policy issues. Too much attention devoted to foreign policy could be seen by the public as irrelevant activity when domestic concerns appear more salient.

The limits of policy set by public opinion vary depending on the nature of the political system. In totalitarian states, those limits may have greater latitude than in a democracy, but dictators can go too far, just as can democratic leaders. These limits or parameters of policy, no matter how broad, do provide a restraint on the policymakers. Decision-makers may see public opposition to their choices as an obstacle to be overcome, but, in so doing, this acknowledgment is recognition that limits are there.

Public opinion is generally described as being volatile, with wide shifts in views possible, particularly for those persons whose opinions are based on sketchy information. While that perspective of public opinion is perhaps correct in regard to specific policy choices, with respect to the broad, general limits of policy the public's view is often relatively steady over time. In the United States, public support of NATO has been consistent, though for a period shortly after the end of U.S. involvement in Vietnam a majority of the American public was willing to defend only Mexico and Canada. Public disillusionment with Vietnam involvement was so pervasive that the public was not even willing to defend our Western European military and trading partners.

Even at this low point of commitment, however, there was no public outcry for the United States to withdraw from NATO.

Despite Japan's reluctance to assume greater responsibility for its defense, no strong move has developed in the United States to drop commitments for the defense of Japan. U.S. membership in the OAS has not been questioned domestically, although Latin American countries have, on occasion, suggested that the organization would be more effective without the United States. In general, the alliances the United States has undertaken have not been questioned by the American public. Nor has the U.S. commitment to deterrence been a matter of general debate. How many delivery systems and how large a stockpile of nuclear weapons are needed to maintain deterrence is discussed, but not the underlying concept. The public is generally supportive of the military's being strong enough to defend the United States, but fluctuates substantially in opinion on the amount of funding for defense. (Russett, and Starr, 1981, 241). The public thus seems to accept the broad, basic principles and concepts of U.S. foreign policy.

While, in general, the American public's support of these parameters of policy changes little, an example of the American public's abandonment of a longstanding position followed the Nixon initiative in improving Sino-American relations in 1972. The public moved from overwhelming opposition to improved relations to overwhelming support. While the American public does form long-term commitments, these, too, can be changed on occasion.

Describing the American public as poorly informed, overall, on foreign policy matters is only generally correct. The public ranges from segments with virtually no information to persons who are well informed. Portions of the public ignore international relations (perhaps about 30 percent of the public) and are virtually unaware of what occurs on the international scene. Another portion is aware of major events as they occur at the international level, but has little knowledge beyond that. This group comprises about one-half of the general public in the United States. The remaining 20 percent of the public reads about and converses with others concerning international events and has at least a general understanding of what is taking place in international relations. This well-informed group also tends to include the better-educated and those having high socioeconomic status. Among the segments of society that are part of this group, substantial disagreement may exist concerning U.S. foreign policy among business leaders, senior military officers, and Republican politicians at one end of the opinion scale; and leaders in the media, labor leaders, and Democratic politicians at the other end of the scale. (Russett and Starr, 225.)

It is difficult to assess just how much restraint is exerted by either the general public or the foreign policy elite on policy-makers. The view presented here is that they do establish a foreign policy consensus beyond which policy-makers risk strong opposition. Another perspective is that public opinion can be so easily manipulated by clever leaders that the public only responds to policy, but has little effect on its creation; thus the public only appears to be a contraint on decision-makers. If the public is a restraint on policy it is, at the same time, an important force in the development of policy. Public opinion both restrains and promotes policy with the decision makers.

Regarding elite opinions, the charge has been made that portions of the foreign policy elite have too much influence on policy; that, in fact, policy is a product of their deliberations, not those of the decision-makers themselves. During the Carter administration, this charge was leveled at the Trilateral Commission (of which Carter had once been a member); earlier, similar charges were made against the Council on Foreign Relations. Since many presidential candidates and secretaries of state had at some time been members of the Council, it was assumed that the Council controlled their actions when they took office.

What is overlooked in such charges is that while the elite opinion-makers share with the public the foreign policy consensus, they exhibit considerable disagreement about policy choices, just as do members of the general public.

Stated in its broadest terms, the foreign policy outlook of either the general public or the foreign policy elite is one of commitment to allies and maintaining security in Western Europe and East Asia, and providing assistance to friendly nations. This internationalist perspective contrasts sharply with the isolationist viewpoint of the American public held prior to World War II. The war reduced the isolationists to a handful, although a neoisolationist sentiment has been held by a portion of the public since the Vietnam War. This means that the foreign policy consensus can change, but does so either because of a dramatic event, such as World War II, or through slow evolution over a long period of time.

In a discussion of the role of either public or elite opinion on policy, one development emerges that runs counter to the foreign policy consensus argument. That is the public's reaction to the Vietnam War. Opposition to U.S. involvement in the war occurred from the beginning, but a majority of the American public supported the war during the early years. This support was consistent with public consensus in favor of containment. Following the Tet offensive in January 1968, opposition to the war increased until a majority of the public opposed involvement. This has given rise to the argument that although the American public possesses little factual knowledge about foreign policy, it does recognize faulty policy in operation (Nathan, and Oliver, 1981). While containment remained a part of the foreign policy consensus in general, it no longer formed the basis for supporting a U.S. presence in Vietnam.

In a very real sense, American presidents who increased U.S. commitment to South Vietnam were operating within the then-accepted foreign policy consensus which called for aid to a country resisting communism. President Johnson thus was continuing that commitment by aiding Viet-

nam even after public opinion turned against his Vietnam policy. The policy, originally consistent with public opinion, was found difficult to change when the American public wearied of the war (Betts, 1979).

The information that serves as the basis of opinions for most members of a national public comes from the electronic and print media; few have any firsthand contact with international events. Consequently, images held by the public are a product of how those events are presented by the media. Whatever biases, intended or not, that are developed in reporting the news become a part of the public's perceptions. In free societies the press theoretically presents several perspectives for the public to integrate or choose from, but in closed societies where the press is state controlled, the press becomes a means by which the state molds public opinion to its own view. Under either circumstance, however, the press is an important influence on public opinion.

The branch of U.S. government most sensitive to public opinion is Congress. Although Congress cannot be thought of as a direct reflection of public opinion, it is clearly the branch most reactive to what the public is thinking. On occasion, Congress is charged with overreacting to pressures from portions of the public that hold strong opinions on foreign policy questions. An ethnic group, if strong in a congressional member's district, can often gain support for its position, or a major economic interest can quickly gain its congressman's support for a trade restriction. Overall, however, studies of voting behavior in Congress do not show a high correlation between how the members of Congress vote and the opinions of constituents. The voting records of members of Congress from marginal districts do show a higher correlation with constituent opinion than do the records of congressmen from safe districts, however (Campbell, Converse, Miller, and Stokes, 1966, 363).

Before the Vietnam War, it would have been difficult to make a case that Congress was a serious obstacle for foreign policy originating in the executive branch. But, as the war was coming to a close in the early 1970s, the congressional attitude toward allowing the executive such free reign changed. Congress feared that the president was making foreign commitments about which Congress was either never informed or informed too late to have any impact. Accordingly, Congress passed the Case–Zablocki Act in 1972, under which the president was forced by law to notify Congress within thirty days of the completion of an executive agreement. In 1973, Congress passed the War Powers Act which, among other things, required the president to notify Congress when he committed U.S. troops to a dangerous situation, and to receive congressional approval if the troops remained there more than sixty days (with an additional thirty days, if necessary, to carry out safe withdrawal). This was clearly an effort to restrain the executive's capacity to create a situation such as Vietnam, wherein the executive made a serious commitment and expected Congress to accept and financially support it. Congress wanted to be in on the "takeoffs," not just the "crash landings," of foreign policy.

In general, Congress has become a more difficult partner in the making of foreign policy, providing greater restraint on the executive. As the principal spokesman for U.S. foreign policy, the president still has considerable power to influence the American people and other countries, but now Congress reviews foreign policy more carefully than in the past. Even so, presidents have not lost very often in Congress on foreign policy questions. Congress is more attentive than before, however, and the executive has to give greater consideration to how Congress will react to its policy choices.

Public opinion polls concerning a president's popularity indicate that his standing with the American people depends heavily on his successes and failures in foreign policy. The president's ability to persuade Congress to pass his domestic program is, thus, indirectly affected by his relationship with Congress on foreign policy

matters. What a president does internationally thus becomes an important aspect of promoting both his domestic and foreign policy programs in Congress.

Presidents tend to pick up in popularity if a crisis develops internationally, but if the crisis continues for very long the president's popularity declines. President Carter discovered this characteristic of public opinion during the long Iranian hostage crisis. A president, therefore, must act prudently on the international scene. If he attends an international conference that does not go well, his popularity will suffer, just as his popularity will be enhanced by a successful conference. The Camp David agreement increased Carter's popularity; the Panama Canal Treaties, a product of thirteen years of negotiation, did not. Major portions of the public opposed the canal treaties throughout the national and Senate debate over their fate. Thus, even if members of Congress do not vote the opinions of their constituents a statistically significant portion of the time, a president's popularity with the public does affect his success with Congress.

The ultimate opportunity for the American public to restrain its national leadership in the making of foreign policy occurs at election time. While President Johnson's decision to not run for reelection in 1968 is generally attributed to his unpopular Vietnam policies, voting behavior studies indicate that foreign policy questions are not major issues in presidential or congressional elections. At election time, the public focuses on domestic economic issues, and foreign policy only occasionally emerges as a campaign issue. An illustration is those senators who voted for the Panama Canal Treaties, even though a majority of their constituents opposed the treaties. In the 1978 and 1980 elections (the treaties were considered in the Senate in early 1978), Senators Church (D.,Id.) and Culver (D.,Ia.), both strong proponents of the treaties, were defeated, but so many other factors played a part in their defeats that it was difficult to assess the electoral damage caused by their support of the treaties.

Domestic restraints on foreign policy-makers exist in other countries, but, due to the enormous task of surveying those restraints, only the domestic restraints found in the United States have been discussed. Certainly, in all democratic systems, the legislative branch is a restraining factor. In nondemocratic systems, restraint is most likely to come from the bureaucracy, although that sort of restraint also seems to be common to all political systems.

THE BUREAUCRATIC RESTRAINT

The bureaucratic conflict model of decision-making has been discussed elsewhere, thus will be mentioned here only to point out that the process of decisions going through a nation's bureaucracy tends to moderate decisions and, in this way, restrain a nation's international behavior. The interaction among bureaucratic units is the process of each unit's presenting its perspective and altering the decision to whatever extent possible to comply with the unit's interests. The direction of these modifications is to dilute the decision to the common factors found among the bureaucratic units. The decision becomes less focused and more general and, in this way, more restrained.

CONCLUSION

Even though it is often difficult to determine the specific underlying restraints on a nation's international behavior, since nations are usually not willing to go to war over any specific interest, restraints exist. Those restraints may originate in the interaction of the nation-states that produces norms of behavior nations are expected to conform to or they can originate in the domestic political system. Deterrence is a restraint on superpower actions, and the Third World is restrained by its dependence on the industrial nations. Domestically, public opinion, the media, the legislative branch, and the bureaucracy can restrain the actions of a government's international behavior. Likely, it is the domestic political system that provides the greatest restriction on a nation's international behavior.

CHAPTER 16

Intergovernmental Organizations and Regimes

For a time after World War II, intergovernmental organizations (IGOs) were a major field of study in international relations. The study of IGOs took essentially two forms. The first, more an act of faith than analysis, promoted the possibilities and hopes of conflict resolution through IGOs, particularly the United Nations. These studies represented considerable idealism concerning the post–World War II world and reflected the sense of need for centralized international conflict resolution. A second type of study, more analytical, concentrated on the behavior of IGOs and examined their decision-making processes and their success in dealing with conflict. Neither sort of study is done often today. The idealism that once supported the United Nations and other IGOs faded as a result of the UN's failure to resolve major conflict situations. The behavioral studies have ceased for the same reason. Why study the behavior of international institutions that no longer are regarded as important because they have failed to carry out their charge?

Even though the United Nations itself receives relatively little attention from scholars in the late 1980s, two valid reasons remain for looking at the role of the organization in the international system. The first is that, although the United Nations has failed to develop into an arena for the *resolution* of major international conflicts, it still plays a role in the *management* of conflict. Conflict management may not produce a solu-

tion, but effective management can limit and control conflict. Secondly, the United Nations has spawned some interesting attempts to resolve conflict by sponsoring various international conferences and establishing several subunits of the UN. These conferences and agencies cover such subjects as the environment, population, food, trade, refugees, economic development, desertification, law of the sea, and women's rights. The success rate for these conferences is low, but no discussion of conflict management and cooperation in the international system is complete without a look at such events and agencies.

EXPANSION OF IGOs

Focusing one's attention on the limited success of the United Nations can produce misleading conclusions about the place of IGOs in the international system. Even if the UN has not lived up to the expectations of its founders, IGOs have increased in number at an astonishing rate during the twentieth century, and particularly since World War II. The first modern IGO came into being early in the nineteenth century and, by World War I, 49 IGOs existed. By the beginning of World War II 90 had been formed. In the late 1980s, the total number of IGOs is over 350. (Jacobson, 1985). The range of activity resulting from so many IGOs responding to the complex needs of the international system has produced what Harold Jacobson describes as a vast "network of interdependence." (Jacobson, 1985, 9-11.) The UN is a part of this network, but is only one organization within it.

CHARACTERISTICS AND FUNCTIONS OF IGOs

IGOs present varied sets of responsibilities, functions, and purposes. Some have broad-based membership on either a regional or worldwide basis, and others are limited in membership by the purpose they serve. Their purposes can be broadly defined or they can be organized to handle a specific and perhaps narrow area of activity within the international system. The UN is the single global, broad-based organization today, although important regional organizations exist that have broadly defined functions, such as the Organization of American States (OAS) and the Association of Southeast Asian Nations (ASEAN). Also, some IGOs have a global membership nearly as large as that of the UN, but have specific purposes such as those of the specialized agencies of the UN, the International Labor Organization (ILO) or the World Health Organization (WHO) being examples. The most common IGOs have both limited membership and limited purposes. It is this type of IGO that has shown the greatest increase in numbers.

While IGOs may have either limited or global membership and either general or specific purposes, certain characteristics are common to all IGOs. All are multinational in membership, and have specified means of adding new members. Each was established by an international agreement that states the purpose of the organization and sets out the limits of behavior for the IGO. For the United Nations the Charter is such an agreement, although it is, in fact, a multilateral treaty approved by each member state following

its domestic procedures for the approval of treaties. Also, each IGO has a permanent staff or secretariat headed by a secretary-general, and a headquarters for the organization. The secretariats vary in size from a few dozen persons to the more than 45,000 employees of the United Nations system. Secretariats provide their IGOs continuity and make the organizations something other than a series of multinational conferences.

Some IGOs hold their meetings at various locations, usually in the capitals of member states, and others meet where they are headquartered. The Organization of African Unity (OAU) and the OAS are examples of organizations that rotate their meetings among national capitals (The OAU is headquartered in Addis Ababa and the OAS in Washington, D.C.). The UN holds most of its meetings in New York City, but the Security Council has met on regional issues elsewhere. The European Community (EC) is headquartered in Brussels, but its legislative body meets in Strasbourg. NATO also has its headquarters in Brussels. The UN's specialized agencies are headquartered in various cities in Europe and North America. The membership of all IGOs is based on the nation-state, but a few transcend the powers of their members and have developed supranational authority. The only well-known IGO of this sort is the EC. Voting within IGOs is usually based on one vote per member, but the World Bank is an exception. There a member's voting strength is proportionate to its monetary investment in the organization.

The specific functions performed by IGOs are nearly as numerous as IGOs themselves, but they all relate to handling conflict or serving a regulatory function in some manner. At a minimum, all IGOs serve as a means of communication among their members. If communications are effective, conflict can be resolved or a confused regulatory problem organized; short of this, communication can at least lead to identifying the nature of the problem more clearly.

Even though IGOs are often unsuccessful in resolving conflict, they at least provide a forum for the articulation of interests by member states. An IGO can also be seen as a substitute for an embassy in another country. If a nation does not have diplomatic relations with a country with which it needs contact, or cannot afford to maintain an ambassador in that country, the framework of an IGO provides that contact. An IGO can also be the forum for countries to negotiate matters they could not discuss on a bilateral basis. Often, bilateral contacts break down in intense international disputes, but an international organization allows those parties to discuss their differences without the appearance that one has sought out the other; an IGO is often seen as neutral ground. An international organization can also provide the additional advantage of being a third party to arbitrate between conflicting nations. The secretary-general of an IGO frequently acts as mediator in such circumstances.

Many IGOs serve as regulatory agencies, which is the function performed by the International Telecommunications Union (ITU) and the World Meteorological Organization (WMO). Such IGOs have the specific assignment to organize what would otherwise be a confusing relationship among nations. The absence of IGOs to regulate telecommunications or weather information would probably not result in any serious international conflicts, but the existence of such IGOs does prevent potentially chaotic situations. The first of the modern IGOs in the nineteenth century were established for regulatory purposes. Other than regulation, some IGOs have a distributive function in that they allocate funds, as do the International Monetary Fund and the World Bank. Still other IGOs are military alliances, such as NATO and the Warsaw Pact. An IGO can, of course, carry out more than one of these functions.

INTERNATIONAL REGIMES

Some attempts at international cooperation have been sufficiently successful that they fall into the category of international regimes. A regime can be an IGO, but some are not formal organizations; the law-of-the-sea negotiations are an example. Traditionally, the term "regime" is applied to domestic political systems, usually authoritarian in nature, or to a particular administration or ruling group. A more recent use of the term is international in scope and refers to those situations in which important conflict exists among nations, but it is to the mutual advantage of the conflicting parties to cooperate with one another. A problem encountered in studying international regimes is determining just what a regime is; as is the case with many concepts in international relations, no single, agreed-upon definition exists.

Two relatively similar definitions useful in studying regimes are that "international regimes are defined as principles, norms, rules, and decision-making procedures around which actor expectations converge in a given issue-area" (Krasner, 1982, 185), and that an international regime is "a set of mutual expectations, rules and regulations, plans, organizational energies and financial commitments, which have been accepted by a group of states" (Ruggie, 1975, 570). Thus, regimes are patterns and rules of behavior in the international system that result in cooperation among nation-states. Whenever two or more nations find that cooperation is a better means of obtaining their interests than trying to force the fulfillment of their interests unilaterally, a regime can develop.

The central concept of a regime is the development of norms and principals that serve as the basis of resolving conflict. Robert Keohane places this in perspective by saying, "We study international regimes because we are interested in understanding order in world politics. Conflict may be the rule; if so, institutionalized patterns of cooperation are particularly in need of explanation" (Keohane, 1982, 325). Examples of international cooperation that are cited as regimes include the General Agreement on Tariffs and Trade (GATT), the International Energy Agency (IEA), the International Monetary Fund (IMF), law-of-the-sea negotiations, and the European

Payments Union (EPU). Each of these examples shares two elements in common. They each have economic conflict as the basic problem they control, which is consistent with a theme that runs throughout this book. Economics, in the late 1980s, comprises a much greater portion of international relations than it did in the immediate postwar period. The second is that these international regimes' expanded influence came after the United States lost its position of hegemony in the international economic system. The United States, before the 1970s, could to a great extent control international economic activity, and regimes thus had no need to develop. Without a dominant nation, the international economic system sought other means of controlling conflict, and international regimes were strengthened.

This chapter examines IGOs in the traditional sense of the term by looking at the role of organizations such as the United Nations, its specialized agencies, and various regional IGOs and, as well, looks at the success of various IGOs as international regimes.

INTERNATIONAL ORGANIZATIONS AND CONFLICT MANAGEMENT

A utopian approach to international conflict resolution is to propose the establishment of a world government. Such an arrangement would be the ultimate IGO in that it would be granted the authority to make decisions that transcended domestic political systems, and, in this manner, abolish the nation-state system. Under such a system, if war were to break out it would by definition have to be a civil war, since nation-states would no longer exist. No attempt has yet been made to organize such a government, nor is there any prospect for such centralized control of the international system in the foreseeable future. Short of having the authority of a world government, IGOs must operate with a more limited capacity to control conflict.

One potentially important tool for managing

conflict is the use of collective security (the details of collective security were discussed in chapter 4). A requirement of collective security is the existence of an IGO to organize the assembly of an international armed force and to identify the nation or nations against which it will be used. This alternative of conflict management has never been fully implemented by either the League of Nations or the United Nations, even though it was an important part of the charge made to each organization. The primary requirement of collective security—that all nations, or at least the major states of the system, join together to punish nations that misbehave—requires an international consensus that has not yet been realized. The UN's decision to send troops to Korea in 1950 resulted in a multinational force, but it was not an overwhelming force as called for in collective security.

Even though an IGO has not successfully mustered the overwhelming force needed for a collective-security operation, multinational military forces for the purpose of separating combatants is possible; these are commonly referred to as peacekeeping forces. Establishing an armed force for this purpose is less difficult for an IGO to agree to than is a collective-security force, since such a decision does not include identifying an aggressor, which is perhaps the most difficult and divisive problem of collective security. Such military forces have been created by the United Nations a number of times, and some regional organizations, such as the Organization of American States, the Organization of African Unity, and the Arab League, have also used this technique for defusing a situation. Minimally, the use of such a force allows time for competing nations to negotiate their problems.

IGOs can play yet another role in the process of containing international conflict. When an international crisis develops, often the first act taken by nations responding to the crisis is to ask an IGO to look into the matter. The United Nations and some regional organizations have received a number of such requests. The typical response, if the crisis involves combat, is for the IGO to call for a ceasefire and, perhaps, issue a request for the conflicting parties to withdraw to the lines they held when the fighting began. Even if the decisions of the IGO are ignored by the combatants, other nations usually delay taking any action until the IGO makes its recommendations. The net effect of such behavior is that nations not directly involved in the conflict have an opportunity to give the matter greater consideration before responding—the international equivalent of "counting to ten."

While each of the possible actions available to IGOs falls short of the sort of behavior expected of a major conflict-resolving organization, IGOs do make an important contribution to conflict management.

DEVELOPMENT OF INTERNATIONAL ORGANIZATIONS

IGOs were discussed by political philosophers for centuries before one was created, and although intergovernmental organizations existed before the nineteenth century the first modern IGO was created by the Congress of Vienna in 1815—the Central Commission for the Navigation of the Rhine. In 1856, a similar commission was established for the Danube. The functions of these and other nineteenth-century river commissions and organizations were primarily regulatory and limited. Organizations with near-universal membership and broad-based functions did not develop until after World War I when the League of Nations was established.

The League was part of an overall peace settlement—spelled out in the Treaty of Versailles— the victors of World War I negotiated in 1919. While the Allied governments had done little to plan the postwar world while the war was in progress, considerable private pressure developed during the war for a postwar universal, international organization. Prominent individuals in France, Great Britain, and the United States promoted the idea.

The League was a product of the optimistic belief following World War I that nations could control conflict and thus avoid not only another devastating world war but wars of a lesser nature. This optimism was, at least in part, a product of desperation. The Western world had suffered millions of fatalities in a war of attrition fought over four years. European politics had lost their nineteenth-century stability, and the map of Europe had been redrawn. Unsure of what caused the war, the planners of the League of Nations designed a new system—collective security—to replace the balance of power system that had failed to prevent the war. Since both the old and new systems were based on the nation-state, the new system was not as revolutionary as it first appeared. Also, as is typical of postwar arrangements, the new system was designed by the victors of that war and imposed on the defeated. The victor-designed nature of the League was to plague the organization throughout its existence.

The heart of the League of Nations was its collective-security role. Conceptually, collective security was deceptively simple, but the League was authorized to use it only as a last resort. The League's primary role was to be a talking place where nations could take their disputes. If a dispute could not be resolved by this method, the debate would at least provide time for the parties involved to cool off. If those steps failed and war broke out, only then was collective security to be implemented.

The assumption of collective security was that in any war some nation or group of nations was the aggrieved party and someone was the offender or aggressor nation. The League had the responsibility of identifying which was which. Once that was accomplished, members of the League were to join together and punish that nation by bringing overwhelming power, economic or military, against it. If such collective action was taken, however, it was as an act of last resort; its use was an indication that the threat of collective security had failed to deter a nation from committing aggression. Since every nation planning an aggressive act would know the consequences—it would face overwhelming force—the hope was that that nations' leaders would think rationally and simply not attack.

The League's use of collective security was largely unsuccessful. Several reasons for the failure existed, among which was that the League had difficulty in keeping as members major states that disagreed with its decisions. Before the beginning of World War II, Germany, Japan, and Italy had withdrawn from the League, and the Soviet Union was expelled after it attacked Finland in late 1939. The United States never joined, and, among the major powers, only France and Great Britain were members from the League's beginning to its end. Without the major states working in concert, collective security could not be an effective deterrent against aggression, and certainly the threat of overwhelming power was not credible if one or more of the major states was labeled the aggressor.

Measuring the success of collective security as a deterrent is difficult, since success, in this instance, is achieved only when something does not happen. Collective security did not, however, deter Japan from committing aggression in Manchuria in 1931, nor Italy from taking similar action in Ethiopia in 1935. In both situations, failure to deter was followed by failure to bring overwhelming power to bear on the aggressors. Both countries, when labeled aggressors, simply withdrew from the League. Labeling the Soviet Union as an aggressor nation after it invaded Finland in November 1939 was a particularly useless act. The only sanction imposed was to expel the Soviet Union from the organization, which meant nothing, since World War II was already under way.

The failures of the League thus were: 1) its inability to retain major powers as members and to bring the United States into the organization; 2) its failure to prevent aggression and, when aggression occurred, to punish adequately those who committed it. To the disappointment of all who supported the League and collective security, the League demonstrated the difficulty of defining what constituted aggression in the international

system and of recognizing that aggression is not necessarily the act of a single nation. Collective security became a dubious proposition when the major states divided into armed camps and one camp saw nothing wrong with an aggressive act.

STRUCTURING THE UNITED NATIONS

While the League failed in major respects, it had its minor successes, thus providing UN planners with precedents both as to what to do and what not to do when establishing a replacement organization. The League's planners had had a more difficult task than had the planners of the UN, since they could not draw upon the experiences of an earlier near-universal-membership organization with broad responsibilities. The only experiences the planners of the League could look to were some limited forms of international cooperation in the nineteenth and early twentieth centuries.

The Concert of Europe, an arrangement among the major powers of Europe, maintained peace in Europe for nearly a century and provided an important precedent for both the League and the UN. Beginning with the Congress of Vienna in 1815, a conference was held whenever the major European powers agreed that a sufficient agenda of conflict situations existed. The last such conference was held in London in 1912–1913. The conferences occasionally included European nations other than the major states, but the diplomacy of the conferences, their agenda, and their outcome were determined by the major powers. These conferences provided peace in Europe through the guarantee of the major powers. The Concert of Europe was not an international organization; rather, it was diplomacy by international conference and an early instance of an international regime (See Krasner, 1983). This arrangement served as the basis of the Council in the League of Nations (which, in theory, was to include all major powers as members) and the Security Council of the UN, with five veto-bearing major powers as permanent members—the U.S., the USSR, France, Great Britain, and China—and six vetoless, nonpermanent members serving two-year terms each. (In 1965, the number of nonpermanent members was expanded to ten to meet the demands of the Third World for more representation.) Since, without a veto for the major powers, the League had difficulty keeping major powers in the organization, the veto was granted the permanent members of the Security Council in order to stop the UN from making decisions that might drive major powers away. (A veto occurs when one or more of the permanent members casts a negative vote when nine or more members of the Council have cast affirmative votes.) On the positive side, what motivated the planners to establish the veto was that if the major powers voted unanimously to carry out an action no means existed by which other nations could counter that combined power. Establishment of the veto also had its practical side; both the United States and the Soviet Union made it a condition of their membership in the UN.

The Hague system, with conferences in 1899 and 1907, also provided precedent for the League and the UN. These conferences were to be followed by a third conference in 1915, but the system failed to develop further due to the outbreak of World War I. The contribution made by the Hague system was the nature of its membership. The first conference included many of the smaller nations of Europe, and the second included a few non-European nations. Conferences with such broad membership had not been held earlier. While many independent nations were not invited to either conference, the concept of an international body with universality of membership was suggested. This concept served as the basis of both the Assembly of the League and the General Assembly of the United Nations, the only bodies of either organization in which the total membership was represented. It should be pointed out that the Hague conferences did not produce any important agreements in their brief history, but did establish the Permanent Court of Arbitration, which still exists.

A third precedent for a universal international organization was the creation of public international unions. In addition to the river commissions established in the nineteenth century, in 1865 the International Telegraph Union (later renamed the International Telecommunications Union) was organized, and in 1874 the Universal Postal Union came in being. Both organizations had broad membership for the purpose of administering a specific international problem. The industrial revolution, advancing technology, and increased contact and trade between the European nations created situations in which the need for regulation of specific problems became evident. The concept of specialized organizations with broad membership and the authority to regulate those problems became the precedent for a number of specialized agencies in the United Nations system.

In addition to the opportunity for drawing on the experiences of the League, another important advantage planners of the UN had over those who designed the League was the manner in which World War II progressed as compared to World War I. In 1918, the Allies knew only during the final weeks of the conflict that they would be in charge of the postwar world; during World War II, however, the Allies knew by 1943 that they would ultimately be victorious. As early as August 1941, even before the United States had entered the war, Churchill and Roosevelt committed their countries to a postwar international organization. The Allied foreign ministers conference held in Moscow in October and November 1943 stated in its closing communique that a general international organization would be negotiated among the victors. As a result, planning for the postwar world began long before the fighting ended. Negotiations among the major powers at Dumbarton Oakes, where much of the UN Charter was written, concluded in December 1944, and the political problems which that conference could not resolve were settled at Yalta in February 1945. The general conference at which the Charter was presented to the lesser powers was held in San Francisco in April and May 1945. Although the war was clearly in its closing months, the conference began before either Germany or Japan had surrendered. This wartime planning of a new universal IGO not only readied the UN to function before the war ended; it also kept the organization separate from any postwar peace settlement. Since the League's Covenant was an article in the Treaty of Versailles, when the U.S. Senate rejected the treaty the League went down with it. Since the Charter was not a part of the peace settlement for World War II, entanglement in postwar negotiations was avoided.

The planners of the United Nations rejected the idea that the UN be a reconstituted League and opted for a new organization. In many respects, however, the two organizations were similar. Several of the UN's institutions were near-copies of those in the League, but important differences were the veto in the Security Council and the requirement of a two-thirds' majority vote in the General Assembly. The Council and the Assembly of the League required a unanimous vote before action could be taken. Also, in the UN, collective security was not considered as important to the success of the organization as it had been to the League.

CONFLICT-RESOLVING TOOLS

In spite of the institutional changes made in the United Nations' Charter that were designed to avoid the mistakes of the League, the UN never met the high hopes of its designers. The UN did attempt a collective security action in Korea in 1950, but the aggressors, North Korea and China, were not forced to face overwhelming power; thus, the war ended in a stalemate in 1953. This version of collective security came closer to fulfilling the design of collective security than did

any of the League's attempts, but it was somewhat less than a success.

The primary reason the so-called Korean "police action" developed into a limited war in which both sides were willing to accept a stalemate was the imposition of bipolarity on the United Nations. The Soviet Union and the United States fought the Cold War wherever they could, and the UN was an important arena for them. Since in the early years of the UN the United States could muster over two-thirds of the votes in the General Assembly, where no nation had a veto, the Soviets protected themselves by frequent use of their veto in the Security Council. The Soviets cast many of their vetoes to block from UN membership nations that the Soviets felt would only enhance the large U.S.–controlled majority. The United States made use of Soviet vetoes to embarrass the Soviet Union by pointing out that the U.S. had never found it necessary to veto a resolution in the Security Council.

In one sense, the veto served its purpose in that it prevented the Security Council from making decisions that might have resulted in one or more of the major powers' leaving the UN; but the veto created a negative attitude about the UN when no consensus developed among the major powers on how to approach postwar problems. Even the UN's decision to send a military force to Korea came about as a matter of happenstance. The Soviets had been boycotting the Security Council at the time of the invasion to protest Beijing's not being seated in the UN, thus were not present to cast a veto. Such Soviet cooperation through absence could not be depended upon if instances similar to Korea were to occur in the future. Since, in 1950, the U.S. had the votes in the General Assembly to do whatever it wished but was frustrated in the Security Council because of the Soviet veto, the U.S. developed a strategy to bypass the Soviets.

In addition to placing the UN's collective-security capability in the Security Council, the Charter vests the Security Council with a wide range of power, including the imposition of

Fig. 16.1 The Structure of the United Nations

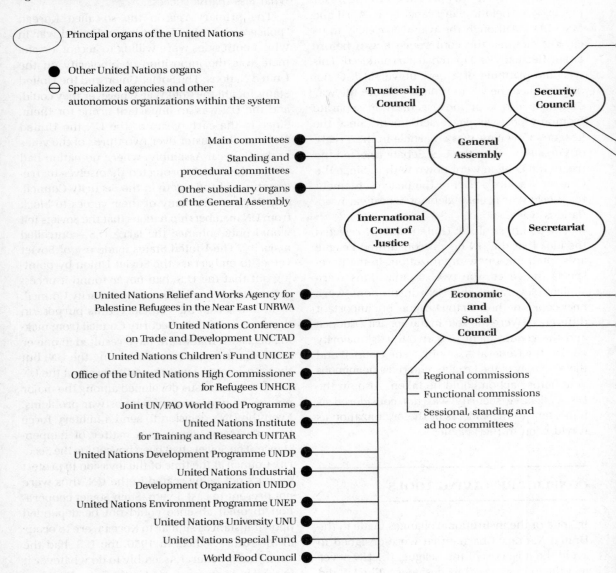

○ Principal organs of the United Nations

● Other United Nations organs

⊖ Specialized agencies and other autonomous organizations within the system

Main committees ●

Standing and procedural committees ●

Other subsidiary organs of the General Assembly ●

Trusteeship Council

Security Council

General Assembly

International Court of Justice

Secretariat

United Nations Relief and Works Agency for Palestine Refugees in the Near East UNRWA ●

United Nations Conference on Trade and Development UNCTAD ●

United Nations Children's Fund UNICEF ●

Office of the United Nations High Commissioner for Refugees UNHCR ●

Joint UN/FAO World Food Programme ●

United Nations Institute for Training and Research UNITAR ●

United Nations Development Programme UNDP ●

United Nations Industrial Development Organization UNIDO ●

United Nations Environment Programme UNEP ●

United Nations University UNU ●

United Nations Special Fund ●

World Food Council ●

Economic and Social Council

Regional commissions

Functional commissions

Sessional, standing and ad hoc committees

SOURCE: United Nations Office of Public Information.

UNTSO United Nations Truce Supervision Organization in Palestine

UNMOGIP United Nations Military Observer Group in India and Pakistan

UNFICYP United Nations Peace-keeping Force in Cyprus

UNEF United Nations Emergency Force
UNDOF United Nations Disengagement Observer Force

UNIFIL United Nations Interim Force in Lebanon

Military Staff Committee

Disarmament Commission

IAEA International Atomic Energy Agency

GATT General Agreement on Tariffs and Trade

ILO International Labour Organization

FAO Food and Agriculture Organization of the United Nations

UNESCO United Nations Educational, Scientific and Cultural Organization

WHO World Health Organization

IDA International Development Association

BRD International Bank for Reconstruction and Development

IFC International Finance Corporation

IMF International Monetary Fund

ICAO International Civil Aviation Organization

UPU Universal Postal Union

ITU International Telecommunication Union

WMO World Meteorological Organization

IMCO Inter-Governmental Maritime Consultative Organization

WIPO World Intellectual Property Organization

sanctions. The General Assembly had no such authority. To overcome the greater authority of the Security Council, where the Soviet veto blocked action, the United States sponsored the Uniting for Peace Resolution. This resolution, passed by a large majority in the General Assembly, stated that when the Security Council was deadlocked, that is, prevented from acting because of the Soviet veto, the General Assembly could take up the matter without the Security Council's permission. The procedure set out in the Charter was that if the Security Council was considering a matter, it could be debated in the General Assembly only if the Security Council permitted; therefore, some argued, the Uniting for Peace Resolution violated the Charter.

Using the General Assembly to bypass the Security Council presented an additional problem. The General Assembly's resolutions are only recommendations, and only the Security Council can take binding action in matters involving threats to peace and security; thus, any action taken under the Uniting for Peace Resolution was really only a statement of the General Assembly's opinion. Parts of the Uniting for Peace Resolution were used several times in subsequent years, but other aspects of the resolution, such as a UN army under the General Assembly's direction, were never implemented. As the United States lost control of the General Assembly during the 1960s when many Third World members joined the organization, use of the resolution declined.

The United States, after so often chiding the Soviet Union for its frequent use of the veto, cast its first veto in 1970. U.S. use of the veto accelerated during the 1970s and early 1980s, until the United States was casting more vetoes than the Soviet Union. Now both superpowers used the veto to protect themselves—the Soviets from Western moves, and the United States from the actions of the Third World and the Soviet Union. In recognition of their mutual need for the veto, the superpowers developed an understanding to consult with one another before introducing a resolution in the Security Council in order to avoid forcing the other to cast a veto. This was a far cry from the early days of the UN, when the U.S. deliberately brought up issues certain to produce a Soviet veto. When the U.S. has cast a veto in recent years, it usually has been against a resolution coming from the Third World.

A United Nations divided by bipolarity and the discussion of essentially only East–West issues was the old UN. The new United Nations that emerged in the 1960s was one of expanding membership, primarily countries that were former colonies. The agenda of the newer members indicated more concern with ending colonialism and neocolonial economic relationships than with how the Cold War was progressing. As a result, the superpowers gradually moved their bilateral diplomacy outside the UN, turned the General Assembly over to the Third World countries, and retreated into the Security Council, where they had the veto to protect them. The U.S. and the USSR still use the organization to embarrass one another when an occasion arises to do so, but not through use of the veto. The agenda of the UN now contains the issues chosen by the newer members.

What these changes in the nature of the UN indicate is that the organization reflects what is going on in the international system as a whole. The issues and conflicts that exist outside the UN are often the ones that divide it. It is not a supranational organization and was not intended to be. The superpowers have never been controlled by the UN, and even the Security Council, where the major powers were to have their greatest influence, has had little success in limiting the activities of its major-power members. Because the UN is a product of the nation-state system, the interests of nations are presented within the UN with about the same intensity that exists elsewhere. As a consequence, the UN can provide no more consensus of policy or resolution of conflict than can the international system it reflects. The organization changed a great deal in its first forty years, and interpretation of the Charter's provisions reflected those changes; but the UN

could be no stronger than its member states allowed it to be. The hope that wartime cooperation among the allies would continue in the postwar world and guarantee world peace almost immediately proved to be invalid, and the conflicts that plagued the international system also plagued the UN.

In one sense, however, the UN has not been reflective of the international system. Since the membership is based on the concept of one-nation, one-vote, the organization is not directly reflective of power relationships among nations. As a result, the UN tends to hear more about the Third World's problems than is heard in the international system at large. Since the Third World feels that the industrial nations pay too little attention to their problems, use of the UN, particularly the General Assembly, as a forum for the Third World may be one of the organization's most significant contributions to international stability.

A disadvantage of this circumstance is that Third World nations, in their unity against the industrial world, are overly protective of the activities of Third World countries. Israel is seen as a Western enclave by much of the Third World, and, therefore, its actions are sharply criticized. Behavior by Third World countries that is similar to Israel's passes unnoticed by the UN. South Africa, with its white-minority government, is frequently and appropriately condemned for its policy of apartheid and its actions in Namibia and Angola, but human rights violations in black African nations elicit no attention from the UN. Whenever Israel responds in the General Assembly to charges from various Third World representatives, it often speaks to a nearly empty chamber. At least, Israel is allowed to speak. South Africa, by vote of the General Assembly, has not been allowed for several years to participate in that body's deliberations. Sentiment against Israel in the UN was so strong during the late 1970s that the General Assembly and other units of the United Nations system passed resolutions equating Zionism with racism. After strong objections from the United States, the 1980s have been free of such resolutions.

Terrorist activity is defined by a substantial portion of the UN's membership as the work of freedom fighters and, instead of condemnatory, as worthy of support. In 1977, the General Assembly did pass a resolution condemning the hijacking of aircraft, but it took this action only after an international organization of airline pilots threatened to go on strike if the UN did not act against hijackings. After years of pressure from Western nations, in 1985 the General Assembly did pass a general antiterrorist resolution.

In the West, one of the most controversial decisions of the UN occurred when, in 1974, Yasser Arafat, head of the Palestinian Liberation Organization (PLO), was invited to speak to the General Assembly. This marked the first occasion when a representative of a nongovernmental organization was allowed to speak to that body. Later, the UN granted the PLO observer status. The PLO contained terrorist elements within its membership, and its new status at the UN was sharply criticized by the U.S. In 1975, Idi Amin, then chairman of the OAU, appeared before the General Assembly and spoke in support of terrorist attacks on Israel. Idi Amin's killing in Uganda of up to 300,000 members of tribes other than his own went uncondemned by the UN, as did Pol Pot's massacre of a quarter of Kampuchea's population. The Third World dominance of the UN has produced what often appears to be a double standard for judging international and domestic behavior.

THE UNITED NATIONS AND CONFLICT MANAGEMENT

Since major-power solidarity, as a means of guaranteeing world peace, never developed, and the General Assembly failed to be an institution in which grand debates of world problems took place, efforts by the UN to maintain peace had

to develop in other ways; even then the organization was not successful in resolving the world's major problems. The organization was unable to prevent the Cold War or to lessen its intensity, and attempts by the UN to play a significant role in bringing about arms control were largely supplanted by bilateral negotiations between the United States and the Soviet Union. The Third World's problems with the industrial nations were voiced strongly in the General Assembly, but little progress in resolving those issues was made. A review of UN accomplishments concerning a central role in resolving conflict, therefore, is discouraging. Even though the UN has not succeeded in dealing with the major issues of the post–World War II era, in other aspects of conflict management the organization has a better record.

The United Nations is often thought of only in terms of the more highly publicized activities of the Security Council and the General Assembly. The United Nations is more than those institutions and, in terms of the total UN system, includes a wide array of additional activities. For example, the Security Council has established a number of agencies to supervise the disengagement of combatants. It maintains a peacekeeping force in Cyprus (UNICYP), a force in southern Lebanon (UNIFIL), and a military-observer group in India and Pakistan (UNMOGIP). A disengagement-observer force (UNDOF) and a truce-supervisory organization (UNTSO) for Israel and its neighbors were also established. The force in Cyprus was formed in 1974 to separate the Turkish–held portion of the island from the Greek Cypriot–controlled section in the south. The force in Lebanon was sent by the UN in 1978 to maintain security in southern Lebanon during the height of PLO activity in that region.

When Israel invaded Lebanon in 1982, Israeli forces simply passed through the UN force. This disregard for the UN probably weakened any future chance of establishing similar forces. The Israelis charged that the force was ineffective, for, had it been effective, the invasion would not have been necessary. The military observers in India and Pakistan have been in place since the first war between those two countries in 1948. Though not a military force, the observers' function is to report to the UN violations of the truce agreement. The UN observers in Israel originally were placed there to supervise the truce between Israel and its Arab enemies in 1948 (UNTSO). Later, UNDOF was added to maintain the cease-fire between Israel and Syria following the October 1973 war.

The UN also has established military forces that subsequently completed their operations. In 1960, the UN sent a military force to the Congo (presently Zaire) to reunite that country, which was then in chaos following its independence. This is the only UN force since the Korean operation that was called upon to do other than separate combatants or supervise a truce. It carried out military operations and settled some of the internal violence, but by the time it was withdrawn in 1964 insurrections in other parts of the country had broken out. The premature withdrawal of the force was necessary because several countries, including the Soviet Union and France, refused to pay their share of the cost of the operation. The resulting debt was so large that the UN faced bankruptcy if it did not withdraw. The Congo operation was approved and supervised by the General Assembly under the Uniting for Peace Resolution. The financial difficulties of this operation were an indication of the need for common agreement among the major powers before approval of such a force, and were a reaffirmation of the rationale for the veto in the Security Council.

Two other instances of military forces no longer operative were forces stationed in the Sinai. In 1957, the UN sent the United Nations Emergency Force (UNEF) to separate the Israelis and Egyptians, following a brief war in October 1956. This force remained in place until Nasser demanded its withdrawal shortly before the Six–Day War in 1967. The force was stationed only on Egyptian soil, and Nasser had permitted its

presence on condition that it would be withdrawn when he requested. UNEF II was established and placed in the Sinai following the 1973 October War. It changed its positions several times as Israel gradually withdrew from the Sinai following the disengagement agreement in 1975. The need for that force came to an end when Israel completed its withdrawal from the Sinai in 1979 and a peace treaty was concluded between the two countries. The UN has also had observers in Greece (1952–1954), in Lebanon (1958), in Indonesia (1962–1963), and in Yemen (1963–1964).

All UN peacekeeping forces have been multinational in composition and none included troops from the two superpowers. While the central objective of a collective security operation is to bring all the major powers together in a collective action, for peacekeeping operations the objective is to keep the major powers out in order to prevent an East–West confrontation. The overall accomplishments of both military forces and truce observers have been limited to keeping disputing parties at arm's length, but the UN has played only a minimal role in settling the disputes that make a UN presence necessary. The UN is, perhaps, not able to prevent wars, but it can and does limit the effects of a war when it breaks out.

While the Security Council and the General Assembly are the best known of the major units of the United Nations, other units also are important to the UN's programs. Because of the growing demands of the Third World nations, a focal point of activities in the UN has become the Economic and Social Council (ECOSOC). This organ of the UN has fifty-four members elected by the General Assembly and is responsible for many of the issues the Third World is interested in. Since those countries clearly have the votes in the General Assembly to establish the agencies they want, the General Assembly has set up a number of agencies that report jointly to ECOSOC and the General Assembly. These include the United Nations Conference of Trade and Development (UNCTAD), which has as its primary focus the negotiation of trade problems among the member states, and, in particular, the trade and development problems of the Third World. As discussed in chapter 6, this has been an active arrangement, and several such UN-sponsored conferences have been held. The United Nations High Commissioner for Refugees (UNHCR) has the enormous task of protecting, feeding, housing, and simply keeping track of the millions of political and economic refugees throughout the world. Also in the realm of refugees, the UN has its Relief and Works Administration for Palestine Refugees in the Near East (UNRWA). In the area of development, the UN has established the Development Program (UNDP) and the Industrial Development Organization (UNIDO). In the realm of food and population problems, the UN has set up the World Food Program and the World Food Council. The UNFPA is the Fund for Population Activities. These and other units of the UN have, in many instances, been an outcome of UN–sponsored conferences such as the conference on the environment held in Stockholm in 1972, the population conference held in Bucharest in 1974, and the food conference held in Rome in 1974. The UN has also sponsored conferences on women's rights (Mexico City in 1975 and Nairobi in 1985).

The United Nations has six major units. Three have been discussed: the General Assembly, the Security Council, and the Economic and Social Council. Another is the Secretariat, the international civil service of the UN. As pointed out earlier, an IGO's secretariat prevents a group of nations that meet periodically from simply engaging in a series of conferences. A secretariat not only provides staff support for the members, but provides continuity for the IGO between meetings. The UN has about 7,000 employees, but the UN system (the UN plus all related and specialized agencies, many of which have their own secretariats) has about 45,000 employees worldwide. With increasing frequency, the complaint is voiced that the bureaucracies of the UN system have grown too large and that the system

exists more for the survival of the bureaucracy than for the promotion of the organizations. Also, critics allege that salaries are too high. These charges were among those voiced by the United States to justify its withdrawal from UNESCO. Another often-heard complaint is that the secretariat is not neutral, as the Charter indicates it should be. The Soviets made this charge in the early years of the UN, but today this sort of complaint is usually heard from the Western nations now that the secretariats of the UN system are dominated by persons from Third World nations.

The UN's secretariat is headed by the secretary-general who, since 1982, has been Javier Perez de Cuellar. He is only the fifth person to hold that position, but each occupant has brought a different perspective to the office. The early secretaries–general (Trygve Lie and Dag Hammarskjold) concentrated more on actively directing the UN's attention to problem areas and providing political leadership than did later secretaries–general (U Thant and Kurt Waldheim). Due to the East–West split, active leadership often resulted in either the United States' or the Soviet Union's taking exception to such initiatives. Following Hammarskjold's death in a 1961 plane crash, the Soviet Union, claiming that Hammarskjold had represented only Western interests, pressed for a three-person, or *troika*, office of secretary–general. The Soviets wanted one representative each from the communist bloc, the Western nations, and the Third World. The plan was not adopted.

More recent secretaries-general have played less of a political and more of an administrative role within the UN. All have been effective behind-the-scenes negotiators, however. Also, all the secretaries-general have been from the lesser powers or neutral countries (Norway, Sweden, Burma, Austria, and Peru). The later secretaries–general have, perhaps, been more realistic than were the earlier ones, since they seem to have realized that the UN can be only as effective as the major powers are willing for it to be. For the secretary–general to feud with one of the superpowers ultimately weakens the organization.

The secretariat and the secretary–general also have the responsibility of administering the budget of the UN, which is about $2.5 billion a year. Several cities and most of the states in the United States have larger budgets. In 1985, the UN's budget was less than 1 percent of the U.S. defense budget. Thus, the UN's budget, when compared to the expenditures of other governmental systems, is not large. The budget is controversial, however, particularly in the manner in which it is funded.

The UN's budget is financed by an assessment of the membership based on ability to pay. The present U.S. assessment is 25 percent of the UN's budget which is, however, fixed by U.S. law, and not the UN's budgetary process. Initially, the U.S. Congress restricted U.S. payments to 33 percent of any IGO's budget, but in 1973 Congress lowered the maximum assessment to 25 percent. The U.S. can pay more voluntarily, however. Even at this reduced level of assessment, as U.S. disillusionment with the UN has grown, portions of the American public and Congress have been critical of even the reduced percentage. One argument that opposes the present U.S. assessment is that it is not healthy for any IGO to be overly dependent on a single nation for contributions, because that nation could wield undue influence within the IGO.

The other two organs of the UN are the Trusteeship Council and the International Court of Justice (ICJ). The Trusteeship Council was designed to oversee the demise of colonialism, but the colonial empires broke up largely without UN supervision. The General Assembly often passed anticolonial resolutions, but most former colonies received their independence directly from their colonial masters. The Trusteeship Council did oversee the granting of independence to trust territories administered by the UN, but that task now is virtually completed, and the Council therefore has little to do. The ICJ (fifteen judges elected for nine-year terms by the General Assembly and the Security Council) also has done little in recent years. Before its decision in 1980 in which the court found Iran in the wrong when it condoned the seizure of the American hostages, the ICJ had not handed down a decision for more than five years. Major disputes rarely have been taken to the court; thus, the infrequent decisions handed down by the court have carried little weight internationally. Discussion of the ICJ's impact on international law will take place in the following chapter.

The specialized agencies, while a part of the United Nations system but not units of the UN itself, function as separate IGOs, although they do report to ECOSOC on their activities. Several of these organizations clearly have a regulatory function, such as the International Civil Aviation Organization (ICAO) and the Universal Postal Union (UPU). The World Health Organization (WHO) has the responsibility for controlling various endemic diseases. Its best-known success was the eradication of smallpox. Other agencies such as the International Bank for Reconstruction and Development (IBRD or the World Bank), the International Monetary Fund (IMF), and the International Development Agency (IDA) have a distributive function for loans to Third World countries. The Food and Agriculture Organization (FAO) is assigned the task of raising the world's nutrition level and improving the production and distribution of food. Each of these dozen or so agencies has its own secretariat, budget, headquarters, and membership.

REGIONAL IGOs

Major military and economic IGOs in Europe—NATO and the Warsaw Pact, and the European Community and COMECON, respectively—were discussed in an earlier chapter. The central theme of that discussion was that each coalition has conflicts that tend to pull it apart and common interests that tend to bring it together. This is, of course, true of any coalition or IGO. These

European IGOs will not be reviewed further here, but it is appropriate to point out that they have been successful organizations within the context in which they were formed. Because of their levels of success, that is, the norms of behavior they have developed, some, such as the European Community, qualify as international regimes. Other European IGOs that could be regarded as regimes are the European Payments Union (EPU) and the Organization of Economic Cooperation and Development (OECD), although the latter IGO's membership is not restricted to European nations alone. Each of these regional organizations has been in existence for twenty-five years or more, and none shows any serious signs of weakening. Regional IGOs outside Europe are generally not as healthy, however, but their survival also depends on how they manage the stresses placed upon them.

The founders of the United Nations anticipated no conflict between regional organizations and the UN, and no serious ones have developed. Article 51 of the UN Charter allows for regional IGOs and permits them to take collective action when a threat to peace and security develops, until the Security Council can respond. If the problem is not referred to the Security Council, or if it is and the Security Council fails to act or is blocked by a veto, the management of the conflict remains with the regional IGO. As with NATO, SEATO, and CENTO, collective actions by a regional organization are often referred to as acts of collective security, which they are not. An action, including the use of military force, may be taken by a number of nations agreeing to act together, but collective security is a system based on global, not regional, response.

The long-term trend has been that if a regional problem develops, the United Nations ordinarily takes no action as long as a regional IGO is looking into the matter. Thus, the UN is seen as a forum of last resort, or is reserved for problems that extend beyond a regional IGO's jurisdiction. Ernst Haas has found that conflicts dealt with by regional organizations are not as serious as those

handled by the UN; in line with this observation, he has also observed that disputes dealt with by regional IGOs involve less combat than do those referred to the UN. Regional IGOs over time have handled about the same number of disputes as has the UN, but the UN has taken up fewer disputes in recent years than have regional IGOs (Haas, 1982, 189–256). While regional organizations, such as the Association of Southeast Asian Nations, the Organization of African Unity, and the Organization of American States, have carried out collective military operations, they have broader responsibilities than that alone.

THE OAU AND AFRICAN PROBLEMS

The OAU is the largest in membership of the regional organizations. While the fifty-nation organization has not experienced great success in resolving conflicts, it has not been reluctant to take up the major political problems of Africa. Several situations it has dealt with, however, have strained the very fabric of its existence.

The OAU held its first annual meeting in 1963, and from the beginning the black African and Arab African nations found themselves at odds. The issue was Pan–Africanism, with Nkrumah of Ghana attempting to control the movement in the name of black Africa and Nasser of Egypt attempting to do the same for the Arab nations. The dispute between the two leaders became so serious that several countries refused to attend the OAU's third annual meeting, held in Ghana in 1965, because Nkrumah, in his zeal to bolster his leadership of the movement, had attempted to overthrow their governments. Neither Nkrumah nor Nasser emerged as Africa's leader, nor did any one else do so subsequently.

The OAU has failed to manage a number of conflicts in Africa, including controlling civil wars in Nigeria (the Biafran War) and in Zaire. The organization was also unsuccessful in taking any action when Zaire was twice invaded from

Angola in the 1970s. On one occasion, French troops, and on the other, Moroccan troops, came to the aid of Zaire. In 1975, however, the OAU did succeed in stopping mass killings in Burundi.

The OAU, in its early years, was beset with several smaller regional groupings within its membership, but those organizations did not bring about a long-term fragmentation of the OAU. The issue that united the OAU was its anticolonial stand and its insistence that all of Africa be granted its independence. During the late 1960s and the 1970s, after most of Africa had obtained its independence, Africa's principal remaining colonial issue was the white regimes of southern Africa—Rhodesia and South Africa. When Rhodesia gained its independence as Zimbabwe in 1980, that episode of white rule was ended, but South Africa continued to be an OAU problem.

Additional conflicts came before the organization when the Soviet Union and Cuba intervened militarily in Angola. The Soviet Union supported the MPLA, one of three liberation movements in Angola; the United States supported the other two movements, the FNLN and UNITA. When Angola received its independence in 1975 after a long struggle with Portugal, the OAU was evenly split between supporting the MPLA to form the new government and supporting all three movements joining together in a coalition government. The problem was resolved when the U.S. Congress, out of fear that a new Vietnam would develop in Angola if the U.S. continued to support any faction, prohibited further aid to forces in Angola. The MPLA was able to consolidate its position and organize the government. This period also marked the beginning of divisions within the OAU over the status of Western Sahara, a former Spanish colony that Morocco and Mauritania claimed. Algeria supported a countermovement, the Polisario Front, that was fighting for the former colony's independence. The OAU's demands for Djibouti's independence also resulted in a conflict with France. France delayed independence on the grounds that a civil war likely would break out between the two principal tribes if the colony were granted independence. France ended the dispute in 1977 by giving Djibouti its independence.

In the 1980s, three important problems still faced the OAU: control of Western Sahara; fighting in Chad, where the rebels received support from Libya; and South Africa's continued resistance to granting Namibia its independence. The OAU had long supported Namibian independence, but South Africa linked its withdrawal from Namibia with the withdrawal of Cuban forces from Angola to the north of Namibia. In response, the OAU demanded that the UN place an economic boycott on South Africa until South Africa agreed to implement UN Security Council Resolution 435, which provided the framework for Namibian independence. While splits existed within the OAU on the Western Sahara and Chad, no division existed over Namibia.

The status of the Western Sahara was particularly divisive because it was linked with other African problems. It was a contributing factor to failures to obtain a quorum at two attempts to hold the 1982 OAU annual summit meeting. The meeting was to be held in Tripoli, Libya, but the Polisario Front had been granted membership in the OAU and a number of nations supportive of Morocco refused to attend. Although a majority of the OAU opposed Morocco's claim to the Western Sahara (Mauritania had given up its claim), a second reason for members' boycotting the meeting was Libya's support of rebels in Chad. The two issues combined to prevent a quorum from attending. Also, the French had sent armed forces to Chad to oppose Libya's forces, which increased the tension further within the OAU, as is always the case when the armed forces of a former colonial power become involved in African affairs. The meeting finally took place in June 1983, after the location was moved to the OAU's headquarters in Addis Ababa. When the Polisario Front occupied its seat at the annual meeting in 1984, Morocco withdrew from the organization. Zaire was the only other country to withdraw its delegation in support of Morocco. These three issues—South Africa and Namibia, Chad, and Western Sahara—plus financial problems, continue to occupy the attention of the OAU.

THE OAS AND LATIN AMERICAN PROBLEMS

In contrast to the heavy involvement of the OAU in African problems, the OAS in the 1970s and 1980s remained on the fringes of Latin American conflicts. The OAS had taken an active role in a number of Latin American problems earlier in its history, such as voting support for the United States during the Cuban missile crisis in 1962 and the Dominican crisis in 1965, and supporting peacekeeping operations in Central America and between Haiti and the Dominican Republic. Also, it was through the structure of the OAS that economic and diplomatic sanctions were imposed on Cuba during the early 1960s. In regard to more recent conflicts, however, the OAS has not played an important role. The Falklands War, the insurgence in El Salvador, conflicts between Nicaragua and its neighbors, the U.S. invasion of Grenada, and the debt issue for several Latin American countries have not been dealt with by the OAS.

One explanation for the current inactivity of the OAS is that the United States is a member. The OAU has no non–African or major-state members, and a number of OAS members feel that if the U.S. were excluded from the OAS the organization would be stronger, particularly since several of the problems in Latin America involve U.S. relations with various Latin American countries. Until the mid-1960s, the United States used the OAS to promote its policy aims in Latin America, but as anti–U.S. feelings grew, the organization became less responsive to U.S. initiatives. Traditional U.S. allies in Latin America, for the most part, now oppose U.S. leadership,

but no Latin American leadership has emerged to replace that of the U.S. Even though the OAU has not resolved many of the issues it has dealt with, it has not sidestepped issues, as has the OAS.

ASEAN AND SOUTHEAST ASIA

ASEAN is an IGO whose initial purpose was to bring about economic development among its members through cooperation. Its six members— Thailand, the Philippines, Indonesia, Malaysia, Singapore, and Brunei—have had some moderate successes in reducing tariffs and other trade barriers, but the biggest problem for the organization has been nonmembers in the region. The mass killings in Kampuchea under Pol Pot went unchecked, even though ASEAN strongly objected, but the organization was equally disturbed by the implications of the Vietnamese invasion of Kampuchea that stopped the killing. ASEAN, while not primarily a security IGO, worries about fighting along the Thai–Kampuchean border between Thai and Vietnamese forces and the larger problem of the superior military force possessed by Vietnam. Concern exists that conflict in the region will spread further among the members of ASEAN. The modest economic gains of the organization have been overshadowed by security problems in the region.

CONCLUSION

An important example of an international regime that was not discussed in this chapter was the series of law-of-the-sea negotiations. Those negotiations do not constitute an IGO as such, but do illustrate the development of norms of behavior to control an area of conflict, although a number of questions concerning U.S. involvement remain. Those negotiations also illustrate the development of international law through an international conference; thus, the discussion of the law-of-the-sea talks is more appropriate to the next chapter on international law.

If a regime is defined as a situation in which norms of behavior develop that control conflict in the international system, examples of success among IGOs are few; but IGOs do carry out a number of important functions even when they fail to achieve major successes. IGOs are a framework for communication, which includes clarifying the scope and severity of a conflict. IGOs can provide a time delay that allows the conflicting parties an opportunity to discuss their differences. An IGO can also serve as a neutral mediator of conflicts; but if all this fails, some IGOs are equipped to serve the policing function of separating combatants from one another with the hope that negotiations will eventually prove fruitful. IGOs can also serve a regulating function. Some international problems are not so much conflict situations as they are situations of confusion, and a number of IGOs have developed to give order to such situations. In brief, successful IGOs provide multilateral diplomacy with a regularized arrangement for attempting to manage conflict.

CHAPTER 17

International Law

While no nation would contend that it does not support international law, various perspectives exist within the international system as to what international law is or ought to be. For example, in certain respects the Western interpretation of international law conflicts with that of the Soviet Union or the Third World. The result is that, when in conflict, each nation can argue that, from its perspective, international law supports its case. In spite of that, a broad but generally accepted definition of international law is that it encompasses the rules, norms, and principles which nation–states accept in their relations with one another, and that these standards of behavior are obeyed because nations feel obligated to do so. Arguments arise as to what these standards of behavior are, but in this respect international law does not differ from any other body of law; the basis of any court case can be a difference over interpretation of the law.

Internationally, while frequent debates take place as to what is morally correct behavior, international law is not international morality. Morality involves how nations should act, not how they feel obliged to act. Neither is international law to be confused with international comity. Comity constitutes the rules of courtesy among nations, but they too are not supported by a sense of obligation to obey.

As is so often the situation in the study of

international politics, the manner in which a concept or area of study is defined determines its relevance to explaining behavior within the system. The study of international law is a particularly valid illustration of that point. Some observers of the international system argue that what is described as international law has so many weaknesses that it cannot be considered to be law. Since international law has only limited means for punishing those nations that violate it, they point out, it falls short of the standards needed to be a body of law. Countering this is the argument that a body of law can exist without sanctions, since fear of sanctions is not necessarily the basis upon which nations obey international law or, for that matter, the reason parties to any other body of law obey legal principles. Rather than the fear of sanctions, most nations most of the time obey international law because they feel that it is in their best interests to do so, and they accept that the principles of international law are a reasonable means of regulating behavior.

If, in fact, obedience to international law were based only on the imposition of sanctions, nations would have little reason to obey international law as frequently as they do, since sanctions are rarely imposed on violators. Even more to the point, the imposition of sanctions requires a central authority, and the international system has no such authority. The United Nations, specifically the Security Council, is the logical candidate for such a role, but, as was demonstrated in the last chapter, the UN is far from having such status. The imposition of sanctions in a self-help international system falls to the nation that feels its rights have been violated. Thus, if the central test for judging whether a set of principles constitutes a body of law is whether sanctions will be imposed on violators, then international law is not law. If, however, the significant test is whether nations see those principles as binding on their behavior, in most circumstances, then international law is law.

Drawing parallels between municipal law (the proper term for domestic law when compared to international law) and international law must be done with some care, since sanctions are more readily available in municipal law than in international law, and domestic systems have a central authority to impose sanctions. It is valid to point out, however, that municipal law also is obeyed for reasons other than the fear of sanctions alone. Drivers may obey a stop sign because they fear a traffic ticket, but drivers are also motivated to stop because it is in their best interests to protect themselves from physical harm even when no policing authority is nearby. Under these circumstances, obeying the law is not a purely voluntary act if a sense of obligation is involved. Nor is obedience to international law to be considered a purely voluntary act, particularly when nations accept the idea that they have an obligation to obey.

Despite the commonly held impression to the contrary, international law is usually obeyed. Exceptions often are important ones that lead to international crises, but, short of that, even those nations holding a view of international law differing from that held by the Western nations adhere to the general principles of international law. Nation-states recognize a need for some order in the international system, and international law provides that order to some degree. An international system in which no standards of behavior existed would be even more disorderly and unpredictable than is the present one.

HOW RELEVANT IS INTERNATIONAL LAW TO THE SYSTEM?

In addition to the argument concerning sanctions, some students of international law contend that international law is largely irrelevant to the manner in which the present international system is organized. This allegation is based on the assumption that international law may at one time have been a regulator of international behavior, but that the international system has changed to such an extent that principles of law that were important in the nineteenth century and earlier are no longer applicable or accepted in the present system (Deutsch and Hoffmann, 1971, 34). This approach to international law argues that the demise of the classical balance-of-power system, the development of bipolarity, and the expansion of the nation-state system have changed the system so much that it is currently impossible to apply nineteenth-century principles of law in the late twentieth century.

A balance-of-power system is considered important to international law because many of its principles were developed when the international system was organized around the European system of balance of power. Therefore, with balance of power gone, the law it spawned has at least been weakened, if not destroyed. Since the current system is a loose form of bipolarity that entails two directly antagonistic and hostile coalitions, international law no longer contains agreed-upon principles of behavior that can control conflict of this intensity. Under bipolarity, coalition leaders are willing to intervene in the internal affairs of lesser members to keep the coalition intact, thus violating one of the basic principles of international law under balance of power—noninterference in the internal affairs of another state. Within the context of this argument, the expansion of the nation-state system also weakened international law because the new nations were colonies at the time many principles of international law were being developed. Since international law was developed by the Western nations, and since many of the new nations reject the international system as organized by the Western nations, the new nations also reject Western interpretations of international law.

The argument that international law is irrelevant in the present system does overlook, however, that even though new nations, as well as the Soviets and the Chinese, have interpretations of international law at odds with those of Western nations, international law is not rejected by the dissenting nations. It is interpreted differently, but even with differing approaches most nations most of the time accept and abide by the long-established, basic principles of that law. Even when balance of power constituted the basis for organizing the international system, the system often did not follow the rules of balance of power, but international law nevertheless continued to play a role in regulating conflict. Thus, international law survived when politics in the nineteenth century functioned outside the rules of balance of power. The successful application of international law, therefore, is not necessarily dependent on a particular means of organizing the international system.

Yet another problem that some observers find with international law is its ineffectiveness in preventing wars. This argument can be answered in two ways. First, the assumptions of international law never implied that wars could always be prevented; otherwise, international law would not have been divided into the laws of peace and the laws of war. International law does offer principles that can be used to prevent wars, if the nations involved wish to use them, such as arbitration, negotiations through a regularized process, and diplomatic protocol. If war breaks out, however, then international law offers principles as to the conduct of war and the behavior of nonbelligerent nations in regard to that war. Secondly, when war breaks out, since international law allows for wars of self-defense, wars

do not necessarily violate that law. Thus, any party to a war can feel it is fighting a just war and is complying with international law. Allowing for wars of self-defense may be seen as a weakness of international law, but such wars are not a violation of that law.

Even in those instances in which war occurs and a nation, in the eyes of world opinion and perhaps in the opinion of an international tribunal such as the International Court of Justice, clearly violated international law, this is not evidence that international law does not exist, but only that the law has been violated. Any body of law incurs violations. A civil war is a violation of municipal law and order just as international wars might be considered violations of international law. No body of law would exist if the standard for its existence were that it not be violated. The issue is, however, how often a body of law can be violated before it is considered to be irrelevant.

The most valid point made by those who contend that international law is irrelevant is that international law has not been applied successfully in recent years to the major disputes occurring in the international system. The Cold War continues, the tensions in the Middle East remain, North-South conflict has escalated, and the twentieth century has produced two world wars. Certainly, the two world wars would have to be considered a breakdown in the regulatory functions of the international system, including international law; but for various reasons, conflicts in the forty years since World War II have not resulted in similar collapses. As was pointed out in the earlier chapter on the use of force, wars have been contained since 1945, and the major powers have not engaged directly in war with one another. The issue is, of course, to what extent international law has played a role in limiting conflict during that forty-year period. Even though nations are restrained in various ways in the use of national power, including the internal restraints of the domestic system and the external restraints of world opinion, international law is, in many instances, also a restraint.

Granting that international law has deficiencies, it may at least be credited with establishing the principles upon which the international system is based, and it has developed the procedures through which nations have contact with one another. Even when conflict is not resolved or even limited, international law is a factor in the attempt to resolve conflict in that it establishes the procedures through which communication can take place and the standards nations employ to deal with one another. In addition, even though international law has failed to resolve the major conflicts of the international system, it is useful in governing the day-to-day contacts between nations that might not escalate into serious conflicts even without international law but that must be dealt with, nevertheless.

In brief, international law, minimally speaking, is a constraint on the activities of nations in that nations usually find it more convenient to obey its principles than to ignore them. It provides the channels for diplomatic contact between nations, and it regularizes and provides standards for settling routine disputes between nations. Even though international law is violated, it is adhered to more often than is generally assumed. Other restraints on nations are also violated; world opinion is often defied by nations, and nations also resist attack even when the power relationship is not to their advantage. The ultimate test of international law must be whether nations behave as though it is law, and this they do much of the time.

THE DEVELOPMENT OF INTERNATIONAL LAW

If the principles of international law are validly described as a constraint on the activities of nations, and if those nations accept those principles as an obligation, then international law is misnamed. The word "international" suggests a law between and among nations, but if nations behave as if obligated to obey, then the law takes on a supranational character. Therefore, even though labeled as international or between nations, international law can be understood to transcend voluntary actions in compliance with international law. The degree to which international law has a supranational character is debatable, but the one body of principles and norms whose supranational character is virtually beyond question are those that regulate the European Community. The Commission of the European Community can make rules that are binding on members, and these rules are enforceable with sanctions imposed by a court set up for that purpose. The European Community is not a political union, however, and the rules are limited principally to economic matters.

The subjects of international law are primarily nation-states. Individuals are protected by this law only through their nationality. If the nation of which an individual is a citizen wishes to protect him or her or further his or her case against another country for a violation of international law, then the nations are the subjects, not the individual. Exceptions to the individual's not being a subject do exist, however. After World War II, war-crimes trials were held in both Germany and Japan in which the leaders of those countries were tried and several found guilty of waging an aggressive war and crimes against humanity. These proceedings operated on the assumption that individuals were responsible for acts they committed in the name of the state; therefore, individuals were made subjects of international law, at least in that instance and in regard to the sorts of crimes with which they were charged.

International organizations are also subjects of international law; but since the membership of IGOs is based on the nation-state, the nation remains the primary subject even when an international organization is involved. Further evidence of the centrality of the nation-state to international law is that international law developed parallel to the nation-state system; both began in the seventeenth century. MNCs, NGOs, insurgency groups, or national liberation movements are not subjects of international law.

While eventually international law developed from several sources, the earliest source was the writers and chroniclers of the law who were the first to note the development of general principles governing the behavior of nations. In a sense, to state these writers were a source of international law is to introduce a "chicken and egg" argument into the question of sources. Observable behavior among nations had to exist before the writers had something to write about; thus, behavior in support of the principles of international law preceded the writers as the original source of international law. Among the early writers on the subject, Hugo Grotius is considered to be the father of international law, publishing his comprehensive treatise on international law, *On the Law of War and Peace*, in 1628. Although he was not the first to write about international law, his treatise gained the respect of national leaders, and he was the first to write about international law in a comprehensive fashion.

Grotius also was among the first to write about the conflict among the early writers concerning whether international law was a God-given law of nature or a law originating with man. Grotius accepted both as sources. Emmerich Vattel and other eighteenth-century writers shared Grotius' view as to the mixed origin of the law. Still other authors, such as Samuel Pufendorf, were among the naturalists who viewed international law as emanating solely from the law of nature. From this perspective, man's task was to discover the law of nature rather than develop the law by observing the behavior of nations. The problem with the naturalist approach was that, since man had to discover what constituted the law of nature, no means existed for deciding when the right discovery had been made.

The other school of thought was that of the positivists, who, after the eighteenth century,

dominated thought concerning the source of international law and is the most generally accepted approach today. This school of thought presents the concept that international law results from nations' behavior and is thus found in the customary practice of nations and the treaties nations draw up among themselves. Early advocates of the positivist school were Cornelius von Bynkershoek and Richard Zouche. To them, commonly agreed-upon forms of behavior, not discoveries about natural law, were binding on nations. The seventeenth- and eighteenth-century writers of international law had considerable impact on the development of international law; as custom, and then treaties, became the principal sources of international law, writers became a less important source.

Yet another approach to international law is to be found in the realist school of international politics which accepts neither the natural law or positivist approach, but rather contends that nations tend to adapt a principle of law to fit their policy choices. Accordingly, policy comes first, then the decision as to how to defend that choice legally. This highly pragmatic approach to international law allows for considerable discretion in the manner in which international law is applied, essentially saying that international law is as flexible as are the policy choices available to a nation. "In the realist view of international relations, international law and organizations totally lack any intrinsic significance within the utilitarian calculus of international decision making" (Boyle, 1985, 7).

This view of international law follows logically from the tenets of the realist school, the main tenet of which is that policy should be judged as to its contribution to a nation's power, not its contribution to morality or law. This approach seems to reflect the tensions that existed among the major powers at the height of the Cold War. In the 1980s, the realist approach reflects the attitude of many of the Third World nations. Non–Western nations tend to see international law as a product of interaction among the powerful

Western nations; thus international law is what the powerful say it is. No nation embraces this approach without question, however, for to do so would mean that any international agreement would be obeyed only as long as the nations involved had the power to impose their will.

In the early positivist approach to international law, custom stood as the principal source of law. Custom as a source of international law develops when a practice is carried on long enough that nations feel a legal obligation to obey the principle. Custom can be discovered by observing the actions of nations, particularly when action is carried out as an obligation. This sort of discovery can be made by examining diplomatic correspondence and judicial decisions in which international law is applied, and clearly is a product of lengthy development.

In the nineteenth century, treaties replaced custom as the most important source of international law. As contact between nations increased, the need arose to develop international law more rapidly than allowed by the slow process of custom. Today, treaties are the main source of law and are, in turn, protected by international law under the long-established principle of *pacta sunt servanda*, which translates as "agreements must be obeyed." Treaties are binding only on the signing nations, and in those instances in which only a few countries are parties no new principle of international law develops. Multilateral treaties, however, which involve many nations, such as the nonproliferation treaty or the limited nuclear-test ban, are the nearest thing to international legislation found in the international system. Nations that do not sign a treaty that receives widespread adherence, while not bound by the treaty, are under considerable pressure to accept its provisions. Examples are the pressures placed on France and China to comply with the nonproliferation and test ban treaties, since neither signed either treaty. Neither country has violated the nonproliferation treaty, and France, because of this pressure, has not conducted tests above ground since 1972. In

1986, China announced that it, too, no longer would conduct above-ground tests. Thus, nonparties to a treaty can indirectly become adherents to it, and the principles expressed in a treaty can have general application.

International law also is thought of as having a source in the precedents of earlier decisions, although less a source, perhaps, than the specific application of general principles developed through custom and treaty. Precedents contribute to the development of international law in that, in applying general principles to specific situations, each decision provides the law with greater detail. Precedents are important also in that international law is not codified; therefore, previous decisions have importance for discovering how to apply the law. While several attempts have been made to codify international law, no generally accepted code exists. Treaties constitute the only source of law with specificity, while custom and general principles are more abstract. Decisions by international tribunals and national courts applying international law can help remove ambiguity from international law.

In summary, the sources of international law contribute to the development of the law in important respects. While no international legislative body exists, several recognized and accepted procedures have developed for the making of international law, particularly custom and treaties. The subjects to which international law are applied are primarily the nation-state and IGOs. International and national tribunals apply and interpret the law when a dispute arises. Among the shortcomings of international law is its uneven development. Some areas of the law, such as diplomatic privileges and immunities, are highly developed, whereas others, such as economic and trade relations, exhibit only rudimentary development. Since international law is based on the nation-state arrangement for organizing the international system, international law encourages and perpetuates that system. The international system supported by international law is seen by some as a means for strong nations to maintain their position of strength over the weak. Despite these challenges, the test of whether international law is important in the system is whether the nation-states think it is important. Since they do behave as though the law is important and as though it governs their behavior, then the law is indeed relevant to the study of international relations.

DIFFERING INTERPRETATIONS OF INTERNATIONAL LAW

The United States, like all nations, has its own approach to international law. Since international law has no universal code, the U.S. State Department periodically compiles a digest that reflects the U.S. position on the many issues of international law. This task of summarizing thousands of documents and situations falls to the editorship of a noted specialist on international law. The most recent editor was Margaret Whiteman, who completed the sixteen-volume *Digest of International Law*. Earlier digests were edited by Wharton, Moore, and Hackworth, all outstanding American experts on international law. This digest is not only important in identifying the U.S. position on issues of international law, but it also is indicative that the United States has its own perspective of the law distinctive from other nations.

Differences in interpretation between the United States and other Western nations do exist, but they are not fundamental. The U.S. and British interpretations are particularly close. Within the Western context, the principal differences exist between the Anglo-American view and the continental European view; these differences are limited to certain jurisdictional issues such as crimes aboard foreign flagships anchored in harbor and the proper location for trying a person captured in a country other than where he committed the crime with which he is being charged. These sorts of issues are not apt to become a major international problem.

While not exclusively the view of Western nations, the basis of Western international law is the survival of the nation-state system and the means by which to make it function more smoothly. Thus the concept of sovereignty, which views each nation as legally equal, is essential. To a skeptical non–Westerner, however, the principle of the equality of nations is applied by Western nations only among themselves, not worldwide. This certainly was the case during the colonial era and, as seen by many Third Worlders, is still true under the present conditions of economic neocolonialism. Sovereignty as an international concern includes noninterference in the internal affairs of another country. Again, this seems more a rule of behavior among the Western countries than between Western and non–Western nations.

The freedom of the seas also was important to the seafaring and trading nations that were, until the nineteenth century, mainly European. Today, for strategic as well as trade purposes, the freedom of the seas remains an important subject of international law and still is hotly debated, with the Western objective being to maximize the freedom of the high seas and allow the fewest restrictions possible on world shipping.

As one would expect, the Soviet view of international law is somewhat different from that found in the West. During the 1920s, one of the issues between the Soviet Union and the United States and Great Britain was the Soviet seizure, without compensation, of Western–owned property in the Soviet Union. The Western view of the law was that the Soviets could legally seize foreign-owned property only if they were willing to compensate for it. Since it was the property of capitalists, the Soviets rejected the concept of compensation for that which had been obtained through exploitation of the working class. In short, the Soviets viewed the Western perspective on international law as an extension of class conflict.

The Soviets also have their own view of the

circumstances under which treaties are binding. The Western practice governing treaties maintains that treaties are made between states, not between governments; thus, even if the government of a nation changes, all treaties remain in force. The Soviets argue that their revolution was so fundamental that not only did a new government came to power, a new state existed as well; thus, treaties entered into by the czarist government were not binding on the Soviet government. This postrevolutionary attitude and subsequent problems between the Western countries and the Soviet Union over the interpretation of various treaties have contributed to the impression that the Soviets are unreliable treaty partners. Since the end of World War II, the United States has charged the Soviet Union with repeated violations of the Yalta Agreements and, more recently, with failure to live up to provisions of the SALT I and II treaties.

A recent example of Soviet use of international law is the Brezhnev Doctrine. Although Western nations have intervened in the internal affairs of other nations from time to time, they profess to place no limits on the concept of a nation's sovereignty. The Soviets also support the concept of sovereignty, but they place limits on it in regard to other communist nations. The Brezhnev Doctrine states that the Soviet Union has the responsibility to intervene in a communist state that deviates beyond the limits of internal and international behavior acceptable to other communist states. The Soviet Union utilized the Brezhnev Doctrine to justify its invasion of Czechoslovakia in 1968, and if the Soviets had militarily intervened in Poland in 1980 and 1981, they doubtless would have done so under the Brezhnev Doctrine.

While the Soviets are critical of Western international law, seeing it as a reflection of the capitalist economic system, they generally obey the basic principles set forth by the West when dealing with the West. They are more apt to reject the Western view of international law when dealing with fellow communist nations, however.

Although important differences exist between Soviet and Western interpretations of international law, the sharpest critics of Western international law are the Third World countries. The basis of their criticism is that Western international law is used to justify the West's maintaining an economic advantage over the Third World. As the Third World sees the situation, this economic advantage has resulted in unfair economic relationships that are protected by international law. Third World countries argue that their sovereignty is violated when Western nations make Third World nations economically dependent upon Western capital, trade, and markets. The MNCs are seen as instruments used by Western nations to penetrate the economies of the Third World. The Western concept that the property of MNCs headquartered in Western nations cannot be nationalized without adequate compensation is challenged by the Third World on the grounds that this is simply a means of maintaining Western economic control of the Third World. The core demand that the Third World makes is that the world economic order be drastically reformed, as has been expressed repeatedly in the General Assembly, ECOSOC, and UNCTAD. The Declaration on the Establishment of a New International Economic Order and the Charter of Economic Rights and Duties of States, both passed by the General Assembly, are manifestations of these attitudes. To the Third World, such resolutions should be principles of international law.

The Third World shares with the Soviet Union the attitude that a new revolutionary government should not be obligated to meet the commitments and debts of previous governments. While the Third World has been successful in voicing its position, it has made little headway in convincing the Western nations that these changes in international law should be made. Despite these variations, whether a Western, Soviet, or Third World view of international law is expressed, many of the rules of international law are shared, at least in principle, by all perspectives.

EXAMPLES OF INTERNATIONAL LAW

The strongest and most highly developed aspects of international law are found in specific areas where detailed rules have developed permitting the avoidance of particular sorts of disputes. The following are examples.

Details of diplomatic privileges and immunities were discussed in an earlier chapter, but the general acceptance of rules protecting the diplomatic process are prime examples of a well-developed area of international law. Practices that first became international law through custom and then were reenforced by a 1961 treaty, the Vienna Convention on Diplomatic Relations, established rules designed to protect diplomats, their papers, and the buildings from which they operate, in order to allow representation between countries to be as unrestricted as possible.

The law protects the status of diplomats stationed in other countries not so much out of concern for the individuals involved as to maintain representation for purposes of communication. Not only is domestic law not to interfere with a diplomat's representative function, the host country has a special responsibility to protect the diplomat and the embassy from domestic groups that may wish to attack either. The host country can, under international law, be held responsible for a diplomat's death or for damage to embassy property if international standards for protection are not met. While several instances can be cited in which such protections have not been provided by the host government, the rules governing diplomatic privileges and immunities generally are adhered to with considerable care.

The rules protecting diplomatic privileges and immunities are complicated and complex, as is much international law, but the single-most blatant violation of those rules was the seizure of U.S. embassy personnel in Tehran in November 1979. Among the Western nations, the violation of the embassy grounds and the taking of diplomats as hostages was seen as a reversion to practices predating the development of international law. While the Iranian government initially insisted that the diplomats were seized by students, the Iranian government was held responsible for their continued captivity. In addition to negotiations with Iran and economic sanctions imposed on that country, the United States took its complaint to the International Court of Justice (ICJ). The Court agreed that Iran violated international law, but could not force Iran to comply with the decision. An indication that Iran had not totally rejected international law was Iran's argument that it was operating within its rights. Iran charged that the embassy had been headquarters for spying and for manipulating the domestic political system; thus, Iran argued, the seizure of the embassy staff was justifiable retaliation.

Another area of well-developed international law concerns the recognition of new states and governments. No matter how long a state delays its recognition of another state, international law has not been violated; nations are not legally obligated to recognize one another. The law is violated, however, if recognition is premature. An example of premature recognition would be recognizing a rebel force as the legitimate government before that force had adequately gained control of the country. French recognition of the United States during the Revolutionary War was considered premature by Great Britain, just as United States recognition of Panama in 1903 was considered premature by Colombia. American and Soviet recognition of Israel came shortly after Israel declared itself a state in 1948, but Great Britain withheld recognition for a time on the grounds that Israel had not yet met the standards of statehood.

A new state must be independent, have a

government with effective authority, and control territory, but the recognizing government makes the judgment as to when those conditions have been met. Recognition can be explicit through a formal act of recognition and the exchange of ambassadors, or it can be implied by entering into direct bilateral negotiations or signing a bilateral treaty. Recognition is not implied if two nations without recognition enter into the same multilateral treaty or belong to a multinational international organization. If doubt exists as to whether recognition was intended, the decision of the recognizing government is final.

International law makes a distinction between recognizing a state and recognizing a government. Once a state is recognized, that status is permanent; but if a new government comes into office by other than constitutionally prescribed means, the new government must be recognized. When countries break diplomatic relations, they continue to recognize each other as states, but their governments no longer have formal diplomatic contact. Perhaps the best-known recent example of delayed recognition among the major states occurred between the U.S. and the Chinese communist government. The United States recognized the state of China, but after the communists won the civil war in 1949, the U.S. continued to recognize the nationalist government on Taiwan as the legitimate government of China. The U.S. argued that the communist government was not prepared to meet China's international obligations, and was, as a result of a UN resolution, an aggressor nation in the Korean War and therefore not deserving of recognition.

Although Sino–American relations improved, beginning in 1971, the U.S. did not recognize the communist government until 1979. The U.S. relationship with Taiwan caused the delay and continued to be a problem after recognition, even though recognition of the Beijing government clarified the legal relationship between China and the United States. After 1979 the status of Taiwan posed interesting questions. China claimed Taiwan as a province and no major Western nation recognized Taiwan as a sovereign nation, but Taiwan nevertheless remained an active trading partner with the West. The United States unilaterally abrogated its mutual defense pact with Taiwan at the request of China, but continued to sell Taiwan arms. China objected to the U.S. continued support of what China considered a break-away province.

International law also has a number of rules concerning boundaries between countries. If a mountain range is designated the boundary, then the exact division of territory is the watershed of the range. If a river is the boundary, then the middle of the main channel is the boundary if the river is navigable; if it is not navigable, then the middle of the river is the boundary. The territory under a nation's control is not limited to land mass. A nation also controls the airspace over its territory, but not the space beyond the atmosphere. Perhaps the most rapidly expanding area of international law is that governing space, since space is considered to be international but had no need for rules of behavior until the comparatively recent exploration of space. Commercial air travel through the air space of another country is regulated by a treaty concluded in 1944, the Convention on International Civil Aviation, plus numerous bilateral agreements concerning landing rights and the discharging and taking on of passengers. The International Civil Aviation Organization (ICAO) takes responsibility for administering the multilateral treaty. Nations also control the waters that touch on their shores out to a certain number of miles. The distance to which a nation controls such waters has been in dispute for several years; of particular concern is the size of the economic zone beyond the territorial waters. This will be discussed in greater detail below in regard to the Law of the Sea Conference.

Nations also regulate the extradition of individuals who commit a crime in one country and are apprehended in another. Extradition once was governed primarily by customary law, but now is largely regulated by bilateral treaties. The basic rules of extradition applied in most treaties state that a person cannot be extradited for a political crime, that the requesting nation must present a *prima facie* case as to the person's guilt, and that the crime must be a crime in both countries.

The areas of international law just discussed are included under the law of peace; the international law of war can be equally complex. A number of treaties exist that regulate the conduct of war, including the Geneva Protocol of 1925 that outlaws poison gas and a 1929 treaty concerning the treatment of prisoners of war, which was updated in 1949 to include wartime treatment of civilians. The laws of war also cover the legal definition of war as to its beginning and conclusion, and the status and protections to be accorded neutral nations during wartime. Rules concerning wartime treatment of enemy aliens allow a country to intern the citizens of any country against which a declaration of war has been issued. During World War II, the United States interned all persons of Japanese ancestry, whether American citizens or aliens. While not violation of international law, the internment of Japanese–Americans has remained controversial as a violation of those persons' rights under the U.S. Constitution.

The areas of international law discussed here are only examples and certainly do not exhaust the extensive concepts, principles, and treaties that make up international law. They do serve to illustrate, however, that international law, often detailed, is a broader body of law than it is ordinarily considered to be. While international law is violated within the system, it is far more often obeyed, because the rules appear to most nations most of the time to be reasonable arrangements for managing conflict. An area of development of international law receiving considerable international attention in recent years is the system of rules concerning territorial waters and economic zones. Questions concerning these rules constituted the agenda of the Third United Nations Conference on Law of the Sea (UNCLOS)

that concluded its deliberations in 1982, a conference that illustrates the development of law through treaties and the problems involved in producing international legislation through multilateral treaties.

DEVELOPMENT OF THE LAW OF THE SEA

A logical approach to the need for negotiations between states is that bargaining is not necessary until significant conflict develops that requires resolution or management. Applying this approach to the United Nations–sponsored Law of the Sea Conference, the conflict that brought it into existence was the breakdown of customary practice as to what constituted territorial waters. Customary law dictated that territorial waters usually ended three miles from shore and roughly followed the coastline, with international waters existing beyond that point. Except for the innocent passage of foreign vessels through territorial waters, domestic law applied as it did on the land. In 1930, at one of several Hague conferences on international law, an attempt to convert that practice into treaty law failed. After World War II, as new nations came into the international system, claims to territorial waters extending out to fifteen miles were made, thus producing a need for agreement as to what constituted territorial waters. The International Law Commission of the United Nations, while setting no common claim for territorial waters, recommended that they not exceed twelve miles.

The troublesome aspect of expanding claims to territorial waters is that wider claims could result in closure of many international waterways. For example, the English Channel, which is twenty-one miles wide at its narrowest point, would cease to be an international waterway if both France and Great Britain claimed twelve-mile territorial waters. In an effort to resolve this problem, the United Nations, in 1958, sponsored the First Geneva Conference on the Law of the

Sea. No conclusive results were forthcoming. A second conference in 1960 foundered in conflicting claims to territorial waters and fisheries beyond those waters. By the 1970s, most countries claimed territorial waters between 3 and 12 miles, though Nigeria claimed 30 miles, Senegal 150 miles, and Brazil 200 miles. During the 1970s, nine other countries, all Latin American except Sierra Leone, extended their territorial waters to 200 miles (von Glahn, 1981, 357).

The issue of control of seas adjacent to a nation's land mass was complicated further when, after World War II, oil was discovered in the Gulf of Mexico beyond the territorial waters of the United States. Subsequently, the United States laid claim to the resources found on or beneath the ocean floor out to the edge of the continental shelf. The claim was rationalized on the grounds that the shelf was an extension of the continental land mass. In general, this claim extended about 200 miles offshore. Other countries laid similar claims, notably Mexico, since it too wanted its fair share of the oil found in the Gulf of Mexico. The west coast of South America, however, had little continental shelf; thus, countries along that coast could make no claims based on the continental-extension argument. In those waters, what was of value were fisheries. When those west-coast countries subsequently extended their economic zones, as opposed to territorial waters, to 200 miles, those fisheries were denied to other nations.

While the United States continued to claim only a 3–mile zone for territorial waters, in 1976 the U.S. did expand its economic zone from 12 miles beyond its territorial waters to 200 miles. This immediately caused problems with Cuba and Canada. An agreement with Cuba was signed in 1977, but the dispute with Canada continues along the west coast. Disputes with Canada off the east coast were settled in 1983. After the United States expanded its economic zone, a number of other countries also established 200–mile economic zones.

What had once been a relatively simple issue—whether territorial waters could be extended beyond three miles but not more than twelve—had become much more complicated. After the 1958 and 1960 failures, a third United Nations-sponsored conference was called in 1974 to sort out the broadening range of problems. After more than eight years of negotiation and with meetings in various cities throughout the world, a treaty was concluded in 1982. The least controversial aspect of the treaty pertained to the matter that had stimulated the negotiations in 1958—territorial waters and economic zones. The treaty allowed nations up to 12–mile territorial waters and a 200–mile exclusive economic zone (EEZ). Innocent passage through territorial waters and the EEZs was guaranteed by the treaty, and straits used as international waterways were to remain open and international. The controversial aspects of the treaty pertained to arrangements for mining seabed resources. The treaty, at the insistence of Third World nations and supported by the Soviet Union, set up the International Seabed Authority (ISBA). ISBA could negotiate contracts with a nation or firm that wanted to mine or explore for seabed re-sources and, in addition, could conduct its own exploration and mining through an agency called the Enterprise. A thirty-six-member Executive Council would set policy for the organization. Regardless of which agency or firm carried out the exploration, if an area of the seabed produced promising results, half the resources would be reserved for the Enterprise to develop and mine. ISBA could also demand the necessary technology from private firms to conduct mining and exploration through the Enterprise. The United States, as well as most of the other industrial nations, objected to the extent of international controls and limitations placed on private firms. While 117 countries signed the treaty immediately, forty-five others refused to sign, including most of the industrial West. In June 1982, the U.S. announced that it would not sign the treaty and in December indicated that it would not pay its share of ISBA's cost. The U.S., in particular, objected to the one-nation, one-vote method of representation on the Executive Council. The United States wanted representation based on financial contribution (Malone, 1984, 53). The U.S. arrangement would have been similar to representation within the World Bank, an arrangement to which the Third World had long objected. In March 1983, the United States announced its own 200–mile EEZ, independent of the Law of the Sea Treaty.

The treaty went into effect after sixty nations signed, but ISBA had no source of financing explorations or of obtaining the technology necessary to explore for or mine resources without the support of the Western countries. The Third World took the view that natural resources found on or under the world's land mass were already under Western control, directly or indirectly, and that the mineral resources of the seabed should be reserved for the development of the Third World nations. The Third World argued that the resources of the oceans were the "common heritage of mankind" and that control of those resources under an international authority was a major step in establishing the New International Economic Order (NIEO). Since the treaty took the form preferred by the Third World, the Third World appeared to have scored a significant victory; the victory was tarnished, however, since no means existed of financing the operation without the West. What began as a promising bargaining process eventually became a confrontation between the industrial West and the Third World. New international law had been created among the signatory nations, but those countries refusing to sign prevented the treaty from having general application and observance.

INTERNATIONAL LAW AND THE INTERNATIONAL COURT OF JUSTICE

The founding fathers of the United Nations planned the organization without arriving at a consensus as to what caused wars; therefore, they built into the organization various institutions each of which would contend with a possible cause of war. If colonialism caused war, then the Trusteeship Council would bring an end to colonialism; if agreement among the major powers could guarantee peace, then the Security Council would provide the framework in which such agreement could develop; if economic problems produced wars, then ECOSOC would be the forum for dealing with such problems. The International Court of Justice (ICJ) was the legal approach to peace. The goals of the court were ambitious, and the underlying assumption was that peace was possible if disputes were adjudicated and international law used to resolve conflict.

The League of Nations' court was the Permanent Court of Justice (PCJ); the structure and charge of the ICJ differed only in minor respects from that court. The close resemblance between the two courts reflected the general feeling that the PCJ had been a success; thus, little change was necessary when the ICJ was established. Of the fifteen judges on the ICJ, no more than one can be from any country, and five of the judgeships are reserved for the permanent members of the Security Council. Since 1971, when the communist government first represented China in the UN, China did not take its offered seat. China's refusal to participate in the court reflected its attitude toward the Western origins of international law. In 1984 China finally did take its position on the court, which probably indicated how much change in attitude toward the West has taken place in China under the Deng regime.

While the judges on the ICJ have, almost without exception, been important and highly respected jurists, the court generally has been considered a failure because of its inability to attract major international disputes for consideration. Before accepting that overall judgment, however, several aspects of the court should be examined, including the types and number of cases brought to the court, the problem of enforcing the court's decisions, and the impact of the qualifications the U.S. placed on its acceptance of the court's compulsory jurisdiction.

The principal reason the PCJ was considered a success was, in addition to the large number of cases it received, its successful adjudication of several cases among major European powers. In the eighteen years the court functioned, it handled sixty-five cases and advisory opinions. In its first thirty years, the ICJ handed down only fifty-seven decisions on cases and advisory opinions. (Agencies of the United Nations and members states can ask the court's advice about legal questions; thus, some of the decisions are advisory only.) While a number of important conflict situations came before the PCJ, the ICJ has had few. (Maechling, 1978–79, 101–103.) Admittedly, the PCJ had a significant advantage over the ICJ in that it functioned essentially within the Western context of nations. Third World countries played only a minor role in the League, and the Soviet Union was struggling for survival during much of the PCJ's history; thus, differing interpretations of international law were less evident in the PCJ than on the ICJ.

The ICJ applies principles of law drawn from those sources from which international law is drawn, such as treaties and custom, but the court, under its statute, must accept only its own decisions as binding on its actions. This narrow approach to the law has produced considerable uncertainty among nations as to what precedents and principles the court will apply to a case. (Maechling, 1978–79, 110–111). Also, since the Western view of international law is not the only interpretation to come before the Court, Soviet, Chinese, and Third World views of international law provide further complications. Normally eight or nine of the positions on the ICJ are occupied by judges from nations in disagreement with the Western view of international law.

Another problem the ICJ has encountered in attracting cases to the court pertains to the Optional Clause, which a nation must approve in order to come under the compulsory jurisdiction of the court. By being a member of the United Nations, a country also subscribes to the statute of the ICJ, but no country is under the compulsory jurisdiction of the court until it separately approves the Optional Clause. Less than one-third of the UN's members have accepted compulsory jurisdiction, and many of those members have attached crippling qualifications on their acceptance. Much of the blame for the limited acceptance of this clause has been placed on the United States. When the U.S. accepted compulsory jurisdiction in 1946, it attached the Connally Reservation, which allowed the U.S. the right to determine when a matter was a domestic matter outside the purview of the ICJ. Ordinarily, the decision as to what is domestic and what is international is left to the court. This reservation allowed the U.S. the means to withdraw a case from the court whenever it chose to label the case a matter of domestic jurisdiction.

The optional clause became an issue again when, in November 1984, the ICJ accepted Nicaragua's case in which the United States was charged with aggression because it had supported the Contras and had mined Nicaraguan waters. The United States withdrew its acceptance of the optional clause in this instance as of April 1986, on the grounds that it would be "contrary to our commitment to the principle of equal application of the law, and would endanger our vital national interests." The U.S. then refused to participate in the proceedings before the ICJ when the Nicaraguan charges were heard. In 1986 the court found the United States guilty of committing acts of war against Nicaragua. The United States did not boycott the court concerning other cases with which it was involved.

This was not the first time a country had refused to accept the jurisdiction of the court. Iceland rejected the ICJ's jurisdiction when Germany and Great Britain challenged Iceland's 50–mile exclusive fishing zone; France rejected the court's jurisdiction when Australia and New Zealand challenged French nuclear tests conducted in the Pacific; India rejected jurisdiction when Pakistan demanded the return of prisoners of war held by India following their 1971 war; and Turkey denied the court jurisdiction in the dispute about whether Greece or Turkey controlled the continental shelf off the Turkish coast.

In addition to jurisdictional issues, when the court receives a case it has had problems implementing its decisions. In the 1949 *Corfu Channel Case*, which concerned a dispute between Great Britain and Albania, both countries accepted the jurisdiction of the court, but Albania refused to accept the court's decision that went in favor of Great Britain. The case most damaging to the court's reputation, however, was the *South West Africa Case* handed down in 1966. Ethiopia and Liberia, the only black African countries belonging to both the League and the United Nations, brought a case against South Africa challenging that country's racist policies in Namibia, the League's old mandate. After years of deliberation, the court decided that Ethiopia and Liberia had no substantial interest in the situation and, thus, had no standing before the court. For the Third World, this case confirmed the Western orientation of the court, in which the Third World believed it could not receive a fair hearing.

The ICJ not only has not developed into a conflict-resolving institution, it also has been criticized for its protracted deliberations before handing down a decision; therefore, the ICJ has been by-passed in favor of direct negotiations. Furthermore, compulsory jurisdiction has been flawed by the many exceptions nations have included in their acceptance of the Optional Clause.

The principal failing of the court, however, is that it has been unable to bring the major disputes of the international system before it. In many respects, the problems of the ICJ are the problems of international law. While much of international law is developed in detail, some areas have shown little development. The development of new areas of international law, such as laws governing the environment, has been slow overall. When attempts have been made to develop new areas, such as law of the sea, the decisions produced have been unacceptable to the Western countries.

CONCLUSION

To some observers of the international system, the role of international law cannot be differentiated from that of international organizations. Although the resolutions passed by the UN have impact on the international system, the General Assembly's actions have not been accepted as making international law. The exception to this practice is the negotiation of a treaty within the framework of the UN, and even then the treaty is subject to the approval of each member's domestic political process. Until such time as a universal organization develops with the capability of making binding decisions in its own right, the roles of international organizations and international law in the international system will remain related, but distinct.

CHAPTER 18

Conclusions and Observations

Conflict and cooperation in the international system have been the central themes of this book. These activities take place among a variety of actors of which the nation-states are the most prominent; but international organizations, multinational corporations, liberation movements, and terrorist groups are also active internationally. The theme that the origins of conflict and cooperation eminate from domestic political systems has been returned to several times. In a strong sense, when nations conflict or cooperate it is the demands of their domestic political systems that bring this about. Whether conflicting or cooperating, nations act in an effort to fulfill as many of their interests as possible.

The power a nation exerts internationally in its attempts to fulfill its interests reflects the combination of its economic capabilities, geographic location, military might, national leadership, form of government, population base, and a variety of other national attributes. The success a nation has in converting those attributes into power depends on how other nations perceive those efforts. A nation's power is limited, however, and distributed among many interests, except in those rare instances in which one interest dominates a nation's activities. Nations usually achieve some of their interests but seldom obtain all that they strive for. Sometimes international diplomacy is a zero sum game with winners and losers, but most of the time it is a non–zero sum game in which nations perceive victories and defeats in marginal terms.

Three additional recurring themes have been the complexity of the international system, the lack of moral clarity concerning international events, and the constant change in the form and substance of the international system.

The international system's complexity often makes international events difficult to understand or explain. Any case study used to explain international behavior is multifaceted and thus can be used to illustrate different aspects of the international system. A particular event can perhaps at one point be used as a case study in international law, later as an example of a superpower in conflict with a smaller power, or even as an aspect of combating international terrorism. A case study of U.S.–Libyan relations in the late 1980s could be utilized in any one of these ways. This does not mean that confusion exists about what a particular case illustrates, but only that few cases have only one point to make.

An outcome of this complexity is difficulty in making moral judgments about international conflict. The problem of drawing moral conclusions becomes more complicated as an observer's knowledge of an event becomes more detailed; moral clarity diminishes as depth of knowledge increases. Events such as World War II, where moral certitude was seemingly with the democracies and the fascists were clearly in the wrong, becomes more difficult to explain when the Soviet invasions of Finland and Poland are included. Also, although the Soviet Union was an ally of the Western democracies, its regime was unmistakably totalitarian. The outcome of the war certainly lacks clarity. West Germany and Japan emerged from the ruins as economic giants despite their military defeat.

Issues less complex than a world war also can be perplexing. The U.S. raid on Libya in April 1986 was, to many people, a fully justifiable act of retaliation for terrorist acts supported and financed by the Libyan government. But to others, including some U.S. allies and many Third World countries, the attack was either the strong picking on the weak or the expansion of an international conflict beyond reasonable dimensions.

Some issues are easier to judge, however. Apartheid in South Africa has few defenders in any context, and even fewer would defend that policy on moral grounds. The actions of the Pol Pot government in Kampuchea found few supporters, but even in this instance most of the Third World and Western nations failed to support the Vietnamese invasion that overthrew that government. Genocide is morally reprehensible in the international community, but such practices in Uganda under Idi Amin or tribal warfare in Rwanda and Burundi in the early 1960s were not condemned by the United Nations or the international community in general.

In addition to its complexity and lack of moral clarity, the international system is undergoing constant change, most of which is difficult to predict. From the perspective of the mid–1970s, it would have been difficult to conclude that within a decade Egypt and Israel would sign a peace treaty and the United States would be supplying arms to both countries. Within the same time frame, it would have been equally difficult to predict the number of new democracies that have flowered in South America after decades of military governments in most of those countries. The debt crisis in the Third World seemed highly unlikely in the 1970s as the economies of

many Third World countries expanded and Western banks sought borrowers for the enormous deposits of OPEC petrodollars they held. The Falklands War came as a major surprise in that it fit none of the categories of post–World War II wars. Change in the international system may be inevitable, but the direction of change is difficult to forecast.

HOW STABLE IS THE SYSTEM?

Peaceful relationships among the nation-states are directly dependent upon the stability of the international system. International stability, however, can be viewed in different ways. From the perspective of actors and organization, the overall system is very stable. The nation-state as the basic unit of the system is well-established and shows no evidence of weakening as the means of organizing the world politically. The expansion of the nation-state system to include 150 percent more members than existed at the end of World War II is strong evidence of the the system's popularity. A nation's form of government may change from democratic to authoritarian and back again, but the nation-state continues on. Nor have any nation-states disappeared since World War II through annexation by neighboring countries, supporting the argument that the nation-state is widely protected by the rules of behavior of the international community. These observations do not mean that the nation-state system will endure indefinitely; the nation-state system itself is an innovation that is only three centuries old. Other systems existed before it; therefore, it is safe to assume that new systems will emerge. At the present, however, the end of the nation-state system is not imminent.

Not that the map of the world does not change; a discerning observer of international politics can usually determine a map's publication date (give or take a year) because so many changes take place. These changes, however, are usually the result of countries gaining their independence or changing their name rather than any fundamental change in the system.

Nor does the strength of the nation-state system mean that reorganization of the system is not possible. The Concert of Europe following the Napoleonic Era was a major shift in the manner in which the system was organized, just as was the development of bipolarity between the superpowers following World War II. The actors that make up the system are stable, but the manner in which those actors are organized may not be.

If stability is judged in terms of peaceful relations among the actors of the system, the system appears somewhat less stable. While conflict among nations may be normal and the use of violence in conflict more than an occasional occurrence, a troublesome problem for students of international relations is assessing whether the nation-state system is becoming more or less violent. Historically, except for brief periods, wars among the nation-states have been occurring at several locations at any given time. If the increase in the number of nation-states is taken into account, wars per nation-state have declined; but, system-wide, wars are occurring at about a normal rate.

Unquestionably, wars since World War II have produced fewer casualties and have had fewer participants than did wars earlier in the twentieth century. Also, the major powers have not engaged in wars against one another, although this development may be the result of nuclear weapons within the system rather than the evolution of a more stable system. A somewhat discouraging observation concerning the stability of relations between the superpowers is that the presence of mass-destruction weapons has made the international system appear more stable. The superpowers now indirectly engage in armed conflict with one another through surrogate nations.

A reflection of how secure nation-states feel themselves to be within the system is the amount of money spent on armaments and the maintenance of armed forces. Arms transfers to Third World countries may be declining, but the military establishments in Third World countries have not been reduced in size. Additionally, the budgets of the superpowers have increased in recent years, particularly the funds expended for military hardware. These aspects of international behavior, too, would indicate no particular trend concerning the stability of the international system.

REGULATING BEHAVIOR

Finding the means to regulate the behavior of other nations is illusive for even the superpowers. Economic sanctions or the threat of military sanctions have not been particularly effective instruments of foreign policy for actors in the international system, whether used by nation-states or international organizations. The superpowers have used military and economic sanctions to maintain the coalitions they head, but such sanctions have not been particularly effective outside those coalitions. The wars in Vietnam and Afghanistan are indications that the superpowers are willing to use military force, though its use has not led to conflict resolution. Nor has the use of economic sanctions had much effect on the behavior of nations. Economic sanctions to force policy changes in Rhodesia, the Soviet Union, Cuba, Nicaragua, and China have all failed.

The international system overall is not necessarily more regulated now than formerly. The UN's failure to develop regulatory powers does not mean that the system is less regulated than before, but only that conflict management by the UN did not develop as the organization's founders hoped. While political conflicts appear as unregulated as ever, economic issues are another matter. The development of interdependence among the Western industrial powers does indicate an important trend in the system—the development of more regulation of the international economy.

HOW ISSUES HAVE CHANGED

The nature of issues in the international system has become more and more economic in the years since the demise of traditional colonialism and the economic growth of the Western democracies. The extent to which this has occurred prompted two important themes of this book—growing interdependence within the industrial West and continued dependence of the Third World on the West. Interdependence is regarded as a positive development in that it led to control of economic conflict among the Western nations. No Western nation dares promote its interests too forcefully with other Western nations without jeopardizing its own economic wellbeing. The extent to which this is true indicates that relations among the Western nations are progressively controlled by interdependence, as opposed to the exercise of power.

Economic dependence of the Third World on the Western industrial nations has changed little, even though territories of the world that once were colonies are now independent nations. The growing demands of the Third World that it now be granted its economic independence are heard with increasing intensity. To the Third World, the growth of Western economies is seen as a threat, particularly when the so-called "developmental gap" between the industrial nations and the Third World continues to widen. While the Third World still holds the view that the primary cause of its dependence is Western policy, the Third World is increasingly seeing both Western and communist industrial nations as a common foe. The domestic organization of the industrial nations' economies is of less concern to much of the Third World than is the impact these economies have on the economies of the less–developed nations.

While the issues that divide the industrial nations and the Third World are many, the one issue that is bringing those problems to an open confrontation is the Third World debt owed Western lending agencies. The Western expectation, when making the loans, was that the economies of the Third World would grow rapidly and the loans would not present an ongoing problem. The world's economy, especially that of the Third World, slowed so dramatically in the early 1980s that many nations are in a nearly continuous state of economic crisis. The West demands payments and is increasingly reluctant to make new loans; at the same time, heavy-debtor nations want lower interest rates, longer repayment periods, and, in some instances, cancellation of loans. The debt issue, while not necessarily the most serious economic issue in the Third World, is surely the most immediate.

Another issue that has arisen in North-South conflict is whether the world's natural resources are plentiful enough to allow the development of additional advanced industrial nations. If resources are not sufficient to develop all nations, then how many can be developed with present resources? Which nations will be left out of the development process? If left out, will they die economically, thus creating a permanent two-class economic arrangement? This latter question would suggest that some nations are beyond hope, and that any efforts by industrial nations to aid the Third World should be done on a selective basis depending on the possibilities of development. The distribution of resources was perhaps the primary issue of the law-of-the-sea negotiations. If the seabed proves to be a major source of raw materials, the Third World wanted to guarantee that those resources would go toward their development and not simply to further expand the economies of the advanced nations.

NEW KINDS OF ISSUES

Although the issues and conflicts that exist at any given time do, of course, differ to some extent from those arising during any other time period, recent years have produced a new category of conflict. This sort of conflict is less the result of nations' having differing objectives for their foreign policies than the result of changing conditions in the international system. These issues are generally identified as Third World problems, but they have little to do with whether the Third World has its political independence. For example, the population problem is an issue that most likely would have been of great concern internationally whether the colonial empires broke up or not; there is little reason to believe that population increase is related in any significant way to the expansion of the nation-state system since World War II. Food shortages fall in the same category. The droughts that have occurred in Africa would have presented the Western world with a major relief problem regardless of the political status of the Third World countries involved.

Environmental issues are a similar sort of problem but present a significant difference from the population and food problems in that the Western nations are held responsible by the Third World. To the Third World, environmental damage is primarily the result of the careless industrialization of Western nations. Environmental issues, whether acid rain or nuclear fallout, would have occurred, however, whether or not the Third World was independent. These issues—food shortages, population control, and environmental damage—are long-term problems and are likely to be with the international system for many years. North and South are in conflict over how the problems are to be dealt with.

FUTURE OF EAST–WEST RELATIONS

The relationship between the Soviet Union and the United States has, in one sense, remained unchanged since the end of World War II; both countries have relied upon deterrence as their means of avoiding a major war. Even though the Soviet Union did not develop an atomic bomb until 1949, it used its superiority in conventional forces to offset the U.S. atomic bombs. The present issue in East–West relations is whether deterrence will continue as the basis for avoiding war between the superpowers or whether a new arrangement will develop. The Reagan administration is attempting to develop a defense system that would remove deterrence as the basis of East–West relations, but it is still to be seen if such a system is technologically possible or whether the American political system is willing to spend the money to build such a system.

An alternative to either deterrence or a strategic defense system is an arms-reduction agreement between the superpowers that would supplant both policies. Short of an arms agreement that produced near-disarmament of nuclear weapons, deterrence would continue to be an aspect of U.S.–Soviet relations, however. Regardless of the level of arms accorded each superpower in an arms agreement, deterrence will survive as long as both nations have a second-strike force capable of destroying the other. As the international system is presently organized, deterrence remains the middle-ground policy between disarmament and a strategic defense system.

CONFLICT AND PERCEPTION

An additional theme that has been emphasized

in this book has been the role of perception. Each nation develops its own perception of how it fits into the international system and, based on that perception, how it will go about promoting its interests. Nations, in turn, interact with one another based on how they perceive each other. National perceptions are developed by a nation's decision makers; therefore, perceptions are the result of both interactions among the nation–states and the actions of the domestic systems of the many nation–states. The manner in which perceptions develop provides the basis of a nation's foreign policy and, to a great extent, serves as the basis of nationalism.

All conflict cannot be attributed to different perceptions, however. Nations have differing interests and even when perceptions are accurately assessed by all parties, the conflict may remain. Ideological or nationalistic differences also can be understood by all, yet the conflict remains unresolved. The diplomatic method may be effective in communicating the interests of all parties accurately, while the result is that the nature of the conflict is merely better understood. The hoped-for goal of the international system, therefore, is to resolve conflict when it can, or at least *manage* conflict despite perception, nationalism, or ideology.

References

Chapter 1.

Alger, Chadwick F., "Comparison of Intranational and International Politics," *American Political Science Review*, Vol. 57, June, 1963.

Banks, Michael, ed., *Conflict in World Society* (New York: St. Martin's Press, 1984).

Boulding, Kenneth E., *Conflict and Defense: A General Theory* (New York: Harper and Row, 1962).

Butterworth, Robert Lyle, *Managing Interstate Conflict, 1945–74: Data with Synopses* (Pittsburgh: University Center for International Studies, University of Pittsburgh, 1976).

Chouchri, Nazli, and North, Robert C. *Nations in Conflict* (San Francisco: W.H.Freeman, 1975).

Fox, William T.R., "World Politics as Conflict Resolution," in Matthews, Robert O; Rubinoff, Arthur G.; and Stein, Janice Gross; eds., *International Conflict and Conflict Management* (Scarborough, Ontario: Prentice–Hall of Canada, 1984).

Franck, Thomas M., and Weisband, Edward, "Panama Paralysis," *Foreign Policy*, Vol. 21, Winter 1975–76.

Grieves, Forest L., *Conflict and Order* (Boston: Houghton Mifflin, 1977).

Holsti, K.J., "Resolving International Conflicts," *Journal of Conflict Resolution*, Vol. 10, September 1966.

Jervis, Robert, *Perception and Misperception in World Politics* (Princeton, N.J.: Princeton University Press, 1976).

Kegley, Charles W., Jr.; Richardson, Neil R.; and Richter, Gunter; "Conflict at Home and Abroad: An Empirical Extension," *Journal of Politics*, Vol. 40, August 1978.

Masters, Roger D., "World Politics as a Primitive Political System," in Rosenau, James N., ed., *International Politics and Foreign Policy* (New York: Free Press, 1969).

Schelling, Thomas C., *The Strategy of Conflict* (Cambridge, Mass.: Harvard University Press, 1960).

Singer, J. David, "The Level of Analysis Problem in International Relations," in Knorr, Klaus, and Verba, Sidney, eds., *The International System* (Princeton, N.J.: Princeton University Press, 1961).

Snyder, Glenn H. and Diesing, Paul, *Conflict Among Nations* (Princeton, N.J.: Princeton University Press, 1977).

Wilkenfeld, Jonathan, ed., *Conflict Behavior and Linkage Politics* (New York: McKay, 1973).

Chapter 2.

Barnet, Richard J., and Muller, Ronald E., *Global Reach: The Power of the Multinational Corporations* (New York: Simon and Schuster, 1974).

Blake, David H., and Walters, Robert S., *The Politics of Global Economic Relations* (Englewood Cliffs, N.J.: Prentice–Hall, 1976).

Deutsch, Karl W., *Nationalism and Social Communication. A Inquiry into the Foundations of Nationality* (New York: Wiley, 1953).

Emerson, Rupert, *From Empire to Nation* (Cambridge, Mass.: Harvard University Press, 1960).

Feld, Werner J., and Jordan, Robert S., *International Organizations: A Comparative Approach* (New York: Praeger, 1983).

Hoffmann, Stanley, *Gulliver's Troubles, or Setting of American Foreign Policy* (New York: McGraw–Hill, 1968).

Huntington, Samuel, "Transnational Organizations in World Politics," *World Politics*, Vol. 25, April 1973.

Jacobson, Harold K., *Networks of Interdependence: International Organizations and the Global Political System* (New York: Alfred A. Knopf, 1979).

Keohane, Robert O., and Nye, Joseph S., Jr., eds. *Transnational Relations and World Politics* (Cambridge, Mass.: Harvard University Press, 1972).

Papp, Daniel S., *Contemporary International Relations: Frameworks for Understanding* (New York: Macmillan, 1984).

Rejal, Mostafa, and Enloe, Cynthia H., "Nation–States and State–Nations," *International Studies Quarterly*, Vol. 13, June 1969.

Rosenau, James N., "Pre–Theories and Theories of Foreign Policy," in Farrell, R. Robert, ed., *Approaches* to Comparative and International Politics (Evanston, Ill.: Northwestern University Press, 1966).

Snyder, Louis, The Meaning of Nationalism (New Brunswick, N.J.: Rutgers University Press, 1954).

Spiegel, Steven L., Dominance and Diversity (Boston: Little, Brown, 1972).

Taylor, Phillip, Nonstate Actors in International Politics: From Transregional to Substate Organizations (Boulder, Colo.: Westview Press, 1984).

Chapter 3.

Bachrach, Peter and Baratz, Morton S., "Decisions and Non–Decisions: An Analytical Framework," American Political Science Review, Vol. 57, September 1963.

Baldwin, David, "Power Analysis and World Politics," World Politics, Vol. 33, January 1979.

Brown, Seyom, "The Changing Essence of Power," Foreign Affairs, Vol. 51, January 1973.

Brzezinski, Zbigniew, "How the Cold War Was Played," Foreign Affairs, Vol. 51, October 1972.

Bundy, William P., "Elements of National Power," Foreign Affairs, Vol. 56, October 1977.

Claude, Inis L., Jr., Power and International Relations (New York: Random House, 1962).

Cline, Ray S., World Power Trends and US Foreign Policy for the 1980s (Boulder, Colo.: Westview Press, 1980).

Dahl, Robert A., Modern Political Analysis (Englewood Cliffs, N.J.: Prentice–Hall, 1963).

Deutsch, Karl W., Nationalism and Social Communication: An Inquiry into the Foundations of Nationality (New York: Wiley, 1953).

Hoffmann, Stanley, "Notes on the Elusiveness of Modern Power," International Journal, Vol. 30, Spring 1975.

Keohane, Robert O., and Nye, Joseph S., Power and Interdependence: World Politics in Transition (Boston: Little, Brown, 1977).

Knorr, Klaus, Military Power and Potential (Lexington, Mass.: Heath, 1970).

Organski, A.F.K., and Kugler, Jacek, The War Ledger, (Chicago: University of Chicago Press, 1980).

Riker, William H., "Some Ambiguities in the Notion of Power," American Political Science Review, Vol. 58, June 1964.

Rosenau, James N., "Capabilities and Control in an Interdependent World," International Security, 1, Fall 1976.

Singer, David, "Inter–Nation Influence: A Formal Model," American Political Science Review, Vol. 57, June 1963.

Waltz, Kenneth N., "International Structure, National Force, and Balance of World Power," Journal of International Affairs, Vol. 21, 1967.

Chapter 4.

Claude, Inis L., Jr., Power and International Relations (New York: Random House, 1962).

Doren, Charles F., and Parsons, Wes, "War and the Cycle of Relative Power," American Political Science Review, Vol. 74, December 1980.

Duetsch, Karl W., and Singer, J. David, "Multipolar Power Systems and International Stability," World Politics, Vol. 16, April 1964.

Garnham, David, "Power Parity and Lethal International Violence, 1969–1973," Journal of Conflict Resolution, Vol. 20, September 1976.

Haas, Ernst B., "The Balance of Power: Prescription, Concept, or Propaganda," World Politics, Vol. 5, July 1953.

Hanrieder, Wolfram F., "The International System: Bipolar or Multibloc?," Journal of Conflict Resolution, Vol. 9, September 1965.

Hoffmann, Stanley H., "International Systems and International Law," World Politics, Vol. 14, October 1961.

Kaplan, Morton A., "Balance of Power, Bipolarity and Other Models of International Systems," American Political Science Review, Vol. 51, September 1957.

_____, and Katzenbach, Nicholas de B., The Political Foundations of International Law (New York: John Wiley and Sons, 1961).

Liska, George, Nations in Alliance (Baltimore: Johns Hopkins Press, 1962).

Masters, Roger, "A Multi–Bloc Model of the International System," American Political Science Review, Vol. 55, December 1961.

Morgenthau, Hans J., Politics Among Nations, 3rd ed., (New York: Knopf, 1956).

Nogee, Joseph L., "Polarity: An Ambiguous Concept," Orbis, 18, Winter, 1975.

Organski, A.F.K., World Politics, 2nd ed. (New York: Knopf, 1968).

Rosecrance, Richard N., Action and Reaction in World Politics (Boston: Little, Brown, 1963).

Rummel, R.L., The Dimensions of Nations (Beverly Hills, Calif.: Sage, 1972).

Siverson, Randolph M. and Sullivan, Michael P., "The Distribution of Power and the Onset of War," Journal of Conflict Resolution, Vol. 27, September, 1983.

Waltz, Kenneth N., The Theory of International Politics (Reading, Mass.: Addison–Wesley Publishing Co., 1979).

Chapter 5.

Aspaturian, Vernon V., ed., *Process and Power in Soviet Foreign Policy* (Boston: Little, Brown, 1971).

Barnet, Richard J., *The Giants: Russia and America* (New York: Simon & Schuster, 1977).

Brzezinski, Zbigniew, and Huntington, Samuel P., *Political Power: USA/USSR* (New York: Viking, 1964).

Graebner, Norman A., *Cold War Diplomacy 1945-1960*, (Princeton, N.J.: D. Van Nostrand, 1962).

Kennan, George F. (X), "The Sources of Soviet Conduct," *Foreign Affairs* 25, July 1947.

——————, *Russia and the West Under Lenin and Stalin* (Boston: Little, Brown, 1961).

Nogee, Joseph L., and Donaldson, Robert H., *Soviet Foreign Policy Since World War II* (New York: Pergamon Press, 1981).

Nye, Joseph S., Jr., ed., *The Making of America's Soviet Policy* (New York: Oxford University Press, 1983).

Rubinstein, Alvin, Z., *Soviet Foreign Policy since World War II: Imperial and Global* (Cambridge: Winthrop, 1981).

Schweitzer, Arthur., "Ideological Strategy," *Western Political Quarterly*, Vol. 15, March 1962.

Spanier, John, *American Foreign Policy since World War II* (New York: Holt, Rinehart and Winston, 1977).

Ulam, Adam B., *Dangerous Relations: The Soviet Union In World Politics, 1970–1982* (New York: Oxford University Press, 1983).

Weisband, Edward, *The Ideology of American Foreign Policy* (Beverly Hills, Calif.: Sage Publications, 1973).

Welch, William A., *American Images of Soviet Foreign Policy* (New Haven, Conn.: Yale University Press, 1970).

Chapter 6.

Arms Control and Disarmament Agency, *World Expenditures and Arms Transfers 1985* (Washington, D.C.: Arms Control and Disarmament Agency, 1985).

Bhagwati, Jagish N., Ruggie, John G., eds., *Power, Passions and Purpose: Prospects for North–South Negotiations* (Cambridge, Mass.: MIT Press, 1984).

Brown, Lester, *World Without Borders* (New York: Vantage Books, 1973).

Caporaso, James A., "Dependence, Dependency, and Power in the Global System," *International Organization*, Vol. 32, Winter 1978.

Cardoso, Fernando Henrique, and Faletto, Enzo *Dependency and Development in Latin America* (Berkeley and Los Angeles: University of California Press, 1978).

Cassen, Robert, Jolly, Richard, Sewell, John W., and Woods, Robert, eds., *Rich Country Interests and Third World Development* (London: Croom Helm for the Overseas Development Council, 1982).

Cline, William R., *International Debt and the Stability of the World Economy* (Washington, D.C.: Institute for International Economics, 1983).

Donaldson, Robert H., *The Soviet Union in the Third World: Successes and Failures* (Boulder, Colo.: Westview Press, 1981).

Gosovic, Branislav, *UNCTAD, Conflict and Compromise: The Third World's Quest for an Equitable World Economic Order Through the United Nations* (Lieden, Netherlands: A.W. Sijthoff, 1972).

Hart, Jeffrey A., *The New International Economic Order: Conflict and Co-operation in North–South Economic Relations 1974-77* (New York: St. Martin's Press, 1983).

Hobson, John, *Imperialism: A Study* (London: Allen and Unwin, 1902).

Keohane, Robert O., *Beyond Hegemony: Co-operation and Discord in the World Economy* (Princeton, N.J.: Princeton University Press, 1984).

Lenin, V.I., *Imperialism: The Highest Stage of Imperialism* (New York: International Publishers, 1939, first published in 1917).

McNamara, Robert S., "Time Bomb or Myth: The Population Problem," *Foreign Affairs*, Vol. 62, Summer 1984.

Murphy, Craig N., *The Emergence of the New International Economic Order* (Boulder, Colo.: Westview Press, 1984).

Organization for Economic Cooperation and Development, *Development Co-operation 1983* (Paris: OECD, 1983).

Snyder, Louis L. ed. *The Imperialism Reader*, (Princeton: Van Nostrand, 1962).

Spero, Joan Edelman, *The Politics of International Economic Relations*, 3rd ed. (New York: St. Martin's Press, 1985).

World Bank, *World Development Report, 1984* (Washington, D.C.: Internatinal Bank for Reconstruction and Development, 1984).

Chapter 7.

Bergsten, C. Fred, "The Cost of Reaganomics," *Foreign Policy*, Vol. 44, Fall 1981.

Blake, David H., and Walters, Robert S., *The Politics of Global Economic Relations* (Englewood Cliffs, N.J.:

Prentice–Hall, 1983).

DeMenil, George, and Solomon, Anthony M., *Economic Summitry* (New York: Council on Foreign Relations, 1983).

Destler, I.M., *Making Foreign Economic Policy* (Washington, D.C.: The Brookings Institution, 1980).

Luard, Evan, *The Management of the World Economy* (New York: St. Martin's Press, 1983).

Keohane, Robert O., *Beyond Hegemony: Co-operation and Discord in the World Political Economy* (Princeton, N.J.: Princeton University Press, 1984).

_____, and Nye, Joseph S., *Power and Interdependence* (Boston: Little, Brown, 1977).

Kindleberger, Charles F., "Dominance and Leadership in the International Economy," *International Studies Quarterly*, Vol. 25, June 1981.

Krasner, Stephen D., "The Tokyo Round: Particularistic Interests and Prospects for Stability in the Global Trading System," *International Studies Quartely*, Vol. 23, December 1979.

Ostry, Sylvia, "The World Ecomomy in 1983: Marking Time," *Foreign Affairs*, Vol. 62, Special Issue 1983.

Reich, Robert B., "Beyond Free Trade," *Foreign Affairs*, Vol. 61, Spring 1983.

Spero, Joan Edelman, *The Politics of International Economic Relations*, 3rd ed. (New York: St. Martin's Press, 1985).

Vernon, Raymond, "International Trade Policy in the 1980s: Prospects and Problems," *International Studies Quarterly*, Vol. 26, December 1982.

Wallerstein, Immanuel, "Friends and Foes," *Foreign Policy*, Vol. 40, Fall 1980.

Chapter 8.

Boulding, Kenneth, *The Image* (Ann Arbor: University of Michigan Press, 1956).

George, Alexander, *Presidential Decision-Making in Foreign Policy: The Effective Use of Information and Advice* (Boulder, Colo.: Westview Press, 1980).

Holsti, Ole R., "The Belief System and National Images: A Case Study," *Journal of Conflict Resolution*, Vol. 6, September 1962.

Janis, Irving L., and Mann, Leon, *Decision Making: A Psychological Analysis of Conflict, Choice, and Commitment* (New York: Free Press, 1977).

Jervis, Robert, *The Logic of Images in International Relations* (Princeton, N.J.: Princeton University Press, 1971).

_____, *Perception and Misperception in International Politics* (Princeton, N.J.: Princeton University Press, 1976).

Kelman, Herbert, *International Behavior: A Psychological Analysis* (New York: Holt, Rinehart, and Winston, 1965).

Lindblom, Charles E., *The Policy–Making Process* (Englewood Cliffs, N.J.: Prentice–Hall, 1968).

Rapaport, Anatol, *The Big Two: Soviet–American Perceptions of Foreign Policy* (New York: Pegasus, 1971).

Chapter 9.

Burton, John W., "The Resolution of Conflict," *International Studies Quarterly*, Vol. 16, March 1972.

Ikle, Fred C., *How Nations Negotiate* (New York: Harper and Row, 1964).

Lall, Arthur S., *Modern International Negotiation: Principles and Practice* (New York: Columbia University Press, 1966).

Lockhart, Charles, *Bargaining in International Conflicts* (New York: Columbia University Press, 1979).

Macomber, William, *The Angels Game: A Handbook of Modern Diplomacy* (New York: Stein and Day, 1975).

Mayer, Martin, *The Diplomats* (New York: Doubleday, 1983).

McCamy, James L., *Conduct of the New Diplomacy* (New York: Harper and Row, 1964).

Nicolson, Harold, *The Evolution of the Diplomatic Method* (New York: Macmillan, 1955).

O'Neal, John R., *Foreign Policy Making in Times of Crisis* (Columbus: Ohio University Press, 1982).

Pillar, Paul R., *Negotiating Peace: War Termination as a Bargaining Process* (Princeton, N.J.: Princeton University Press, 1983).

Poullada, Leon P., "Diplomacy: The Missing Link in the Study of International Politics," in McLellan, D.S., Olsen, W.C., and Sondermann, F.A. eds., *The Theory and Practice of International Relations* (Englewood Cliffs, N.J.: Prentice–Hall, 1974).

Thayer, Charles W., *Diplomat* (New York: Harper, 1959).

Watson, Adam, *Diplomacy* (New York: McGraw–Hill New Press, 1982).

Webster, Charles Kingsley, *Art and Practice of Diplomacy* (New York: Barnes and Noble, 1962).

Wood, John R., and Serrs, Jean, *Diplomatic Ceremonial and Protocol* (New York: Columbia University Press, 1970).

Zartman, I. William, "The Political Analysis of Negotiation: How Who Gets What and When," *World*

Politics, Vol. 26, April 1974.

_____, and Berman, Maureen, *The Practical Negotiator* (New Haven, Conn.: Yale University Press, 1982).

Chapter 10.

Betts, Richard K., *Surprise Attack: Lessons for Defense Planning* (Washington, D.C.: The Brookings Institution, 1982).

_____, "Surprise Despite Warning: Why Sudden Attacks Succeed," *Political Science Quarterly*, Vol. 95, Winter 1980–81.

Brecher, Michael, and Wilkenfeld, Jonathan, "Crises in World Politics," *World Politics* Vol. 34, April 1982.

Gelb, Leslie H., with Betts, Richard K., *The Irony of Vietnam: The System Worked* (Washington, D.C.: The Brookings Institution, 1979).

Gochman, Charles S., and Maoz, Zeev, "Militarized Interstate Disputes, 1816–1976: Procedures, Patterns, and Insights," *Journal of Conflict Resolution*, 28, December 1984.

Handel, Michael I., *The Diplomacy of Surprise: Hitler, Nixon and Sadat* (Cambridge, Mass.: Center for International Affairs, Harvard University, 1981).

Janis, Irving L., *Groupthink: Psychological Studies of Policy Decisions and Fiascoes*, 2nd ed. (Boston: Houghton Mifflin, 1982).

Lebow, Richard Ned, *Between Peace and War: The Nature of International Crisis* (Baltimore: Johns Hopkins University Press, 1981).

Morrow, James D., "A Spatial Model of International Conflict," *American Political Science Review*, Vol. 80, December 1986.

Williams, Phil, *Crisis Management* (New York: Wiley, 1976).

Young, Oran, *The Politics of Force* (Princeton, N.J.: Princeton University Press, 1968).

Chapter 11.

Alexander, Yonah and Meyers, Kenneth A., eds., *Terrorism in Europe* (New York: St. Martin's Press, 1982).

Art, Robert J., and Waltz, Kenneth N., eds., *The Use of Force* (Boston: Little, Brown, 1971).

Atlas of NATO, United States Department of State, Bureau of Public Affairs, Washington, D.C., February, 1985.

Beer, Francis A., *Peace Against War: The Ecology of International Violence* (San Francisco: W.H. Freeman, 1981).

Blechman, Barry M., and Kaplan, Stephen S., *Force Without War: U.S. Armed Forces as a Political Instrument* (Washington, D.C.: Brooklings Institution, 1978).

Chan, Steve, "Mirror, Mirror on the Wall: Are the Freer Countries More Pacific?," *Journal of Conflict Resolution*, Vol. 27, December, 1984.

Clausewitz, Carl von, *On War* (Princeton, N.J.: Princeton University Press, 1976).

Grieves, Forest L., *Conflict and Order* (Boston: Houghton Mifflin, 1977).

Howard, Michael E., *The Causes of War* (Cambridge, Mass.: Harvard University Press, 1983).

Huntington, Samuel P., ed., *Changing Patterns of Military Politics* (New York: The Free Press of Glencoe, 1962.

Livingstone, Neil C., *The War Against Terrorism* (Lexington, Mass.: Lexington Books, 1982).

Mills, C. Wright, *The Causes of World War III* (New York: Ballantine, 1958).

North, Robert, Hoch, Howard, Jr., and Zinnes, Dina, "The Integrative Functions of Conflict," *Journal of Conflict Resolution*, Vol. 3, September 1960.

Organski, A.F.K., and Kugler, Jacek, *The War Ledger* (Chicago: University of Chicago Press, 1980).

Papp, Daniel S., *Contemporary International Relations: Frameworks for Understanding* (New York: Macmillan, 1984).

Richardson, Lewis, *Arms and Insecurity* (Pittsburgh: Boxwood, 1960).

Rummel, R.J., "Libertarianism and International Violence," *Journal of Conflict Resolution*, Vol. 27, March 1983.

_____, "Testing Some Possible Predictors of Conflict Behavior Within and Between Nations," *Peace Research Society Papers* Vol. 3, 1963.

Russett, Bruce M., and Monsen, R. Joseph, "Bureaucracy and Polyarchy as Predictors of Performance: a Cross–national Examination," *Comparative Political Studies*, Vol. 8, April 1975.

Sivard, Ruth Leger, *World Military and Social Expenditures 1979* (and *1983*), (Leesburg, Va.: World Priorities, 1979, 1983).

Small, Melvin, and Singer, J. David, *Resort to Arms: International and Civil Wars, 1816–1980* (Beverly Hills, Calif.: Sage, 1982).

Tanter, Raymond, "Dimensions of Conflict Behavior Within and Between Nations, 1958–1960," *Journal of*

Conflict Resolution Vol. 10, March 1966.

Weede, Erich, "Democracy and War Involvement," *Journal of Conflict Resolution,* Vol. 28, December 1984.

Wilkenfeld, Jonathan, "Domestic and Foreign Conflict Behavior of Nations," *Journal of Peace Research,* Vol. 5, No. 1, 1968.

Wright, Quincy, *A Study of War* (Chicago: University of Chicago Press, 1942).

Chapter 12.

Baldwin, David A., *Economic Statecraft* (Princeton, N.J.: Princeton University Press, 1985).

Bergsten, C. Fred, *The Future of International Economic Order* (Lexington, Mass.: Heath, 1973).

Bertsch, Gary K., and McIntyre, John R., eds., *National Security and Technology Transfer: The Strategic Dimensions of East–West Trade* (Boulder, Colo.: Westview Press, 1983).

Cabwell, Robert, "Economics Sanctions and Iran," *Foreign Affairs,* Vol. 60, Winter 1981-82.

Caldwell, Lawrence T., and Diebold, William, Jr., *Soviet–American Relations in the 1980s: Superpower Politics and East–West Trade* (New York: McGraw–Hill, 1981).

Cline, William R., *International Debt and the Stability of the World Economy* (Washington, D.C.: Institute for International Economics, 1983).

Cottam, Richard; Schoenbaum, David, Shahram Chubin, Moran, Theodore H., and Falk, Richard A., "The United States and Iran's Revolution," *Foreign Policy* Vol. 34, Spring 1979.

Doxey, Margaret P., *Economic Sanctions and International Enforcement* (New York: Oxford University Press, 1980).

Goldman, Marshall I., *Detente and Dollars: Doing Business with the Soviets* (New York: Basic Books, 1975).

Krasner, Stephen D., "The Tokyo Round: Particularistic Interests and Prospects for Stability in the Global Trading System," *International Studies Quarterly,* Vol. 23, December 1979.

Nincic, Miroslav, and Wallensteen, Peter, eds., *Dilemmas of Economic Coercion: Sanctions in World Politics* (New York: Praeger Publishers, 1983).

Olson, Richard S., "Economic Coercion in World Politics: With a Focus on North-South Relations," *World Politics,* Vol. 31, July 1979.

Paarlberg, Robert L., "Lessons of the Grain Embargo," *Foreign Affairs,* Vol. 59, Fall 1980.

Spero, Joan Edelman, *The Politics of International Economic Relations,* 3rd ed. (New York: St. Martin's Press, 1985).

von Amerongen, Otto Wolff, "Commentary: Economic Sanctions as a Foreign Policy Tool," *International Security,* Vol. 5, Fall 1980.

Weintraub, Sidney, ed., *Economic Coercion and U.S. Foreign Policy* (Boulder, Colo.: Westview Press, 1982).

Chapter 13.

Harkavy, Robert E., and Newman, Stephanie G., eds., *Arms Transfers in the Modern World* (New York: Praeger Special Studies, 1979).

Hollist, W. Ladd, "Alternative Explanations of Competitive Arms Processes: Tests on Four Pairs of Nations," *American Journal of Political Science,* Vol. 21, May 1977.

Keohane, Robert O., and Joseph S. Nye, Jr., *Power and Interdependence: World Politics in Transition* (Boston: Little, Brown, 1977).

Pierre, Andrew J., ed., *Arms Transfers and American Foreign Policy* (New York: New York University Press, 1979).

_____, *The World Politics of Arms Sales* (Princeton, N.J.: Princeton University Press, 1982).

Platt, Alan, and L.D. Weiler, eds., *Congress and Arms Control* (Boulder, Colo.: Frederick A. Praeger, 1978).

Rattinger, Hans, "From War to War: Arms Races in the Middle East," *International Studies Quarterly,* Vol. 20, December 1976.

Scott, Andrew M., *The Dynamics of Interdependence* (Chapel Hill: University of North Carolina Press, 1982).

Sivard, Ruth Leger, *World Military and Social Expenditures 1983* (Leesburg, Va.: World Priorities, 1983).

U.S. Arms Control and Disarmament Agency, *World Military Expenditures and Arms Transfers 1972–1982* (Washington, D.C.: U.S. Arms Control and Disarmament Agency, 1984).

_____, *World Military Expenditures and Arms Transfers 1985* (Washington, D.C.: U.S. Arms Control and Disarmament Agency, 1985).

Wallace, Michael D., "Armaments and Escalation: Two Competing Hypotheses," *International Studies Quarterly,* Vol. 26, March 1982.

Chapter 14.

Barton, John H., *The Politics of Peace: A Evaluation of Arms Control* (Stanford, Calif.: Stanford University Press, 1981).

Bueno de Mesquita, Bruce, *The War Trap* (New

Haven, Conn.: Yale University Press, 1981).

Clark, Duncan L., and Brauch, Hans Guenter, *Decisionmaking for Arms Limitation* (Cambridge, Mass.: Ballinger, 1983).

Coffey, Joseph I., ed., "Nuclear Proliferation: Prospects, Problems and Proposals," *Annals of the American Academy of Political and Social Science*, March 1977.

Cusick, Thomas R., and Ward, Michael Don, "Military Spending in the United States, Soviet Union, and the People's Republic of China," *Journal of Conflict Resolution*, Vol. 25, September 1981.

Gray, Colin S., and Payne, Keith B., "Victory Is Possible," *Foreign Policy*, Vol. 39, Summer 1980.

International Institute for Strategic Studies, *Military Balance, 1984–1985* (London, 1985).

Keeny, Spurgeon M., Jr., and Panofsky, Wolfgang K.H., "MAD Versus NUTS," *Foreign Affairs*, Vol. 60, Winter 1981–82.

Kolkowicz, Roman, and Loeck, Neil, eds., *Arms Control and International Security* (Boulder, Colo.: Westview Press, 1984).

Moll, Kendall D., and Luebbert, Gregory M., "Arms Race and Military Expenditure Models," *Journal of Conflict Resolution*, Vol. 24, March 1980.

NATO Information Service, *NATO and the Warsaw Pact: Force Comparisons* (Brussels, 1984).

Nincic, Miroslav, *The Arms Race: The Political Economy of Military Growth* (New York: Praeger, 1982).

Rattinger, Hans, "Armaments, Detente, and Bureaucracy: The Case of the Arms Race in Europe," *Journal of Conflict Resolution*, Vol. 19, December 1975.

————, "War to War: Arms Race in the Middle East," *International Studies Quarterly*, Vol. 20, December 1976.

U.S. Department of State, *Western Defense. The European Role in NATO* (Washington, D.C., 1985).

Wolfe, Thomas W., *The SALT Experience* (Cambridge, Mass.: Ballinger, 1979).

Chapter 15.

Betts, Richard, *Vietnam: The System Worked* (Washington, D.C.: Brookings Institution, 1979).

Cohen, Raymond, *International Politics: The Rules of the Game* (London and New York: Longman, 1981).

Gamson, William, and Mosigliani, Andre, "Knowledge and Foreign Policy Opinions: Some Models for Consideration," *Public Opinion Quarterly*, Vol. 30, Summer 1966.

Henkin, Louis, *How Nations Behave: Law and Foreign Policy* (New York: Council on Foreign Relations, Inc., 1979).

Krasner, Stephen, *In Defense of the National Interest: Raw Materials, Investments, and U.S. Foreign Policy* (Princeton, N.J.: Princeton University Press, 1978).

Miller, Warren E., and Stokes, Donald E., "Constituency Influence in Congress," in Campbell, Angus; Converse, Philip E.; Miller, Warren E.; and Stokes, Donald E.; eds., *Elections and the Political Order* (New York: Wiley, 1966).

Nathan, James A., and Oliver, James K., *United States Foreign Policy and World Order*, 2nd ed. (Boston: Little, Brown and Co., 1981).

Robinson, John P., *Public Information About World Affairs* (Ann Arbor, Mich.: Institute for Social Research, 1967).

Russett, Bruce, and Starr, Harvey, *World Politics: The Menu for Choice* (San Francisco: W.H. Freeman and Co., 1981).

Scammon, Richard M., and Wattenberg, Ben J., *The Real Majority* (New York: Berkeley Publishing, 1970).

Sick, Gary, *All Fall Down* (New York: Random House, 1985).

Chapter 16.

Eichelberger, Clark M., *Organizing for Peace* (New York: Harper, 1977).

Franck, Thomas M., *Nation Against Nation* (New York: Oxford University Press, 1985).

Goodrich, Leland, *The United Nations in a Changing World* (New York: Columbia University Press, 1974).

Haas, Ernst B., "Regime Decay: Conflict Management and International Organizations, 1945–1981," *International Organization*, Vol. 36, Spring 1982.

Jackson, Richard L., *The Non–Aligned, the U.N. and the Superpowers* (New York: Praeger, 1983).

Jacobson, Harold K., *Networks of Interdependence: International Organizations and the Global Political System*, 2nd ed. (New York: Alfred A. Knopf, 1985).

Jordan, Robert S., "What Has Happened to Our International Civil Service? The Case of the United Nations," *Public Administration Review*, Vol. 41, Spring 1981.

Keohane, Robert O., "The Demand for International Regimes," *International Organization*, Vol. 36, Spring 1982.

Kim, Samuel S., *China, the United Nations, and World*

Order (Princeton, N.J.: Princeton University Press, 1979).

Krasner, Stephen D., *International Regimes* (Ithaca, N.Y.: Cornell University Press, 1983).

_____, "Structural Causes and Regime Consequences: Regimes as Intervening Variables," *International Organization*, Vol. 36, Spring 1982.

Meron, Theodor, *The United Nations Secretariat* (Lexington, Mass.: Lexington Books, 1977).

Olson, Robert K., *U.S Foreign Policy and the New International Economic Order* (Boulder, Colo.: Westview Press, 1981).

Rikhye, Indar Jit; Harbottle, Michael; and Egge, Bjorn; *The Thin Blue Line: International Peacekeeping and Its Future* (New Haven, Conn.: Yale University Press, 1974).

Riggs, Robert E., "The United States and the Diffusion of Power in the Security Council," *International Studies Quarterly*, Vol. 23, December, 1979.

Ruggie, John Gerard, "International Responses to Technology: Concepts and Trends," *International Organization*, Vol. 29, Summer 1975.

Scott, George, *The Rise and Fall of the League of Nations* (New York: Macmillan, 1974).

Chapter 17.

Barkun, Michael, *Law Without Sanctions: Order in Primitive Societies and the World Community* (New Haven, Conn.: Yale University Press, 1968).

Boyle, Francis Anthony, *World Politics and International Law* (Durham, N.C.: Duke University Press, 1985).

Cohen, Jerome A., ed., *China's Practice of International Law: Some Case Studies* (Cambridge: Harvard University Press, 1973).

Deutsch, Karl W., and Hoffmann, Stanley, eds., *The Relevance of International Law* (Garden City. N.Y.: Doubleday-Anchor, 1971).

Gross, Leo, ed., *The Future of the International Court of Justice* (Dobbs Ferry, N.Y.: Oceana, 1976).

Higgins, Rosalyn, "Policy and Impartiality: The Uneasy Relationship in International Law," *International Organization*, Vol. 23, Winter 1969.

Hollick, Ann L., *U.S. Foreign Policy and the Law of the Sea* (Princeton, N.J.: Princeton University Press, 1981).

Kaplan, Morton A., and Katzenbach, Nicholas, *The Political Foundations of International Law* (New York: Wiley, 1961).

Levi, Werner, *Law and Politics in the International Society* (Beverly Hills, Calif.: Sage Publications, 1976).

Maechling, Charles, "The Hallow Chamber," *Foreign Policy*, Vol. 33, Winter 1978–79.

Malone, James L., "Who Needs the Sea Treaty?" *Foreign Policy*, Vol. 54, Spring 1984.

Osakwe, Chris, "Socialist International Law Revisited," *American Journal of International Law*, Vol. 66, No. 3, 1972.

Ramundo, Bernard A., *Peaceful Coexistence: International Law in the Building of Communism* (Baltimore: Johns Hopkins University Press, 1967).

von Glahn, Gerhard, *Law Among Nations*, 4th ed. (New York: Macmillan Publishing Co., 1981).

Weston, Burns, Falk, Richard A.; and D'Amato, Anthony A.; *International Law and World Order* (St. Paul, Minn.: West Publishing, 1980).

Wright, Quincy, *Contemporary International Law: A Balance Sheet* (New York: Doubleday, 1955).

Index